DURESS

A JOHN HOPE FRANKLIN CENTER BOOK

Ann Laura Stoler

DURESS

IMPERIAL DURABILITIES IN OUR TIMES

Duke University Press   Durham and London   2016

Designed by Courtney Leigh Baker
Typeset in Quadraat Pro by Westchester Publishing Services

Library of Congress Cataloging-in-Publication Data
Names: Stoler, Ann Laura, author.
Title: Duress : imperial durabilities in our times / Ann Laura Stoler.
Description: Durham : Duke University Press, 2016. |
"A John Hope Franklin Center Book." |
Includes bibliographical references and index.
Identifiers:L CCN 2016024770
ISBN 9780822362524 (hardcover : alk. paper)
ISBN 9780822362678 (pbk. : alk. paper)
ISBN 9780822373612 (e-book)
Subjects: LCSH: Europe—Colonies—Historiography. | Europe—Colonies—
Race relations-History—20th century. | Imperialism—Historiography. |
Postcolonialism—Historiography.
Classifi cation: LCC JV151 .S75 2016 | DDC 325/.34—dc23
LC record available at https://lccn.loc.gov/2016024770

Cover art: Photograph by Tessa Hirschfeld-Stoler

THIS BOOK IS DEDICATED to those living contained and constrained in two places I have been honored to teach: Palestine and at the Eastern Correctional Facility in Napanoch, New York. In their different ways, these colleagues, students, and friends have sharpened my capacity to look and feel for the forms that duress takes and the endurance it demands. Their insights—critical, conceptual, visceral, and acute—have clarified both those questions worth attending to and why they matter for those living in the shadows and glare of imperial formations.

CONTENTS

Use of the term "colonial studies" or "(post)colonial studies" rather than "postcolonialism" may call for some explication. I have avoided the term "postcolonial" for some time. Despite the warnings of those who rightly insist that it is not a time period but a critical stance. In practice, however, the term "postcolonial" often references a critical perspective on a past colonial situation (too easily made distinct from our own) or on those who bear the costs of living in a space that was once colonial and is no more. However finessed, the bottom line is something that this book attempts to tackle: the temporal and affective space in which colonial inequities endure and the forms in which they do so.

I have addressed these temporal difficulties here in several ways. No matter how "post" one's stance may be, the fact of living both colonial relations that are alive and well and postcolonial predicaments at the same time should command our political work and analytic attention. In arguing for a recursive history and the uneven sedimentation of colonial practices in the present, I intend to retain the "post" as a mark of skepticism rather than assume its clarity. I choose to avoid the artifice that makes the "cut" between the colonial and postcolonial before asking how those temporalities are lived. I prefer "(post)colonial" studies to emphasize a colonial "presence" in its tangible and intangible forms and to acknowledge that there are colonial "presents"—as those who work in Australia and the Americas would argue and those concerned with a Palestinian/Israeli context would contend.

For a more informal discussion of the trajectory of this book and the concerns that have informed its writing, see the interview done by Valentine Daniel for *Public Culture* (24, no. 3 [Fall 2012]: 487–508). I thank Val for crafting an interview that allowed movement among personal anxieties, political investments, and conceptual blockages, concerns that more often are submerged in formal genres of exposition. In the end, this remains a project in formation with more to unlearn and to change.

APPRECIATIONS

I think of appreciations to underscore the privilege and accrued value—rendered in a flash or in longer gestation—of thinking with colleagues, students, and friends. My hope is that their patience and persistence have made the arguments clearer, the arc of the book more accessible, and its form traceable to those who have inspired me along the way.

I thank Larry Hirschfeld, who persistently demanded a simpler word, a cleaner statement, a better parsed phrase, and Adi Ophir, with his fine-grained thinking about concepts (despite and because of my adherence to "conceptual labor" and his to "conceptual performance"), who has been such a generous presence and inspiration and who provided detailed comments on a condensed version of chapter 3. I thank Lila Abu-Lughod for her incisive comments on chapter 2. For help with chapter 4, I especially thank Didier Fassin, Eric Fassin, Larry Hirschfeld, Achille Mbembe, Richard Rechtmann, Janet Roitman, and Miriam Ticktin for their insights and comments. A shorter version of that chapter appeared in *Public Culture* (23, no. 1 [Winter 2011]).

Chapter 5 profited from close readings by Frederick Cooper, Fernando Coronil, Fasail Devji, Larry Hirschfeld, Amy Kaplan, Claudio Lomnitz, Ussama Makdisi, and the anonymous reviewers for *Public Culture*. The latter part of the chapter was thought through with graduate students in my first seminar at the New School for Social Research and especially with David Bond, who urged me to further specify what I meant by any particular term and often offered an explication that was better than my own. An earlier version of this chapter appeared in *Public Culture* (18, no. 1 [Winter 2006]).

A first version of chapter 6 was prompted by an invitation from New York University's humanities initiative in the lecture series "Exporting Enlightenment: The Local Careers of a Global Idea" in 2008 and expanded with the comments of those, especially Allen Feldman and Robert Young, who engaged my incipient formulations. I thank Graham Huggan for his comments on an earlier version of chapter 4, published in *The Oxford Handbook of Postcolonial Studies*, which he edited. Chapter 7 first appeared as "Racial Histories and Their Regimes of Truth," in *Political Power and Social Theory* (Stamford, CT: JAI Press, 1997).

Chapter 8 is based on research done in the south of France in 1997–98 with the help of Frederic Cotton, Chantal Février, and Annie Roquier. Research in 1999 was carried out with Delphine Mauger, who at the time was an undergraduate in anthropology at the University of Michigan. The Literature, Science and Arts faculty fund, the Office of the Vice President, and the Institute for Research on Gender at the University of Michigan generously provided funding. A synoptic version of the chapter was published in the *Journal of the International Institute* (7, no. 1 [Fall 1999]). And a version of chapter 9 appeared in Anne Berger, ed., *Genre et postcolonialismes* (Paris: Éditions des Archives Contemporaines, 2011). The project that prompted chapter 10 was originally conceived with my former colleagues at the New School for Social Research, Adriana Petryna and Vyjayanthi Rao, in fall 2005. I thank both of them for thinking with me about the politics of scarred tissue, debris, and exposures. The chapter itself appeared in partial form in *Imperial Debris: On Ruins and Ruination* (Durham, NC: Duke University Press, 2013).

Finally, I thank Ken Wissoker, who has always been the consummate editor and gently makes me know that revisions based on readers' responses, however trying, make things better. Both Charles McDonald and Katie Detwiler read through the essays, as the manuscript became a book in formation. Both of them, in their eminently incisive ways, pushed me to make explicit sensibilities that they each reminded me were my own. Finally Kevin Swann took on the task of preparing the manuscript for publication, at a time that it was not easy for him to do so and Erick Howard kindly and skillfully finished the preparation and rendered the index, what I always think of good references to be, a conceptual roadmap, attentive to those connectivities that most matter as readers cull what is useful to think with—for adjacent efforts or different tasks.

I. CONCEPT WORK

FRAGILITIES AND FILIATIONS

CRITICAL INCISIONS
ON CONCEPT WORK AND COLONIAL RECURSIONS

How do colonial histories matter in the world today? Are not these histories of a past that is over and done with, as former imperial polities and those once subject to them deal with more pressing issues: epidemics, disaster management, persistent racial inequities, ecological catastrophes, forced dislocations and refugee populations, humanitarian failures, border regimes, and security protocols that impinge on their everyday and future possibilities? Did not decolonization confer sovereignty and autonomy nearly fifty years ago on most of the world that was once colonized, making postcolonial disorders and globalization the issues at hand? And do not these histories matter more to a bevy of academics than they do in a contemporary world in which the past is something that needs to be reckoned with so younger generations can be freed to move on?

It is one premise of this book that these are indeed issues of the day but that many of the most urgent ones—be they toxic dumping in Africa, devastated "waste lands," precarious sites of residence, ongoing dispossession, or pockets of ghettoized urban quarters—are features of our current global landscape whose etiologies are steeped in the colonial histories of which they have been, and in some cases continue to be, a part. It is the contention of this book that many of these conditions are intimately tied to imperial effects and shaped by the distribution of demands, priorities, containments, and coercions of imperial formations.

Those connectivities are not always readily available for easy grasp, in part because colonial entailments do not have a life of their own. They wrap around contemporary problems; adhere in the logics of governance; are plaited through racialized distinctions; and hold tight to the less tangible emotional economies of humiliations, indignities, and resentments that may manifest in bold acts of refusal to abide by territorial restrictions imposed or in the flare of burning tires in "sensitive" urban quarters. Colonial counterinsurgency policies rest undiluted in current security measures. Molten in their form, colonial entailments may lose their visible and identifiable presence in the vocabulary, conceptual grammar, and idioms of current concerns. It is the effort of this venture to halt in the face of these processes of occlusion and submersion, to ask about how they work, their differential effects; and on whom they most palpably act.

COLONIAL PRESENCE

Tyranny is a pedagogic scenario of pure loss. . . . The question of education is no longer the question of how to transmit knowledge but of how to suspend it.—Martin Heidegger, The Art of Teaching, 1945

Some work in the field of (post)colonial studies has assumed that the connectivities joining colonial pasts to "postcolonial" presents are self-evident and unproblematically identified and accessed. This book starts from the premise that more often they are not. Many of the "vestiges" of colonial constructions seem as though in easy reach. Local and regional administrative units may be kept in place, albeit outfitted with new agents; the segregated divisions of colonial urban planning may be demolished but still mark the social geography of where upscale housing clusters and where dense settlements of privation remain. While many of the roads, railways, bridges, and canals built under colonial engineering projects with forced local labor may be in disrepair or bombed out, elsewhere they have been refurbished to move people and produce to service new profit-sharing ventures between national elites and foreign multinationals. Oil palm plantations may no longer serve to transform peanut butter into a U.S. staple. Indeed, they now do much more as their acreage has expanded to supply one of the major biofuels in the world today. Plush shopping malls built over razed squatter settlements with police dogs guarding their gates are the Janus face of the "postcolony" from Johannesburg to Jakarta.

But colonial constraints and imperial dispositions have tenacious presence in less obvious ways. The geopolitical and spatial distribution of inequities cast across our world today are not simply mimetic versions of earlier imperial incarnations but refashioned and sometimes opaque and oblique reworkings of them. Colonial pasts, the narratives recounted about them, the unspoken distinctions they continue to "cue," the affective charges they reactivate, and the implicit "lessons" they are mobilized to impart are sometimes so ineffably threaded through the fabric of contemporary life forms they seem indiscernible as distinct effects, as if everywhere and nowhere at all. The preserved disrepair of colonial buildings are top selling points in tourist excursions throughout the world: colonial homes refitted as colonial-era hotels confer the nostalgic privilege of those who can pay their price; girls' boarding schools are turned to the profit of "educational tourism"; slave quarters are now assigned as World Heritage sites; colonial ministries are updated as archival depots for the dissertation industry; plundered objects are refashioned as ethnological museums in metropolitan centers to valorize cultural difference. All are comforting affirmations that colonialisms are over, initiatives and gestures that firmly and safely consign those places and sometimes the people who once inhabited them as frozen icons of a shamed and distanced past.

But leftovers are not what most interest me here. Connectivities to those colonial histories that bear on the present can escape scrutiny: some of those that are most pressing evade recognition. I ask why and how that may be so. The analytical tools we use to identify either historical continuities or, alternatively, profound ruptures from the past may be obstacles rather than openings. Colonial archives can impede the task: They have a way of drawing our attention to their own scripted temporal and spatial designations of what is "colonial" and what is no longer, making it difficult to stretch beyond their guarded frames. Qualified and celebrated memories black out censored ones. Environmental effects of colonial agribusiness are renamed and compressed into more generic ecological hothouse phenomena in our climatically sensitized anthropocentric world, sharply cut off from the history of imperial mandates that set them on their damaging course. *The acrid smell of industrial rubble masks, and is often more palpable than, the toxins of imperial debris.*

Or perhaps there is a problem with our vocabularies. The scholarly romance with "traces" risks rendering colonial remnants as pale filigrees, benign overlays with barely detectable presence rather than deep pressure points of generative possibilities or violent and violating absences. The "haunting" trace seems too easily unmoored from material damages and disseminated landscapes, or from border barricades installed as colonialism's parting gestures, now hardened and more intractable than stone. Duress, as I shall argue, has temporal, spatial, and affective coordinates. Its impress may be intangible, but it is not a faint scent of the past. It may be an indelible if invisible gash. It may sometimes be a trace but more often an enduring fissure, a durable mark. One task, then, is to train our senses beyond the more easily identifiable forms that some colonial scholarship schools us to recognize and see.

Not recognizing these colonial genealogies, however, may have as much to do with what the connectivities between past and present are *expected* to look like—what are imagined as the dominant features of colonial formations, the attributes assigned to what colonial governing strategies are thought to have encompassed, or what colonial racism is thought to have looked like (always posed as so much fiercer than they are today)—how tangible or intangible those effects are expected to be.

Here I consider what methodological renovations might serve to write histories that yield neither to too smooth continuities nor too abrupt epochal breaks. Each chapter attempts to capture the uneven, recursive qualities of the visions and practices that imperial formations have animated, what they have both succeeded and failed to put in place. Each works through a set of conceptual and concrete reconsiderations of the logics and sensibilities that pervade our imperial present, that evade easy access and still carve out the jagged lineaments, political scissions, and some of the deep fault lines of the world today.

ON THE LINEAMENTS OF DURESS

Duress (n.) *early 14 c., "harsh or severe treatment," from Old French duresse, from Latin duritia "hardness, severity, austerity" from durus "hard" (see endure). . . .* —Online Etymology Dictionary, 2014

French dure-r, to last, continue, persist, extend < Latin durare to harden, be hardened, hold out, last. Sense of "coercion, compulsion" is from 1590s.—Dictionary.com, 2016

1. *Hardness, roughness, violence, severity; hardiness of endurance, resistance, etc.; firmness.*
2. *Harsh or severe treatment, infliction of hardship; oppression, cruelty; harm, injury; affliction.*
3. *Forcible restrain or restriction; confinement, imprisonment.*
4. *Constraint, compulsion; spec. in Law, Constraint illegally exercised to force a person to perform some act.*—Oxford English Dictionary, 1989

"Duress" figures in the title of this book to capture three principal features of colonial histories of the present: the hardened, tenacious qualities of colonial effects; their extended protracted temporalities; and, not least, their durable, if sometimes intangible constraints and confinements. *Duress, durability,* and *duration* in this work all share a politically inflected and afflicted historical etymology. But *endurance* figures here, as well, in the capacity to "hold out" and "last," especially in its activated verb form, "to endure," as a countermand to "duress" and its damaging and disabling qualities.

How one chooses to address imperial duress depends in part on where and among whom it is sought, how it is imagined to manifest, the temporalities in which it is lodged, and the sensory regimes on which it weighs. As an object of inquiry, it demands that we ask how we know it and what the political consequences are of knowing in certain ways. One founding premise of this book is that the concepts called on to identify and make sense of the durabilities of colonial duress may be inadequate to the task. An excursion through the politics of conceptual labor is the meat of the chapters that follow. The political effects and practices that imperial formations impose and induce are its marrow.

Duress, then, is neither a thing nor an organizing principle so much as a relation to a condition, a pressure exerted, a troubled condition borne in the body, a force exercised on muscles and mind. It may bear no immediately visible sign or, alternatively, it may manifest in a weakened constitution and attenuated capacity to bear its weight. Duress is tethered to time but rarely in any predictable way. It may be a response to relentless force, to the quickened pacing of pressure, to intensified or arbitrary inflictions that reduce expectations and stamina. Duress rarely calls out its name. Often it is a mute condition of constraint. Legally it does something else. To claim to be "under duress" in a court of law does not absolve one of a crime or exonerate the fact of one. On the contrary, it admits a culpability—a condition induced by illegitimate pressure. But it is productive, too, of a diminished, burned-out will not to succumb, when one is stripped of the wherewithal to have acted differently or better.

In recounting his life as an invisible, racially marked man in the mid-twentieth century United States, Ralph Ellison described his writing as an effort to access "the lower frequencies" of human experience.[1] Duress may be one elemental attribute of that very domain: not manifest in the scenes

1. Ralph Ellison, *Invisible Man* (New York: Random House, 1952), 579.

of high-pitched drama but what is borne at "lower frequencies," the quotidian defamations of personhood inflected at an insistent pace, or punctuated, mercilessly, in non-verbal registers. If duress is borne, we might ask what forms it takes, the conditions that produce the silenced exertions it demands, encumbered possibilities, relations of power incrementally imposed. Situations of imperial duress might be measured by the force embodied in it and the frequency by which it is applied, by the limits on endurance and the refusals it produces in its wake. Duress as I conceive it is a relationship of actualized and anticipated violence. It bears on those who are its perpetrators, produces anxieties, and expanding definitions of insecurities that are its effect, a demolition project that is eminently modern, and as Franz Fanon conceived it, a form of power that slashes a scar across a social fabric that differentially affects us all.

Not least, the landscape of duress depends on the concepts we call upon, those seen as available and construed as relevant, those that call on us and command our attention.[2] Conceptual conventions may do more than get in the way. Such conventions can hamper our capacities to re-vision those histories and dislodge what we imagine already to know. At issue are the ready-made concepts on which we rely and what work we call on them to do; less obvious may be an adherence to an implicit notion of the stability of concepts, more fixed than are concepts themselves.

My interests are threefold: in the distributions of inequities that concepts condone, inscribe, and inhabit; in the challenges of writing new colonial histories that press on the present; and, not least, in unlearning what we imagine to know about colonial governance and why those understandings and misrecognitions should continue to concern us now.

In identifying the sinews and sites of duress, concepts emerge as seductive and powerful agents. They invite appropriation, quick citation, promising the authority that such invested affiliations are imagined to offer. They also invite unremarked omissions when their capacities to subsume are strained, a setting aside of what seems uneasily, partially, or awkwardly to

---

2. My use of the "we" here is not meant to assume a unified "we" or a striated unified one but to signal a disparate and dispersed "we" of those who each deal in our different ways with colonial histories and colonial presence. I make no assumptions that the "we" is shared in terms of intent, content, location, or form, but do contend that anyone working on imperial formations must grapple with the conceptual conventions and the currency of vocabularies called upon.

"fit" within the analytic repertoire of "cases" that confirm both disciplinary protocols and ready analytical frames.

The sort of conceptual labor I work through here attempts a venture unyielding to easy fit, one that is about neither the "usage" of concepts nor acts of "borrowing." It is, rather, an exercise in attentiveness and vigilance in a provisional, active mode. The challenge is both to discern the work we do with concepts and the work that concepts may explicitly or inadvertently exert on us. Rather than acquiesce to the resolute security that concepts may be marshaled to confer, we might better look to the unmarked space between their porous and policed peripheries, to that which hovers as not quite "covered" by a concept, as "excess" or "amiss," that which cannot be quite encompassed by its received attributes, when "portability" is not self-evident, to that which spills across its edges.

How to think otherwise (*penser autrement*)—a project that Michel Foucault took as his own task—is always the critical challenge. In an effort to do so, these chapters make two entwined moves: one to examine a set of concepts familiar to those concerned with colonial histories and imperial formations and to ask how well these concepts have worked; and two, to ask what sorts of rethinking and reformulations might allow a better understanding of the political grammar of colonialism's durable presence, the dispositions it fosters, the indignities it nourishes, the indignations that are responsive to those effects. The latter move is not necessarily offered as a replacement for those concepts, on some of which colonial regimes avidly called. Rather, thinking otherwise is to inhabit them differently, to envision how to recast the resilient impingements and damages to which imperial forms give rise. Not least, the task is to recognize the force field of colonialism's conceptual web in which many more of us than often acknowledged remain entangled. Some are elements in what I have elsewhere argued are the "imperial dispositions of disregard": that which makes it possible—sometimes effortlessly and sometimes with strenuous if unremarked labor—to look away.[3]

Each of these chapters is an intervention of sorts that reflects on the conceptual vocabulary and interpretive categories that might open to the occluded, alternative genealogies of imperial effects. Each seeks to think

3. For an earlier effort to capture what it is both to know and not know the imperial strictures to which one is tethered, and the demands to which one is bound, see Ann Laura Stoler, "Imperial Dispositions of Disregard," in *Along the Archival Grain: Epistemic Anxieties and Colonial Common Sense* (Princeton, NJ: Princeton University Press, 2009), 237–78.

through the conceptual habits we bring to the study of colonial presence, not least the assumption of "confident access" to what that presence entails: how it manifests and on whom it most impinges. These are the assumptions that these essays attempt to identify and from which conceptual conventions may turn us away.

DIS-ARMING CERTITUDES AND COLONIAL OCCLUSIONS

Each certitude is only sure because of the support offered by unexplored ground.
—Michel Foucault, The Politics of Truth, 1997

"Duress" is central to this venture. "Occlusion" is, as well. In broaching what I call the occluded histories of empire, I intend to invoke acts of obstruction—of categories, concepts, and ways of knowing that disable linkages to imperial practice and that often go by other names. To occlude is an act that hides and conceals, creates blockage, and closes off. Underlying these chapters is an effort to treat occlusions as subjects of inquiry in their own right, not as obstacles on a predetermined track. That which occludes and that which is occluded have different sources, sites of intractability, forms of appearance, and temporal effects. They derive from geopolitical locations as much as they do from conceptual grammars that render different objects observable, that shape how we observers observe our chosen observers (as Niklas Luhmann might put it), and thereby construe the proper "lessons of empire" and what count as the salient "historical facts."[4]

Occlusion is neither an accidental byproduct of imperial formations nor merely a missed opportunity, rendered visible to a critical witness "after the fact." They are not just neglected, overlooked, or "forgotten." Occluded histories are part of what such geopolitical formations produce. They inhere in their conceptual, epistemic, and political architecture. One sense of occlusion comes particularly close to what I have in mind: "a line drawn in the construction of a figure that is missing [or more accurately 'disappeared'] from the finished product."[5]

Occluded histories in this book take varied forms. Sometimes they manifest as "benign" mislabelings, dissociating the social distribution of

4. Niklas Luhmann, *Theories of Distinction: Redescribing the Descriptions of Modernity* (Stanford, CA: Stanford University Press, 2002), 98–99.

5. "Occlusion," in *Online Etymology Dictionary*, 2014, http://www.etymonline.com /index.php?term=occlusion&allowed_in_frame=0.

contemporary privations from their ongoing histories of colonial effects. Chapter 2, "Raw Cuts," takes as its charge the occlusion of Israel as a colonial state in the field of (post)colonial studies, where it remained impolitic to discuss, eviscerated from any connection to U.S. imperial pursuits for so long. Israeli occupation of Palestine was treated as a Zionist issue, relegated as a "shatter zone" in international politics, as a salutary history of democratic nation making, as a liberation struggle from British rule. Only now are Israeli policies publicly and loudly enunciated as the combined ferocity of high-tech and lowly, daily creations and reorderings of ever more present distinctions and discriminations, as cumulative and amplified accretions of colonial presence, violently, deliberately, and carefully designed.

Much of my previous work has been tightly bound to colonial documents. The sites of the imperial landscape pursued here veer further afield in time and space from the colonial archives proper. Pursuit of these other sorts of documents offers openings to counterintuitive genealogies of imperial breadth. Sometimes at issue is a different sort of reading from within official colonial archives. But as often analytical traction comes from what resides on their edges and outside their received frames, the seemingly innocuous comparisons made to contexts that seem radically distinct from what count as part of the imperial world, attentiveness to the ways of knowing on which they relied, from which only certain narratives could be crafted with smooth coherence and authority. Chapters 2 and 3 take as their task a redrawing of a "virtual" colonial archive through a re-visioned conceptual map.

In that pursuit, some chapters might seem distant from, even only loosely tied to, the prevailing themes of colonial history as we know it, with an associative resonance that may, at best, seem tenuous. Working with and through these dissociations is at once my subject and opens to the brunt of the questions I ask. Sometimes occlusion is broached from reimagining how an imperial network otherwise might be thought and drawn. Such is the case in chapter 3, which looks to the children's agricultural colonies (les colonies agricoles) for wayward youths in mid-nineteenth century France that Foucault identified in Discipline and Punish as the signature sites of "the art of punishing that is still more or less our own."[6] Long relegated (as Foucault did) to the history of social reform in Europe, these colonies have been

6. Michel Foucault, Discipline and Punish: The Birth of the Prison (New York: Random House, 1977), 296.

severed from the broader imperial history of military intervention and installations, colonial recruitment and settlement, disentangled from the political matrix that joined the unsettled confinements of colony and camp, of which the redistributions of containments were a crucial part.

Chapter 4 on colonial aphasia seeks to make sense of how long and how viscerally colonial entailments have been absented from French national history and rendered outside its proper bounds. It addresses the issue of occlusion in a particular site, France, and specifically with respect to its racial register. It attempts to ask not why its colonial history has been so repeatedly effaced but, rather, how it is that such a history can be rendered irretrievable, made available, and again displaced.

Conceptualizing this striking irretrievability as *aphasia* is an effort to address what John Austin so famously articulated in his essay, "A plea for excuses," when some "abnormality or failure" signals a "breakdown" in conduct and when the retreat to ignorance, forgetting, or amnesia is not "excuse" enough.[7] Aphasia is a condition in which the occlusion of knowledge is at once a dismembering of words from the objects to which they refer, a difficulty retrieving both the semantic and lexical components of vocabularies, a loss of access that may verge on active dissociation, a difficulty comprehending what is seen and spoken. Colonial aphasia as conceived here is a *political condition* whose genealogy is embedded in the space that has allowed Marine Le Pen and her broad constituency to move from the margin and extreme—where her father was banished—to a normalized presence in contemporary France.

But colonial aphasia is not peculiar to France. A blog by Dutch activists embraced the term in protesting the continued celebration of what they saw as the racist image of "Black Pete"—the helper of Sinterklass and a Dutch national icon. The politics of aphasia clearly has had wider resonance.[8] In 2012, a young woman who had served in the Israeli army, after hearing my lecture on the subject, was palpably agitated when she blurted out that I had just described both her spliced self and the untenable contradictions in which she lived. This capacity to know and not know simultaneously renders the space between ignorance and ignoring not an etymological exercise

7. J. L. Austin, "A Plea for Excuses: The Presidential Address," *Proceedings of the Aristotelian Society* 57, new series (January 1, 1956), 1–30.

8. For their use of the term, based on an earlier version of this essay, see John Helsloot, "*Zwarte Piet* and Cultural Aphasia in the Netherlands," *Quotidian* 3, 1 (February 2012). http://www.quotidian.nl/vo103/nro1/ao1.

but a concerted political and personal one. "Self-deception" does not do justice to the ways we each find to turn away.[9]

Chapter 6, "Reason Aside," treats conceptual occlusion from a very different angle that seeks to reorient how the political rationalities of imperial forms have been conceived. It considers how a focus on the "supremacy of reason" as the master trope of colonial critique has displaced the enduring affective work that such rationalities perform. Here the concept-work is around the sentiments and sensibilities that notions of security produce; on the subjects they endeavor to create; on the manipulations of space they condone; and on the objects of fear they nourish, reproduce, and on which they depend.

One might argue that these are simply a few among many of the histories that we have inevitably "missed," were innocent and ignorant of, have not gotten around to writing, or just could not possibly know. Some may be, but as a research strategy I suspend that judgment. Nor do I think we can assume that what escapes inquiry is "unthinkable," epistemologically out of reach, as Michel-Rolph Trouillot once so cogently argued that the Haitian Revolution was for French colonials.[10] I would argue instead that the forms of counter-violence and refusal were *too* politically thinkable, eminent potentialities in wait—not that they were not.[11] I am more convinced that our conceptual currencies may be curtailed by political logics and epistemic assumptions that render some events, contexts, and comparisons easily dismissed as forced and counterintuitive, as too difficult to track, as interpretive stretches that reach beyond what we can really know.

The occluded histories that concern me are not those that bear on redeeming the past. My assays push in another direction: to ask how the uneven sedimentations of colonial reason and the affective sensibilities on which they depend—whether under the rubrics of "security," "terrorism," "defense of society," or "race"—participate in shaping the possibilities for how *differential futures* are distributed and who are, and will be, targeted as those to be exposed, both external and internal enemies in the making. Rendering these histories to their contemporary valence, then, is as much

9. On the "politics of disregard" see Stoler, Along the Archival Grain, 237–78.

10. Michel-Rolph Trouillot, *Silencing the Past: Power and the Production of History* (Boston: Beacon, 1995).

11. Dale Tomich makes a related point in "Thinking the 'Unthinkable': Victor Schoelcher and Haiti," *Review* 31, 3 (January 1, 2008): 401–31.

about the inequities inscribed in how common sense is forged as it is in anticipatory dangers in the conditional and future tense.

Some features of this occlusion stem from assumptions of (post)colonial studies itself. After some thirty years studying colonial governance and the racialized techniques and intimate practices that provided its relay and support, I am increasingly convinced of a slippage, an unremarked analytical gray zone, between what we who devote ourselves to discerning the machinations of colonial practice think we know about those practices and how we imagine they manifest now. Embarking on a tracking of these occlusive processes with an expectation of a repetition of earlier colonial policies is a misguided task. The chapters that follow reflect on that expectation or, alternatively, on the assumption of a clean temporal break. Critique here is not about "fault finding" and judgment but about restoring the forms that occlusion takes and the questions that its effects may lead us to ask.[12] Thus, the effort is to understand that occlusion is an ongoing, malleable process, sometimes in a form already congealed and seemingly over as it acts on the present, making of us unwittingly compliant observers, nearly always belated in identifying just how it works.

ON THE FRAGILITY OF CONCEPTS

Every concept arises from the equation of unequal things.—*Friedrich Nietzsche*, On Truth and Lies in a Nonmoral Sense, 1873

In pursuing this venture, I find challenge in a number of commanding questions: How might we trace new genealogies of imperial governance that are not constricted and policed by the colonial archives themselves—or by the dominant readings of them? As I ask in chapter 5, what are the effects of Victorian India providing the quintessential form of imperial sovereignty when such stark evidence should lead to other sites and in other directions? What imperial history is being rehearsed with this model in mind when more gradated forms of sovereignty have been equally effective and perva-

---

12. I think here with Judith Butler's invocation of Raymond Williams's and Michel Foucault's rejection of "fault finding" as foundational to critique, replaced with an investment in the "specificity of the response" as "a practice": see Judith Butler, "What Is Critique? An Essay on Foucault's Virtue," in *The Political: Readings in Continental Philosophy*, ed. David Ingram (Malden, MA: Blackwell, 2002): 212–28.

sive (think of Morocco, Palestine, Puerto Rico, and Vieques) and make up not the exception to imperial governance but such a widespread norm? This range of occlusions may seem to address disparate issues, incommensurate misrecognitions, unique arrangements, and legal confusions. It is my contention that they do not.

What has long made the U.S. military base of Diego Garcia in the Indian Ocean a "secret history," or the nuclear test sites that have ravaged large swaths of reservation land in the United States a "Native American problem," or consigned the Mariana Islands as outside the field of (post)colonial work? Why have these not been considered nodal points of an imperial history rather than grist for the case that the U.S. remains an imperial exception?[13]

Again, some occlusions derive from colonial scripts: some derive from the *conceptual habits* we bring to them and the implicit assumptions that our conceptual repertoires leave unaddressed. Sometimes that distinction is hard to draw. Occlusions have multiple sources not easily untangled. Some occlusions are the disparaged remainders cast out from the categories and concepts of colonial narratives. Some derive from how we inadvertently call on colonial logics, treated simultaneously as both worthy of scrutiny and suspect. What catches us within the confines of those very rubrics as we move awkwardly against and along their grain?

Identifying imperial fields of force is a multiplex exercise: it entails seizing on the comparisons—of visions and practices—imperial architects and agents themselves performed, locating their temporal and spatial coordinates, and only then recharting the shadowed zones of governance—smudged and effaced, rendered illegibly blurred—on imperial maps. To compare is a situated political act of discernment, a virtual performative that can implicitly confirm the pre-emptive rationale for future violences (as in "imperial lessons" to learn) and create the fears that strategic comparisons only profess to name. The paradox of comparison is that judgment of pertinence rests on "the equation of unequal things;" and it is precisely around the *equivocations* about the adequacy of those *equivalencies* that the political weight of comparison, like that of concepts, depend.

One task is to identify what for some time I have referred to as the "epistemic politics" that often sever colonial pasts from their contemporary

13. David Vine, *Island of Shame: The Secret History of the U.S. Military Base on Diego Garcia* (Princeton, NJ: Princeton University Press, 2009).

translations—sometimes simply dismissed, sometimes with more finesse.[14] The historical epistemologies of race used to distinguish colonial racism from contemporary racism examined in chapter 7 are exemplary of what I have in mind. The sweeping turn to "ontology" in current anthropology and the contention that epistemological concerns just get in the way seems to miss a crucial point. Ontologies are accessible only if we engage how a category such as race is secured and made credible and on which its effects rely. These need not be mutually exclusive analytical strategies.[15] Here I ask the reader to reconsider how "racial regimes of truth" and our historiographic narratives of them have produced recurrent declarations of "new" racisms. In an essay that has had several incarnations, I examine what I see as the hardened assumptions about what colonial racism once looked like, arguing that these characterizations make little room for the *mobile essentialisms* that produce racism's protean qualities.

Chapter 8 reckons with the common sense of the French radical right in the late 1990s—and how those characteristics have morphed into a broader, normatively endorsed racialized common sense in Europe today. The chapter is not a "snapshot" of another time. Rather, I treat it as a diagnostic to argue that the French extreme right has not been an aberrant or unique development, as it has sometimes been cast, but part of the deep, racialized features of colonial and contemporary France. Throughout this work, the reader is asked to reconsider the subject of "relevance" as a political issue and to reflect on the implicit measures both we and those we study use to assess it. On what grounds has "intimacy" become shorthand for domestic relations, affections, child care, and sex but used less often to refer, as I ask in chapter 9, to other forms of bodily exposure: to intimate violence and humiliation in the nondomestic space of prisons, checkpoints, and immigration offices that open to embodied and affective injuries of a different intensity?

The final chapter on imperial debris turns to other sites that are sometimes off the radar of (post)colonial studies as once conceived to ask explic-

14. Ann Laura Stoler, "Epistemic Politics: Ontologies of Colonial Common Sense," *Folk Epistemology* 39, 3 (Fall 2008): 349–61.

15. Ethnography's "ontological turn" subsumes a wide range of adherents, from Eduardo Viveros de Castro's formative work to that of Phillipe Descola, and Martin Holbraad. For a careful critique of its assumptions and political effects, see Lucas Bessire and David Bond, "Ontological Anthropology and the Deferral of Critique," *American Ethnologist* 41, 3 (2014): 440–56.

itly how the "slow violence" of imperial formations is dislodged from the politics of its making and renamed.[16] It addresses the toxic consequences of imperial debris and duress on matter and mind; of what is left and what people are left with, as it attends too to the resurgent resentments marshaled as a critique of those histories, not as acquiescence. I look to Agent Orange—the spreading of twenty million gallons of deadly herbicides across Vietnam by U.S. forces from 1961 to 1971—long studied as part of the history of warfare and combat zones and as environmental history but rarely joined with the enduring violence of compounded forms of imperial governance. It is far from the only one. We might look to Vasiliki Touhouliotis's trenchant account of the continued violence of undetonated bombs supplied by the United States that Israel sprayed across southern Lebanon in the war of 2006, impaling a civilian population with shrapnel and cancers that do not go away.[17] An account of the imperial commensurabilities that produced the blueprints for Bantustans in South Africa, designed on the model of Canadian native reserves that South African officials culled on their reconnaissance trips to Canada in the 1950s, has yet to be written.

WHAT IS CONCEPT-WORK?

I consider this project one of "concept-work" for colonial histories and for "our times" to underscore the sort of analytical and methodological exercises that I see concept-work demanding and enabling, and the political entailments it requires engaging, the labor to be performed. Cognitive psychologists tell us that concepts are organizing guides that provide stability to our conceptual world. In the abstract they may be right, but what they typically fail to address are the relations of force in which concepts are embedded, the fictions of their "stability" that entail violences of their own. Stability is not an a priori attribute of concepts. Concepts are construed as more stable and made more stable than they are—as are the distinguishing features of the members assigned to them. There is work that goes into

---

16. Rob Nixon, *Slow Violence and the Environmentalism of the Poor* (Cambridge, MA: Harvard University Press, 2011).

17. I thank Vasiliki Touhouliotis for allowing me to draw on her dissertation, "Weapons between Wars: Cluster Bombs, Technological Failure and the Durability of War in South Lebanon," Ph.D. diss., New School for Social Research, New York, 2014.

securing that stability and into their repeated and assertive performance.[18] As Nietzsche insisted, the stability of concepts is a false one. His observation that "every concept arises from the equation of unequal things" offers more than a warning: If stability is not an intrinsic feature of concepts, then one task must be to examine how their stability is achieved, how unequal things are abstracted into commensurabilities that fuel our confidence in those very concepts that then are relegated as common sense.

Concept-work as I conceive it demands "mobile thought," Foucault's term, in advocating an "ethics of discomfort."[19] He invoked both terms in the context of reviewing the fearless writing of Jean Daniel, an Algerian-born Jewish journalist who founded and remains executive editor of one of the most widely read French weeklies, Le Nouvel Observateur, and who was largely condemned for his support of Palestinian rights during and after the Arab-Israeli war of 1967. What was "mobile" about Daniel's writing in Foucault's account was his capacity "to never cease to think about the same things differently."[20] But there was also something more: Daniel's capacity (and Foucault's, because in many ways the essay was a statement about his own endeavor) to reflect on how "an obvious fact gets lost." It is not regained, he writes,

> when it is replaced by another which is fresher or cleaner, but when one begins to detect the very conditions that made it obvious: the familiarities which served as its support, the obscurities on which its clarity was based, and all these things that, coming from afar, carried it secretly and made it such that 'it was obvious.' "[21]

This is more than a methodological invitation; it is an alert, a challenge, and a political demand. Imagining that we know how different colonial racism is from racism today, that we know what a "colony" is, or that we readily recognize what the "legacies" and "vestiges" of colonialism looks like renders each too "obvious" to elicit scrutiny when they could be seized as analytic provocations, prompting moments of arrest. "Mobile thought," here, opens to what concepts implicitly and often quietly foreclose, as well as what they

18. For his development of the performative quality of concept formation, see Adi Ophir, "Concept," trans. Naveh Frumer, in Political Concepts: A Critical Lexicon 1, 1 (2014). http://www.politicalconcepts.org/issue1/concept.

19. Foucault, The Politics of Truth, 122.

20. Foucault, The Politics of Truth, 136.

21. Foucault, The Politics of Truth, 145.

encourage and condone.[22] It entails keeping the concepts with which we work provisional, active, and subject to change; it entails retaining them both as mobile and as located as they are in the world.[23] In *The Archaeology of Knowledge*, Foucault chides his readers from the outset for being duped by the appeal of vacuous historical terms (such as the "spirit [of an age]" or "[Western] influence"), which are endowed with a "virtual self-evidence" that should sound an alarm rather than warrant the trust too quickly invested in them.[24] Most pointedly, he cautions that concepts are no more than "ready-made syntheses."[25] The task is "to free the problems they pose." Nor are concepts "tranquil," stable configurations in a resting mode but in restive agitation.[26] Concepts are moving targets. They act in concert, as Gilles Deleuze and Félix Guattari repeatedly remind us.[27] A concept accumulates force from the other concepts that congeal, collide, and rearrange themselves around it. Replacing a concept not only displaces another. It breaks up contiguities and can render invisible the mutual dependencies (such as that between "colony" and "camp," as I argue later) that join them to a problem, the articulations through which they do their work.

Such a venture raises methodological challenges, not least because concepts and the processes of occlusion they afford and the misrecognitions to which they give rise, are not external to the durabilities of imperial formations. Nor can we assume that what endures in distorted, partial, or derisive form—whether conventions of locution and turns of phrase; forms of disregard, subjugation, or acquiescence; techniques of containment; security measures; or sites of enclosure—are merely unwelcome "leftovers,"

22. A case so well made in Janet L. Roitman, *Anti-Crisis* (Durham, NC: Duke University Press, 2013), with a different referential matrix from the one I draw here.

23. Paul Rabinow's rich formulations of concept work are formative, important, and complementary in this regard. His projects over the years foster an exemplary care for concepts in a collaborative mode that entails genealogical, ethical, and diagnostic labor. Some of this work is spelled out by him and by those with whom he has worked at www.anthropos-lab.net and is discussed in various of his books, usually with reference to whatever specific concept is under consideration. See also Anthony Stavrianakis and Gaymon Bennett, "On Concept Work: Somatosphere," September 25, 2012, http://somatosphere.net/2012/09/on-concept-work.html.

24. Michel Foucault, *The Archaeology of Knowledge* (New York: Pantheon, 1982), 26.

25. Foucault, *The Archaeology of Knowledge*, 22.

26. Foucault, *The Archaeology of Knowledge*, 26.

27. Gilles Deleuze and Félix Guattari, *What Is Philosophy?* (New York: Columbia University Press, 1994), 18.

dim traces of dismantled colonial systems, shorn of their potency and commanding force.

TOUCHSTONES OF POLITICAL CONTEST

Imperial formations prodigiously produce specialized lexicons of legal, social, and political terms, concepts, and enduring vocabularies that both innocuously and tenaciously cling to people, places, and things. The narratives in which they are habitually embedded do so, as well, unevenly irrupting in spasmodic expressions of unaccountability, disparagement, and blame.[28] Paradoxically, these expressions are neither only available as the armature of those political pundits who celebrate colonial policies of the present or past or the property of those who condemn it. Like racial discourse and practice, they can be mobilized for different projects; they have "polyvalent" signatures, their potentialities undecided and unfixed, yielding different agendas and possibilities.[29]

28. When Eric Fassin was recently asked in a French televised forum who was to blame, or culpable (coupable), in the brutal beating of a sixteen-year-old Roma boy in one of the "hot" outskirts of Paris, Fassin did not hesitate for a moment: the question was not who was *coupable* but who and what was *responsible* for the relentless tying of "insecurity" to the Roma presence, to their behavior and to their "nature": see Eugénie Bastié, "Roms: Pas, ça, Fassin!" Causeur, June 18, 2014, http://www.causeur.fr/roms -lynchage-racisme-28125.html#; Éric Fassin Carine Fouteau, Serge Guichard, and Aurélie Windels, Roms et riverains: Une politique municipale de la race (Paris: Fabrique, 2014).

29. We might take Kwasi Kwarteng's The Ghosts of Empire: Britain's Legacies in the Modern World (London: Bloomsbury, 2011) as an example, where he argues that much of the British empire's spread to its "possessions"—Iraq, Sudan, Burma, and Nigeria—had nothing to do with central planning or design but was appropriated "unintentionally" and haphazardly by "men on the spot,":28. Kwarteng, described in reviews as an "old Etonian" with a Cambridge doctorate in history, commanded ephemeral attention with his composite cultural capital—Tory member of Parliament, Oxbridge, from Ghana, black. Despite laudatory reviews, his account was as problematic as the ad hoc history of imperial acquisitions he chronicled.

More disturbing was the appeal of his narrative. Not one review questioned his recourse to "individual" initiatives, neither to the connections made to the ad hoc forms of authority and sovereignty he claimed nor to his attribution that colonial violence was confined to the activities of "men on the spot." Kwarteng's book was a minor moment, and a tedious rehearsal of a familiar plot. Still, it was one of those small events that signal the appeal of "lessons" the United States should learn from its British predecessors, who, with the "goodwill" of "well-meaning" and well-heeled colonial civil servants, carried out imperial initiatives. British empire here remains no more than a "series of improvisations and haphazard policy-making," a formula for the "instability"

Few would take these occluded sites of blockage any longer as the perennial and pedestrian problem of historical retrieval hampered by disappeared documents, traumatized memory, and inevitable loss. But could we not take them as opportunities instead? Here I treat them as productive *touchstones of political contest* and subjects of analysis—*as occasions rather than obstacles* to ask how conceptual claims assert themselves; as entry points of inquiry into racism's multiplex genealogies; into the historiography of reason, colony, "legacies," "colonial intimacies," and imperial sovereignty. We need not partake in the high drama Foucault accords the task of banishing the deceptive work of concepts as "ready-made syntheses" or his (Enlightenment) quest to "drive [them] out from the darkness in which they reign." Still, we may profit from taking seriously what goes into their "ready-made" quality and the attributes that make them "obvious."[30]

Epistemic, legal, and political clarity have rarely been defining features of colonial polities. It is in the messy, troubled spaces of ambiguous colonial lineages that this book's venture uneasily rests. Rather than dismiss these sites as exceptional, marginal, or quasi-imperial space, here I treat them as key points of access to imperial logics that depend on the differential allocation of resources and rights—and the racialized distinctions in which they are cast.

Attending to these occlusions is a lesson that an immersion in the paper trails of colonial documents underscore, one that those who wrestle with the restricted rubrics of colonial official documents confront at every archival turn. The challenge of archival labor is to resist the reversion to received terms or the retreat to those in our ready repertoire—when one knows (in those dark conversations with oneself) that one has compromised, too quickly finessed what matters, and impatiently settled for a gloss. At issue could be any number of conceptual terms held too tightly and deactivated, depleted of their relational predicates and visceral force. What were the idioms in which "security" was flagged on colonial terrain; when and where do dangers appear; and what might their placement tell us about what

---

bequeathed to the former territories of empire. Kwarteng got it right and wrong: wrong that these partial sovereignties were not by design, right that they were far more varied than the favored imperial model of clear cut imperial borders suggests. His rendering simply rehearsed the welcome fiction that ambiguous forms of sovereignty were unintended consequences of individuals, not part and parcel of colonial histories and contemporary formations.

30. Foucault, *The Archaeology of Knowledge*, 22.

required "defense" as it was conceived in the nineteenth century and as it is redeployed today? Is a "paradigm of security" really, as Giorgio Agamben wrote, the hallmark of modern states any more than it has been foundational to the very installments of imperial authority and racial formations for so long?[31]

The concepts focused on here are those that have disrupted what I once assumed were obvious, fixture features about how imperial governance works. Warding off certainty is partly about prolonging how long one can admit to an unresolved space of one's own doubt—and, not least, the doubts and insisted-on certitudes of those whose perceptions and practices we imagine to comprehend. Attending more closely to how doubt manifests, is placated, soothed, dismissed, or remains dissonant puts strain on conceptual habits and methodological conventions. At its productive best, doubt opens to disruptive genealogies, truncated possibilities, and sharper questions about how those possibilities were foreclosed.

Not least, warding off certainty provides opportunities to ask what implicit knowledge makes up colonial common sense and why certain kinds of colonial situations have been taken as patent and prototypical and not others. In that pursuit, I think repeatedly throughout this book with how Foucault so acutely and sparingly defined an "event": as "the breach of self-evidence," as those moments in which what is taken as common sense no longer works, in which clarity gives way to doubt, in which epistemic habits fail to do their work, in which, even for a brief moment, what once seemed "normal" and "obvious" is open to reflection and no longer looks the same.

In these chapters, I take a number of different tacks in working to identify these occluded genealogies and identify their recursive qualities. Chapter 5, "On Degrees of Imperial Sovereignty," attempts to rethink the ambiguous zones of imperial governance, not as inert residuals, but as troubled geopolitical and social forms. Chapter 10, "Imperial Debris and Ruination," works cautiously in an experimental mode between the lively materiality of debris and "rot"—and their intangibilities. Here I take these metaphors as a provocation, as the anticipatory indistinct zone that may capture more than available concepts do and that may enable new conceptual purchase if still

31. Agamben makes this claim in a number of places and in different ways, such as where he writes that the "state of exception has been replaced by an unprecedented generalization of the paradigm of security as the normal technique of government": see Giorgio Agamben, *State of Exception* (Chicago: University of Chicago Press, 2005), 14.

evasive clarity. Each chapter asks what to do when colonial effects are literally dismembered from the conditions that made them possible, from their content and context, and called by other names. The terms substituted may not be problematic in themselves, but they are not innocuous. As subjects of conceptual politics, these other names condone the distractions of other attentions.

THE METHODOLOGICAL INSIGHTS OF GENEALOGY

Each of the chapters thinks in different ways with the work that Foucault's treatment of genealogy might help us do. I take genealogy to be not an abstract, "theoretical" program but a grounded, enabling political methodology. Genealogy has been subject to more than overexposure. And despite efforts, such as those of Wendy Brown, to underscore its political acuities and the traction it can offer to think history as a "field of eruptions, forces, emergences and partial formations," genealogy too often remains invoked as a fashionable substitute for "history," stripped of its opening to displaced histories as a political force and potential resource.[32]

Here I treat genealogy as a working strategy—a conceptual alert, if you will—that is responsive to historical roads not taken, to brazen and impossible alternatives proposed and squashed, to muted dissensions and suspended plans. Genealogy advocates for attention to messy, bellicose beginnings rather than originary moments for beginnings that seem to be re-marked and effaced over and again. Its focus on dissension and dispersion underscores contingencies as it avoids the assumptions of thinking historical trajectories as a coherent and singular master plan. As method, it insists on more than a refusal to search for distilled origins. It attends to differential histories (of battles lost or won) as the products and productive potentials that emerge from tracking unrealized possibilities, arrested and failed experiments that commonly remain unmarked as "proper" historical events because they were never fully realized and thus were not understood to have been possible or to have "happened."

This particular notion of history attuned to unachieved visions and interrupted imaginaries, attends to more than dispersion. It demands alertness

32. Wendy Brown, "Genealogical Politics" in Politics out of History (Princeton, NJ: Princeton University Press, 2001), 117. But see also Martin Saar, "Understanding Genealogy: History, Power and the Self," Journal of the Philosophy of History 2, 3 (September 2008): 295–314.

to those haphazard moments when narratives are revised, when dissension is demoted or displaced—to those small gestures that have made some historical accounts more cited, speakable, credible, and amenable to recounting than others. It demands a vigilant watch over what is strategically excised from the imagined colonial order of things and what is affirmed as clear, reasonable, and common sense. It reminds us to pause in the face of how we read for "relevance." One might take genealogy as a priming to the unsettled features of common sense, to differentials of worth embedded in the most seemingly innocuous interstices of words, intimacies, and things. It insists on perspectival agility—and thus a questioning of those histories that are imagined as more pressingly present than others.

Chapter 3, "A Deadly Embrace," is perhaps the clearest and most challenging genealogical work I have in mind. It begins with nineteenth-century documents in which colony and camp appear and reappear as distinct, substitutable, adjacent, and interdependent forms of containment: barbed wire, walls, checkpoints, internment camps within the colony, refugee camps that produce new (and expanded) borders for the colony, military camps outfitted with potential settlers.

Here the genealogies splay in different directions; the logics circle back and implicate one another again, with "defense" of society and security producing ever more sweeping containments and movement and enclosure. Tracking colony and camp in this way addresses what such a genealogy might look like that bridles against the convention of treating "colony" as a commonplace noun. It accredits its diffuse and seemingly disparate course through histories positioned as nonaligned. What emerges is not only the "colony" as a subjacent political concept. The "camp" also emerges as if in double exposure or, alternatively, as its twin, on its edges, not merely its mirror but its other face. The politics of confinement and containment emerge not on the fringes of that which defines it but as constitutive of its suffocating closures.

ON RECURSIVE HISTORIES: BEYOND RUPTURE AND CONTINUITY

Imperceptible moments of change, displacements, slidings, cracks, turn-abouts, gaps that increase, decrease, paths that get far, cave in and suddenly turn back.—Michel Foucault, The Politics of Truth, 1997

One distinctive, troubled feature for those of us whose research and pedagogy revolve around colonial histories of the past is how to convey how those histories remain present. Two distinct postures could be said to inform the contested and troubled fields in which colonial history figures. One analytic posture treats colonial history with clear temporal and spatial demarcations—well-documented histories whose violence has been scrupulously described; whose agents and subjects can be relatively clearly discerned; and whose disparate dispositions as colonizer and colonized are relatively clear, if not unproblematic. Such a posture often assumes that we know the colonial past and can now move easily to identify the more complex contemporary machinations of racial inequities as "colonial vestiges" or (unwelcome) "legacies" in the (post)colonial present. Within such a frame, colonial agents were distinctly different from those who manage politics today, committed to an imperial world that they wholeheartedly (but those who see themselves as critical world citizens decidedly would not) embrace. That moral high ground often turns the writing of colonial histories in Euro-American, French, German, and Dutch academe into a self-congratulatory tale, safely "Other" and distant, a purifying, redemptive exercise that distinguishes "us" from a distant "them."

The other posture refuses that clear break, insists on a more seamless continuation of colonial practices that pervade the present. But here the invocation can come in different historical and political semantic forms that slide between tenses and may implicitly or explicitly draw on metaphor, simile, or analogy to make a case. Thus, something may be designated "colonial" which is not to say that it is colonial but to say that it is like, akin to, or as oppressive as a colonial situation. Some may take the form of (1) analogic comparison to prior colonial practices (insinuating a future [desired or feared] trajectory); (2) condemnation of contemporary discriminatory practices (with the term "colonial" hurled more as an epithet, metaphorically hurled to cast blame); or (3) assertion that the present is the site of colonial practices in the active tense and that some populations are still subject to instantiations of those practices themselves.

The first stance depends on rupture; the latter, more on continuity. Both, I would argue, get us in trouble, leaving unaddressed (if not directly evading) the most difficult issues around the durability and distribution of colonial entailments that cling—vitally active and activated—to the present conditions of people's lives. The answers may be elusive in part because we have not yet even sufficiently formulated a workable set of questions about the multiple temporalities in which people live: what is past but not over; how the articulation of past and present may recede and resurface; how colonial relations are disparately and partially absorbed into social relations and ecological disparities and are productive of very distinct dispositions toward how—and, indeed, whether those histories matter today. Can we provide an adequate vocabulary to identify what a "colonial presence" looks like? Is it lodged in the figure of the stateless migrant, the killing machine of the drone, ashen landscapes, or the global philanthropic industry? Overarching "Theory" may not be the way to go. Recharting imperial effects seems to demand another sort of labor on another scale: one that attends to their partial, distorted, and piecemeal qualities, to uneven and intangible sedimentations that defy easy access in the face of the comforting contention that there really is no imperial order of things.

Interpretations of Foucault's historical analytics may be both part of the problem and an entry point for thinking beyond the bifurcated alternatives that continuity and rupture invite. While his treatment of historical transformations have been central to writings of colonial history, on this particular issue of historical ruptures, what has been borrowed from his analytical lexicon has been selective, at best. Discontinuity and rupture have long been taken as key features of Foucault's innovation, a rejection of the smooth continuities of the sorts of Braudelian history against which his interventions were aimed.[33]

But there is a more productive feature to his work on historical transformations, one that is rarely given the due it should rightly claim—namely, attention to what I call, for lack of a better term, "recursive analytics," or history as recursion. This sort of history is marked by the uneven, unsettled, contingent quality of histories that *fold back on themselves* and, in that refolding, reveal new surfaces, and new planes. Recursion opens to novel contingent possibilities.[34] "Recursion" in mathematics is a process of

33. See, e.g., Judith Revel, *Foucault, une pensée du discontinue* (Paris: Mille et Une Nuits, 2010). Revel offers a subtle analysis of Foucault's "strange singularity" and a nuanced treatment of "discontinuity" as his signature feature, 14. Pointing to the complex ways in which discontinuity figured for Foucault, she aptly quotes Foucault's introduction to a text of Canguilhem, republished in the late 1970s, "The history of discontinuity is not acquired once and for all. It is itself 'impermanent' and discontinuous." It is this element of his thinking with and about history as a deeply philosophical project to which her work is addressed: Revel, *Foucault, une pensée du discontinue*, 19–20.

34. "Recursivity" and "recursive functions" are mathematical concepts that figure in Niklas Luhmann's understanding of information systems but do different work from that I do here with a focus on historical movement: see Luhmann, *Theories of Distinction*, 98–99; Heinz von Foerster, "For Niklas Luhmann: How Recursive Is Communication?" trans. Richard Howe, in *Understanding Understanding* (New York: Springer, 2003), 305–23 (originally published in German as *Teoria Soziobiologica*, 2 [Milan: Franco Angeli,

"repeating items in a self-similar way." As I use it here, though, recursion is precisely *not* to imagine that social and political processes ever play out in a repetitive and mimetic fashion.[35] These histories are marked less by abrupt rupture or by continuity and not by repetition of the same (a point on which Foucault was to insist). Rather, they are processes of partial reinscriptions, modified displacements, and amplified recuperations.

There are some explicit moments in which Foucault underscored this approach, but more often these moves are gestured toward, more pronounced in his choice of vocabulary, and demonstrated rather than commented on. I was first struck by these "recursions" nearly twenty years ago. Vocabulary, as I said, is key. Thus, in volume 1 of *The History of Sexuality*, he wrote about an earlier symbolics of blood that is not replaced but, rather, "reanimated" and "converted" into a modern analytics of sexuality, the former "lending its weight" to a power exercised through the "deployment" of the latter.[36]

The force of that "weight" remained opaque, but its consequences for the analysis become increasingly clear. One has the sense that Foucault was in the midst of working these recalibrated techniques through for himself. Recursion seemed to underwrite both an analytics of historical process and a description of his own style of work. It makes its appearance most forcefully in the mid-1970s, but even in *The Archaeology of Knowledge*, where his concerns are so discursively bound, he sought "recurrent redistributions [that] reveal several pasts."[37] Jonathan Goldberg, commenting on the same "conversion" from

1993], 61–88). In a book about the generative work that anthropology can do by making room for other conceptualizations of truth and verification to subvert anthropological conventions of analysis, truth, and concept formation, Martin Holbraad uses the term "recursive anthropology" in what I see as a complementary but different venture. Both his and my own efforts are designed to unsettle the stability assigned to, and imagined to be, what concepts do: see Martin Holbraad, *Truth in Motion: The Recursive Anthropology of Cuban Divination* (Chicago: University of Chicago Press, 2012).

35. "Recursion," *Wikipedia, the Free Encyclopedia*, August 3, 2015. https://en.wikipedia.org/w/index.php?title=Recursionandoldid=674378167.

36. As I wrote at that time, "At issue here is not rupture, but the tension between rupture and recuperation. Thus, just as a reader may think that the thematic of blood disappears with the analytics of sexuality, Foucault reveals the symbolics of blood as a living discourse that 'lent its weight' to a power exercised through the deployment of sexuality": Ann Laura Stoler, *Race and the Education of Desire: Foucault's History of Sexuality and the Colonial Order of Things* (Durham, NC: Duke University Press, 1995), 38–39. See also Michel Foucault, *The History of Sexuality, Volume 1: An Introduction*, trans. Robert Hurley (New York: Vintage, 1990), 38.

37. Foucault, *The Archaeology of Knowledge*, 5.

a symbolics of blood to an analytics of sexuality, also noted a "*strange continuity with the old supposedly outmoded regimes of alliance*."[38]

"Strange continuity" is precisely the point about colonial presence. The colonial configurations are different, as are the actors, but the tactics of instantiating difference and forging an "internal enemy" are colonial reverberations with a difference—and with more than a distant semblance to earlier racial logics, engendered fears, and counterinsurgent tactics from which they gained their support. There is neither abrupt disappearance of the one nor clean and clear emergence of the other. At issue is how their force is exercised and reanimated. It is their weighting, combination, and recruitment of earlier idioms of practice and perception that map the configurations of change.

Recursion is a more explicit analytic strategy and description of how things work in the Collège de France lectures of 1976 on racism and biopolitics. In *Race and the Education of Desire*, I suggested that "what occupies Foucault (with respect to racisms) are the processes of recuperation, of the distillation of earlier discursive imprints, remodeled in new forms."[39] "Displacement" of certain elements and "conversion" of others are methodological linchpins to these processes and his analysis of them.[40] The alert is pivotal but suggests what *not* to expect (a return, a repetition, a clean break) more clearly than what to look for, leaving us to discern what is subject to conversion and what is displaced.[41]

Still, this is a far more challenging historical analytics than what came before—one that is emphatic about multiple forms of power operating not sequentially but simultaneously. Moreover, it opens to that "reflective prism," that "practico-reflexive system" Foucault sought to isolate in the lectures that would follow.[42] The adjective "reflexive" does important work, for it insists on

38. Jonathan Goldberg, *Sodometries: Renaissance Texts, Modern Sexualities* (New York: Fordham University Press, 2010), 16; emphasis added. This quote remains as a footnote, a measure of my tentative register of the issue at the time, in Stoler, *Race and the Education of Desire*, 40, fn. 53. But Matthew Kurtz deftly builds on that tentative claim: see Matthew Kurtz, "Ruptures and Recuperations of a Language of Racism in Alaska's Rural/Urban Divide," *Annals of the Association of American Geographers* 96, 3 (September 2006): 601–21.

39. Stoler, *Race and the Education of Desire*, 68.

40. Stoler, *Race and the Education of Desire*, 71.

41. In 1995, frustrated with his opacities, I simply noted that "what remains unclear . . . are the mechanisms that account for the selective recuperations of some elements and not others": Stoler, *Race and the Education of Desire*, 89.

42. Michel Foucault, *Sécurité, territoire, population: Cours au Collége de France, 1977–78* (Paris: Gallimard/Seuil, 2004), 282.

asking how something has come to be reflected on, has become made "real" as a discernible knowledge-thing epistemologically (how do we know what we know; how did they think they knew what they knew?) and politically (what are its effects and how does a set of reflexive, reflective strategic alignments in the making of knowledge create that which is purported only to be described)? The "prism" signals a crucial reworking, as well, because it is this "prism" that elsewhere comes to be vaguely designated as a "set of correlations" that will mark this analytic moment as different from what came before.

This is a more compelling analytics that not only makes more room for multiple forms of power operating simultaneously but also accounts for the reflexive thinking that their co-presence demands, the mechanisms weighing differently, recombining, and producing new calibrations and configurations with different effects. Foucault will state this most clearly in the lectures of 1978, but I would hold that is already operating as a strategy of historical analysis in the lectures of 1976 in how a much earlier "perception of the war between races" will reconfigure as a grid of intelligibility and operate differently when working through a biopolitical form.[43] In *Security, Territory, and Population* he puts it more boldly:

> So there is not a series of successive elements, the appearance of the new causing the earlier ones to disappear. There is not the legal age, then disciplinary age, and then the age of security. Mechanisms of security do not replace disciplinary mechanisms which would have replaced juridico-legal mechanisms. In reality you have a series of complex edifices . . . in which *what changes is the dominant characteristics, or more exactly, the system of correlations* between juridico-legal mechanisms, disciplinary mechanisms, and mechanisms of security.

And if this is not difficult enough, he strains our analytic capacities even more, noting that "there is another history . . . more general, but of course much more fuzzy history of the correlations and systems of the dominant feature which determine that, in a given society and for a given sector . . . a technology of security will be set up, taking up again and sometimes even multiplying juridical and disciplinary elements and redeploying them within its specific tactic."[44]

43. Michel Foucault, *Society Must Be Defended: Lectures at the Collège de France, 1975–76* (New York: Picador, 2003), 88.
44. Foucault, *Sécurité, territoire, population*, 8–9.

Thus, it is sometimes "reutilization," such as within state racism, of an earlier anti-Semitism, "which had developed for other reasons." Or, as we find with the new technology of power in the second half of the eighteenth century, it "is not disciplinary" Still, it "does not exclude disciplinary technology, . . . but dovetails into it, integrates it, modifies it to some extent, and above all uses it by sort of infiltrating itself, embedding itself in existing disciplinary techniques."[45] Here Foucault compels us to turn away from totalizing regimes and analysis and toward the ways in which new techniques "exist at a different level, on a different scale," with a "different bearing/surface area" (*une autre surface portante*) and "using different instruments."[46]

To my mind, this insight is enormous. We no longer ask about the definitive break between "new" and "old" forms of power replacing each other wholesale; "colonial" as opposed to "postcolonial" makes much less sense, with the former "leftover," dead matter in a wholly new present. We are asked instead to cut a different swath through the given rubrics for macropolitics—democratic, colonial, fascist, and their conceptual knowledge-bearing supports, those "ready-made syntheses," that conceal so much more than they reveal, that confer common features contrived as shared. Instead we are urged to attend to scaling, to co-temporalities, to the specific sites where they are threaded through one another; not to what particular forms of governance are and call themselves but what a sedimented set of governing techniques with a different distribution do.

In this "recursive analytics," there is no question of an earlier historical discourse called on in toto, but rather in strategically altered, piecemeal combination. Again, what is retrieved is not a matter of mere recurrence. It can never look the same. And again, too, the language is crucial to the analytics: at issue are amplified reinscriptions, "retranscriptions," and recuperations.[47] Deleuze offers a related observation on Foucault's analytics: reactivations and traces are rarely isomorphic with what came before. They can cross thresholds, occur at different levels, cut transversal swaths on a diagonal axis—or, as Foucault would express it, in "orthogonal articulation."[48] This is a luminous insight and again is methodologically and historically difficult

45. Foucault, *Society Must Be Defended*, 89, 242.
46. Foucault, *Society Must Be Defended*, 216; Foucault, *Sécurité, territoire, population*, 242.
47. Foucault, *Society Must Be Defended*, 216.
48. Gilles Deleuze, *Foucault*, repr. ed. (London: Continuum, 2012), 22; Foucault *Sécurité, territoire, population*, 253.

to track and discern. If colonial "reactivations" do not occur at the levels at which they once appeared, on the planes of social relations in which they were once activated, how do we identify their morphings and morphologies? How do we cipher the readjustments that activate familiar forms on new planes?

Such protean forms with moving parts require those charged with governance—their practitioners—to be opportunistic, to reflect on the consequences of readjustments in calculated consideration of more direct pressure or less, less discipline or more "self-cultivation." Such recursive moves invite us to refuse the quick resort to "before" and "after"—and even to work against the wooden, if all too common, conceptual containers of "past" and "present."

This recalibration of Foucault's thought makes crucial sense of his understanding of the "reflective" quality of governance (how they thought about how they thought). For imperial governance, where disciplinary, sovereign, and biopolitical power quintessentially meet in the administering of security, these perceptions and practices prompt an avid concern not only for what is but for *what might be*. As we shall see in chapter 6, "Reason Aside," the temporal thrust of the biopolitical state, with racism buttressing its logic, manifests in an obsessive concern for the protection of society from itself, its internal threats, producing an ever amplified attention to the conditional, subjunctive, and future tense. Predictive assessments join here with preemptive angst in the name of security for (a Euro-colonial) society's defense. "Security" has long been the conceptual and political nexus of the expulsions and containments in which imperial formations invest. They are decidedly not the same as—but they are embedded in—the consolidated and honed technologies of security that thrive today.

There is no methodological programmatic plan in Foucault's projects— an endeavor he adamantly refused, a conceit he claimed to abhor. Nevertheless, this quality of recursion is at once an analytic thread and a methodological incitement to work more closely in the obscured folds of history and not to assume, with all due respect to Marx, that earlier imperial practices were tragic and that the distilled, revised, and reassembled techniques in which that history bears on the present are merely repeated as farce.

Foucault's struggle with the nature of recursive history, as a history that builds on earlier strategies of governance without rehearsing what became before, offers the closest rendition I know of how to think about how colonial histories are taken up and "recombined" with enduring presence today.[49] They alert us to avoid the assumption that they should appear in the same locations and with the similitude of easily identifiable forms. Few studies of Foucault explicitly seize on the specifically historical implications of his insight or work through how these recuperations, reactivations, and recombinations of familiar forms pre-adhere to new practices while obscuring relational histories that have been pulled apart.[50] Recursion surfaces in both what is rendered as imperial aftermath and what is discerned as active imperial forms. Thinking with the processes to which a recursive sense of imperial history attends may be an opening to alternative ways to understand what imperial debris might look like, as I explore in chapter 10; how racialized dispositions are entrenched and refigured; how people's capacities are disabled or incited; and how colonial pasts are mobilized to matter as political acts of the present. As Luhmann reminds us, what we take to be objects of those whom we observe in their acts of observing are "nothing but" products of the very observing systems of which they are a part that use and reuse their previous distinctions. The formulation is unduly involuted, but I think it captures something fundamentally similar to what I hope to pursue in the chapters that follow.

49. On Foucault's sustained concern in later years, not with epochal breaks but with "redeployments" and "recombinations," see Stephen J. Collier, "Topologies of Power: Foucault's Analysis of Political Government beyond 'Governmentality,'" *Theory, Culture and Society* 26, 6 (November 1, 2009): 78–108, whose incisive treatment of Foucault's analysis makes a complementary observation from a different vantage point. See also Paul Rabinow's earlier insistence that Foucault would turn away from "epochal" thinking in his later work: Paul Rabinow, *Anthropos Today: Reflections on Modern Equipment* (Princeton, NJ: Princeton University Press, 2003), 14. Both note this later modification. I would argue that his commitment to "ruptures" was a strategic intervention from the start, responsive to the prevailing modes of historical narrative at the time, never one that he categorically embraced *tout court*.

50. For an important exception (but oriented to a very different argument about the relationship between philosophical and historical inquiry), see Phillipe Artières and Matthieu Potte-Bonneville, *D'après Foucault: Gestes, luttes, programmes* (Paris: Contemporary French Fiction, 2012). Artières and Potte-Bonneville describe *Discipline and Punish* as a text with a "relatively linear trajectory" that nevertheless, from a "historical point of view is broken/interrupted in the middle of the book" in such a way that "Foucault carries out a striking turn back (*retour en arrière*). . . . He goes back, from the 18th century to the 17th century, and . . . retraces at the same moment the historical period that he just finished analyzing." As they so keenly put it, "At the same time, Foucault complicates the supposed unity of each period, showing that the classical age, in a sense, while organized by the political figure of the sovereign, is simultaneously penetrated by the implementation of another type of power relation." They call this feature a "double dispersion": Artières and Potte-Bonneville, *D'après Foucault*, 100–101.

Recursion as both a mode of history making and a mode of historical analysis speaks to a problematic that threads throughout this book and for which each chapter seeks to find an adequate vocabulary. Is it possible to dispense with the sharply defined temporalities that past, present, and future invoke as discrete time frames? Can we use these terms but still understand that they are not sequential ways of living time and colonial duress, but they can exist simultaneously, recessed and seized on, with different weightings?

For my purposes here, I make a distinction between a "colonial present" in the sense that Derek Gregory so appropriately uses that term to describe Iraq and Palestine today, and a colonial *presence* that I see marking the interstices of what once was and what is, reworking both.[51] Thinking with the multiple tenses that "colonial presence" intends to invoke is one of the ways in which I try to distinguish between a past that is imagined to be over but persists, reactivates, and recurs in transfigured forms. But it is also to argue that colonial sensibilities, distinctions, and discriminations are not just leftovers, reappointed to other time and place. Nor are they abstract "legacies." Colonial presence is an effort to make room for the complex ways in which people can inhabit enduring colonial conditions that are intimately interlaced with a "postcolonial condition" that speaks in the language of rights, recognitions, and choices that enter and recede from the conditions of duress that shape the life worlds we differently inhabit.

These temporal overlays and the sensory regimes (of sound, touch, and taste) that can bring the persistence of a past to the immediacy of the present are issues that Henri Bergson and Maurice Merleau-Ponty so famously articulated in their work and that subsequent philosophers have called on to rethink duration and temporalities.[52] The philosopher Alia Al-Saji makes a powerful case for this simultaneity of past and present with a vocabulary shared with Merleau-Ponty and Bergson, drawing on Merleau-Ponty's

51. Derek Gregory, *The Colonial Present: Afghanistan, Palestine, Iraq* (Malden, MA: Blackwell, 2004). For an interesting and resonant, if somewhat different, treatment of "presence" as a "theoretical paradigm," see Ranjan Ghosh and Ethan Kleinberg, eds., *Presence: Philosophy, History, and Cultural Theory for the Twenty-First Century* (Ithaca, NY: Cornell University Press, 2014).

52. For a very different engagement with Bergson's understanding of "duration," see Souleymane Bachir Diagne, "Bergson in the Colony: Intuition and Duration in the Thought of Senghor and Iqbal," *Qui Parle* 17, 1 (October 1, 2008): 125–45.

"*simultaneité passé-present*" to describe the "now," but with a precision that is distinctively her own. Joseph Massad, as we shall see in chapter 2, signals that those subject to colonial conditions live in a different temporality from those who are protected and secured from their damaging effects.[53] I am more convinced that few selves are properly "buffered" from the weight of colonial relations. But in attending to the quality of that distribution and the intensity of what has to be borne and by whom, I call on his insights to amend his claim. Raphaëlle Branche, the French historian of the violence of colonial Algeria, similarly writes about the "coexistence" rather than the "division" that produces a historicity that cannot be untangled from its historical ontology—a historicity shaped by its colonial formation.[54]

Sometimes at issue might be what Merleau-Ponty referred to as "*un passé qui n'a jamais été present* (a past that has never been present), calling on the possibility of activating those elements and sensibilities of a past that could not be realized or "actualized" at an earlier moment but that "adhere"—shadowed or amplified in the present in new and unexpected ways.[55] The issue of how to think about and imagine the past and the metaphors called on to invoke it—its very stability—is crucial to the political and affective practices that speak to colonial presence today. Al-Saji insists on recognizing the "instability" of the past to attend to what gets released, transformed, activated, and clogged within contemporary situations. "Instability" of the past is a good starting point for thinking about what is mobilized of the past and what features of earlier relationalities are requisitioned for new projects and thereby rendered more durable than others.

"Memory" may be inadequate to account for these quixotic regroupings. Memory suggests that the past resides predominantly in how we find to remember it, rather than in the durable and intangible forms of its mak-

53. Joseph Andoni Massad, "The 'Post-colony' Colony: Time, Space, and Bodies in Palestine/Israel," in *The Persistence of the Palestinian Question: Essays on Zionism and the Palestinians* (New York: Routledge, 2006), 13–40.

54. Raphaëlle Branche, *La torture et l'armée pendant la guerre d'Algérie, 1954–1962* (Paris: Gallimard, 2001). See also David Lloyd's thoughtful work in *Irish Times*, where he writes about "multiple and often incommensurable temporalities for which the terms 'tradition' and 'modernity' are only partial and certainly inadequate designations": David Lloyd, *Irish Times: Temporalities of Modernity* (Dublin: Field Day and Keough-Naughton Institute for Irish Studies, University of Notre Dame, 2008), 6.

55. Maurice Merleau-Ponty, *Phenomenology of Perception* (New York: Routledge, 2013), 242; Maurice Merleau-Ponty, *The Visible and the Invisible* (Evanston: Northwestern University Press 1968), 244.

ing. Colonial entailments endure in more palpably complicated ways. As Al-Saji puts it, "The past . . . overflows that which can be consciously recollected."[56] Arguing that "the past retains the trace of its own temporal becoming," she demurs from the notion that the modality of pastness implies "irreversibility," "immutability," and completion. Instead, she reaches for another formulation that sees the past "so close to the present as to be its lining." It is here that she, too, draws on Merleau-Ponty's enigmatic phrase "a past that has never been present" in *The Phenomenology of Perception*, written at the tail end of one catastrophic Holocaust moment and on the cusp of another: the Nakba.[57]

A "past that has never been present" is not a phrase that Foucault cited, but the genealogical method could be construed as attempting to capture just that: to think about sites of confluence and cohabitations in abeyance, about the muffled possibilities that defy the fixed divisions so deeply etched in the incompatible common sense of categories of people pitted against one another in colonial situations as they attempt to extricate themselves from those social derangements. These cleavages may be built and demolished with mortar and stone, but they are not fixed once and for all by them.

The resonant call on recursion here is hard to miss. Recursive histories may be about not only how imperial formations call on their earlier manifestations but, more importantly how those who live them move in and around the constraints imposed—the visions failed and the desperate, indignant, and defiant acts that duress can produce. My responses to the quandary of an impoverished political lexicon for describing this retroactive and refractive pull that presses on the present are provisional, at best. This response merely underscores that the convention of past, present, and future are not only inadequate. They occlude how imperial regimes work and what they do to those living the subaltern and privileged sites within them.[58] We need to do better to understand the nature of imperial duress,

56. See Alia Al-Saji, "The Past," in *Political Concepts: A Critical Lexicon* at www.political concepts.org. Forthcoming.

57. I thank Alia Al-Saji for sharing her reflections on Merleau-Ponty's treatment of history and especially her essay " 'A Past Which Has Never Been Present': Bergsonian Dimensions in Merleau-Ponty's Theory of the Prepersonal," *Research in Phenomenology* 38, 1 (September 2008): 41–71. I also thank Keith Whitmoyer, on whose dissertation defense in philosophy on Merleau-Ponty I assisted in 2013, and who introduced me to Al-Saji's work.

58. A bibliographic accounting for the various ways in which students of colonialism have attempted to reckon directly or indirectly with these temporalities would call for another essay. But they might be tracked through the range of historically inflected

the anxieties and fears it produces, the potentialities it short-circuits, the possibilities it enables, and the force it galvanizes to ensure that viable futures are not foreclosed. Accounting for what duress looks like needs the poetics of thought to make its case. Whether this entails calling on poets or finding that poetics are already central to concept formation, as both George Steiner and Giorgio Agamben rightly claim, the sensorial insights are crucial to the critical impulses that hover unarticulated on our tongues and that flourish in what some are already saying and others of us cannot hear.[59]

---

ethnographies that have also struggled to come up with a language adequate to the task. A very incomplete list might include Richard Price, who writes that "time . . . is like an old–fashioned Martiniquan concertina—alternately being squeezed and pulled apart, compressing some things, stretching out others": Richard Price, *The Convict and the Colonel* (Boston: Beacon, 1998), xi. It might also include Heonik Kwon, *Ghosts of War in Vietnam* (Cambridge: Cambridge University Press, 2008); Jennifer Cole, *Forget Colonialism? Sacrifice and the Art of Memory in Madagascar* (Berkeley: University of California Press, 2001); the contributions in Ann Laura Stoler, ed., *Haunted by Empire: Geographies of Intimacy in North American History* (Durham, NC: Duke University Press, 2006); David Scott, *Omens of Adversity: Tragedy, Time, Memory, Justice* (Durham, NC: Duke University Press, 2014); Gary Wilder, *Freedom Time: Negritude, Decolonization, and the Future of the World* (Durham, NC: Duke University Press, 2015). Both Scott and Wilder identify their central concerns to be "with temporality" and Wilder, to be with "utopian potentiality"—to name but a very few.

59. Perhaps our resources are already abundant and available in the explosive power of poetry and literature and the generative conceptual forms they enable: see, e.g., Mahmoud Darwish, *In the Presence of Absence*, trans. Sinan Antoon (Brooklyn, NY: Archipelago, 2011), which has so figured for those writing on the long colonial present in Palestine; Raja Shehadeh, *A Rift in Time: Travels with My Ottoman Uncle* (London: Profile, 2010). The spare, piercing prose in Assia Djebar, *Algerian White: A Narrative* (New York: Seven Stories, 2000), evokes how it feels to lose one's dearest friends to a colonial war and then to an internal Algerian one. Or we might look to the dark description of a ruinous colonial past as "the rot [that] remains when the men are gone"—my opening to thinking the politics of metaphor, concept-work, and imperial debris in the final chapter: Derek Walcott, "The Antilles: Fragments of Epic Memory," in *Nobel Lectures in Literature: 1991–1995*, ed. Sture Allen (Amsterdam: Elsevier, 1997), 20.

RAW CUTS

PALESTINE, ISRAEL, AND (POST)COLONIAL STUDIES

If there is good reason to think with the production of occlusions, histories of colonial recursions, and the durabilities of imperial duress, the treatment of Palestine in (post)colonial studies offers a prominent site and dramatically disturbing exemplar of the need to do so. One could argue that (post) colonial studies as an academic field, in fact, emerged precisely around such issues, excising from the start the very forms of colonial governance and imperial presence that motivated one of its founding moments in Edward Said's work—with respect to Palestine. This chapter in part addresses an irony: the crucial role *Orientalism* played in launching (post)colonial studies and the failure of *The Question of Palestine* to animate an appraisal of Israeli state policies as understood in colonial terms. In so doing, it opens to a broader set of questions about the constrictions that have informed studies of colonial situations and the temporalities of imperial formations.

While this book reflects on what we know about the social and political ecologies on which colonialisms thrive, it has been more immediately shaped by the celebrations of a "benevolent" U.S. empire since 9/11, the war in and on Iraq, and most forcefully over the past six years as I have been making my way to Palestine:[1] to Nazareth, Haifa, Jaffa, Nablus, and to refugee camps squeezed on their borders, through tracts of farmland severed from their owners' homes by the "security wall" as it was expanded to slice through ever larger swaths of Palestinian villages cut off from one another,

---

1. Robert Kagan, "The Benevolent Empire," *Foreign Policy* III (July 1, 1998): 24–35.

from access roads, and from their own gardens and agricultural land; to Hebron, where Israeli soldiers surveil the dark and bolted market from above the quieted hub of activity through a net to shield Palestinian inhabitants from the garbage and heavy objects thrown on them by Hebron's Israeli settlers; to Ramallah, again and again, while lecturing and teaching at Birzeit University, where checkpoints and roadblocks can make getting to classes for faculty and students not only unpredictable but a noxious, humiliating, and failed effort; and then to Bil'in (two miles east of the Green Line on the outskirts of Ramallah) to join Abdullah Abu Rahmah, his children, and the throngs of local and international supporters in the weekly demonstration against Israeli state policies that since 2005 has cut the village off from 60 percent of its land.[2] Immediacy and colonial history collude and collide in this site of colonial presence.

TO PALESTINIANS AND Middle East scholars, none of this is news. Bil'in garnered the attention that so many more villages marginal to Israeli security forces have not. Still, it is business as usual in the expansive and calibrated strategies of dispossession practiced by the Israeli state and its settler enclaves. The fact that this is no longer news to a much broader readership today is also strikingly new over the past fifteen-odd years (a subject I return to later in this chapter). But for those of us who have studied colonial histories and comparative colonialism elsewhere for decades, the fact that

2. "MAG Closes File in 2009 Killing of Bassem Abu Rahmeh," press release, B'Tselem, September 10, 2013, http://www.btselem.org/press_releases/20130910 _bassem_abu_rahmeh_killing_file_closed. Abdullah Abu Rahmah's brother, Bassem, was killed in Bil'in in 2009 by a high-velocity tear gas grenade that hit his chest. While Wikipedia is always a suspect source for those who imagine themselves careful scholars, the entry for Bil'in, and the fifty-four references to court proceedings and newspaper coverage of the events is an excellent place to get a sense of how far Israeli state officials have been willing to go. Since 2005, Abdullah Abu Rahmah has led a weekly Friday demonstration to the hilltop bordering the security wall where Israeli soldiers, in an effort to break up the nonviolent throngs of villagers, international demonstrators, and photographers, shoot rubber bullets and tear gas bombs. Some of that is now over. The area between the Israel barrier and village has been declared a closed military zone: Bil'in, and Abu Rahmah, who was imprisoned for fifteen months, have been the subject of documentaries and books and have been at the center of an ongoing set of cases against Israel in the International Court of Justice in The Hague. The case against the Israeli state in Bassem Abu Rahmah's death was dismissed by Israel's military advocate general (MAG) four and a half years after his death because of "lack of evidence."

Israel's colonial profile and politics have been visible and documented for so long but not widely "recognizable" as a colonizing project as it is increasingly viewed today deserves some reflection and renewed attention.

While some of the chapters of this book were written before those visits, virtually each of them speaks back in some uncanny way through a set of conditions that crystallize in the Palestinian/Israeli situation. This is not to argue that Palestine is the key to a new colonial studies, but it is to argue that the decades in which it has been held at bay and relegated to the margins—especially by those of us who might otherwise claim some alliance with some version of critical colonial studies—is symptomatic of a broader set of conceptual and political elisions in the field as a whole.

In attending to Palestine's "colonial situation," the possible "lessons" are at once meager and too many and hard to choose among.[3] One obvious choice would be to offer a comparative perspective that takes its cue from the insights of colonial and postcolonial studies, the cumulative methodological and conceptual cautions that a particular "we" have considered to heed about the forms that colonial governance takes; to learn from the creative strategies of refusal marshaled by colonial subjects and by students of colonialism who have sought to redraw and revamp the archival field, challenging the authoritative truth claims on which command over the facts of imperial matters for so long have continued to rest. But even a brief perusal of the subjects and sites to which (post)colonial studies has attended seems to hinder such a pursuit, for as a field of critical scholarship, it has produced an archive that, not unlike colonial archives themselves, is ironically selective, evasive, and problematic.

The most striking fact, should one think to profit from the ample drove of colonial histories tracked elsewhere for their insights in thinking through the Palestinian/Israeli situation, is that for so long Israel and

---

3. I refer to "lessons" here using shudder quotes to note the profusion of lessons talk that emerged among U.S. and European political pundits and their favored historians after 9/11 with respect to what we might all learn from empires past (so often imagined to be "good lessons" to follow). But even "lessons" in a critical vein, as in the Social Science Research Council's conference of that title in 2003, in which I took part, is a demanding enterprise. It entails making explicit the commensurabilities on which comparisons are made and the "politics of comparison" in which different approaches to empire invest. For some of the problems confronted in imagining that lessons are easily drawn, see the contributions in Craig Calhoun, Frederick Cooper, Kevin W. Moore, and Social Science Research Council, eds., *Lessons of Empire: Imperial Histories and American Power* (New York: New Press, 2006). See also chapter 5 in this volume.

Palestine's colonial history of the present has remained systematically out of sight, largely absent from what long remained the canon. One could even argue that lessons are difficult to draw because the dominant definition of what constituted colonial and postcolonial conditions circumvented—and, indeed, seemed defined to exclude—Palestine/Israel and the U.S. presence as sites of inquiry. One could go further. The case could be made that much of (post)colonial studies actually defined its critical project as a venture whose analytic space circumvented the conceptual and political inclusion of Israeli politics. Instead it submitted to Israel's "exceptional" status, despite the fact that it was in just these fractious spaces that Said's work developed and, that long before Said's interventions, marked the sites of colonial intervention.

This might be construed as an exaggerated claim. It is *not* to argue that those of us who have been participants in the field intended to embrace its exclusions and unstated strictures; nor is it to argue that there have not been those who have produced work that has meticulously analyzed the historical and ongoing practices and principles of Israeli strategies and identified the Israeli state as a colonial one. Numbers of journalists, scholars, and activists—Palestinians and others from around the world— have done just that for decades, from the 1960s onward. Still, it remains more significant that Palestine has not been present as one of the places where we might identify the recursive qualities of colonial interventions in their contemporary and vividly violent form. The colonial principles that underlie Israeli governance have not been treated until recently by those who have self-identified with "post-colony theory" or among a broader field of historical and anthropological scholarship for whom neither the Nakba nor the expulsion of 750,000 Palestinians from their homes deserved mention.

Densities of scholarship accumulate and bear weight, as it were, beyond our backs. Looking to the initial formation of (post)colonial studies as a recognizable field, the evidence at the very least demands that we ask what happened when the field was launched to generate its selective directions. In questioning both what stabilized the core concerns of (post)colonial studies and what was pushed to its edges, I have found myself seeking over the past decade to turn the obvious question around: to ask not what the quintessential and privileged sites of colonial practice might tell us about Palestinian/Israeli histories of this present but, instead, how an examination of the politics of scholarship and the recursive history of colonial impositions on Palestinians might challenge what we imagine we know about colonial situations and imperial formations.

Resituating Palestine/Israel not on the fringes of colonial studies but at its *fulcrum* places focus on the sustained, cumulative, modular pedagogy that colonial states and imperial formations have shared and the knowledge production, strategic practices, weaponry, and people (military, arms manufacturers, intelligence "experts") that have circulated in these domains. It stretches our capacities to grapple with imperial forms—that of the United States, most notably, not only with respect to its "own" colonies, recognized as such, of the Philippines, Samoa, or Puerto Rico. At issue are the multiple ways in which U.S. interventions in other polities have shaped the distributed destitutions of our times. Thus, it opens not least to a point I repeatedly have made and that underwrites this venture, fleshed out more fully in chapter 4 on degrees of imperial sovereignty—namely, that uncertain domains of jurisdiction; sliding scales of rights; and ad hoc exemptions from the law on the basis of racial, cultural, and religious differences produced and protected in the name of a relentless demand for ever broader scales of "security" are guiding and defining principles of imperial policy and colonial situations. These are not exceptions to colonial norms; nor are they ad hoc, reactive measures. They are the very coordinates of how these polities work. Inside and outside, visibility and invisibility, public and private are bifurcations that colonial situations scramble, reinsert, and transgress. As important, imperial regimes have long been contingent on partial visibility, sustaining the capacity to remain unaccountable ones. Each of these features is part of the very fabric of Palestinian/Israeli relations. These bifurcations are not only inherent in the multilevel socio-technological features of Israel's security regime. Sliding scales of rights, legal opacities, and the protections and privileges provided to Israeli settlers sometimes take forms that are even starker and more carefully guarded than those in the earlier histories that stand as the prototypes of colonial domination.

EXCISIONS: COLONIAL STUDIES IN ITS FORMATION

The questions I pose are these: Why has consideration of Palestine/Israel remained absent for so long from the field of (post)colonial studies, and what has changed to figure it as appropriately open to colonial comparison now? Why did it seem aberrant for so long to the study of colonial situations, and what were the conditions that rendered it so? The first thing to observe is that whatever the answer might be, what is glaring is the circumspection around *the very question,* how easily it has been muted in some quarters and elsewhere assumed as obvious. More troubling has been the ways in which key issues have been formulated so that the question need not be posed.

Let us begin at one "beginning" among many: the commonly shared emergence of (post)colonial studies as a designated field. The year is 1978. Turning back to the moment that *Orientalism* hit the shelves and seemed almost singlehandedly to spawn what was to become the cross disciplinary field of (post)colonial studies, a curious and disturbing set of elisions was there from the start. A sharp partition—a wall, if you will—separated the uptake of Said's work on the historical, cultural coordinates of Orientalism as a "configuration of power" (one of the many definitions on which he insisted) from his simultaneous work on the recursive and current history of colonization and U.S. empire that figured so centrally in his book *The Question of Palestine,* written during the same year *Orientalism* went to press.

The elision was not only with respect to *The Question of Palestine.* There was selective treatment and appeal of the issues to which *Orientalism* itself was imagined to speak and those aspects of it that garnered scholarly attention. One could argue that the profusion of scholarship that *Orientalism* generated across the disciplines carefully avoided some of its most central claims—namely, that it was "not only about French and British empire in the eighteenth and nineteenth centuries, but as Said insisted throughout the book, about the U.S."[4] As he was to remind his audience in 2003, "*Orientalism's* first page opens with a 1975 description of the Lebanese Civil War."[5] It did not begin with a literary analysis of *Middlemarch* or *Jane Eyre.*

Said's book was not just a study of how colonial "traces" permeated British literature of the nineteenth century.[6] His powerful analysis of literature was never an end in itself but a means to establish a located problematization and political argument. It was about how "large political concerns" of

4. Ann Laura Stoler, "A Tribute to Edward Said," quoted in Nadia Abu El-Haj, "Edward Said and the Political Present," *American Ethnologist* 32, 4 (November 1, 2005): 550.

5. Edward Said, "Orientalism Once More," lecture delivered on the occasion of the awarding of the degree of Doctor Honoris Causa at the Institute of Social Studies, The Hague, Netherlands, May 21, 2003.

6. Nadia El-Haj also made the crucial point that "readings of Orientalism . . . effectively both elevated and neutered Said's contribution by stripping it of its specific history and politics": El-Haj, "Edward Said and the Political Present," 539.

"three great empires—British, French, American" shared the "intellectual and imaginative territory" such writing produced.[7] More important, it was a "history of the present" and about our contemporary world. If many heard the call to attend to "the present," curiously—and in what can only be called a patterned fashion—even treatments of U.S. empire made a relatively wide berth around the United States in the Middle East (a subject seen more as the domain of "diplomatic history" and "foreign relations") and the sustained Israeli degradation of the conditions of Palestinians. There was nothing new about these circumventions, either. As Tim Mitchell cogently argued in his analysis of the emergence of Middle East studies in the then popular paradigm of "area studies," as early as 1962 Middle East studies "deliberately excluded the state of Israel (and thus the Palestine question), in part to limit "controversy" among the region's "experts" who thus were able to avoid "sensitive" issues of which the Arab-Israeli war was central.[8] Strikingly, this occurred at an intellectual and political juncture in which the politics of knowledge was prominent—as a left-leaning swathe of academe was condemning counterinsurgency operations in Vietnam and Project Camelot and a significant portion of academic regional experts were collaborating with the U.S. Central Intelligence Agency (CIA), the protective wall around Israel remained unbreached.[9]

In this context, *Orientalism* became one of the most cited books across academe, enabling a multidisciplinary assault on "the West" as a concept, on the politics of high European literature and its surface and subjacent racialized plots. More broadly, those of us pursuing colonial histories turned to the work of nineteenth-century European mapmakers, voyagers, geographers, and botanists as "handmaidens" (the term Kathleen Gough famously used to condemn the field of anthropology a decade earlier) to document these imperial pursuits and their civilizing projects—subjects that confirmed a "critical" stance toward colonial historiography while leaving untouched the contemporary "persistence and the durability of saturating hegemonic

7. Edward Said, *Orientalism* (New York: Vintage, 1979), 15.

8. Timothy Mitchell, "The Middle East in the Past and Future of Social Science," in *The Politics of Knowledge: Area Studies and the Disciplines*, ed. David L. Szanton (Berkeley: University of California Press, 2004), 74–118.

9. For a recent history of "Project Camelot," the counterinsurgency study begun by the U.S. Army in 1964, and the response of academics working in Latin America when they learned about it, see Joy Rohde, *Armed with Expertise: The Militarization of American Social Research during the Cold War* (Ithaca, NY: Cornell University Press, 2013).

systems" that exemplified Israel's unfettered colonizing project and instantiations of U.S. support.[10]

The Question of Palestine, by contrast, not only received little of the acclaim accorded to Orientalism; rather it was almost hushed as though unseemly and indiscreet, relegated in academic vernacular to the "Other (politically committed) Said." Hardly a nod was made to the fact of the proximity of—and confluence between—the two books.[11] The lines were drawn without much ado and with hardly any critical comment. But one could approach their separation differently: The intellectual work and political evasions that made that division so "easy to think" and readily accepted defined the geopolitics of a critically emergent field—a field that otherwise and elsewhere took pride in defining its task as progressive, unshackled from political conventions—a signature of its claim to subversive scholarly intervention.

Aijaz Ahmad was one of the few to argue that The Question of Palestine would be the work for which Said would and should be remembered (deeming Orientalism "deeply flawed").[12] Ahmad was roundly disparaged by many colleagues when he made this claim in a book published in 1992. His first claim was simply ignored, overshadowed by his virulent critique of Orientalism. But one could ask whether his insight about The Question of Palestine was too quickly dismissed, for it is considering The Question of Palestine and Orientalism as conjoined projects that might have served to point to the global network of power relations that linked British colonial history, the Israeli occupation of Palestine, and the former's alignments with western European and U.S imperial agendas meant to manage Middle East politics and "contain" Islam. Had this been appreciated in (post)colonial studies, colonization might not have remained a description of a historical phenom-

10. Kathleen Gough, "Anthropology and Imperialism," Monthly Review 19, 11 (April 2, 1968): 12–17, 12; Said, Orientalism, 14. In 1971, seven years before Orientalism came out, Arghiri Emmanuel, a Marxist economist who was born in Greece, then lived in Belgian Congo before moving to France, named Israel a "spearhead of imperialism" and a "secessionist colonial state": see Arghiri Emmanuel, "White-Settler Colonialism and the Myth of Investment Imperialism," New Left Review 1, 73 (June 1972): 35–57. The original essay in French is Arghiri Emmanuel, "Le colonialisme des 'poor-whites' et le mythe de l'impérialisme d'investissement," L'Homme et la Société, 22, 1 (1971): 67–96.

11. As Said notes in the introduction, The Question of Palestine was written "during 1977 and the early part of 1978": Edward Said, The Question of Palestine (New York: Vintage, 1979), xxxv.

12. Aijaz Ahmad, In Theory: Classes, Nations, Literatures, repr. ed. (London: Verso, 2000), 160.

enon; nor would colonial governance of Palestine have been reserved only to describe British colonial rule and thus remained relegated to the past, in the more comforting *passé composé*.

RETHINKING THE "EVENT"

I would argue that the resounding "event" here is not the much hailed publication of *Orientalism*, frequently invoked as the acclaimed moment, but the disclaimed one: the radical sundering, severing, and decoupling of the two political, conceptual, and empirical projects. If a historical event is, as Michel Foucault thought it, "a breach of self-evidence"—a moment in which common sense fails to do its work, when singularities become visible, and when people rethink what they imagine they know, how they know it, and what they take knowledge, epistemology, and the political to be—this failure to see Said's two studies as pieces of a singular effort was a diagnostic rupture and, potentially, a first order event. Granted, one could argue that it was only so for a specific corner of the reading public—namely, the intellectual and academic quarters of the Anglophone and Francophone world (although the book was translated into twenty-six languages, as Said noted when it appeared to much praise in Vietnamese).[13] But given the politically critical capital with which Said was endowed, it reached far beyond those who saw their work as addressing what he identified as a hegemonic vision of "the Arab" in visual and literary culture. As his friend and interlocutor Eqbal Ahmad put it, *Orientalism*'s achievement was "to put imperialism at the center of Western civilization."[14] Although Ahmad's appraisal of *Orientalism*'s import was perhaps overstated, colonial projects of all kinds did become the legitimate subject and target of academic study. Still, U.S. imperialism largely disappeared from these endeavors and remained less a part of colonial studies than it did for a cohort of scholars whose trajectories were more emphatically Marxist, and whose intellectual and political roots ran from Lenin to Fanon, Arghiri Emmanuel, Andre Gunder Frank, and Immanuel Wallerstein, a tradition to which Said saw himself as only marginally relevant and aligned.

13. Edward Said, "Orientalism Once More," *Development and Change* 35, 5 (November 2004): 869–79.

14. Eqbal Ahmad, *Confronting Empire: Interviews with David Barsamian* (Cambridge, MA: South End, 2000), 39.

It would be hard to claim that The Question of Palestine was a book of comparable import, portability, style, or breadth.[15] It was designed for a (Euro) American public, at the time still resistant to using the word "Palestine" or examining what Zionism and its entanglement with U.S. imperialism meant to Palestinians. However, the strikingly limited consideration of the relationship between Orientalism and The Question of Palestine, or reflection on the two as companion pieces (given their timing and the cross-references throughout the latter to the former) seem more deliberate than oversight or accidental. I take it as a diacritic of a set of excisions that defined colonialism in a highly constricted way that removed contemporary Palestine, the Israeli state, and U.S. imperial practice in the Middle East as sites in which the contemporary nature of colonialism could and should be pursued. Orientalism was made "safe" for scholarship; The Question of Palestine was not.[16]

The consequences for the field of (post)colonial studies as it has developed over the past thirty odd years are evident in a number of ways. What counted as colonialism in its quintessential form were British and French colonialism of a particular sort. Imperialism was a political concept of a Marxist past: "Colonial culture" and "imperial knowledge" were historical

15. Reviews of The Question of Palestine were far fewer, as well. It was treated as a "defense of Palestinians" but not as an analysis of a colonial imperial project in which the United States was implicated. None commented on the relationship between the two books. In "The Heart of the Matter," Journal of Palestine Studies 9, 3 (Spring 1980): 137–42, for example, Hilton Obenziner noted that he could find only two reviews (albeit prominent) prior to his own. Also see, Christopher Lehmann-Haupt, "Books of the Times: Case for the Palestinians," New York Times, January 4, 1980; Nicholas Bethell, "Edward W. Said: The Question of Palestine," New York Times, January 20, 1980); Joel Migdal, "Review of The Question of Palestine," Political Science Quarterly 95, 4 (December 1, 1980): 726–27; Stu Cohen and Beshara Doumani, "Contesting Zionism: Two Views of the Question of Palestine," MERIP Reports 100–101 (October 1, 1981): 44–48; M. Nasr Mahanna, "Review of The Question of Palestine," Third World Quarterly 6, 2 (April 1, 1984): 506–8. In a radically different vein—a diatribe against both books' submission to Said's "political ideology"—see Cameron S. Brown, "Answering Edward Said's The Question of Palestine," Israel Affairs 13, 1 (January 2007): 55–79.

16. Ironically, one of the few places where they are treated as an insidious political package is in Philip Carl Salzman and Donna Robinson Devine, eds., Postcolonial Theory and the Arab-Israel Conflict (London: Routledge, 2008). One essay in the collection opens with a diatribe against "Edward Said's ridiculous polemic, The Question of Palestine": Salzman and Devine, Postcolonial Theory and the Arab-Israel Conflict, 144. As for the tenor of the collection, one might refer to the contention by its co-editor, the anthropologist Philip Salzman, that "the Arab Middle East has remained largely a pre-modern society, governed by clan relationships and violent coercion": Philip Salzman, Culture and Conflict in the Middle East (Amherst, NY: Humanity, 2008), 194.

artifacts that were readily documentable by scrutinizing any number of colonial archival collections. Imperialism in this sense was not an ongoing and active global project shaped by the opacities it produced. It lacked the requisite currency and caché. In the work that *Orientalism* generated, one is hard pressed to find the nature of contemporary "imperialism" as a geopolitical and affective formation analyzed, much less U.S. imperialism and its relationship to Israel.[17] When "the New Imperial History" as it was called, took off, the subjects were different, as were the politics. I am not the first to note that "U.S. imperialism" and imperialism more generally were distinguished from "empire," as the practices and spectacles of "colonial culture" moved to center stage. If Said distanced himself from the revolutionary solutions that Frantz Fanon invoked—and, as some claimed, from Fanon's Marxist bearings—he also distanced himself pointedly from much of the domesticated genre of "postcolonial studies" that lost its political edge as it selectively followed in his wake.[18]

"UNBEARABLY HISTORICAL"

Within the constrained topography of (post)colonial studies, the United States, which had long remained outside the picture of "real" colonialism with its limited "colonies," was set aside as the "exception." Israel was cordoned off, as well, long granted a sacred exceptional status on so many po-

17. It is not insignificant that the first volume that named the "new imperial history" defined its time period between 1660 and 1840 and was confined to the "cultural history of British expansion." Only one of the contributing essays located the time of its writing at the moment that "the United States is bombing Afghanistan" and that of "state-sponsored terror in Israel," the author's opening to a history of Atlantic slavery in which no further reference to that "location" is mentioned: see Kathleen Wilson, ed., *A New Imperial History: Culture, Identity, and Modernity in Britain and the Empire, 1660–1840* (Cambridge: Cambridge University Press, 2004); Walter Johnson, "Time and Revolution in African America: Temporality and the History of Atlantic Slavery," in *A New Imperial History: Culture, Identity, and Modernity in Britain and the Empire, 1660–1840,* ed. Kathleen Wilson (Cambridge: Cambridge University Press, 2004), 197. This is not a fault with the volume. Rather, it is indicative of the shifting and wider—less political—terrain on which studies of "empire" took hold.

18. Robert Young argues that neither Islam nor Said's concerns with Palestine was "a major preoccupation of postcolonial studies" in part because "the Caribbean model of creolization and hybridity" had little traction as a "way to move forward." But this does little to account for their systematic exclusion, particularly for the many scholars for whom "hybridity" was never a prevailing reference point or relevant frame: see Robert J. C. Young, "Postcolonial Remains," *New Literary History* 43, 1 (2012): 28.

litical fronts, by academics and by the public at large, on the "global stage."
It is true that a handful of progressives in the 1970s and 1980s, in and outside academe and from Palestine, Israel, South Africa, the United States,
and Europe, made the lonely and unpopular case that "Israeli occupation"
was a euphemism for "Zionist colonialism," as Fayez Sayegh boldly put it
early on.[19] Ibrahim Abu-Lughod was a central figure in this move, publishing critical volumes on Israel as a colonial state while encouraging Said to
write more directly about the portrayal of "the Arab."[20] But for the most
part, scholars emphasized the temporary status of Israeli occupation rather
than—if they mentioned at all—the long-term effects of dispossession.
Indeed, the very term "temporary" obscured a history of the strategically
planned migration of Israeli "settlers recruited for colonization in its modern form."[21] The French journalist Jean Daniel (referred to in Chapter 1)
in a book published in 1979 and in an essay that had appeared ten years
earlier, did name "Israeli colonialism" condemning "the exception" that it
was conferred—most notably, by the outspoken luminary of France's war
against Algeria, Jean-Paul Sartre, who remained a staunch supporter of Israel, to Said's "disappointment."[22]

19. See Fayez A. Sayegh, *Zionist Colonialism in Palestine* (Beirut: Research Center, Palestine Liberation Organization, 1965). Sayegh's work is not widely known outside those
who work in the region, although an excerpt from the book was recently published with
an introduction to his work in Fayez A. Sayegh, *Settler Colonial Studies* 1 (January 1, 2012):
206–25.

20. I thank Lila Abu-Lughod for conveying to me some of the nature of the relationship between her father, Ibrahim Abu-Lughod, and his friendship with Said: see esp.
Ibrahim A. Abu-Lughod, *The Transformation of Palestine: Essays on the Origin and Development
of the Arab-Israeli Conflict* (Evanston, IL: Northwestern University Press, 1971); Ibrahim A.
Abu-Lughod and Baha Abu-Laban, eds., *Settler Regimes in Africa and the Arab World: The
Illusion of Endurance* (Wilmette, IL: Medina University Press International, 1974). Also
see Maxime Rodinson, *Israel: A Colonial-Settler State?* trans. David Thorstad (New York:
Pathfinder, 1973); Ian Lustick, *Arabs in the Jewish State: Israel's Control of a National Minority*
(Austin: University of Texas Press, 1982), and his subsequent *For the Land and the Lord:
Jewish Fundamentalism in Israel* (New York: Council on Foreign Relations, 1988).

21. Ella Shohat's incisive insights on postcolonial studies as a space in which "contemporary power relations" had little place emerged in the early 1990s: see Ella Shohat,
"Notes on the 'Post-Colonial,'" *Social Text* 31–32 (January 1, 1992): 99–113, and the seething essays collected in Ella Shohat, *Taboo Memories, Diasporic Voices* (Durham, NC: Duke
University Press, 2006).

22. Jean Daniel, "Une terre à tous promis," in *L'ère des ruptures* (Paris: Grasset and
Fasquelle, 1979), 116. Daniel recounts how he was lambasted by members of the French
intelligentsia and subjected to a psychological analysis for being a self-hating Jew,
thereby dismissing the language he used and the questions he raised. Acknowledging

Still, for political reasons that are all too evident today, colonialism in Palestine was treated as a thing of the past that ended with the British Mandate and David Ben-Gurion's raising of the Israeli flag. Israelis and Palestinians could be studied as players embroiled in a contemporary "Arab-Israeli conflict" and as a "problem" for U.S. foreign relations. Students of comparative colonialism and imperial circuits of knowledge production—subjects that have flourished over the past two decades—stayed clear of the Israeli state and the violence it engendered. This avoidance was as much the case for those whose political affiliations were with anticolonial movements elsewhere. Anthropology is a case in point, one that Khaled Fulani and Dan Rabinowitz have examined in detail and Talal Asad was to indict in 1973 for its continuing functionalist focus on "tradition" and its "disregard for the colonial dimension of the Palestinian predicament."[23] Anthropology in the region confined itself to drawing cultural portraits of "ethnic" Jews, tribal populations (Bedouins), and the artifacts of their cultural distinctions.[24]

---

that the title of his editorial, "Must Israel Be Destroyed?" was admittedly "in bad taste," in the genre of "Should we burn Kafka?" he insisted that even raising the issue of Palestinian rights in France, where the subject was so assiduously avoided, prompted "rage" and "indignation" that would not have been the case for another subject. Jean-Luc Godard was one of the very few to commend Daniel for what he was fearless enough to say.

On Said's acerbic take on his disconcerting encounter with Sartre, De Beauvoir, and Foucault in 1979, see Eugene Wolters, " 'A Bitter Disappointment': Edward Said on His Encounter with Sartre, De Beauvoir and Foucault," Critical-Theory, August 26, 2014, http://www.critical-theory.com/a-bitter-disappointment-edward-said-on-his-encounter -with-sartre-de-beauvoir-and-foucault, originally published as Edward Said, "Diary," London Review of Books, June 1, 2000, 42–43.

23. See Khaled Furani and Dan Rabinowitz, "The Ethnographic Arriving of Palestine," Annual Review of Anthropology 40, 1 (2011): 481, and Dan Rabinowitz's survey of early Israeli anthropological studies of Palestinians, "Oriental Othering and National Identity: A Review of Early Israeli Anthropological Studies of Palestinians," Identities 9, 3 (July 1, 2002): 305–25; Talal Asad, ed., Anthropology and the Colonial Encounter, repr. ed. (Amherst, NY: Humanities Press, 1973).

24. Israel was so off limits as a colonial state that even a revered Israeli ethnographer such as Henry Rosenfeld (lauded for his anti-Zionist stance in later work) could write in the 1970s about the "proletarianization" of Palestinians in an analysis abruptly cut off in 1948 only to the note that ". . . we do not find a mass movement back to the villages as an aftermath of the [Second World] war. This state of affairs terminated drastically with the Israeli-Arab War of 1948, when, among other things, approximately 650,000 Arabs left the area that became Israel and fewer than 150,000 remained," Shulamit Carmi and Henry Rosenfeld, "The Origins of the Process of Proletarianization and Urbanization of Arab Peasants in Palestine," Annals of the New York Academy of Sciences 220, 6 (March 1, 1973): 470–85, 477; emphasis added.

Consider some of the major edited volumes that appeared in the twenty years that followed the publication of *Orientalism* and *The Question of Palestine*. Palestine and the Israeli occupation were given wide berth in Bill Ashcroft, Gareth Griffiths and Helen Tiffin's *Empire Writes Back* (1989) and their jointly edited *The Postcolonial Studies Reader* (1995), Nicholas Dirks's *Colonialism and Culture* (1992), Ann McClintock's *Imperial Leather* (1995), Padmini Mongia's *Contemporary Postcolonial Theory* (1996), my *Tensions of Empire*, with Frederick Cooper (1997), and Amy Kaplan's *The Anarchy of Empire in the Making of U.S. Culture* (2002). Palestine is absent from nearly every one of these volumes, as well as from virtually every edited volume that republished the "canonical" essays that put (post)colonial studies on the academic map. Gyan Prakash's *After Colonialism* (1995), subtitled, *Imperial Histories and Postcolonial Displacements*, would have seemed a likely place for inclusion of an essay on contemporary Palestinian displacements, but the one essay on the region, a fine-grained analysis of the part played by Palestinian workers in labor Zionism by the historian Zachary Lockman, ends its treatment in 1929.[25] "Postcolonial displacement" in Prakash's introduction is not to be found in Palestine.

Can we really take seriously a purported study of proletarianization that shows a glaring refusal to reference the land confiscations and military assaults that produced that process, which Rosenfeld eclipsed with the pallid euphemism that Arabs "left the area"? But, then, Rosenfeld was in esteemed myopic company. A recalcitrant refusal to address the political situation in which one worked was not unusual for anthropology's most eminent practitioners—Clifford Geertz notably among them. Geertz could write about "thinking as a moral act," the "ethical dimensions of fieldwork," and "the need to put social science not in the dock, where it belongs, but on the witness stand" in 1968, with no mention of the slaughter in Indonesia in 1965–1966 of hundreds of thousands of alleged communist sympathizers, neither a "forgotten" nor "unthinkable" history, from which he so assiduously looked away: see Clifford Geertz, "Thinking as a Moral Act: Ethical Dimensions of Anthropological Fieldwork in the New States," *Antioch Review* 28, 2 (July 1, 1968): 139–58.

25. This is not to suggest that Lockman should have done otherwise. His careful analysis of "the way in which elements of a national project, a colonial-settler project and a socialist or working-class project interpenetrated" offers precisely the sort of history on which we might think to draw, and I do in "A Past That Was Never Present," paper presented at European University, Florence, March 2012. My point, instead, is that the relevant comparative colonial situation is a historical one, and "imperial histories" in the contributions are not drawn from the United States: see Zachary Lockman, "Exclusion and Solidarity: Labor Zionism and Arab Workers in Palestine, 1897–1929," in *After Colonialism: Imperial Histories and Postcolonial Displacements*, ed. Gyan Prakash (Princeton, NJ: Princeton University Press, 1995), 211–40.

Within American studies, the occlusion was similarly stark. When the American studies field sprinted in the direction of rethinking the nature of U.S. empire as distinct from earlier literature on U.S. imperialism, what emerged were indictments and sharply critical analyses of U.S. colonial situations in Samoa, the Philippines, and Cuba. Military installations in the U.S. imperial archipelago came into prominent view, particularly after 9/11, and they are ubiquitous sites of work by geographers, historians, and anthropologists today. Even the scholarship that Subaltern Studies prompted, when it reached outside its initial location in South Asia (where it was to dovetail with the critical impetus of *Orientalism*), was devoted to the underclasses in the postcolonies of the rest of the world—again, excepting the colonial saturation of Palestine. Israeli-U.S. cooperation, investments, shared technologies, and strategies of surveillance—in short, military, cultural, and economic traffic and the filiations they secured—still largely avoided the Israeli colonial state and its U.S. nexus.[26] It was the unlikely writing of Chalmers Johnson, China specialist and consultant to the CIA from 1967 to 1973, who made the case for a U.S. empire of military bases maintained throughout the world. Writing for an audience that consisted of a general public for whom the existence of a U.S. empire was hardly a given, he argued that "neither formal colonialism nor the neocolonialism of the chartered company or multinational corporation exhaust[s] the institutional possibilities of imperialism," naming Israel as the U.S.'s "client state"—dependent for munitions and world validation for support.[27]

26. See the important intervention in Amy Kaplan and Donald E. Pease, eds., *Cultures of United States Imperialism* (Durham, NC: Duke University Press, 1993), for its expanded but still limited range of sites of U.S. imperialism. Contrast this with Kaplan's more recent project on Zionism in American culture, discussed in Amy Kaplan, "In Palestine, Occupational Hazards," *Chronicle of Higher Education*, November 7, 2010, http://chronicle.com/article/In-Palestine-Occupational/125246. See also Douglas Little's important book on the "special relationship" between the United States and Israel: Douglas Little, *American Orientalism: The United States and the Middle East since 1945* (Chapel Hill: University of North Carolina Press, 2002). Although Little is a "diplomatic historian," the terms "imperialism," "colonialism" (except when quoting Henry Kissinger), and "empire" do not appear in the book as relevant to identify these "special" relations.

27. Chalmers A. Johnson, *The Sorrows of Empire: Militarism, Secrecy, and the End of the Republic* (New York: Henry Holt, 2005), 31. Johnson's analysis of the history of American bases in Latin America that derived from the Monroe Doctrine of 1823 and others that followed the Spanish American War of 1898 is brilliant and unprecedented. I remember reading Johnson's work as an undergraduate working on the rural roots of the Chinese

Johnson put it succinctly when he wrote, "A nation can be one or the other, a democracy or an imperialist, but it can't be both."[28] If his statement almost reads as revelatory, those who had been studying the two together in imperial contexts have long made the argument that the "interior frontiers" of liberal democracy and empire were woven from the same well-armed and exclusionary cloth.[29]

I draw on the treatment of Palestine and Israel to examine the politics of occlusion, not to rehearse a colonial history that has been, and continues increasingly to be, researched from ever new vantage points by a wide range of Palestinian, Israeli, and international scholars. Nor am I arguing that identification of Israel as a colonial state was unavailable, not acknowledged by an albeit small swathe of public intellectuals, political thinkers, and activists in various parts of the world. On the contrary, it is the very availability of those analyses and the cumulative knowledge they represent that was censored, as if an invisible *cordon sanitaire* was around Israel, as though acknowledgment of Israeli aggression and recognition of the familiar and unique forms in which it was manifest would diminish and demean the sacrosanct history of the Holocaust as **the** genocide that has most mattered in, and to, "our" world. Again it is not ignorance that is at issue but self-censorship and a regime of truth-telling that made Israeli aggressions appropriate to ignore. Such treatment underscores the selective sites and subjects of those of us who have pursued an academic quest for how colonial pasts and colonial presences matter, and how they recursively act on people whose possibilities for the future are, as Said once put it, so "unbearably historical."[30]

As important, the observation prompts another question about the limits of critique that a critical (post)colonial studies has pursued, a ques-

---

revolution and imagined him at the time as part of the staunchly conservative academic mafia that was adamantly opposed to communist China: see also Chalmers A. Johnson, *Blowback: The Costs and Consequences of American Empire* (New York: Henry Holt, 2004).

28. Amy Goodman, "Chalmers Johnson, 1931–2010: On the Last Days of the American Republic," interview transcript, November 22, 2010, http://www.democracynow.org /2010/11/22/chalmers_johnson_1931_2010_on_the.

29. See Uday S. Mehta, "The Liberal Strategies of Exclusion," *Politics and Society* 18, 4 (1990): 427–54; Ann Laura Stoler, "Sexual Affronts and Racial Frontiers," in *Carnal Knowledge and Imperial Power: Race and the Intimate in Colonial Rule* (Berkeley: University of California Press, 2002), 79–111.

30. Edward Said, *Reflections on Exile and Other Essays* (Cambridge, MA: Harvard University Press, 2002), 174.

tion similar to one Dirks posed more than two decades ago when he asked whether (post)colonial studies had become "safe for scholarship."[31] I would pose it differently. Was not the field of (post)colonial studies (and an entire multidisciplinary initiative to document colonial situations and their effects) made safe for scholarship from its very beginning by an occlusive process that, among other things, held the two texts, *Orientalism* and *The Question of Palestine*, apart? And what would colonial studies look like today if the two texts had been given the same analytic weight to define what constitutes critique and what a critical postcolonial studies might look like that abjures its self-imposed limits and earlier canon?

After a talk on this subject at Columbia University in spring 2015, an eminent scholar in the audience asked, with a wry smile, whether I was perhaps too easy on Said; that it was Said who positioned himself as the elegant, mobile cosmopolitan New York intellectual and as the belligerent exiled Palestinian advocate, (too) deftly gliding between the two. He may be partially right. Perhaps Said's juxtapositions made it too easy for some scholars to partake in the agility of his literary insights, less as a means than as an end in itself. But I would demur from my interlocutors's assessment and place as much of the onus on us, his avid and selective readers. Politics was dead center for Said, as was the politics of epistemology—a point that Dipesh Chakrabarty's *Provincializing Europe* was to make with breathtaking force from his imperial archive on European epistemologies.[32] The politics of knowledge reverberated across academe—it just was not to be touched with respect to Palestine.

"LESSONS" TURNED AROUND: ON PALESTINE AND COLONIAL STUDIES

Rather than drawing on the insights of colonial and postcolonial studies, as well as their critical interventions, my impulse is to do something else that moves in a different direction—namely, to look at some of the questions that colonial studies long set aside, at the sorts of questions not asked and the conceptual frames that made it easy do so. Further, I want to track what has more recently shifted in scope and scale as problematics have ·

31. Nicholas B. Dirks, ed., *Colonialism and Culture* (Ann Arbor: University of Michigan Press, 1992).

32. Dipesh Chakrabarty, *Provincializing Europe: Postcolonial Thought and Historical Difference*. Princeton, NJ: Princeton University Press, 2000.

been reformulated to open to colonial sites that were once seen as outside the pale or, at least, outside the canonical colonial forms. Both moves call into question what long served as the prevailing model of colonial sovereignty.

As I discuss in chapter 3, an alternative attention to "degrees of imperial sovereignty" and sliding scales of rights—and to what I elsewhere have called "the politics of comparison"—may help make sense of the nonexceptional ways in which the "rule of law" has not been an antidote to unbridled acts of dispossession but, instead, has been deployed to maximize, in Yoav Mehozay's words, the "fluid jurisprudence" of Israel's emergency powers that has served those ends.[33] "Semblances of sovereignty," impromptu removal of entitlements, suspension of property rights, reinstatement of partial ones—these are all within the normal functional bounds of how colonial governance has operated and the strategies in which imperial formations normally invest. Ahmad H. Sa'di's *Thorough Surveillance* (2014) draws on extensive documentary evidence to make the case that "systematic thinking and consistency in the [Israeli] state's actions" were not ad hoc strategies but were affected as early as the 1920s by protracted and deliberate design.[34]

Might we think of the *conceptual politics* of colonial studies that has shaped what has not been available to think about colonial pasts and about what has long remained on the policed edges of (post)colonial studies as a field and fashion of inquiry?[35] But what was it that was condoned and condemned? For one thing, students of colonialism often have subscribed to the very distinctions made by colonial polities themselves in defining what was a colony and what was not. Exceptionalism reigned. As Said once pointed out, and as I discuss in chapter 5, every empire has imagined itself as an exception for which the use of force is a "last resort."[36]

Said was right, but one could take that observation further. As I have argued for some time, colonial states operate as states of exception that vigilantly produce exceptions to their principles and exceptions to their

33. Yoav Mehozay, "The Fluid Jurisprudence of Israel's Emergency Powers: Legal Patchwork as a Governing Norm," *Law and Society Review* 46, 1 (March 2012): 137–66.

34. Ahmad H. Sa'di, *Thorough Surveillance: The Genesis of Israeli Policies of Population Management, Surveillance and Political Control towards the Palestinian Minority* (Manchester: Manchester University Press, 2014).

35. I borrow the term "conceptual politics" from Lawrence A. Hirschfeld, "The Conceptual Politics of Race: Lessons from Our Children," *Ethos* 25, 1 (March 1, 1997): 63–92.

36. Said, *Orientalism*, xxi.

laws. Exceptionalism was homegrown on Israeli terrain. And here, as else-where, the exceptionalism served its own purposes: to sanction and le-gitimate the rationale for destroying Palestinian homesteads, confiscating property, and literally burying Palestinian towns. Exceptionalism with re-spect to democratic principles, international law, and the most basic tenets of citizenship condoned deeply distorted marshaling of material artifacts and symbolic capital in the name of a Jewish homeland and crafting a dis-torted history of Israel's own making.[37]

One could argue that (post)colonial studies made no conceptual place for the very forms of colonial governance that motivated Said's work. Reading The Question of Palestine alongside Orientalism might have provoked a different set of questions that are more present in a vastly reconfigured colonial studies now: about the relations among imperial formations; about the network of power relations that joined British colonialism, Eu-ropean racism, U.S. investments in the Middle East, and the persistent encroachment of Israeli settlements on working Palestinian land and lives. It is in The Question of Palestine, as Abdul-Rahim al-Shaikh has rightly noted, that Said drew "a connection between the project of Orientalism and that of Zionism."[38]

Again, what might the study of imperial formations have looked like if the Israeli state had not been off-limits, if comparable analytic weight had been given to define what colonialism looks like today, a subject that has come increasingly to the very center of a range of work that exceeds the confines of (post)colonial studies and its circumscribed space? It was, after all, in The Question of Palestine more directly than in Orientalism that Said set out a line of inquiry into what he called "the moral epistemology of imperialism."[39] As Robert Young notes, when Said was queried in an interview about postcolonial studies in 1997, he tersely responded, "I don't

37. El-Haj's Facts on the Ground was considered so bold when it came out that it became a cause célèbre beyond the embroiled politics of Columbia University, where it almost cost her tenure: Nadia Abu El-Haj, Facts on the Ground: Archaeological Practice and Ter-ritorial Self-Fashioning in Israeli Society (Chicago: University of Chicago Press, 2001). See the trenchant defense of El-Haj in Jane Kramer, "The Petition," New Yorker, April 14, 2008.

38. Abdul-Rahim al-Shaikh, "Palestine: The Tunnel Condition," Contemporary Arab Affairs 3, 4 (October 1, 2010): 482. Scott Atran argued that Zionism itself was an explicit colonial project from its conception, a "surrogate colonialism" of Britain's from the start: Scott Atran, "The Surrogate Colonization of Palestine, 1917–1939," American Ethnologist 16, 4 (November 1, 1989): 719–44.

39. Said, The Question of Palestine, 18.

think colonialism is over, really, I don't know what they are really taking about."[40] In *Reflections on Exile*, published a few years later, he described his own position as one of "opposition to empire."[41]

Where might a historicized (post)colonial studies have gone? For one, the paradigmatic case of colonial "domination without hegemony," South Asia, might not have had the centrality it was conferred and claimed. True, Subaltern Studies developed in India, and there is no surprise that Anglophone archives have had more attraction for Anglophone doctoral students scrambling to finish their dissertations within the ever decreasing time limits that U.S. universities impose. Still, that does not wholly account for why the range of imperial forms that have emerged over the past 150 years as distinct from the Victorian Indian model of empire have not been adequately conceptualized as non-exceptional imperial forms rather than cast on its outer margins.

In an effort to press on the limits of the "empire" concept, I use the term "imperial formations" throughout this book to register the ongoing quality of processes of decimation, displacement, and reclamation that endure beyond the formal exclusions that legislate against equal opportunity, commensurate dignities, and equal rights.[42] As an a alternative to "empire," it is to signal the temporal stretch and recursive recalibrations to which we could be looking.

Both of Said's books placed the United States within an imperial constellation. As I have insisted, it is not, then, that U.S. imperial pursuits in the Middle East were not present in *Orientalism*. In fact, Said's political intervention was directed precisely at the United States as an imperial force and its well-funded flank of official and unofficial American "social scientists" who

40. Quoted in Robert J. C. Young, "Edward Said: Opponent of Postcolonial Theory," in *Edward Said's Translocations: Essays in Secular Criticism*, ed. Tobias Döring and Mark Stein (New York: Routledge, 2012), 37. I thank Mark Stein for pointing me to Young's essay in Stein's co-edited volume that had just come out, on the occasion of a keynote address I gave in Bern in spring 2012, based on an early and much condensed version of this chapter.

41. Said, *Reflections on Exile and Other Essays*, xxvi, quoted in Young, "Edward Said," 37.

42. This concept is first formulated in Ann Laura Stoler, "On Degrees of Imperial Sovereignty," *Public Culture* 18, 1 (Winter 2006): 125–46. A revised version of the article is included as chapter 5 in this volume. It is also elaborated in Ann Laura Stoler and Carole McGranahan, "Refiguring Imperial Terrains," in *Imperial Formations*, ed. Ann Laura Stoler, Carole McGranahan, and Peter C. Perdue (Santa Fe, NM: School for Advanced Research Press, 2007), 3–44.

conferred upon themselves "an intellectual authority" marked by a "ponderous style of expertise."[43] French and British literary texts were crucial to his argument, but it was Orientalism as a "strategic formation" and a *transnational* one that methodologically guided his work, with Islam figured as the "lasting trauma" for Europe. In *The Question of Palestine*, what Said called the "outright intellectual terrorism" against those in the United States who might have thought to defend Palestinian rights was a challenge that an expanded field of (post)colonial studies would only later more persistently and directly pursue.[44]

PALESTINE AS FULCRUM: ON COLONIAL PRESENCE TODAY

The issue of a Palestinian absence from (postcolonial) studies was dismissed or deferred by some, and for others the reasons for its absence were too obvious to articulate. Yet another question remains unaddressed: What accounts for the unprecedented explosion of work on the Israeli colonial state that took off with such density and determination on the cusp of the twenty-first century? Never before has so much been published by Palestinians, Israelis, and others on the Israeli state's techniques of torture and surveillance; the conditions of those living in Palestinian refugee camps; the daily, systematic, and systemic violence against Palestinians living within the Green Zone, in exile, cordoned off in Gaza and under siege and deprived of basic services in the Occupied Territories.

What has brought attention to Palestine and the Israeli project as a colonial one demands collective reflection about the conditions that have produced that effect. At issue is not an "originary" moment so much as a mounting momentum of critical assessment coming from different quarters, a conjuncture that some might call "overdetermined."[45] One might argue as so many have that 9/11 unleashed an intensified regime of security

43. Said, *Orientalism*, 19.
44. Said, *The Question of Palestine*, 50.
45. I think here both with Freud's early use of that term and Althusser's later adaptation—in Freud's sense, both with respect to the lasting traumas that give rise to the subjects of dreams and the local "residue of the day" that produces their content and effect. At issue is not causality (*pace* Freud and Althusser) but the multiple conditions that account for a particular effect. In Althusser's use, overdetermination served to underscore opposed *forces active in and acting upon the emergence* of a political situation. If the claim that any particular political situation is overdetermined too often has been a way to couch what cannot be accounted for, we might take it elsewhere—to point to

and relentless targeting of Islam, and a subsequent response by those who rallied against these impulses. Still, one can find numbers of (post)colonial edited volumes that sought to take up the charge to include Israel and Palestine before that event.[46] Some might point to the failure of the Oslo Agreement and the subsequent "breakdown" of peace negotiations. Others might argue that the writing was on the wall and that the "breakdown" was already well in progress, evident in the emergence of the second intifada in July 2000. The construction of the euphemistically named "separation barrier" (or "wall of apartheid," as it is rendered in Arabic) begun in 2002 (proposed by Yitzhak Rabin in 1992) and that now runs some 450 miles, twenty-six feet high and nine feet thick, gave concrete and barbed-wire material force to a sequestering to which Palestinians and their supporters have been calling attention for much longer. The decision of the International High Court in The Hague in 2004 to condemn the wall as a breach of international law confirmed that it served to blockade the Palestinians and laid bare that its twists and turns are a blatant embodiment of unabated and future Israeli encroachments. The boycott movement launched the following year, in 2005, was modest to begin with but has since brought the issue of boycott, sanctions, and Israeli policy into mainstream discussion in a way that had escaped scrutiny before. The increasing numbers of artists, musicians, and academics who have declined to appear in Israeli state-sponsored and funded venues have made frequent headlines in the press. They have been joined by prominent senior scholars across the academy whose primary work is neither in Arabic nor on Palestine and make it more possible for others, like myself, to reflect on, speak to, and sometimes act on the Boycott, Divestment, and Sanctions (BDS) movement's platforms and claims.[47]

---

the forms in which dissensus takes hold and the situated knowledges from which those effects are viewed.

46. Notable among them is Fawzia Afzal-Khan and Kalpana Seshadri-Crooks, eds., *The Pre-occupation of Postcolonial Studies* (Durham, NC: Duke University Press, 2000), 4, which explicitly addresses an "inadequately enunciated notion of the margin" and of critique in (post)colonial studies as it was manifest at the end of the twentieth century.

47. On the changing political academic landscape of U.S. anthropology with respect to Israel and Palestine and the "self-protection strategies" that shielded many anthropologists from writing about Palestine, see the superb analysis and comprehensive data gathered in Lara Deeb and Jessica Winegar, *Anthropology's Politics: Disciplining the Middle East* (Stanford, CA: Stanford University Press, 2015). Deeb and Winegar provide us with the climate in which those who deigned to work on Palestine (such as Ted Swedenburg

No one seems quite sure where to locate the impetus. One Palestinian scholar opined that "this time Israel went just too far," with too many successive strategic assaults over the previous decade: Operation Cast Lead in 2008–2009; Operation Pillar of Defense in 2012; and, most recently, Operation Protective Edge in 2014. Given these relentless assaults, some might see no need to rehearse further what has given Palestinian dispossession and demands more credence and visibility than it could sustain before.

Realignments within academe were precipitators, as well. Some observers have argued that the escalation of Zionist groups targeting Jewish and non-Jewish faculty on listservs as anti-Semitic has had a sobering and mobilizing effect, activating questions of ethics and "freedom of speech" for a broader academic constituency. Others have made the case that the "demystification of states and hegemonic groups that control them," coupled with the bombing of Lebanon, broke through "Israel's sanctity in the West."[48]

But the impetus has come equally from elsewhere. The events of 9/11 prompted a reassessment of U.S. empire—its technologies and its reach—that has underscored the deeply entrenched ties between the U.S. and Israeli political investments and capital. Students of colonialism, border regimes, detentions, and confinements were already broadening their net to think harder about what was once called "internal colonialism" and sought a way to make comparative sense of "settler colonialism" as a specific and particularly violent colonial form. Patrick Wolfe in Australia, Olivier Le Cour Grandmaison in France, and a new generation of Native American scholars have persuasively argued for an equation between colonization and extermination.[49] The conceptual and political weight of "settler colonialism"

---

and Ilana Feldman) did so earlier on and discuss the explosion of work since by a younger generation that refuses to abide by the earlier gatekeeping and self-censoring restrictions. I thank both for sharing their manuscript with me before it was released. But many came before: see, e.g., Rebecca L. Stein and Ted Swedenburg, eds., *Palestine, Israel, and the Politics of Popular Culture* (Durham, NC: Duke University Press, 2005); Joel Beinin and Rebecca Stein, eds., *The Struggle for Sovereignty: Palestine and Israel, 1993–2005* (Stanford: Stanford University Press, 2006).

48. Fulani and Rabinowitz, "The Ethnographic Arriving of Palestine," 476.

49. See Patrick Wolfe, *Settler Colonialism and the Transformation of Anthropology: The Politics and Poetics of an Ethnographic Event* (London: Cassell, 1999), and his more recent "Settler Colonialism and the Elimination of the Native," *Journal of Genocide Research* 8, 4 (December 2006): 387–40; Olivier Le Cour Grandmaison, *Coloniser/exterminer: Sur la guerre et l'état colonial* (Paris: Fayard, 2005). See also the analysis of "cultures of exterminability" in Ghassan Hage, *Alter-Politics: Critical Anthropology and the Radical Imagination* (Carlton, Victoria, Melbourne University Press, 2015).

has mobilized and provided a resonant vocabulary to a larger number of scholars who had not actively worked on colonialism per se to recognize and name a condition as colonial in a way that they could not before. For some it has opened inquiry into long-term damage to populations, abandoned and displaced to the margins of the nation to address the velocity of assault and the incremental "slow violence" on infrastructure, economy, resources, and values. Refusal to accept the very frame of debate rather than the recognition of rights draws together a demand for what pan-Africanism once sought and what Mohawks straddling the U.S.-Canadian border seek today.[50] Indigeneity movements in Australia, Canada, the United States, New Caledonia, and elsewhere have had potent force, bringing political and environmental decimation together with questions of self-determination.[51]

My reservation about the enthusiastic embrace of settler colonialism as a description of Israel's relationship with Palestinians has less to do with the political concept itself than with the fact that it is often invoked as an ontological state rather than a fractious historical condition. "Settler colonialism" is a protracted moment in colonial statecraft but far less fixed and unsettled than it sometimes portrayed. Colonizing projects moved between failed visions, as in Indochina of French settlement on a large scale and a small "expatriate" community preening its "sleek and fragile pelts," as Marguerite Duras put it; between visions of British India populated by large numbers of impoverished Scottish farmers that was reduced to a relatively well-heeled bureaucratic staff, as David Arnold has shown; of "poor whites" whom colonial authorities were never quite sure would turn their backs on the metropolitan center or invest in the imperial project as loyal settlers. These are battles won and lost.[52] Settler colonialism is no more fixed and

50. See Gary Wilder, *Freedom Time: Negritude, Decolonization, and the Future of the World* (Durham, NC: Duke University Press, 2015); Audra Simpson, *Mohawk Interruptus: Political Life across the Borders of Settler States* (Durham, NC: Duke University Press, 2014).

51. A surge of work has galvanized around indigeneity and native studies; see, e.g., J. Kehaulani Kauanui, *Hawaiian Blood: Colonialism and the Politics of Sovereignty and Indigeneity* (Durham, NC: Duke University Press, 2003); Audra Simpson and Andrea Smith, *Theorizing Native Studies* (Durham, NC: Duke University Press, 2014); Noenoe Silva, *Aloha Betrayed: Native Hawaiian Resistance to American Colonialism* (Durham, NC: Duke University Press, 2004).

52. Duras, quoted in Stoler, *Carnal Knowledge and Imperial Power*, 15; Carnegie Commission, quoted in Ann Laura Stoler, "Tense and Tender Ties: The Politics of Comparison in North American History and (Post)colonial Studies," *Journal of American History* 88, 3 (December 2001): 829–65; David Arnold, "White Colonization and Labour in

given than are any colonial formations that assert their illegitimate claims. Settler colonialism might better be understood not as a unique "type," but as the effect of a failed or protracted contest over appropriation and dispossession that is not over when the victories are declared, killings are accomplished, and decimation is resolved as the only "solution." Settler colonialism is only ever an imperial process in formation whose security apparatus confirms that it is always at risk of being undone.

What is striking about these trajectories of intellectual and political labor is how much they call for historicized accounts and a critical politics of comparison—two moves from which much of (post)colonial studies in its earlier incarnations had turned away with respect to Palestine. The cascade of new work depends not just on identifying silenced histories but also on tracking new genealogies that place suspended histories as resources for new possibilities. These recent revisions have been predicated in part on reassessing what constitutes contemporary colonial practice and what counts as imperial pursuit as they distinguish between geopolities that rest on emergent rather than residual imperial forms.[53] They give credence to the argument that "security," "intelligence," and the production of fear and expectant danger

---

Nineteenth-Century India," *Journal of Imperial and Commonwealth History* 11, 2 (January 1, 1983): 133–58.

53. The range of more recent books on the subject is overwhelming: see Afzal-Khan and Seshardri-Crooks, *The Pre-occupation of Postcolonial Studies*; Ariella Azoulay, *The Civil Contract of Photography* (New York: Zone Books, 2008); Rashid Khalidi, *Brokers of Deceit: How the U.S. Has Undermined Peace in the Middle East* (Boston: Beacon Press, 2013); Hagar Kotef, *Movement and the Ordering of Freedom: On Liberal Governances of Mobility* (Durham, NC: Duke University Press, 2015); Adi Ophir, Michal Givoni, and Sari Ḥanafi, eds., *The Power of Inclusive Exclusion: Anatomy of Israeli Rule in the Occupied Palestinian Territories* (New York: Zone, 2009); Ilan Pappé, *The Ethnic Cleansing of Palestine* (Oxford: Oneworld, 2007); Ahmad H. Sa'di and Lila Abu-Lughod, *Nakba: Palestine, 1948, and the Claims of Memory* (New York: Columbia University Press, 2007); Nadera Shalhoub-Kevorkian, *Militarization and Violence against Women in Conflict Zones in the Middle East: A Palestinian Case-Study* (Cambridge: Cambridge University Press, 2009), and *Security Theology, Surveillance and the Politics of Fear* (New York: Cambridge University Press, 2013); Yehouda Shenhav, *The Arab Jews: A Postcolonial Reading of Nationalism, Religion, and Ethnicity* (Stanford, CA: Stanford University Press, 2006), and *Beyond the Two States Solution: A Jewish Political Essay* (Cambridge: Polity, 2012); Gianni Vattimo and Michael Marder, eds., *Deconstructing Zionism: A Critique of Political Metaphysics*. New York: Bloomsbury, 2014).

But see also the defense of Israeli politics presented as a measured critique of the "compromises" and shortcomings of postcolonial "theory" generally and specifically with respect to Arab-Israeli relations in Salzman and Divine, *Postcolonial Theory and the Arab-Israel Conflict*.

on which the crafting of these concepts are based shift in concert and have long been at the center of imperial governance.

But if times have changed with respect to the placement of Palestinians within a number of fields in which it had not been present before—I think here of the cascade of new work among geographers—this is not the case across the board.[54] Amir Eshel's subtle study of the power of poetry to offer a new vocabulary and vision of how possibilities are opened and made thinkable, and that seeks to go beyond what might have been imagined as conceivable before, confines his study to Jewish Israeli writers on the argument that inclusion of the "poetry and prose of history's victims and their descendants" would have "exhausted the framework of his study." How do we understand such a sentence and the politics of knowledge to which it subscribes? What "exhausts" a "framework"? On what political grounds is such exhaustion invoked? Could it not be similarly argued that the distorted "past" of Jewish Israelis has "exhausted the framework" of the contemporary situation, making obsolete its restrictive frame?

IMPERIAL TEMPORALITIES

Joseph Massad's insight that Palestinian-Israeli relations encompass at one and the same time both a colonial and postcolonial situation may arguably be used to endorse what makes Palestinian-Israeli relations an "exception."[55] But it also may not. In rejecting the simple bifurcation of fixed colonial past and unmoored postcolonial present, Massad may actually have touched on a more prevalent and telling colonial condition. In his analysis, the coterminous presence of colonial and postcolonial conditions is assigned to differentiated populations subject to different relations to the past and living under widely different legal strictures, economic conditions, and political possibilities in the present.

But one may also think of this congested colonial/postcolonial space to be the experience not of different populations but of the *same* people, living both of those conditions at the same time. We might even think of

54. Craig A. Jones, "Frames of Law: Targeting Advice and Operational Law in the Israeli Military," *Environment and Planning D: Society and Space* 33, 4 (2015): 676–96.

55. Joseph Andoni Massad, "The 'Post-colony' Colony: Time, Space, and Bodies in Palestine/Israel," in *The Persistence of the Palestinian Question: Essays on Zionism and the Palestinians* (New York: Routledge, 2006), 13–40.

Israel-Palestine and the restrictions that are arbitrarily placed on people's movements and relations as a situation that typifies the confused, imbricated lived space to which a colonial presence gives rise more generally today, not only for Palestinians, but in the distorted, schizophrenic material and mental landscapes of postcolonial refuge. We might look to the Martinique Richard Price describes in *Convict and Colonel* or to the plushly financed extra-state territories that Keller Easterling so eerily conveys as unearthly pleasure domes of finance and tourism buttressed by the labor of displaced undocumented workers who are available only because they had hoped to escape something worse.[56]

In Israel and Palestine, a colonial presence messes with temporalities: It is not one context but many in which what is most technologically advanced (surveillance) is predicated on deeply honed colonial practices and where what are imagined as most intractably divisive—"primordial loyalties" and identity politics anchored to territorial attachments—are equally trained dispositions, part of the apparatus of modern governance, of the arts and crafts of nationalist projects and of modern invention.[57]

It may now be commonplace to speak of colonialism as a history of the present, but how such a venture is understood—what work needs to be done to track such a history and what features of the present demand renewed scrutiny—differs in content and form. It is left for us to to grapple with an impoverished vocabulary to account for the contractions, expansion, and accordion reach of these histories' spatial, temporal, and intimate effects. Students of colonialism in the 1970s and 1980s attended to metropolitan "imports" of modernity, civility, technology, and science on colonial terrain—or to colonies as "laboratories" of what were once construed as signature features of European political culture, such as state bureaucracies, urban surveillance techniques, and the architectures of containment. That moment

56. See Richard Price, *The Convict and the Colonel* (Boston: Beacon, 1998); Keller Easterling, *Extrastatecraft: The Power of Infrastructure Space* (London: Verso, 2014). Easterling writes of neither empire nor colonialism, but her study invites us to ask who these displaced workers are and about the imperial conditions that produced their abundant numbers and "availability."

57. Martin Thomas makes this important point in *Empires of Intelligence: Security Services and Colonial Disorder after 1914* (Berkeley: University of California Press, 2008). See the pointed and perceptive analysis of what Bashir Doumani calls the "identity/territorial/ sovereignty matrix," which I take to be a core set of historical constructions with disabling effects: Bashir Doumani, "Palestine versus the Palestinians? The Iron Laws and Ironies of a People Denied," *Journal of Palestine Studies* 36, 4 (July 1, 2007): 49–64.

has passed. These forms of duress are increasingly found to be ricocheting back and forth across the imperial world. Israeli-Palestinian relations may be one of the most vital and active instantiations of how the currencies of knowledge, commerce, technology, military, and other expertise are converted; of how they travel and work.[58] This is not to argue that Palestine is the Ur-colonial situation or that Israel is the quintessential colonial state. Instead, it is to see how the dispossession of Palestinians articulates the so carefully crafted and normalized segregrationist policies used to achieve it, providing a window onto forms of duress that are less visible elsewhere, forms that in Palestine are being made acutely resonant and recognizable.

As a field of inquiry, (post)colonial studies still wrestles with the "evolved" hypermodern forms in which imperial pursuits and colonial relations, practices, and conceptual software garner their force and thrive. From this vantage point, Israeli-Palestinian relations may offer less a unique site in which colonial relations bear on the present than a critical location to examine a networked colonial sphere of ongoing occupation—allegedly interim and "provisional" (as the term "occupation" has been used to imply); a sphere that is high-tech, dense, amplified, and compact, relentless in its multifaceted scope of vertical and territorial operation.[59] As such, what characterizes the relationship between Palestinians and Israelis could be seen as neither limited to the typological fixity of "settler colonialism" nor reduced to a "colonial

58. Olivier Le Cour Grandmaison argues that extermination was a fundamental visionary feature of French colonial policy in Algeria. His book *Coloniser/exterminer* was panned, as was he, for not being proper archivally based. The debate on German colonial policy about the site of the first German concentration camps for the Herero has followed on much earlier work on Spanish camps and British camps for Boers during the Boer War. On the ricocheting of military intelligence infrastructure and expertise, see Jones, "Frames of Law." Bashir Abu-Manneh similarly argues that U.S.-Israeli relations are not confined to the temperate domains of "cultural and religious exchange" but realized in the support that the United States provides to Israeli colonial policies: Bashir Abu-Menneh, "Israel in the U.S. Empire," *Monthly Review* 58, 10 (2007), http://monthlyreview.org/2007/03/01/israel-in-the-u-s-empire; Lisa Bhungalia, " 'From the American People': Sketches of the U.S. National Security State in Palestine," *Jadaliyya*, September 18, 2012, http://www.jadaliyya.com/pages/index/7412/"from-the-american -people"_sketches-of-the-us-nati.

59. See the now ubiquitously cited Eyal Weizman, *The Hollow Land: Israel's Architecture of Occupation*. London: Verso, 2007, and, most recently, *Forensis: The Architecture of Public Truth*, edited by Forensic Architecture (Berlin: Sternberg Press, 2014), Weizman's research agency at Goldsmith's College.

extreme," a twenty-first-century variant of the overtly sharp and stringent exclusions of South African apartheid.

Settlement is at issue, but "unsettledness" is at colonialism's heart (as argued in chapter 3). Illicit, regulated, surreptitious, policed movement is an animating force and productive of cultivated fears.[60] Macro and minutely intrusive forms of surveillance and security are posited as a response to unruly movement rather than the very practices that create ever new "potentially dangerous" subjects, "transgressions," and potential threats. Expanding regimes of security are installed as responses, "to defend society" with a moral fervor that endorses whatever means are professed to be required.[61]

Peculiarities in the historiography, however, remain. The "imperial footprint" in the Middle East is often still seen as more "ambiguous" than that of high British, French, and Dutch colonialism in Africa, South Asia, and Southeast Asia. Such a perception may point to a problem about what colonial projects are imagined to look like and which situations are taken as their exemplars. "Ambiguity" only makes sense if one assumes, as argued in chapter 5, that some crisply clear model of discrete borders and transparent criteria for citizenship are the imperial norm somewhere else.

While the nature of the colonial past under British rule goes uncontested, the use of the term "colonial" for the contemporary situation still is not. Comparative nationalism once provided the preferred frame of critical history for the region; now it is, in Rashid Khalidi's words, "resurrected empire."[62] Colonialism in an active mode is called on by a range of scholars to describe what Israeli-Palestinian social geographies look like today: military actions, surveillance techniques, exemptions and exclusions that endorse and finance Israeli settler expansion, discriminatory labor laws, and skeletal social services. Multiple forms of enclosure, "relocation" camps, and dispossession are not unfamiliar to those of us who have tracked the political rationalities of colonial regimes in other time and place. As we shall see

60. On this production of fear, see Shalhoub-Kevorkian, *Security Theology, Surveillance and the Politics of Fear*.

61. Foucault's description of this precise phenomenon is the thrust of *Il faut défendre la société: Cours au Collège de France, 1975–1976* (Paris: Gallimard and Seuil, 1991), and *Sécurité, territoire et population: Cours au Collège de France, 1977–1978* (Paris: Seuil and Gallimard, 2004).

62. "Everything that has followed in that conflict-riven land has flowed inevitably from [the Balfour Declaration of 1917]": Rashid Khalidi, *Resurrecting Empire: Western Footprints and America's Perilous Path in the Middle East* (Boston: Beacon, 2004), 118.

in the next chapter, containments in multiple forms—of settlers protected by military stations, of penal colonies surrounded by barbed wire—have a history that is written in meshed steel, cement blocks, and crushed stone.

British rule is removed enough to be a benign academic issue, but the description of a contemporary situation as "the colonial present," as Derek Gregory expressly refers to Palestinian-Israeli relations, is not.[63] Naming these relations features of a "colonial present" has been disparaged by the facile and frequently deployed critique that what he offers is a political intervention, not a scholarly (measured and "objective") one. If some defenders of Israeli state policy would dismiss the "colonial present" as an oxymoron as a declaration of political war, an inappropriate deployment of political concepts for strategic use, that is precisely Gregory's provoking point. Much of the public sphere in the United States and Israel still confers a unique status to Israel, but for an increasingly broad range of scholars its colonial signature is bold and decidedly not exceptional.[64]

CONCEPTUAL CURRENCIES

One need not invoke Foucault or Said to ask when and how conceptual frames are constrained by political investments or how and when political clarity is disabled by the conceptual frames endowed with the greatest currency. Nowhere are the two more imbricated than in the historical and contemporary treatment of Palestinian-Israeli relations. Analytical categories may frame what is politically relevant, but political pressure in academe (and beyond) dictate what can be said and by whom about Zionism in the present tense (without being labeled anti-Semitic) or about the role of U.S. military and domestic interests in Israel's treatment of Palestinians.[65] It is telling that a story that accounts for the political parameters that have shaped the canon of acceptable critique in (post)colonial scholarship is yet to be written. What Mahmoud Darwish called "the presence of absence" ap-

63. Derek Gregory, The Colonial Present: Afghanistan, Palestine, Iraq (Malden, MA: Blackwell, 2004).

64. Imperial "exception," U.S. exception, and Israeli exception feed on one another in multiple forms: exoneration from international law, on human rights issues, and with respect to what constitutes a "democracy." For one view, see John Felfer, "The Israeli Exception," Foreign Policy in Focus, May 4, 2010, http://fpif.org/the_israeli _exception.

65. Deeb and Winegar, Anthropology's Politics.

plies to more than the abyss that divides Israel and Palestine.[66] It describes most of the history of (post)colonial studies, as well.[67]

When observers posit colonialism "in an active voice," it is not always clear whether the reference is to a form of governance *reactivated* on an earlier colonial model or to a newly fashioned set of refracted colonial practices that build creatively and transformatively to redefine what colonialism looks like today. The temporal stretch, the uneven sedimentation of expanded and contracted forms of colonial effects, the grossly disparate ways in which that presence adheres to some bodies compelled to remember, as Didier Fassin might put it, constitute one horizon of work to be done.[68]

66. Mahmud Darwish, *In the Presence of Absence*, trans. Sinan Antoon (Brooklyn, NY: Archipelago, 2011).

67. Censorship around these issues differs by location. In France, a conference scheduled in 2011 on Palestinian-Israeli relations at one of the University of Paris locations was banned by the administration based on the argument that this was a "political issue," not an intellectual one. In Germany, a lecture on Israeli colonialism elicited neither a query nor discussion from the audience—just awkward silence—and the issue was not entertained. In the United States, the terrain is divisive. One can teach on these issues, but university-sponsored invitations are blocked or rescinded if a prominent speaker is known to support BDS. The subject of the boycott need not be raised.

A broad community of academics can easily reckon with the fact that the history of nineteenth-century liberalism was founded on a politics of exclusion and that imperial pursuits and liberalism have been tightly implicated, complementary projects. It is still hard for the same majority to agree that Israel is a racially defined polity—only a democracy in the most distorted sense of the term if one counts only the "select" Jewish population and not Palestinians.

Comparative work on what I call "colonial ruination" in chapter 10 passes muster in a broader academic sphere when directed at the postcolony in Africa. It is less easily seen to apply to what Abdul-Rahim al-Shaikh argues is the "failure to move towards the post-colonial" in Palestine: The Tunnel Condition," *Contemporary Arab Affairs* 3, 4 (October-December 2010): 480–94, 41.

68. Didier Fassin, *When Bodies Remember: Experiences and Politics of AIDS in South Africa* (Berkeley: University of California Press, 2007).

A DEADLY EMBRACE
OF COLONY AND CAMP

Every concept arises from the equation of unequal things.—Friedrich Nietzsche, "On Truth and Lies in a Nonmoral Sense," 1873

Concept formation is an opaque process; concept recognition, a deceptively simple act. Both obscure how readily we assign to concepts the appearance of stable things. How many times do we need to remind ourselves (as Derrida warned) that concepts conceal the scenes of their making?[1] How often do we need to reiterate that naming them offers only a temporary and false security—namely, that we know that to which they refer and hence can thereby manipulate their use and count on and assure ourselves of their portability?

Both concept formation and concept recognition are radically contingent on what we differently imagine concepts are, what they do, what are taken to be the distinguishing features that differentiate them from the common nouns that name them. They shape the parameters of research, stretch across unexpected sites of inquiry, constrain the viability of comparisons, and point to what we might consider exemplary "cases" or "exceptions." Sometimes they are placeholders for what one is not yet equipped to spell out or willing to say. Sometimes they are shorthand and signposts

---

1. Jacques Derrida, "White Mythology: Metaphor in the Text of Philosophy," trans. Alan Bass in *Margins of Philosophy* (Chicago: University of Chicago Press, 1982), 207–71, 213.

that tell the reader—and ourselves—that we are eligible interlocutors in high-profile debates (about "neoliberalism," "imperial formations," "biopolitics," and so on) and have the competence to participate in those coveted conversations. We bristle at those concepts that get in our way and eagerly (if anxiously) celebrate those that take us to places we otherwise would not have thought to go. We may speak of and with concepts all the time, leveraging them to our service, but that is decidedly different from addressing explicitly the force they command and recognizing how they do so.

Cognitive psychologists tell us that concepts are mental representations, "units of thought" that connect those representations to entities in the world, that provide us with a secure hold on the chaos of the worlds around us.[2] But this characterization skirts their very protean qualities, the multiple tasks they perform, how they detach partially or wholly from the entities to which they are imagined to refer and career beyond the sensibilia from which they are thought to emanate, askew to the entities in the world they are commissioned to order and capture. It is the motility of concepts that concerns me here—their capacity to expand and contract, to be capacious and constricting, and, with respect to this chapter, my effort is to trace their restive qualities. As Warren Montag writes so perceptively of Pierre Machery's work with concepts, it is their filiations and fragilities as much as their mutations to which we need to attend.[3]

Concepts that are not endowed with clarity, resolute reference, and a commanding space might be considered "quasi-concepts" that lack the full criteria that the prevailing definition as concept confers. But such a term already implicitly subscribes to a notion that concepts, when they are in their

2. Edward E. Smith and Douglas L. Medin, *Categories and Concepts* (Cambridge, MA: Harvard University Press, 1981), 1. See also the consummate work in Susan Carey's *The Origin of Concepts*, a synthesis of a career devoted to understanding, in her own words, "the human conceptual apparatus—what it is like, what it is good for, and how it arises, especially over ontogenetic and historical time": Susan Carey, *The Origin of Concepts* (Oxford: Oxford University Press, 2011), vii. Cognitive science has done a good job of showing that concepts stabilize a world that is not and that concepts provide the psychic boundaries to phenomena that are vague and varying. They have also shown how concepts change, as now witnessed by the massive literature in cognitive development. While very small pockets in psychology have addressed how concepts (such as race and caste) change in coordination with changing political location and landscapes, this is not an interest of general concern.

3. See Warren Montag, "Pierre Machery: Between the Quotidian and Utopia," *Décalages* 1, 3 (January 1, 2013). http://scholar.oxy.edu/decalages/vo11/iss3/10.

proper form, do not vacillate in a gray zone between common nouns and a condition and context that gives them more conceptual force and organizing weight. To replace a focus on the stable feature of concepts with a sense of their "fragility" turns analytic and political energies elsewhere—namely, to their capacity to morph, to identify what might otherwise construe as peripheral sites of their making or as uncertain, wayward, deviating features, set aside because they seem to lead us astray.

Concepts occur in constellations; they draw other concepts into their fold.[4] As Gilles Deleuze and Félix Guattari provocatively define a concept, it is "a point of coincidence, condensation and accumulation."[5] Political concepts do something more: They intervene in the allocation of power. They authorize and sanction what is deemed political and survey what counts as a political situation or a political event.

Here my interest is in the noun "colony," which acquires its critical force precisely because it is not commonly considered a political concept at all, because it has been so long considered benign and removed from the domain of contemporary politics. One way to make its import felt is to glean its potency from the veiled fashion in which it crafts subjects, requisitions objects, and couches its command. I seize on it because of the counterintuitive traction it affords: It innocuously grabs conceptual hold by offering a way to think otherwise about what is assigned as common usage and common sense about the places and people to which it refers. "Colony" as I pursue it here scrambles received associations; it counters the silence of political decorum and the distracting din of analytic convention.

"Colony" inhabits an ambiguous sort of conceptual space. It oscillates, perhaps more than some other political concepts, veering more toward the still neutrality of a common noun than assuming its status as a political concept charged with potentiality. We might think of it as a political concept-in-waiting. Philosophers tend to bypass it.[6] As a common noun with no con-

---

4. This feature of concepts, their occurrence in "constellations," is considered basic in cognitive psychology, as well. See Susan A. Gelman and Cristine H. Legare (2011), "Concepts and Folk Theories," *Annual Review of Anthropology* 40, 1 (2011): 379–98.

5. Gilles Deleuze and Félix Guattari, *What Is Philosophy?* (Columbia University Press, 1994), 20.

6. But see the exceptional work on the *colonie* by the philosopher Seloua Luste Boulbina, who also argues that "*il faut travailler philosophiquement autrement et penser la colonie*" (we must work philosophically otherwise and think the colony): Seloua Luste Boulbina, *Le singe de Kafka: Et autres propos sur la colonie* (Lyon: Parangon, 2008), 9.

ceptual caché, "colony's" referents fall too easily into unproblematic and manifest place. Political theorists prefer to grapple with the more compelling "isms" of which "the colony" is typically considered a product. Colonizer and colonized are generally agreed to be the principal parties to which it gives rise. Definitional authority over what colonialism is or is not is perceived as a contest with higher political stakes. For students of societal forms, too, "a colony" warrants little intellectual work. Sociologists and anthropologists, who have tended to favor delineated contexts and concrete moments, offer descriptive profiles of a particular colony (be it a settler colony or a penal colony) and proceed to compare a particular "case" with others that already meet the received requirements for inclusion and validate that designation.

Among those of us who work in a sociohistorical mode, a colony tends to be treated as transparent. It describes a physical and social location, a geographical place distinct from its metropole, a specified disaggregated population of colonizer and colonized and those caught in between. These distinctions are productive of and dependent on unequal entitlements to resources and rights, on conquest as dispossession, on dispossession as progress, and, not least, on a requisite set of embodied racialized and sexualized relations of dominance.

But this is only one version of its manifestation and its capacious political career. None of these points of entry broach the force fields in which the term "colony" has operated or the global, geopolitical, and historical breadth of the political visions embedded within it. Each approach assigns an essence rather than following its range of coordinates, ascribing rather than questioning what a colony is. Such starting points are poorly positioned to address its range of mutations. Nor do they compel its treatment as a non-obvious entity. Not least, a foundational if shadowed feature is lost—namely, that "the colony" (the penal colony; the military colony; the settler colony; the nineteenth-century agricultural colonies in England, the Netherlands, Belgium, and France) is marked by the *instability of its morphology and the instability of the political mandates* to which its architects and agents subscribe.

Such points of departure are ill poised to address what Hannah Arendt called the "wild confusion of historical terminology" to which imperial formations give rise.[7] Few (Arendt among them) have asked whether this

7. Hannah Arendt, *The Origins of Totalitarianism* (1951) (New York: Harcourt Brace, 1979), 131.

"wild confusion" is significant in itself. Already knowing what a colony is precludes asking whether ambiguous nomenclatures, competing visions, repeated failures, and reversals of course (and the violence and fortressed settledness they engender) prefigure "the colony" as something else—rather than a site of *settlement*, an always unstable and precarious project, plagued by the expectant promise (and fear) of its becoming something other than which its visionaries prescribed.

COLONY: COMMENSURABILITIES CALLED FORTH AND UPON

With this in mind, in this chapter I turn to one of the fundamental challenges raised in the introduction: What might a genealogy of imperial practices look like that neither succumbs to a teleology of the present nor is restricted to the policed categories of colonial archives themselves? How might we broach the recessed spaces of imperial entailments whose recognition may be obscured by unfamiliar associations, ambiguous terminology, and other names? In treating these often subjacent durabilities as objects of inquiry, not as given facts, what once figured as received distinctions of colonial and metropolitan contexts not only reconfigure in unexpected ways. In short, they challenge conceptual and comparative conventions.

Such a venture might resist the urge to distinguish "old" from "new" empires, a starting point that much historiography was once inclined to accept. The occluded, ambiguous qualities of imperial formations are not attributes of more modern imperial forms. The tensions between their evasive and blatant practices are constitutive of the political concepts that have long supported imperial logics of security and surveillance and their anxious orientation toward a preemptive, predictive "taming of chance."[8]

Imperial formations are macropolities of deferral and postponement, as we shall see in chapter 5. But they are something more. They produce recursive, restless recalibrations and redistributions of detentions and confinements, of mobilizations and restricted passages. Mapping these movements demands refusal to succumb to the ease with which colonial documents might otherwise carry out that task: Official colonial archives can constrict that possibility and obstruct the tracks of displacement. As technologies of rule, colonial archives are products of what we cannot easily identify or see—what is censored or deemed irrelevant—in omissions

8. Ian Hacking, *The Taming of Chance* (Cambridge: Cambridge University Press, 1990).

and the relations they refuse to make. Colonial archives create lines of severance, boundaries of jurisdiction, categories of persons who ostensibly fall outside the clear-cut rubrics of colonizer and colonized, excised from the polity of nation or empire, categories of persons pulled in and expelled from colonial locations as they are transported and immobilized across imperial domains. Severed, disabled histories are what imperial formations produce; these are the opacities in which they invest, that they nourish, and on which they depend.[9]

One dominant response to these severed histories and to the insistent sequestering of national from colonial histories has been to turn the tables on the conventional wisdom that once dictated the directionality of development of the institutions and technologies of modern governance: where they were first honed and whether structured violence is inherent in them. The exclusionary principles and practices of liberalism have come under scrutiny for some time as the foundation of British empire; today, it is the exterminating and genocidal colonial policies that are seen to have provided the "precursors," "incubators," and "models" for the technologies and visions that have been the cornerstones of European nation-states. German policies in Africa, it has been argued, were preparation for the Holocaust, rendering it not a unique event but part of what Sven Lindqvist, among others, now identifies as a "common European heritage."[10] On French terrain, the imperial shaping of national history is under revision as well: Algerian internment camps of the 1840s and France's genocidal colonial policies are no

9. See Ann Laura Stoler and Carole McGranahan, "Introduction: Reassessing Imperial Terrain" in *Imperial Formations*, ed. Ann Laura Stoler, Carole McGranahan, and Peter C. Perdue (Santa Fe, NM: School for Advanced Research Press, 2007), 3–44.

10. See Uday S. Mehta, *Liberalism and Empire: A Study in Nineteenth-Century British Liberal Thought*. Chicago: University of Chicago Press, 1999; Sven Lindqvist, *"Exterminate All the Brutes": One Man's Odyssey into the Heart of Darkness and the Origins of European Genocide*, trans. Joan Tate (New York: New Press, 1997), 9. For literature that has exploded in the past decade on the colonial template for the Holocaust, see "Forum: The German Colonial Imagination," *German History* 26, 2 (April 1, 2008): 251–71; Isabel V. Hull, *Absolute Destruction: Military Culture and the Practices of War in Imperial Germany* (Ithaca, NY: Cornell University Press, 2006); Jürgen Zimmerer, "The Birth of the Ostland out of the Spirit of Colonialism: A Postcolonial Perspective on the Nazi Policy of Conquest and Extermination," *Patterns of Prejudice* 39, 2 (June 1, 2005): 197–219. On how German South West Africa "incubated" ideas and methods adopted by the Nazis, see Benjamin Madley, "From Africa to Auschwitz: How German South West Africa Incubated Ideas and Methods Adopted and Developed by the Nazis in Eastern Europe," *European History Quarterly* 35, 3 (July 1, 2005): 429–64.

longer cordoned off as aberrant perturbations, apart from the national order of things, but recognized as traceable systemic violence—part of the deep if unwelcome history of racial France today.[11] For England, the strong case has been made for an extensive and deadly system of detention camps instituted by the British in Kenya in the 1950s, where as many as 320,000 persons were detained and many more were isolated in military zoned villages. Here, too, "genocide" and the characteristic technologies of a "gulag" are decoupled from their "originary" European sites, relocated as the common but acknowledged workings of racially defined imperial states.[12]

These new histories have effectively "provincialized" Europe, but whether or not they have allowed for the full breadth across which colonies, camps, and their containments have circumscribed the imperial globe is still open to question. The tethering of any particular metropole to the set of colonies under its aegis suggests that circuits of knowledge, coercion, and policies moved largely along the metropole-colony axis and can be tracked by the archives that joined them. Ferreting out the originary moments of the technologies of incarceration, detention, and inquisition is one way to make the case that what were once conceived as wholly European political projects were in fact imperial ones. But we also know that shared visions and knowledge underwrote the spread of political logics across imperial terrains, suggesting a scale of exchanges, transpositions of political projects, and conceptual frames that moved neither from colony to metropole alone nor only the other way around.

Here I take up a second task raised in chapter 1: to consider those methodological renovations needed to write histories that capture what imperial formations animated, the range of practices their architects both imagined as possible and succeeded, failed, and tried again to put in place. There is

11. See Marc Bernardot, "Les mutations de la figure du camp," in *Le retour des camps: Sangatte, Lampedusa, Guantanamo*, ed. Olivier Le Cour Grandmaison, Gilles Lhuilier, and Jérôme Valluy (Paris: Autrement, 2007), 42–57; Raphaëlle Branche, *La torture et l'armée pendant la guerre d'Algérie, 1954–1962* (Paris: Gallimard, 2001); Marnia Lazreg, *Torture and the Twilight of Empire: From Algiers to Baghdad* (Princeton, NJ: Princeton University Press, 2008); Olivier Le Cour Grandmaison, *Coloniser/exterminer: Sur la guerre et l'état colonial* (Paris: Fayard, 2005), and *La république imperiale: Politique et racisme d'état* (Paris: Fayard, 2009).

12. On Britain's "gulag" in Kenya, see Caroline Elkins, *Imperial Reckoning: The Untold Story of Britain's Gulag in Kenya* (New York: Henry Holt, 2006); David M. Anderson, *Histories of the Hanged: Britain's Dirty War in Kenya and the End of Empire* (New York: W. W. Norton, 2005).

obviously no single preferred way to track them. Here I pursue this work in two registers that are methodologically and analytically joined. In the first register, I pursue, quite literally, the citational referents of a document from the mid-nineteenth century that includes kinds of colonies that seem to bear little resemblance to the more common use of that term. I adhere closely to the unsure filiations it recognizes between different sorts of colonies that seem incommensurate in motive and kind. The second register attempts to make sense of how the terms colony and camp morph, what concepts congeal around them and the political logics they sustain.

Such filiations sometimes converge in specific content and at other times converge in visionary form. Pursing them extends and refigures Foucault's founding concept in *Discipline and Punish*, the "carceral archipelago," in time and place across a broader imperial map that rebinds the genealogies of penal colonies, settler colonies, detention camps in France and Algeria, a prison in Philadelphia, poor colonies in the Dutch countryside, Russian orphanages, camps that were refitted as sites for potential colonial settlers, and failed settler colonies that were militarized with soldiers as settlers. Each marks zones of exclusion and enclosure through mutations rather than correspondence, through filiations rather than fixities, through urgent and partial borrowings, through congruences sought rather than through discretely marked relations.

What emerges from such a tack is a notion of a colony as a political concept with multiple and unstable valences. Michel de Certeau might have included it among those "displaced" histories, contrary and suspended, on the fringes and *beyond* the colonial archive's long shadows. Such a strategy presses on the uncertainties, the self-evident features of what we imagine a colony is, how we recognize one, and how we come to understand what it "does." Here we are poised to take up Foucault's methodological insight that a historical event is "the breach of self-evidence." In such moments, as Paul Rabinow has succinctly put it, knowledge-things are being assembled. My interest centers on a somewhat different set of moments in that making: how "knowledge things" are *disassembled*, reassembled, fail, or fall apart.[13] It is in these breaches (of short-lived or long-term duration and of weak or

13. Michel Foucault, "Table Ronde du 20 mai 1978," in *Dits et écrits: 1954–1988, Volume 4: 1980–1988*, ed. Daniel Defert and Francois Ewald (Paris: Gallimard, 1980), 20–34, 23; Paul Rabinow, *Anthropos Today: Reflections on Modern Equipment* (Princeton, NJ: Princeton University Press, 2003), 85.

strong intensity) that we might locate the tenuous and tenacious qualities of what a colony and a camp could be, their oscillations in form, the political rationalities that underwrote them, their deployments in policy and practice between charged political concept and innocuous common noun.

Genealogical work as critical methodology alerts us to stay on the track of dispersions rather than unities, of "the dissension of other things."[14] Abstractions offer little help. Our course is "patiently documentary." It calls into question concepts, those "ready-made syntheses" taken to be settled and true. It opens up words at those moments in which things tear from their earlier incarnations.

For some who inhabit them, a "colony" is both a promise and the anticipation of a future. For others it is the suspension of time; the ordinary is reordered in a cordoned-off, designated space—in a holding pen that constricts which forms of public sociality are allowed and manages the forms of sociality that are conferred. It cultivates some within it to clarify and invest in its internal frontiers and others to abide by those distinctions as it monitors and bars their use of public space. It nourishes suspicion and further confines the recalcitrant.

A "colony" criminalizes dissidence, disassembles and punishes those who refuse its terms, and suppresses contestatory and participatory politics. It produces and identifies enemies within and outside, eagerly invests in the hunt for those targeted as a threat, anxiously celebrates the ever false and short-lived security that follows the repeated rites of capture.[15] Internally, the colony's agents are emboldened by the fervent search for those who elude its strictures by disguise and feigned acquiescence. The disdained and most held in contempt are those whose speech, class, and comportment have been educated to "fit," those who threaten to, and almost, "pass."

---

14. Michel Foucault, "Nietzsche, Genealogy, History," in *The Foucault Reader*, ed. Paul Rabinow (New York: Pantheon, 1984), 79.

15. On the centrality of the trope of predator and prey, the hunt and the hunted through the history of political philosophy (and our contemporary moment), see Grégoire Chamayou, *Manhunts: A Philosophical History* (Princeton, NJ: Princeton University Press, 2012), originally published as *Les chasses à l'homme: Histoire et philosophie du pouvoir cynégétique* (Paris: Fabrique, 2010). But see also Marc Bernardot, *Captures* (Bellecombe-en-Bauges, France: Croquant, 2012), who draws on a history of wars to capture slaves as a model for understanding the constraints, expulsions, and confinements of those subject to migration politics today.

The concept of security, as Foucault argued, works on "possible events" as much as on events that are current and operative. Thus, the colony as a political concept is in part defined by its *potentiality*.[16] The problem of security may be muted or manifest, confronted or quelled with different degrees of rigor and intensity. But the incitement to create and leverage security is at its heart. Giorgio Agamben insisted that security has become "the veritable paradigm of government" today, but it has been paradigmatic and elemental for the practices of imperial governance for far longer than he suggests.[17]

That discrepancy raises an issue that both eluded Foucault's treatment of the carceral archipelago (from which he excluded the penal colony as too early and the camp as too extreme) and Agamben's treatment of the (refugee) camp as the exception that has become "the nomos" of the modern: *The colony and the camp are both containments, enclosures, and unsettled encampments that are more closely allied than we may have imagined.* They are not mere inversions or mirror images, as one might expect. As historical formations, they feed off each other, are porous components of a political matrix that seep into each other—until they are strategically and violently torn apart. One might argue for their "family resemblance" (in Ludwig Wittgenstein's sense), not any one essential, shared core feature so much as sharing a partially and "overlapping," "crisscrossing" set in "a complicated network of similarities."[18] That resemblance, however, varies in scale. It may register as a similarity in infrastructure or planning or veer toward the minute protocols of detail.

Colony and camp make up a *conjoined conceptual matrix*, twin formations that give rise to social deformations with different effects. The concept of security shaped the imperial coordinates of polities long before it took over how national logics of security operate. As Foucault described the aim of his work on security in his Collège de France lectures of 1978–79, "This technology of security consists in large part in a reactivation and transformation of juridico-legal techniques and of disciplinary techniques," recursively calling on those tactics in place much earlier.[19] Colony and camp borrow and

16. Michel Foucault, *Sécurité, territoire, population: Cours au Collège de France, 1977–1978* (Paris: Seuil and Gallimard, 2004), 22.

17. Giorgio Agamben and Andrea Cortellessa, "Le gouvernement de l'insécurité," *La Revue Internationale des Livres et des Idées*, February 24, 2009, http://www.revuedeslivres.net /articles.php?idArt=118.

18. Ludwig Wittgenstein, *Philosophical Investigations* (1953), trans. G. E. M. Anscombe, 3d ed. (Englewood Cliffs, NJ: Prentice Hall, 2000), parts 66–67, 32.

19. Michel Foucault, "Leçon du 11 janvier 1978," in *Sécurité, territoire, population*, 11.

blend essential features of their protective, curative, and coercive architecture. They are in a deadly embrace from the start.

Such a treatment fundamentally alters the carceral archipelago, expands its political coordinates in time and space. For Foucault, the carceral archipelago served as a conceptual metaphor to identify a "carceral continuum that diffused penitentiary techniques to the most innocent of disciplines, transmitting disciplinary norms to the very heart of the penal system" and, more important, "to the depths of the social body." However, its web was cast both more literally and more widely than he in fact sought to pursue.[20] As we shall see, refiguring that concept as a "carceral archipelago of empire" does more than widen to an imperial net. It refigures and demands reassessment of the historical projects to which it gave rise—and of which it was, in turn, an effect. It re-visions the material and virtual "archipelagos" traversed. Not least, such a refiguration calls into question the multiple political logics it incited and amplified across the globe.[21] Agricultural colonies, penal colonies, resettlement camps, detention centers, island military bases, and settler communities (temporary and permanent) were nodes in an imperial network—nodes that were strategically connected and detached to produce unique and unanticipated effects.

THE COLONY AND ITS FILIATIONS

The conceptual work marshaled to maintain the colony as a political principle renders a colony protean, transitory, and provisional in its very formation. Although a colony stands apart, as a political entity it is part of, and attached to, something else. Ontologically, it exists in virtue of its dependent political status as a subset of another, prior, more substantial polity that wields authority over it. Those who inhabit a colony stand in relationship to a broader biopolitical norm and legal status that those in a colony are imagined to aspire to and desire but, by design, cannot attain. A separate (and often disparaged) social status is assigned to its habitants; its subjects are relegated to a different and distinctive legal positioning. Conceptually, the colony is a tenuous, illegitimate, conditional political formation that can sustain itself only

20. Michel Foucault, *Discipline and Punish: The Birth of the Prison* (New York: Random House, 1977), 297, 301.

21. For an initial abbreviated discussion of the "carceral archipelago of empire," see Ann Laura Stoler, *Along the Archival Grain: Epistemic Anxieties and Colonial Common Sense* (Princeton, NJ: Princeton University Press, 2009), 130–34.

by enforcing differences that turn people into other social kinds. The political subordination and apartness of the colony invariably augurs subservience to, and the imposed quest for, an unachievable and unachieved racialized norm.

Rather than assuming unity, I begin elsewhere—not with a formal etymological exercise or with the word's firm founding in the Latin *colonus* (farmer) or the verb *colere* (to till), but with what Foucault and Ian Hacking might underscore as its historical ontology.[22] This tack is tightly bound to the historical coordinates of the conceptual and physical landscapes a colony inhabits. Such an approach favors the seemingly peculiar associations "a colony" calls forth, the disparate and convergent uses to which the term was put and those sites it named.

One strategy is to follow the trajectories of the term itself. The other is to track what colonies were understood to do and the adjacencies their management elicited. Such a strategy attends especially to the reflections made by their "social engineers" (as Rabinow once called them), to the comparisons they made with spatial arrangements of people that were not necessarily named colonies but on whose logics of security and control they called. It attends to the political imaginations of those high and low charged with making real a colony's ideal workings. Such a strategy registers petty ascriptions of distinction and worth, the tactics of recruitment, the criteria of expulsion, abrupt revisions in what might count as effective implementation.[23]

Thus, a crucial methodological point: *Such a strategy follows the contour of the colony and its relationship to the camp by the range of commensurabilities it called forth and called upon.* Modular, modified and minute variations are to be not distilled and dismissed but retained, close at hand. Such a treatment might render historical labor less the enumeration of "cases" (as the empirical groundwork of concept formation is so often construed in the philosophical field) than a privileged, generative site where concepts come into creation. For this analytic venture, I call on "fieldwork in philosophy," a term that the philosopher John Austin first used for his linguistic work, that Pierre Bourdieu was to adopt to mark his sociological enterprise, and that Paul Rabinow would deploy to describe his ethnographic projects, thus thinking

22. Ian Hacking, *Historical Ontology* (Cambridge, MA: Harvard University Press, 2002), 26.

23. On "social engineers," see Paul Rabinow, *French Modern: Norms and Forms of the Social Environment* (Chicago: University of Chicago Press, 1989), 91.

the term differently yet again. For me, fieldwork in philosophy is meant to render the effort both to track reference and to trace how commensurabilities are conceived as conceptual, political, and epistemic labor.[24]

A PROTEAN ARCHIVE

We should recall here that concepts, for Deleuze and Guattari, are condensed "centers of vibration."[25] Nowhere is that resonance more palpable than in the pulse of the archive that the colony concept produced, in the paper trails that track the obvious and oblique connectivities to entities imagined to share relevant features, and to other concepts that cling around it. Let me be clear. My starting point is *not* a colonial archive as we have come to understand it as a thing and as a term. It is not a prior, bounded collection of official colonial documents with policed categories, with inclusions and excisions shaped by the exigencies of imperial governance and the acquisitive bureaucracies that paperwork sustained.[26] Rather, what I have in mind is a virtual archive, more like a nodal network or a *dispositif* as Foucault developed the term, "gradated," "compact and diffused," freed of the "house arrest" that keep archives sequestered and in place as Derrida imagined.[27] More important, the archive as I see it is *protean*, born out of the imagined yet real, blueprinted, studied, dismissed, and cross-referenced articulations that have emerged from its own filiations. Like the colony itself, this archive-in-the-making thrives on and registers its assessments in the future conditional tense.

It is a protean archive in another sense: constituted by a spread of disparate and related documents of island and landlocked colonies that stretched across the coercive and curative carceral and humanitarian globe. It is an

24. On archival work as conceptual labor, see Ann Laura Stoler, "On Archival Labor: Recrafting Colonial History," *Diálogo Andino*, 46 (March 2015): 153–65. See also Ann Laura Stoler, "Fieldwork in Philosophy: Refiguring Social Inquiry's Conceptual Labor," Jensen Memorial Lectures delivered at the Frobenius Institute, Johann Wolfgang Goethe University, Frankfurt, Germany, June 2014.

25. Deleuze and Guattari, *What Is Philosophy?* 23.

26. See Stoler, *Along the Archival Grain*, 1–17.

27. Foucault develops the concept of a *dispositif* throughout his works. It first appears in *Discipline and Punish* with little specificity or elaboration and is more clearly articulated several years later in "The Confession of the Flesh," in *Power/Knowledge: Selected Interviews and Other Writings, 1972–1977*, ed. Colin Gordon (New York: Pantheon, 1980), 194–228. I return to the concept of a *dispositif* later in this chapter.

archival web sprawled across the hundreds of agricultural colonies for delinquent youth established throughout France and the Netherlands in the
1840s and 1850s; the pioneer colonies on the Russian steppe; the domestic
"farm colonies" in England and then the United States; the leper colonies
of Trinidad, Tobago, and Hawaii; the fortressed camps of French Indochina
turned into penal colonies; the penal colonies of the French Antilles and
British Guiana (the *bagnes*), which were always proximate to the white settlers' sugar colonies off their shores; the New Caledonian penal colonies
that brought Maghrebian political agitators together with exiled *communards*; the Algerian prison colonies where French dissidents were deposited
after the revolutions in 1848; the agricultural colonies in the same Algerian
countryside designed to remove from Europe, and resettle, the numbers of
urban poor who were considered increasingly dangerous.[28] Not least, it is
an archive that moves across different scales: It may include refugee camps
within colonies such as those Palestinians have inhabited for decades; it may
include prison camps within colonies, as well as enclave colonies of containment, such as those planned but not realized for poor Indo-European
mixed-bloods in the Netherlands Indies, ranging from the outreaches of

28. On New Caledonia as a penal colony, opened in 1863 with four thousand persons
condemned for their participation in the Paris Commune of 1871, see Alice Bullard,
Exile to Paradise: Savagery and Civilization in Paris and the South Pacific, 1790–1900 (Stanford,
CA: Stanford University Press, 2000). Bullard carefully tracks how "each expansion of
the penal colony caused further encroachments on Kanak lands" in the mid-nineteenth
century with reservations first established in 1876, often on non-arable land: Bullard,
Exile to Paradise, 168. For a view of New Caledonia's bagne based on a visit that came just
after the period covered in Bullard's study, see Jean Carol, "Le bagne," *Le Revue de Paris*,
November–December 1901, 10–31. See also Mélica Ouennoughi, *Algériens et maghrébins
en Nouvelle-Calédonie: Anthropologie historique de la communauté arabo-berbère de 1864 à nos jours*
(Algiers: Casbah, 2008). Much has recently been written about the recruitment of the
increasing numbers of "new urban poor" to Algeria in the 1840s. Among the earlier
studies in English on that initiative, see Michael J. Heffernan, "The Parisian Poor and
the Colonization of Algeria during the Second Republic," *French History* 3, 4 (December
1, 1989): 377–403. Heffernan describes this as a "remarkable episode" [that] "has been
largely forgotten": Heffernan, "The Parisian Poor and the Colonization of Algeria during the Second Republic," 377. On the "domestic colonies" that included farm colonies
and labor colonies in England and Canada, and their relationship to sterilization campaigns in the United States—and, not least, their centrality for "liberal colonialism"—
see Barbara Arneil, "Liberal Colonialism, Domestic Colonies and Citizenship." *History
of Political Thought* 33, 3 (2012): 491–523. Arneil, too, draws on the establishment of
domestic colonies within Britain and British settler states "to challenge the scope and
definition of 'colonialism' in previous literature": Arneil, "Liberal Colonialism, Domestic Colonies and Citizenship," 491.

New Guinea in the 1930s to the heartland of nineteenth-century Java. The archival web is predicated on the associations called forth. It is mobile; it is reactive to changes in governing strategies; and it cuts across the boundaries of any one polity.

I track part of this virtual archive through one particular document, with the multiple filiations drawn between these different sorts of "colony." It is a document that made precisely those connections. The "life" of this document may be sought not in how often it was cited (rarely) but in the kinships it recognizes, the genealogies it ignores, and the alliances it calls up and commands. Its "life" resides in its lively node of connectivities, concerns, and preoccupations shared and exchanged; commensurabilities sought and assumed; proximate and distant affiliations affirmed. It passes through futures aborted and tenacious attachments that may no longer be. Its framing strains our conceptual categories and chronologies, confounding what might be imagined as properly "in" or "out" of place.

Most striking, it casts what was hailed as one of the most successful and famous social reformist projects of mid-nineteenth-century Europe—the agricultural colonies (les colonies agricoles) for orphaned, abandoned, and delinquent children and youth—through linkages that prompt us to reconsider them in a broad arc of imperial governance rather than as carceral institutions confined to social reform projects in Europe, as they most often have been portrayed.

What might otherwise be construed as this minor node identifies exemplary if unexpected connections. It allows us to plot a geopolitical topography that joined policies, visions, institutions, and practices directed at the containment of people, the strategies of displacement, the definitions of security, the tactics of defense, and, not least, the ever present doubts about what combination and balance of restrictions and license would work best. Together they make up what I call the emergent nexus of the "imperial modern." I take the imperial modern as a heuristic to underscore that global regimes of security and the management of colonies share a deep temporal and spatial history of their own. But it is also to insist that concentrated containments and voluntary enclosures are the Janus face of imperial logics and the anxious sensibilities they nourish—and with which they must then contend.

It is worth remembering here Foucault's insistence that "you don't have mechanisms of security which take the place of disciplinary mechanisms which would have taken the place of juridico-legal ones."[29] These forms of governance are persistent and recombined, predicated on redrawing the common sense of those categories of people against which society must be defended; redrawing the trajectories of circulation; reshuffling membership and the relevant attributes to decide on suitable membership as situations changed. Relations of force and philanthropy, racism and social reform, curative and punitive instruments were forged, fumbled, dismissed, replaced, and reworked. These foundational sites of imperial formations produce an archival map of the imagined and realized; failed experiments and visions should not be set aside as irrelevant or discarded. They were insistent reminders of the dangers to be defended against, part of the cumulative archive of imagined and real threats, giving reason to the urgency of vigilance in the face of dangers and fears that could go viral.

So what is this exemplary document? First of all, it is not to be found in the colonial archives. It is a treatise of some five-hundred pages, in four volumes, written by a certain Count A. de Tourdonnet and printed in Paris in 1862 under the title *Essais sur l'éducation des enfants pauvres: les colonies agricoles* (Essays on the Education of Poor Children: The Agricultural Colonies).[30] It was neither an exceptional treatise nor the first of its kind; it was merely one work in a proliferating, if minor, genre of reformist writing from the corridors of law, penality, and philanthropy between the 1830s and the 1870s, especially preceding and following the political storms of 1848. Some were crafted as responses to pauperism in France, with precursors drawn from the Netherlands, Belgium, England, and Australia. Others focused specifically on France, as de Tourdonnet's did, advocating proposals for newly envisioned penal institutions.

The number of detailed commissions, reports, and multisite surveys carried out during these years is staggering. Many ran to several hundred pages as their authors set out to review, assess, project, and give substance to the viability and widely shared conviction that an attachment to land, life

29. Foucault, *Sécurité, territoire, population*, 10.

30. A. de Tourdonnet, *Essais sur l'éducation des enfants pauvres: Des colonies agricoles d'education* (Paris: Brunet, 1862). Details about de Tourdonnet's "career" as a consultant to the government and about his noble family's genealogy still remain elusive. He is always referred to as "A." de Tourdonnet. For other such treatises, see also Raymond Théodore Troplong, "La proposition concernant les enfants confiés à l'assistance publique," Commission de l'Assemblée Législative, session de 1865, Paris.

in the countryside, and manual (especially agricultural) labor would provide the economic, political, and moral solutions to the "problems" as they were posed: to alleviate urban pauperism; to quell the revolutionary potential of Europe's urbanizing poor; and to avert a new generation of wayward, abandoned youth who would otherwise turn to revolt and crime. Colonization in its multiple forms, through forced and persuasive recruitment of convicts, political detainees, and poor, abandoned children or delinquent youths were imagined as feasible ways to protect European society and make productive those seen as a burden and social danger in the making.

The *colonies agricoles* were cast as reformist enterprises to extricate children from adult prisons and rescue them from moral harm. In historiography, this has marked the constricted frame in which they were viewed. Some historians have traced their advent to an eighteenth-century romance with the restorative, morally rehabilitable qualities of the countryside; to conservative Catholic philanthropic initiatives invested in the regenerative power of labor; and to the communal and cooperative vision of utopian agrarian settlements.[31] Other historians trace them further back, to Greek city-states; others, to the French Revolution; and still others, to Malesherbes and Rousseau. Some linked them to a modernizing penitentiary system, in which houses of corrections were expanded with *colonies agricoles* attached to them or turned, in the 1830s, into *colonies pénitentiaires* (penitentiary colonies). Although some celebrated their new pedagogic goals, the *colonies agricoles* were also depicted as "depots of mendacity" and "prisons in the fields," as they would be parodied and condemned in the early twentieth century.[32]

31. See Ceri Crossley, "Using and Transforming the French Countryside: The 'Colonies Agricoles' (1820–1850)," *French Studies* 45, 1 (1991): 147, 160; Luc Forlivesi, Georges-François Pottier, and Sophie Chassat, eds., *Eduquer et punir: La colonie agricole et pénitentiaire de Mettray (1839–1937)* (Rennes: Presses Universitaires de Rennes, 2005).

32. See, e.g., Christian Carlier, *La prison aux champs: Les colonies d'enfants délinquants au Nord de la France au XIXe siècle* (Paris: Éditions de l'Atelier and Éditions Ouvrières, 1994). Carlier offers one of the most detailed histories of the "rise and fall" of the *colonies agricoles* in France. He traces the earlier studies on which the *colonies agricoles* were based, the extensive debates among those who were for and against them, the latter holding that the *colonies*, in practice, bore little resemblance to the lofty descriptions on the basis of which French authorities endorsed them with the law of August 5, 1850. Still, Carlier's meticulous study makes no mention of, and gives no analytic space to, the imperial politics, circuits, and places so imbricated in that history. The sorts of filiations traced by de Tourdonnet (who is not referenced) have no place.

Colonies agricoles came in many forms, and it is no surprise that social reformers rarely agreed about how to distinguish among them. But their discrepant taxonomic work and the debates about how the *colonies* should best be viewed are neither misunderstandings of what *colonies agricoles* were nor mere mislabelings. Instead, the discrepancies serve as a diacritic of the multiple political logics to which the *colonies* were subjected and to the contested politics of conceptual frames. A pedagogic model of "[poor] relief" joined principles and practices of incarceration: both passed through a "dressage" of the body, and varying intensities of punitive violence if training was resisted, and acquiescence was not achieved.[33]

Graphing their changing taxonomic grids yields a striking observation: What de Tourdonnet would distinguish as religious colonies, military colonies, settler colonies (*colonies de défrichement*), and "charitable agricultural colonies for children" were sustained by a set of precepts and procedures that he imagined could be fruitfully borrowed and exchanged. Even among *colonies agricoles* designed for children, the distinctions were fluid—embraced, erased and redrawn. Thus, de Tourdonnet sought to devise his own typology, differentiating those devoted to poor relief from those designed for repression and both from those that stressed education. Such sorting efforts were not his alone; principles and practices that morphed and meshed were key features of how this knowledge was assembled, reassembled, and disseminated across the globe.

De Tourdonnet's essay is not so much representative as exemplary in one specific sense. I treat it as *a diagnostic of dissensions—an opening to the multiple logics* that underwrote what constituted "colonies" and who should inhabit them. An orphan, a child who stole a loaf of bread, and a child caught sleeping under a Parisian bridge fell under the same rubric and were assigned to the same system of internment, in part because they were subsumed under the same constellation of overlapping political frames: to deter a new generation through rehabilitation and labor from becoming enemies of the state; to defend society from the potential threat they represented; and to secure France's colonies with productive and loyal settlers.

33. On Mettray in the 1920s, the deprivations endured by the young colonists on their "ravaged bodies," and their responses to the multiple forms of daily duress imposed on them, see Myriam Bendhif-Syllas, "Les 'corps perdus' de Mettray," *Revue d'Histoire de l'Enfance "Irrégulière,"* 8 (November 15, 2006): 133–48.

RESITUATING METTRAY

Among the most famously successful of the children's colonies was the *colonie agricole et pénitentiaire* of Mettray, its very title reflecting the ambivalence of its curative project. Opened in 1840, Mettray was lauded as exemplary from its founding. Throughout Europe, none was more often visited, written about, or discussed by dignitaries from Britain, Belgium, Germany, the Netherlands, and the United States. In its initial years, social reformers across the political spectrum were its supporters. By 1851, Mettray was so renowned that the Académie Française devoted the theme of its poetry competition to "La colonie de Mettray."[34] Mettray's founder, the former magistrate, Frédéric-Auguste Demetz, subscribed to and advocated a moral mission: Abandoned and delinquent children should be not just punished but also redeemed as citizens through strict discipline, agricultural labor, and a familial model of supervision designed to train and care for children's bodies and souls. Mettray's reputation was to last. As Demetz was to write proudly in a report on his *colonie* from 1862, there was no need to repeat the well-known story of its success.[35]

Mettray's prominent status was not accidental. Demetz encouraged visitors from highly placed people and had so many come to witness the working of his venture that he built a Hotel de Colonie just outside the colony's gates. More than sixty such *colonies* were created over the next decades, all claiming to follow Mettray's organizational model and moral mandate.[36] As with the Dutch agricultural colonies on which Mettray was partially modeled, such *colonies agricoles* were to be "seedbeds" to raise honest citizens and hardworking laborers with limited aspirations.[37] Its young inmates were never referred to as "prisoners" but as "*colons*." They were to invest their time and energy in labor and the land. For de Tourdonnet, too, Mettray

34. Forlivesi et al., *Eduquer et punir*, 154.

35. Frédéric-Auguste Demetz, "Société d'économie charitable." In *Revue d'Économie, Chrétienne*, Tome 7 (Paris: Adrien Le Clerc, 1864).

36. On the tension between "confinement" of children and the supposed educational and redemptive virtues of performing agricultural labor in the case of *colonies agricoles* administered by the Clairvaux prison, see Jean-François Condette, "Entre enfermement et culture des champs, les vertus éducatives supposées due travail de la terre et de l'atelier. Les enfants de Clairvaux (1850–1864)," *Le Temps de l'Histoire* 7 (November 15, 2005): 41–75.

37. Gabriel De Lurieu and Hippolyte Françoise Marie Romand, *Etudes sur les colonies agricoles de mendicants, jeunes détenus, orphelins et enfants trouvés (Holland, Suisse, Belgique, France)* (Paris, Dusacq, 1851), 2.

was a benchmark against which to measure all others. Three decades after Mettray's founding, the New York Times was still lauding its purported ambition that "children should be 'educated' . . . not simply reared."[38]

Foucault brought renewed attention to such colonies in the last chapter of Discipline and Punish, where he marked Mettray's opening as "the completion of the carceral system" and, more forcefully, as the condensation of "the art of punishing that is still more or less our own."[39] For Foucault, Mettray marked "a new era"—concentrating all the coercive technologies of comportment and behavior through meticulous and multiple forms of training—for its staff and its "colonists," the children themselves. With characteristic hyperbole, he dubbed Mettray "the first training college in pure discipline" and in the "art" of "power relations."[40]

But Mettray and other, similar colonies agricoles were also something more, which was central to Foucault's larger analytic project. He seized on Mettray in particular as an opportunity to identify "a whole series of institutions" that constituted the carceral archipelago—a "far-reaching" network of "compact and diffuse" institutions and methods "that were to be both curative and punitive." The carceral archipelago was "a subtle, graduated, carceral net . . . part of a new dispositif"—a set of techniques for modern discipline that turned away from the spectacle of punishment to the isolation of the cell.[41] As important, it was an emergent vehicle in the power of normalization that collapsed into a single entity the "multiple dangers of social disorder, deviance, madness, and crime." If these children's colonies represented the soft end of the carceral spectrum, Foucault's choice of Mettray was intentional, selected precisely, as he put it, because "it was somewhat unjust."[42] It was where his favored site for analysis would rest, on "the frontiers" of techniques that erased distinctions between the undisciplined and the dangerous and that extended to the "lower reaches of criminal law."[43]

Foucault's analytic sweep is characteristically compelling, but it is also partial, schematic, and skewed in time and place. Mettray was a node in a

38. "Model Prisons," New York Times, August 25, 1873.
39. Foucault, Discipline and Punish, 302.
40. Foucault, Discipline and Punish, 295.
41. Foucault, Discipline and Punish, 297; Michel Foucault, Surveiller et punir: Naissance de la prison (Paris: Gallimard, 1975), 349.
42. Foucault, Discipline and Punish, 296; Foucault, Surveiller et punir, 347.
43. Foucault, Discipline and Punish, 297; Foucault, Surveiller et punir, 347.

sprawling network, many of whose linkages and abutments Foucault by-passed, was unaware of, or had not yet sought to name. What was dramatically "new" in his estimation was not only how effectively Mettray combined multiple models outside and within institutions, but their dispersal across a broad societal domain. When *Discipline and Punish* was first published, French historians quickly took issue with his generalizations, noting that if Mettray was unique, its practices were almost never followed. He quipped that they missed the point.[44]

Foucault's response when asked why he chose the prison as the center of a new penal system, and not deportation or the penal colonies, is curious. He insisted that he liked to dwell not in "universals" but in work that takes place between "unfinished abutments and anticipatory strings of dots" (*pierre d'attente et des points de suspension*).[45] But if "unfinished abutments" were his sites of choice, and genealogy turns precisely to those conceptual and concrete sites where plans and practices remained unfinished or failed to materialize, the genealogy he pursued seems oddly selective. Despite his emphasis on *gradations* of punitive and curative arrangements within the carceral archipelago, the massive network of colonies outside northern Europe remained barely in his peripheral vision and had little interest for him. *Colonies militaires* housing French soldiers in Algeria, labor camps of Europeans serving colonial public works projects, and, most notably, penal colonies such as those of New Caledonia, French Indochina, and French Guiana were scattered across the topographies of Europe's empires. Indeed, Peter Redfield has called penal colonies not "marginal spaces on the edge of the nation," as Foucault sometimes located them, but central technologies of it.[46] So why these refused and severed connections?

At one level, the answer is obvious. Foucault was intent on showing that even the most seemingly benign social projects were riddled from the outset with forms that did not take the prison model in whole but "utilized some of its carceral mechanisms: societies of patronage, moralizing proj-

44. Jacques Julliard and Michel Winock, eds., *L'impossible prison: Recherches sur le systeme penitentiaire aux XIXe siècle* (Paris: Seuil, 1980).

45. Michel Foucault, "Questions of Method," in *The Foucault Effect: Studies in Governmentality, with Two Lectures by and an Interview with Michel Foucault*, ed. Graham Burchell, Colin Gordon, and Peter Miller (Chicago: University of Chicago Press, 1991), 73. Also see Foucault, "Table Ronde du 20 mai 1978," 41.

46. Peter Redfield, *Space in the Tropics: From Convicts to Rockets in French Guiana* (Berkeley: University of California Press, 2000), 64.

ects, offices that at once distributed aid and assured surveillance, workers' compounds, all retained marks of the penitentiary system" and were spread throughout society at large. But in avoiding the moralizing missions of expansive networks of punitive institutions, of which colonialism itself could be considered the quintessential form, his very project becomes oddly distorted, for it was about not "discipline and punishment," as the English translation would lead us to expect, but surveillance and punishment, as in the French title. Thus, the range of imperial, racialized subjects against which society was encouraged to defend itself, and to which his later work would direct us, remain outside "*la trame carceral*"—and the very modern and global coordinates of the carceral frame. Indeed, it is precisely his striking invocation of a "return/boomerang effect" (*effet de retour*) of the practices of colonization that he would identify in his 1976 Collège de France lectures (there only addressed with respect to the end of the sixteenth century) that one could imagine exploding the constraints of his nineteenth-century—and our twenty-first-century—carceral map.[47]

RESEARCH TRIPS IN THE ARTS OF GOVERNANCE

Mettray did get enormous press, and its name was known more widely than that of many other, similar institutions at the time. Still, a concerted genealogy of its making could tell a story in the arts of governance that belies its designation and distinction as the quintessential site of modern society and punitive reform. From the detailed and profuse range of documents prior to, during, and subsequent to its establishment, Mettray—as a vision and set of practices—points to vectors of political affiliation and infrastructural contiguity that sprawl across a broad map. Mettray was the product of a cumulative set of transatlantic, trans-European, and trans-imperial, largely government-financed research projects. Between the late 1830s and the 1860s, that production was prolific: New multi-tome reports appeared every few years reviewing these initiatives. Some made a case for the success of particular *colonies agricoles*, documenting their precedents; others commented on the isolation-cell model in Philadelphia or commended the

47. Michel Foucault, *Society Must Be Defended: Lectures at the Collège de France, 1975–76* (New York: Picador, 2003), 103. For a discussion of this extraordinary passage, see Ann Laura Stoler, *Race and the Education of Desire: Foucault's History of Sexuality and the Colonial Order of Things* (Durham, NC: Duke University Press, 1995), 75.

Auburn prison, established in New York in 1816, which combined isolation, silence, and "congregate labor."[48] Some observers countered both options with recommendations for military or work camps as more reasonable and relevant models on which to draw.

These commissioned reports were not based on expeditions that collected flora, fauna, and ethnographic exoticisms across the seas, although we know that these, too, were critical nodes in shaping the qualified knowledge used to make colonial projects work. Rather, the reports that prepared the ground for Mettray and that followed were reconnaissance trips of another sort. These were studies in the mobile and tactical arts of governance and in the varied organization of clustered, policed settlements that would be most likely to actualize these multipurpose governing forms. These were projects that detailed appraisals of building design, obstructions to escape, topography, the materials used for enclosure, and the organization of labor and life that would most economically and efficiently make profits, colonization, surveillance, and security possible. *One might even see them as the percipient emergent features of a proto-intelligence pacification industry.*

In 1836, Mettray's founder, Demetz, and the already well-known architect of carceral institutions, Guillaume Blouet, made a commissioned trip to England, and then to the United States to investigate the new "Philadelphia system" in Pennsylvania. They were not the first French contingent to do so. Gustave de Beaumont and Alexis de Tocqueville had made a similar investigative trip five years earlier to Philadelphia, to the New York sites of Auburn and Sing-Sing, and other institutions in the United States. De Tocqueville's two consulting trips to Algeria, in 1841 and 1847, the basis for his own proposals for *colonies agricoles*, were to come after.[49]

48. For the Philadelphia model and Auburn as a "history of the present" of incarceration in the United States, see Jonathan Simon's excellent account, "Rise of the Carceral State," *Social Research* 74, 2 (July 1, 2007): 471–508.

49. Gustave Auguste de Beaumont de la Bonninière and Alexis de Tocqueville, *On the Penitentiary System and Its Application in France, with an Appendix on Penal Colonies and also Statistical Notes* (Philadelphia: Carey, Lea and Blanchard, 1833). De Tocqueville's support for colonization in Algeria actually preceded his first visits and only strengthened when he did visit and endorsed Bugeaud's brutal massacres, which he deemed "unfortunate necessities which cannot be escaped by any people at war with Arabs": quoted in Melvin Richter, "Tocqueville on Algeria," *Review of Politics* 25, 3 (July 1, 1963): 379. De Tocqueville was eventually to condemn the French army's tactics and instead proposed civilian settler colonization and *colonies agricoles*: see Alexis de Tocqueville, "Second Report on Algeria, 1847," reproduced in *Writings on Empire and Slavery*, ed. Jennifer Pitts (Baltimore: Johns Hopkins University Press, 2001), 174–98. See also the discussion of de Toc-

Thus despite Mettray's fame, Demetz was one among a steady stream of social reformers and government officials charged with assessing the potential of various models for vacating the metropole of *les misères*. Michel Heurne de Pommeuse's 1,200 page report on Belgian and Dutch rural penal institutions published in 1832 was the product of a similar investigative inquiry in search of other penal and curative templates. Pierre Nora cites Heurne de Pommeuse's report, commissioned by the French minister of agriculture, as "the most complete" of those on agricultural colonization.[50] It was certainly the longest and wordiest, largely concerned with the possibility of applying what its author considered the "highly successful" Dutch model. The aim, as he put it, was to offer "comparative examples" from other countries that demonstrated, with respect to *colonies agricoles*, "more civilized" options than the forms of confinement then current in France.

De Tourdonnet's proposal, too, was to create a docile and mobile laboring class equipped with industry and experience and "guided by the lessons that their experience in the *colonies agricoles*" conferred on them. His favored examples were the welfare *colonies agricoles* of Belgium and Holland, particularly those created in 1818 by Johannes van den Bosch under the aegis of his newly created Dutch Benevolent Society (which Heurne de Pommeuse also considered most promising.) De Tourdonnet was also attracted to the Netherlands' example in encouraging colonial expansion, a project that he saw could be applied most notably in Algiers.[51] Here the "lessons" wind back to colonial models, not those for Europe alone. The Dutch historian Albert Schrauwers makes the strong case that van den Bosch's experiments in poor relief were not sui generis: the string of agricultural colonies that the Dutch Benevolent Society had established by 1827 bore "striking resemblance to the organization of labor" adopted for the onerous and infamous Cultivation System that van den Bosch created, implemented, and imposed on small farmers in Java. By Schrauwers's account, the Cultivation System that made a "para-penal colony"

---

queville's writing on Algeria in Tzvetan Todorov, "Tocqueville et la doctrine coloniale," in *De la colonie en Algérie* (Paris: Complexe, 1988), 9–36.

50. Pierre Nora and Lawrence D. Kritzman, *Realms of Memory: Rethinking the French Past* (New York: Columbia University Press, 1996), 537.

51. See Michel Heurne de Pommeuse, *Des colonies agricoles et leurs avantages* (Paris: Huzard, 1832), 148, 194.

of Java, showed "remarkable continuity" through "the coercive use of the underutilized labor of paupers."[52]

Others studies followed. Le Baron de Gérando's report of 1839 on rural institutions for the poor carefully investigated Swiss and German colonies, as well as those in Holland.[53] Just after Mettray opened, and before de Tourdonnet's treatise went to press, the pros and cons of *colonies agricoles* in Algeria received extensive and critical treatment by the Saint-Simonian disciple Barthélemy Prosper Enfantin, newly appointed to yet another research commission to collect ethnographic and historical data in Algeria. Condemning the French army's "pure acts of destruction," he proposed instead colonization by French civilians and *colonies agricoles* that would retain the positive features of the earlier *colonies militaires;* he lauded their "esprit de corps," and "collective character."[54] Enfantin's five-hundred-page report was rejected, deemed too political and too tangential to the subject about which he was commissioned to write, not least because it was one of the few studies to insist that prospective *colons* be skilled cultivators as well as soldiers and "take their inspiration" from "*des habitudes arabes,*" and that Arab sobriety should serve as a model for them.[55]

Most of these studies were indeed inscribed in a national frame, but as the Dutch historian Jeroen Dekker notes, they were transnational as well, entailing communication across Europe among its privileged elites. And should one imagine that the French Revolution removed the aristocracy from power, one need only read the prefixes of the commission authors: among them were counts, barons, and those conferred high ranks in the Legion of Honor. These architects, planners, and agents of *colonies agricoles* were the purveyors of what Rabinow might call "new knowledge things" and how they would be assembled. This is a global history documented on a micro-scale.[56] But it was

52. Albert Schrauwers, "The 'Benevolent' Colonies of Johannes van den Bosch: Continuities in the Administration of Poverty in the Netherlands and Indonesia," *Comparative Studies in Society and History* 43, 2 (April 2001): 298–328.

53. Joseph Marie de Gérando, *De la bienfaisance publique* (Bruxelles, Hautman, 1839).

54. Prosper Enfantin, *Colonisation de l'Algérie* (Paris: P. Bertrand, 1843), 153.

55. For an exuberant endorsement of the *colonies agricoles* from a passionate accolade of Charles Fourier, see François Cantagrel, *Mettray et Oswald: Étude sur deux colonies agricoles* (Paris: Librairie de l'École Sociétaire, 1842). His recommendation was to give "the young detainees, if not liberty, at least the appearance of liberty": Cantagrel, *Mettray et Oswald*, 40.

56. Jeroen J. H. Dekker, "Punir, sauver et éduquer: La colonie agricole 'Nederlandsch Mettray' et la rééducation résidentielle aux Pays-Bas, en France, en Allemagne

also a conceptual and concrete working archive in which expansionist imperial design was honed and, not least, where that "wild confusion of terminology" (to which Arendt alluded) was produced, where the appellations for colonies and camps and types of confinement were scrambled, transposed, superimposed, and replaced. *Colonies militaires, colonies agricoles,* and *colonies pénitentiaires* were not so much homonyms as contiguous, contingent elements in imperial formations.

Many of the treatises on *colonies agricoles* explicitly celebrated their philanthropic outreach, with the moral regeneration of abandoned children of the urban poor and the welfare of delinquent and orphaned children. But this emphasis belies other associations: their citations, cross-references, and borrowed elements make the distinctions between the curative work of the *colonies agricoles* and other forms of detention and isolation hard to draw. "*Colonies pénitentiaires*" was a term and a concept that moved across multiple domains. It could designate children's rural institutions, rural sections of prisons in France, or the penal colonies of empire. The expansion and contraction of force and isolation might better be viewed as differences in quality than in kind.[57]

The term and sites for *bagnes* are usually totally distinct in historiography, but here, too, there were elements that blurred. In their earliest incarnation, "*bagne*" referred to domestic prisons and, more commonly, the shipyard work camps for convicts in the late eighteenth century and early nineteenth century. When these *bagnes* within France were phased out and partially replaced with "transport" to forced labor camps, the term *bagne* was used to refer to penal colonies overseas. Colonial *bagnes* in their various forms all were sites of exclusion and enclosure for political prisoners, common criminals, and, after new legislation in the second half of the nineteenth century, those who were considered "hardened" criminals—that is, irremediable recidivists with recurrent infractions against them. Hard labor was to be their final fate in the service of punishing crime and building and expanding colonial infrastructure.[58]

---

et en Angleterre entre 1814 et 1914," *Le Mouvement Social* 153, 3 (September 1, 1990): 63–90.

57. Thus, see Demetz, "Les colonie agricole de charité," 1.

58. The most common use of the term after 1852 was reserved for transport, or deportation with specific terms designating those who were terminal and those who could be converted to life sentences (*relegués*). For a particularly rich study of them, see Stephen A. Toth, *Beyond Papillon: The French Overseas Penal Colonies, 1854–1952* (Lincoln:

Historians of the colonial *bagnes* often remind us that in 1852, just as British authorities ended their penal colonies, the French invested in theirs. The contrast makes for a good story but is not wholly accurate. It is true that as the transportation of convicts to Australia ended, French transport to Guiana began. Although this was suspended in 1867, with the new Relegation Law of 1885 transport of convicts began anew to New Caledonia.[59] While common criminals did leave the shipyard bagne, one could argue that Algeria served the French military as an *unmarked* penal colony earlier and for a longer time. By Dominique Kalifa's graphic telling, "Biribi" was the name given to an unspecified complex, a "punitive archipelago" of military penal colonies run by *les corps speciaux* of the French army, which inflicted torture and severe forms of discipline on those deemed resistant to military recruitment and on those considered recalcitrant within the battalions. Operative in Algeria, Morocco, and Tunisia (and later in New Caledonia and Guiana) between 1830 and 1962, when the last unit of prisoners was transferred from Tunisia to France, Kalifa estimates, anywhere from 600,000 to 800,000 men (condemned for a disparate set of minor infractions and political offenses) went through an abusive and sadistic disciplinary and penitentiary system of which *ateliers de travaux publics* (workshops for public works), operating as forced labor camps for the building of roads, sewage systems, and ports, were only one version.[60] According to Colin Forster, Botany Bay was heavily researched by French authorities from the tail end of the eighteenth century

---

University of Nebraska Press, 2008). The vast historiography on French *bagnes* has been facilitated by the equally extensive archives devoted to the subject. See Archives Nationales d'Outre-Mer, "Les archives des bagnes," *Criminocorpus: Revue d'Histoire de la Justice, des Crimes et des Peines*, January 1, 2008, http://criminocorpus.revues.org/144, http://criminocorpus/revues.org/167, http://criminocorpus.revues.org/173.

59. As Marc Renneville writes, the "colonial *bagne* . . . were born out of a convergence of two utopias: that of the regeneration of individuals through work, and that of colonization by forced exile": Marc Renneville, "Les bagnes coloniaux: De l'utopie au risque du non-lieu," *Criminocorpus: Revue d'Histoire de la Justice, des Crimes et des Peines*, January 1, 2007, http://criminocorpus.revues.org/173.

60. Dominique Kalifa, *Biribi: Les bagnes coloniaux de l'armée française* (Paris: Grand Livre du Mois, 2009), 10. Kalifa makes a similar point to mine, but with respect to the "military subtleties" (which have distinguished various forms of forced labor and detention camps) he notes "more than by their singularities, it is [the] similarities [of] these diverse unities" that should retain our attention. Biribi became the name for the excesses of military discipline and torture in the public imagination. It was then an imaginary place and real at the same time, a sort of penitentiary *archipel*: Kalifa, *Biribi*, 11.

and after, with the Department of the Navy initiating two failed expeditions for French penal colonies in Australia.[61]

It would be hard to claim that the overseas penal colonies for political deportees and criminals were the same as those imagined for the children's *colonies agricoles* overseas. But their shared features, with respect to political vision, military aim, designs for colonization, and techniques of containment, make it equally difficult to place one set outside the carceral archipelago and the other as its quintessential form. When the inveterate royalist Comte Portalis submitted his *mémoire* of 1854 on the benefits of establishing *colonies agricoles* in Algeria to be made up of abandoned French children, arguing, "In short, that [a French] orphanage could serve in many respects as the model for an imperial colony," that model was only part of his plan. He looked as much to the Russian military colonies, Transylvanian colonies for itinerant Roma groups, and those on the provincial buttressed frontiers of Austria.[62] De Tourdonnet, as we shall see, looked to these, as well.[63] They are what Roland Barthes might call the "punctum" of these narratives (the "shock" of unexpected details that alters one's vision); in the case of these varied camps and colonies, the "prick" comes in the form of the seemingly incommensurable comparisons and lessons that the visionaries of these containments repeatedly would draw.

At one point in *Discipline and Punish*, Foucault dismisses the penal colonies, but in Alan Sheridan's English translation they seem to reappear twenty pages later, precisely when the term "carceral archipelago" is introduced. Foucault explains that he will not "reconstitute the whole network [of the carceral archipelago]" but, rather, offer "a few references and dates that should give some idea of the breadth and precocity of the phenomenon," with the "penal colonies envisaged by the law of 1850" among his chosen examples.[64] But Sheridan's translation of Foucault's term *"les colonies pénitentiaires"* as "penal colony" confuses the issue and misses a critical historical and conceptual point.[65] Foucault's pairing of the 1850 law on *colonies agricoles* with *colonies pénitentiaires* and

61. Colin Forster, *France and Botany Bay: The Lure of a Penal Colony* (Carlton South, Australia: Melbourne University Press, 1996).

62. Comte Portalis, "Mémoire sur un projet de loi suivi d'un Senatus—Consulte sur la création de colonies agricoles en Algérie pour les enfants trouvés et abandonnés et les orphelins pauvres de France âgés de 12 à 21 ans," 1854, 59–60.

63. Portalis, "Mémoire sur un project de loi suivi d'un Senatus," 60, 66.

64. Foucault, *Discipline and Punish*, 297.

65. Foucault, *Discipline and Punish*, 298.

Sheridan's translation as "penal colony" are misleading because Foucault's use of the term refers to the domestic *colonies pénitentiaires*, not the overseas penal colonies. But perhaps the confusion is telling. Foucault may not have been concerned with colonial locations, but here the avoidance seems too forced, both absence and artifice, a suspended genealogical path he chose not to take.

To underscore the point again, *colonies agricoles* across the imperial archipelago remained outside Foucault's territorial, political, and analytic frame. In brief mention of the possibility of a broader carceral net in *Discipline and Punish*, he writes that "the example of colonization comes to mind," but then discards it as "not the most convincing example."[66] But colonization is "not the most convincing example" of what? Of how surveillance and reform were imbricated? Or of the "softer" forms of discipline in the broader social body in which these disciplinary practices were lodged? In the only direct reference to colonialism, he discounts the projects that were drawn up "for the delinquent, undisciplined soldiers, prostitutes and orphans to take part in the colonization of Algeria, as well as those in Guiana or later to New Caledonia" because they "had no real economic importance."[67]

But this reasoning, for Foucault, is also strange. When did he ever discount technologies of governance because they were not profitable? Economic efficacy was never a sufficient measure to account for the political imaginaries he sought to name. Failed projects were the very fabric of experimentation and crucial sites of what Foucault himself called "political dreams," indices of the anxieties and fears that produced the very formation of enclosures and categories of people to be contained.[68] One crucial methodological insight of genealogy is precisely to consider not only the implemented but the productive qualities of the failed and imagined. It is Foucault who urged a tracing of histories "in a piecemeal fashion from alien forms."

DE TOURDONNET'S CITATIONAL MAP

And this is exactly what de Tourdonnet did—not because he was endowed with prophetic foresight or was more astute than Foucault but simply

66. Foucault, *Discipline and Punish*, 279.
67. Foucault, *Discipline and Punish*, 279.
68. Foucault, *Discipline and Punish*, 117.

because he inhabited the prevailing political logic in which security, containment, and the dangers of an amorphously defined underclass were thought to work. Consider Foucault's claim that Algeria was formally excluded as an overseas penal colony in 1854.[69] It was, indeed. But that would be neither the beginning nor the end of the story. De Tourdonnet makes clear that Algeria was a strategic location for children's *colonies agricoles* in the same years. He was hardly alone in promoting Algeria as a renewed and excellent site.[70] De Tourdonnet's proposal was for the *colonies agricoles* to be spread throughout rural France to raise strapping youths with a love of the "sweat of labor" and a ready love of the land. Ultimately, the children in the French *colonies agricoles* would become able fodder for colonizing and securing Algeria for France's expanding empire. The ties between children's agricultural colonies and the settlement of Algeria are threaded through de Tourdonnet's essay; through the logics of colonization, punishment, and the rehabilitation of youth and their moral education. Ironically, perhaps, they are drawn, as Foucault insisted they should be understood in pursuing a genealogy, in "a piecemeal fashion" from "alien forms."[71]

Placing Mettray in a broader constellation of institutional forms than Foucault did, de Tourdonnet notes that the "transplantation of welfare children in Algeria was nothing new" in the 1860s. Earlier commissions from 1832, 1852, and 1856 had also sought "to bind" destitute French children to Algeria. The St. Ilan orphanage in Brittany proposed such a project to the emperor in 1830. In 1851, more than two hundred children were sent from Paris to Ben Aknoun, an orphanage outside Algiers run by the Catholic priest Father Brumaud. The *département* of the Seine financed the initiative (receiving boys of

69. Foucault writes, "Despite all the projects that were drawn up under the July monarchy for delinquents, undisciplined soldiers, prostitutes and orphans to take part in the colonization of Algeria, that colony was formally excluded, by the law of 1854, from becoming the overseas penal colonies": *Discipline and Punish*, 279.

70. A member of the private counsel to the emperor, the jurist Raymond Théodore Troplong, drafted a proposal in 1856 that newborns abandoned at convents and municipal hospitals would make excellent candidates for the *colonies agricoles* in Algeria. Organized around a central colony with branches in Algiers, Oran, and Constantine under the direction of the governor-general, the *colonie agricole* would house the children until age fifteen or sixteen, when they then would be sent to work and live with farmers and adult *colons*: see Raymond Théodore Troplong, "Développements présentés par M. Le Premier Président Troplong à l'appui de la Proposition Concernant Les Enfants Confiés à l'Assistance Publique," 1856, http://www.youscribe.com/catalogue/livres/litterature/developpements-presentes-par-m-le-premier-president-troplong-a-302251.

71. Foucault, "Nietzsche, Genealogy, History," 142.

age ten to thirteen who were to learn to cultivate the soil and their souls).[72] Eleven more regional departments were granted subsidies to do the same. Forty-six more children were sent under Father Abram, director of the Algerian orphanage at Misserghin, with the "warmest support from the war ministry." Like many other *colonies agricoles*, Misserghin had little success, attributed to the fact that the children were too young to work and were ill prepared for the climate. From Brumard's *colonie agricole* established in 1852 fifty-eight of the two hundred children ran away.

Algeria was envisioned as part of a solution to the fact that many of the children's *colonies agricoles* in France had failed to prosper and that among those that were established, some lasted fewer than twenty years. By 1860, only six hundred children were installed as colons in eighty-six French departments, not including those in Algeria. An inquiry opened by the minister of interior that year seized on what was posed as a fundamental question: Why were there only six hundred children as colons across France?

Commissioners sought obvious answers in obvious sites. On leaving the *colonies*, boys were said to end up incarcerated; the girls, in prostitution (although there is no documentation to substantiate that this was so). Despite initial enthusiasm, the Ministry of Interior's report spelled out why the prospect was futile, suggesting that the young colons were neither docile nor without their own forms of refusal and critique. Adolescents released from the *colonies agricoles* and orphanages in France were said to resent the constant surveillance and lacked the experience needed to run the small concessions they were granted. The Algerian *colonies agricoles* did poorly, as well. However theoretically feasible, the commission opined, Brumard's "remarkable report" described why the situation was otherwise. Providing a rare glimpse of what prevailed among the young colons themselves, Brumard insisted that they were constrained by too many rules, with insufficient freedom weighing too heavily on them. Moreover, they were too regimented to develop the requisite "personal initiative" for the project to work.[73]

So de Tourdonnet proposed another solution: Arguing against taking small children from their nursemaids (and arguing that French colo-

72. Gilles Merien, "La colonization de l'Algérie ou le Pied Noir sans foi," *Histoire, Économie et Société* 6, 3 (1987): 427–32.

73. Ministère de l'Intérieur, *Enfants assistés. Enquête générale ouverte en 1860 dans les 86 départements de l'empire. Rapport de la Commission instituée le 10 Octobre 1861* (Paris: Imprimerie Impérial, 1862).

nial authorities in Algeria would be unable, in any case, to handle their needs), he proposed a three-stage process to better prepare children for a tropical climate and strenuous labor. They would be sent first to "preparatory colonies" (with nursemaids) in France from age one to twelve, then to "colonies of transition" for those age twelve to fourteen, where adolescent bodies might be first "bronzed by the sun of Provence or Languedoc." In a third stage, those age fifteen to twenty-one would be sent to "colonies of application" in Algeria, "labor-ready" and equipped with acclimated bodies and cultivated self-discipline. The goal, as an earlier report (from 1851) expressed and de Tourdonnet opined, was "not to produce flabby townsmen but to form robust workers, hardened to fatigue, with the will to work, for whom labor is the life of their organs and who conceive progress as the well-being that comes from the fruit of their sweat and the harvest of their own efforts."[74]

ENTANGLED PROJECTS IN 1848

Algeria was cast into the carceral net long before de Tourdonnet and others reanimated the debate with proposals for reformed *colonies agricoles*. Those established there morphed among permanent agricultural colonial villages, detention centers, and temporary military settlements. Just how intimately these projects were superimposed and overlapped in the 1840s and 1850s defies even the rudiments of a clear or linear narrative.

Striking is the sheer flux of movement in proposed plan and policy. Occupying French military authorities headed by the army's chief military officer, Thomas Bugeaud, newly appointed as the governor-general, devised an ill-conceived plan to place former soldiers, allegedly already acclimatized, to settle on confiscated Algerian land. Most of these efforts failed. The number of civilian colonists, recruited at the same time, rose tenfold, from more than seven thousand in 1833 to more than seventy thousand a decade later, despite huge losses to disease and departures.[75] By 1846, there was a French settler community of more than 100,000. In 1848, the number of new recruits was estimated at 13,500.[76]

74. De Lurieu and Romand, *Etudes sur les colonies agricoles de mendiants*, 192.
75. Heffernan, "The Parisian Poor and the Colonization of Algeria during the Second Republic," 380.
76. Heffernan, "The Parisian Poor," 380.

These, too, had little success. When Parisian workers arrived, they were housed in military barracks; the land was not partitioned among them as promised; and virtually nothing promised (in public advertisements) to prepare their new homesteads was in place. In addition to military veterans and the Parisian poor many of whom returned to France, there were involuntary settlers with whom they were "confounded"—namely, participants in the revolts of June 1848, several months earlier.[77] If there was "nothing in common" between those condemned to transport and colons who came months later (as they and their descendants have insisted), there was, on the contrary, much shared in the visionary regime of security and colonization to which they were subjected. Botched planning prevailed, as did an uneasy and often unworkable balance between protection and surveillance. These waves of transported and freely recruited colonists were joined in the 1850s by "insurgents" from France, deported to at least six former *colonies agricoles* that had been newly converted into *colonies pénitentiaires* (penal colonies).

Inconsistent and confused accounts of the number of colonists who left for Algeria between 1848 and 1851—and the conditions under which they went—should command our attention. The accounts reflect the multiple streams of influx, the unstable sense of what these colonies and converted military camps were for, and their rapid change of function.[78] By some counts, fourteen thousand Parisian workers were ordered to Algeria in September

77. Maurice Bel, *Les colonies agricoles de 1848* (Nice: Maurice Bel, 1997). Bel's personal account of his family's experience is an unusual one. Tracking their voyage from Paris on November 5, 1848, with the eighth Algeria-bound convoy headed for Damiette, Lodi, and Medea, he describes how workers were recruited in September of that year. Posters plastered across Paris announced "Colonisation de l'Algérie: Avis aux ouvriers," specifying the terms of departure, the costs covered, and the allocations of two to ten hectares for bachelors and married couples. See also Fernand Rude, *Bagnes d'Afrique: Trois transportés en Algérie après le coup d'état du 2 décembre 1851* (Paris: Maspero, 1981). It includes the letters of the French feminist and socialist Pauline Roland, one of the few women for whom there is a written record, with a detailed account of the preparations that were *not* made for her confinement with fifteen other women. Tortured, starved, and chained to a rock, she celebrated her own insolence to refuse the one franc that the French authorities gave her per day: Rude, *Bagnes d'Afrique*, 129, 135. She died a year after George Sand secured her release.

78. Jeannine Verdès-Leroux, *Les français d'Algérie de 1830 à aujourd'hui: Une page d'histoire déchirée* (Paris: Fayard, 2001), 195; J. P. T. Bury, *France, 1814–1940* (London: Routledge, 2003), 77; Catherine Belvaude, *L'Algérie* (Paris: Karthala, 1991), 36. Each offers a different estimate.

1848, only some of whom were political deportees. By the time of Louis Napoleon's coup in 1851, what had been the model Algerian village of 1848 was deserted.[79] By some accounts, three thousand republicans were sent to Algeria in 1851. Others put the number of deported republicans much higher, at twice that number—six thousand (out of nearly fifteen thousand people arrested).[80]

Take the Algerian penal colony of Lambesc. It was reserved for 450 political deportees. Colonists from Malta, Italy, and Spain (and even Germany and Russia) were encouraged to emigrate voluntarily, joining the mix of French soldiers established earlier in *villages-militaires*. Failed villages-militaires were turned over to voluntary Parisian recruits to buttress the *colonies agricoles*, and defunct *colonies agricoles* were requisitioned for incarceration. Even as late as 1875, new proposals were made to institute the "military colonization" of Algeria, again taking up Bugeaud's earlier, poorly received, and failed project.[81]

It might be claimed that the Algerian situation was an exceptional case, condensed as it was into two decades of trial and error during which the conquest of Algeria, rebellion in Paris, and anticipated increasing numbers of urban poor in France were conjoined. But the confused conceptual architecture of what constituted a colony and what should be a camp may not be unique at all. Nor was it purely by French design. As we know, de Tocqueville's proposals for *colonies agricoles* in Algeria came after his research trip to the United States, as did de Tourdonnet's. The latter's account attests to these morphings. When in 1856 the director of Algerian affairs was commissioned to establish a large farm made up of five hundred colonists housed in "concentrated buildings," the farm was under military protection and surveillance but also "inspired" by military colonies from elsewhere.

79. For a detailed account of the Algerian context in which these transformations of *colonies agricoles* into *colonies pénitentiaires* took place, see Stacey Renee Davis, "Turning French Convicts into Colonists: The Second Empire's Political Prisoners in Algeria, 1852–1858," *French Colonial History* 2, 1 (2002).

80. For a meticulous tracking of the changing terms that were used for those "transported" and then designated "deported" in 1848, see Louis-José Barbançon, "Transporter les insurgés de juin 1848," *Criminocorpus: Revue d'Histoire de la Justice, des Crimes et des Peines*, January 1, 2008, https://criminocorpus.revues.org/153.

81. See "De la colonization militarie en Algérie," letter from Monsieur Buzelin, a former soldier from Nantes, to the President de la République, Duc de Magenta, August 28, 1875.

This is a truncated account, but the point should be clear: This *shift of function* produced an experimental space in which an agricultural colony could serve as a militarized zone not unlike a camp with varied degrees of unfreedom, and a penal institution could be transformed into a "normalized" civilian colonial settlement. Law is not suspended; it is minutely tailored and underwritten by the racialized requirements that it produces and to which it responds.

Transpositions of function brought penality, philanthropy, social welfare, and imperial conquest and intervention into proximity and adjacency, mixing strategies that have lasted long past the mid-nineteenth century. Sometimes these transpositions scrambled the distinctions between "colon" (in the sense of a penal colony inmate) and "colon" as a newly crafted settler. Sometimes, as in French Guiana during the second half of the nineteenth century, the hard labor needed to open concessions (to clear land and carve out roads) was imposed on convicts, and the lighter labor was allocated to those "worthy of being a colon," who nevertheless were often given nonarable plots on land studded with quartz.[82]

Le Cour Grandmaison argues that *colonies agricoles* were part of a dual system to disgorge France's carceral institutions and protect the political order through colonial deportation.[83] Marc Bernardot documents a sedimented, layered history of internment that used the legalities of psychiatric internment in 1838 and the vagabond laws from 1912 as a model for future decrees of political internment within France.[84] These fused traditions of protection and surveillance treated successive waves of targeted populations in the very same sites—most notably, colonial subjects—at least until the 1960s. Riversaltes was created in 1935 as a military center; in 1939, as a transit center; in 1940, as a center for "foreign workers"; in 1941, as a center for "familial

82. E. Abonnenc and M. Abonnenc, "Le bagne de la Guyane française durant les années 1856 à 1872," *Bulletin de La Société de Pathologie Exotique* 74, 2 (1981): 246.

83. Le Cour Grandmaison, *Coloniser/exterminer*, 295–99. Le Cour Grandmaison's work has been criticized for its claims about extermination and more directly for dependence on secondary sources rather than colonial archival documents. I, however, am unaware of archival work that contradicts his observations.

84. Bernardot, "Les mutations de la figure du camp," 45. Bernardot's last decade of books and essays on the genealogies of internment, "security," and the sedimented history of camps in France is a crucial source but as yet unavailable in English. See also Marc Bernardot, "Les camps d'étranger, dispositif colonial au service des sociétés de contrôle," *Revue Projet* 308, 1 (January 1, 2009): 41–50.

regroupement"; in 1942, as a center for Jews; and from 1957 to 1962, as an internment site for militant Algerians.

And, of course, France was not the only site where the sedimented history that joined camps and colonies and the common currencies in political logics were joined. Tarrfal was a Portuguese penal colony on Cape Verde Island that first housed antifascist dissidents of António Salazar's right-wing regime; it closed in 1954 and reopened in the 1970s to house Africans fighting Portuguese colonialism.[85]

And should we think to trace the sedimented histories of colony and camp, the Andaman Islands, established as a British penal colony for political prisoners in 1858, is an important example. Although British accounts once emphasized the redemptive features of farm labor, free medical care, and schools for the prisoner's children, the Cellular Jail at Port Blair included nearly seven hundred cells for solitary confinement. Some redeemed prisoners may have become self-supporting cultivators in a revised version of a colonie agricole, but the medical records from the 1870s tell another story of political dissidents who continued to be tortured through the 1930s. The facility was finally closed in August 1947.[86]

The first workers' colony established in East Westphalia, Germany, in 1882 and in East Africa, as the historian Sebastian Conrad notes, shared far more than methods of labor compliance. As projects, their history is deeply entwined: Initiatives to deport the "work-shy" to German South-West Africa may have failed, but its twisted genealogy ties it at the end of the nineteenth century to "fact-finding missions to New Caledonia, the Andaman Islands, Australia, and China"—and, four decades later, to the failed

85. See Timothy J. Coates, Convicts and Orphans: Forced and State-Sponsored Colonizers in the Portuguese Empire, 1550–1755 (Stanford, CA: Stanford University Press, 2001); "Preliminary Considerations on European Forced Labor in Angola, 1880–1930," Portuguese Literary and Cultural Studies 14–15 (2010): 79–105; and Social Exclusion: Practice and Fear of Exile (Degredo) in Portuguese History (Lisbon, Edições Universitárias Lusofonas, 2005), 122–24.

86. For a popular account, see Cathy Scott-Clark and Adrian Levy, "Survivors of Our Hell," The Guardian, June 22, 2001, http://www.theguardian.com/lifeandstyle/2001/jun /23/weekend.adrianlevy; Clare Anderson, "Legacies of a British Penal Colony: Adivasis in the Andaman Islands," University of Leicester: Carceral Archipelago, December 8, 2014, http://staffblogs.le.ac.uk/carchipelago/2014/12/08/legacies-of-a-british-penal-colony -adivasis-in-the-andaman-islands; and New Histories of the Andaman Islands: Landscape, Place and Identity in the Bay of Bengal, 1790–2012, eds. Clare Anderson, Madhumita Mazumdar, Vishvajit Pandya (New York: Cambridge University Press, 2016).

"Madagascar Plan" of the Third Reich government to forcibly relocate the entire Jewish population of Europe to Madagascar.[87]

But there are also other sorts of colonies that are more counterintuitive to the sorts described here. Warwick Anderson's important work on the Culion leper colony in the Philippines reminds us that even such a medically insidious form of disease as leprosy and the leper colony designed to serve those suffering from it was modeled on what in this chapter has been a refrain—namely, as he put it, "The colonial reformatory [for lepers] . . . excelled in fashioning estranged, marginal men and women, in making contaminated bodies and second-class citizens" who themselves complained about "forced labor on public works."[88] There are reservations of Canada's native Indian population, visited repeatedly by South Africa's British government officials as early as the Boer War and later, in the 1950s, taken as models of design for what would become the Bantustans.[89] Australia's infamous beginnings as a convict colony has been rehearsed perhaps more than any other, but more remains to be asked about it, not only as the consequences of "settler colonialism," as it is so often viewed, but as one exemplary node in a global network of shared knowledge concerning containment and demarcation in the carceral archipelago of empires.

These deeply dependent genealogies of "colony" and "reservation" beg for renewed consideration. While an abundance of work has addressed their carceral features, as in the case of the relationship between Tasmania's penal colony and its aboriginal population, the nexus of colony and camp

87. Sebastian Conrad, *Globalisation and the Nation in Imperial Germany* (Cambridge: Cambridge University Press, 2010).

88. Warwick Anderson, *Colonial Pathologies: American Tropical Medicine, Race, and Hygiene in the Philippines* (Durham, NC: Duke University Press, 2006), 159, 173.

89. Ron Bourgeault argued that "the South African Land Settlements Act of 1912 and 1913 were patterned after Canada's Dominion Lands Act," in Ron Bourgeault, "Canada/Indians: The South African Connection," *Canadian Dimensions* (January 1988): 8. John Saul, who relies heavily on Bourgeault's analysis, wrote "Canada's Dominions Land Act of the 1870s (after which the South African Land Settlement Act of 1912 and 1913 was actually patterned, according to Bourgeault), and related acts including our very own Indian Act, restricted Indians, as they were then termed . . . from acquiring property or trading their goods off the reserves. They also deprived Indians of the vote, and even established a kind of pass system for exit and re-entry to reserves. Small wonder that apartheid South Africa was interested": John S. Saul, "Two Fronts of Anti-Apartheid Struggle: South Africa and Canada," *Transformation: Critical Perspectives on Southern Africa* 74, 1 (2010): 136.

has not received the same attention.[90] Coercive containments produced colonies besieged by their own brutalities, internments within and outside their borders, barbed wire that bordered colonies as camps, and camps as the sites of potential colonists.

THE ARTS OF PUNISHMENT THAT "ARE STILL VERY MUCH OUR OWN"

Such observations make more troubling Foucault's insistence that he sought to write a history of the present "of the arts of punishment that are still very much our own."[91] His history not only abruptly stopped short of these exemplary instruments to cordon off specific populations under modern governance. Foucault's genealogy excises the abundance of forms of containment that "are still very much our own" and threaded through our social fabric. Agamben has famously called the paradigmatic "political space of modernity"—the camp, not the prison—a "new and stable spatial arrangement," the hidden matrix of our time, born out of a state of exception that became a norm.[92] But Agamben's purview is spatially selective, geopolitically narrow, and historically thin. Like Foucault, Agamben circumvents the deeper history of empire (leaving historians to quibble over the "trivial" point of whether the first camps were those of the Spanish in Cuba in 1896 or those in which the British herded Boer families in southern Africa at the turn of the twentieth century).[93]

90. See Benjamin Madley, "From Terror to Genocide: Britain's Tasmanian Penal Colony and Australia's History Wars," *Journal of British Studies* 47, 1 (January 2008): 77–106.

91. Foucault, *Discipline and Punish*, 296.

92. Giorgio Agamben, *Homo Sacer: Sovereign Power and Bare Life*, trans. Daniel Heller-Roazen (Stanford, CA: Stanford University Press, 1998), esp. 119–23. He notes that Foucault's analysis of modern biopolitics stops short of the concentration camp. See also Giorgio Agamben, "What Is a Camp?" in *Means without End: Notes on Politics* (Minneapolis: University of Minnesota Press, 2000).

93. Agamben, *Means without End*, 37. Although most originary accounts of the European "concentration camp" cite the internment camps of the Spanish in Cuba in 1898, one might also look to an earlier history where "the expansion of penal reforms in the Iberian metropole had as their counterpart an increase in . . . penal servitude, peonage, impressment, and generalized confinement in the Spanish Antilles": Kelvin Santiago-Valles, " 'Bloody Legislations,' 'Entombment,' and Race Making in the Spanish Atlantic: Differentiated Spaces of General(ized) Confinement in Spain and Puerto Rico, 1750–1840," *Radical History Review* 2006, 96 (September 21, 2006): 33–34. Santiago-Valles makes the important point that carceral techniques of the early nineteenth century

Agamben's invocation of a state of exception-turned-norm misrepresents how gradations of containment worked and misses the deeper history in which the forms were lodged. Rehabilitation camps, re-concentration camps designed for "protection" and immobility, forced labor colonies, and agricultural colonies for children were only as provisional and exceptional as imperial formations themselves. They were forms of enclosed habitation that were part of the very architecture of empire, neither vestiges of earlier systems of order and control, as Foucault would have it, nor exceptions that became the norm, as Agamben claimed. Imperial formations, as I have argued elsewhere, "create new subjects that must be relocated to be productive, dispossessed to be modern, disciplined to be independent, converted to be human, stripped of old cultural bearings to be citizens, coerced to be free."[94] These geographic arrangements are fundamental to defining and maintaining the racial distributions and durabilities of imperial duress today.

That Foucault never touches on the camp as a singular carceral entity is not an inadvertent lapse. The inspiration he acknowledged for his use of the term "carceral archipelago" was a direct reference to Aleksandr Solzhenitsyn's *The Gulag Archipelago*, published the year before *Discipline and Punish*.[95] *The Gulag Archipelago* was at the forefront of French public intellectual life when it appeared, dividing the left on "totalitarianism" and Soviet camps and marking the moment that many leftist intellectuals turned away from the Communist Party.[96] Foucault shared that "disappointment" but was not

---

already "overlapped with the carceral forms more associated with political-economic liberalism": Santiago-Valles, " 'Bloody Legislations,' 'Entombment,' and Race Making in the Spanish Atlantic," 39.

94. Ann Laura Stoler, "Considerations on Imperial Comparisons," in *Empire Speaks Out: Languages of Rationalization and Self-Description in the Russian Empire*, ed. Ilyā Gerasimov, Jan Kusber, and Alexander Semyonov (Leiden: E. J. Brill, 2009), 40. See also chapter 5 in this volume.

95. Aleksandr Isaevich Solzhenitsyn, *The Gulag Archipelago, 1918–1956: An Experiment in Literary Investigation* (New York: Harper and Row, 1974).

96. *The Gulag Archipelago* (1974) sparked heated debate in France when it came out. A visceral attack from the French Communist Party (FCP) accused Solzhenitsyn of mounting an anti-Soviet campaign, with major French leftist intellectuals responding to the FCP by setting out their "antitotalitarian" position, distancing themselves more than ever from Soviet policy. Jean Daniel, then the director of *Le Nouvel Observateur*, whom Foucault so admired, was at the center of the confrontation. On the very different reception of the book in France and in other countries, see Michael Scott Christofferson,

a major voice in those divisive conversations.[97] When queried in 1976 about the geographical metaphors he used, he had only this to say: "There is only one notion here that is truly geographic, that of an archipelago. I have used it only once, to designate via, the title of Solzhenitsyn's work, the carceral archipelago; the way in which a form of punitive system is physically dispersed yet at the same time covers the entirety of a society."[98]

Yet the question remains: If the carceral archipelago was so preeminently embodied by *colonies agricoles* such as Mettray, why did it exclude so many of the models on which those *colonies* drew, their imperial coordinates, and their colonial variants? One could imagine that Foucault chose not to confuse the normalizing processes of coercive and curative surveillance with the more easily condemnable brutality of Soviet camps. But, then, why use the metaphor of archipelago (with the "gulag" as its silent but so prominent partner) if not to make the case that incarcerations of modernity are the inequitable fate of us all—in which we as subjects are shaped into participating agents?

One could also imagine that, given what some have construed as Foucault's sharp distinction between the "classical" and the "modern" age, penal colonies—as we know, not a modern invention—were not appropriate to his subject at hand. But even here, where the historical discontinuities are strategically asserted, there are equivocations in his adherence to ruptures and abrupt breaks. As Paul Rabinow and Stephen Collier rightly have contended, "epochal" distinctions were to become less pivotal to him in his later work. But *Discipline and Punish* allows us to see that equivocation is already evident in his gestures to a subtler and recursive set of social technologies that selectively recuperate and redeploy established ones. And what if Foucault had taken the penal colony not as a vestige of another age but as the converted/diverted template of our own?

"The Gulag as a Metaphor," in *French Intellectuals against the Left: The Antitotalitarian Moment of the 1970s* (New York: Berghahn, 2004), 89–111.

97. Jan Plamper argues that partly because of Foucault's "Eurocentricism," the gulag "remained a paradox to Foucault," not sure whether to classify it "as a premodern or a modern phenomenon, though never 'in between'" and thus arguing for the problems in applying a Foucaldian analysis "outside the West": Jan Plamper, "Foucault's Gulag," *Kritika* 3, 2 (2002): 268–69. I disagree. Foucault's geopolitical frame was limited, but this in no way hampers our capacity to call on a genealogical method (which Plamper identifies as hampering Foucault) across a broader imperial plane.

98. Michel Foucault, "Questions on Geography," in *Power/Knowledge: Selected Interviews and Other Writings, 1972–1977*, ed. Colin Gordon (New York: Pantheon, 1980), 68.

Thinking with a carceral archipelago of empire does more than extend the geographic scope of Foucault's analysis. If a key issue is to identify the conditions "that have made [certain] practices possible and to establish the grounds on which they depend for their intelligibility," then an imperial vantage point would extend Foucault's carceral continuum to new political and analytic space and, not least, to a conceptual matrix in which a politics of security has figured centrally in the policing of imperial borderlands and ambiguous frontiers.[99]

What might come into our purview by doing so? The carceral archipelago would include the labor camps of empire, the Texas penitentiaries that developed out of slavery and housed the forced labor mobilized for the American South's heavily protected coal and iron mining industries and its major public works.[100] The relationship between the carceral archipelago of empire and public works in colony and metropole are evident over a long time span and at different nodes. Other sites and connections would come back into view, as well: the detention and prison camps instituted in Kenya under British rule whose inmates supplied the forced labor for airport construction and public works. The "labor camp" here is the colony—the normalized excess of the imperial modern. It makes sense of Michel-Rolph Trouillot's offhand remark that "Port-au-Prince was like 'a camp of tartars'—a port of call, an assemblage of forts, the temporary shelter for its seamen, soldiers, slaves, civil servants and tradesmen."[101] Or it might return us to the Banda Islands of the Netherlands Indies, already established as a forced labor camp for the production of spice commodities in the eighteenth century and turned into a penal colony for anticolonial dissidents by the Dutch in the 1930s.[102] It would not omit the military-run agricultural colonies of Algeria, the convict cultivators in New Caledonia in the 1860s, or the island reformatories and colonies for the poor established as "good works" in the 1840s just off what is now part of the tourist

99. Paul Rabinow and Nikolas S. Rose, "Foucault Today," In *The Essential Foucault: Selections from Essential Works of Foucault, 1954–1984* (New York: New Press, 2003), xiii.

100. See the powerful account of the welding of slavery, colonialism, and incarceration in Robert Perkinson, *Texas Tough: The Rise of America's Prison Empire* (New York: Metropolitan, 2010).

101. Michel-Rolph Trouillot, "Port-au-Prince, Haiti l'état d'un siège," *Lire Haiti* 1, 1 (December 2000): 5–13.

102. I thank James Fox for alerting me to this long-term, layered history of Dutch colonial internments.

haven of France's Mediterranean coast, the Îles d'Hyères, once home to its *bagnes*.[103]

At issue in all are what Michel Agier calls the logistics of camps in the world today, a logistics riveted on "the control of flux" that joins "islands of retention" and "interior exile" via a thick corridor of containments that are at once transitory and have "no exit."[104] Nor would the isolated forest hamlets where Algerians who served as auxiliary military for the French during the Algerian War (the Harkis) be outside our virtual imperial archives and the carceral archipelago's geopolitical breadth. The squalid clustered dwellings throughout rural France where Harkis were sequestered for decades were at once sites of enclosure, exclusion, privation, and abandonment.[105]

Nor might we overlook the history of successive waves of populations housed in internment camps throughout rural France—Larzac, Riversaltes, and Marzargues—a history Marc Bernardot insists is not captured by envisioning a "reappearance" of such sites but, rather, by envisioning an enduring set of confinements from the early twentieth century.[106] As he underscores for the camps in France, and Redfield so rightly insists for the penal colony, multiple logics were always at play that "shift[ed] between the need to colonize, the need to punish and the need to reform."[107] This, too, describes some of the *colonies agricoles* and the visions for them out of which installations such as Mettray were established.

A new cartography entails a new conceptual map. If we return yet again to Foucault's definition of a historical event as the "breach of self-evidence," the opening of Mettray in this altered political cartography appears barely to be a breach at all; neither were the *colonies agricoles*. Both were products of an amplifying and transforming carceral network that cut across colony and metropole and joined protection and repression, "good works" and surveillance, containment and defense. James Walston makes a similar observation about Italian concentration camps immediately after the Second World War and their relationship to prior policies of internment used in Africa.

103. Adrien Egron, *Le livre du pauvre* (Paris Librairie des Livres Liturgiques Illustrés, 1847).

104. Michel Agier, *Le couloir des exilés: Être étranger dans un monde commun* (Bellecombe-en-Bauges, France: Croquant, 2011), 55.

105. See Vincent Crapanzano, *The Harkis: The Wound That Never Heals* (Chicago: University of Chicago Press, 2011).

106. Bernardot, "Les mutations de la figure du camp."

107. Redfield, *Space in the Tropics*, 64.

Although most Italian historiography distinguishes between two different kinds of camps—those for protection and those for repression—their histories were joined, and their practices meshed.[108]

De Tourdonnet's extended essay on *colonies agricoles* alerts us to just this, as it endeavors to situate such *colonies* as one of the potential resources for securing imperial frontiers and the dispossession of land. Not least, children in the agricultural colonies and freed penal colony inmates would be a front line of settler colonialism. The adult colon was to provide a reserve army for defense.

Foucault's concept of *dispositif*, which first appears in *Discipline and Punish*, is strikingly resonant in describing the protean quality of this archipelago and its arrangements. Although English-language renditions have more commonly translated *dispositif* as a "social apparatus," in many ways this misses the very mobile and mutating connectivities that a *dispositif* came to convey. One of the more productive, later terms Foucault used to define it was as *réseau* (network), a "heterogeneous ensemble of institutions, discourses, architectural forms, scientific statements, moral and philanthropic propositions." A *dispositif*, then, is not a thing but the system of connections among this ensemble of arrangements.[109] As important—and here is a critical feature less often noted—it is an active response to "urgency." A *dispositif* is not a steady state; it is marked by constant "readjustment of different elements that surface at various points . . . a perpetual process of strategic elaboration."[110] Its key feature is plasticity, an "interplay of shifts of position and modifications of function which can vary widely."

If Foucault rejected the use of geographical terms, Deleuze's description nevertheless finds them at the very center of Foucault's conceptual project. As Deleuze describes a *dispositif*, "[It's] like drawing up a map, doing cartography, surveying unknown landscapes and this is what [Foucault] calls 'working on the ground.' . . . One has to position oneself

108. James Walston, "History and Memory of the Italian Concentration Camps," *Historical Journal* 40, 1 (March 1997): 169–83. See also Nicola Labanca, "Italian Colonial Internment," in *Italian Colonialism*, ed. Ruth Ben-Ghiat and Mia Fuller (Basingstoke, U.K.: Palgrave Macmillan, 2008), 27–36.

109. See Giorgio Agamben, *Qu-est ce qu'un dispositif?*, trans. Martin Rueff (Paris: Payot and Rivages, 2014), 1. Agamben moves between "apparatus" and "network" in commenting on this "decisive technical terms in the strategy of Foucault's thought."

110. Foucault, "The Confession of the Flesh," 195.

on these lines themselves , . . . which do not just make up the *dispositif* but run through it. These lines of force act as arrows that continually cross between words and things."[111] The concept seems to emerge both from the metaphor and from a concrete geographical form that Foucault dismissed as irrelevant. But might not we do better to treat the carceral archipelago materially and through its spatial coordinates? This is something de Tourdonnet seemed so readily to grasp.

BACK TO DE TOURDONNET'S CONCEPTUAL MAP

De Tourdonnet's essay begins not with the children's *colonies agricoles* in northern France but with a prelude to comparisons across the imperial world. He looks to the initiatives of Catherine II and her imperial successor to create a fortified empire within Russia's interior frontiers and on its external borders; to establish colonies on Russia's vulnerable frontiers, as well as on the outskirts of Moscow; to house abandoned children in rural colonies on the fringes of St. Petersburg, as well as in the "remarkable Russian colonies of Saratoff in the Volga basin," made up of German immigrants recruited to settle and colonize Russia's steppes.[112] The colonies at issue for de Tourdonnet, the *colonies agricoles*, were already part of what Willard Sunderland has called "a new sort of imperialism" that emerged from the settling of the Russian steppe with " 'land-militia regimes' made up of retired soldiers, state peasants, willing commoners, and the forced settlement by Catherine the Great that followed to the imperial borderlands."[113] Should we imagine that the comparisons to other colonial projects are merely overextensions of our own scholarly making, we might note that by the 1860s, when de Tourdonnet was writing, Russian reformists were

---

111. Gilles Deleuze, "What Is a Dispositif?" in *Michel Foucault, Philosopher: Essays*, trans. Timothy J. Armstrong (New York: Harvester Wheatsheaf, 1992), 159–68.

112. De Tourdonnet, *Essais sur l'éducation des enfants pauvres*, 32.

113. See Willard Sunderland's astute analysis of the changing comparative frames in which colonization was viewed and the making of Russian colonies in the mid-eighteenth century for which the term "colony" was never used. As he writes, "The European steppe as a whole was never described as a colony. . . . The Russians . . . began their most intense period of steppe colonization by invoking much of the rhetorical style of European colonialism, *yet without clearly identifying the colony in question as a colonial place*": Willard Sunderland, *Taming the Wild Field: Colonization and Empire on the Russian Steppe* (Ithaca, NY: Cornell University Press, 2006), 89; emphasis added.

writing about the colonization of the Caucasus as "our Russian Algeria" and about the Amur as "a Siberian Mississippi."[114]

De Tourdonnet also makes such implicit comparisons, taking note of the penal colonies in Guiana, New Caledonia, and both the Siberian colonies and the *colonie agricole* in Algeria at Lambessa for political dissidents. The very connections circumvented in Foucault's carceral archipelago are placed full front on de Tourdonnet's cognitive, visionary, and political maps. Each of these sites fueled his argument that, of all the means of moralization, agricultural work is the most powerful and least costly.

De Tourdonnet uses the terms "colonists" and "colonies," with telling referents. His purview includes religious colonies, military colonies, failed eighteenth-century pauper colonies, and those active in the mid-nineteenth century. Children's agricultural colonies are compared to retirement colonies for the military or infirm. A colonist could be a new French settler in Algeria, an adult inmate in a pauper colony outside Paris, a penal colony inmate in French Guiana, or an orphan in a *colonie agricole* in Provence. His account finds relationalities and defies the incommensurabilities that we as students of those histories have since drawn.

De Tourdonnet's cartography spills across institutions of care and correction, protection and repression, dotted across a vast imperial space. A historian of eighteenth-century imperial expansions might find it evocative of the well-trafficked networks within and among empires themselves. Relocations of populations, dislocation of dangerous elements, and deportation of dissidents were fundamental features of imperial governance of a *longue durée*. The historian Kerry Ward describes "an imperial network of forced migration" in the 1700s, with multiple circuits from Java to Ceylon and the Cape of Good Hope, networks that were critical "to maintain[ing] civic and political order in the posts, settlements, and colonies that comprised the East India Company's territorial nodes."[115]

Not least, de Tourdonnet's reference to these disparate forms captures something that contemporary studies of empire have since lost: How dif-

114. Sunderland, *Taming the Wild Field*, 158. Plamper reminds us that "Siberia was used as a place for convict labor [from] the 16th century, long before the French established penal colonies in New Caledonia and other places. Siberian colonization and relegations à la ruse, were intertwined before the French Revolution": Plamper, "Foucault's Gulag," 266.

115. Kerry Ward, *Networks of Empire: Forced Migration in the Dutch East India Company* (Cambridge: Cambridge University Press, 2011).

ferent notions of a colony should be organized and who should rightly be in them were shared, compared, and subject to change, reflection, and re-evaulation. Imperial modes of confinement, resettlement, and recruitment were not separately conceived; nor did de Tourdonnet take them as wholly interchangeable or all the same. He, too, asked whether pioneer colonies should be treated alongside long-settled agricultural colonies and together with colonies of rescue for foundlings, repression for criminals, and the education of potential colonial settlers. But while carceral concerns and care for the poor were the emphasized goals, they were equally understood as connected and sometimes contiguous sites for experimenting with, and implementing, convergent tactics of security, social order, and territorial control.

De Tourdonnet teaches us something else. French blueprints for agricultural and pauper colonies alert us to imperial rearrangements of people that depended on strategic mobilities and imposed immobilities of persons recruited, directed, or forced into and out of colonies and camps by imperial design. Ambiguous nomenclatures, substitutable populations, and partial appropriations were the very substance of movements of people and things that secured the viability of imperial formations. That de Tourdonnet could look at once from the Crimean colonies in the Russian south to those in the Amur basin on the Chinese frontier underscores not the sweep of his personal vision but two more important things: first, an already shared and contested sense of what a colony might look like; and second, what constituted colonization and settlement could be conceived with or without use of the term. Rather than a furtive poaching of practices, or what might otherwise be construed as an incomprehensible amalgam of disparate things (not unlike that passage from a "certain Chinese encyclopedia" with which Foucault opened The Order of Things), de Tourdonnet's references mark "reasoned" connections that were part of a constellation of what were deemed relevant cross-imperial knowledge practices, acquisitions, and applications.

If "history is for cutting"—for severing received categories, as Foucault so fiercely claimed—de Tourdonnet's essay slices our common sense with sharpened shears.[116] It underscores the subjacent lineaments of governance that the prevailing distinctions between "colony" and "camp" pull apart. In the sections on Algeria, he expressed his hesitant attraction to the central logic of "displacement" (déplacement) of children and made his temperate

116. Foucault, "Nietzsche, Genealogy, History," 88.

case for how *colonies agricoles* could one day make Algeria a "second continental France."

He was not alone in imagining the *colonies agricole*'s curative powers. In Java during the same years, Dutch colonial authorities found a favored "solution" for dealing with what were perceived as the rapidly increasing "wavering classes" of destitute mixed-blood people in an explicitly Mettray model: It, too, prescribed a return to the land for those who had never lived off it and the instilling of bodily discipline, limited aspirations, love of the soil through closely supervised surveillance, and care for the soul.[117] It also failed. Mettray's founder, Demetz, as de Tourdonnet noted, drew his inspiration from the Dutch former colonial official van den Bosch already mentioned, whose first private agricultural colonies for the criminalized poor in the Netherlands were so resonant with his forced cultivation system for Javanese farmers that lasted some thirty years. Although the latter was infamously oppressive on Java and the former in the Netherlands failed, still de Tourdonnet notes van den Bosch's efforts with admiration. From Heurne de Pommeuse to Tocqueville to Demetz to de Tourdonnet, and so many before them and after, an expandable set of political logics joined the children's colonies to colonization and both to the domestication of the poor, the dissident, and new subjects of empire.

FIGURE AND GROUND

The carceral archipelago of empire could be conceived not as a prelude to the modern but the gradated sites of its instantiation. New concepts, Deleuze and Guattari write, provide "the conditions under which not only subject and object are redistributed but also figure and ground, margins and center, moving object and reference point, transitive and substantial, length and depth."[118] De Tourdonnet's essay takes shape in those recursive reflections noted in chapter 1, those reflections on governance that Foucault so emphasized in his historical analytics. De Tourdonnet instantiates precisely that reflective mode in the comments and critiques he makes about a range of containments and enclosures, in the commensurabilities he turned from and those he claimed.

117. For how these visions and practices played out in Java, see Ann Laura Stoler, "Developing Historical Negatives," in *Along the Archival Grain*, 105–39.
118. Deleuze and Guattari, *What Is Philosophy?* 18.

For Foucault, the carceral archipelago was a conceptual metaphor of a modern phenomenon, but if Deleuze is right that Foucault was after a new cartography, it would seem that the metaphor had more material substance than Foucault initially acknowledged. That slippage might prove to be an enabling one for us. As Keller Easterling writes in her remarkable work on the politics of global architecture,

> Spatial products act not only as glyph or monument to an overt political text, but as heavy information that becomes a nuanced, unexpressed subtext of action or practice. . . . Spatial products perhaps resist semiotics but offer other precise expressions of value and exchange stored in arrangement and presence.[119]

Literal and figurative islands, atolls, and enclosed and cordoned off mainland encampments were not only key sites of deportation, "transport," and internment in an earlier, premodern age. Britain may have renounced formal deportation in 1878, but Republican France never closed their penal colonies, reviving new ones seven years later, some of which lasted late into the 1930s. Permanent banishment for petty delinquents was reactivated in France in 1885. And as in France's *colonies agricoles*, it was not hardened criminals but "petty delinquents" and those who might be redeemed who were their major offenders.

By the time Richard Price began pursuing the peregrinations of the extraordinary personage of Médard—convict, artist, madman—who lived in the French colony of Martinique when he was not incarcerated at the penal colony of St. Jean, in French Guiana, in the 1930s, he was counted as the 15,930th convict logged in since the penal colony had opened—and not the last.[120] In the midst of a campaign against Guiana's penal colonies, the French minister of colonies established a new camp/colony in South America for Indochinese political prisoners and convict labor, not unlike the earlier camps in Algeria, combining the exile of political dissidents with the colonization of new territories. As the historian John Frow writes, Tasmania's Port Arthur penal settlement, established in 1830, may have belonged to the old regimes of spectacular punishment on the body, but

---

119. Keller Easterling, *Enduring Innocence: Global Architecture and Its Political Masquerades* (Cambridge, MA: MIT Press, 2005), 6–7.

120. Richard Price, *The Convict and the Colonel* (Boston: Beacon, 1998).

it also spoke to new humane regimes of moral inculcation, operating on the soul.[121]

These carceral networks were literal archipelagos but also figurative in more senses than Foucault envisioned. They were zones of semi-extraterritorial status, legally secured but exempt from certain laws, inside and outside the nation proper. Like the detention and refugee camps in Europe today, which Didier Fassin describes as removed from the polis proper, *colonies agricoles* in their many forms were clusterings of types of people who were both "of" and "at" biopolitical risk. Some were relegated to the edges of legality, to the outskirts of the nation and on the edges of the former empire, but such spaces and people were not outside the law, a point that Miranda Spieler makes with such clarity in the case of French Guiana: "They live under the law as it threatens and unmakes them."[122] They are not outside imperial networks of security, surveillance, and intelligence or the visionary bounds of governing bodies. In many ways, camps and colonies are precisely where regimes of security have taken their modern forms. Colonies, like camps, are predicated not always on the making of "bare life" but on the arbitrary and quixotic shift in technologies that unevenly suspend rights, sustain privation, and diminish capacities for political life. But the suspension of rights is not the suspension of law. As we have learned from the case of Guantánamo in our times, and from New Caledonia's expansion as a penal colony in the late nineteenth century, "The space of the camp (and penal colony) is governed by norms rules and even laws . . . not a space being governed outside the law, but from within the law, by regulations and practices that authorities within the state enact."[123]

MANAGED MOBILITIES

Much of this history of the agricultural colonies and the models for them in Europe were described in detail at the time of their making and have been

121. John Frow, "In the Penal Colony," *Journal of Australian Studies* 24, 64 (January 1, 2000): 1–13.

122. See the subtle treatment of the ways in which indeterminate legal status defines the carceral space between citizen and noncitizen, traced through a history of France and its colonies that created both: Miranda Frances Spieler, *Empire and the Underworld: Captivity in French Guiana* (Cambridge, MA: Harvard University Press, 2011), 15.

123. See Claudia Aradau, "Law Transformed: Guantánamo and the 'Other' Exception," *Third World Quarterly* 28, 3 (January 1, 2007): 489–501.

described by successive waves of social reformers and historians. However, little in this corpus has addressed the multiple contiguities and conceptual lines that were drawn between what today we take to be such fundamentally different experiments and governing projects. Even a glimpse at their connectivities should humble our assessments of what we know about the carceral, imperial, and curatival arrangements that were conceived in collaboration and contest and by political rationalities of security, reform, and managed mobilities that remain submerged within our own.

This is not an archive in which a "colony" is secured as a political concept once and for all. Distinctions between the staid life of "colony" as a common noun and its vibrant life as a political concept molts and moves as now should be obvious. Nor is "colony" immediately recognized as a "governing concept" that organizes the bounty of a thick conceptual field. We might think of it more as a *subjacent political concept* that exerts surreptitious command. It resonates but does not cohere. It invites us to follow its "movable bridges" (as Deleuze suggests concepts do), and the detours through which it unfolds, in short-lived projects, borrowed technologies, blueprints realized and scraped, revised projections, and aborted plans.

A "colony" does not announce itself as a political concept but exerts its force nonetheless. It organizes visions and imaginaries. It never stands alone. It is always relational, measured against and distinct from a broader and more stable normative physical, political, and social space: distinct from the conventions of a normal population (of those not exiled, excommunicated, diseased, politically contagious, socially unfit, vagrant, disabled, or abnormally disposed). A "colony" as a common noun is a place where people are moved in and out; a place of livid, hopeful, desperate, and violent *circulation*. It is marked by unsettledness, and forced migration.

A "colony" as a political concept is not a place but *a principle of managed mobilities*, mobilizing and immobilizing populations according to a set of changing rules and hierarchies that orders social kinds: those eligible for recruitment, for resettlement, for disposal, for aid, or for coerced labor and those who are forcibly confined. Some were holding pens and returned to that function in later times; some take as their goal the making of new social kinds sculpted from those who have been cajoled, seduced, chosen, or forced to be there.

A "colony" as a political concept *assesses the value of human kinds*. It organizes activities of labor and leisure and who is assigned them. It metes out punishment and defines transgressions by the goals it has set for itself.

Many die in colonies in pursuit of a better life; many die or starve there crushed by the quest of a better life of others. As such, a "colony" as a political concept not only identifies recurrent problematizations. It is the crystallization of one problematization that always gives way to many more. They are insistently reposed, reformulated, and reworked: Who should be there, how many, who will do the manual work, and what kinds of punishments will be meted out to which of its inhabitants? Who will be charged with letting some out and others in are pragmatic problems of the everyday that can change the colony's profile and course. But such arrangements are also feats of agentive social engineering designed to monitor how much pressure to apply and where to apply it: on the social body, on the comportments of some, or on strategic points of a person's flesh.

Concepts of "security," "fear," expendability," "risk," and "reform" make up the shared vocabulary of those charged with a colony's pragmatic and conceptual care. If security can in part be defined by access to "freedom of circulation or freedom of movement," a colony is never secure.[124] The filiations drawn in this virtual archive between an agricultural colony for wayward boys and a prison in the fields, between a military camp turned into an agricultural settlement in Algeria in 1845, are not unreasoned fabulations. These forms suggest kinships that are uncontained by the distinctions between metropole and colony and are poorly served if we gloss over their spatial scope and interchangeabilities.

In this virtual archive of the colony that joins penal colonies, settler colonies, and agricultural colonies of delinquent youth one is struck by several things. First, virtually all forms of the colony, no matter the intent, location, or designated population, are *artifacts of deliberate and concerted design*. As with camps, design is key; it announces how much the colony as a political concept commands the preemptive, calculates malintent, and assesses future transgressions and potential breaches of security. Design works in the subjunctive mood and gravitates to the possible. "Colony" as common noun and political concept, as a place and a potentiality, is imagined, implemented, and lived in this anxious future tense.

If the concept is, once again, "the contour, the configuration, the constellation *of an event to come*," "the colony" anticipates that event in its very making. It is a provisional configuration that promises something else: the

124. Michael Dillon and Andrew W. Neal, eds., *Foucault on Politics, Security and War* (Basingstoke, UK: Palgrave Macmillan, 2011), 97.

recalcitrant, impoverished poor white colon who will be reformed. Young thieves roaming Europe's plush avenues will be quarantined in Provence until they are "made ready" to reinhabit France's depopulated countryside or adapted for work in a hotter clime, to settle the colony and defend the empire. Such visions had a long life. The colony of Southern Rhodesia between the wars was a place imagined for the placement of Britain's poor white children in resettlement schemes, dependent on a belief in the inherent "malleability" of children of the poor, just as were the *colonies agricoles*.[125]

The colony and camp assess social kinds but also inscribe their factuality in everyday implementation and design—in who gets how much cloth or meat and their quality; in the distribution of shelter, services, privileges, water, and land. This meticulous partitioning is not a sign of the success of the colony. Even indelible inscriptions on the body, as Franz Kafka so graphically described, are no guarantee that the planning will work.[126] On the contrary, they register the anxious counter-movements of the colony's subjects and how they maneuver those precarities. The political concept of the colony does not foretell a future colony held in place by design. Rather, it underscores the unstable morphology of its provisional remaking again and again.

Second, despite that deliberate design, there is no one commanding logic that can account for content or form. Dissension, refusal, and conflict animate these colonies' beginnings and their permutations into what might go by another name. This, then, is not only the archive of a different history from those of penal histories, colonial histories, and histories of social reform that have stood apart for so long. The archive of the "colony" condenses what Foucault identified as the prime subject of genealogy and the mobile conceptuality that a genealogy allows us to track. It is one entry point to a *differential history* that recuperates the lines of force, relational histories, and "the dissension of other things" and disparities. Doing so opens to the calibrated minute and large-scale interventions designed to ward off unidentified dangers in a thickly embattled space.

125. See Ellen Boucher, "The Limits of Potential: Race, Welfare, and the Interwar Extension of Child Emigration to Southern Rhodesia," *Journal of British Studies* 48, 04 (October 2009): 914–34.

126. Franz Kafka, *In the Penal Colony* (Leipzig: Kurt Wolff, 1919). Margaret Kohn argues that Kafka's *In the Penal Colony* should be read as more than a "morality tale": Margaret Kohn, "Kafka's Critique of Colonialism," *Theory and Event* 8, 3 (2005), https://muse.jhu.edu/journals/theory_and_event/voo8/8.3kohn.html.

Warren Montag describes this fragility and "wandering" (*errance*) of the concept that pervades Pierre Machery's work with concepts in ways that speak to the "wayward" movement of "the colony" in its historical and conceptual instantiations:

> The concept appears in all of its fragility, as if it was always on the verge of becoming something other than itself . . . as if it went out of its way in vain to avoid the contagion that it has touched, as if it attacked itself in attempting to reject its other. To follow a concept in its *errance* (wandering) is to perceive that the very means by which a concept searches for its truth, compels it to evade itself, as if it could only exist in fleeing itself. It is this *fuite en avance* [evasive rush forward] by which the concept seeks its proper identity.[127]

Rather than imagining a typology of colonies that emerged clean and well demarcated out of whole cloth—a settler colony, a penal colony, an entrepôt with few colonists at all—we see the tangled projects and investments that defined their distinctions, as well as their convergences. Consensus on how they should be managed and who should be in them were always provisional, at best. Settlements of abandoned children, unemployed Parisian families in the Algerian bled, impoverished North African Jews sent to the borderlands of Israel's declared borders or deposited squarely in the heartland of Palestinian territory, and Spanish reconcentration settlements for Cuba's volatile and recalcitrant urban poor cannot be charted on a linear or developmental scale. There is no originary moment or foundational tale to tell.

What is more striking is how many of these disparate settlements were conceived as political projects with interchangeable parts and substitutable populations. Degrees of unfreedom joined them; "education for work" and "work for education" distinguished and melded their forms. Penal colonies in the 1930s were not vestiges of earlier forms of disciplinary control, as Foucault would have it. In the virtual archive of the colony there is no clear line to be drawn. Even this supposedly defunct form of a colony displays recursive elements and enduring properties.

As a political concept designed to distribute power, "a colony" is doomed to fail. Inside and outside are mobile locations that cannot be maintained as viable borders once and for all. Interior frontiers stretch obliquely across

127. Montag, "Pierre Machery," 3.

and within their guarded space. Enclosure, gated enclaves, and sequestered populations produce imagined and real threats—transgressions of the private, intrusions on the safe, a storming of the gates. They take the form of enclosure and containment, but what and who must be kept out and what and who must stay in are neither fixed nor easy to assess. Internal enemies are potential and everywhere. To protect those within or contain them, or to protect those outside who might be disturbed, at risk, or endangered by exposure, were not mutually exclusive projects. Nor were, and are they, opposing ones. Being "at risk" and "a risk" is a fuzzier political line than most colonial histories allow us to imagine. Being protected is not designated only by who is within the colony and who is not. This quality of and quest for boundedness within and outside produces both its desired and unwelcome effects: transgressions, escapes, flight, detention, suspicion, illicit border crossings, entrapment, and more surveillance. But who is the "hunter" and who is "hunted" are not fixed ontologies in this furtive, bellicose space, but unstable ones. Who is "hunted" may turn into the hunter for despite the dissymmetry of material force and resources, the installment of fear can work the other way around.[128]

From inside and out, a colony mobilizes fear, insecurity and force. No one is immune. Colonies, designed as safety nets and havens, are never safe. Such settlements called "colonies" are nodes of anxious, uneasy circulations; settlements that are not settled at all. A colony is a ravaged home for some; an unsettled one for others; and both for the very same people at different times. Albert Memmi held that there is no going home from a colony. One is never again the same. But that is not really the case. The colony is rendered unhomely for those on whom it is imposed, those dispossessed by it, and those to whom it is offered as a stolen gift. There is no "being at home," only unsettled waiting for something else, for release from that anxious labor.

128. On the interchangeability of predator and prey and the manhunt as an enduring nexus of political philosophy again, see Chamayou, La chasse à l'homme.

COLONIAL APHASIA
DISABLED HISTORIES AND RACE IN FRANCE

Today it is possible that France will have to choose between attachment to its empire and the need once more to have a soul. . . . If it chooses badly, if we ourselves impel it to choose badly, which is only too likely, it will have neither one nor the other, but simply the most terrible affliction, which it will suffer with astonishment, without anyone being able to discern the cause. And all of those capable of speaking or of wielding a pen will be eternally responsible for a crime.—Simone Weil, 1943

Colonial histories possess unruly qualities. Sometimes they may remain safely sequestered on the distant fringes of national narratives where they have long been deemed to belong. Sometimes they transgress the proprietary rules of historiographic decorum, trample manicured gardens, uproot precious plants, ignore trespassing signs and zoning ordinances. Colonial histories may violently register the tensions of the moments in which they are recalled or slip surreptitiously into the faded patina of irrelevance. They can be rendered to the present as vestige—or pressingly at hand. They can be made unavailable, unusable, safely removed from the domain of current conceivable human relations, with their moorings cut from specific persons, time and place. They are histories that can be disabled and deadened to reflective life, shorn of the capacity to make connections. Not least, they raise unsettling questions about what it means to know and not know something simultaneously, about what is implicit because it goes without saying, or because it cannot be thought, or because it can be thought and is known but cannot be said.

At issue is neither stubborn ignorance nor sudden knowledge. It is the confused and clogged spaces in between in which my queries rest. This chapter reflects on the conceptual processes, academic conventions, and affective practices that both elicit and elude recognition of how colonial histories matter and how colonial pasts become muffled or manifest in contemporary France. My interest is in the peculiar conditions that have rendered France's colonial history alternately irretrievable and accessible, at once selectively available and out of reach. Intimately imbricated is a more basic issue: the political, personal and scholarly dispositions that have made the *racial* coordinates of empire and the racial epistemics of governance so faintly legible to French histories of the present.

THE RIP-OFF

Albert Camus's *The Stranger* is a "swindle." So writes Kamel Daoud in his extraordinary novel *The Mersault Investigation* (*Mersault, contre-enquête*), published in 2013 in Algiers and in 2014 to enormous acclaim in France.[1] In response and retort to Camus's *The Stranger*, published sixty-six years earlier, Daoud makes central and seizes on the emptied space of "the Arab" who in Camus's novel is shot by the Frenchman, Mersault, on a blazing afternoon on an Algerian beach in the summer of 1942. In contrast to Camus, Mersault's victim is no longer a non-person shorn of even a shadow, but "Musa," endowed with a family who mourn him; a village of origin, Bab-el-Oued, where he grew up; a lover, Meriem; friendships—in short a life, a body, and a name.

Told in the words of Musa's brother, Harun, Daoud's dark, spare, and seething prose explodes Camus's celebrated story of a vacant, ahistorical, existentialist act. Transforming it from the white-heat-ridden scene of a generic, senseless crime, Daoud assaults the reader with a killing that consumes and ravages Harun and their mother, both of whom are tortured by Musa's phantom presence, by a body that Camus's novel merely disappears. It is the story of the duress of living in the wakeful nightmare of an incomprehensible death and the murderous existence of living in colonial Algeria, in the violence of independence, its aftermath, and the contemporary ruination of those who have lived the effects of them all.

---

1. Kamel Daoud, *The Mersault Investigation*, trans. John Cullen. New York: Other Press, 2015), originally published in French as *Mersault, contre-enquête* (Arles: Actes Sud, 2013).

In Daoud's telling, Algeria is a place of entrenched despair and random deaths: when Musa was killed in 1942; again in 1962, when Harun and his mother take over the home of a fleeing French family; and yet again when Harun kills a Frenchman on the cusp of independence. He does so not as a freedom fighter, he insists, but in retribution for a French court that in Camus's novel condemns Mersault for not weeping over his mother's death rather than for killing an "Arab." In this obscene colonial world, the "killer-writer" Mersault, as Daoud calls him, is judged for his lack of a son's tears, not for the murder.

So much more could be said, but there is no recounting Daoud's narrative. Like Borge's mapmaker, one would need to repeat every phrase; every boundary transgressed; every bold, hazardous, and fragile move; every sequence that refuses the facile distinctions of colonial past and postcolonial present; every word that strikes at the colonial core of what Camus, and most of his public, never sought to question or see. For Daoud, Camus's *The Stranger* is a "swindle," a rip-off, entrapment in a blinded world in which Musa's tattoos and Algeria's colonial sentence have no place.

So the "Stranger" is replaced. He is not Camus's invisible, disappeared "Arab." The Stranger is the vacuous French colonial—and the summons is to Daoud's readers who still refuse to ask and cannot see. As the now old man Harun puts it, watching a group of French tourists at an airport, they are "mute specters" watching "us Arabs—in silence, as if we were nothing but stones or dead trees."[2] It is their silence that stops Harun and us, his readers, short. "Nevertheless, that's all over now. That's what their silence said." For Daoud, nothing is over. Like Ralph Ellison's *Invisible Man*, Daoud reaches to the "lower frequencies"—in this case, of an Algerian life reduced to "the Arab," repeated twenty-fives times over, in Camus's novel.

What follows is an effort to address not Camus's nor Daoud's novels in particular but why and how it took sixty-six years for such a story to be heard when the colonial history on which it builds has been told and retold. It seeks to address the unstable movement between a French press today rightly enamored with Daoud's terse prose, the numerous prizes he has won, the book's showing as a theatrical piece at the Avignon Festival in August 2015, its making into a movie to be released in 2017, its proposed banning in Algeria—and the continued warped reckoning with the colonial histories that saturate the fabric of contemporary France.

2. Daoud, *The Mersault Investigation*, 11.

Some fifteen years ago, in preparation for what was hailed as the first "transatlantic" conference on "the colonial situation" in honor of the esteemed anthropologist of Africa Georges Balandier, I was struck by two things: (1) by the celebratory effervescence of interest in, and proliferating work on, France's colonial history, evident in both U.S. and French scholarship; and (2) the curiously unreflective idioms in which earlier treatments of colonial issues were being framed.[3] It was a "forgotten history," a "memory hole," "collective amnesia"—a history that somehow got "lost" in the decades following the Algerian War and armed battle in Vietnam and as a French public digested revelations about Vichy and Nazi sympathies that stretched far beyond those previously indicted as its most infamous collaborators.[4]

For many of us who had long worked on France's racially charged colonial history and the breadth of its documentation, the exuberance seemed odd, almost feverish, and misplaced. It was not only belated, as students of French colonialism now so readily note. In light of the staggering surge in publication and debate of the past few years, the excitement could be seen as just one in a series of renewed claims to exposure of the discrepant histories that divide Republican principles from systemic, targeted, and sustained forms of privation in the making of modern France.

At issue, of course, has not been "discovery" of torture in the colonial history of France; nor are these new revelations that there were indeed camps of coercive settlement, detention, and concentration throughout the empire's carceral archipelago. In 1927, André Gide condemned the deadly labor regimes that accompanied the building of Indochina's railway.[5] Simone Weil

3. This chapter only references the U.S. scholarship on French empire, a field that also has exploded in the past fifteen years, where the author provides access to a French debate on the issue at hand. While it would make sense to examine the now high-velocity circulation and exchange between French colonial historians in the United States and France, a comprehensive review of this literature is not my subject here.

4. For a fine English-language review of what Henry Russo called the "Vichy Syndrome," see Rosemarie Scullion, "Unforgettable: History, Memory, and the Vichy Syndrome," *Studies in 20th and 21st Century Literature* 23, 1 (January 1, 1999): 11–26. Examples of the use of "amnesia" and "forgetting" are many: see, e.g., Helene Champagne, "Breaking the Ice: A Burgeoning Post-Colonial Debate on France's Historical Amnesia and Contemporary 'Soul Searching,'" *Modern and Contemporary France* 16, 1 (February 1, 2008): 67–72.

5. André Gide, *Voyage au Congo suivi de le retour du Tchad. Carnets de route* (Paris: Gallimard, 2004). There were many others I do not quote here. For a history of French

produced a steady stream of anticolonial texts in the 1940s, up until the year of her death. In 1958, the militant communist Henri Alleg published *La Question*, a graphic account of his own torture at the hands of the French military.[6] *La Gangrene*, which appeared in June 1959 and was immediately banned, documented the intimate technologies of brutal indignities French soldiers inflicted on Algerian women and men.[7] Pierre Bourdieu was writing about Algerian workers and "the colonial system" throughout the early 1960s.[8] Simone de Beauvoir and Gisèle Halimi's account of the torture and rape of twenty-three-year-old Djamila Boupacha received worldwide attention when it was published in 1962.[9] Extensive evidence of detention camps in Algeria and within France proper has been available to historians in easily accessed sources for a long time.

And then there was Alain Resnais's film *Muriel* (1963), a shattering effort to convey the unspeakable experience of Bernard, a young Frenchman of twenty-two, awkward and ill at ease, who, as we slowly learn, had spent twenty-two months fighting in the Algerian War. "Nothing happens" in the first half of the film; the world he now inhabits in a provincial French urban anywhere, is banal, still, and gray. There is nothing to represent. It is only nearly one hour into the film before we learn that "Muriel" is the name of the young Algerian woman he participated in torturing and watched as his comrades tortured her over the course of days. He recounts the intimate violence with unswerving precision—the blows to her hips, the ripping off of her clothes, the cigarettes lit between repeated blows that are ever harder when she vomits, crumbles, and is left in a pool of blood.[10] Reviews of the film at the time are remarkable for what they did not say: François Truffaut opined that it had stylistic resonance with films of

---

"anticolonial" writings and the different forms those writings took, see Jean-Pierre Biondi and Gilles Morin. *Les anticolonialistes, 1881–1962* (Paris: R. Laffont, 1992).

6. Henri Alleg, *La question* (Paris: Minuit, 1961).

7. Béchir Boumaza and Jérôme Lindon, *La gangrène* (Paris: Minuit, 1959), seized and banned in France by the government, was subsequently translated by Robert Silvers and published in English as *The Gangrene* (New York: Lyle Stuart, 1960).

8. See, e.g., Pierre Bourdieu, "Guerre et mutation sociale en Algérie," *Études Méditerranéennes* 7 (1960): 25–37, and "Les sous-prolétaires algériens," *Les Temps Modernes* 199 (December 1962): 1030–51.

9. Simone De Beauvoir and Gisèle Halimi, *Djamila Boupacha* (Paris: Gallimard, 1962).

10. See the incisive rendition of the film and of Resnais's efforts to convey the unrepresentable quality of extreme violence in Raphaëlle Branche, "La torture dans *Muriel* d'Alain Resnais, une réflexion cinématographique sur l'indicible et l'inmontrable," *L'Autre* 3, 1 (2002): 67–76.

Alfred Hitchcock; the *New York Times* reviewer Bosley Crowther found the film "bewildering and annoying"; Susan Sontag found it "difficult." None of the reviews even noted that the film was about the colonial violence of an unnamed war.[11]

Nor can it be claimed that racially targeted colonial violence in the making and maintenance of the republic was absent from scholarship and popular literature or confined to the exigencies of wartime alone. Aimé Césaire, Frantz Fanon, Albert Memmi, and Jean-Paul Sartre all underscored the "sordidly racist" and "systemic" compartmentalized violence that colonialism animated, the "lines of force" it created, and the "degradations" it instilled in the colonies and in Europe—among both colonizer and colonized.[12] Abdelmajid Hannoum rightly argues that historiography played a key role in making North Africa a European territory "in the minds of the French people" following the formation of a settler society in the 1870s.[13] But French historiography had a lot of help. Historiography has been only one branch of a broader field of French academic and popular culture, whose favored concepts and concerns have carefully excised Algeria, as well as France's other colonies, protectorates, and possessions, from the national purview not once, but again and again.

Gérard Noiriel once used the phrase "collective amnesia" to reference the studied absence of immigration from French historiography and school curriculums.[14] Similarly, "colonial amnesia" and "historical amnesia" are often used pointedly to describe the public and historiographic evasion of colonial history in France.[15] Kristin Ross saw the "keeping [of] two stories

11. François Truffaut, *The Films in My Life* (New York: Da Capo, 1994), 327–28; Bosley Crowther, "Review of Muriel," *New York Times*, October 31, 1963; Susan Sontag, "Review: *Muriel: Ou le Temps d'un Retour* by Alain Resnais." *Film Quarterly* 17, 2 (December 1, 1963): 23–27.

12. See Anne Mathieu, "Jean-Paul Sartre et la guerre d'Algérie, *Le Monde Diplomatique*, November 2004, 30–31.

13. Abdelmajid Hannoum, "The Historiographic State: How Algeria Once Became French," *History and Anthropology* 19, 2 (June 1, 2008): 91–114.

14. Gérard Noiriel, *The French Melting Pot: Immigration, Citizenship, and National Identity* (Minneapolis: University of Minnesota Press, 1996), esp. 1–9.

15. See Anne Donadey, "Between Amnesia and Anamnesis: Re-membering the Fractures of Colonial History," *Studies in 20th and 21st Century Literature* 23, 1 (January 1, 1999): 11–26. See also Todd Shepard, *The Invention of Decolonization: The Algerian War and the Remaking of France* (Ithaca, NY: Cornell University Press, 2008), esp. 101–35; Benoît de l'Estoile, "L'oubli de l'héritage colonial," *Le Débat* 147, 5 (2007): 91–99.

apart [those of modern France and of colonialism] as another name for forgetting one of the stories or for relegating it to a different time frame."[16]

But forgetting and amnesia are more than misleading terms (even when used with irony which it is often not) to describe this guarded separation and the procedures that produced it. As I argue here, very little of these histories has been or is actually forgotten: it may be displaced, occluded from view, or rendered inappropriate to pursue. It may be difficult to retrieve in a language that speaks to the disparate violence it engendered. But it is neither forgotten nor absent from contemporary life. *Aphasia*, I propose, is perhaps a more appropriate term, one that captures not only the nature of that blockage but also the feature of loss. Calling this phenomenon "colonial aphasia" is *not* an appeal to organic cognitive deficit among "the French"; nor is it a phenomenon confined, as we know too well, to France. We could look to Japanese colonial initiatives in Korea, the U.S. imperium, as I do in the next chapter; Israel's colonial settlements, as in chapter 2; or the many years in which Portugal's "colonial war" remained off its public radar. Rather, calling the phenomenon colonial aphasia emphasizes both the loss of access and active dissociation. In aphasia, *an occlusion of knowledge* is the issue. It is not a matter of ignorance or absence. Aphasia is a dismembering, a difficulty in speaking, a *difficulty in generating a vocabulary that associates appropriate words and concepts to appropriate things*. Aphasia in its many forms describes a difficulty in retrieving both conceptual and lexical vocabularies and, most important, a difficulty in comprehending what is spoken.[17]

ON ACCESS AND RETRIEVABILITY

In the opening decade of the twenty-first century, the number of scholarly works published on France's colonial history was nothing short of astounding. Pierre Vidal-Naquet's *La torture dans la république* (2000), Marc Ferro's

16. Kristin Ross, Fast Cars, Clean Bodies: Decolonization and the Reordering of French Culture (Cambridge, MA: MIT Press, 1996), 8–9.

17. David Swinney, "Aphasia," in The MIT Encyclopedia of the Cognitive Sciences, ed. Robert Andrew Wilson and Frank C. Keil (Cambridge, MA: MIT Press, 2001), 31–32; Jonathan D. Rohrer, William D. Knight, Jane E. Warren, Nick C. Fox, Martin N. Rossor, and Jason D. Warren, "Word-Finding Difficulty: A Clinical Analysis of the Progressive Aphasias," Brain 131, 1 (January 1, 2008): 8–38; Wikipedia, "Aphasia," http://en.wikipedia.org/wiki/Aphasia; Harold Goodglass, Understanding Aphasia (San Diego: Academic Press, 1993); Free Dictionary, "Aphasia," http://medical-dictionary.thefreedictionary.com/aphasia.

Le livre noir du colonialisme (2003), Christelle Taraud's *La prostitution coloniale* (2003), Claude Liauzu's *Colonisation, droit d'inventaire* (2004), Olivier Le Cour Grandmaison's *Coloniser/exterminer* (2005) and *La république impériale* (2009); Catherine Coquery-Vidrovitch's *Enjeux politique de l'histoire coloniale* (2009); and Pascal Blanchard, Nicolas Bancel and Sandrine Lemaire's steady stream of edited volumes, which include *Culture coloniale* (2003), *Culture impériale* (2004), *Culture post-coloniale* (2005), *La fracture coloniale* (2005), *Culture coloniale en France* (2008), *Ruptures postcoloniales* (2010), represent only some of the titles emerging in this refigured academic and political space occupied by those who have long written on French colonial rule and by a new generation avid to re-view that colonial history through a different critical lens.[18] The number of journals, academic and lay, that have taken up the "postcolonial question" and its relationship to urban violence and immigration, and to what Benjamin Stora called "ethnoracial regulation," have all the earmarks of endowing the colonial past with a politically active and progressive voice in the present.[19]

---

18. Pierre Vidal-Naquet, *La torture dans la république: essai d'histoire et de politique contemporaine 1954–1962* (Minuit, [1972] 2000); Marc Ferro, ed., *Le livre noir du colonialisme, XVIe–XXIe siècle: De l'extermination à la repentance* (Paris: Robert Laffont, 2003); Christelle Taraud, *La prostitution coloniale: Algérie, Tunisie, Maroc 1830–1962* (Paris: Payot, 2003); Claude Liauzu, ed., *Colonisation, droit d'inventaire* (Paris: Colin, 2004); Olivier Le Cour Grandmaison, *Coloniser/exterminer: Sur la guerre et l'état colonial* (Paris: Fayard, 2005) and *La république impériale: Politique et racisme d'état* (Paris: Fayard, 2009); Catherine Coquery-Vidrovitch, *Enjeux politiques de l'histoire coloniale* (Marseille: Agone, 2009); Pascal Blanchard and Sandrine Lemaire eds., *Culture coloniale 1871–1931* (Paris: Autrement, 2003) and *Culture impériale: Les colonies au coeur de la République, 1931–1961* (Paris: Autrement, 2004); Pascal Blanchard and Nicolas Bancel eds., *Culture Post-Coloniale 1961–2006: Traces et Memoires Coloniales en France* (Paris: Autrement, 2005); Pascal Blanchard, Nicolas Bancel, and Sandrine Lemaire eds., *La fracture coloniale: La société française au prisme de l'héritage colonial* (Paris: Cahiers Libres, 2005); Pascal Blanchard, Sandrine Lemaire, and Nicolas Bancel eds., *Culture coloniale en France: De la Révolution française à nos jours* (Paris: Autrement, 2008); Nicolas, Bancel et al, eds., *Ruptures postcoloniales: Les nouveaux visages de la societe francaise* (Paris: La Découverte, 2010).

19. For special issues of journals devoted to these questions, see "Empire et colonialité du pouvoir," *Multitude* 26 (2006); "Postcolonialisme et immigration," *Contretemps* 16 (2006); "Pour comprendre la pensée postcoloniale," *Esprit* (December 2006), http://www.esprit.presse.fr/archive/review/detail.php?code=2006_12; "La question postcoloniale," *Hérodote* 120 (2006); "Qui a peur du postcolonial? Dénis et controversies," *Mouvements des Idées et des Luttes* 51 (November 2007); "Réflexions sur la postcolony," *Rue Descartes* 58 (2007), http://www.ruedescartes.org/numero_revue/2007-4-reflexions-sur-la-postcolonie; "Relectures d'histoires colonials," *Cahiers d'Histoire* 99 (2006).

Tony Judt was able to easily assign only eight pages to colonial engagements in a much praised history of postwar French intellectuals that appeared in 1992. It would be hard to do that now.[20] What has changed is how that history is thought to matter to people's present choices, future possibilities, and, not least, how divisions are drawn in contemporary politics. What is being rethought is how the social policies of systemic and systematic exclusions figure in the grammar of Republican values and thus how centrally the imperial entailments of national history are framed.

Earlier forays into colonial history are clearly distinct from those that animate debate today. As current precipitants, many commentators see a turning point prompted by the virulent response to the proposed law of February 23, 2005, to require public schools to teach "the positive values of the French colonial presence overseas, particularly with respect to North Africa."[21] One might imagine that such a bold state injunction was a backlash, a response to widespread negative treatment of France's colonial past in school curricula. But French colonialism has never been part of the national curriculum. It has been assiduously circumvented, systematically excluded from the pedagogic map.

20. Tony Judt, *Past Imperfect: French Intellectuals, 1944–1956* (Oakland: University of California Press, 1995), 174–75, 179–89, 282–88, 330–31. A decade later, Judt's review of a new edition of *La Peste* (*The Plague*), with a translation by Robin Buss, was precisely about whether it could (and should) be read as a "simple allegory of France's wartime trauma" or as a situated and personal account of what it was to attempt to live "decently" among "the coming of the rats" in war-torn colonial Algeria. In the essay, Judt notes that Simone de Beauvoir and Roland Barthes, among others, condemned his "antihistorical ethic": see Tony Judt, "On 'The Plague,'" *New York Review of Books*, November 29, 2001, http://www.nybooks.com/articles/archives/2001/nov/29/on-the-plague.

21. For some sense of the intensity of the responses to the law and the range of those who mobilized against it, see "Un appel à l'abrogation de la loi du 23 février 2005, initié par la LDH et rendu public le 13 avril 2005," *Section de Toulon de la LDH*, April 18, 2005, as well as the archived articles available at http://www.ldh-toulon.net. See also Philippe Bernard and Catherine Rollot, "Les interrogations des manuels scolaires," *Le Monde Dossières et Documents* 357, October 2, 2006; Julio Godoy, "Recasting Colonialism as a Good Thing," *Global Policy Forum*, July 2005, https://www.globalpolicy.org/component/content/article/155/25987.html; Sandrine Lemaire, "Une loi qui vient de loin," *Le Monde Diplomatique*, January 2006; Claude Liauzu, "Une loi contre l'histoire," *Le Monde Diplomatique*, April 2005. As reported in the international press, see "France Orders Positive Spin on Colonialism," Associated Press, October 21, 2005. Among the many who have since written about the proposed law and the controversies around it, see Romain Bertrand, *Mémoires d'empire: La controverse autour du fait colonial* (Bellecombe-en-Bauge, France: Croquant, 2006); Catherine Coquery-Vidrovitch, *Enjeux politiques de l'histoire colonial* (Marseille: Agone, 2009).

Others have looked elsewhere to account for the postcolonial surge in academic and political forums, particularly to what was cast as an unprecedented "explosion" of violence in November 2005, when more than ten thousand cars were burned and two hundred public buildings were torched in towns and cities throughout the country. The crass description by former President Nicolas Sarkozy (then the minister of the interior) of the protesters as *racaille* (rabble) recalled a rich lexicon of racialized terms, but his vocabulary was not the only colonial evocation.[22] The imposed "state of emergency" drew on colonial-era legislation from 1955 that had been used to squash protests against the Algerian War. The "riots" on the urban peripheries (*banlieues*) were in the *cités* of sequestered and dilapidated tenements built in the 1960s where a majority of former colonial immigrants and their descendants still live. Unemployment rates among youth in these government-labeled "sensitive quarters" reached 40 percent in 2005, four times the national average, and remains with that same disparity a decade later.[23]

This information was neither revealing nor new. Nearly every commentary seeking to account for the riots began with such a description. Nor has the intensity of segregation or unemployment, contrary to popular perception, in fact changed much over the past twenty-five years.[24] Sociologists have been documenting this territorial segregation and its consequences for decades. What has changed, perhaps, is not what is known about these colonial lineaments but how *uncontainable* the "degradations" that Césaire described as inflictions on Europe have since become.

The repeated deflection and activation of that history is not unrelated to another well-honed and familiar narrative—one that is now charged with ever more urgent currency: that "security" rests on social segregation and spatial containment, and, when possible, deportation.[25] All are silent partners in a structure of feeling and force embraced not by a fringe right

22. Robert Aldrich, "Colonial Past, Post-Colonial Present: History Wars French-Style," *History Australia* 3, 1 (2006): 14.1–10. Riva Kastoryano also notes that "nothing is new with the last riots in France, they just lasted longer"; Riva Kastoryano, "Territories of Identities in France," *Riots in France*, Social Science Research Council, June 11, 2006, http://riotsfrance.ssrc.org/Kastoryano.

23. James Graff, "Why Paris Is Burning," *Time*, November 2, 2005, http://content .time.com/time/world/article/0,8599,1125401,00.html.

24. Eric Maurin, *Le ghetto français: Enquête sur le séparatisme social* (Paris: Seuil, 2004).

25. See Laurent Bonelli, *La France a peur: Une histoire sociale de "l'insécurité"* (Paris: La Découverte, 2010).

wing but by a broad population who has held that the colonial past is not its history and that those involved in the latest protests and earlier ones were not, and subsequent ones, should not be part of France. As Étienne Balibar suggests, a "regime of dis-memberment" has produced its opposite: "the proximity of extremes."[26]

The referents of the recent highly fueled colonial debate have also changed. Fanon, Senghor, Sartre, Césaire, and Memmi have provided founding texts of an earlier moment. They all have been republished and called on to make sense of the voltage around colonial issues today. But the proliferation of research in and around the colonial past has turned as much to a vocabulary and set of questions generated elsewhere. Anglophone "postcolonial studies" and its South Asian Subaltern Studies variant have hit the (academic) shelves. Ignored for nearly two decades, both quickly became the subject of hotly contested assessments about what they profess, who count among their practitioners, and, most important, whether their analytical categories are applicable to France.[27] Islam, the headscarf debate, and "the colonial past" have each been taken as potent, condensed signs that have mobilized and renewed condemnations of universalist claims and exclusionary practices.[28] Multiple meanings arise at these signs' edges, in the intervals be-

26. Étienne Balibar, "Uprisings in the 'Banlieues,'" *Constellations* 14, 1 (March 1, 2007): 48, 60. For what was an ongoing discussion of responses related to the 2005 events in the *banlieues* and critiques of these responses, see www.ldh-toulon.net, and, among others, Achille Mbembe, "La république et sa bête," Section de Toulon de la LDH, November 7, 2005, http://ldh-toulon.net/la-Republique-et-sa-Bete-par.html. See also Theodore Dalrymple, "The Barbarians at the Gates of Paris," *City Journal* 12 (Autumn 2002), http://www.city-journal.org/html/12_4_the_barbarians.html (2002); Remy Herrera, "Three Moments of the French Revolt" *Monthly Review* 58 (2006), https://monthlyreview.org/2006/06/01/three-moments-of-the-french-revolt.

27. Anglophone (post)colonial studies has been recounted many times by French scholars in recent years, and there is no need to do so here. For one version, see Marie-Claude Smouts, ed., *La situation postcoloniale: Les postcolonial studies dans le débat français* (Paris: Fondation Nationale des Sciences Politiques, 2007).

28. Joan W. Scott's *The Politics of the Veil* (Princeton, NJ: Princeton University Press, 2010) captures in a masterly way the anxieties, tenor, and subtexts of the arguments that preceded and followed the banning of the headscarf in French public schools in 2004. See also Caitlin Killian, "The Other Side of the Veil: North African Women in France Respond to the Headscarf Affair," *Gender and Society* 17, 4 (August 1, 2003): 567–90; Stewart Motha, "Veiled Women and the Affect of Religion in Democracy," *Journal of Law and Society* 34, 1 (March 1, 2007): 139–62; Charlotte Nordmann and Étienne Balibar, *Le foulard islamique en question* (Paris: Amsterdam, 2004). On the recently "resurfaced" debate on the headscarf at public universities and the response of young French Muslim women to

tween words and at the political intersections of linguistic gestures.[29] In those unspoken and unheard intervals are colonial genealogies of political disenfranchisement, uneven efforts to link colonial dispossession to "postcolonial urban apartheid" and to a legal system that distinguishes between those who should and those who should not have political rights and be eligible for social services.[30]

Still, each of these moments—the surge in rethinking the colonial in 2000, after 2005, and again now—attend little to the ambivalent treatment of colonial issues in preceding decades. French scholarship careened between a deafening silence on the nature of colonial governance and critical recognition of its resilient structures, if not its contemporary effects. This is not a linear history or one that was formerly obscured and is only now emerging from darkness to light. It has *repeatedly* come in and out of focus, has more than once been represented as "forgotten" and then rediscovered. It is a history that erupted at the center of French politics, then was remanded out of public debate, the nation, and its scholarly bounds. This is about more than malicious intent, historical illiteracy, or the bad faith of individual actors. It is about the very nature of political thinking within and outside fortressed French academe that has valorized only some formats for considering questions of human dignity—as though abstractions from France's own racial history confers privileged philosophical worth. Not least, what has been left persistently unaddressed is why one of the global heartlands of critical social theory and the philosophies of "alterity" and difference has so rarely turned its acute analytic weapons to the deep structural coordinates of race in France.

Opening to this question provides different valence to the repeatedly revelatory tenor of colonial history and its relationship to "the riots" in 2005. The public outcry at the "unexpectedness" of the riots belies the fact that they were not in "any significant respect new."[31] Loïc Wacquant was

it, see Justin Gest, "To Become 'French,' Abandon Who You Are," Reuters Blogs, January 16, 2015, http://blogs.reuters.com/great-debate/2015/01/16/to-become-french-leave-your-identity-behind.

29. Maurice Merleau-Ponty, *Signs* (Evanston, IL: Northwestern University Press, 1964), 41.

30. Paul A. Silverstein and Chantal Tetreault, "Postcolonial Urban Apartheid," *Items and Issues*, newsletter of the Social Sciences Research Council 5, 4 (2006): 8–15.

31. Alec Hargreaves, "An Emperor with No Clothes?" *Riots in France*, Social Science Research Council, November 28, 2005, http://riotsfrance.ssrc.org/Hargreaves.

not alone in asking why protests on this scale did not happen earlier.[32] One need not look far in the sociological literature to find that these banlieues have been zones of containment and abandonment for decades, punctuated with intensifying state surveillance and daily humiliations. The same is true for state strategies that have repeatedly created compartmentalized space in the colonial past and (post)colonial present, a point that prompted Didier Fassin to ask why French anthropologists neither foresaw what happened nor subsequently had much to say about it.[33]

Some parties have had much more to say. The manifesto of the ever expanding activist movement that calls itself *Les Indigènes de la République* (Natives of the Republic), created in 2005, has held that the banlieues are zones without rights, inhabited by an "indigenized" population subject to "colonial mechanisms" of control.[34] By its account, the French state remains a colonial one. Ten years later, it is more visible, active, and vocal than ever before.[35] Achille Mbembe went elsewhere, to an observation that we have long shared: Governance in France rests on the logos and pathos of a racial state honed in a history of empire.[36] It is a state whose strategies of separation and exclusion structure more than state institutions. Racial distinctions permeate the unspoken rules and "choices" of residence, the charged debates on secularism, the valuations that distribute moral disgust and sensory distaste, the explanations of sexual violence, and, not least, the unspoken sense of who can walk with ease on what streets and in which quarters.

32. Loïc J. D. Wacquant, "L'état incendiaire face aux banlieues en feu," *Combats Face au Sida* 42 (2005), loicwacquant.net.

33. Didier Fassin, "Riots in France and Silent Anthropologists," *Anthropology Today* 22, 1 (February 1, 2006): 1–3.

34. See their manifesto: Houria Bouteldja, Sadri Khiari, and Félix Boggio Évanjé-Épée, *Nous sommes les indigènes de la République* (Paris: Amsterdam, 2012).

35. See Clemens Zobel, "The 'Indigènes de la République' and Political Mobilization Strategies in Postcolonial France," *E-Cadernos Ces* 7 (March 1, 2010) http://eces.revues.org /390; Houria Bouteldja, "Au-delà de la frontière BBF (Benbassa-Blanchard-Fassin[s])," Les Indigènes de la République, June 30, 2011, http://indigenes-republique.fr/au-dela-de -la-frontiere-bbf-benbassa-blanchard-fassins. Bouteldja's piece is a manifesto of sorts, refusing that Les Indigènes de la République be located at the cleavage of the right and left or annexed by the French left but, rather, as firmly situated "on the racial and colonial cleavage" in France today. For Bouteldja's most recent statement, celebrating the tenth anniversary of the formation of the Parti des Indigènes de la République, see Houria Bouteldja, "What Will Become of All This Beauty?" *Les Indigènes de la République*, June 23, 2015, http://indigenes-republique.fr/what-will-become-of-all-this-beauty.

36. See Mbembe, "La république et sa bête."

But racialized regimes of truth have refracted through a more fundamental and durable epistemic space. They shape which issues are positioned at the fulcrum of intellectual inquiry and at what counts as a recognizable frame of reference in scholarly and public debate.

In the landscape of racialized sentiments, the word "race" need not be spoken—certainly not in "Republican" France, where race is not a legal category. But a state need not refuse race as legal category for race to find no easy enunciation and to remain unspoken and unnamed. Racial states can be innovative and agile beasts, their categories flexible, their classifications as protean and subject to change. They thrive on ambiguities and falter on rigidities, as we shall see in chapters 7 and 8. Students of the racial history of empire have some lessons to teach—and to learn. Racial formations have long marked differences by other names. Racial formations distribute specific sentiments among social kinds; they assign who are made into subjects of pity and whose cultural competencies and capital are deemed inadequate to make political claims.[37] As such, they demand that we ask who and what are made into "problems," how certain narratives are made "easy to think," and what "common sense" such formulations have fostered and continue to serve.

DERACINÉ: THE WEEDING OUT OF COLONIAL ROOTS

How colonial past and presence have figured in the work of France's leading intellectuals is now open to more scrutiny, but it remains striking, even with the onslaught of new work on France's colonial history, how long it has taken to address how one might even pose that question. I am thinking here not about the mobilizations in the 1950s of Sartre, Weil, and other French intellectuals against the Algerian War, about which so much has been written, but about subsequent elisions that have been evident between political and conceptual work, between "French theory" and scholarship, with respect to colonialism's personal, affective, and political histories.[38]

37. See Miriam Iris Ticktin, *Casualties of Care: Immigration and the Politics of Humanitarianism in France* (Berkeley: University of California Press, 2011).

38. For an early essay in English on Sartre's avid engagement, see Tony Smith, "Idealism and People's War: Sartre on Algeria," *Political Theory* 1, 4 (November 1, 1973): 426–49. For those unfamiliar with his oppositional stance, read Jean Pouillon's editorial, "Et bourreaux, et victimes" [Torturers and victims], *Les Temps Modernes* 15 (December 1946): unpaginated editorial, which is often taken as a signature statement of the *Les*

When Bourdieu insisted on a call for a *savoir engagé* (engaged scholarship) at a speech in Athens in 2001, just months before his death, and condemned the "artificial" division between scholarship and commitment, his assault was directed at the debate over globalization, not at the issue of race or the detritus of colonial relations that so mark former French colonies and contemporary France.[39] Perhaps he had no need to say it there. It had taken him some thirty years to speak once again about the anxious *bouleversement* (confusion) that his work in Algeria had instilled in him and of the academic conditions that for years separated his "theoretical" production from the early war-torn colonial sites of his ethnographic work.[40] *Le Monde Diplomatique*'s editorial insert on the piece referred nostalgically to such an engagement during the Algerian War, but it was *Le Monde Diplomatique*, not Bourdieu, who drew that connection.

Bourdieu's strong anticolonial stance has since been redeemed by a barrage of studies documenting "his unswerving advocacy of Algerian independence" and the confidence he garnered among "those Muslim Algerians he interviewed in Algiers."[41] But despite the insistence by his former devoted student, Loïc Wacquant, and others that Bourdieu's early works—notably, *Sociologie de l'Algérie*—was already a politically engaged book when it was published in 1962, as Jane Goodman and Paul Silverstein note, Bourdieu himself described it as a "project arising from a civic, more than political impulse."[42] One can appreciate the impulse in various publications since his death that

---

Temps Modernes collective. See also his public intervention from a meeting in Paris in January 1956: Jean-Paul Sartre, "Nous sommes tous des assassins" [We are all assassins], *Les Temps Modernes* 145 (March 1958): 1574–76, and "Vous êtes formidables" [How tough and impressive you are], *Les Temps Modernes* 135 (May 1957): 1641–47.

39. Pierre Bourdieu, "Pour un savoir engagé," *Le Monde Diplomatique*, February 2002.

40. See esp. the interview with Franz Schultheis that opens Pierre Bourdieu, *Images d'Algérie: Une affinité elective* (Arles: Actes Sud, 2003), 9–46.

41. See Jane E. Goodman and Paul A. Silverstein, eds., *Bourdieu in Algeria: Colonial Politics, Ethnographic Practices, Theoretical Developments* (Lincoln: University of Nebraska Press, 2009). The collection provides a measured assessment of the fact that Bourdieu served with the Army Psychological Services in Versailles and that "once in Algeria, Bourdieu was initially part of a unit charged with guarding air bases and other strategic sites": Goodman and Silverstein, *Bourdieu in Algeria*, 8. Also see Nirmal Puwar, "Sensing a Post-Colonial Bourdieu: An Introduction," *Sociological Review* 57, 3 (August 1, 2009): 371–84; Tassidit Yacine, Loïc Wacquant, and James Ingram, "Pierre Bourdieu in Algeria at War: Notes on the Birth of an Engaged Ethnosociology," *Ethnography* 5, 4 (December 1, 2004): 487–510.

42. Goodman and Silverstein, *Bourdieu in Algeria*, 12.

hail a "postcolonial" Bourdieu and his invention of an "engaged ethnosociol-ogy" and still want to question the nature of that intellectual field in which he developed his concept of habitus as "sedimented history." What is strik-ing is that even when Bourdieu examined what he called the "reinvention of a new system of dispositions under the pressure of economic necessity" in the early 1960s—and named "colonization" and "imperialist power" as giv-ing rise to a "situation of economic dependence (of which the colonial situa-tion is the extreme)"—the analysis itself was never about the nature of those political impositions. The terms themselves appear only two or three times in 150-odd pages. Dispositions are not analyzed as the making of an histori-cal ontology. There are only "old-fashioned peasants" and "urban subpro-letarians." Colonialism is not subject to an analysis of its content or form.

Nowhere is the elision of race and its colonial coordinates more pro-found than in Bourdieu's acclaimed *Distinction*, in which his subtle exca-vation of the nuances of French bourgeois sensibilities so assiduously sidestepped the racial distinctions that produced the habitus of modern bourgeois France.[43] How much concerted or unconscious work did it take to steer a collective research project and write a six-hundred-page book on the social origins and cultural practices of the French middle class—one that attends so minutely to food tastes learned in childhood, "exotic" potlucks, and sensory distastes—without mentioning, even once, the colonial sites and racialized dispositions to which they responded and in which they were forged? At issue is not what Bourdieu could or should have done but once again the "configuration of a scientific field" that gave little room to, or im-petus for, such assessments.

It is the same field in which Jacques Derrida, born in El-Bar, Algeria, to a *pied-noirs* family of small-town pharmacists, whose appreciation of "archive fever" has had such analytic force across academe and with respect to the "archival turn," who chose, for most of his career, not to examine his own feverish resistance to examining the racialized colonial situation into which he was born. He did eventually convey some of that dis-ease of growing up a Jew in colonial Algeria (in later interviews and in his biography). But evi-dence of his strong personal and political identification as a young man with "our African empire" (with "our" being "French") makes it difficult to ignore

43. Pierre Bourdieu, *Distinction: A Social Critique of the Judgement of Taste* (London: Rout-ledge and Kegan Paul, 1986), first published as *La distinction: Critique sociale du jugement* (Paris: Minuit, 1979).

his belonging among "the French Algerian liberals" whom, as Edward Baring notes, his *lycée* comrade Pierre Nora was to so viciously attack.[44] Both Bourdieu and Derrida divorced their sharp critiques of scholastic knowledge and its conceptual armor from the racial milieus of French empire that they knew intimately and on the ground.[45]

Then there is Derrida's intellectual and political comrade in arms, Hélène Cixous, French feminist writer par excellence, who rarely mentioned that she was born in Oran, Algeria, to a Jewish family. Cixous first writes about her impoverished, "clandestine" childhood as a nomad and "outsider"; of her French passport as a "forgery" in an autobiographical declaration of expulsion as a Jew; and of her disavowal of "allegiance" to any place and anywhere—and decidedly not to Algeria—in *Mon Algériance*. The book appeared some four decades after she arrived in France and two decades after she had become the famous "French" author.[46] It is severed ties on which she insists and depends. As Anne Norton has put it so well, "She remembers that she is the child of a refugee; she forgets that she is the child of colonialism."[47]

Or one might consider Jacques Rancière, born in Algiers, whose masterly work on philosophy's poor, dissensus, and politics as the "suspending of all logics of legitimate domination," who has offered analytical interventions designed to tear us from our assigned places. But when asked about postcolonial studies and its political concerns in an interview in 2008, answered that he did not need to address these issues because there was no

44. See Edward Baring, "Liberalism and the Algerian War: The Case of Jacques Derrida," *Critical Inquiry* 36, 2 (January 1, 2010): 239–61; Pierre Nora, *Les français d'Algérie* (Paris: Julliard, 1961). As has occurred with so many early "sources" on French colonialism, *Les français d'Algérie* was just republished with a long, "moving letter" from Derrida, who chided Nora for his assault on the French Algerian liberals: see Pierre Nora, *Les français d'Algérie* (Paris: Bourgois, 2012). The avid interest accorded the book (radio and television interviews and a slew of written reviews) are all part of this "rediscovery" of, and reckoning with, France's colonial history and those contemporary luminaries who have lived it.

45. Lee Morrissey argues the case that Derrida's conceptual terms should be seen with respect to his positioning as a Jew in Algeria: see Lee Morrissey, "Derrida, Algeria, and 'Structure, Sign, and Play,'" *Postmodern Culture* 9, 2 (1999).

46. See Hélène Cixous, "My Algériance: In Other Words, to Depart Not to Arrive from Algeria," *TriQuarterly*, 100 (1997): 259–79. Also see Lynn Penrod, "Algériance, Exile, and Hélène Cixous," *College Literature* 30, 1 (Winter 2003): 135.

47. Anne Norton, "The Red Shoes: Islam and the Limits of Solidarity in Cixous's *Mon Algériance*," *Theory and Event* 14, 1 (2011).

postcolonial studies in France.[48] It is not that Rancière has not directed his analytics of dissensus to speak out about state racism in France. As he reminded his audience at a colloquium on the expulsion of Romas as a group in fall 2010, fifteen years ago he wrote about racism not as a popular passion, as often misconstrued, but as "cold racism," an intellectual racism, one largely a "creation of the state."[49]

And there are many others. One might also look to the philosopher Alain Badiou, born in Rabat, Morocco, whose insistence that philosophy is "the thought, not of what there is, but of what is not what there is (not of contracts, but of contracts broken)" would almost seem to offer explicit invitation to position these ventures within the folds of France's occlusions around its own colonial past and its present debris—but there is not even a pale trace.[50] Or might we look to Julia Kristeva, whose extraordinary analysis of Marguerite Duras's writing in The Malady of Grief—on Duras's "melancholia as an explosion of history," on her "aesthetics of awkwardness"—seems to retreat from the very formative colonial sites in which Duras's most powerful work took shape.[51] We are left with only a vague reference to the "exotic eroticism" of The Lover and a subordinate clause on Duras's "journalistic account of colonial destitution," as if Duras's force could be wholly unmoored from the anxious labor of being a petit blanc (poor white) in Indochine, the always "awkward," resentful condition and tense site in which she grew up.

One could raise an annoyed objection similar to Mary Louise Pratt's some thirty-five years ago against a common claim.[52] In the case of Camus's stories (and one could include Duras's, as well as Kristeva's writing): These

48. See Sudeep Dasgupta, "Art Is Going Elsewhere and Politics Has to Catch It: An Interview with Jacques Rancière," Krisis 9 (2008): 70–76. See also Jacques Rancière, Dissensus: On Politics and Aesthetics, ed. Steve Corcoran (London: Continuum, 2010), 33; and The Philosopher and His Poor, ed. Andrew Parker (Durham, NC: Duke University Press, 2004).

49. Jacques Rancière, "Racism, a Passion from Above," September 23, 2010. http://mrzine.monthlyreview.org/2010/ranciere230910.html.

50. Alain Badiou, "Thinking the Event," in Alain Badiou and Slavoj Žižek, Philosophy in the Present (Cambridge: Polity, 2009), 15.

51. Julia Kristeva, "The Malady of Grief," in Black Sun: Depression and Melancholia (New York: Columbia University Press, 1989), 225, 230, 234.

52. Mary Louise Pratt, "Mapping Ideology: Gide, Camus, and Algeria," College Literature 8, 2 (April 1, 1981): 158–74. On Camus's "unfinished business" with respect to his "vexed relations to his Algerian terre natale," see Emily S. Apter, "Out of Character: Camus's French Algerian Subjects," MLN 112, 4 (1997): 499–516, and the references therein.

stories are fundamentally moral parables and have been (and should be) read that way, because it is ideas that matter more than place. So why belabor the colonial location? Pratt utterly destroys what seems like such an innocuous claim, nailing the fact that virtually every disposition described—from the *disponible* (available) Arab to the leisured Frenchmen in the colonies—is a product of and dependent on the colonial situation. Scholarly critiques aside, it is Daoud's *The Mersault Investigation* that now should make it impossible to read *The Stranger* without its *contre-enquête* and without locating the violence of colonial Algeria as its *contre-histoire*.[53]

I think Mary Louise Pratt and I would concur on not arguing that we should all now embark on biographical studies of the colonial itineraries of France's intellectual luminaries and the colonial situations in which they lived and into which some were born. In fact, that is already being done, and some have made that case for a long time.[54] And the inquiry I propose here is only in part to underscore how many of those whose conceptual work we call on in colonial studies systematically have set their analytic work apart from the situated histories in which they were at least partly shaped. It is rather to take this submerging of enduring colonial relations as symptomatic of how colonial critique is positioned and effaced. It is to ask why the Second World War, Nazism, and the communist-socialist divide have all been engaged and deemed relevant to contemporary societal conditions, while France's colonial and racial histories seem so easily to evade mention, to fall outside the bounds of relevance and the focus of otherwise politically informed scholarship?[55]

COLONIAL DIS-EASE IN FRENCH ANTHROPOLOGY

Some sixty-five years ago, Balandier advocated for a critical anthropology that would put a historical sensibility at the center of its theoretical project. The challenge he posed was to confront rather than circumvent the

53. Daoud, *The Mersault Investigation*.

54. See, e.g., Conor Cruise O'Brien, *Albert Camus* (New York: Viking, 1970).

55. The cases of exclusion of the colonial are too numerous to cite. See, e.g., Leonard Lawlor, *Thinking through French Philosophy: The Being of the Question* (Bloomington: Indiana University Press, 2003), in which the notion of even thinking the colonial genealogy of France's diffracted philosophical history seems so far afield that it is not even a possibility. One could argue that this is an irrelevant demand. I would question why it is so easy to dismiss and so obviously so.

conflicted universe of colonizer and colonized and to track the "social distortions" of race and the "pseudo-reasons" for it that had shaped African societies under French colonial domination.[56] He was not alone in making that call. In 1950, Alfred Métraux wrote about "a fatal contradiction" at the "heart of our [European] civilization"; in 1945, Bronislaw Malinowski chided anthropology for being too committed to "one-column entries" and urged instead the study of "the aggressive and conquering" European communities in conjunction with native ones; in 1951, Michel Leiris wrote scathingly about a genre of ethnography that committed itself to irrelevance if it "closed its eyes to the colonial problem."[57] These scholars and others were outspoken in denouncing the value of race as a scientific category, but the colonial institutions and practices that eviscerated the social lives and economic prospects of French colonial subjects were rarely registered as core features of their analysis. Although there were exceptions, these warnings in the imperative tense rarely translated into new conceptual formulations of what ethnographers studied, the questions they asked, and where they studied on the ground.[58]

When in 1987 Frederick Cooper and I sought to consider "tensions of empire" that cut across metropole and colony and through the political logics that joined liberalism, racism, and social reform, it was Balandier's foundational essay, "La situation coloniale: Approche théorique" (The Colonial

56. Georges Balandier, "The Colonial Situation: A Theoretical Approach," in *Social Change: The Colonial Situation*, ed. Immanuel Maurice Wallerstein (New York: John Wiley, 1966), 38, 45.

57. Alfred Métraux, "Race and Civilization," UNESCO *Courier* 3, nos. 6–7 (August 1950), 8; Bronislaw Malinowski, "Dynamics of Culture Change," in *Social Change: The Colonial Situation*, ed. Immanuel M. Wallerstein (New York: John Wiley, 1966), 14–15; Michel Leiris, "L'ethnographie devant le colonialisme," *Les Temps Modernes*, 58 (1950), reprinted in his *Cinq études d'ethnologie* (Paris: Gallimard, 1968).

58. Among the most prominent of these exceptions was Claude Meillassoux, who in 1958–59, under Balandier's supervision, undertook a six-month collective research project in central Ivory Coast that dealt in part with "the most profound" effects of a "particularly brutal" policy of dispossession and "*regroupement*" of the Gouru ethnic group that was carried out under French colonial rule in 1928 and destroyed 3,271 settlements in one district alone. As Meillassoux wrote at the time, their study of change worked off the descriptive (if not the interpretive) ethnographic baseline offered by L. Tauxier in 1924, carried out "only eleven years after the conquest": see Claude Meillassoux, *Anthropologie économique des Gouro de Côte d'Ivoire: De l'économie de subsistance à l'agriculture commerciale* (Paris: Mouton, 1964), 9.

Situation: A Theoretical Approach) that partly inspired that turn.[59] Anglophone colonial scholarship was then in hot pursuit of just those connections, spurred by scholars on both sides of the Atlantic, from the global North and South, French social science, however, seemed inured, if not impervious, to a rethinking that brought metropole and colony—much less, racism and Republicanism—into a single analytic frame. What Cooper and I failed to note at the time was that Balandier himself never really took up his own charge.[60]

The marked borders of disciplinary expertise could be invoked to account for that lapse, but, then, disciplines are porous, shaped by those who are powerfully positioned within them, and their fulcrums change. In an interview in 1995 with Marc Augé and other Africanist colleagues, Balandier described his intellectual itinerary, offering an oblique, disquieted, and personal response. He situated himself in a generation that was "liberated, but not entirely, that was decolonized but not fully, that thought about the University differently but did not construct it in a different way." As he poignantly put it,

> I am not going to do a sort of masochist balance sheet, but I will say that I have learned for my part, at my own expense and with pain, that being present to History is not an easy presence, that it is a costly effort, that it comes with costly disillusionment and disenchantment but it demands to be continued and to be done.[61]

59. Balandier, "The Colonial Situation" 45. See also Frederick Cooper and Ann Laura Stoler, "Between Metropole and Colony," in *Tensions of Empire: Colonial Cultures in a Bourgeois World*, ed. Frederick Cooper and Ann Laura Stoler (Berkeley: University of California Press, 1997), 1–56, republished in French as Ann Laura Stoler and Frederick Cooper, *Repenser le colonialisme* (Paris: Payot, 2013).

60. Marxism, which in some strands of U.S. and British anthropology generated an intensive turn in the 1970s and early 1980s to ethnographic histories of the "colonial legacies" that shaped the world capitalist system, had a wholly different career in France, where it was called on more often to query theories of exchange, class, and social evolution: see, e.g., Maurice Bloch, *Marxism and Anthropology: The History of a Relationship* (New York: Oxford University Press, 1983); Maurice Godelier, *Horizon, trajets marxistes en anthropologie* (Paris: Maspéro, 1973); David Seddon, ed., *Relations of Production: Marxist Approaches to Economic Anthropology* (London: Frank Cass, 1978); Emmanuel Terray, *Marxism and "Primitive" Societies: Two Studies* (New York: Monthly Review, 1972).

61. Georges Balandier, *Une anthropologie des moments critiques: Entretien avec Georges Balandier* (Paris: MSH, 1996), 8. The text reads, "Je ne vais pas faire une sorte de bilan masochiste mais je dirai que j'ai appris à mon compte, à mon débit et avec peine d'une certaine manière que la présence à l'Histoire n'est pas une présence facile, qu'elle coûte de l'effort, qu'elle coûte de la désillusion, qu'elle coûte des désenchantements, mais qu'elle contrainte à

The translation is awkward and only poorly captures what is strange and elusive in the original French text. When Balandier writes about being "present to" History with a capital H, modified with the preposition à, he conveys a sense of personal accountability before History and the ongoing psychic expenditure and loss that such self-reflection requires. The text approaches what Foucault called an "ethics of discomfort"—a refusal to let one's certainties "sleep," a mobile vision that is "close-up and right around oneself."[62] Balandier's discomfort seems to register a personal and political reflexivity that comes from the struggle to give what Judith Butler would call an "account of oneself."[63]

"Disenchantments" in the face of one's earlier affiliations (communist or otherwise) are common fare among French intellectuals. But while the repentant mode of memoirs, autobiographies, and national self-flagellation over Vichy silences and collaborations have been staples of postwar French society, critical personal reflections (as opposed to what are now national auto-critiques) of participation in France's "overseas" ventures have not.[64]

Today the landscape is undergoing some significant, if still measured, change. Biographies of intellectual icons of French culture such as Camus and Duras are now relocated in the colonial worlds that shaped their writerly lives.[65] Camus's *Chroniques algériennes*, first published in 1958 on the desirability of an "Algeria of federated peoples tied to France," is deemed misdirected and out of favor by some, but avidly consumed in the public domain.[66] In 2010, President Nicolas Sarkozy decided it would be a deft

continuer, à 'faire.'" I thank Janet Roitman for helping me think through the subtleties of Balandier's phrasing.

62. Michel Foucault, "For an Ethics of Discomfort," in *The Politics of Truth* (New York: Semiotext(e), 1997), 135–45.

63. Judith Butler, *Giving an Account of Oneself* (New York: Fordham University Press, 2005).

64. One such personal account that became a public event and an opportunity to express shocked ignorance and innocence by those who read it was General Paul Aussaresses's newspaper interview in 2001 and subsequent best-selling book describing his participation in systematic torture of Algerians during the Algerian war—and, more important, his defense of the torture tactics he and others used: see "L'accablante confession du général Aussaresses sur la torture en Algérie," *Le Monde*, May 3, 2001; Jean Guerrin, "Les aveux du général Aussaresses réveillent les cauchemars des anciens d'Algérie," *Le Monde*, May 21, 2001. Others, such as General Maurice Schmitt, former chief of staff of the armed forces, pronounced several years later that the accusation of torture used in Algeria was *"pure affabulation"* (pure fabrication): Le général Schmitt nie toute torture à Alger en août 1957," *Le Monde*, March 22, 2005, 9.

65. See, e.g., Laure Adler, *Marguerite Duras* (Paris: Gallimard, 2014).

66. Albert Camus, *Chronique algériennes, 1939–1958* (Paris: Gallimard, 1958).

political move and a "wonderful symbol" to honor Camus's memory by moving his remains to the Pantheon, where France's heroes are buried. He was mocked as soon as the announcement was made for so blatantly trying to "cash in" on Camus's popularity despite his own right-wing politics.[67]

Duras's *Cahiers de la guerre* (2006) supplements the snide gaze on Indochina's French colonials "as great beasts of prey" in her novels with accounts of an even more virulent racialized rule that she saved for her notebooks.[68] Both are feted and re-feted multiple times a year in revues and the press. It was only in 2001 that Bourdieu sought to discuss the ceaseless ill-ease and sense of the "tragic" he experienced as a young sociologist doing research and taking photographs in Kabyle villages during the Algerian War.[69] And only after his death have his early essays on the politics of Algeria come to be seen as central to his corpus and the basis of his sociological theory of *habitus*, not mere case studies for his analytic lexicon or conceptual imagination.[70]

The call on colonial idioms, references, and comparisons has now been ironic, insistent, critical and strong for some time. In the mid-1980s and 1990s, *métissage*, a term long associated with colonial contempt for those who were "mixed," became a way to talk about the public embrace and promise of a multicultural France while turning away from the structures of racial inequalities. Since its formation in 2005, the *Indigènes de la République* movement references the racist colonial policies of the *Code de l'Indigenat* in its

---

67. See Arnaud Leparmentier, "Sarkozy souhaite faire entrer Albert Camus au Pantheon," *Le Monde*, November 19, 2009, http://www.lemonde.fr/politique/article/2009/11/19/sarkozy-souhaite-faire-entrer-albert-camus-au-pantheon_1269540_823448.html. The press in France and elsewhere gloated over the fact that he was rebuffed by Camus's son and the French left. See, among others, Lizzy Davies, "Nicolas Sarkozy Provokes French Left by Honouring Albert Camus," *The Guardian*, November 22, 2009, http://www.theguardian.com/world/2009/nov/22/nicolas-sarkozy-albert-camus-pantheon.

68. Marguerite Duras, *Cahiers de la guerre et autres texts* (Paris: POL and Imec, 2006), and *The Sea Wall* (New York: Perennial Library, 1986), 135–36.

69. Bourdieu, *Images d'Algérie*.

70. See, e.g., Yacine et al., "Pierre Bourdieu in Algeria at War"; Enrique Martín-Criado, *Les deux Algéries de Pierre Bourdieu* (Broissieux, France: Croquant, 2008); Goodman and Silverstein, *Bourdieu in Algeria*. Goodman and Silverstein note, "The theoretical constructs that Bourdieu developed in [his] work, most notably, *habitus*, misrecognition, and symbolic domination . . . , have entered the mainstream of social thought independently of the North African and French political and social contexts in which they were initially developed. . . . The colonial location of [his] work is nearly impossible to discern from the *Outline of a Theory of Practice*, the primary ethnographic study in which the notion of *habitus* was brought to maturity": Goodman and Silverstein, *Bourdieu in Algeria*, 2.

name,[71] reappropriating the disparagements attached to the term *indigène* to recognize and refuse racial discriminations and the fictions of a society that is "too" republican to legally recognize race.[72]

Colonialism and empire now appear as thickened threads in the nation's unraveling republican fabric. There has been intense disagreement about how they figure, whether a focus on the "colonial continuum" strengthens urgent demands for social equity or is an irrelevant distraction from them, whether repentance and guilt have shaped politics or politics has replaced "sound" scholarship.[73] Some would argue that the republic and the empire are now difficult to view as mutually exclusive categories. What had been a patent oxymoron, *la république coloniale*, is still repugnant to some, but for others it represents the pulse of a protracted moment, an opportunity to revise a decorous, whitewashed French history that has never acknowledged that its own convulsive storming of the Bastille was met in the colonies by political demands that challenged the hypocrisy of its universalist claims.[74] Still, some scholars are uncomfortable with the politicization

71. The Code de l'indigénat was adopted in 1881 for French Algeria and expanded to all French colonies six years later, only abolished in 1962. It instituted a set of racially discriminatory restrictions on the "native" populations (night curfews, imposed taxes, and a deprivation of virtually all political rights.) Transgressions were severely punished by imprisonment or deportation.

72. See Sadri Khiari, *Pour une politique de la racaille: Immigré-E-S, indigènes et jeunes de banlieues* (Paris: Textuel, 2006). Khiari is one of the founding members of the Mouvement des Indigènes de la République (Movement of the Indigenous of the Republic; MIR). He and Houria Bouteldja are the authors of many of the essays on the MIR website.

73. Among the trenchant interventions on this subject, see those already cited, as well as Patrick Weil, *Liberté, égalité, discriminations: L'identité nationale au regard de l'histoire* (Paris: Grasset, 2008). Weil's work has a brief seven pages on the "forgotten history" of Muslims in Algeria: Weil, *Liberté, égalité, discriminations*, 151–58. Daniel Lefeuvre claims that the turn to the colonial past has been embraced as a "repentant" gesture alone: Daniel Lefeuvre, *Pour en finir avec la repentance colonial* (Paris: Flammarion, 2008). See also Marc Ferro, ed., *Le livre noir du colonialism, XVIe–XXIe siècle: De l'extermination à la repentance* (Paris: Robert Laffont, 2003); Jane Burbank and Frederick Cooper, "Review of *Le livre noir du colonialism*," *Cahiers d'Études Africaines* 44, 173–174 (January 1, 2004): 455–63. Benjamin Stora offers his sharpest critique of what cannot be claimed to be "new" or "forgotten": Benjamin Stora, *La guerre des mémoires: La France face à son passé colonial* (La Tour-d'Aigues, France: Aube, 2007). On colonial citizenship, see Laurent Dubois, *A Colony of Citizens: Revolution and Slave Emancipation in the French Caribbean, 1787–1804* (Chapel Hill: University of North Carolina Press, 2004).

74. See Pascal Blanchard, Nicolas Bancel, and Françoise Vergès, *La république coloniale: Essai sur une utopie* (Paris: A. Michel, 2003).

of the colonial past by a "militant" left wing.[75] Repentance with respect to France's colonial history is a subject of disdain.[76] While this is rarely explicitly expressed, others seem impatient with a harping on the colonial past because it is seen as a distraction from the social matters at hand and, in its present politicized from, is better not to be pursued at all.

In less than a decade, postcolonial studies and its relevance to France emerged as a flashpoint of debate among academics and of acerbic tension between activists and scholars.[77] Over the last decade, lines have been drawn between those who are bona fide historians and those who dabble in selective and spotty colonial historiography for "political" purposes. In a somewhat strange assault on the new French colonial scholarship, Jean-François Bayart condemned what he called "the sudden vogue" for postcolonial studies as often superficial, superfluous forays that render the analyses both improbable and useless, creating a France "perhaps existing only in [the] imagination" of some its advocates.[78]

When Bayart lamented the "often exaggerated overgeneralizations" among those who label all and everything a "post-colonial situation," he was not all together wrong. Freshly new academic consolidations—memory studies, science studies, feminist studies, (post)colonial studies—have all produced overextended metaphoric appropriations, as well as boldly creative, critical, and counterintuitive ones. Bayart's call that French scholars need to do it their way and, in fact, have been doing similar work for a long time informs his account of why French scholars have been so "reticent" to embrace postcolonial studies. By his account, that reticence reflects a reasonable and measured response in what he called a "different configuration of the scientific field."[79]

75. Emmanuelle Saada reflects that unease, arguing that to "attribute everything to colonization risks rendering invisible the political and fundamental social issues, like the problem of inequalities. . . . If a debt exists, it is an intellectual one. We need to better understand what colonial relations were and to make those results available to those whose personal and family histories have been marked by colonization": Emmanuelle Saada, "Il faut distinguer travail historique et positions militants," Le Monde, January 21, 2006, 8.

76. For Pascal Bruckner, the violence of French colonization is only one node in a "repentance epidemic": Pascal Bruckner, La tyrannie de la penitence: essai sur le masochisme occidental (Paris: Librairie Générale Française, 2008), 59.

77. See Bertrand, Mémoires d'empire.

78. Jean-François Bayart, "Les études postcoloniales, une invention politique de la tradition?" Sociétés Politiques Comparées 14 (April 2009): 1–46, followed by his longer statement in Les études postcoloniales: Un carnaval académique (Paris: Karthala, 2010).

79. Bayart, "Les études postcoloniales," 7, 15.

But to focus on the "delayed" embrace or rejection of Anglophone post-colonial studies misses the point and misdirects the question. Those who study colonial histories of the present do not have a monopoly on the politics of epistemology or on critiques of causal arguments, as Bayart imagines they have claimed. The more important question is precisely what has constituted the "configuration of the scientific field" and what conventions of knowledge production have made France's history of a racialized polity so marginal to so many of France's cherished intellectual elite. Rada Ivekovic saw new possibilities in the "delay," the potential to fashion a history in its own right, one inviting the reconfiguration of a field and perhaps even the "creation of new disciplines."[80]

The territorial battles are sometimes positioned under the sign of disciplinary norms: over who knows the colonial archives, who has a right to write about that history, and who does not. The vitriolic attacks on Le Cour Grandmaison's *Coloniser/exterminer* is a case in point.[81] Few of his critics failed to note his lack of proper credentials: he did not do his archival homework, and was not trained as a historian, much less a colonial one. Nevertheless, his arguments about the French politics of extermination and prolonged privation in Algeria in the 1840s are not difficult to corroborate in published sources from the period and in the colonial archives themselves.

"Discovery" sometimes has ceded to a moral ledger of crimes and condemnation. It has also produced unsettling genealogies that carve deep colonial tracks through the structures of violence, through the geographies of containment and detention, through the unequal distribution of state services—housing, schools, and civic resources. Affective space is not immune: Humiliation and contempt have colonial etiologies, as do inequitable recourse to alleviation from them. Resentment has its virtues that speak to far more than rage and revenge.[82] Vincent Crapanzano makes an apposite point in his work on the "temporal stretch" of the emotional landscape of the Algerian auxiliaries (the Harkis) who fought in the French army during

80. Rada Ivekovic, "Langue coloniale, langue globale, langue locale," *Rue Descartes* 58, 4 (2007): 26–36, 26.

81. Olivier Le Cour Grandmaison, *Coloniser/exterminer: Sur la guerre et l'état colonial* (Paris: Fayard, 2005).

82. This is the crux of the argument in Thomas Brudholm, *Resentment's Virtue: Jean Améry and the Refusal to Forgive* (Philadelphia: Temple University Press, 2008).

the Algerian War and among whose descendants anger has given way to social outrage, despair, and political demands.[83]

Sarkozy's presidential campaign in spring 2006 made explicit colonial connections that were heavy in the air: In a campaign speech in the Lot-et-Garonne region, he denounced those "who choose to live off the labor of others," told those who do not like France that nothing was obliging them to "remain on national territory," and castigated those who "prefer to search in *the folds of history* for an imaginary debt that France owed them."[84] Then, during a visit to Senegal in July 2007, there was his equally artful (and now infamous) reference to Africa as the "wounded" continent and a reminder to the Senegalese youth in his audience that "the real tragedy of Africa is that it has not sufficiently entered history."[85] At issue is not just what Sarkozy said but the common sense on which he called that gave him, as he put, *"la franchise et la sincerité"* (the right and the sincerity)—and his pride in saying it. Although it elicited indignation on the margins of French public culture, much of the "true" French audience to whom it was largely directed (in absentia) regarded it as innocuous, for he called on a common sense with familiar associations and "self-evident" truths that fixed his referents and his narrative. The notion that "self-hate" (*cette haine de soi*) among Senegalese youth was something he had the "franchise" to assess drew on an unedited colonial lexicon of "uplift" so endemic to his thinking and to his coterie of speechwriters that they never even sought to couch it in other terms.[86] In short, he marked "the folds of history" as a danger zone, prompting an exhortation to his listeners not to expect "repentance" from French society today for the crimes of their (often well-meaning) forefathers. The warning was clear: Neither Africa nor France would do well to ferret in those folds. But they are: As Alain Ruscio has argued for *la France sarkozyste*, many of the major media-catching French politicians and intellectuals bear

83. Vincent Crapanzano, "From Anger to Outrage: The Harki Case," *Anthropologie et Sociétés* 32, 3 (2008): 121–38, and *The Harkis: The Wound That Never Heals* (Chicago: University of Chicago Press, 2011).

84. See "La recidive. Sarkozy invite 'ceux qui n'aiment pas la France' à partir," June 24, 2006, http://www.indigene-republique.org/spip.php?rubrique16. Italics added.

85. See the outpouring of responses to Sarkozy's comments—most notably, Achille Mbembe, "Nicolas Sarkozy's Africa," *Africultures*, August 8, 2007, http://www.africultures.com/php/?nav=articleandno=6816. Other responses are at http://www.liberation.fr/rebonds/discoursdesarkozydakar.

86. "Allocution de Nicolas Sarkozy, prononcée à l'Université de Dakar," July 29, 2007, http://www.afrik.com/article12199.html.

more than colonial nostalgia. They have really never left behind an *esprit colonial*.[87]

The fact that Benjamin Stora felt compelled in 2010 to defend both the film *Hors-la-loi* (*Outside the Law*), a selection in the Cannes film festival that year, and its maker, Rachid Bouchareb, against a stream of attacks on his "biased," "anti-French," "anti-national" portrayal of the massacres in Setif, summary executions, and repression carried out by French forces and the foreign legion—some ten thousand Algerians and "one hundred three" Europeans were killed (note the precision of the second number)—is indicative of what remains a touchstone of widely disparate political divisions in contemporary France.[88]

IN THE FOLDS OF COLONIAL HISTORY

One need not resort to Sarkozy's clichés, however, to ask what work is being done in the folds of colonial history today. The rush to unmask, to divulge, and to claim the truth of the colonial past raises new questions. One cannot help but think back to the 1980s, when the ebullient cry to recognize and celebrate *le droit à la différence* (the right to difference) and antiracism saturated the airwaves of academe, public culture, and the press. Harlem Désir, the head of SOS Racisme, was made into a pop hero. Movie stars and public figures celebrated their birth homes in the colonies (Yves Montand and Isabelle Adjani, also known as "Yasmina," among them). François Cusset captured the tone when he described the 1980s as a "lyrical elegy to mixed-ness" and "a tireless sarabande to hybridity."[89] Public culture and racialized structures of power worked off each other in complex ways. Denunciations of racism did not translate into better public services in the banlieues or into better treatment by the police of French youth who "looked" North African. French citizens with North African first names continued to feel the need to

87. See Alain Ruscio, *Y'a bon les colonies? La France Sarkozyste face à l'histoire coloniale, à l'identité nationale et à l'immigration* (Paris: Le Temps des Cerises, 2011).

88. Béatrice Vallaeys, "On assiste à une regression mémorielle" (interview with Benjamin Stora), *Libération*, May 2010, 4, http://next.liberation.fr/cinema/2010/05/22/on-assiste-a-une-regression-memorielle_653693. Stora refers to an "amnesia" of cinema with respect to the Algerian War both in Algeria and France, despite the fact that the documentary *Chronique des années de braise* (1975), by the Algerian filmmaker Mohammed Kakhdar-Hamina, won the Palme d'Or and was met with no protest at the time.

89. François Cusset, *La décennie: Le grand cauchemar des années 1980* (Paris: La Découverte and Poche, 2008), 104.

"Frenchify" their names on job applications, as they still do today. Perhaps the most glaring political effect of the multicultural celebration, which ran into the 1990s, was what we see in chapter 8: the "unexpectedly" large percentage of votes that the Le Pens (first the father and now the daughter) and the Front National (FN) continue to win in regional and national elections.

"Forgetting" that Harki families were placed in forest hamlets under military surveillance throughout the provincial countryside takes hard work when it is those men and women who have swept the streets, tended the gardens of Parisian summer homes in Provence, and provided the agricultural labor in the breadbaskets of France. It is those invisible men whom one comes across in urban and out-of-the way places on Sunday mornings when the shops are all closed, and one is dreadfully reminded of how much they have been rendered "out of place." And what do you do: Speed up your pace to the bakery when you know too well they have nowhere to go?[90] The matter is not a simple one. As Fanon wrote in 1952, "The European knows and does not know."[91] It was Sartre, however, who reminded us that people know and do not know not sequentially but *at the very same time*.[92] It is worth saying again: like the noun "ignorance," which shares its etymology with the verb "to ignore," forgetting is not a passive condition. "To forget," like

90. Tahar Ben Jelloun registers the intense distress of that solitude: see Tahar Ben Jelloun, *La plus haute des solitude: Misère affective et sexuelle d'émigrés nord-africains* (Paris: Seuil, 2003). But it is Abdelmalek Sayad who offers the powerful account of what it was to live the impossible condition of being "a perfectly integrated foreigner and perfectly unassimilable": Abdelmalek Sayad, *La double absence des illusions de l'émigré aux souffrances de l'immigré* (Paris: Seuil, 1999), 11. Sayad devoted decades of work to this issue and, in this text, nearly thirty pages of a direct narrative from the Algerian manual laborer caught in the seductive embrace that France promised to offer. Sayad referred to this register of self-reflection and critique as an "*auto-analyse*," and he was, of course, right: Sayad, *La double absence des illusions de l'émigré aux souffrances de l'immigré*, 257–84. On Sayad's "decentering of immigration," by which Saada accounts for Sayad's "relative absence" from the immigration debate among researchers who became far better known than he, and for why he remained virtually unknown to the Anglophone public, see Emmanuelle Saada, "Abdelmalek Sayad and the Double Absence: Toward a Total Sociology of Immigration," *French Politics, Culture and Society* 18, 1 (April 1, 2000): 28–47. It is Sayad who sought to bring "the long term effects of colonization" to these issues: Sayad, *La double absence des illusions de l'émigré aux souffrances de l'immigré*, 32, 35.

91. Frantz Fanon, *Peau noire, masques blancs* (Paris: Seuil, 1952), 108.

92. For a discussion of Sartre's understanding of the politics of *mauvaise foi* (bad faith), see Ann Laura Stoler, "Imperial Dispositions of Disregard," in *Along the Archival Grain: Epistemic Anxieties and Colonial Common Sense* (Princeton, NJ: Princeton University Press, 2009), 236–78.

"to ignore," is an active verb, an act from which one turns away. It is an achieved state. As one of the extraordinary students in the seminar I taught on colonial histories and global inequalities at a maximum security prison in upstate New York in spring 2015 put it, "Couldn't we argue that systematic forgetting is a form of structured violence?"[93]

The conditions of possibility for the constrictions on colonial history are perhaps obvious by now. Herman Lebovics persuasively argued that the foundational myths of French cultural identity disallowed genealogies of empire as part of the true France, that the "political blueprint" relegated "empire to a national extension" so that "native cultures" could be incorporated in the first half of the twentieth century only if they were wrapped "within the high culture of European France."[94] Noiriel was among the earliest to underscore a unitary myth of France that supported a notion of Frenchness that systematically excluded its immigrant population. Twenty years later, in 2007, on the occasion of the publication of his book on the deep history of racism and anti-Semitism in France, he observed that in his earlier work he "deliberately set aside the colonial question" and wondered whether his *refus* was "perhaps an unconscious one to broach a past that touched [him] too closely."[95] Noiriel's insight about his own dis-regard, like Balandier's, complicates what goes into "choice" and what it means to know and "know better." Here recognition of refusal blurs epistemic sense and affective sensibilities. The unruliness of colonial history in France may be that it is too proximate and touches so many too intimately and up close.[96]

French scholarship may have been "ready" and willing to confront Césaire's claim that colonialism is never done innocently—as many did—but what is more disturbing is how little of France's high-powered theoretical energy across the disciplines (so incisive about political culture, totalitarianisms, capitalism, state structures, and class interpellations) was aimed

93. Under the conditions stipulated by the Bard Prison Initiative, I am not allowed to supply the name of this extraordinary student. In lieu of doing so, I express my appreciation for the perceptive readings and commentaries of this student and each of the seminar participants and for sharing with me their acute conceptual and political insights in class discussions.

94. Herman Lebovics, *True France: The Wars over Cultural Identity, 1900–1945* (Ithaca, NY: Cornell University Press, 1994), 57.

95. Gérard Noiriel, *Le creuset français: Histoire de l'immigration XIXe–XXe siècle* (Paris: Seuil, 1988), 16.

96. Gérard Noiriel, *Immigration, antisémitisme et racisme en France, XIXe–XXe siècle: Discours publics, humiliations privées* (Paris: Hachette Littératures, 2009), 16.

at the racialized foundations of the French state, at France as an imperial formation, or at what Marnia Lazreg has called French empire's "structural imperative" for militarized terror.[97] "Readiness," or the lack thereof, is a description of a disposition, not an explanation. Few passions are excited today in the face of that other divisive memory work for the same period that incessantly has accounted for—and recounts—who actively supported Petain and Vichy politics, who hid whom and where, who was really part of la Résistance.

"Readiness" is an issue of how relevance is construed. France could be exonerated because anti-Semitism could be folded into a history of war and exception while retaining a national narrative of republican virtue and a principle, if not a practice, of inclusion. Evidence of systemic and structured racialized policies written into the patrimonial parchments of the French Revolution could possibly be dismissed, as well, if such evidence remains historically sequestered there, "contextualized" and contained in the trope that "history is a foreign country"—not a genealogy of what permeates the social fabric of France.

The refusal to acknowledge eager complicity with Vichy and the avid embrace of physical and social violation in Algeria and elsewhere in France's "possessions" have something in common. Both contexts have been largely understood not as central features of the republic but as its very negation. When the socialist Lionel Jospin in 1997, then the prime minister, declared that Maurice Papon's trial (for the deportation of more than 1,600 Jews during the Second World War) was the trial "of a man and not that of a period," and that France was not culpable because Vichy was "the negation" of both the Republic and France, he not only received a standing ovation; he bestowed what Achille Mbembe so rightly calls a blameless "secular sainthood" on both.[98] This is, of course, the same Maurice Papon who in 1961, as

97. On the militarization of the French colonial state and torture not as an "epiphenomenon" but as an explicit and central feature of policy, see Marnia Lazreg, *Torture and the Twilight of Empire: From Algiers to Baghdad* (Princeton, NJ: Princeton University Press, 2008), 15.

98. I thank Achille Mbembe for making this point and for directing me to Jospin's speech. See Antoine Guiral and Vanessa Schneider, "Le procès Papon met le feu à la droite. Lionel Jospin est intervenu à l'Assemblée pour calmer la polémique," *Libération*, October 1997. On Papon's trial and his defense attorney's efforts to have the American historian Robert O. Paxton's testimony struck out as "irrelevant," see Bernard Frederick, "Robert Paxton donne une accablante leçon d'histoire," *L'Humanité*, November 1, 1997, http://www.humanite.fr/node/169724.

Paris's prefect of police, ordered the massacre of peaceful Algerian National Front (FLN) demonstrators, for which he was never indicted.[99]

In recent years, the press has brought colonial torture to the public domain before most French historians made their way to it.[100] In 2000, *L'Express's* featured cover story, "Torture in Algeria: An Unpublished Testimony," offered a sensationalist report on colonial violence and violation that seemed to anticipate the testimonial pleasure of the photos taken at Abu Ghraib.[101] From soldiers' private collections came "snapshots" of corpses and heads severed by both the French army and the FLN. One image was of a naked Algerian girl standing in the full sun in Constantine, her wrists held by two armed French soldiers, one with a small smile and the other with a cigarette dangling from his mouth; she faces front, with her breasts and pubic area blocked out in black. Such "coverage" may have conveyed the sins of an unjust war, but it also conveyed ambiguous messages about what was being confessed, what was being revealed, and who was to blame. In 2001, several years before Jacques Chirac's attempt to put into legislation the "positive role" of French colonial pursuits, *Le Monde Diplomatique* profiled the previous forty years of the teaching of history in French public schools to argue that "colonial history itself, and the resistances it created . . . were expurgated from school curriculums" to produce a generation with a warped knowledge of Algeria and an "expunged, bowdlerized history" of the Algerian War.[102] The omission occurred not because teachers had no time or because there were too many required courses but because, as Jean-Pierre Rioux, then the inspector-general of national education explained his own reluctance to

99. See Paulette Péju, *Ratonnades à Paris* (Paris: La Découverte, 1961), republished with an epilogue by François Maspero. The postface, titled "Les mensonges grossiers de M. Papon," originally appeared on February 24, 1990, in *Le Monde*. Sartre's attempt to publish a piece on the "pogrom" in *Les Temps Modernes* was blocked by Papon, who had the volume seized: see Charles Masters, "Papon 'Ordered Secret Paris Massacre of 1961,'" *Sunday Times*, October 12, 1997, http://www.fantompowa.net/Flame/algerians _sunday_times.htm.

100. This is not because they had no access to it. Sartre, among others, wrote about the torture in the 1940s and Second World War–period departmental and national archives became available in the 1990s: see Marc Bernardot, *Camps d'étrangers* (Bellecombe-en-Bauges, France: Croquant, 2008), 51n15.

101. Jacques Duquesne, "Torture en Algérie: Un témoinage inédit," *L'Express*, November 30, 2000, 56–61. See also "Torture: Une Honte Française," *Jeune Afrique* 41, 2105 (May 15–21, 2001).

102. Maurice Maschino, "L'histoire expurgée de la guerre d'Algérie," *Le Monde Diplomatique*, February 2001, 8–9.

give it too much emphasis, "The Algerian War was not very easily placed in a politically correct vision, especially after Auschwitz."[103] It is against such a refusal that Benjamin Stora repeatedly, and relentlessly, made the case to give that war a name.[104] But colonial history was not and cannot be reduced to the Algerian War. Systematic violations against people and property occurred far before "the war" and continues to spill far beyond its edges.

Perhaps the question for students of colonialism is not "Why this memory and not another?" Or "Why some invocations of the colonial but not others?" Rather, these invocations and evacuations of colonial history raise a question prompted by Nietzsche's warning against "idl[ing] in the garden of knowledge."[105] What animates effective rather than idle colonial history is not its timeliness—how well it fits current policies, political maneuvers, and the stories long rehearsed—but how deeply it disrupts the stories we seek to tell, what untimely incisions it makes into received narratives, how much it refuses to yield to the pathos of moral outrage or of new heroes—subaltern and otherwise. Nietzsche's warning leads us back to one of the questions raised in chapter 2 on the occlusion of Israel's policies with respect to Palestinians and with respect to whether colonial studies was hot in the Anglophone academic world because it had become (too) "safe" for scholarship.[106] If the parallel stands, so would a concomitant question: Is colonial history really a charged terrain, or is it somehow safer to reexamine now?

Some confessions are safe; some are not. When President François Hollande (whose father was an ardent supporter of French Algeria) delivered his carefully crafted speech in Algiers in December 2012 denouncing French colonialism "without dissimulation" or "denial" and called for a "truce on memory for French and Algerians alike, the progressive French press could

103. Maschino, "L'histoire expurgée de la guerre d'Algérie" (2001), 8.

104. Among his many efforts to rewrite that history, see Benjamin Stora, La gangrene et l'oubli: La mémoire de la guerre d'Algérie (La Tour-d'Aigues, France: Aube, 1991), and Le transfert d'une mémoire: De l' "Algérie française" au racisme anti-arabe (Paris: Découverte, 1999).

105. Friedrich Nietzsche, Untimely Meditations, trans. R. J. Hollingdale (Cambridge: Cambridge University Press, 1997).

106. Nicholas B. Dirks, ed., Colonialism and Culture (Ann Arbor: University of Michigan Press, 1992), 5. Arif Dirlik placed the onus elsewhere, attributing the surge to the increased presence of self-identified postcolonial intellectuals in England and the United States seeking to "constitute the world in [their own] self-image": see Arif Dirlik, "The Postcolonial Aura: Third World Criticism in the Age of Global Capitalism." Critical Inquiry 20, 2 (January 1, 1994): 329.

not offer enough praise for him and his choice of words.[107] It was almost as if Hollande had given a collective Christmas present to the French public: that of a humble and morally just absolving of guilt, with peace to all. Nothing in subsequent years suggests that it has been so. Indeed, confessionals around French Algeria may be "safe" because they redeem those willing to speak and the memory of what long remained dismissed and unheard, if not unspoken. Shocked moral outrage may suggest the innocence of those who were duped, ignorant, and not to blame. Exposés create their own politics of truth, suggesting unknown and then "revealed" genealogies. Feature stories on colonial war atrocities may be "safe" because they have the perverse effect of suggesting that there are always bad seeds among the virtuous majority and that such *individuated* truths are redemptive. Exigencies of war leave unquestioned sustained violence and the threat of violation as structured features of state racism, "normal" colonial operations, and colonial presence today.

What is more, so conceived these are construed as finished acts that can be relegated to the *passé composé*. Wrong was done; we all live with regrets: beginning and end of story. Regrets themselves can be soothing and safe. Those depicted in the French film *Indochine* were not a counter-history to the chic, cool white linen nostalgia Catherine Deneuve wears with such pathos in the film or that portrayed in the steamier pedophilic pleasures of the blockbuster movie adaption of Marguerite Duras's *The Lover*. Both have perversely fed Vietnam's attraction as one of France's most popular (sex) tourist and honeymoon destinations. But it is for students of colonialism to register and analyze how certain kinds of queries are *rendered* safe for public consumption and scholarly inquiry.

Moral outrage, like compassion, has a history of its own. As Fassin has argued, compassion is a poor substitute for political entitlements and claims.[108] This raises more troubling questions: Might this inundation of intellectual and political labor on the colonial past serve as an act of closure and of completion, as a new benchmark of virtue, much as compassion for

107. See, e.g., "La 'paix des mémoires,' se construit à deux," editorial, *Le Monde*, December 21, 2012; Vincent Jauvert, "Hollande l'Algérien," *Le Monde*, December 13, 2012; Isabelle Mandraud and Thomas Wieder, "Le panthéon anticolonialiste du président français," *Le Monde.fr*, December 21, 2012, http://www.lemonde.fr/a-la-une/article/2012/12/21/le-pantheon-anticolonialiste-du-president-francais_1809368_3208.html.

108. Didier Fassin, "Compassion and Repression: The Moral Economy of Immigration Policies in France," *Cultural Anthropology* 20, 3 (August 1, 2005): 362–87.

refugees and not political rights for "illegal immigrants" serves today? Does this "filling out" of French history do other kinds of political work? Does this making whole proffer a "new" moral narrative—not a repentance, as so many claim, but a renewed pride that to be French is to rise above one's past prejudices and history?[109] Does reclaiming that history confer a new sense of moral and national conscience—precisely when the borders of Europe and who belongs in it are contested and racism across Europe is at once denied and celebrated as not more or less racialized, but with reconfigured sites of intensity, folded into new current issues in ways it had not been before?

RACE AND APHASIC STATES

There are then, in short, diverse tones of mental life, or, in other words, our psychic life may be lived at different heights, now nearer to action, now further removed from it, according to the degree of our attention to life. . . . [In the case of aphasia] it is actual movements which are hindered, or future movements, which are no longer prepared: there has been no destruction of the memories.—Henri Bergson

Some psychologists refer to aphasia as a "comprehension deficit"; others, as a partial "knowledge loss" or "disruptions to comprehension and production of language in both oral and written form." Aphasics are often "a-grammatic," displaying difficulty comprehending "structural relationships"—an anomaly that reveals more widespread and fundamental cognitive and epistemic (dis)organization.[110] In his intriguing work on the faculty of recognition and aphasia, first published in 1898, Henri Bergson argued that in the case of aphasia, "Memories are no longer able to find a fulcrum in the body, a means of prolonging themselves in action."[111] But the still more striking feature on which Bergson insists is that such disturbances to psychic life as aphasia are not inner disorders but, rather, "an unloosing or a breaking of the tie which binds this psychic life to its motor accompa-

109. Thus, the virulently anticolonial spokesman against torture and the treatment of Algerians as a "sub-humanity," Jean-Paul Sartre, reemerges on the pages of *Le Monde Diplomatique* not only as national icon—as he had long been placed—but as the "real" face and conscience of what it is to be truly French: see Mathieu, "Jean-Paul Sartre et la guerre d'Algérie."

110. Swinney, "Aphasia."

111. Bergson, *Matter and Memory*, 108.

niment, a weakening or an impairing of our attention to outward life."[112] Materiality, memory, and worldliness are here entwined.

Whether or not one fully accepts the claim that French history has gone through an impaired state that one associates with aphasics, one thing is clear: aphasia highlights—far more than does "forgetting"—important features of the relationship among French historical production, the "immigrant question," and the absent presence of colonial relations. At issue is the irretrievability of a vocabulary, a limited access to it, a simultaneous presence of a thing and its absence, a presence and the misrecognition of it. As Roman Jakobson reminds us, in aphasia the "context is the indispensable and decisive factor."[113]

Not least, what I call colonial aphasia has produced misrecognitions such as the well-worn claim that racism is an organic American problem, not a French one, as the sociologist Emmanuel Todd repeatedly insisted in Le destin des immigrés. Nancy Green's parsed his categorical argument: "The United States has a major problem with race, France does not."[114] Within what political logic could Todd have made sense of such a statement? It was one in which racism was "a peculiarly American institution" that he held to be an American import "thrust on French history."[115] I doubt more than a decade later that he would take much pride in that claim.

As a concept, colonial aphasia speaks directly to the film Caché (Hidden), in which George Laurent, the successful host of a TV literary program, and his family find their bourgeois lives unraveled by a series of videocassettes placed at the door of their home.[116] Childhood memories of an Algerian boy, Majid, whose mother and father worked as servants for Laurent's parents and who lived with Laurent and his family, are punctuated by their murder in 1961 during the massacre in Paris of supposed members of the FLN and Majid's departure for an orphanage. "Hidden" in Caché is at once the

112. Bergson, Matter and Memory, 14–15.

113. Roman Jakobson, Studies in Child Language and Aphasia (The Hague: Mouton De Gruyter, 1971), 56.

114. See Emmanuel Todd, Le destin des immigrés: Assimilation et ségrégation dans les démocraties occidentales (Paris: Seuil, 1994); Nancy Green writes, "There is one category that has been conspicuously absent from most French discourses about minorities: race": Nancy L. Green, "Le Melting-Pot: Made in America, Produced in France," Journal of American History 86, 3 (December 1, 1999): 1205.

115. Green, "Le Melting-Pot," 1205.

116. Michael Haneke, dir., Caché, film, 2006.

camera, the memory, and the photographer—a history of dispossession, counterinsurgency, and the French empire.

Nothing is "forgotten" by either of the two grown men. The film tracks a "disconnect" between words and things, an inability to recognize people and things in the world and assign proper names to them. Nor did the film fare better than French historiography. None of the laudatory reviews of *Caché*'s "brilliant" treatment of hidden pasts commented on or even alluded to the colonial watermark of the film, the violent history it reenacts, or the "proximity of extremes"—as Balibar puts it—that divides their adult lives.[117] Here duress is a colonial condition inscribed in the flesh.

There are other sites of colonial aphasia that cut deeply into the politics of dissociation. Why, for example, throughout the 1980s and 1990s, when French historians were so taken with Pierre Nora's turn to *les lieux de mémoire* (memory sites) in his multi-volume celebration of national sites of remembrance, were the more than five million square miles of France's colonial "possessions" and protectorates, much less French immigrants, absent from it?[118] The only colonial *lieu de mémoire* in Nora's first five thousand pages were viewed not from Saigon, Dakar, or the homesteads that French settlers carved out of confiscated Algerian orchards, fields, and farms but through the imperial prism of the *exposition coloniale* of 1931 in Paris.[119] Why was there such ample room to remember the "division of space-time" (*partage de l'espace-temps*) that divided Paris from its provinces but no reference to that pervasive political distinction that still divides archival storage, history writing, and popular memory between what was *Outre-Mer* (Overseas) and what was France? Noiriel confronted Nora on just that, as did Catherine

117. See Roger Ebert, "*Caché* Movie Review and Film," January 13, 2010, http://www.rogerebert.com/reviews/great-movie-cache-2005; Jake Meaney, "*Caché*," *Stylus Magazine*, January 27, 2006, http://stylusmagazine.com/articles/movie_review/cache.htm; Wesley Morris, "*Caché* Keeps Its Secrets Brilliantly," *Boston Globe*, January 13, 2006, http://www.boston.com/ae/movies/articles/2006/01/13/cache_keeps_its_secrets_brilliantly; Faizan Rashid, "Dubai Film Festival 2005: Day 4: Caché," Emirates Network, 2005, http://movies.theemiratesnetwork.com/diff/2005/reviews.php?mv=REVIEW-1164; Kevin Yeoman, "Caché," *Celebrity Cafe*, April 17, 2006, www.thecelebritycafe.com/reviews/cache.

118. Noiriel, *The French Melting Pot*, 3.

119. Pierre Nora, *Les lieux de mémoire*, 3 vols. (Paris: Gallimard, 1984–1992). Volume 1, published in 1984, is titled *La république*; volume 2, published in 1986, is titled *La nation*. After a public exchange between Noiriel and Nora on that absence of any reference to immigrants in these first two volumes, Nora invited Noiriel to contribute an essay to the third volume (a decade after the first two appeared): See Gérard Noiriel, "Français et étrangers," in *Les lieux de mémoire*, ed. Pierre Nora (Paris: Gallimard, 1997), 2433–65.

Coquery-Vidrovitch. She recounts asking him about the absence of colonial *lieux de memoire* in those volumes. His answer was that there were none.[120]

There is nothing that Nora "forgot." Nor did he not know about the expunged places. On the contrary, Nora's construction of what he deemed relevant to French national memory defied his own career path and biography. Nora came from a family of *la grande bourgeoisie Parisienne* (the well-heeled French upper class) and was schooled in history at the Sorbonne. His first teaching assignment, at twenty-seven, was at a lycée in the Algerian city of Oran, where he remained between the summers of 1958 and 1960. When he returned to Paris, he spent the next few months writing his first book, *Les français d'Algérie*.[121] In its preface, the eminent colonial historian Charles-André Julien praised his disciple's craftsmanship: Nora's "acute" skills of observation joined with a "strict historical education" that allowed him to stand apart from those who embraced the excesses of "anticolonial totalitarianism." By Julien's account, Nora was "committed to understanding the milieu in which he lived, one that required a will to sympathy without excluding the liberty of judgment and, when necessary, severity."[122]

And judgmental it was. Nora's nationalistic disdain, class contempt, and disparagement of French Algerian liberals who made up *les français d'Algérie* figured on nearly every page and most clearly in his description of the shared characteristics of the "ambiguous French community" in Algeria. The members of that community had three traits in common: All were psychologically *declassé* from their own nations; all had left behind a *manqué* life in Europe; and all were products of 120 years of "Europe's sporadic ejection of undesirables."[123] Nora's story is one of Algeria's colonists who were political deportees and malcontents—the first wave, condemned after the failed coup d'état in 1851; the second wave, defeated *communards* in 1871; and the third wave, a "proletarian flow" from southern Europe between 1881 and 1901 that brought Algeria's European population to 365,000. Most were legally naturalized as French in 1889.[124]

Nora's criticisms of French Algerian liberals has been remarked on (by Derrida, as we saw earlier, among others). That is not the case for his pointed disdain for the working-class Spanish, Italian, and Maltese. They,

120. Pierre Nora, personal communication, New York, May 2001.
121. Nora, *Les français d'Algérie* (2012).
122. Nora, *Les français d'Algérie* (1961), 8–9.
123. Nora, *Les francais d'Algérie* (1961), 83, 85.
124. Nora, *Les français d'Algérie* (1961), 83, 85.

he protested, were not *français de souche* (of real French stock), and their only claim to being French, as he saw it, were "their identity cards."[125] The problem with colonization for Nora was the conflict between the French immigrants and what he called the *néo-français*, who "had lost their footing in Europe but who did not know France." Anti-Semitism, repression, brutality, and the systematic destruction of Arab villages, he argued, were perpetrated by these tawdry sorts of French and European immigrants, a product of their inferiority complex, a question of "classic transference"— of their contrivance alone. Like so many other "classics" in French colonial history, *Les français d'Algérie* was republished recently to much praise, with the fifty-two-page "strange and magnificent letter" Derrida addressed to Nora when it was first published in 1961.[126] Once again, while Nora's disdain for the French "liberals" in Algeria was underscored, what was not commented on was his dismissal of the "French of Algeria" who were not "really French."[127] Ironically, Nora's condemnation of the inherently racist community of French Algerian liberals was to overshadow his own racially inflected nationalistic categories. The fact that the former issue garnered attention

125. Nora, *Les français d'Algérie* (1961), 83.

126. See Baring's thoughtful analysis of Derrida's torn allegiances and "tortured political stance" as "a French Algerian liberal": Baring, "Liberalism and the Algerian War," 241. In a personal communication, Baring suggests that Derrida's position is "relatively unreadable today," in part because his position at the time was to counter the intellectual environment of 1965–1968, in which Louis Althusser was so prominent and when the notion that any idea of science could be free of ideology. As Baring noted, "The question wasn't whether the French tradition was structurally racist (they all agreed on that), but whether there was a tradition that was not. The central debate was whether it was possible to step once and for all outside of this tradition, yet another form of occlusion in Derrida's eye, or whether one had to combat it from within." I thank Ed Baring for allowing me to quote from this e-mail conversation from March 20, 2010. Despite Baring's sensible defense of Derrida, that context still does not account for how easily Derrida completely bypassed Nora's denigration of those who were not "*Français de souche.*"

127. See the interviews with Pierre Nora on the occasion of the reprinting of the book, as well as the various commentaries on it, none of which note the nationalist fervor with which he defined the "really" French: Pierre Nora, "La gauche a eu du mal à accepter l'indépendance de l'Algérie," *Bibliobs*, December 19, 2012, http://bibliobs .nouvelobs.com/essais/20121219.oBS2948/pierre-nora-la-gauche-a-eu-du-mal-a -accepter-1 -independance-de-1 -algerie.html; Pierre Nora, "Les français d'Algérie," *France Culture*, December 19, 2012, http://www.franceculture.fr/oeuvre-les-francais-d -algerie-de-pierre-nora.

and not the latter (to this day) says as much about the nationalistic common sense of French intellectual society as it does about Nora.

Given this narrative, the absence of colonial memory sites in *Les lieux de mémoire*, of both the Algerian War and *les français d'Algérie*, was neither an oversight nor blindness. Again, nothing was forgotten. As Freud wrote, those afflicted with aphasia have severed, "interrupted" links in "pathways" and "systems of association."[128] For Nora these "pathways" were blocked by the categories in which he operated and thus how he associated words with people and things. Dissociations served his racialized accounting of a failed colonial project. And he knew whom to blame. Even the title *Les français d'Algérie* is misleading. It is really an ironic inverted reference—as if (and often) in scare quotes in the text—for folk he never counted as French at all. Indeed, one could argue that there really is nothing contradictory about these two moments in Nora's narrative. One was about real Frenchmen, and one was not.

A similar argument—that French *colons* were not really French—informed Charles-André Julien's introduction to Césaire's *Toussaint L'Ouverture: La révolution française et le problème colonial*, published in the same year as Nora's *Les français d'Algérie*. Julien notes that the *préjugés racistes* (racist prejudice) of white *habitants* in Saint-Domingue were those of men who "did not transport their *patrie* on the soles of their shoes," men who spoke of Louis XVI not as "their sovereign" but "with the same indifference they would have to a foreign prince."[129]

Such aphasia would have admitted little room for Eric Jennings's study that challenges the notion that under Vichy rule, French authorities allowed Germans to run French colonies "behind the scenes." Instead, he argues for a fulsome and "native" French ultraconservative authoritarianism in Madagascar, Guadeloupe, and Indochina.[130] It would also leave little room for

128. Sigmund Freud, *Contribution à la conception des aphasies: une étude critique* (1891) (Paris: Presses Universitaires de France, 1983), 51, 61. I thank the psychiatrist and anthropologist Richard Rechtmann for long discussions about aphasia chez Freud and others. For an incisive use of Freud's notion of "denial" with reference to race in France, see Didier Fassin, "Du déni à la dénégation: Psychologie politique de la représentation des discriminations," in *De la question sociale à la question raciale: Représenter la société française*, ed. Didier Fassin and Eric Fassin (Paris: Découverte, 2009), 133–57.

129. See Charles-Andre Julien's preface to Aimé Césaire, *Toussaint L'Ouverture: La révolution française et le problème colonial* (Paris: Présence Africaine, 1961), 9.

130. Eric T. Jennings, *Vichy in the Tropics: Petain's National Revolution in Madagascar, Guadeloupe, and Indochina, 1940–44* (Stanford, CA: Stanford University Press, 2001).

Hee Jung Ko's work on Nazis in the French Indochina War.[131] Concerned with understanding the representations through which the French occupation of Indochina was made comprehensible to a metropolitan audience, Ko examined the stories from 1947 of "Nazi-like" atrocities committed by French troops in Indochina and looked at how these brutalities joined with those of the Germans. She documents a colonial elite that celebrated and honored Pétain, posters of whom plastered Saigon's streets, and a colonial elite that subjected Jews and Freemasons to the same discriminatory laws to which they were subjected in occupied "free" France. French colonists did more than "sympathize" with Japanese and Nazi racist policies; the French Foreign Legion was full of former Nazi Schutzstaffel (ss) officers and soldiers, of what one former French *parachutiste* described as "an army of pirates, malcontents, men somewhere between the S.S. and cavemen."[132]

This hyperbolic language should give us pause. Former French officers reported that as many as 40–60 percent of some French Foreign Legion units in Indochina consisted of those "of German origin."[133] What is the parachutist's point here: that the barbarisms were committed by Nazi thugs and not Frenchmen? Ko questions whether some Germans joined for the same reason many French soldiers did: to fight against totalitarianism, not to fight a colonial war. Or was it that those Germans who joined units in Indochina were running from war crimes for which they would have been prosecuted had they remained in Germany? What is clear is that the racialized violence of French rule and Vichy enthusiasts joined forces on common colonial ground, a point left unexplored in French historiography. Vichy and post-Vichy right-wing politics did not eclipse imperial priorities. They were a vital part of them, something about which French historians have had nothing to say.[134] Could this be attributed to a conceptual and political

131. Hee Jung Ko, "Nazis in the French-Indochina War: The Vichy Syndrome and the Politics of Memory," paper presented at the Mass Political Violence in Twentieth-Century Southeast Asia conference, University of California, Berkeley, March 2001. I thank Hee Jung Ko for sharing this part of her dissertation in progress when I was working through a first presentation of these issues in 2000.

132. Philippe Arnoulx de Pirey, "Operation-Gachis," *Les Temps Modernes* 92 (July 1953), 100, quoted in Ko, "Nazis in the French-Indochina War," 21.

133. Ko, "Nazis in the French-Indochina War," 23.

134. On the part Vichy played in colonial politics, see Frederick Cooper, *Decolonization and African Society: The Labor Question in French and British Africa* (Cambridge: Cambridge University Press, 1996), esp. 141–49. With respect to labor policy in French colonial Africa, he notes that Vichy ideology "had a longer life than Vichy's four years," with

case of misrecognition among scholars? Were these categorical errors that produced distinctions that did not matter as they missed those that did? Or has this been an effect of what Bayart called the peculiarly French "configuration of the scientific field," one that makes it difficult to conceive of the French colonial state and the metropolitan one as synthetic pieces of a racially inflected imperial formation?

There is another possibility: that some of the charged force of the French postcolonial academic and political maelstrom does not turn on a colonial *past* at all. Rather, it is much more firmly based on the fundamental ways in which racialized epistemologies have long permeated French political thinking, knowledge production, and public debate and on how centrally these political logics, if not their grammars, figure today. As Nancy Green once observed, not only was race long disparaged as an imported American category, but also, "for many years, the majority of French researchers simply ignored the subject of racism in France."[135]

The treatment of Foucault's work in the 1970s on the racial state is a case in point.[136] Despite the renewed interest in his Collège de France lectures (delivered between 1970 and 1984), virtually everything he wrote about the racial inflections of biopolitics remained "unremarkable" in a literal sense—and systematically ignored. When the lecture from February 1976 was published as "The Birth of Racism" in *Les Temps Modernes* in 1991, French scholars, so otherwise attentive to his insights, had little to say.[137] And again, when the first of his annual lectures was published in 1997, what was chosen was *Il faut défendre la société* (*Society Must Be Defended*), the lectures that so carefully outlined a theory of the racial state. Although it was hailed as among his most important statements on biopolitics, virtually no com-

---

"considerable overlap in personnel as well as ideas": Cooper, *Decolonization and African Society*, 142. For a more comprehensive study of Vichy's colonial politics, see Jennings, *Vichy in the Tropics*. For earlier efforts to make these connections, on Vichy's unrealized program to stage a "revival of France through maritime and colonial resources, alongside a great continental Germany," see Robert O. Paxton, *Vichy France: Old Guard and New Order, 1940–1944* (New York: Columbia University Press, 2001), 114. On implementation of the Jewish quota system in 1941, in which the French Ministry of Colonies, like other ministries, voiced "no objections," see Michael Robert Marrus and Robert O. Paxton, *Vichy France and the Jews* (Stanford, CA: Stanford University Press, 1995), 125.

135. Green, "Le Melting-Pot," 1205.

136. See Ann Laura Stoler, *Race and the Education of Desire: Foucault's History of Sexuality and the Colonial Order of Things*. Durham, NC: Duke University Press, 1995), esp. 55–94.

137. Michel Foucault, "Faire vivre et laisser mourir: La naissance du racisme," *Les Temps Modernes* 535 (February 1991): 37–61.

mentaries noted how central a genealogy of state racism was to that project.[138] When the four-volume compiled corpus of Foucault's writings and
interviews, Dits et écrits, appeared in 1994, "race" had no index entry. Six
years later, a special issue of Cités: Philosophie, Politique, Histoire devoted to
"Michel Foucault: De la guerre des races au biopouvoir" (Michel Foucault:
From the War of Races to Biopower) contained not one essay tackling his
analysis of state racism. No one thought to pose the obvious question, a
question Foucault himself did not raise in 1976 but one that is difficult not to
pose two decades later—namely, "What was the society that demanded defending in contemporary France?"[139] Similarly, in Penser avec Michel Foucault,
an otherwise fine collection devoted to his key concepts of critique, security, governmentality, and biopower, not one contributor broaches either
his argument that "racism is the condition that makes it acceptable to put
[certain people] to death in a society of normalization" or his counterintuitive insight that racial discourse consolidates not on the imperial periphery
but within the borders of Europe itself.[140] Something remains amiss when
the connective tissue that Foucault sought between colonial genocide and
the internal distinctions forged by a European racial state commands reflection neither on the location from which he was writing nor on the il-
lustrious and iconic figures of French republican history on which he drew.

French political theory, so salient to how scholars across the globe think
and write about colonial history elsewhere, has rarely been called on to
critically reflect on France's racial order of things, on the historical speci-
ficities that have created a French racial reality over a longue durée. And even
the philosopher Elisabeth Roudinesco, with her laser-like dissection of philosophy "in turbulent times," never once asks why Gilles Deleuze, who so
insisted on the "fascism in us all," left the racial architecture of France and
its empire unaddressed.[141] As Serguei Oushakine has argued in his treatment of aphasia in post-Soviet society, at issue is a "certain inability to sym-
bolize the experience that is present or that has been lived through . . . a

138. Michel Foucault, Il faut défendre la société: Cours au Collège de France, 1975–1976 (Paris:
Gallimard and Seuil, 1997).

139. Yves Charles Zarka, ed., "Michel Foucault: de la guerre des races au biopouvoir,"
Cités: Philosophie, Politique, Histoire 2 (2000).

140. Marie-Christine Granjon, ed., Penser avec Michel Foucault: Théorie critique et pratiques
politiques (Paris: Karthala, 2005), 53.

141. Elisabeth Roudinesco, Philosophy in Turbulent Times: Canguilhem, Sartre, Foucault,
Althusser, Deleuze, Derrida (New York: Columbia University Press, 2008), 142.

persistent attempt not to notice [or] to perform an operation of symbolic substitution . . . constitutive for one's collective or group identity." In both contexts, the historicity of these forms of substitution is key—when they occur, how they are secured, for whom such substitutions work, and what kinds of work they do.[142]

So where is race in this *affaire colonial* that has so permeated the intellectual and political landscape over the past decade and has been eclipsed only by the debate over secularism, Islamophobia, and the fears of Islamic fundamentalism in France today? Didier and Éric Fassin argue that the confused space in which questions of race have been placed represents a "new era" in which the discourse, public and vernacular, about racial recognition and social distribution have moved from the shadows to the spotlight, from "absence to presence," from the taciturn to the loquacious, from the occluded to center stage. Rather than take the mobile space in which race appears to show how little is understood, they take the protean language of race as an accurate representation of the contemporary reality—not as a representation of a misunderstood semantics but as a faithful register of the quotidian problematics with which people grapple and the social quandaries in which they live.[143]

What has changed, as they argue, is the particular way in which French society represents itself to itself. It is not that race was not a topic of political analysis and conversation earlier. In the late 1980s through the 1990s and at the height of the FN's campaign for a "national preference," racism and xenophobia were on research agendas and publishing charts as never before. The multiple works of Pierre-André Taguieff on "racism and its doubles"; Patrick Weil's works on the politics of immigration; Michel Wievioka's *La France raciste* (1992); the 1994 National Commission on the Rights of Man; Michel Winock's history of nationalism, anti-Semitism, and fascism in France; Tzvetan Todorov's reflection on French universalism and racism; Hervé Le Bras's demographic work on racial exclusion; special issues of high-profile journals devoted to "exclusionary France"; and,

142. Serguei Oushakine, "In the State of Post-Soviet Aphasia: Symbolic Development in Contemporary Russia." *Europe-Asia Studies* 52 (2000): 991–1016. The discussion of symbolic substitution is from an e-mail exchange with Oushakine on the similarities and differences we found in our use of aphasia, August 26, 2001. I thank him for allowing me to quote from our correspondence.

143. Didier Fassin and Eric Fassin, *De la question sociale à la question raciale: Représenter la société française* (Paris: Découverte, 2009).

not least, Étienne Balibar's repeated interventions that have increasingly taken on racism as a core feature of Europe's contemporary politics—all appeared before the renewed attention to a postcolonial frame.[144] Many invoked colonization in passing, but few offered sustained analyses of how it mattered.[145] Now race talk is everywhere, as I have noted, but its relationship to scholarship on colonialism remains severed from an analysis of a contemporary racial state. Balibar's emphasis for more than a decade on the extension of institutionalized racism as a "form of European apartheid" has been taken up by others since the riots in 2005.[146] Less clear is whether his reasoning about the emergent present and near future would be equally shared: that Europe's "different types of racisms" are "more vivacious and more deadly" than ever.[147]

ON THE BRINK OF ANXIETY

Colonial aphasia is a political disorder and a troubled psychic space. As Oliver Sacks described it, aphasics fail "to see the whole, seeing only details."[148] Schemas might be identified with the "confabulating of non-existent fea-

144. See Pierre-André Taguieff, *La force du préjugé. Essai sur le racisme et ses doubles* (Paris: La Découverte, 1988); Pierre-André Taguieff, *Face au racisme*, Tome 1 and 2 (Paris: La Découverte, 1991); Patrick Weil, *La France et ses étrangers* (Paris: Gallimard, 1991); Michel Wierviorka, *La France Raciste* (Paris: Seuil, 1992); La Commission nationale consultative des droits de l'homme, 1994, *La lutte contre le racisme et la xénophobie* (Paris: La documentation Française, 1995); Michel Winock, *Nationalisme, antisémitisme et fascisme en France* (Paris: Seuil, 1982); Tvetan Todorov, *Nous et les autres* (Paris: Seuil, 1989); Hervé Le Bras, *Le démon des origines: démographie et extrême droite* (Paris: L'aube, 1998; and esp. Etienne Balibar, "Y a-t-il un neo-racisme?" in *Race, nation, classe: Les identités ambiguës*, ed. Etienne Balibar and Immanuel Wallerstein (Paris: La Découverte, 1988), 27–41; Étienne Balibar, "Racism as Universalism," *New Political Science* 8 (1–2) 1989:9–22; Etienne Balibar, *Les frontières de la démocratie* (Paris: La Découverte, 1992); Etienne Balibar, *Droit de cité: Culture et politique en démocratie* (La Tour-d'Aigues, France: Aube, 1998).

145. Balibar has been among the few to call on both Marx and Foucault to distinguish between the state's imposition of *sécurité* and popular entitlements to civic *sureté* and thereby to underscore how much that distinction determines from whom French "society must be defended" today. On that distinction, see Balibar, *Droit de cité*, 29.

146. See, e.g., Dominque Vidal, "Casser l'apartheid à la française," *Le Monde Diplomatique*, December 2005, 20–21.

147. Balibar, *Droit de cité*, 24.

148. Oliver W. Sacks, *The Man Who Mistook His Wife for a Hat and Other Clinical Tales* (New York: Simon and Schuster, 1998), 10–11, 19.

tures" but "without the reality being grasped at all."[149] They become not only incapable of connecting words and things but, as Sacks put it, "incapable of judgment."[150] As a metaphorical concept, aphasia does only so much work. We need a better understanding of how inaccessibility to knowledge is achieved and more about the political, scholarly, and cognitive domains in which knowing is disabled, attention is redirected, things are renamed, and disregard is revived and sustained. At issue is both disabled knowledge as a political form and "knowing" as a cognitive and affective act.

In struggling to describe these disabling and disabled states over the past decade, I frequently turned to Foucault, not imagining when I began writing about colonial aphasia some fifteen years ago that he, too, had been drawn to its strange effects on knowledge, to its unsettling categorical clusterings and confabulations. But that is precisely where he turned to convey, in the preface to *Les mots et les choses*, the unique quality of the venture in which he was then engaged: to understand how "things are laid, placed, arranged in sites so very different from one another that it is impossible to find a place of residence for them."[151] He called such disturbing sites "heterotopias," sites that "shatter or tangle common names," that cause words and things to pull apart, that "stop words in their tracks."[152]

For Foucault, the dilemma of aphasiacs provided a critical metaphor with which to think how categories are formed and dispersed, how aphasiacs disassociate resemblances and reject categories that are viable.[153] Aphasia, as he described it, produces endless replacements of categories with incomprehensible associations that collapse into incommensurability. Aphasia is an anxious state of malaise, as those afflicted feverishly seek new categories to assemble people and things. As he put it,

> Within this simple space in which things are normally arranged and given names, the aphasiac will create a multiplicity of tiny, fragmented regions in which nameless resemblances agglutinated things into unconnected islets; . . . but no sooner have they been adumbrated than all these groupings dissolve again, for the field of identity

149. Sacks, *The Man Who Mistook His Wife for a Hat and Other Clinical Tales*, 11, 15.
150. Sacks, *The Man Who Mistook His Wife for a Hat and Other Clinical Tales*, 19.
151. Michel Foucault, *Les mots et les choses: Une archéologie des sciences humaines* (Paris: Gallimard, 1966), 10.
152. Foucault, *Les mots et les choses*, xviii.
153. Foucault, *Les mots et les choses*, 10.

that sustains them, however, limited it may be, is still too wide not to be unstable; and so the sick mind continues to infinity, creating groups then dispersing them again, heaping up diverse similarities, destroying those that seem clearest, splitting up things that are identical, superimposing different criteria, frenziedly beginning all over again, becoming more and more disturbed, and teetering finally on the brink of anxiety.[154]

Foucault's concern was with the epistemic order of things, not the colonial disordering of the present world. But his insights point to methodological openings. They invite us to track the formation and dissolution of social kinds and the unspoken and mobile attributes assigned to them. They invite us to pursue how questions of security have morphed into what Didier Fassin calls "racial security" and to ask how such words have become glued in common sense to specific people, places, and things. Not least, they make *sense* of a political *déraison* (unreason) that splits and disperses colonial from contemporary categories and disassembles the features that make them part of similar governing logics.

Imperial formations are infamous for fostering these fragmenting processes and for creating fractured space. Fernando Coronil captured a crucial feature of colonial projects when he argued that an enduring "privilege of empires" is to make their "histories appear as History . . . *predicated on dissociations that separate relational histories.*"[155] Imperial formations thrive on the capacity to assign to their systems of demarcation innocuous intentions and appellations. Rights are "temporarily" suspended for the greater public good; acts of state violence are reclassified as preemptive and protective; and circuits of knowledge production that connect the protection of privilege and the violence of disenfranchisement are blocked. Exclusions are

154. Foucault, *Les mots et les choses*, xviii. The French text reads, "Il parait que certain aphasiques . . . forment, en cet espace uni ou les choses normalement se distribuent et se nomment, une multiplicité de petits domaines grumeleux et fragmentaires ou des resemblances sans nom agglultinent les choses en îlôts discontinus. . . . Mais à peine esquissés, tous ces groupements se défont, car la plage d'identité qui les soutient, aussi étroite qu'elle soit, est encore trop étendue pour n'être pas instable; et à l'infin, le malade rassemble et sépare, entasse les similitudes diverses, ruine les plus évidentes, disperse les identités, superpose les critères differents, s'agite, recommence, s'inquiète et arrive finalement au bord de l'angoisse."

155. Fernando Coronil, "After Empire: Reflections on Imperialism from the Americas," in *Imperial Formations*, ed. Ann Laura Stoler, Carole McGranahan, and Peter C. Perdue (Santa Fe, NM: School for Advanced Research Press, 2007), 245.

posited as responsive and exceptional rather than quotidian and systemic. Imperial formations, as already noted, have long been skilled at calling their selective refusal to recognize demands for justice by other names.

That privilege comes with others. When anthropologist Emmanuel Terray, with intentional perversity, argued that the task today is not to harp on or rehearse memories nor to identify hereditary culprits and victims but to forget, one can understand that impulse. But Terray missed what colonial genealogies of the present should be about and are about for those who so vigorously dissent from how occluded colonial histories have been portrayed.[156] *The dissensions are not about the past; nor are they about settling scores.* As he rightly asserts, they cannot be about the "instrumentalisation" of a "duty to remember" spurred by a "competition of victims."[157]

Confronting the imperial privilege to render some histories as History demands not historical shortcuts to show that every contemporary injustice can be folded into an originary colonial tale. Rather, it demands specific and located histories of the present that retain the complexities and ambiguities of colonial entanglements—and equal attentiveness to when they no longer matter at all. History in an active voice is only partly about the past. More important, it is about how *differential futures* are distributed. It requires assessing the resilient forms in which the material and psychic structures of colonial relations remain both vividly tactile to some in the present and, to others, events too easily relegated to the definitive past.[158] Foucault's definition of critique as "reflective or intractable insolence" and his calling on the ancient Greek understanding of truth as "fearless speech" once again invites us to ask how—and in what forms—France's histories of colonialism have realized some connections and repeatedly turned away from others. In this recursive movement, both ruptures and recuperations make up the lineaments of what people inequitably are now living—whether they want to or not.

As we shall see in the final chapter, to imagine that the durabilities of colonial duress and the expectations they harbor are known and self-evident is a political fiction and an intellectual conceit. Colonial "common sense," colonial racial epistemologies, and the psychic structures of power cannot

---

156. Emmanuel Terray, *Face aux abus de mémoire* (Arles: Actes Sud, 2006).

157. Terray, *Face aux abus de mémoire*, 43.

158. Achille Mbembe, "Décoloniser les structures psychiques du pouvoir," *Mouvements* 51 (October 2007): 142–55.

be rendered as mere vestiges. They do not just benignly remain. In new force fields they are reactivated at different paces, and strategically, they are part of the fabric that shapes the liveliness of racialized ascriptions and the often livid affective states tied to them.

Skin color has never been the only baseline of racism, and it certainly is not in France now. As I argue in chapter 7 on regimes of racial truth, there is no need to add the adjective "cultural" to racism to account for the passions so animated against French citizens whose parents or grandparents may have been of Tunisian, Moroccan, or Algerian origin. Better understanding of the history of colonial racism in France, Germany, the Netherlands, South Africa, Israel, and the United States can be called on to tell very different stories—ones that are patterned but not the same, ones that press close to how threats to "security" are now being framed. These, too, are histories that "line" the present. They speak to how new subjects are produced and what they refuse, to the state apparatus and its multiplex supports that make people into "problems." They speak to the quotidian abrasions at the "lower frequencies" in which duress manifests, encumbering potentials and spawning indignation at how rights and resources are distributed throughout the world today.[159]

159. For an astute analysis of the creation of "the immigration problem" in France and Europe more broadly, see Éric Fassin, "L'immigration, un 'problème' si commode," Le Monde Diplomatique, November 2009.

II. RECURSIONS IN A COLONIAL MODE

ON DEGREES OF IMPERIAL
SOVEREIGNTY

We don't do empire.—Donald Rumsfeld, 2003

Concepts, as this book argues throughout, do work and work on us to authorize some questions, to refigure what questions are worth asking, and, not least, to foreclose others. Concepts have a force of their own whose gravitas can be measured, in part, by the spaces they are called on to inhabit and by the constellation of concepts that congeal around them. With respect to imperial practice, they shape the parameters of what can be construed as the "facts of the matter"—in this case, imperial presence and what counts as evidence of it.

In 2004, Harry Harootunian called "the recent and aggressive resurfacing of imperialism as both an older, historical category and as a concept and description employed in contemporary political discussion and scholarly opinion . . . an event of such overdetermined magnitude" that it was "threatening to exceed even 9/11 as a symptom of what it says about our current situation."[1] Harootunian's observation was one shared by

Epigraph: Donald Rumsfeld, quoted in Roger Cohen, "The Ends of Empire," *New York Times*, July 4, 2004, http://www.nytimes.com/2004/07/04/weekinreview/world-ends -empire-strange-bedfellows-imperial-america-retreats-iraq.html. Cohen seems to have confused two of Rumsfeld's statements: "We don't do diplomacy" and "We don't seek empire." The latter was Rumsfeld's response to a reporter for Al Jazeera who asked him whether the Bush administration was "bent on empire building." He answered, "We

many of us poised on the sidelines or directly involved in those heated and pressing conversations. But the force of the concept, I would argue, spoke to far more than the "current situation." What was equally striking was the implicit conceptual and historical architecture attributed to colonial empires, the conceptual conventions on which the received accounts implicitly relied, and the endorsement of specific understandings of empire threaded through them. The conceptual and historical scaffolding rested on very particular understandings of what was assumed to be imperial practice in its "true form" (sometimes referred to as the "classical imperial mode" or "high imperialism"), in contrast to what has been imagined as distinctive and "new" about contemporary imperial visions, practices, and technologies.

THE POLITICS OF "EMPIRE TALK"

If "empire" could be hailed as a watchword of the times in 2003 and as "suddenly hot intellectual property" in the corridors of Washington, D.C., that is no longer the case today.[2] "Empire" became such a common term among critics and advocates of U.S. policy, as well as across academe, that it is difficult to imagine how recently it was without resonance—and then in a prolonged flash, positioned as a charged public commodity and at political center stage. The urgency of use of the term—either to celebrate the "war on terror" and preemptive counterinsurgency policies or to condemn unilateral intervention in the name of peace—has passed, but the analytic and political quandaries that accompanied its invocation and the range of historical referents called on to make either case have not.

What is striking in retrospect is not that "empire" was strategically deployed and revitalized for public consumption to garner support for a war on Iraq but how unprepared, and initially removed, those of us academics who have long studied the nineteenth-century and early twentieth-century instantiations of imperial authority and colonial situations were from those public conversations. As the "lessons of empire" careened between outra-

---

don't seek empire. We're not imperialistic. We never have been. I can't imagine why you'd even ask the question."

1. Harry D. Harootunian, *The Empire's New Clothes: Paradigm Lost, and Regained* (Chicago: Prickly Paradigm, 2004), 7.

2. Martin Sieff, "Analysis: Arguments against U.S. Empire," United Press International, July 15, 2003, http://www.upi.com/Business_News/Security-Industry/2003/07/15/Analysis-Arguments-against-US-empire/23201058291958.

geous and measured assessments of what were considered "reasonable" comparisons to make between those earlier instances of European colonialism and the U.S. exception at the start of the twenty-first century, something more than a whitewashed vision of the United States as an imperial force emerged from the fray. What became more than evident was an implicit, bare-boned and simplified template of early imperial governance often culled from a historiography drawn from imperial scripts themselves.

There are any number of insights we might gain from examining this crescendo and timing of empire talk and the convergent conditions that brought about its amplification. But that is not the task that concerns me here. Instead, I draw on this moment of dense and strategic definitional fervor to do something else: to identify and call into question the assumptions that have informed the comparisons deemed viable, the commensurabilities called on, and the attributions assigned to what counts as imperial practice that were, and often continue to be, made.

In this chapter, I argue a number of related points. First, and most important, much of the earlier work in (post)colonial studies and that which falls on its edges has long subscribed to a myopic view of empire. It is a view that sidelines a wide range of imperial forms as anomalous; it casts their political and territorial ambiguities as idiosyncratic or accepts that their indeterminate legal status is common to the peculiar conditions that create "quasi-imperial" zones.[3] On this view, the United States is one of several exceptions, at the edges of empire proper. I would hold to the opposite, as would an increasing number of others now who address these more varied imperial forms.[4] These partial forms of sovereignty, opaque legal

3. On "quasi-American Empire," see Charles S. Maier, "Forum: An American Empire," *Harvard Magazine*, December 2002, http://harvardmagazine.com/2002/11/an-american-empire.html. Martin Shaw makes a point that is related to, but different from, mine, critiquing the international relations field's lack of attention to contemporary empire. In my view, the appellation "quasi-imperial" misses the fact that a historical genealogy of imperial formations would show clearly that there is nothing "quasi" about such forms: Imperial formations in their range of modalities have been constituted by these plural arrangements of control and distributions of sovereign authority and rights: see Martin Shaw, "Post-Imperial and Quasi-Imperial: State and Empire in the Global Era," *Millennium* 31, 2 (March 1, 2002): 327–36.

4. For helpful accounts of the political history of the United States and the crafting of its exceptional status, see Ian Tyrrell, "American Exceptionalism in an Age of International History," *American Historical Review* 96, 4 (October 1, 1991): 1031–55; Paul A. Kramer, "Empires, Exceptions, and Anglo-Saxons: Race and Rule between the British and United States Empires, 1880–1910," *Journal of American History* 88, 4 (March 2002): 1315–53.

terms of jurisdiction, illegible rights to intervention in the intimate spaces of people's lives, and the continuing right to intervention make up not the impromptu responses of imperial governance in decline, renewal, or withdrawal, but, rather, exemplary conditions created and protected by a far broader range of imperial forms themselves.

Nor is it only the "imperial United States" that is at issue: treatment of the U.S. empire provides an entry point for rethinking a wider set of sites and scenes in which colonial infrastructures and arrangements, be they legal, pedagogic, military, or territorial, have continued to exert their force far beyond formal "transfers of sovereignty"—and, indeed, in places such as Israel and Palestine, where dispossession in the name of security, as discussed in chapter 2, refuses reference to, or recognition of, the colonial nature of these relations at all. The legal machinations and concerted planning that have created this messy and opaque political space are exceedingly well documented, as we shall see. These are neither leftovers of empire nor the awkward arrangements that emerge as stopgap measures in times of "crisis," "transition," or urgency. Nor are they temporally confined to the ends of empire, mere legal confections intended to extend the conditions of imperial control.

As Ahmad Sa'di argues in the case of Israeli control over Palestine, the mechanisms of partial disenfranchisement for Palestinians within what Zionist leaders considered their rightful domain were initiated systematically as early as the 1920s.[5] Antony Anghie, contra the convention that imagines international law as based on the "sovereign equality of states," makes the crucial point that international law itself was created from its early incarnations in the nineteenth century to instantiate and fix the unequal status of territories (on the basis of racially defined civilizational failures and achievement) that were under colonial control.[6] By his account, sovereignty was not a benign concept created in and for Europe and

5. Ahmad H. Sa'di, *Thorough Surveillance: The Genesis of Israeli Policies of Population Management, Surveillance and Political Control towards the Palestinian Minority* (Manchester: Manchester University Press, 2014).

6. Antony Anghie, *Imperialism, Sovereignty and the Making of International Law* (Cambridge: Cambridge University Press, 2007), 6. Jean L. Cohen addresses the question of "sovereign equality" in "Sovereign Equality versus Imperial Right: The Battle over the 'New World Order,'" *Constellations* 13, 4 (December 1, 2006): 485–505. For her more extended discussion, see Jean L. Cohen, *Globalization and Sovereignty: Rethinking Legality, Legitimacy and Constitutionalism* (Cambridge: Cambridge University Press, 2012).

then extended beyond its borders. Sovereignty was a concept created and "improvised out of the colonial encounter" as much as "trusteeships" depended on a civilizational hierarchy that required tutelage and beneficently coercive surveillance.

Anghie's sense of sovereignty accords with mine. For some time, I have been working with what I identify as an organizing principle of imperial governance—what I call "degrees of imperial sovereignty"—with the intention of turning away from the hard-and-fast distinction between those who have sovereignty and those who do not. "Degrees of sovereignty" describes a principle of governance that convenes a contested political relation. It resituates focus on an embattled space and a longer temporal stretch, in which gradations of rights, deferred entitlements, and incremental withholding or granting of access to political and economic resources shape the very conditions that imperial formations produce and productively sustain. With this conceptual formulation, temporary exclusions, partial inclusions, and legal exemptions are not occasional and ad hoc strategies of rule but the racialized modus operandi of imperial states. Oscillation between coercion and persuasion—and the always "preserved possibility" of violence—underwrite these strategic practices by design.[7]

Second, rather than rehearsing the political history that produced American exceptionalism and its subsequent reinventions, I start from a premise that construes exceptionalism differently, as a fundamental feature of what I refer to as "imperial formations." I take imperial formations, as alluded to in earlier chapters, to be macropolities whose technologies of rule thrive on the production of exceptions and their uneven and changing proliferation. Territorial ambiguity, legal categories of belonging that produce quasi-membership (and ambiguous rules of access to that membership), and geographic and demographic zones of partially and indefinitely suspended rights are defining features.

Third, I argue that imperial formations are not now and rarely have been clearly bordered and bounded polities. We might think of them better as scaled genres of rule that in their very making thrive on opaque taxonomies that produce shadow populations—liminally tethered second-class citizens, citizens-in-waiting, threatened with expulsion if they do not sub-

---

7. I borrow the term, "preserved possibilities" from Lawrence Hirschfeld, who develops it for a very different context: see Lawrence A. Hirschfeld, "Art in Cunaland: Ideology and Cultural Adaption," *Man*, new series, 12, 1 (April 1, 1977): 104–23.

mit to a devil's pact for access to basic rights. Imperial formations are productive of social kinds: of ever improved measures to manufacture enemies and install regimes of security to protect the common good against those deemed a current or potential threat.

As organizing principles, exclusion is fundamental and exemption is key. Imperial formations give rise both to new zones of exclusion and new sites of—and social groups with—privileged exemption. But it is in the ambiguous and partial forms in which legal rights to property, employment, marriage, residence, and mobility are unevenly distributed that political traction of imperial governance lies. Reckoning with and recognizing these systemic features is at the heart of how imperial formations transform and thrive.

Rethinking the conceptual conventions that made certain comparisons viable and others counterintuitive is a project that students of colonialism from a range of disciplines have been questioning for some time—and long before 9/11. The conjuncture coincided with (post)colonial studies expanding into new regions and temporal domains over the past fifteen years, in what one might think of as the "second wave." Still, the profusion of new work disrupting the neat categories of colonizer and colonized and challenging the notion that colonialism is a finished story, as we saw in the case of Palestine, remained sequestered on the outer rim of the constricted archive from which "relevance" was construed and comparisons were drawn. At issue was never really just one of "cases." What became increasingly clear was that the working concepts were not doing enough work and that students of colonialism were not doing enough work with them.

EXCLUSION IS FUNDAMENTAL, EXEMPTION IS KEY

Certainly, empire was not "hot" in 2003 because it was new—or because the United States does not "do empire," or because the United States has just acquired one. Scholars, politicians, and public intellectuals have vehemently disagreed about imperial practice and abuse, about imperial stretch and "overstretch" of the U.S. polity, since the mid-nineteenth century.[8]

8. The relevance of academic expertise to political strategy does not in itself make intellectual property "hot." On the contrary, the use of ethnographic knowledge for U.S. military projects was once deemed classified, covertly gathered and studied, and decidedly not available to popular scrutiny. The surreptitious requisition of what academics knew about Vietnamese populations and their deep affiliations in the 1960s by U.S. mil-

Favored examples include Mark Twain's anti-imperialist satire in 1867 on government plans to buy the island of St. Thomas, his outrage at the U.S. initiative in 1884 to recognize the Congo Free State in the wake of King Leopold's campaign of carnage in the name of progress, and his relentless condemnations at the turn of the twentieth century of the U.S.-Philippine War.[9] Some point to W. E. B. Du Bois's appraisal in 1915 that the First World War was not a battle in Europe but a war over black bodies and imperial contests over Africa.[10] William Appleman Williams's insistent arguments in the 1950s against American exceptionalism in which he traced U.S. imperial interventions to the 1780s is familiar to students and scholars of U.S. expansion.[11] Similarly, students of U.S. interventions in Latin America, the Middle East, and Southeast Asia have never hesitated to call the structured violence of occupation; annexation; inter-imperial scrambles for access to ports, raw materials and cheap labor, and new sites for capital expansion; and the dislocations that followed—despite the United States' lack of "colonies proper"—by their imperial name.

What changed, then, was not the declaration of empire but the force field in which it operates, the breadth of its metaphoric extensions, and the invocation of a ready historical frame of comparison for an American public for whom it has been readied for consumption. What changed dramatically with the "war on terror" was not only the currency of empire and the historical referents called on but the cross-section of, and crossover between,

---

itary operations for "strategic hamlet studies"; about Latin American guerrilla tactics in 1964–65 by the U.S. Army for Project Camelot; and about counterinsurgency operations in Thailand in the 1970s by Defense Department strategists all raised the political stakes of ethnographic knowledge, but not as front-page news. Ethnographic terms were not vetted as public commodities. See, e.g., Irving Louis Horowitz, *The Rise and Fall of Project Camelot: Studies in the Relationship between Social Science and Practical Politics* (Cambridge, MA: MIT Press, 1967); Eric Wakin, *Anthropology Goes to War: Professional Ethics and Counterinsurgency in Thailand* (Madison: University of Wisconsin, Center for Southeast Asian Studies, 1992).

9. See, e.g., Jim Zwick, *Confronting Imperialism: Essays on Mark Twain and the Anti-Imperialist League* (West Conshohocken, PA: Infinity, 2007), which lists hundreds of newspaper articles from the 1890s by such well-known anti-imperial figures as William James and Jane Addams.

10. W. E. B. Du Bois, "The African Roots of War," *The Atlantic*, May 1915, 707–14.

11. William Appleman Williams, *Empire as a Way of Life: An Essay on the Causes and Character of America's Present Predicament, along with a Few Thoughts about an Alternative* (London: Oxford University Press, 1982).

scholars and policy advisers moving between both disparate and shared understandings of how a common language of empire could be used.

For (post)colonial studies—a field devoted (at its best) to the changing rationales, technologies, and representations of imperial rule and to how those subjected to imperial impositions have creatively refused and recast the strictures imposed on them—thinking critically about empire after 9/11 could have raised some pointed questions: Did our conventions of colonial scholarship hinder intervention in public debates? Why did we seem ill equipped to identify what imperial practice looks like and what imperial polities do?

Political pundits and Euro-American scholars of the long nineteenth-century "age of empire" have been alternately at odds and in agreement over whether British imperial strategies in Asia and Africa have useful lessons to teach. Washington's political advisers—like scholars—deftly have crafted strategic historical comparisons. But the former seemed to be reorienting their gaze to consider those peoples long off their radar, in places rarely acknowledged as figuring on their working political maps. Thus, nearly fifty years later, the exercise of French colonialism in Algeria became a renewed source of reflection for the U.S. State Department, directly pertinent to the tactics of torture and moral ethics of intervention. In fall 2003, in a call for papers on the "lessons of empire," Craig Calhoun, then the director of the Social Science Research Council, rightly identified a disconnect between what academics do and the discourse that pervades public domains. But what constituted that disconnect was less than clear. In noting that students of colonialism were not at the forefront of these debates, we may in retrospect rightly ask whether our conceptual vocabulary has been more brittle and constrained than imperial forms themselves.

ACADEMIC PACING AND PUBLIC DEBATE

If those working on imperial history and presence once worried that the field lacked the tools to deal with the most pressing questions about empire today, in its current configuration it may be seizing the opportunity to do so now.[12] But right after 9/11 and with the "war on terror," the terms of debate were being formulated in other quarters. Conservative journals

12. Nicholas B. Dirks, ed., *Colonialism and Culture* (Ann Arbor: University of Michigan Press, 1992), 5.

that tend to feature celebrants of empire, such as the *National Interest*, shared with students of imperial history an effort to define the perils and promises of empire past and present, while policy makers pondered what a measured imperial vision might destroy or ably serve in Afghanistan or Iraq. Eric Hobsbawm wrote forcefully in *Le Monde Diplomatique* that today's American empire "has little in common" with the nineteenth-century British empire and dismissed point by point any productive comparison between the two, but seemingly with little impact on which comparisons mattered and why certain comparisons were being used.[13] Others, such as the imperial historian A. G. Hopkins, declared that the lessons of the "civilizing mission" ("underestimated" difficulties, unrealistic plans, wrong-headed premises) were unlearned at the time and should be better learned today.[14]

Few have missed the fact that the dominant rhetoric of an American imperium celebrated a geopolitical form once denied, if not condemned. Critics long have claimed that the United States is an empire in denial, but both critics and advocates not surprisingly offered contrary assessments about the celebration. On both sides was a new set of descriptive referents. Thus, Robert Kagan, a member of Ronald Reagan's Department of State, referred to a "benevolent empire" ("a better international arrangement than all realistic alternatives"), and Robert Cooper, adviser to Tony Blair, declared it a "new liberal empire" and a "cooperative" one. The equally applauded terms "voluntary empire," "humanitarian imperialism," and "empire by invitation" hailed the advent of a beneficent macropolity endowed with consensual rather than coercive qualities.[15] Not everyone who mattered agreed: James Atlas noted in the *New York Times* that the avid "new empire builders," as he called many of the Bush administration's key interlocutors, were acolytes of Leo Strauss, indebted to his classicist admiration for the "natural right

13. Eric Hobsbawm, "Où va l'Empire americain?" *Le Monde Diplomatique*, June 11, 2003, https://www.monde-diplomatique.fr/2003/06/HOBSBAWM/10188.

14. A. G. Hopkins, "Lessons of 'Civilizing Missions' Are Mostly Unlearned," *New York Times*, March 23, 2003, http://www.nytimes.com/2003/03/23/weekinreview/lessons-of-civilizing-missions-are-mostly-unlearned.html.

15. Robert Kagan, "The Benevolent Empire," *Foreign Policy* 111 (July 1, 1998): 24–35; Robert Cooper, "Why We Still Need Empires," *The Observer*, April 7, 2002; Daniel Vernet, "Postmodern Imperialism," *Le Monde*, April 24, 2003. These are echoed by Niall Ferguson, who approvingly invoked "an imperial preference," which he called the favored term of late nineteenth-century Britain's most self-consciously authentic imperial politician, Joe Chamberlain: Niall Ferguson, *Empire: The Rise and Demise of the British World Order and the Lessons for Global Power* (New York: Basic, 2004), 284.

of the stronger" in their celebration of "high-tech warfare" and " 'smart' precision-guided bombs." As William Kristol virtually boasted, "If people want to say we're an imperial power, fine."[16]

Empire's critics also sought new modifiers. Michael Mann described an "incoherent empire" that could not "control occupied territories like the Europeans used to" because practices in Afghanistan and Iraq were "too rudimentary to be considered imperial."[17] Others insisted on the U.S. empire's "invisible" qualities, stressing its new, more secretive technologies and forms of surveillance—prompting the obvious questions: Less visible than what, and invisible to whom? "Humanitarian imperialism," "the arrogant empire," "the conceited empire," "the quasi-empire," "the invisible empire," or, alternatively, the "global" empire: each is contingent on an absent presence, tacit features of what European empires were imagined to exhibit as defining traits (to be coherent, full-blown, visible, blatantly coercive, overtly exploitative, territorially distinct, and decidedly not committed to humanitarian intervention).[18]

One, cynically, could dismiss these caricatures, but it would be more productive to ask about the model from which these designations were so easily drawn. Such conceptual efforts do specific kinds of work that couch the constitutive power of a concept and the historical narratives on which they depend. Nietzsche's counsel to be suspect and untimely again seems an appropriate stance to guide our queries: to question these received features of imperial forms and remain wary of the definitional angst that accompanied the term, the politics of these comparisons and their consolations.[19]

16. James Atlas, "A Classicist's Legacy: Empire Builders," New York Times, May 4, 2003, 3–4.

17. Michael Mann, The Incoherent Empire (London: Verso, 2005), 29.

18. Martin A. Senn and Felix Lautenschlager, "The Conceited Empire," The Dominion, July 6, http://www.dominionpaper.ca/features/2003/07/26/the_concei.html; Nicholas Mirzoeff, "Invisible Empire: Visual Culture, Embodied Spectacle, and Abu Ghraib." Radical History Review 95 (Spring 2006): 21–44. Charles Maier, former director of Harvard University's Center for European Studies, wrote about a "quasi-American empire" that "we believed was an empire with a difference—a coordination of economic exchange and security guarantees welcomed by its less powerful member states, who preserved their autonomy": Maier, "Forum," 1. Students of Latin American history have long argued that the face of Spanish and U.S. imperial projects have borne little resemblance to either model.

19. Friedrich Nietzsche, "On the Uses and Disadvantages of History for Life" (1876), in Untimely Meditations, trans. R. J. Hollingdale (Cambridge: Cambridge University Press, 1997), 101.

Amplified assertions of empire as an appropriate scale of analysis and model of practice for contemporary global politics have posed challenges to academic know-how and the relevance of historical and ethnographic expertise. Striking in these escalating debates on the "new imperialism" was how little they initially drew in—or on—the close-up witnesses to imperial history that many students of colonialism claim to be. Disputing whether public figures and the media use the vocabulary of empire "correctly" is not the point. Rather, it is to ask *how* it matters that in the public domain imperial metaphors and analogies are conflated with historically grounded comparison. Is the task to provide alternative histories of the present or studied appraisals of what empires supposedly once condoned or condemned that are now rendered salient, common sense, politically efficacious, and therefore "true"? Both questions are about imperial presence, about what constitutes current ecologies of belief and practice, the sedimented histories through which these notions of empire circulate, and about what imaginaries fed these notions among colonial authorities and what imaginaries nourish them now.

WHAT HISTORY LESSONS

History lessons have a way of morphing in both scholarly and journalistic hands. In September 2003, the *New York Times* reported on the Pentagon's summer screening of Gillo Pontecorvo's *The Battle of Algiers* (1965), a fictional documentary that quickly became the "gold standard for *cinema vérité*."[20] Focused on terrorist acts and the brutal interrogations of Arab suspects in the Algerian War of the 1950s, the film—once requisite viewing as a "teaching tool for radicalized Americans and revolutionary wannabes opposing the Vietnam War"—was called on to offer a disquieting vision of the Pentagon's priorities and goals.[21] The forty attending officers and civilian experts "urged to consider and discuss the implicit issues at the core of the film" were asked to address "the advantages and costs of resorting to torture and intimidation in seeking vital human intelligence about enemy plans." If the lessons to be learned were not clearly spelled out at the time,

20. Liza Bear, "On the Frontlines of the 'Battle of Algiers,' http://www.indiewire.com /article/on_the_frontlines_of_the_battle_of_algiers.

21. Michael T. Kaufman, "What Does the Pentagon See in 'Battle of Algiers?' " (*New York Times*, September 7, 2003), http://www.nytimes.com/2003/09/07/weekinreview/the -world-film-studies-what-does-the-pentagon-see-in-battle-of-algiers.html.

they have since been played out in gruesome detail: torture is an acceptable "antiterrorist" practice against possible "terrorists," against those who could potentially become terrorists, those designated as "terrorists," as well as against "terrorists" acts.[22] Only months later, what had struck some observers as examples of the dangerous extremes to which the United States might go to combat "Islamic terrorism" emerged as documented incidents of a sustained pattern of circumventing the Geneva Conventions. Over the past decade, the evidence has been overwhelming, attesting to implicit and explicit directives for torture in Afghanistan, in the "legal black hole" of Guantánamo Bay, and in U.S. detention centers in Iraq.[23]

One could focus on the oddity of the film showing at the Pentagon, but more significant is why it was not an oddity at all. What made the Algerian War so relevant to U.S. policy makers is part of a much longer history of shared counterinsurgency strategies across the imperial world.[24] The showing of *Battle of Algiers* merely made explicit the lessons that have guided the graduates of the School of America and appeared in its torture manuals since 1946.[25] *Battle of Algiers*, long banned in France for exposing what French nationalists and most French nationals preferred to deny, had

22. See Philip Gourevitch, "Winning and Losing," *New Yorker*, December 12, 2003, http://www.newyorker.com/magazine/2003/12/22/winning-and-losing.

23. George Monbiot, "Backyard Terrorism," *The Guardian*, October 29, 2001, http://www.theguardian.com/world/2001/oct/30/afghanistan.terrorism19. On Abu Ghraib, see Reed Brody, "The Road to Abu Ghraib," June 2004, https://www.hrw.org/report/2004/06/08/road-abu-ghraib; Mark Danner, "Abu Ghraib: The Hidden Story," *New York Review of Books*, October 7, 2004, http://www.nybooks.com/articles/archives/2004/oct/07/abu-ghraib-the-hidden-story. Some, including me, were haunted by other comparisons that linked the photogenic unabashed "trophy shots" of torture to smiling young white girls picnicking at lynching parties in the 1930s: see Luc Sante, "Tourists and Torturers," *New York Times*, May 11, 2004, http://www.nytimes.com/2004/05/11/opinion/tourists-and-torturers.html.

24. See Martin Thomas, *Empires of Intelligence: Security Services and Colonial Disorder after 1914* (Berkeley: University of California Press, 2008).

25. Michael Kaufman reported a "civilian-led organization" run by the person who was then the assistant director of defense, who, Kaufmann was told by an official with the U.S. Department of Defense (DOD), was responsible "for thinking aggressively and creatively" on issues of guerrilla war. As the DOD's Special Operations and Combating Terrorism website of the DOD described, the members of the Special Operations Forces (SOF) are "versatile, . . . diplomatic warriors" whose specialty is "unconventional warfare"—that is, low-visibility, covert, or clandestine operation: www.dod.gov/olicy/solic. The SOF is an "organic staff element" within the Office of the Secretary of Defense. Note that the SOF's website has since been taken down.

become a serviceable colonial lesson for the State Department's consideration of counter-terrorist strategies. At a time that much of the French public still refused to recognize that colonial rule in North Africa was more than an unseemly episode outside national history—as evinced in the preceding chapter—*Battle of Algiers* became a feature film in the United States.[26] Fueled by the Pentagon screening, film clubs across the country billed it as a "suspenseful thriller" with "astonishing immediacy"—"as relevant today as it was in 1965."[27]

Not everyone agreed. Christopher Hitchens "challenge[d] anybody to find a single intelligent point of comparison between any of these events and the present state of affairs in Iraq," on the argument that in 1956, Algeria "was not just a colony" but a "department of metropolitan France" and the French sought to "retain it as an exclusive possession."[28] Note that for Hitchens, the comparison partly floundered because France sought exclusive rights to Algeria; in Iraq, on the contrary, the United States by his reckoning, did not.[29]

26. Nostalgia for French Algeria has been common fare for some time, but few have shared Benjamin Stora's searing condemnation of the relationship between that memory and anti-Arab racism as it exists in France today. On the nostalgia, see Jeannine Verdès-Leroux, *Les Français d'Algérie de 1830 à aujourd'hui: Une page d'histoire déchirée* (Paris: Fayard, 2001). Stora's prolific work include *Le transfert d'une mémoire: De l' "Algérie française" au racisme anti-arabe* (Paris: La Découverte, 1999).

27. J. Hoberman, "Revolution Now (and Then)!" *American Prospect*, December 15, 2003, http://prospect.org/article/revolution-now-and-then; Rialto Pictures, "Critics on *The Battle of Algiers*," http://www.rialtopictures.com/eyes_xtras/battle_quotes.html; Peter Rainer, "Prescient Tense," January 12, 2004, http://nymag.com/nymetro/movies/reviews/n_9697.

28. Christopher Hitchens, "Guerrillas in the Mist," *Slate*, January 2, 2004, http://www.slate.com/articles/news_and_politics/fighting_words/2004/01/guerrillas_in_the_mist.html.

29. How might critical scholars otherwise treat the comparison? Should we have required our undergraduates to watch the film and study what produced the conditions for French license to torture and the tactical violence of the Algerian response? Or should we have noted that what Pentagon officials thought to compare (tactics of terrorism) was very different from the focus of comparison—torture techniques—almost a year later, in the wake of the Abu Ghraib scandal? By May 2004, the posed images of a proud, smiling, cherry-cheeked Lyndie England pointing to the genitals of Hayder Sabbar Abd, the hooded Iraqi prisoner, and the subsequent reports on the Abu Ghraib prison recast the comparison again. It made the Pentagon showing of *The Battle of Algiers* not a history lesson but a chillingly prescient portrayal of what was actually transpiring in U.S.-controlled prison complexes in Iraq.

The lessons to learn and teach could be geared in any number of directions. They might convey that categories imposed by imperial rule do matter, but precise definitions of empire do not. They might consider that imperial states and their administrative apparatus never achieved command over the shifting terrain of categories they helped to create or over what often seemed arbitrary shifts in the membership of who "belonged." Or the lesson might issue a warning to proceed with caution, underscoring that an anthropology of empire is about the critical and alternative reflections of those who pushed on imperial limits, lived both on their margins and squarely within them.[30] When James Kurth, political science professor at Swarthmore, wrote in the National Interest that American empire is based on "ideas more than empires of the past," it was hard to identify his historical referents.[31] Colonial empires have always been dependent on social imaginaries: blueprints unrealized, borders never drawn, administrative categories of people and territories to which no one was sure who or what should belong.[32]

EMPIRE VERSUS HUMANITARIAN REPUBLIC

For those of us schooled in the working of nineteenth-century and twentieth-century imperial formations, the framings were familiar—and not. Republican liberty versus imperial reach and responsibility, violent intervention in the name of humanitarian sympathies, the proper weighting of consent versus coercion, and the "soft" versus "hard" tactics of empire were all contrasts and connections that students of colonialism have schooled themselves to treat not as contradictions of empires but as part of their standard grammar. Still, how these terms appeared seem at once resonant with and oddly askew to conventional definitions of empire in their usage and form.

Take Michael Ignatieff's feature article "American Empire: The Burden" from the New York Times. The essay appeared both brazen and historically

30. See John D. Kelly, Beatrice Jauregui, Sean T. Mitchell, and Jeremy Walton, eds., Anthropology and Global Counterinsurgency (Chicago: University of Chicago Press, 2010).

31. James Kurth, "Migration and the Dynamics of Empire," National Interest (Spring 2003), 5–28.

32. On imperial blueprints, see Ann Laura Stoler, "Developing Historical Negatives," in Along the Archival Grain: Epistemic Anxieties and Colonial Common Sense (Princeton, NJ: Princeton University Press, 2009), 105–40.

discordant when it appeared in January 2003. It acknowledged the previously unacknowledged: that the deep denial of empire is a major part of early twentieth-century American history and that U.S. foreign policy was, and remains, about "enforcing [a global] order."[33] But Ignatieff's "empire lite" depended on a caricature of what empire once was and what it looks like today. The latter's "grace notes," he wrote, are now "free markets, human rights, and democracy," as if these liberal impulses were new imperial inventions.[34] Ignatieff's insistence that his "Empire lite" was "no longer in the era of the United Fruit Company" was an assessment which those participating in a strike of United Fruit workers contesting the continued use of insecticides banned in the United States (reported in the *Times* of the same week) would undoubtedly have not agreed.

Ignatieff's story hinged on what he identified as "the real dilemma"— "whether in becoming an empire [the United States] risks losing its soul as a republic"—as if these were ever mutually exclusive categories. Even Chalmers Johnson, who offered an insider's critique of American empire, with its more than 735 (acknowledged) military bases throughout the world, lamented the "end of the Republic" as if these were incompatible political projects.[35] Students of empire have argued otherwise: that colonial empires have long coexisted with metropolitan republics and in dynamic synergy with them. The grace notes of human rights are not embellishments. To posit that the impulses that guided this form of imperial rule in a postimperial age are confusing because they are "contradictory" rehearses both a fictive model of colonialism and a misconceived one. Civic liberties and entitlements such as those lauded in the making of republican France were forged through the extension of empire. Racial distinctions and inequalities were written into the very definition of democratic liberties in the United States, as well as in England, the Netherlands, Germany, and Belgium. In France, the "color of liberty" was decidedly white, not North African, not Vietnamese, and in Haiti, it was creole but not black.[36] That "America's empire is not like those of times past, built on conquest and the

33. Michael Ignatieff, "The American Empire: The Burden," *New York Times*, January 5, 2003, 24.

34. Ignatieff, "The American Empire," 24.

35. Chalmers Johnson, *The Sorrows of Empire: Militarism, Secrecy, and the End of the Republic* (New York: Henry Holt, 2005).

36. Sue Peabody and Tyler Edward Stovall, eds., *The Color of Liberty: Histories of Race in France* (Durham, NC: Duke University Press, 2003).

white man's burden" would have no traction in the Philippines, Samoa, or Vietnam. It would be hard to spin as anything but false.[37]

Appeals to moral uplift, compassionate charity, and appreciation of cultural diversity were based on imperial systems of knowledge production enabled by and enabling coercive practices. These were woven into the very weft of empire—how control over and seizure of markets, land, and labor were justified, worked through, and worked out. Treating humanitarianism as the ruse, the mask, or "the packaging" of empire, as have some of empire's critics, misses a fundamental point that over the past decade had been forcefully made in many quarters.[38] Compassionate imperialism and the distributions of pity it produced and condoned did not constitute objections to empire. Nor were these just false advertising for what were inherently exploitative projects. Social hierarchies were produced and nourished by sympathy for empire's downtrodden subjects.[39] Sympathy conferred distance; bolstered inequalities of position, privilege, and possibility; and was basic to the affective economy of empire as well as founding and funding of imperial enterprises. These were core features of imperial formations that the elaboration of such affective dispositions helped to create.[40]

One could argue that these debates about what constitutes empire—who has one and who does not—were short-lived; that they have now slipped off the public radar and fed a historically ill-formed public discourse; that a measured response would be to fight what Du Bois labeled "educated igno-

37. Ignatieff, "The American Empire," 24.

38. Anatol Lieven, "The Empire Strikes Back," *The Nation*, July 27, 2003. The arguments made by Didier Fassin, Miriam Ticktin, and those in the new journal *Humanity* make this point unnecessary to rehearse here.

39. Amit Rai, *The Rule of Sympathy: Sentiment, Race, and Power, 1750–1850* (New York: Palgrave, 2002). See also Luc Boltanski, "The Politics of Pity," in *Distant Suffering: Morality, Media, and Politics* (Cambridge: Cambridge University Press, 1999), 3–20.

40. But Ignatieff knew that all too well. As he was quick to point out, humanitarian intervention is another name for war and "an imperial exercise of power": Michael Ignatieff, *Empire Lite: Nation-Building in Bosnia, Kosovo and Afghanistan* (London: Vintage, 2003). Students of colonial studies have sought to describe the racialized inflections of an imperial politics of sympathy; Ignatieff, however, directed his critique in the opposite direction, against Médecins sans frontières, spending thirty pages of a 125 page text to accuse its founder, Bernard Kouchner, of self-promoting, noisy, interventionist, dripping liberal, moralistic imperial aspirations—in short, the peacock and "pro-consul of an imperial exercise in nation-building and pacification": Ignatieff, *Empire Lite*, 59. We might call this hoisting the liberal left by its own petard but also ask about the politics of Ignatieff's comparison when he concludes that "imperialism doesn't stop being necessary just because it becomes politically incorrect": Ignatieff, *Empire Lite*, 106.

rance," to shake the United States out of what Edward Said called its "atemporal present" to rectify the record for a broader audience.[41] Said criticized the North American public, schooled to be passionate about the history of the American Revolution, quilt making, and small-town heroes but silent about the "sacrosanct altruism" of U.S. innocents abroad and their well-meaning, do-good state.

Students of colonial empires could easily substantiate that claims to universalism are founding principles of imperial inequalities; that the United States is no less or more an empire because it claims that its folk theories are human universals. Histories of imperial pursuits do more than resonate with contemporary racial formations in the world. They set the conditions of possibility for the uneven entitlements such polities foster.[42] We might step back and ask not what is new (as many have) but why newness, like racism, is so frequently a part of imperial narratives, a query raised more fully in chapter 7 on racial regimes of truth. The U.S. empire was considered new at the turn of the twentieth century, "new" by Du Bois in 1920, and again by Hannah Arendt and others in 1948, an "entirely new concept in the long history of political thought and action."[43] With all due respect to those revered, we might instead question what model of the "classical form" was so entrenched, whether a more appropriate adjective might be "renewed" to describe the recursive histories of imperial forms today.

TUNNEL VISION: RETHINKING IMPERIAL FORMATIONS

The analytic tools of colonial studies clearly have helped us think how humanitarian interventions and the distribution of compassion are worked through imperial projects. But other, more tacit notions that inform treatment of the very logic of how colonial governance works have led us astray

41. W. E. B. Du Bois, *Darkwater: Voices from within the Veil* (1920) (Mineola, NY: Dover, 1999), 23; Edward W. Said, "L'autre Amerique," *Le Monde Diplomatique*, March 2003, 1, 20, 21.

42. See, e.g., Anne Foster, *Projections of Power: The United States and Europe in Colonial Southeast Asia, 1919–1941* (Durham, NC: Duke University Press, 2010). Foster shows with precision that the U.S. presence in Southeast Asia "as a colonial power was instrumental in creating the type of imperialism which existed during the period 1919–1941": Foster, *Projections of Power*, viii.

43. Brooks Adams, quoted in Neil Smith, *American Empire: Roosevelt's Geographer and the Prelude to Globalization* (Berkeley: University of California Press, 2004), 10; Hannah Arendt, *The Origins of Totalitarianism* (1951) (New York: Harcourt Brace, 1979), 125.

in identifying imperial formations and their nature. One has been a fixation on empires as clearly bounded geopolities, as if the color-coded school maps of a clearly marked British empire, designed and traced with linear precision, were renderings of real distinctions and firmly fixed divisions.[44] Why maintain this focus when so much of the historical evidence points less to neat boundaries than to troubled, ill-defined ones?

Imperial formations have never been "steady states" in any sense of the phrase. They are not securely bounded and are not firmly entrenched; they are neither regular nor well regulated. Imperial formations should be considered what the term suggests: processes of becoming rather than being, macro-polities in constant (re)formation. The historian Thongchai Winichakul once said it with a simplicity that underscores the weight of his point: imperial maps were a "model *for* rather than a model *of* what [they] purported to represent."[45] Imperial cartographies were projected imaginaries for, rather than instantiations of, reality, performatives that only barely did their envisioned work. Imperial ventures are and have been both "deterritorialized" and reterritorialized, both more and less marked, opaque and visible in ways scholars have not always registered or been able to foresee.[46]

A second problem: (post)colonial studies has predominantly focused on northern European empires, with France, Britain, Belgium, and the Netherlands establishing the prototypes for what constitute the foundational strategies of rule.[47] What Arendt called "continental imperialisms"

44. I make this point in Ann Laura Stoler, "On Degrees of Imperial Sovereignty," *Public Culture* 18, 1 (Winter 2006): 125–46. Lauren Benton made a similar point, with a broader and rich range of instantiations, when she wrote several years later, "While an iconic association with empire is the pink shading of British imperial possessions in nineteenth- and early twentieth-century maps, that image, and others like it, obscures the many variations of imperial territories": Laura A. Benton, *A Search for Sovereignty: Law and Geography in European Empires, 1400–1900*. Cambridge: Cambridge University Press, 2010), 2.

45. Thongchai Winichakul, *Siam Mapped: A History of the Geo-Body of a Nation* (Honolulu: University of Hawai'i Press, 1997), 130; emphasis added.

46. Zygmunt Bauman makes a related argument that the paradoxical effect of the globalization of economy is a new and enhanced defense of place, "the necessary concomitant of the assault against the impermeability of established borders and locally grounded sovereignty": Zygmunt Bauman, "Wars of the Globalization Era," *European Journal of Social Theory* 4, 1 (February 1, 2001): 19.

47. When Spanish empire and U.S. intervention in Latin America are brought back into the colonial studies equation, the multiplex arrangements of empire and their genealogies look very different. Among those who make this argument most forcefully, see Fernando Coronil, "Latin American Postcolonial Studies and Global Decoloniza-

or contiguous empires—the Hapsburg, Russian, and Ottoman empires—were long treated both by students of these regions and by those who study colonial empires proper as incommensurate kinds.[48] This is no longer the case today.[49]

A third problem: European empires have been equated with their colonial variants and reduced to only certain features of them. Thus, outright conquest, European settlement, and legalized property confiscation are taken as their defining attributes. Deviations from that norm become just that: aberrant, exceptional cases, peripheral forms. But "quasi-sovereignty," "quasi-states," and quasi-autonomies have been excavated and analyzed by legal historians of empire for some time. Martin Thomas's meticulous history of imperial intelligence should be called on more than it has been to make the case that the "edges of empire" in the Middle East and North Africa, where "the dread word colony [was] scrupulously avoided," were only the edges in a limited sense: these were the sites in which imperial intelligence was honed as carefully as the oft-cited fingerprinting technologies of the British Raj.[50] Not least, prevailing vocabularies have long been misleading and inadequate. "Internal colonialism" already presupposes a form located apart from the more "authentic" and dominant version. Elsewhere, scholarly vocabulary defers to the terms of empires themselves: "Indirect rule" and "informal empire" are colonial designations and misleading euphemisms, not working concepts of critical analysis.

---

tion," in The Cambridge Companion to Postcolonial Literary Studies, ed. Neil Lazarus (New York: Cambridge University Press, 2004), 221–40; Walter Mignolo, Local Histories/Global Designs: Coloniality, Subaltern Knowledges, and Border Thinking (Princeton, NJ: Princeton University Press, 2012); Irene Marsha Silverblatt, Modern Inquisitions: Peru and the Colonial Origins of the Civilized World (Durham, NC: Duke University Press, 2004).

48. Arendt, The Origins of Totalitarianism, 222–66.

49. See, e.g., Willard Sunderland, Taming the Wild Field: Colonization and Empire on the Russian Steppe (Ithaca, NY: Cornell University Press, 2006, an analytically sophisticated and historically fine-grained study referred to in the preceding chapter. Sunderland takes on the difficult issue of how comparisons were and were not drawn between the "Russian takeover of the mostly Islamic world of the Volga and trans-Volga steppe in the sixteenth century as the tsardom itself took an important step toward becoming a colonial empire": Sunderland, Taming the Wild Field, 17. See also the historically rich account in Jane Burbank and Frederick Cooper, Empires in World History: Power and the Politics of Difference (Princeton, NJ: Princeton University Press, 2010).

50. Thomas, Empires of Intelligence, 4–5.

Some have argued that the "stable canon" of colonial and postcolonial studies has been "overly committed to literary and historical perspectives."[51] I would argue that these fields have not been historical enough. They tend to homogenize the range of forms in which modern empires have flourished. Some imperial forms are marked by distinctly rendered boundaries, transparent transfers of property, and even clear distinctions between colonizer and colonized. But these represent only one end of the spectrum and a narrow range of their orientations.[52]

Although students of the colonial embrace the notion that racial categories were murky and porous, they do not extend this insight as fully to rethink the concepts of protracted imperial jurisdiction as well. Michael Hardt and Antonio Negri's now well-known characterization of nineteenth-century European empires as those that "forged fixed separate identities, forged fixed, distinct castings" is a caricature more than an accurate description of how they worked.[53] This fixity never described nineteenth-century empires, and they are right that it does not characterize imperial forms today. The legal and political fuzziness of dependencies, trusteeships, protectorates, mandates, and unincorporated territories were all part of the deep grammar of partially restricted rights in the nineteenth-century and twentieth-century imperial world that were contested again and again. Legal historians have been documenting this fact for some time, yet their insights seem to have made little dent in the conceptual convention that posits that there are "real" imperial forms and then only quasi variations on them. Most important, those who inhabited those indeterminate spaces and ambiguous places were rarely beyond the reach of imperial will and force. That force was carved into entrenched legal systems and, as Achille Mbembe would argue, into the arbitrary implementations of power for

51. C. Richard King, ed., *Post-colonial America* (Urbana: University of Illinois Press, 2000), 3.

52. On hybrid forms of empire, see George Steinmetz, "Return to Empire: The New U.S. Imperialism in Comparative Historical Perspective," *Sociological Theory* 23, 4 (December 1, 2005): 339–67.

53. Michael Hardt and Antonio Negri, *Empire* (Cambridge, MA: Harvard University Press, 2000), 199. See George Steinmetz's helpful discussion of the useful and less than illuminating ways in which Hardt and Negri draw on Carl Schmitt's "state of exception" to understand the policies of the contemporary United States: George Steinmetz, "The State of Emergency and the Revival of American Imperialism Toward an Authoritarian Post-Fordism," *Public Culture* 15, 2 (2003): 323–45.

which certain African postcolonies are so well known.[54] They were not out of imperial bounds.[55]

In short, much contemporary work on imperial presence has produced a prototypical archive of empire that seems to mimic that of well-bounded nation-states, in part because empire is seen as an extension of nation-states, not as another way—and sometimes prior way—to organize a polity. Boundaries matter to nation-states in ways that for vast imperial states in expansion they often could and did not. What if one starts from another premise: that this model of empire represents a tunnel vision, one scripted, limited, and endorsed by imperial states themselves? What if the notion of empire as a steady state (that may "rise or fall") is replaced with a notion of imperial formations as supremely mobile polities of dislocation, dependent not on stable populations so much as on highly moveable ones, on systemic recruitments and "transfers" of colonial agents, on native military, on a redistribution of peoples and resources, on relocations and dispersions, on contiguous and overseas territories? What if we begin not with a model of empire based on clearly delineated imperial cartographies but with one dependent on shifting categories and moving parts whose designated borders at any one time were not necessarily the force fields in which they operated or their operative limits?[56]

The point is a simple but critical one: Imperial forms of rule are dependent on moving categories, technologies of surveillance that have to be adaptable, productive of and responsive to populations frozen in place or summarily displaced. Imperial forms are geared to the contingent movements and restrictions between camp and colony and their "managed mobilities," as discussed in chapter 3. These forms locate themselves not with fixed boundaries and clearly demarcated borders culled from models based on nineteenth-century nation-states, but by wide thresholds of partial sovereignties and territorial claims that produce contradictory legal entitlements

54. Achille Mbembe, *On the Postcolony* (Berkeley: University of California Press, 2001).

55. I owe the phrase to Carole McGranahan: see her "Empire Out of Bounds: Tibet in the Era of Decolonization," in *Imperial Formations*, ed. Ann Laura Stoler, Carole McGranahan, and Peter C. Perdue (Santa Fe, NM: School for Advanced Research Press, 2007), 173–210.

56. As Carl Schmitt wrote, "True empire around the world has claimed a sphere of spatial sovereignty beyond its borders . . . a space far exceeding the boundaries of the state proper": Carl Schmitt, *The Nomos of the Earth in the International Law of the Jus Publicum Europaeum* (1950), trans. G. L. Ulmen (New York: Telos, 2003), 281.

and ambiguous human rights. Even such carefully guarded borders as those of Israel have permeable walls and ever changing borders. And the infamous checkpoints are not only those between Palestine and Israel but also those within the Occupied Territories, a massive cement block cutting off a Palestinian village on any particular day or two or three and disappearing on another.

Expansion and conquest, intervention and force should not be overlooked because they lack easy recognition and are called by other names. Considering what makes the "Nuclear Pacific," Bikini Island, Guam, Samoa, Guantánamo, Puerto Rico, and Native American reservation lands both part of the United States and decidedly outside it; what gives some of their inhabitants rights to vote in local elections but not in federal ones; what produces nomenclatures that indicate "national" but not "citizen" is to confront a basic feature of imperial formations—namely, that modern empires thrive on such plasticities and reproduce their resilience through the *production* of announced and unscheduled exceptions and exemptions.

Nor is the disclaimer of sui generis status a Euro-American imperial invention. Ottoman, Russian, and Chinese empires, like those of France, the Netherlands, and the United States, have all insisted at different moments that their raison d'être was different, that their violence was temporary and that their humanitarian visions excused or distinguished their interventions as responsive measures, not sustained excesses.

In 2000, Hardt and Negri defined the new Empire with a capital E as one marked by "circuits of movement and mixture," but there were no colonial empires that were not.[57] *Blurred genres of rule are not empires in distress but imperial polities in active realignment and reformation.* "Semblances of sovereignty" and contestation and congressional debate over the application of U.S. law beyond the territory of the United States, as the legal historian Alexander Aleinikoff has so powerfully argued, are enduring features of U.S. history. "Sovereignty," he writes, "meant more than the control of borders. It also implied power to construct an 'American people' through the adoption of membership rules."[58] By attending to attenuated sovereignties rather than citizenship alone, Aleinikoff could not but trace the joined legal histories

---

57. Hardt and Negri, Empire, 197.
58. Thomas Alexander Aleinikoff, *Semblances of Sovereignty: The Constitution, the State, and American Citizenship* (Cambridge, MA: Harvard University Press, 2002), 6.

that conferred limited political rights on Native Americans and the residents in U.S. "possessions" overseas.

"Transfer of sovereignty" is a phrase that connotes a finite act of decolonization. But semblances of sovereignty were not annulled by such transfers. Such semblances cut across U.S. imperial history before, after, and without outright colonization. Nor was the British model of an imperial formation ever the British Raj alone; Britain's imperial forms can be traced through a genealogy that passed through Wales, Scotland, Protestant Ireland, Palestine, the Caribbean, and North America.[59] French empire, as Frederick Cooper argues, was not located only in the colonies; French empire was a single but differentiated France in which Napoleon's continental expansion was part of an older and more recent pattern of expansion overseas.[60]

None of these are new insights. They are well documented in historiographies across the globe. What is worth underscoring, however, is not the absence of these liminal and disparate zones (and debates about them) but the scant conceptual treatment of them as fundamental features of how imperial governance works. Ambiguous zones, partial sovereignty, temporary suspensions of what Arendt called "the right to have rights," provisional impositions of states of emergency, promissory notes for elections, deferred or contingent independence, and "temporary" occupations—these are conditions at the heart of imperial projects and present in nearly all of them.[61] We need only look to the history of the British Mandate in the early twentieth-century Middle East; to contests over the Falkland Islands; to the terms of the Moroccan French protectorate; to the "unincorporated territory" of Puerto Rico, the Virgin Islands, or the Mariana Islands, to the "temporary acquisition" of Guantánamo Bay in 1903 (or to the allegedly "law-free zone"

59. David Armitage, The Ideological Origins of the British Empire (Cambridge: Cambridge University Press, 2000), 6–7. See also David Lloyd, Ireland after History (Notre Dame, IN: University of Notre Dame Press and Field Day, 1999).

60. Frederick Cooper, "Provincializing France," in Stoler et al., Imperial Formations, 341–77.

61. Aihwa Ong develops a related concept of "graduated sovereignty" to grasp "sovereignty in practice" and the "different mechanisms of governance beyond the military and the legal powers." Her interest, however, is neither in imperial formations nor in their deeper genealogies. She uses the term to describe a specific historical shift in the early 1970s onward to describe a "system of graduated sovereignty" that came "into effect as the government has put more investment in the biopolitical improvement of the Malays , . . . awarding them rights and benefits largely denied to the Chinese and Indian minorities": Aihwa Ong, "Graduated Sovereignty in South-East Asia," Theory, Culture and Society 17, 4 (August 1, 2000): 58–59.

of Guantánamo that the Supreme Court ruled unconstitutional in 2008); or to American Samoans who are considered U.S. nationals but not U.S. citizens.[62]

All are founded on multiplex criteria for inclusions and sliding scales of basic rights. Each generated imperial conditions that required constant judicial and political reassessments of who was outside and who within at any particular time. Each required frequent redrawing of the categories of subject and citizen, fostering elaborate nomenclatures that distinguished among resident aliens, naturalized citizens, nationals, immigrants, and U.S. citizens without federal voting rights—as in the case of Guam.[63] All produced scales of differentiation and affiliation that exceeded the clear division between ruler and ruled. These sliding scales that placed both those born into Native American tribes and those in overseas territories as "owing allegiance to the United States but not entitled to political rights" define the common architecture of imperial rule.[64] They represent enduring forms of empire, force fields of attraction and aversion, spaces of arrest and suspended time. Imperial discourses have framed these as unique cases, but they are only "exceptions" in a context in which such exceptions are a norm. Assuming that agents of empire were intent on clarifying borders, establishing "order," and reducing the zones of ambiguity misses a crucial point. They were equally invested in, exploited, and demonstrated strong stakes in the proliferation of geopolitical gray zones, destabilizing and shattering the common sense of who belonged.[65] Puerto Rico, "inside and outside the constitution," and Guantánamo, "both belonging to [and] not part of the United States," index only a U.S. mastery of a shared feature of imperial forms.[66]

62. See, e.g., C. T. Sandars, *American's Overseas Garrisons: The Leasehold Empire* (Oxford: Oxford University Press, 2000), esp. 142–45 (on Guantánamo's history). See also "The Falklands," in Ian Hernon, *Massacre and Retribution: Forgotten Wars of the Nineteenth Century* (Stroud, UK: Sutton, 1998); Louise Richardson, *When Allies Differ: Anglo-American Relations during the Suez and Falklands Crises* (New York: St. Martin's Press, 1996).

63. Robert F. Rogers, *Destiny's Landfall: A History of Guam* (Honolulu: University of Hawai'i Press, 1995), 225–27; Penelope Bordallo Hofschneider, *A Campaign for Political Rights on the Island of Guam, 1899–1950* (Saipan: Commonwealth of the Northern Mariana Islands, Division of Historic Preservation, 2001).

64. Aleinikoff, *Semblances of Sovereignty*, 50.

65. For one protracted contest over degrees of sovereignty, see Thomas J. Osborne, *"Empire Can Wait": American Opposition to Hawaiian Annexation, 1893–1898* (Kent, OH: Kent State University Press, 1981).

66. Amy Kaplan, *The Anarchy of Empire in the Making of U.S. Culture* (Cambridge, MA: Harvard University Press, 2005), 3, and "Prisoners and Rights: Guantánamo's Limbo Is

Students of colonial history should know this well. As noted in chapter 2, Said long insisted that the discursive and material configuration of power that defined Orientalism describes not only a cultural enterprise in France and England but also a current political enterprise in the United States. As he asserted in his preface to the twenty-fifth anniversary edition of Orientalism, "Every single empire in its official discourse has said that it is not like all the others, that its circumstances are special, that it has a mission to enlighten, civilize, bring order and democracy, and that it uses force only as a last resort."[67]

These are consequential claims: One dismisses U.S. exceptionalism, while the second, more importantly, holds that discourses of exceptionalism are part of the material apparatus and conceptual grammar of imperial ventures themselves. Said's insight opens to another: Imperial states by definition operate as states of exception that vigilantly produce exceptions to their principles and exemptions to their laws.[68] From this vantage point, the United States is not an aberrant empire but a quintessential one, a consummate producer of excepted populations, excepted spaces, and its own continuously reiterated exception from international and domestic law.

Some political theorists have defined sovereign power not as the monopoly to sanction or to rule but as the right to decide when laws are suspended and when they are not.[69] One could argue that the formation and redistribution of zones of ambiguity just as accurately describes a long history of imperial contest and expansion. Whether we look to the Netherlands Indies, French Indochina, French Algeria, or British Malaya, each of their legal histories tracks prolonged exercises in forms of incorporation and differentiation that reshuffled and attenuated which populations and which

Too Convenient," New York Times, November 24, 2003, http://www.nytimes.com/2003/11/24/opinion/24iht-edkaplan_ed3_.html.

67. Edward W. Said, Orientalism (New York: Vintage, 1979), xxi.

68. Stephen Rosen, professor of national security and military affairs at Harvard's Olin Institute for Strategic Studies, makes a similar point when he argues that "the organizing principle of empire rests on the existence of an overarching power that creates and enforces the principle of hierarchy, but is not itself bound by such rules": Stephen Rosen, "An Empire, If You Can Keep It," National Interest (Spring 2003), http://nationalinterest.org/article/an-empire-if-you-can-keep-it-947.

69. The "state of exception" with respect to imperial forms is not a subject that either Carl Schmitt or Giorgio Agamben sought to address: see Carl Schmitt, The Concept of the Political (1927) (Chicago: University of Chicago Press, 2007); Giorgio Agamben, Homo Sacer: Sovereign Power and Bare Life, trans. Daniel Heller-Roazen (Stanford, CA: Stanford University Press, 1998).

social kinds (and in what distribution of spaces) at any specific moment had a "right to have rights"—or rather to some rights and not others—to education, labor protection, health care, or housing. Protracted debates over who was to be classified as white, European, mixed-blood, or native Christian; who was subject to land tax and who was not; and who could hold property and for how long were exercises in developing regulations for specific populations and in setting out special conditions for the suspension and reinvention of the laws applied to them.

Imperial formations and the varied degrees of sovereignty they provide could be understood as extended and extensive examples of macro-polities that thrive on the thick or thin thresholds of vague political and legal status and territorial autonomy.[70] Imperial architectures are not wholly visible or wholly opaque. Oscillation among the visible, secreted, and opaque structures of sovereignty are common features.[71] Creative and seemingly ambivalent lexicons provide a more comprehensive picture of the varied and changing criteria by which empires sanction appropriations, occupations, and dispossessions.

The notion that the "new U.S. empire" of the early twenty-first century is in fact an old one is argued by several scholars. Oscar Campomanes holds that U.S. global power has long embraced peculiar forms and formulations of territoriality. This feature is what partly "helps to explain the extreme difficulty of making it critically accountable."[72] In this frame, the non-territorial "virtual" expansion of the United States was and remains its distinguishing feature. What might be considered "new" in 1898 may not be the explicit and full-blown imperial interests of the United States as expressed in the occupation and annexation of the Philippines (the case most frequently invoked to prove U.S. empire commensurable with its European variants). Rather, what distinguishes that moment may be the accentuated, amorphous forms of power that the United States assumed—and the justifications for "just war" based on them. But even then, it was not new.

---

70. Whether "our age" increasingly foregrounds the state of exception as the "fundamental political structure . . . that ultimately becomes the rule" is hard to sustain for the history of imperial formations: see Agamben, *Homo Sacer*, 20.

71. Arendt was among those who noted "the intimate traditional connection between imperialist politics and rule by 'invisible government' and secret agents": Arendt, *The Origins of Totalitarianism*, xx.

72. Oscar V. Campomanes, "1898 and the Nature of the New Empire," *Radical History Review*, 73 (Winter 1999): 132.

One could argue that the invisible boundaries outlining the "Western Hemisphere" drawn by the Monroe Doctrine in 1823 set the conditions of possibility for a geopolitical zone to be subject not to European empire but to a still emergent North American one.[73]

Students of imperial history depend on having a solid archival trail to track, on elaborated cultures of documentation for which agents of empire were rewarded and in which they invested their careers. We are less skilled at identifying the scope of empire when the contracts are not in written form, when policies are not signaled as classified or spelled out as confidential, secreted matters of state.[74] The absence of a "scrap of paper being signed that might involve the United States in legal obligation to the world at large or to any part of it" has a long history that runs through the earliest alienation of indigenous rights written into the Declaration of Independence.[75] Being an effective empire has long been contingent on partial visibility—sustaining the ability to remain an unaccountable one.

THE ENEMY OUTSIDE AND WITHIN

Hannah Arendt argued that what distinguished totalitarian from imperial expansion was that the former recognized no difference between a home and foreign country while the latter depended on it.[76] But Arendt did not anticipate certain effects of decolonization or how much the changing face of capital investment would bring the empire back home, collapsing some of that distance and difference. One profound imperial effect is a reconfigured space of the homeland, its defense, and who has what rights in it.[77]

Internal enemies are one of the most prolific products of imperial formations, sustenance for the elaborate technologies of identification and surveillance that their potentiality demands. Proudly conservative political

73. Schmitt, *Nomos of the Earth in the International Law of the Jus Publicum Europaeum*, 281–94.

74. On archival secrets as colonial history, see Stoler, *Along the Archival Grain*, 25–28.

75. Anthony J. Hall, *The American Empire and the Fourth World* (Montreal: McGill-Queen's University Press, 2003). For Robin Matthews' review of Hall, see http://www.shunpiking.org/ol0111/Hall_review.htm.

76. Arendt, *The Origins of Totalitarianism*, 131.

77. David Harvey makes the point that "the new imperialism" joins a state project targeting "the evil enemy without" to a "new sense of social order at home"—an exorcising of the "devils lurking within." Whether this is "new," and how, deserves to be questioned: David Harvey, *The New Imperialism* (Oxford: Oxford University Press, 2005), 17.

science professor James Kurth made the case in bald terms in an essay from 2003, envisioning the advent of a Europe internally divided as if it were "two nations"—one white, "secular, rich, old and feeble," and the other an "anti-European nation" of colonial peoples, "Islamic, poor, young and virile."[78] In his version, the "foreign colonizing nation will be the *umma* of Islam, and the colonized entity will be Europe" itself. In Kurth's social imaginary, the enemy was to the south and east but increasingly internal and domestically located, displacing whites in the north and west. His "melancholy tale of empire and immigration" was a sober "warning" and "prophesy" for America that transposed terror into an explicitly racialized formulation. And so he asked whether "imperial immigration" might cause the United States also to become two nations, with "the coming of a Latino nation" that would be "poor, young and robust," accompanied by a "widespread fear of Latino terrorism." His hero, Samuel Huntington, rehearsed a well-known and similar argument, playing on fears of a dark demographic tidal swell: "The most immediate and most serious challenge to Americans' traditional identity comes from the immense and continuing immigration from Latin America, especially from Mexico, and the fertility rates of these immigrants."[79]

That modern state projects are designed to defend society against its enemies outside and within confronts the disturbing logic of such arguments, making sense of how macro-polities enlist their own citizens to police themselves and accept the deaths of their soldier-children in the name of the greater good.[80] Michel Foucault's identification of a racial state as one in which "society must be defended" situates the moral right to murder those "outside," as it produces disenfranchisements, persecutions, and internments as protections for the common good. It also produces a dangerous participation in popular profiling as required of "good citizens." Foucault may have

78. Kurth, "Migration and the Dynamics of Empire," 10–11. "Two nations" is, not inconsequently, the term Andrew Hacker used a decade earlier to characterize what it meant to be black in white America—namely, separate, hostile, and unequal: see Andrew Hacker, *Two Nations: Black and White, Separate, Hostile, Unequal* (New York: Charles Scribner, 1992).

79. Samuel Huntington, "The Hispanic Challenge," *Foreign Policy* (October 28, 2009), https://foreignpolicy.com/2009/10/28/the-hispanic-challenge. See also Roberto Lovato, "White Fear in Wartime—Samuel Huntington Brings His 'Clash of Civilizations' Home," *Pacific News Service*, May 17, 2004.

80. Michel Foucault, *Society Must Be Defended: Lectures at the Collège de France, 1975–76* (New York: Picador, 2003), 254–56.

framed the racism that "society will practice against itself" as a nation-state project, but security regimes, as we know, are equally relegated to international legal jurisdiction. "Humanitarian intervention" and the "responsibility to protect" by some accounts provide "simply the discourses and deformalized mechanisms by which empire aims to rule (and to legitimate its rule) rather than ways to limit and orient power by law."[81]

If categorization is theory-driven, as students of cognition often argue, then we should be more attentive to the changing grids in which those categories are framed. Progressive scholars are concerned about rethinking the parameters of the new empire, but I am not convinced we know the inhabited space—the weathered sites, the material deposits, the sedimented histories and social etymologies—of imperial forms of duress that have long been there. What different polities have been willing to call themselves and how they have sought to compare themselves to and label others are part of the affective space of empires themselves. These are strategically malleable active ingredients, not dead metaphors in the making of consensus, in the building of popular support, in the making of what counts as benevolence and what passes—when and for whom—as legitimate rule. One sobering lesson we have learned about key symbols and powerful discourses in and out of colonial contexts is that they are resilient to contrary evidence. Like racism, they thrive smugly unchallenged by empirical claims. Some of the "lessons" may stretch us to find new ways to demonstrate that imperial effects are intimately bound to who is doing the looking and from where and for what anticipated interventions those questions are asked.

UNTIMELY COMPARISONS IN HARSH TIMES

If the security state made its presence felt in the wake of 9/11, it is ensconced today. We are no longer being warned to inspect UPS packages or suspect those who deliver them. Nor is the Orwellian report in 2005 by the Homeland Security Council on the "Universal Adversary" (a simulation model that offered fifteen detailed scenarios of "emergency preparedness" against an outside enemy, including "disgruntled employees") as much in the antiterrorism spotlight today—although in 2009, Sotera Defense

81. Jean L. Cohen, "Whose Sovereignty? Empire versus International Law," *Ethics and International Affairs* 18, 3 (December 2004): 1–24.

Solutions garnered a $1.5 million award to support DHS's Universal Adversary program.[82] This sci-fi fantasy is still operative, part of the embedded logic, however unrealized, and ever more authorized through newly updated technologies. Such imaginaries make demands on critical history, not to provide lessons as soothing and tame distractions, but to attune one's sensibilities to how such imaginings can be crafted into common sense, to attend to how dissonant events and arrested projects are refigured as constituent parts of the present. At issue is not the identification of conspiracy theories but ways to untangle a set of political rubrics imbued with a widely resonant moral vocabulary that reframes and redefines what counts as imperial intervention and what does not.

Those terms that signal the unclarified sovereignties of U.S. imperial breadth are not, as I have insisted, the blurred edges of what more "authentic," visible empires look like but their empowered variants.[83] Expanded and contracted "thresholds" between inside and out and who will be caught and cordoned off within them are part of a more pervasive affective apparatus, a flourishing of what Giorgio Agamben and Ghassan Hage so rightly call a fictive sense of a "state of siege" that Hage holds is no longer as it once was the privileged modality of settler colonial dispositions alone[84] When the U.S. Department of Homeland Security was inaugurated after 9/11, it was dedicated to redefining not overseas "Others" but U.S. interior frontiers and to expanding that defensive corridor. Such an understanding invites students of empire to redraw their maps across internal distinctions and external ones and across those widening pockets of people caught in between. It demands comparisons that are counterintuitive, what imperial archives and historiographies would render as jarring incommensurabilities and that continue to make up a colonial inflected common sense.

---

82. U.S. Department of Homeland Security, "TOPOFF 3 Frequently Asked Questions," March 2005, http://www.dhs.gov/xprepresp/training/editorial_0603.shtm.

83. See Chalmers Johnson, "America's Empire of Bases," Wisdom Fund, January 15, 2004, http://www.twf.org/News/Y2004/0117-Empire.html.

84. Giorgio Agamben, *State of Exception* (Chicago: University of Chicago Press, 2005). See also Ghassan Hage, "Etat du siège: A Dying Domesticating Colonialism?," *American Ethnologist* 43, 1 (2016): 38–49. Hage is absolutely right that besiegement characterizes a much wider geopolitical sensibility today but I would argue that it was equally the case historically for many more colonial formations that were not of a settler variant.

SILENT HEMORRHAGING OF PUBLIC LIFE:
INAUDIBLE INTIMACIES, MUTED MOMENTS

To defeat an enemy that lurks in the shadows and seeks relentlessly for some small crack through which to slip their evil designs—such a victory requires the vigilance of every American, the diligent preparation of every community, and the collective will of our entire nation.—Tom Ridge, St. Louis, 2004

Michel de Certeau once argued that domains of the intimate represent "the dark reign of a non-distinction, a kind of 'matter' that never makes it into the analytical taxonomies of social form." He writes of the intimate as "a silent hemorrhaging of public life by an uncontrollable individual mobility."[85] Such notions of the intimate splice through prison cells, as well as through homes, holding centers, the shared knowledge of border vigilantes and their prey, of women serving shell-shocked occupying forces in army barracks.[86] It reorients toward those caught in metropolitan zones of ambiguous rights, as well as toward those caught on empire's geographic margins.

The "silent hemorrhaging of public life" has a political etymology of a long imperial *durée*. Technologies of truth production—torture, confession, humiliation, isolation, and the threat of death—are honed inquisitional skills in the arts and crafts of imperial intelligence.[87] Detecting "fraudulent, fabricated Europeans in the nineteenth-century Netherlands Indies" and "hidden enemies" of the right hue but wrong blood; those Christianized but with secreted affiliations and native mothers; those who took imperial rhetoric about equality too literally (and imagined it was applicable to them) were both the subjects and products of empire's truth-producing experts.[88]

85. Michel de Certeau, *Heterologies: Discourse on the Other* (Minneapolis: University of Minnesota Press, 1986), 154–55.

86. On the sexual service for empire's military barracks, see Kenneth Ballhatchet, *Race, Sex, and Class under the Raj: Imperial Attitudes and Policies and Their Critics, 1793–1905* (London: Weidenfeld and Nicolson, 1980); Cynthia H. Enloe, "It Takes More than Two," in *The Morning After: Sexual Politics at the End of the Cold War* (Berkeley: University of California Press, 1993), 142–160; Hanneke Ming, "Barrack Concubinage in the Indies, 1887–1920," *Indonesia* 35 (April 1, 1983): 65–94.

87. See Silverblatt, *Modern Inquisitions*; Michael Taussig, "Culture of Terror—Space of Death: Roger Casement's Putumayo Report and the Explanation of Torture," *Comparative Studies in Society and History* 26, 3 (July 1, 1984): 467–97; Sylvie Thénault, *Violence ordinaire dans l'Algérie colonial: Camps, internements, assignations à résidence* (Paris: Jacob, 2012).

88. See Ann Laura Stoler, *Carnal Knowledge and Imperial Power: Race and the Intimate in Colonial Rule* (Berkeley: University of California Press, 2002), 79–111.

Trained to identify what could not be seen, and rewarded for amassing evidentiary knowledge, colonial agents produced their truths—measuring and making up differences that mattered (sexual, moral, medical, and otherwise) and that indexed the "true" interior dispositions of those "dangerous" subjects they marked.

What hemorrhages public life is a sensory alert that demands attention to minute difference, that prescribes a guard against differences that matter and those that do not. These are not new intimacies of empire. Rather, they are ones that should help us think differently about empire's zones of exception that spill outside the spaces cordoned off as holding pens by barbed wire. In the twenty-fifth-anniversary edition of *Orientalism*, Said reminded us insistently about the breadth of the configuration he sought to engage. He wrote about the stereotyping of Arabs, caricatures of terrorists, urging scholarship not to be "about" the world but squarely in it. If "differential knowledge" owes its critical force "to the harshness with which it is opposed by everything surrounding it," in these harsh times we would do well to attend to the subjacent and capacious forms in which imperial visions and practices so unevenly and unequally permeate what counts as "security" as we shall see in the following chapter, what counts as intimate space.[89]

89. Michel Foucault, "Two Lectures," in *Power/Knowledge: Selected Interviews and Other Writings, 1972–1977*, ed. Colin Gordon (New York: Pantheon, 1980), 82.

REASON ASIDE

ENLIGHTENMENT PROJECTS AND EMPIRE'S SECURITY REGIMES

This chapter puts genealogy to work to think through an "obvious" imperial truth, as it draws a counterintuitive arc. It traverses what has often been taken to be the prevailing import of Enlightenment precepts for colonial governance—"the supremacy of reason"—to question how that focus has skewed the imperial history of security regimes as they emerged and look today. Arguing for an *affective genealogy of security*, it traces how a ready distinction between sentiment and political rationality occludes the work that sensibilities have been, and are, called on to do in shaping the governing principles and practices of imperial formations.

One need not be well versed in the field of (post)colonial studies to attest that the glare of the Enlightenment pervades historiographies of nineteenth-century European imperial formations and their analytic space. Some notion of "an Enlightenment project" (as Alasdair MacIntyre first called it) features as a core conceptual frame for understanding why and how what is commonly referred to as "universal reason" and "totalizing systems of knowledge" underwrote European colonial expansions and made possible the regimes that claimed sovereignty over the non-European world.[1] It is in these terms that imperial projects have been understood: the agents they recruited, the dispositions they cultivated, the subjects they

---

1. Robert J. C. Young, *White Mythologies: Writing History and the West*. London: Routledge, 1990), 9; Alasdair C. MacIntyre, *After Virtue: A Study in Moral Theory* (Notre Dame, IN: University of Notre Dame Press, 1981), esp. 51–78.

created and coerced, and the domains they privileged for intervention. Implicit or explicit, "the Enlightenment" is cast as an organizing principle for understanding the epistemological scaffolding of imperial governance—what political lessons we need to learn from its prescriptive mandates and their durable effects, and what of those commanding logics surreptitiously work on and through us so differently now.

Inspiration for this assessment comes from many philosophical quarters, and not least from the scripted narratives of scientific progress that some colonial architects rehearsed among themselves.[2] Variations abide, but the ubiquity is clear. The Enlightenment with a capital E appears almost seamlessly to map onto the capital E of Empire. For that master of Enlightenment scholarship, Jonathan Israel, it is a postmodern camp that has been guilty of portraying the Enlightenment as "biased, facile, self-deluded, over-optimistic, Eurocentric, imperialistic and ultimately destructive."[3] But Israel's assault is misleading: The Enlightenment has been far more pluralized by students of empire than his derisive statement would suggest. If anything, it is the sprawl of the Enlightenment's impact and the features underscored to define its most prominent concerns that need qualification.[4]

The choice of verb to describe its effect on imperial principles may serve as an alert to the scope of that spread. The Enlightenment has been argued to provide the vehicle of imperial domination, buttress empire, inaugurate the exploratory verve that opened to its voracious agrarian enterprises and ambitious scientific projects, shape the dispositions of empire's practitioners, preen imperial arrogance, prime anticolonial nationalist movements, and, not least, animate and justify the toxic mix of coercive and curative in-

2. These "inspirations" (of Kant and Hegel, Theodor Adorno and Max Horkheimer, Michel Foucault, Edward Said, and Jean-François Lyotard) are not my focus here.

3. Jonathan Irvine Israel, *Enlightenment Contested: Philosophy, Modernity, and the Emancipation of Man, 1670–1752* (Oxford: Oxford University Press, 2008), v. Interestingly, Israel significantly toned down his dismissal of postmodern scholarship after *Enlightenment Contested* went to press, noting instead of its practitioners "their partially correct (but too narrow) critique, and a thinking 'with' rather than against them": see Jonathan Irvine Israel, "Enlightenment! Which Enlightenment?" *Journal of the History of Ideas* 67, 3 (2006): 523–45.

4. See also Russell A. Berman, *Enlightenment or Empire: Colonial Discourse in German Culture* (Lincoln: University of Nebraska Press, 1998). Berman impatiently condemns those who insist on collaboration between Enlightenment and empire. By his account, students of empire have gotten it all wrong by endorsing "a blanket refusal of reason—and, by extension of science, progress, and a normative universalism": Berman, *Enlightenment or Empire*, 8.

terventions and reforms that have served the installation of European sovereignties across the globe. The notion of "Enlightenment-as-imperialism" and the "epistemic violence" that fusion enabled (as Gayatri Spivak has charged) have dominated scholarship over the past few decades, just as its imaginary is said to have once instrumentally colonized so much of the world.[5]

Here I invite us to look more carefully at what this fit between imperial formations and Enlightenment precepts looks like, between the workings of one imperial body politic—that of the nineteenth-century and early twentieth-century Netherlands Indies—and the loose, ill cut of its Enlightenment clothes. At issue is more than the discrepancy between prescription and practice; rather, an attempt to make room for what constituted the lived epistemic space in which different forms of knowledge were combined, contested, reflected on, and compared.

In that pursuit, three underlying, if tacit, assumptions deserve examination and frame my concerns. One is the unquestioned identification of empire with a "rule of reason." That equation seems to take little account of what was often a more cobbled and messy colonial order of things that ricocheted between standardization and arbitrary protocols, bureaucratic precisions and unrealistic visions, large-scale planning and gross failures of foresight. Not least, the conditions and practices of governance often contravened what a commitment to reason might otherwise have required and a commitment to rational knowledge would have disallowed.

The second assumption is tacit, as well. It leaves unquestioned whether European colonials actually shared clarity (if not consensus) about the kinds of knowledge that mattered to them. I would argue that they did not. With respect to the making of social kinds, to the production of racial categories, and to the strategies of security and surveillance that empire's architects and agents sought to put in place, their confidence was often compromised and troubled by an uncertain epistemic space.

The third assumption, that the Enlightenment is best designated as the "Age of Reason," goes unremarked among students of empire, as it does in so many other fields. But here it is a convention with unique effects on how scholars have understood the domains that empire's practitioners saw as their proper province, the kinds of knowledge they deemed "relevant," and

---

5. Patrick Williams and Laura Chrisman, eds., *Colonial Discourse and Post-Colonial Theory: A Reader* (New York: Columbia University Press, 1994), 15.

ultimately what they thought they needed to know—and thus took to be their primary tasks.

One could start from another premise—namely, that an overarching commitment to reason in fact poorly describes the compendium of the Enlightenment's core considerations and the prevailing concerns of many of those taken as Enlightenment exemplars. Albert Hirschman and Susan James offer compelling arguments that in matters of governance and statecraft, the sentiments and passions—states of feeling and disposition usually opposed to the rule of reason—were central to Enlightenment thinking. They were central to colonial dispositions and the practices they served, as well.[6] Such a genealogy might find its ballast in another direction. Seventeenth-century French philosophers understood that the art of governance entailed "the art of knowing men."[7] It was John Locke, after all, the author of what some have considered "the 'Bible' of the Enlightenment," who set out so meticulously those affective sensibilities that made one eligible to be a proper citizen.[8] Hume identified the contagious quality of sentiments, and later Adam Smith worried over the problematic careers of the moral sentiments in usefully or abusively shaping a state's agendas and political priorities.[9]

Under Dutch colonial rule, attention to sentiments marked out the domains targeted for scrutiny and surveillance; the attachments and proximities seen as problematic; and the "habits of heart" that both were demanded for governance and, alternatively, could countermand the attachments that secured its control. Efforts to assess other people's "interior states," and the kinds of affective and psychological knowledge on which those assessments relied, were both critical for identifying who and what constituted a

6. Albert O. Hirschman, *The Passions and the Interests: Political Arguments for Capitalism before Its Triumph* (Princeton, NJ: Princeton University Press, 1977).

7. See Ann Laura Stoler, *Along the Archival Grain: Epistemic Anxieties and Colonial Common Sense* (Princeton, NJ: Princeton University Press, 2009), 77, 101; Susan James, *Passion and Action: The Emotions in Seventeenth-Century Philosophy* (Oxford: Clarendon, 1997), 2.

8. See Katharine M. Morsberger, "John Locke's 'An Essay Concerning Human Understanding': The 'Bible' of the Enlightenment," *Studies in Eighteenth-Century Culture* 25, 1 (1996): 1–19. See the discussion of the "passions," which Uday Mehta took to "underlie Locke's concern with self-discipline and self-mastery": Uday S. Mehta, *The Anxiety of Freedom: Imagination and Individuality in Locke's Political Thought* (Ithaca, NY: Cornell University Press, 1992), 137.

9. On the contagious quality of sentiments in Hume, see esp. Adela Pinch, *Strange Fits of Passion: Epistemologies of Emotion, Hume to Austen* (Stanford, CA: Stanford University Press, 1999).

present threat to colonial polities and, as important, who might constitute a threat in the future. This was neither a diminutive nor derivative problem in the pragmatics of governance. A limited capacity to recognize political sentiments and personal attachments *that could not be measured* was understood as one of the most vulnerable nodes in the craft of rule. Efforts to discern affective differences permeated the seemingly benign and more brutal strategies of defense, security, and segregation. Not least, it underwrote a quest for affective knowledge about intuitions and inclinations; attentiveness to the bodily, tactile, and intimate sites of intervention and control (see chapter 7).

I address these questions through the archival field I know best: that of the nineteenth-century Netherlands Indies. It would be easy to see such a specific focus as peculiar and unique.[10] Although the Indies architecture of authority was singular, the epistemic predicaments it reveals and repeats were not. The concern is specific; the archive particular to the Indies; the aims, both narrow and broad: to offer an alternative inflection on imperial dispositions that opens to more "disorderly" genealogies of the present. The focus is on the making of social categories and the conceptual work (both epistemological and political) that went into the ascription of racial kinds.

One might imagine such a domain to provide a contrived invitation to illustrate how the logic of scientific rationality was invoked to authorize such distinctions and secure the rigid categories that clarified those who were white and inherently superior from those who were not. Indeed, nineteenth-century race sciences sought and claimed to have found universal laws of racial classification derived from biologically blatant patterns of human physical variation.[11] But science often came up short. It is in this

10. According to Jonathan Israel, the Dutch Enlightenment had its strongest influence on the European Enlightenment and was of "diminishing" importance and increasingly "marginal" throughout the eighteenth century. Israel's notion that the establishment of the Maatschappij tot Nut van 't Algemeen (Society for the Public Good) was a significant example of Dutch Enlightenment projects is problematic. As discussed in chapter 3, not only was it an institution based on punitive care and coercive instruments of reform, but it became one of the models of what Michel Foucault called "the carceral archipelago": see Jonathan Irvine Israel, *The Dutch Republic: Its Rise, Greatness, and Fall, 1477–1806* (Oxford: Clarendon, 1995), 1038–66. On the Dutch Enlightenment in Java, see Jean Gelman Taylor, *The Social World of Batavia: Europeans and Eurasians in Colonial Indonesia* (Madison: University of Wisconsin Press, 1983), 78–95.

11. The historical accounts that track this story of racism's rise are too numerous to list here. The next chapter discusses the problematic argument that "cultural" racism is a relatively new phenomenon.

quintessential and critical space of race making—in which colonial regimes were so vitally invested and dependent—that the elusive, ambiguous qualities of social kinds called into question the sorts of knowing on which those distinctions could and should be made. If Enlightenment precepts and concepts mattered, they did so not because they provided the firm principles of colonial rule or because they were wholly convincing and exhaustive. On the contrary, they mattered precisely because they were understood at the time to offer inadequate sources of epistemic authority for the pedagogy of empire's governing tasks.

THE RULE OF REASON

Even if the Enlightenment has been a very important phase in our history, and in the development of political technology, I think we have to refer to much more remote processes if we want to understand how we have been trapped in our own history.—Michel Foucault, "Omnes et Singulatim," 1981

Progress, reason, scientific rationality, liberalism, and secularism are among those many political concepts (and the institutional formations they animated) claimed to have a genealogy rooted in Enlightenment thinking. Such thinking is claimed to have made it possible for empire's advocates to conceive of their ventures as ennobling enterprises, to school its agents and architects to value their moral missions, if not relish their bureaucratic tasks. Foundational Enlightenment priorities find in empire what Uday Mehta writes about liberalism, its iconic descendant: "the concrete space of its dreams."[12] In Partha Chatterjee's incisive account, it is the tyrannical universality of Reason that sets passions to work in its service while keeping "itself in the background, untouched, unharmed [and] unscathed.[13] He locates "the story of the Enlightenment in the colonies" in "the hands of the policemen and . . . in the station-house when the cunning of reason turns against particular ethical values of the nation."[14] Gyan Prakash identifies the subtle ways in which scientific reason became "a multivalent sign" that exerted force in a wider social and political domain. In British India, rea-

12. Uday S. Mehta, *Liberalism and Empire: A Study in Nineteenth-Century British Liberal Thought* (Chicago: University of Chicago Press, 1999), 37.

13. Partha Chatterjee, *Nationalist Thought and the Colonial World: A Derivative Discourse* (Minneapolis: University of Minnesota Press, 1993), 168.

14. Chatterjee, *Nationalist Thought and the Colonial World*, 168.

son was the syntax of reform for British colonials and Indian intellectuals. "Universal reason" was not only "a means of rule adapted to other guises and other language; science was the grammar of modern power with its fullest expression in the state."[15] On the terrain of Latin America, Walter Mignolo tracks an earlier genealogy of imperial authority that also asserted a "hegemonic epistemological imaginary" and "a planetary epistemological standard" that valued scientific authority and its credibility above other ways to know the world—with Reason supporting a new global design.[16]

Such claims identify an imperial veneration of Reason and rational knowledge, and implicitly something more: empire as a crystalline embodiment of the way both permeated the infrastructure of authority, the hierarchies of credibility, and the prioritized policies in colonial relations. In this view, colonial circumstances offered a new sense of, and sites for, the uses of rational knowledge to tame nature and control subject populations, fueled by those convinced of its power, its transformative qualities, and in the pragmatics of governance, its efficacy and worth. Peter Gay reminds us in *The Enlightenment: The Science of Freedom* that it was Francis Bacon who, in breaking with the historical fatalism that preceded the Enlightenment, insisted that knowledge was power.[17] It is students of colonialism who have attributed that insight, so differently mobilized, to Foucault. For Dipesh Chakrabarty, the master narrative of the European Enlightenment has been, and continues to be, the "silent referent" that organized the Eurocentric epistemics of imperial knowledge production.[18] As Chatterjee has shown, India's elite nationalists shared its premises and were entrapped by it.[19] For Chakrabarty that narrative has enforced a pernicious teleology, a sequential temporality, and a form of historical progression that captured colonial agents and, more pointedly still, governs our writing of history and continues to unknowingly bind us all.

If what falls under the Enlightenment project is sometimes encompassing and broad, it is the elevation of a parochial, local, and culture bound

15. Gyan Prakash, *Another Reason: Science and the Imagination of Modern India* (Princeton, NJ: Princeton University Press, 1999), 9.

16. Walter Mignolo, *Local Histories/Global Designs: Coloniality, Subaltern Knowledges, and Border Thinking* (Princeton, NJ: Princeton University Press, 2012), 59.

17. Peter Gay, *The Enlightenment: An Interpretation*. New York: W. W. Norton, 1977), 6.

18. Dipesh Chakrabarty, *Provincializing Europe: Postcolonial Thought and Historical Difference* (Princeton, NJ: Princeton University Press, 2000), 2.

19. Chatterjee, *Nationalist Thought and the Colonial World*, xx.

sense of reason to a universal standard against which critical colonial studies has been rightly aimed—against epistemological commitments that have partitioned the world into unequally deserving and differentially capable social kinds, plotted on a grid that divides those who are either committed to and capable of reason from those who are not. Dorinda Outram puts it clearly: "The Enlightenment itself often seemed to devote as much energy to designating entire social groups, such as women or peasants, as impervious to the voice of reason, as it did to constructing a better world for [some] human beings."[20] This deeper critique targets less implementation than the structural entailments of the exclusions built into knowledge production.

Rethinking of this tableau has come from within and outside the quarters of colonial historians. Sankar Muthu contends that the foes of empire were among the most prominent Enlightenment intellectuals and that by ignoring their anti-imperial arguments we diminish our own ability to track the diverse effects of its force.[21] Prakash has argued that India's colonized intellectuals mounted their assault by asserting "another reason," thereby "opening colonialism's normalizing myth . . . to questioning and contention [and to] a space for the negotiation of science's status as truth."[22] Richard Shweder attributes to anthropology a long-standing appreciation of cultural difference that refused the normative uniformity of mankind under the "dictate of reason and evidence."[23]

No one who has spent time in French, British, Dutch, or German colonial archives would deny that scientific and technological inquiry and innovations were fundamental to the organizational apparatus of imperial ventures, or that colonial administrations called on and encouraged European experts and amateurs of all kinds—botanists, economists, geographers, architects,

20. Dorinda Outram, The Enlightenment (Cambridge: Cambridge University Press, 2005), 21–22.

21. Sankar Muthu, Enlightenment against Empire (Princeton, NJ: Princeton University Press, 2003).

22. Prakash, Another Reason, 72. Aamir Mufti insists that it is a "false perception to view the colonial reenactment of the modern bourgeois Enlightenment as entirely the imposition of an external (European) form": Aamir Mufti, Enlightenment in the Colony: The Jewish Question and the Crisis of Postcolonial Culture (Princeton, NJ: Princeton University Press, 2007), 24.

23. Richard A. Shweder, "Anthropology's Romantic Rebellion against the Enlightenment, or There's More to Thinking than Reason and Evidence," in Culture Theory: Essays on Mind, Self, and Emotion, ed. Richard A. Shweder and Robert Alan LeVine (Cambridge: Cambridge University Press, 1984), 7–66.

doctors, epidemiologists—to ply their trade, refine their instruments, and, indeed, to imagine and to attempt to make of colonized places their comparative "laboratories of modernity" on a micro and macro scale.[24]

Still, three decades of work in the French and Dutch colonial archives produce a dissonance with these accounts and a query about what is missed and amiss in how these mappings of the Enlightenment on empire are framed. The epistemic commitments that are supposed to have governed colonial visions seem too capacious in the ready lineup of governing practices with the Enlightenment's abstract claims.[25] Nor do they accord with the "epistemic politics" of empire, the constellation of conceptually articu-

24. See, e.g., Lewis Pyenson, *Empire of Reason: Exact Sciences in Indonesia, 1840–1940* (Leiden: E. J. Brill, 1989). For a nuanced treatment of the collusion and conflicts between the Netherlands Indies administration in Java and the botanists who worked there, see Andrew Goss, *The Floracrats: State-Sponsored Science and the Failure of the Enlightenment in Indonesia* (Madison: University of Wisconsin Press, 2011). On the term "laboratories" of modernity, see Paul Rabinow, *French Modern: Norms and Forms of the Social Environment* (Chicago: University of Chicago Press, 1989) and Gwendolyn Wright, "Tradition in the Service of Modernity," *Journal of Modern History* 59, 2 (June l987): 291–316.

25. Let me be clear: My focus is not primarily on science and empire. I have no intention to contradict the finely grained historical work in so many colonial contexts on the synergy that imbricated scientific and imperial pursuits across so many domains, exemplified in Richard H. Grove, *Green Imperialism: Colonial Expansion, Tropical Island Edens and the Origins of Environmentalism, 1600–1860* (Cambridge: Cambridge University Press, 1995). And, of course, colonial bureaucracies across the globe drew on science to collect statistics, to dam up rice fields for export crops, to convert sugar beet machines into those for Javanese cane sugar, to conceive imperial maps (and reorder space to fit them) in the name of imperial sovereignty and under the sign of giving "value," and in the name of progress and profit, social welfare, and peace.

Nor is my subject Enlightenment thinking among colonial subjects, popular or elite visionaries who appropriated its emancipatory lexicon of freedom for themselves. Others are pursing those projects with finesse. I think, among others, of David Scott's considered reading of Toussaint L'Ouverture and C. L. R. James's early attention to him; of Michel-Rolph Trouillot's and Laurent Dubois's reading of the French and Haitian revolutions; of Partha Chatterjee's rendition of a Bengali middle-class elite smitten with Enlightenment precepts; and of Akeel Bilgrami's treatment of Gandhi's prophetic warnings against a "liberal democracy" that India's elite were so eager to embrace as part of the dissenting "radical enlightenment": see David Scott, *Conscripts of Modernity: The Tragedy of Colonial Enlightenment* (Durham, NC: Duke University Press, 2004); C. L. R. James, *The Black Jacobins: Toussaint L'Ouverture and the San Domingo Revolution* (New York: Vintage, 1989); Michel-Rolph Trouillot, *Silencing the Past: Power and the Production of History* (Boston: Beacon, 1995); Laurent Dubois, *A Colony of Citizens: Revolution and Slave Emancipation in the French Caribbean, 1787–1804* (Chapel Hill: University of North Carolina Press, 2004); Partha Chatterjee, ed., *Texts of Power: Emerging Disciplines in Colonial Bengal* (Minneapolis: University of Minnesota Press, 1995), 93–117; Akeel Bilgrami, "Occiden-

lated and inchoate understandings of what the arts and crafts of governance entailed on the ground, on the ways of knowing that guided its practitioners, and on what made up the unstable coordinates of colonial common sense.[26] Might we not question, then, how much is assumed about what colonial agents did, how they did it, and, not least, how successfully they achieved—and how much they were convinced of—their taxonomic goals?

WHAT DO WE KNOW AND HOW DO WE KNOW IT?

The science of order is the science of a lie.—Jacques Rancière, The Philosopher and His Poor, 2004

"Reason," as so many have argued, is an elusive—indeed, moving—target, mobile in meaning, unfettered by scale, historically contingent, radically altered by context.[27] In its movement between common noun and commanding concept, it may silently traverse the analytic heights of philosophy, detail the precise procedures of scientific inquiry, or ratify that which constitutes the thoughtful grounds for the most mundane acts. Reason with a capital R represents at once a European philosophical tradition of truth production, both the form and content of the kind of knowledge valorized in it. As a verb, "to reason," it often loses its philosophical command and epistemic weight. As an adjective to modify an action considered "reasoned" and "reasonable," it parses shared understandings and prosaic requirements. As a modifier of "knowledge," the adjective "rational" stands in its place to indicate either subsumption by a set of norms and procedures or conceptual schemes already in place, independent of what any practitioner may find on the ground. If sometimes these different senses of the

talism, The Very Idea: An Essay on Enlightenment and Enchantment," *Critical Inquiry* 32, 3 (2006): 381–411.

26. See Ann Laura Stoler, "Epistemic Politics: Ontologies of Colonial Common Sense." *Folk Epistemology* 39, 3 (Fall 2008): 349–61, with which some parts of this argument overlap.

27. As Talal Asad notes, when people make claims about the concept of rationality (and religion), it is not always clear what concept of rationality they are using: see Talal Asad, *Genealogies of Religion: Discipline and Reasons of Power in Christianity and Islam.* Baltimore: Johns Hopkins University Press, 1993), 235fnn57–58. On the use of a concept of rationality in current debates that is "wider than mere scientific truth," see Chatterjee, *Nationalist Thought and the Colonial World*, esp. 14–17.

term are distinguished, they often were, and still are, not.[28] As students of empire have argued, the conflation of Reason as a mental faculty, Universal reason as a specific European logic, and reason—as opposed to emotion— as that required to make good judgments is no historical or semantic accident.[29] Their interchangeability has been understood to form part of the unspoken epistemological matrix of European superiority, the Enlightenment's legacy, a conflation that helped secure the hierarchical racial order of the imperial world.

Still, the archival record for this period of Dutch rule in its colonial heartland of Java and Sumatra sits uneasily with a rule of reason as its operative frame. If "reason" was "the syntax of reform," it was a grammar that yielded neither a clear political semantics nor straightforward rules of application. Chakrabarty takes the task of examining European rationalism in the history of empire to be "a matter of documenting how its 'reason,' which was not always self-evident to everyone, has been made to look obvious far beyond the ground where it originated."[30] I agree. Our points of entry and sites of query are complementary. But they are not the same. Chakrabarty's are posed against what he sees as the warped, constraining optic of European colonial archives and the unspoken logic and forms of history that underwrote their implicit truth claims. My points of entry are the documentary forms and the political content subjacently lodged within them. Gaston Bachelard's quest for a history of "epistemological detail" resonates with what I have in mind: attentiveness to those conceptual and political perturbations that disperse and hug close along the

28. Akeel Bilgrami offers one enabling way to clarify our use of the concept of rationality in this affected epistemic and historical space, suggesting a distinction between a "thin" sense of rationality as that which is "uncontroversially possessed by all" and a "thick" sense of rationality that "owes to specific historical developments in outlook around the time of the rise of science and its implications for how to think ('rationally') about culture and politics and society." It is the "thick" notion of scientific rationality against which Gandhi's critiques were aimed, a position he shared with many proponents of the Radical Enlightenment: see Bilgrami, "Occidentalism, The Very Idea," and responses to it.

29. While much of the contrast was between reason and the authority of religious sentiments, of faith, it is the more general distinction between the calculus of reason and the capricious, unpredictable power of the sentiments that has had such lasting post-Enlightenment resonance.

30. Chakrabarty, Provincializing Europe, 43.

ragged edges of the European colonial archival grain.[31] Or inflected somewhat differently, threats to colonial common sense come in many forms. Some breaches of evidence are pressed by colonial subjects; others erupt from within the protocols of governance itself, those moments "when the certainties are lost" among those Europeans often taken as Reason's disciples and advocates.[32]

The "minor" histories, to which Chakrabarty and I turn, converge and diverge, as well. Both "cast doubt on the 'major' " and reflect on the ways in which the " 'rationality' of the historian's methods necessarily makes [relationships to the past] 'minor' or inferior, as something 'nonrational' . . . as a result of, its own operation."[33] His focus probes other ways to know "subaltern pasts" that are excluded from what counts as history in a European mode. Mine rest with the unquiet minds of colonialism's European practitioners to invoke what I think of as "history in a minor key." Such a history initiates a rereading of the anxious and anticipatory states that imperial governance engendered to better understand the regimes of security that it produced and the expectant, affective economies on which imperial formations continue to depend.

The force of reason swells and recedes in the making of rule, in how Dutch colonial civil servants in the Netherlands Indies understood their tasks and how those social, industrial, legal, and medical technicians who worked directly for them or on the outskirts of their authority intervened in colonial policy and set the tenor of the debates about those interventions. Both groups palpably struggled with the criteria to use in assigning racial categories and evaluating moral dangers and political threats—and with how to make their assessments convincing and credible. They questioned not the validity of empire so much as the kinds of knowledge that served what they were counted on to know. Epistemic clarity eluded them—what

31. Gaston Bachelard, *La philosophie du non: Essai d'une philosophie du nouvel esprit scientifique* (Paris: Presses Universitaires de France, 1940), 12. The term "epistemological detail" is actually Hans-Jörg Rheinberger's beautiful translation of Bachelard's methodological entreaty to turn away from "un seul point de vue fixe" and instead imagine a "une méthode d'analyse très fine" (method of arranged dispersion); see Hans-Jörg Rheinberger, *Toward a History of Epistemic Things: Synthesizing Proteins in the Test Tube* (Stanford, CA: Stanford University Press, 1997), 23.

32. Michel Foucault, "Table Ronde du 20 mai 1978," in *Dits et écrits: 1954–1988, Volume 4: 1980–1988*, ed. Daniel Defert (Paris: Gallimard, 1984), 27, and Michel Foucault, "For an Ethics of Discomfort," in *The Politics of Truth* (New York: Semiotext(e), 1997), 143.

33. Chakrabarty, *Provincializing Europe*, 101.

a deep confidence in a "calculus of reason" and science as "the measure of men" might be imagined to bestow.[34]

To say that what constituted "reason" for them was not self-evident is not to suggest that they were closet anti-imperialists, renegades to European colonial society, or unheralded descendants of the counter-Enlightenment. On the contrary, they were colonialism's "social technicians"—both fledgling and seasoned bureaucratic soldiers of empire whose reports had to be comprehensible and convincing to their superiors, legible and intelligible assessment about who was a danger, what threatened security, and what was a risk.[35] To make credible their recommendations, they needed to be versed in the categories that demonstrated a skilled adherence to the repertoire of narratives deemed appropriate and in the selective choice of contexts that accorded with those conventions. Such prosaic features of reportage were subject to the "political rationalities" of rule but never dictated by the mandates of "reason" alone.

WHO HAS A "FEAR OF PHANTOMS"?

A ruler who is himself enlightened has no fear of phantoms, yet who likewise has at hand a well-disciplined and numerous army to guarantee public security, may say what no republic would dare to say: Argue as much as you like and about whatever you like, but obey!—Immanuel Kant, "What is Enlightenment?," 1784

Whether construed as a period, a "cultural climate," an intellectual phenomenon, a political legacy, or a disposition toward the world in Immanuel Kant's sense, the work Enlightenment thinking has been enlisted to perform may account for both less than its evocation promises and its accusers profess: less in that classificatory zeal is often taken as evidence of its definitive imprint on colonial epistemology; less in that historical emphasis on the regulative "architectonics" of reason privileges prescriptive categories rather than the fractious epistemic work and uncertainties of those who wrestled with them on the ground.[36] As with any commanding term elevated to a concept, the Enlightenment is a "point of condensation"

34. Michael Adas, *Machines as the Measure of Men: Science, Technology and Ideologies of Western Dominance* (Ithaca, NY: Cornell University Press, 1989).

35. Rabinow, *French Modern*, 13.

36. On Kant's "architectonics of reason," see Jacques Derrida, *Rogues: Two Essays on Reason* (Stanford, CA: Stanford University Press, 2005), 120.

that gathers in its components, as it draws around it affiliate concepts that provide resonance and make it "work."[37] It prescribes a directionality, preempts and prompts certain lines of inquiry. Most important, it forecloses and precludes others. It promises access and legibility, generalizations that comfort as they bind and arrest.

Peter Gay, who sought to remind us of the diverse and acrimonious currents within the Enlightenment, still celebrated it as a period marked by "the recovery of nerve," a ubiquitous and irresistible commitment to an ardent and unshackled spirit of inquiry.[38] Many historians might agree that nineteenth-century imperial projects relished that encyclopedic quest for knowledge and displayed that nerve, in brash and destructive ways. But one might be equally struck by how much imperial management produced and displayed the opposite: a nervous reticence about what to know; distrust of civil servants who knew too much; a bureaucratic shuffling that regularly moved officials from one region or district to the next in relatively short intervals, favoring a bracketed know-how, stupefied states of ensured ignorance (as Avital Ronell might call them) and, ostensibly to curb collusion and corruption with local rulers, truncated local ties and thin familiarities.[39] Local knowledge was filtered through and schooled in Dutch institutions in the Netherlands, a requirement for access to all but the lowest civil service positions. Only then was knowledge of Java brought back to Java. Valorized and relevant local knowledge, as I have long argued, could not be really local at all.

During the opening of East Sumatra's plantation belt in the 1870s, such strategies served them poorly. In the final chapters of *Along the Archival Grain*, I recount the story of the abrupt dismissal of a certain newly transferred district officer, Frans Carl Valck, who, confronted by an unprecedented series of murders of European planters and their family members in the months before his arrival, was unprepared (and some thought, unhinged) not only by the multiple instances of violence in and around the estates but also by the wooden categories in which he was schooled to make sense of them. Outraged at the false facts imparted by planters, he was ultimately undone by what he knew, what he asked, and what he did not then know about the

37. Gilles Deleuze and Félix Guattari, "What Is a Concept?" in *What Is Philosophy?* (New York: Columbia University Press, 1994), 20.
38. Gay, *The Enlightenment*, 11.
39. Avital Ronell, *Stupidity* (Urbana: University of Illinois Press, 2003).

principles of imperial disregard expected of civil servants stationed near the European estates.[40] He gave native rumors credibility over the confected facts plied to him by planters committed to maintaining their unencumbered control. Valck was ousted from the service and excised from colonial hagiographic history not only for knowing too little and too much but also for his sense of what counted as evidence and from whom he sought it.

The iconic Enlightenment motto "dare to know" may have animated some of the new "self-consciously scientific Orientalists" that Christopher Bayly described in his study of British political intelligence in northern India in the 1790s.[41] And Andrew Goss may be right that the "floracrats" in Java who collected and classified plants "strove for" an Enlightenment ideal of ordered knowledge. But such quests and bravado were hardly typical of Dutch colonial practice in the Netherlands Indies. Massive compilations of statistics, scientific initiatives, and political intelligence were joined with a circumspect disposition toward knowledge of the world in which colonial civil servants lived. Someone like Frans Carl Valck was not alone in having to reckon with the failure of that which he was schooled to take as prevailing common sense. It proved to be a poor guide for when and from what he should have properly turned away. Trust, the backbone of civil service collegiality, was strained in a social environment in which people could not be sure to belong to the legal (European) status they claimed or to be whom they morally claimed to be. Or perhaps distrust was more deeply carved into colonial relations among Europeans by the compounded illegitimacies of the profits and privileges accrued from their ventures.

The notion that the Enlightenment enforced a reduction to the "calculability of the world" had more success in some domains of Indies administration than others. If the moral sciences were born of Enlightened Reason, the Dutch colonial archives tell other tales—ones in which the tools of marking racial categories proved too blunt to do their work, inadequately sharpened to read those "invisible ties," affective bonds, and moral proclivities for which physical attributes provided poor access. Intuitions about comportment, habits, and affiliations filled in that with which more scientific criteria and measurements could not contend. And if statistics was designed to subject social relations to the 'sweet despotism of reason,' as Ian Hacking

40. Stoler, *Along the Archival Grain*, 181–236.
41. Christopher Alan Bayly, *Empire and Information: Intelligence Gathering and Social Communication in India, 1780–1870* (Cambridge: Cambridge University Press, 1996), 118.

argues, it was a tool of limited use.[42] It could not predict the political aspirations of those who threatened the state's projects nor could it identify the abnormally strong and willful sentiments among them. It could not distinguish true Europeans from those who sought sundry means to claim that status. Not least, it could not identify those who would remain reliably loyal from those whose sentiments might turn them recalcitrant, stubbornly resistant to higher command, or subversive.

Let me underscore a critical point: At issue was not a "failed" project of reason that nevertheless held dominant sway. There were successes and failures, to be sure. My point is that rational, scientific ways to know the world were insufficient for governance. They inadequately describe the temperament of rule, and they poorly capture how it worked.

In an incisive study of Britain's "covert empire" in the Middle East, Priya Satia argues that intuition guided intelligence strategies precisely because rational knowledge could not. This "intuitive mode" may have been a "radical departure from the dogged empiricism of earlier and contemporary efforts to gather information" within the British Empire, as she argues. Still, it was neither an invention that emerged with the Great War, nor was it specific to British intelligence operations, as she insists.[43] Intuitive knowledge directed not only early twentieth-century spies on the edges of empire. In the Netherlands Indies, it shaped the archives of security that document nineteenth-century imperial governance; the imagined and real threats on which those intuitions fed; and the intimate, secreted domains of bedroom and nursery into which the quest for "security" invariably sought to reach.[44] What separated grounded intuitions from extravagant fabrication was not always clear. However one might describe that space in between, it would not be captured by a commitment to "rational knowledge."

Nor was this the case just for the Indies. Thomas Richards locates an "epistemological paranoia" that "conflated knowledge and terror" as the hallmark of a British "corporate subject" in whom that paranoia "can be seen

42. Ian Hacking, *The Taming of Chance* (Cambridge: Cambridge University Press, 1990), 35.

43. Priya Satia, *Spies in Arabia: The Great War and the Cultural Foundations of Britain's Covert Empire in the Middle East* (Oxford: Oxford University Press, 2010), 6.

44. For discussion of these sorts of "security" issues, see Ann Laura Stoler, *Race and the Education of Desire: Foucault's History of Sexuality and the Colonial Order of Things* (Durham, NC: Duke University Press, 1995), esp. 137–64.

as part of a larger and systematic phenomenology of rearmament." Richards's insights about "epistemological panic" draw on colonial fiction, but these are descriptions that make sense of a much wider imperial phenomenon across the globe.[45] From what was then the Indies to South Asia, the "supremacy of reason" might better be termed a fantasy of reason applied to the phantoms of empire.

Already figured as a key diacritic of the Enlightenment and of Empire, Reason is something whose authority we as colonial historians are quick to question, but not its authority among colonial agents themselves. Doing so exposes equivocations that otherwise would have no rightful place. If we take one common definition of "rational knowledge" as that which allows one to order categories, recognize viable categories, and include or exclude members from them, its preeminent authority seems more tenuous, more fragile, less suited to bear its authoritative weight. Among empire's agents, category errors were rampant and markers of difference were fluid and vexed. Directors of orphanages had only vague guidelines when confronted with light-skinned children who chose to stay with their native mothers or fathers. Colonial lawyers filled their briefs on the regulation of mixed marriage with densely footnoted exegeses on the barrage of claims to European rights and membership (or outright rejection of them) that laws could not help them assess.[46]

"Rational knowledge" did not always fail its purveyors and practitioners, but in situations in which it did, it tended to do so again and again. Decisions about who counted as a European and by what measure—whether racial attributes derived from the tainted milk of a native woman who was or was not an infant's mother; at what age a child of mixed parentage could be lost or redeemed as European; whether Maltese or Italians in colonial Algeria were really French or merely "neo-French," as the historian Pierre Nora disparagingly called them (only designated French by their "identity papers" as he wrote and as we saw in chapter 4)—relied on multiple ways to apprehend and evaluate what Clifford Geertz once called "the tonalities and temper" of the common sense of their social world.[47] Reasoning,

45. Thomas Richards, The Imperial Archive: Knowledge and the Fantasy of Empire (London: Verso, 1993), 114.

46. See the Vereenging Pro Juventute, Jogykarta, Verslag over het jaar 1934, Pro Juventute society, which documents the choices that parents of "mixed-blood" children, and the choices of those children, that were contra the expectations of their desires.

47. See Pierre Nora, Les français d'Algérie (Paris: Bourgois, 2012), and discussion of Nora's selective "lieux de memoire" in chapter 4.

the philosopher Susan James asserts, is "arduous." By popular Enlightenment notions of reason, it was "severe, rigorous, strict, exact, and above all
unpersuasive."[48] In the Indies, intuition and the "considered thought" of common sense, conveyed in "temper" and "tonalities," could sometimes have
more purchase in the gray borderlands of race and in the invisible networks
of "the enemy" that imperial intelligence was charged to trace.[49] Racialized
exemptions and exclusions depended not on a fixed set of essentialisms but
on protean and strategic rearrangements of them.[50] The Enlightenment notion of reason—that James describes as "strict" and "exact"—did not.

Intuition, as Aristotle imparted to his disciples, was the basis of reasoned wisdom, but colonial intuition was turned to other ends. It emanated
from an elaborately imagined world of potential enemies in the making,
poised to storm Europeans' guarded privilege and sequestered space. Colonial functionaries and agents were more aware than we, who feverishly cull
their archived inscriptions, of their piecemeal knowledge and how much
evaded what they were charged to count, measure, anticipate, and control.

If these tasks were usually seamlessly carried out, as my first distracted
readings of the Dutch colonial archives' formulaic narratives seemed to suggest, in repeated returns to those documents, I have come to see more the
uneasy labor that could appear as surface tremors through tedious reports
and rote refrains. Contexts were never givens. The choice of one rather than
another could give credence to one set of truth claims, dismiss the validity
of another, or frame the parameters and thus the "causes" sought to explain
an "event." Choices of context imply epistemic commitments, how they are
contested and change. Whether the slashing of a European planter and his
family was attributed to an Aceh-based Islamic assault on European rule
or to the idiosyncratic passions of an abused and vengeful estate worker
marshaled both different kinds of "proof" and different ways to assess
emotionally charged cognitive states. What emerges as a choice of context
indexes both how people imagine they know what they do and the affective
grids of intelligibility on which they draw.

How words are used and repeated in these archives draws us close to this
epistemic unease to broach something more than the strictures of bureau-

48. James, *Passion and Action*, 215.
49. Clifford Geertz, "Common Sense as a Cultural System," in *Local Knowledge: Further
Essays in Interpretive Anthropology* (New York: Basic, 1983), 84.
50. On racial "essences" as protean rather than fixed, see chapter 7.

cratic conventions. Phrases and wording sometimes adhered to protocol; sometimes they marked faltering about the suitability and proper use of received designations. Such hesitancies unsettle the sure-footed criteria of what "goes without saying" so central to the force of common sense and to the fictive clarities of a taxonomic state.

The intensity and density of the debates that came to a crescendo in the late nineteenth century around one particular social category, that of the *inlandsche kinderen* (who were neither natives [*inlandsche*] nor children [*kinderen*], as a literal translation would suggest), offers a "paradigmatic" site of this unease in the sense that Giorgio Agamben understands a paradigm, where the contradictions are on the surface—acute and exposed.[51] What colonial agents had to say about the category of *inlandsche kinderen* (a designation that constantly slipped among "poor whites," Indo-Europeans, *déclassé* Europeans born in the Indies, and those who were mixed and veered more toward native cultural sensibilities than European ones), and who officials differently imagined they were, is a story about the making and unmaking of that crafted clustering in the Indies' racial history. But it is not about that alone. It is also about the competing intelligibilities that racial regimes called forth and on. Hesitance about social labels and uncertainty about their use provides entry points to identify moments of doubt and perturbation, what Foucault might have defined as a historical "event."[52] These are moments of discernment, when colonial common sense and convention failed them, when what people thought they knew, and how they might know it, they found they did not.

Inlandsche kinderen was a mobile designation about social milieu, an appellate, and a political fact. That many Eurasian children were raised in "respectable" families made no difference to the reams of colonial literature, newspaper articles, and confidential official documents that worried incessantly about the micro-environments in which they lived: whether children were acquiring the dispositions and cultural competence to be European

51. Giorgi Agamben, "What Is a Paradigm?" *The Signature of All Things* (New York: Zone Books, 2009), 9–32.

52. Foucault, "Table Ronde du 20 Mai 1978," 23. Foucault's phrase is actually "rupture des évidences," but I prefer Rabinow's rendering of it as a "breach of self-evidence," which better captures (than would a literal translation) something between a "break" and a "gap" and Foucault's identification of that which at one moment seems so obvious and at another no longer is so: see Paul Rabinow, *Anthropos Today: Reflections on Modern Equipment* (Princeton, NJ: Princeton University Press, 2003), 41.

or, in the case of poor, mixed-blood children, whether they were properly schooled in the unspoken rules that would limit their aspirations. Racialized perceptions and practices are rarely diminished or deterred by contrary empirical evidence. These are the complex social imaginaries that shape the emotional economies and sensory regimes by which people distinguish "us" from "them."

Displaced histories are folded within the changing contours of who "fit" or refused the labels assigned to them. No colonial mind-set is lurking in the pen's shadow; no overarching *mentalité* is floating in the ether of colonial space. We would do better as historians of colonial governance to attend to the ground that lies between the resilience and fragility of categories, to the moments in which reasoning went awry, when the rubrics of "poor whites" and "mixed bloods" made little sense because people and things were not what and where they ought to be. Under such conditions, the "ought" could waver—either reassert its authority or dissolve in the face of its contradictions; a term might be abandoned, substituted, and changed. The contested epistemics of race emerge in these moments, the explicit and oblique ways on which the knowledge of social kinds relied. Social ontologies (and, specifically, racial ones) were reassembled and remade. Uncertainty provided its coordinates. As I argued in *Along the Archival Grain*, a Weberian model of bureaucratic might, driven by rationality and accredited knowledge, filters out the complex managed sentiments on which it was based.[53] I fleshed out parts of this argument there and will not do so here. But it might be useful to reiterate one key point: "The political rationalities of Dutch rule—strategically reasoned forms of administrative common sense informing policy and practice—were grounded in the management of such affective states, in assessing both appropriate sentiments and those that threatened to fly 'out of control.' "[54]

SENSIBILITIES IN POLITICAL RATIONALITIES

One defining feature attributed to the Enlightenment project was the normative guide it is said to have offered for subordinating individual passions to their rightful place in the social realm and for the clear and principled distinctions it made between reasoned judgment and affective life. Both features have been subject in recent scholarship to critical reevaluation. As

53. Stoler, *Along the Archival Grain*, 57.
54. Stoler, *Along the Archival Grain*, 59.

students of seventeenth-century and eighteenth-century philosophy, such as Susan James, now argue, the passions deserve to be placed central to early modern Enlightenment philosophy.[55] Governance required a fine-tuned knowledge of the affections. Members of the Indies administration understood that well. Colonial statecraft took seriously the force of affect and strove for its mastery. And as Albert Hirschman reminds us, the harnessing of individual passion was at once a concern of seventeenth-century political thinking and a flourishing feature of nineteenth-century liberalism. It was also a central diacritic in designating race.

Following Hirschman's genealogy allows us to work differently through the politics of the darker sentiments and sensibilities that imperial projects of the twentieth century and twenty-first century continued to produce and on which they have continued to depend: anxiety, fear, and paranoia. These were fundamental to forging the technologies of security that cordoned off people and space, those strategies that forced migration or restricted movement and legitimated expulsions, manhunts, and incarceration. It is these affects that might be considered among those "slow violences" that rational knowledge could not explain or wholly help us comprehend.[56]

Gertrude Himmelfarb contends that it is misleading to imagine that the Enlightenment belonged to the French or that their "ideology of reason" faithfully captures what the Enlightenment was about. By her account, its more "enlightened" expression emerged from the analytic and political impulses of British and Scottish moral philosophers, with their attention to the "social affections."[57] She is right to point to the affections but grossly misconstrues the sorts of political work those affections were enlisted to do. Her account of the beneficent virtues does not stray from Europe or the United States. But the distribution of compassion, sympathy, and pity—who had them and to whom they were rightly directed—was pivotal to the workings of imperial formations. Each was part of the architecture of empire—with exacting exclusions and inequities structured through them. They charted the affective grid that separated true Europeans and their colonized Others and provided the affective grounds on which racially distinguished

55. James, *Passion and Action*, 2–3.

56. Rob Nixon, *Slow Violence and the Environmentalism of the Poor* (Cambridge, MA: Harvard University Press, 2006).

57. Gertrude Himmelfarb, " 'Social Affections' and Religious Dispositions," in *The Roads to Modernity: The British, French, and American Enlightenments* (New York: Vintage, 2005).

"benevolent" institutions were formed. Social hierarchies, as I have argued, were not only created and bolstered by sympathy for empire's subjects; such sentiments were judgments in themselves.[58] Pity demanded distance and preserved it as forcefully as did segregated housing, pools, and schools.[59]

Himmelfarb's chosen exemplar of an Enlightenment legacy makes precisely this point, despite her own intention. She found it alive and well in George Bush Sr.'s solution to curb welfare and social services for the poor. His call on "compassionate conservatism" was an aggressively punitive social project that she praises for "encourag[ing] the social affection of the one while respecting the moral dignity of the other." On the contrary, compassionate conservatism was boldly marked by a racialized principle of distinction between those who deserve public welfare and those who do not. As Hannah Arendt parsed pity, it is the pleasure of "being sorry without being touched in the flesh."[60]

Partha Chatterjee has held that Reason with a capital R went "untouched and unscathed in the colonial project," following Hegel's lesson that because reason does not work directly on the subject or lower itself to becoming a particular thing, it cunningly makes the individual's passions work in its service. Some of the British colonial elite may indeed have seen empirical science as universal, rational knowledge, free from prejudice and passion. But as Johannes Fabian makes the case, the practices of British scientific explorers in Africa showed otherwise. In *Out of Our Minds*, a "critique of imperialist reason," Fabian argues that the accumulation of ethnographic knowledge was inseparable from the prejudices and passions that equally guided these men.[61] Affective and emotional registers of experience were prerequisites, not hindrances, to what they sought to know and how they were able to know it.[62]

58. See Amit Rai, *The Rule of Sympathy: Sentiment, Race, and Power, 1750–1850* (New York: Palgrave, 2002), and my discussion of the imperial politics of sentiment in chapter 5. On emotions as appraisal and judgment see Robert Solomon, "On Emotions as Judgments," American Philosophical Quarterly 25 (1988): 183–91.

59. Luc Boltanski, "The Politics of Pity," in *Distant Suffering: Morality, Media and Politics* (Cambridge: Cambridge University Press, 1999), 3–19.

60. Hannah Arendt, *On Revolution* (1963) (New York: Penguin, 2006), 80.

61. Johannes Fabian, *Out of Our Minds: Reason and Madness in the Exploration of Central Africa* (Berkeley: University of California Press, 2000), 54.

62. It is hard not to notice that many of those most concerned with this relationship are eminent students of South Asian history, and of British empire in particular. I would only note that just as our understanding of the gradated degrees of sovereignty

Knowledge production among some scientific explorers was dependent on affective knowledge; the art of governance was as well. Dutch colonials wrote incessantly of the *stille kracht* (the hidden force of the Indies) that could destroy their collective project, the European community's security, an individual's sense of composure—what counted to maintain a European self and soul. This is not to rehearse *Heart of Darkness* but, rather, to underscore a point Edward Said made in his study of Conrad's letters.[63] Conrad and those Europeans about whom he wrote lived not with the assurance of Reason at their backs, but with a troubled relationship to what they knew—or, as Said put it, with a "problematic knowledge" of themselves. The syntax of reason was found wanting, an impoverished grammar of intelligibility for what they needed to do and to act on. It thus was not only in the allegedly mystical, tradition-bound world of the colonized other where passions ran amok and where people were animated by spectral visions and fears. Panivong Norindr is not alone in claiming that it was "phantasmic Indochina" rather than anything else that most French thought they knew so well.[64]

It was not just the failures of reason that disrupted the coherence of colonial agents and the policies they were charged to enforce but an exuberant imaginary that produced a commitment to something else, what one might argue was a fundamental and frequent turn away from reason that organized a spectrum of nervous, expectant, protective small and large-scale instances of violence, interdictions, and gestures: infeasible blueprints for colonial projects; improbable security measures; and a continually shifting set of confinements, detentions, and displacements that were to reorder and bind the social and spatial partitions of their privileged, profitable, and insecure world and could never do so enough.

EPISTEMIC PRACTICE

Recent thinking about the politics of epistemology and empire leave little room to examine the *practical-epistemic space* in which empire's architects and

---

on which imperial formations have been based do not coincide with the South Asian template, Dutch, French, U.S., German, and Spanish historiography has been far less bent on granting a Rule of Reason—or assaults on it—such a prominent place.

63. Edward W. Said, *Joseph Conrad and the Fiction of Autobiography* (New York: Columbia University Press, 2008).

64. Panivong Norindr, *Phantasmatic Indochina: French Colonial Ideology in Architecture, Film, and Literature* (Durham, NC: Duke University Press, 1996).

agents operated. What colonial actors imagined they could know and, more important, *what epistemic habits they developed to know it* required competing, often implicit and changing, epistemic frames. Rather than treating epistemology as a domain of the foundational, architectural, and fixed, I share a premise of historical and social epistemology: epistemic considerations are neither transcendent nor abstract. They are squarely of the colonial world. Treating epistemology as a navigational strategy alters field and ground and what questions we ask. People sought to identify that which they knew they could not see: "racial membership" or political desires that were unavailable to ocular evidence. They sought to distinguish politically motivated passions from private ones, to know when the latter could turn into the former—and to know when they needed to act on them.

In the Indies, the project and problems of "making up people" pervaded the administrative archives, the Dutch-language press, and a century of colonial fiction and fed the epistemic anxieties that eddied around them.[65] The production of social kinds entailed the codification of self-evident measures to distinguish social privilege and political exclusion. In a colony where the legal stipulation for being granted European equivalent status entailed evidence of being "at home" in a European milieu, what counted as adequate knowledge went beyond the preparatory courses for a civil service career. In distinguishing race, upbringing could be given more weight than paternity; comportment, more credence than color; and cultural competence, more weight than birth. In this trained and strained social space, colonial agents relied on an intuitive reading of sensibilities more than science, on a measure of affective states of affiliations and attachments more than origins, and on assessments of moral civilities that were poorly secured by color-based taxonomies or visual markers.

Surface perceptions were deemed unreliable, producing what the Dutch called fabricated and fictive Europeans; Europeans in disguise; and what French officials in Indochina most feared, natives and *métis* who fraudulently were legally recognized and passed as European. These categorical errors could be accessed only by another kind of knowledge, probabilistic predictions about the political consequences of people's affective and moral states.

---

65. Ian Hacking, "Making Up People," in *Historical Ontology* (Cambridge, MA: Harvard University Press, 2004), 99–114.

Prolific in producing the feared, the unrealized, and the ill-conceived, such assessments point to sites of troubled social topographies and agitations of a peculiar kind that prompted infeasible plans that could not be carried out, and if they were, that could not be sustained.[66] The fact that political scientists today can posit the obsession with the anticipatory future tense in contemporary security regimes as a hallmark of our current political moment belies more than a historical myopia. It does more than truncate the historical depth of these imaginaries. It misses the imperial coordinates of the quest to specify the interior states of those whose reasoned affects remain unintelligible to the sorts of reason defined by imperial control.

Following these breaches and this faltering renders the panoptic state based on rational knowledge a frail conceit. Even in such a quintessential product of bureaucracy and reasoned procedure as the state commission, preconceived protocols repeatedly failed. For the European Pauperism commissions of 1901, "objective" data never told them enough. What they resorted to were commonly intuited notions of who belonged where; how people spoke to their young, sat, ate, and dressed. For such commissions on race, scientific procedures were only one limited way for science to read and render what distinguished social kinds.

One is reminded of Max Weber's contention that bureaucracies excise those domains they cannot measure by eliminating from official business love, hatred, and all purely personal, irrational, and emotional elements that escape calculation.[67] But Weber knew better, as his later interlocutors have shown: Weber's work on rationality, as Alan Sica has argued, was "a study in tension" between rationality and what Julien Freund argues was at the core of Weber's thinking, "the empire of the irrational."[68] I would put it otherwise. In the Dutch colonial bureaucracy, emotional elements bore epistemic and political weight. These were as much the grammar of rule as anything else. Disdain, contempt, and envy were instantiations and performatives of relations of power, judgments, and interpretations of the social and political world. They served as incisive markers of rank,

66. On these plans, see Stoler, *Carnal Knowledge and Imperial Power*, 106–8.

67. Max Weber, "Legitimate Authority and Bureaucracy" (1922), in *Economy and Society* (2013).

68. Alan Sica, *Weber, Irrationality, and Social Order* (Berkeley: University of California Press, 1988), 12, and Julien Freund, quoted in Sica, 13.

of privileges being lost or won—the unstated rules of expulsion and exemption.

SECURITY: BETWEEN REASON AND *DÉRAISON*

Any reading of Dutch colonial literature astounds one with its obsessive concern with a (supposedly fragile) orde.—Benedict R. O'G. Anderson, "The Languages of Indonesian Politics," 1966 (emphasis added)

This line, written by the eminent Indonesianist scholar Benedict Anderson, in 1966 would seem to warrant little rewriting. But when it was republished twenty-four years later, the crucial parenthetical phrase, "(supposedly fragile)," disappeared and was replaced by "menaces to order."[69] For Anderson it might have been a trivial revision (with the snide adverbial remark "supposedly fragile" perhaps excised as redundant, given that a reference to Dutch "obsessive concern" with order already nailed the critique). But I would argue something else: It is in the slippage between the adjectival phrase "supposedly fragile" and the noun "menace" that much of the workings of Dutch colonial governance operated and that its "security" concerns and the affective charge they animated took shape. If *rust en orde* (peace and order) were keywords of the Dutch colonial state's vision of its tranquilizing task, what constituted a threat both exceeded its tools of measurement and was more incipient and veiled than its tools could assess. Implying that Dutch authorities only imagined their rule to be fragile (as a rationale to justify their intelligence apparatus) flattens a more complicated story. It turns away from what we might learn from that troubled space about what Dutch authorities knew and how they knew it. As John Austin might have suggested in his "Plea for Excuses," the phrase "supposedly fragile" dismisses the question before it is asked.[70] It obscures how reasons were crafted; how good Reason was affirmed; and how much unreason informed, not aberrant moments in the arts of governance, but the phantoms produced, the fears circulated. Not least, it glides past how violence was rendered as an appropriate response when reasonably framed.

69. Cf. Anderson, "The Languages of Indonesian Politics," 98, and Benedict R. O'G. Anderson, "The Languages of Indonesian Politics," in *Language and Power: Exploring Political Cultures in Indonesia* (Ithaca, NY: Cornell University Press, 1990), 133.

70. J. L. Austin, "A Plea for Excuses: The Presidential Address," *Proceedings of the Aristotelian Society* 57, new series (January 1, 1956): 1–30.

Rust en orde was an incantation and a political concept that drew other concepts into its frame and fold. Along with it came the invariable iteration of the threat to "security" (veiligheid) and the fear of "insecurity" (onveiligheid), which, perhaps, better captures the unquiet affective space Dutch colonials inhabited and the shapes of the phantoms with which they lived. In the corridors of imperial authority and in the lives of Europeans who sought to be "at home" in the colonies, security was a common noun that worked as a political concept. It could expand and extend, slide between scales, and, not least, create subjects—and their ascribed proclivities—to be defended against and contained. As Thomas Moore has argued, security regimes operate between contractual claims to protect and the demand for "obedience," both making "real" how a security regime produces its own authorization.[71]

"Security" is an epistemic object that occupies the conceptual and concrete space between "what is thought to be known and what is beyond imagination."[72] As a feature of imperial governance, "security" is put to work in multiple domains to call forth its object. The quest for security and the safeguarding of it could mobilize the deployment of Dutch battalions readied with arms on the outskirts of Batavia in 1848; produce a demand for treatises on colonial household management (minutely attentive to where servant quarters were placed and who cared for one's young). "Security" hovered in the interstices of the legal codes that separated mixed-blood children from their native mothers; it was splayed across the repeated commissions on impoverished whites and blurred into the "moral safety" of the young, confirming the necessity of nurseries for European children for "reasons of state."[73]

Imperial practice and imperial knowledge were, in part, "predicated on making common sense of the categories of persons against which society had to be defended and reshuffling this membership as situations changed."[74] A broader genealogy of security as a concept would not be an

71. Thomas Moore, "Epistemic Security Regimes," n.d., https://www.researchgate.net/publication/228802295_Epistemic_Security_Regimes.

72. Rheinberger, Toward a History of Epistemic Things, 11.

73. I use the term "reasons of state" here not with reference to a specific state apparatus of a particular moment in European history, as Foucault uses it, but instead with reference to the connotation of the prevalent term used in colonial documents, rust en orde.

74. Ann Laura Stoler, "On Archival Labor: Recrafting Colonial History," Ketelaar Annual Lecture delivered at the National Archive, The Hague, 2011, 157.

inexorable teleology of the present. It would attend to how political common sense gets forged, how related histories are severed, how specific places are retooled with substitutable populations in them. Such a genealogy would ask how imperial displacements continue to shape the sensibilities and logics that underwrite the distribution of containments and managed mobilities of our world today.[75]

THE UNDERSIDE OF REASON

As Ian Hacking writes in his preface to the now complete version of Foucault's *History of Madness*, the key term *déraison* quickly dropped out of the abridged French editions after 1961 and never appeared in the English translation. Hacking nevertheless argues that déraison was the central and elusive concept that defined Foucault's project.[76] Although Hacking is tentative about what Foucault meant by it, he knows what it is not: Déraison is neither the opposite of reason nor is it reduced to madness alone. But I think Foucault's treatment of déraison suggests something else, a particular sort of analytic move that runs through much of his work. Déraison might be better understood not as a fixed noun with assigned attributes, but as a relational concept, as a methodological entry point, a diagnostic of sorts that registers historical movements, the subtle shifts, imperceptible substitutions and boldfaced reversals between what was once deemed reasonable and then was not. Déraison seems to operate as a relational concept with respect to a changing norm, to those practices and perceptions that were once deemed reasonable and then slip to its outer shores. Déraison may be a way to mark that which recedes from and rejects convention's demands, when unquiet minds can no longer be trusted to be predictable, when they or we become unreliable guardians of common sense.

This relational quality of déraison is close to what Michel Serres also describes as central to Foucault's work. For Serres, déraison works as a displacement that produces "the closed insularity of reason" to track how

75. One part of this project is described in chapter 10.

76. Ian Hacking, "Foreword," in Michel Foucault, *History of Madness*, ed. Jean Khalfa (New York: Routledge, 2006), ix–xii. This is more fully explored in Ian Hacking, "Déraison," paper presented at Foucault across the Disciplines conference, University of California, Santa Cruz, March 2, 2008 and published in James Faubion, ed., *Foucault Now: Current Perspectives in Foucault Studies* (Cambridge: Polity, 2014), 38–51.

that insularity "slowly takes shape."[77] As Foucault expressed it, "Unreason slowly creeps back to that which condemns it, imposing a form of retrograde servitude upon it, where recognition of this unreason is the mark, the sign and almost the emblem of reason itself."[78]

Unreason, then, is not reason's opposite. Rather, unreason is reason's repeatedly incited and verifying moment, shaped by its normative and changing truths. Nowhere is the force of Reason more vulnerable than at its center, among its staunchest and most insistent advocates. Architects and agents of empire might be seen as those who occupy this unstable, normalized place. To live in and off empire entails a complex set of distorting psychic dispositions, warped sensibilities that ricochet between obsessional attentiveness to imagined sources of insecurity, "revulsions" cultivated (as Albert Memmi described them), and studied, protective disregard.[79] Imperial dispositions have been and continue to be marked by a negative space—that from which those with privilege and standing could excuse themselves—an assertion of the "necessity" of violence when reason is too pallid to justify their exemption and not sufficient to allow them to do so.[80] Unreason in these colonial archives is a distinguishing mark attributed to those who do not abide by colonial common sense, ascribed to those off-

77. Michel Serres, "The Geometry of the Incommensurable," in *Foucault and His Interlocutors*, ed. Arnold I. Davidson (Chicago: University of Chicago Press, 1997), 51.

78. Foucault, *History of Madness*, 345.

79. Albert Memmi, *The Colonizer and the Colonized* (1957) (Boston: Beacon, 1991), 27.

80. Studies of "security" and its inscribed animation of "insecurity" as concepts, regimes, and political technologies of governance—and not least, as a key feature in the magic making of imperial states—has spawned a multidisciplinary literature at a velocity and reach far too vast to summarize here. Among the work I have found the most helpful to think with are Michael Dillon's Foucauldian-inspired work on security and biosecurity over the last decade: see esp. Michael Dillon, *Politics of Security: Towards a Political Philosophy of Continental Thought*. London: Routledge, 1996), and "The Sovereign and the Stranger," in *Sovereignty and Subjectivity*, ed. Jenny Edkins, Nalini Persram, and Véronique Pin-Fat (Boulder, CO: Lynne Rienner, 1999), 117–40. For a discerning treatment of security (with a decidedly non-Foucauldian bent) as a political concept and its deep genealogy in political thought, see John T. Hamilton, *Security: Politics, Humanity, and the Philology of Care* (Princeton, NJ: Princeton University Press, 2013). For a focus on "insecurity" in particular, see Josefina Echavarría Alvarez, "Re-thinking (In)security Discourses from a Critical Perspective," *Asteriskos* 1–2 (2006), 61–82, as well as the contributions in Michael Dillon and Andrew W. Neal, *Foucault on Politics, Security and War* (Basingstoke, UK: Palgrave Macmillan, 2011)—notably, the contribution by Didier Bigo, who writes incisively on the subject.

guard, uncommon, unauthorized critical reflections that emerge when one does not look away.

But unreason may take another course: bursting the seams of reason with proliferating efforts to contain and manage what cannot be predicted and known. In so doing, insecurity and demands for ever more demonstrations of security—and ever more vigilance directed at potential sites of security breaches and where techniques of detection may be lax—produce sensory derangements, intuitive hunches, structures of feeling that perforate the hyper-rationalized technologies on which security regimes and defense of society come to depend.[81]

Imperial histories and the violence they condoned operate within and are dependent on the force derived from the conditional, anticipatory tense. Imperial polities engender an *unheimlich* world of those imagined possibly to be masking their intentions, potentially hiding their "real" attachments— those whom empire's agents took their external and most proximate threats to be. Such an approach turns us from the ready-made synthesis of Reason to expansions, contractions, and reversals of its making. Concepts do not come fully hatched but, as Hans-Jörg Rheinberger notes, from "spatio-temporal singularities," more like "auxiliary organs of touch," smell, and premonition in the flesh.[82] Importantly, a history of such epistemic things arrives at no point of completion, because there is "no possibility of anticipating the future object constellations that accrue from it."[83]

The universals that have been regarded as organizing imperial taxonomies were breached from the start. Challenges came from those within the radical strands of the Enlightenment, those from outside its Europe-bound philosophical orbit, among those who reworked its principles—and invented their own—across the imperial globe, and from many more who never

81. Rebecca Lemov broaches this issue from another fascinating angle in a study of a set of scientific projects in Micronesia, the "Nuclear Pacific," and elsewhere during the late 1940s and 1950s, initiated just two years after the U.S. occupation and trusteeship of Micronesia was established. Under the rubric of the Coordinated Investigation of Micronesian Anthropology, a multidisciplinary team set out to develop "projective techniques" that "promised access to new areas of the human psyche," in a quest for an "automatic transparency" about "what the individual doesn't want to tell and what he himself does not know": see Rebecca Lemov, "On Being Psychotic in the South Seas, circa 1947: Making a Science of the Human," in *Colloquium at Max-Planck-Institut für Wissenschaftsgeschichte*, Berlin, 2010.

82. Rheinberger, *Toward a History of Epistemic Things*, 14.

83. Rheinberger, *Toward a History of Epistemic Things*, 14.

thought about it at all.[84] Frantz Fanon was not alone in identifying colonialism and racism as European afflictions that would cut off its breath. Unreason organized the political grammar of empire at its beginning—and perhaps not least as it has been concentrated in the rationales for torture in the name of curbing violence, in the "standard operating procedures" of the U.S. presence in Iraq, in the U.S. Department of Homeland Security's billion-dollar initiatives to identify people's propensities for "Violent Intent" (prior to any act) with "non-invasive brain scans" and by calculating the tautness of their posture and body temperatures.[85] It takes privileged shelter in a colonizing Zionist "reason" about an authentic Jewish homeland in Palestine that underwrites the relentless Israeli incursions into Palestinian land. Unreason organizes the continued singling out of French citizens whose parents may be of North African origin. It displays its force not least in the U.S. State Department's surreal endeavor to identify the attributes of a "Universal Adversary."[86] It is in the simulation model of the "Universal Adversary"—with its seven scenarios and four major targets ranging from Islamic terrorists to "disgruntled workers"—that some of the most fantastic imaginaries of U.S. preparedness conjure an amalgamated enemy of state and society in a political logic out of control.

84. See the historical account of the Enlightenment not as a European-generated movement or "thing" but as "the work of historical actors around the world": Sebastian Conrad, "Enlightenment in Global History: A Historiographical Critique." *American Historical Review* 117, 4 (October 1, 2012): 1001.

85. See A. P. Sanfilippo and F. G. Nibbs, "Violent Intent Modeling: Incorporating Cultural Knowledge into the Analytical Procedure," Pacific Northwest National Laboratory, U.S. Department of Energy, August 2007, http://www.pnl.gov/main/publications /external/technical_reports/PNNL-16806.pdf; Ian Sample, "Security Firms Working on Devices to Spot Would-Be Terrorists in Crowd," *The Guardian*, August 9, 2007, http:// www.theguardian.com/science/2007/aug/09/terrorism; Mike Richards, "Comments on 'Project Hostile Intent Plans "Non-Invasive" DHS Brain Scan,'" *The Register*, August 9, 2007, http://forums.theregister.co.uk/forum/1/2007/08/09/no_not_the_mind_probe _again; Allison Barrie, "Homeland Security Detects Terrorist Threats by Reading Your Mind," FoxNews.com, September 23, 2008, http://www.foxnews.com/story/2008/09/23 /homeland-security-detects-terrorist-threats-by-reading-your-mind.html. See also "If Looks Could Kill: Surveillance Technology," *The Economist*, October 23, 2008, http://www .economist.com/node/12465303; "Deception Detection: Identifying Hostile Intent," *Science and Technology*, U.S. Department of Homeland Security, May 2007, http://www.dhs .gov/science-and-technology/deception-detection.

86. David Howe, "National Planning Scenarios: Executive Summaries," iv, Homeland Security Council, July 2004, https://www.facs.org/~/media/files/quality%20programs/trauma/disaster/wmd_dhs_planning.ashx.

Such projects produce their predators and prey, ever more people assigned attributes relevant to security, which in turn amplify what the conceptual and political matrix around "security" must broach and breach. Security regimes play off generic fears that are widely shared and then concentrate and direct those fears to particular sites and situations.[87] Security regimes requisition the protocols of common sense (beware of strange, unfamiliar behavior and people around you), define and then sanctify what is normal, and recruit sensory intuitive knowledge as crucial features of intelligence expertise.

The practices that flourish in the pursuit of "things as they might be" have long undone the "supremacy of reason" as a mark of the Enlightenment and a hallmark of empire, as they each once looked and in the forms they manifest today. What remains striking in this prolific field around security, insecurity, and preparedness is how little it reckons with (beyond just recognizing the fact of an installment of fear) how much work is performed on sensibilities, sensory regimes, and the micro-affective space in which predator and prey are compelled to live. Increased duress is part of its architecture. These are not the supplemental effects of security as a governing project but the very lineaments of its possibility to move so effortlessly between minute and globalizing instantiations, to adhere to flesh and feeling, to make fear a requirement of life, and for it to expand and thrive.

87. Daniel Goldstein has called for a "critical anthropology of security," rightly arguing that " 'security' calls on the power of fear." But his contention that "security" fills "the ruptures that the crises and contradictions of neoliberalism have engendered" misses that the "paradigm of security" has a deeper imperial history and cannot be reduced to a neoliberal effect or invention: Daniel M. Goldstein, "Toward a Critical Anthropology of Security," *Current Anthropology* 51, 4 (August 1, 2010): 487.

RACIAL REGIMES OF TRUTH

"Racial Histories and Their Regimes of Truth" at its first rendition in 1995 was an impatient and perhaps impolitic response to the several fields in which I worked, marking my unease with how race was construed in them. My research was then in the Dutch colonial archives on how categories of race were devised, debated, reworked; my teaching was on colonialism and the plurality of racism's histories. A South African philosopher friend, Windsor Leroke, and I were rereading Nietzsche's "Use and Abuses of History," aloud with the German text by our side, in boisterous weekly sessions, arguing over what an "effective history" of race might look like. *Race and the Education of Desire* had just been published that fall, but I saw more work still to be done, not on colonial racial practices, but on the "grids of intelligibility" that gave them resilience and sustenance. It was the overt and subjacent politics of racial truths—those of the archives and of us who studied them—that grabbed my attention.

Some of the essay's questions were prompted by what I saw as a sharp discrepancy between the contested concepts of race in those nineteenth-century colonial archives and the straightforward manner in which race was treated in contemporary historiography. My questions about the politics of racial epistemologies were prompted both by the fraught debates in those archives about what constituted racial membership and by a decade of following the widening popular appeal of France's National Front (discussed in chapter 8). But it was also a generative moment of confluence with cognitive psychologists, historians of science, and philosophers about the making of "social kinds." My interest was in the sources of the durability of some social (racial) kinds and the effervescence of others. I was perplexed by the epistemological confidence about race and racism in scholarship and the kind of knowledge on which those assured assessments relied.

Politically, the mid-1990s was also a confident moment for (post)colonial studies with a rethinking of colonial representations of difference and new insights about the contemporary cultural dynamics of race. For those working on racial formations in colonial contexts, social-constructionist research agendas felt subversive by their very nature. If racial categories were invented, not given, they could be undone. There was political satisfaction in such accounts—but disquiet, as well. Those working on (post)colonial conditions seemed too convinced of the clarity of colonial racism, too sure of what the racial order of things looked like on colonial ground and in the past tense.

This essay was a reaction to that trend, an effort to question the neat historical narratives that portrayed the "new racism" as rooted in culture, as opposed to the "purer" and earlier biological racism that was not. I admittedly painted the canvas broadly, but the fact of a flattening out of colonial histories is one to which I still hold. I was convinced that we knew less than we thought about colonial and contemporary kinds of racism, their plasticity, and their recursive genealogies.

Also, it was a response to a conceptual and pedagogic dilemma. In teaching on the histories of racism, I found that my graduate seminars designed to explore racism's changing properties, each year, became more difficult to teach and problematic: neither was there a clear trajectory (and certainly not a linear one), in the historical arguments for racially formatted forms of governance, nor did the contemporary historiography—so bent on seeking originary and linear narratives for racism's rise—seem capable of capturing its recuperative course. The essay, then, in part was an effort to make sense of, rather than dismiss or finesse, the profusion of conflicting claims that circled around racism's "origins" and its historical qualities.

But that was only part of the task. "Effective history" in a genealogical mode invited attentiveness to the "minute deviations" in what was agreed to be "true," to the "reversals" in the criteria of what counted as a truth claim about racial logics and what did not. The lines drawn between those pursuing an analysis of discourse and those who saw themselves as committed to the analysis of grounded political and economic relations of power seemed to be a disabling artifice that missed a crucial point: that the making and

imposition of political rationalities was (and remains) part of how categories of people are rendered "real" and acted on—these racial grammars are
the very grit of inequities, the silent partner in the distribution of affect and
at the heart of my attempt to join the subsumption of racial logics and political economy.

Reactions to the essay by those invited to comment by the journal where
it was first published ranged from one who assessed it as "gutsy" to another
who saw it as "too discursive."[1] But what I took to be its most singular argument went basically unaddressed—namely, that despite the ardent critiques of essentialist thinking (across the disciplines at the time), relatively
little attention was given to how such essentialisms actually worked. My
argument was simple: Racial essences, I contended, are made up not of a
fictively fixed and finite set of features but of an essentialized malleable and
substitutable range. Racial essentialism may be constant but its content
is not. Saying that racism "is easy to think" is not necessarily so because
essences stay the same. Racial formations combine elements of *fixity and
fluidity* in ways that make them both resilient and impervious to empirical,
experiential counterclaims.

One could ask why it matters if we (incorrectly) caricature racism in
the past as long as we deal squarely with subverting the power of those racial illusions that are so active today. Part of the answer might be sought
in Foucault's critique of originary histories as those that efface embattled
beginnings. Originary histories found and constrict current and potential
political claims. To suggest that liberalism or colonialism is the foundational
"source" of racism is an argument not only about the past but also about
what subversive strategies can be imagined as effective and viable. Critical
scholars disproving the correspondence between race and intelligence, between physical type and cognitive endowment, as in *The Bell Curve* genre, may
still subscribe to a notion that if really "good science" can prove race to be
nonbiological and nonscientific, it will disappear as a social category and
political force.

Imagining that "race" can be retired from the popular, public, or academic lexicon was as utopian in the past as it is now. The notion that by
scholarly sleights of hand or legal fiat racism can be erased from analytical

1. See the commentaries by Virginia R. Domínguez, Uday Singh Mehta, David
Roediger, and Loïc J. D. Wacquant in Diane E. Davis, ed., *Political Power and Social Theory*
(Greenwich, CT: Emerald Group, 1997), 11.

and popular discourse would be to miss the tactical political practices in which race talk and discourses continue to be mobilized—as a technology of governance at one moment and in defiance of those governing projects at another. As is all too clear today, race remains a salient category, an ever potent and active political one. Whether we look to the "peremptory challenges" by which black jury members now can be and are dismissed for "having dreadlocks" or "bad posture," for making "poor eye contact," or for living in a "poor part of town"—or to the steady stream of shootings of blacks in 2015 by the police (black and white) because of the assumed violent actions that they might perform, the mobile essentialisms attached to race are alive and well, and despite the new configurations of what some take to be a "post-racial" present, they have not gone away.[2] Reckoning with these mobile essentialisms that are not secured by skin color alone, that are seen "through," as W. J. T. Mitchell has put it, is an issue of our times, a history threaded through the racial present.[3]

———————

Before World War II, before the rise of Nazism, before the end of the great European empires . . . race was still seen as an essence, a natural phenomenon, whose meaning was fixed, as constant as a southern star.—Michael Omi and Howard Winant, *"On the Theoretical Status of the Concept of Race"* (1993)

This chapter is about concept work in a charged colonial and contemporary space. It is about the historical narratives provided to account for forms of racism in current scholarship and the epistemological assumptions about race that have long underwritten those arguments. My terrain of inquiry draws on two locations: one from colonial archives of the nineteenth century and early twentieth century, where Dutch and French architects and agents of colonial governance debated the attributes they could assign

2. Adam Liptak, "Exclusion of Blacks from Juries Raises Renewed Scrutiny," *New York Times*, August 16, 2015, http://www.nytimes.com/2015/08/17/us/politics/exclusion-of -blacks-from-juries-raises-renewed-scrutiny.html. And see David Theo Goldberg, *Are We All Postracial Yet?* (Cambridge, UK: Polity, 2015), who swiftly and effectively dispels any notion that postracialism describes the logics and inequities we live with now.

3. On race as a "medium" that we do not look "at" but "through," see W. J. T. Mitchell, *Seeing through Race* (Cambridge, MA: Harvard University Press, 2012), xii.

to identify racial membership and assess its salient and essential qualities; the other from depictions in contemporary scholarship of what racialized distinctions once looked like and how differently they are imagined to manifest now. At issue is a fundamental paradox: on the one hand, sharply divergent truth claims that underpin racism's historical trajectories; on the other hand, a striking and common thread of epistemic principles on which those historical accounts depend. Here I ask what epistemic features and conceptual coordinates hold these narratives in place, how racisms are imagined to be secured, and what originary myths are assigned to them. What truth claims inform these accounts, and on what grounds are some taken to be more credible than others?

Contemporary scholarship insists that there is no single object called racism. It is a plurality—not rehearsals of one another but distinct grammars of perceived differences construed to matter in organizing the acute relational inequalities of our different social worlds.[4] Different meanings are attached to the concept of "race" and the situated racisms they entail. Recognition of plurality in part stems from the attribution of racism's conditions of origin to those distinct events and historical contexts deemed to amplify and solidify unequal distributions of power. More surprising are the features these varied accounts share that, in view of their disparate moments and sites, would seem unlikely to recur. So a basic question: Are these recurrences derived from the fact that these accounts have a common object—that is, racism—as we might expect, or are they derived from the common epistemic assumptions about how race is known that underlies that scholarship? Perhaps more troubling: Are even those critical histories of racism, despite intention, subject to racialized regimes of truth?

I start from a basic observation: that the profusion of historical research on the emergence of what Michael Omi and Howard Winant aptly have referred to as "racial formations" has turned on specifying the changing political semantics of race and how the race concept has been mobilized differently in structuring specific racisms and their hierarchies of difference.[5] Some have sought to identify the convergence of racism with specific

4. When referring to "this scholarship," my focus is on accounts produced largely by academics trained in Euro-American theoretical and methodological traditions and on those convergences and contradictions that dominate much of the contemporary Euro-American historical field.

5. Michael Omi and Howard Winant, *Racial Formations in the United States: From the 1960s to the 1980s* (New York: Routledge and Kegan Paul, 1986).

labor regimes (of slavery or indenture), with colonial conquest and expansion, with the advent of capitalism and globalized wage labor markets, or with the bureaucratic normalizing technologies of modern states. Some have identified racism not as an aberrant feature in the establishment of liberalism and democratic rights but as one of its founding principles.[6] Different chronologies and points of origin follow: the seventeenth century for some; for others, the nineteenth century to designate racism's congruity with nationalism and ascendant bourgeois hegemony in its modern form.[7] My interest is not in the "accuracy" of these depictions and varied dating but in what makes such a range possible.

I offer several arguments: one, that some of the patterned ways in which contemporary racism is understood are predicated on flattened, thinned-out histories of what racism once looked like, so that, two, when scholars distinguish between forms of racism past and present, colonial racism is construed to have existed in more overt and pristine form. Third, I take this "flattening" not to be arbitrary but contingent on a basic and historically problematic contrast between a biologized, somatic racism of the past held up as fundamentally distinct from a more nuanced, culturally coded, and complex racism of the present. This contrast is central to how "new racism" is identified as a more "insidious," "silently sophisticated," "subtle," and "novel" phenomenon.[8] But is it? This disposition toward the past

6. For a close historical examination of this process, see Thomas C. Holt, *The Problem of Freedom: Race, Labor, and Politics in Jamaica and Britain, 1832–1938* (Baltimore: Johns Hopkins University Press, 1992); Edmund S. Morgan, *American Slavery, American Freedom: The Ordeal of Colonial Virginia* (New York: W. W. Norton, 1975); David R. Roediger, *The Wages of Whiteness: Race and the Making of the American Working Class* (London: Verso, 1991); Cornel West, *Prophesy Deliverance! An Afro-American Revolutionary Christianity* (Louisville, KY: Westminster John Knox Press, 1982). For a synthetic treatment of the relationship among racism, liberalism, and modernity, see David Theo Goldberg, *Racist Culture: Philosophy and the Politics of Meaning.* Cambridge, MA: Blackwell, 1993); Uday S. Mehta, "The Liberal Strategies of Exclusion," *Politics and Society* 18, 4 (December 1, 1990): 427–54.

7. George L. Mosse, *Nationalism and Sexuality: Respectability and Abnormal Sexuality in Modern Europe* (New York: H. Fertig, 1997).

8. On contemporary racism as distinguished by its "invisibility," "color-blindness," and subtle but strong cultural coding, see Eduardo Bonilla-Silva, " 'New Racism,' Color-Blind Racism, and the Future of Whiteness in America," in *White Out: The Continuing Significance of Racism,* ed. Ashley Doane and Eduardo Bonilla-Silva (New York: Routledge, 2003); Paul Gilroy, *"There Ain't No Black in the Union Jack": The Cultural Politics of Race and Nation* (Chicago: University of Chicago Press, 1991); Pierre-André Taguieff, *La force du préjugé: Essai sur le racisme et ses doubles* (Paris: La Découverte, 1994). Gilroy writes, "It will be argued [that the new racism's] novelty lies in the capacity to link discourses of

rests on a scholarly quest for origins, for the "original" moment in which the die of race was cast. That search shapes the particular forms that antiracist histories take: sometimes written as narratives of "original sin" and sometimes as narratives that describe innocuous cultural representations of difference "before the (racial) fall."[9] Both promise exit strategies, inoculation, and redemption.

RACIAL EPISTEMOLOGIES: ON THE SENSORY AND THE SOMATIC

This quest for origins affects content as well as form—thus, the profusion of histories that track the Portuguese, Spanish, or French etymology of the word "race" and its first appearance, or those that trace the deep symbolic import of the color "black" and its biblical referents. Etymological exercises are privileged over epistemic ones—that is, reflection on the ways of knowing in which scholars participate and imagine racism to rely. For those who take racism to be first and foremost a "visual ideology," the visible and somatic confirms the "truth" of the racialized self. But this is only one epistemological stance. For others, racial thinking historically counts on visual markers to index distinct hidden properties of different human kinds. The observation may be obvious, but the consequences for how race is assumed to be knowable and racism is assumed to be secured are not.

The concept of race thus operates according to two distinct epistemic claims: in one, the "truth" of race is understood as grounded in somatically observable, *dependable* differences; in the other, the "truth" of racial membership is not visually secured at all. Sometimes surface perceptions are paramount and thus have to be measured, described, or calculated according to an assumed, prescribed, or prevailing norm. In the other, surface perceptions are unreliable. Here, assessment of racial membership depends on a distinctly different form of knowledge that can be considered intuitive and privileged—sensibilities imagined, unarticulated desires that

---

patriotism, nationalism, xenophobia, Englishness, Britishness, militarism and gender difference into a complex system which gives 'race' its contemporary meaning": Gilroy, "There Ain't No Black in the Union Jack," 43.

9. As Nietzsche so famously put it and Foucault drew on for his own genealogical analytics, origins are not endowed with purity or "perfection"; nor are they the most "precious" and pristine moments. They are wrought by conflict and dissensions, and it is these to which we should pay heed and attend: Michel Foucault, "Nietzsche, Genealogy, History," in *The Foucault Reader*, ed. Paul Rabinow (New York: Pantheon, 1984), 77.

cannot be adequately measured, propensities as yet unrealized and masked. Or it may call on "expert" knowledge about "hidden properties" of particular populations in a social body, of those secreted in their depths.

These epistemic standpoints on race yield different stories. Racism is either so pervasive because difference is so palpable and "obvious," or it is lethal and always potentially dangerous and arbitrary because it is not. Critical race histories may either seek to expose the nineteenth-century fiction of physiological perceptible fixities or the nonvisual blood-based fiction of essentialist ones. In both cases, the target is racism's reliance on the artifice of fixed and immutable racial types. Both accounts turn on "proving" the porousness of race as a concept or the permeability of racial categories. Both accounts aim their analytical (and political) assault at the false stability of racial taxonomies on the premise that debunking the fixity of racial categories is necessary, if not sufficient, to dismantle racism that depends on those fabulated distinctions.

The critique of immutability is often shared. An "ocular obsession" often is shared, as well. Here, racism is argued to reside in visual "common sense." It is the power of the gaze on which racial knowledge is conceived to build and on which its resiliency is imagined to rest.[10] But in either historical or contemporary perspective, it is hard to support such a claim. Racism may call on the visual, but the certainties of visual recognition are never as secure as professed. Visual "common sense" is not a historical constant. It has played a minor part in some folk and scientific theories of race and a more prominent one in others. One thing is clear: Popular conceptualizations of racial difference are as *sensory as they are somatic*. They are rarely, if ever, grounded in the latter alone.

Colonial efforts to distinguish and demarcate who would be considered "white," "native," "mestizo," or "black"—and the entitlements to which some would have access, or the housing and jobs from which some would be barred—suggest shifting criteria of assessments, a *changing* set of features from which the essence of race was sought and derived. Among these

---

10. But on the "profound suspicion of vision and its hegemonic role in the modern era," see Martin Jay, *Downcast Eyes: The Denigration of Vision in Twentieth-Century French Thought* (Berkeley: University of California Press, 1993), 14. On the nonvisual features of racial thinking, see Ann Laura Stoler, *Race and the Education of Desire: Foucault's History of Sexuality and the Colonial Order of Things* (Durham, NC: Duke University Press, 1995). See also the cognitive account in Lawrence A. Hirschfeld, *Race in the Making: Cognition, Culture, and the Child's Construction of Human Kinds* (Cambridge, MA: MIT Press, 1998).

criteria, as I have long argued, were cultural competencies, moral codes, vague measures of civilities, emotive proclivities and sensibilities that were poorly secured by chromatic indices—by neither color-based taxonomies nor visual markers.[11] Racial distinctions were profoundly tethered to sensory distinctions of smell, sound, and comportment, "ways of being," assessments of what was deemed in good or bad "taste." They are not so different from those that remain unspoken or underwrite the vernacular idioms in which racialized assessments are "validated"—in hushed speech or blasted across social media in the "new" racism today.

Rather than choose between these approaches, we might better explore the disparity between the "seen" and the "unseen," the interpretive and political space such a tension provides and what it enables. One line of my argument should be clear: The ambiguity of those sets of relationships between the physically apparent and the inner self, the phenotype and the genotype, pigment shade and psychological sensibility are not slips in, or obstacles to, racial thinking and practices but the very conditions for their proliferation and possibility.

ORIGINARY MYTHS AND COMMON SENSE

Competing theories about racism's emergence, coupled with the striking commonalities that different approaches to racism share, invite what should be an obvious question: Why do such contradictory accounts pervade historical narratives? But perhaps the question is off the mark. At issue may not be the incompatibility of these accounts but a basic feature of a race as a concept and configuration of power—what Foucault called its "tactical polyvalence" (la polyvalence tactique) and what I have morphed as its "polyvalent mobility."[12]

Historians' narratives reveal two characteristics: a wide range of dates for the emergence of various forms of racism and multiple explanations for them. A small sample: Harry Bracken offered that seventeenth-century empiricism "and the rise of manipulative models of man" made it more possible to think about different species of humans and was "decisive" in racism's

11. See Ann Laura Stoler, *Carnal Knowledge and Imperial Power: Race and the Intimate in Colonial Rule* (Berkeley: University of California Press, 2002), 79–111.

12. Michel Foucault, *La volonté du savoir* (Paris: Gallimard, 1976), 100. On "polyvalent mobility" see Stoler, *Race and the Education of Desire*, 69.

historical emergence.[13] Cornel West has contended that the "idea of white supremacy" emerged from the power of a modern discourse to "produce and prohibit, develop and delimit forms of rationality, scientificity, and objectivity . . . which draw boundaries for the intelligibility, availability and legitimacy of certain ideas."[14] Étienne Balibar has claimed that universalism and racism are more than "complementary"; they are "contraries affecting one another from the inside."[15]

Collette Guillaumin located racism's origins in the emergence of individuality, in a bounded notion of the "ownership of the self" that "gave rise to the legal expression of racial membership."[16] By her account, the decline of monarchy, and destruction of the naturalized social hierarchies that absolutism endorsed, prompted new naturalized collectivities and new disciplines accounting for them, the latter giving credence to the belief that group membership was organic, based on distinct somatic and psychological traits that differently (but still naturally) "carved nature at its joints" (as Plato, not Guillaumin, put it). John Rex, too, has attributed racist beliefs to the decline of a legal system that upheld inequalities and the sanctions to back it, positing that "the doctrine of equality of economic opportunity [of economic liberalism] and that of racial superiority and inferiority are complements of one another."[17]

George Mosse traced racism's "foundations" to "the Enlightenment"—as do many others—and to "the religious revival of the eighteenth century."[18] For Uday Mehta, racism is an exclusionary principle theoretically inherent in, and crucial to, the development of a liberal polity.[19] Zygmunt Bauman contends that extreme racism, modernity, bureaucratic culture, and the

13. H. M. Bracken, "Essence, Accident and Race," *Hermathena*, 116 (December 1, 1973): 81–96.

14. West, *Prophesy Deliverance!*, 49.

15. Étienne Balibar, "Racism as Universalism." *New Political Science* 8, 1–2 (September 1989): 9–22.

16. Colette Guillaumin, "The Idea of Race and Its Elevation to Autonomous, Scientific and Legal Status," in *Racism, Sexism, Power, and Ideology* (London: Routledge, 1995), 61–98.

17. John Rex, "The Theory of Race Relations: A Weberian Approach," in *Sociological Theories: Race and Colonialism*, ed. UNESCO (Paris: UNESCO, 1980), 131.

18. George L. Mosse, *Toward the Final Solution: A History of European Racism* (New York: H. Fertig, 1985), 3.

19. Mehta, "The Liberal Strategies of Exclusion."

civilizing process are historically and organically bound.[20] David Goldberg, too, locates race as "one of the central conceptual inventions of modernity," embodying the "liberal paradox" that as "modernity commits itself to progressive idealized principles of liberty, equality and fraternity, [it gives rise to] a multiplication of racial identities and the sets of exclusions they prompt and rationalize, enable, and sustain."[21] For Foucault, modern racism not only allows for the establishment of biopower but is the sine qua non of a governing technology that introduces "a fundamental division between those who must live and those who must die," establishing a positive relation between the right to kill and the assurance of life. By Foucault's account, racism is the condition that makes it acceptable to put (certain) people to death in a society of normalization.[22]

This is hardly an exhaustive list. The reader may choose other examples. But the crucial point should not be lost. How can the "emergence," "articulation," "development" of empiricism, universalism, capitalism, modernity, liberalism, the Enlightenment, state structure, and slavery all account for the rise of racism?[23] Racial "theory" in these accounts is systemic and infused through the social body, but thought and articulated by those who truck in high science and high politics, by and large confined to those who explicitly think racial theory with a capital T. There is little agreement about which forms of knowledge and political organization are critical to the making of racism and which are not. For liberalism, universalism and cultural relativism—while frequently seen as the enablers—rarely occupy the same explanatory ground. Sometimes they are treated as bodies of belief and practice whose conceptual architecture gives rise to racism; at other times, they are treated as conjunctural moments that allow for prior practices of subjugation to be

20. Zygmunt Bauman, *Modernity and the Holocaust* (Ithaca, NY: Cornell University Press, 2000).

21. Goldberg, *Racist Culture*, 3.

22. On the wedding of state racism to biopower, see Michel Foucault, *Society Must Be Defended: Lectures at the Collège de France, 1975–76* (New York: Picador, 2003), 254.

23. In contrast to most myths of origin, and to the originary tales of race, timing is specified rather than people or place. Racism is discussed as if its conditions of appearance and reception were contingent on the prior valorization of particular forms of erudite knowledge (as in Philip Curtin's distinction between the fact that "there has always been instant recognition of race" and "the full-blown pseudo-scientific racism" that emerged in the 1840s) or precipitated by conjunctural shifts in economic and political relations (the decline of absolutism, the rise of capitalism): see Philip D. Curtin, *The Image of Africa: British Ideas and Action, 1780–1850* (Madison: University of Wisconsin Press, 1973), 28–29.

realized in consolidated and intensified form. Elsewhere the emphasis is on progressive political principles gone awry (here it is not the principles but their "misuse" that is raced) that retain the potential, when righted, to yield plausible strategies for racism's eradication.

What is at issue here? Either these scholars are not talking about the same phenomenon (their definitions of race and racism differ) or these are indeed complementary correlations, not causal connections. Or is it that the propensity to think in racial terms is a "preserved possibility," a potentiality ready to be activated, but not accounted for, by these historical sightings?[24] Or is it that racism calls up and on a uniquely potent configuration of knowledge and power that facilitates its capacity to weld to varied projects?

Assessments of racism's "true emergence" differ, as well. Whether that date coincides with the advent of slavery, as Barbara Fields has suggested, or with the decline of slavery, as Thomas Holt has argued, or whether it coincides with the bureaucratic procedures of the Spanish Inquisition, with the emergence of modernity and liberalism, or with the making of modern nation-states, in each of these moments racism is characterized as "new."[25] "Newness" may be more than a case of scholarly misrecognition and mistaken identity.[26] "Newness" may index something more basic to the ease with which racial discourse and practices harness to realigned relations of power and production and their institutionalized supports.

This points to another quandary. If racism so often appears new, it also appears as frequently *renewed* for the same contexts, if not for the same authors. As often as scholars recount the uniqueness of racism's invention, they remind us that these forms of racism can be called "new" only because there are earlier ones from which they emerged and that fuel them.[27] Even when the "newness" of racism is heralded, for some commentators, racisms

24. Lawrence A. Hirschfeld, "Art in Cunaland: Ideology and Cultural Adaption," *Man*, 12, 1 (April 1, 1977): 104–23.

25. Cf. Barbara J. Fields, "Ideology and Race in American History," in *Region, Race, and Reconstruction: Essays in Honor of C. Vann Woodward*, ed. J. Morgan Kousser and James M. McPherson (New York: Oxford University Press, 1982), 143–77; Holt, *The Problem of Freedom*.

26. Quests for origins are not unique to racism's histories. They are ubiquitous in how Euro-American religious and secular scholarly traditions have made credible the "facts" on which truth claims are based. What is the case is how committed critics of racism remain to such originary quests and what political narratives they uphold and embrace.

27. See, e.g., the introduction in Tore Bjørgo and Rob Witte, *Racist Violence in Europe* (Basingstoke: Macmillan, 1993).

are treated as systems of thinking and practice that build on primordial loyalties, entrenched conflicts with deep and tenacious historical roots. Leon Poliakov's *Aryan Myth* is a strong case in point. But so is Winthrop Jordan's repeatedly cited argument in *White over Black* that U.S. racism tapped into "deep-seated unconscious needs of at least some white men," atavistic psychological associations of color, contamination, and pollution made readily available to service new social stratigraphies and classifications.[28]

Rather than reconciling these contradictory claims, it may be more useful to take another tack: to question whether these competing claims are not evidence of a fundamental feature of what Barbara and Karen Fields call racecraft itself—namely, its capacity and potential to work though sedimented and familiar cultural representations and relations of subjugation that simultaneously tap into and feed the emergence of new ones. Thus, the very "relevance" of racial distinctions, what makes them speakable, common sense, comfortably incorporated, and ready to be heard, may derive from the dense set of prior representations and practices on which they build and that they in turn recast.[29]

We might take again the racially charged political debates about "mixed bloods" in the Dutch East Indies discussed in chapter 6. No historian of the Indies would suggest that the notion of "the mixed blood" was invented in the late nineteenth-century out of whole cloth. "Mestizo" was rendered a problematic category for the East Indies Company in the seventeenth century, as was the category *inlandsche kinderen*, that amorphous designation in the second half of the nineteenth-century for those Europeans born in the Indies and of those with dubious "real" European affiliation. At issue is not whether "mixing" appeared earlier but what kinds of discrimination were intensified in the process of naming some unions "mixed" and thereby defining some people as part of the "mixed-blood problem" but not others.[30]

28. For the most frequently invoked account of this sort, to which subsequent histories of racism frequently refer, see Winthrop D. Jordan, *White over Black: American Attitudes toward the Negro, 1550–1812* (Chapel Hill: University of North Carolina Press, 1968), esp. 252–57; Karen E. Fields and Barbara J. Fields, *Racecraft: The Soul of Inequality in American Life* (London: Verso, 2014). For the Fields, "Racism is first and foremost a social practice . . . an action and a rationale" for it: Fields and Fields, *Racecraft*, 17.

29. On theories of relevance, see Dan Sperber and Deidre Wilson, *Relevance: Communication and Cognition* (Oxford: Blackwell, 1988).

30. On the ubiquity and subsequent decline of the term *inlandsche kinderen*, see Ann Laura Stoler, *Along the Archival Grain Epistemic Anxieties and Colonial Common Sense* (Princeton, NJ: Princeton University Press, 2009), 105–39.

By any contemporary criteria, the *metis* "problem" in French colonial Indochina and the "Indo" problem in colonial Java were discourses of racial exclusion. But these colonial debates were never about "inherited traits," physiological difference, and phenotype alone, features often associated with racism's nineteenth-century fluorescence. These were contentious anxious debates about racial profiles that were deemed inadequate to police who could claim Dutch national citizenship. The "fit" between class, residence, marriage choice, physiology, and race being messy at best, European attachments, skin color, and middle-class affiliations only loosely overlapped— far less so than those architects and agents managing the distribution of colonial privileges and profits sought them to be.[31]

And a whole set of new techniques and institutions were called on to manage who would have access to what: kindergartens and nursery schools that were hailed as progressive inventions of forward-looking liberal states, as in Germany where they were first established, were made into tight-fisted racist ones in the colonies, where those children allowed to enter them were schooled in the protocols of what it meant to be white.[32] In the Indies, those who advocated the urgent need for better measures of racial distinction—doctors, schoolteachers, low-ranked civil servants, and high-level bureaucrats (those endowed with qualified knowledge and what they saw to be strong intuitive knowledge about other social kinds)—debated environmental contagions on child development, psychological contaminations of human character and racial type, more than they emphasized biological immutability. Lamarckian notions of racial susceptibility—fears of sexual, moral, and affective contamination (of white children by native servants and the native children with whom they played) were readily available and easy to grasp. These assessments were both new and renewed, well worn and innovative, geared to limiting the entitlements of specific populations and safeguarding the privileges of the "real" European population in the near and imagined future.

Race as a concept performs in a mobile field. It animates vacillating discourses with dynamic motility. Racial lexicons accumulate recursively, producing new racial truths as they requisition and reassemble old ones.[33] Foucault was not alone in noting this mobile quality. Barbara Fields has

31. See Stoler, *Carnal Knowledge and Imperial Power*, 79–111.
32. See Stoler, *Carnal Knowledge and Imperial Power*, 112–39.
33. See Stoler, *Race and the Education of Desire*, 62–94.

called racism a "promiscuous critter," just as George Mosse underscored the "very broadness" of its claims.[34] Ralph Ezekiel held that U.S. racist movements "hitchhike" on other political programs.[35] For David Goldberg, the race concept is an "empty vacuum"—an image that conveys both its "chameleonic" quality and its ability to ingest other ways to distinguish social categories and incorporate ostensibly competing ones.[36] This mobility is recognized, but few have explored its epistemic properties or effects. If Foucault was right that one of the defining features of racism is its tactical mobility—that it may be embraced by those opposed to and beleaguered by the state at one moment and refolded to serve the state governing tactics at another (so vividly demonstrated in his Collège de France lectures of 1976), an important point follows: that race is invoked by, and coexists with, a range of political agendas is not a contradiction but a fundamental historical feature of its multiplex political genealogies.

Foucault offers something more. In underscoring mobility, he signaled a compelling reason for it: Racial discourses are built out of both "erudite" knowledges and "subjugated" knowledges submerged within them. Genealogy's project is to locate those "tattered" and "disorderly" narratives that "reactivate" alternative ways of knowing, that disrupt qualified knowledge and the authorized accounts it commands.[37] Racial discourse may serve those allied with state power at one moment and convert to a counter-history (contre-histoire) at another, as an irruptive stance contesting the credibility of erudite knowledge's very truth claims. Within this frame, historical accounts of racism matter very much, for they are not

34. Fields, "Ideology and Race in American History," 155–59; Mosse, Toward the Final Solution, xxvi.

35. Raphael S. Ezekiel, The Racist Mind: Portraits of Neo-Nazis and Klansmen (New York: Penguin, 1996), xxxii.

36. Goldberg, Racist Culture, 3.

37. Some students of racism's histories refer to racial discourse's "imperialistic" qualities in that it is taken up by, and takes over the content of, other constructions of difference (such as that of caste in India, where the contemporary debate on caste is so often framed in racial terms). Thus, to underscore racism's "tactical mobility" is to address not only how it tethers to European structures of dominance, as Stuart Hall put it, but how it is mobilized by subaltern social movements to validate and substantiate their claims. Anthony Appiah directed us to the hazards of doing so and argued that the Negritude movement in Africa "begins with the assumption of the racial solidarity of the Negro" and with a notion that "racism . . . could only be countered by accepting the categories of race": Kwame Anthony Appiah, My Father's House: Africa in the Philosophy of Culture (New York: Oxford University Press, 1993), 6.

outside racism's relations of power but are what Foucault would call the "relays" of their relations and fundamental to their making.[38] Race as a political concept has tactical qualities that are more quixotic still, for it moves as easily between different political projects as it seizes piecemeal on *different* elements of earlier discourses reworked for new and revised political ends.

Some political concepts ("equality," "freedom," "individual rights," "social justice") are potent by definition if they are capacious enough to remain resilient over space, context, and time and are not "lost' in local translation. Race as a concept may be exemplary in its capacity to adhere to new discriminations, *not as a superimposition that can later be unpeeled or as a general principle diluted in a specific context.* Race operates instead as an embedded nexus of speech acts and practices that adhere to other names for difference and work through the logics on which they mutually thrive.

Edmund Morgan still stands out for long arguing that American republican notions of freedom were forged by asserting the distinctions of race.[39] David Roediger, too, has shown that a discourse on "whiteness" enabled nineteenth-century working-class formation with "assertions of white freedom" and struggles against capitalist disciplinary strategies mounted in the language of race.[40] These remain exceptions: Racial discourse still somehow is seen to belong to those "with power" (or those trying to maintain their hold) rather than providing (as Foucault might have put it) a particularly "dense transfer point"—the site and idiom—in which relations of power are defended and fought. In scholarly inquiry, racists are too easy to reduce to ill-educated, closed-minded conservatives or ill-intentioned but well-heeled ones (a point I return to in chapter 8). Pierre-André Taguieff was broadly criticized in the 1980s when he made the astute and unpopular case that much of French antiracist discourse posited racism as a pathological response of those labeled "racist" by simply inverting racist claims, de-

38. For Foucault on racial discourse as a *contre-histoire*, see Stoler, *Race and the Education of Desire*, 68–69, 73–80.

39. See Morgan, *American Slavery, American Freedom*. George Fredrickson, like Edmund Morgan and John Rex, argued that "the rejection of hierarchy as the governing principle of social and political organization and its replacement by the aspiration for equality . . . has to occur before racism could come to full flower": George Marsh Fredrickson, *Racism: A Short History* (Princeton, NJ: Princeton University Press, 2003), 47.

40. Roediger, *The Wages of Whiteness*, 49.

flecting attention from the "well-meaning" larger society in which racism was well nourished and devoutly maintained.[41]

The identification of racists as damaged and disturbed personalities (and thus not "healthy" citizens) has a long history in which psychoanalysis and social psychology are called on to make the case.[42] Here racism is construed historically as a set of social practices embraced by thwarted and threatened, reactionary members of a changing body politic. Even those who see liberalism as giving rise to racialized exclusions may posit racism as a *reactive* strategy, cemented by those upper or lower classes tenaciously guarding themselves against incursions on their privilege or limited power (i.e., "poor whites"). But Eduardo Bonilla-Silva is right to reassert the argument that one does not need self-proclaimed racists to sustain a polity in which racism thrives.[43]

RACIST EXCESS AND UNRULY MEN

Paradoxically, then, racism may be treated as a set of power relations instigated by those who rule but embraced in its more virulent forms by those who do not. Thus, another foundational fiction emerges: that racist excess, like sexual excess, results from the unbridled passions of ordinary folk, not from those endowed with the civilities of respectable, educated white women and men.[44] Such a view does more than substitute individual for social pathologies, and vice versa. It prompts an analytic move that histories of racism embrace: association of its emergence with "disorders" of

41. As Taguieff writes, some antiracisms feed the illusion that "racism only exists among 'racists,' patently, labeled, declared or recognized as such in public space. Situated, localized, identified in the singular figure of the political 'barbarian' of the late 20th century, racism thus can be combated in the same way one fights against organized groups menacing the public order: i.e., through police repression and by judicial sanction": Pierre-André Taguieff, *Les fins de l'antiracisme* (Paris: Editions Michalon, 1995), xi.

42. On the pathological outcome of a dysfunctional childhood, see Theodor W. Adorno, Else Frenkel-Brunswick, Daniel Levinson, and R. Nevitt Sanford, eds., *The Authoritarian Personality* (1950) (New York: W. W. Norton, 1982).

43. Eduardo Bonilla-Silva, *Racism without Racists: Color-Blind Racism and the Persistence of Racial Inequality in the United States* (Lanham, MD: Rowman and Littlefield, 2006).

44. In Dutch colonial documents, poor, *decivilisé* whites are targeted as both the most ardent supporters of racism and subversive of it. For debates on this issue, see Stoler, *Carnal Knowledge and Imperial Power*, 130–33. On the "unbridled passions" of subaltern European men, see Stoler, *Race and the Education of Desire*, 179–80.

the underclasses—"disorders" that may take social, moral, political, or economic form. When strongly put, the causal arrow from "disorder" to racism is directly drawn. Thus, Karen Newman has attributed the racialized discourse in Shakespeare's Othello to the fear of people out of place, "masterless men," and of those challenging "traditional notions of order and degree."[45] Michael Banton drew on Winthrop Jordan to point to a seventeenth-century British society "in ferment," to the preponderance again of "masterless men" who provoked anxieties about the "apparent dissolution of social and moral controls."[46] Hannah Arendt saw racialized accounts of the social order emerging among an aristocracy whose privileges were fast being encroached on by an increasingly mobile and masterful bourgeoisie, commanding both positions of power and authority over what defined morality.[47]

Both colonial assessments and this historiography converge on a similar point: that intensified racism reflects the sexual appetites and insecurities of subaltern white men.[48] Accounts of the "new racism" stand on similar grounds, as a response to social and economic disorders, dislocations and anonymities produced by postmodern capitalism, and neoliberalism and reactive to a disjuncture between expectations and an attenuation of entitlements.[49]

These narratives may accurately mark the particular moments that intensify racialized accounts, but "disorder" accounts for too little—and too much. How can a key term and justification for exclusionary, racialized policies provide for an account of that which it sets out to explain? As Bauman argues, the image of the "conceptual Jew" in Nazi Germany as *visqueux*

45. Karen Newman, " 'And Wash the Ethiop White': Femininity and the Monstrous in Othello," in *Shakespeare Reproduced: The Text in History and Ideology*, ed. Jean Elizabeth Howard and Marion F. O'Connor (New York: Routledge, 1990), 130.

46. Michael Banton, *The Idea of Race* (London: Tavistock, 1977), 14. See also Jordan, *White over Black*.

47. Hannah Arendt, "Race-Thinking before Racism," in *The Origins of Totalitarianism* (1951) (New York: Harcourt Brace, 1979). See also Stoler, *Race and the Education of Desire*, 77–78. I, too, have argued that consolidated racialized policies in colonial Indonesia responded to "crises of control," to the state's fear that disorderly moral conduct signaled subversive political trends: see Stoler, *Carnal Knowledge and Imperial Power*, 58–59.

48. In a similar vein, Joe Feagin and his colleagues note that racial violence may be perpetrated by "less-educated whites," while the conditions for it are managed by the white middle class: Joe Feagin, Hernan Vera, and Pinar Batur, *White Racism: The Basics* (New York: Routledge, 2001), 166.

49. Goldberg, *Racist Culture*, 70.

(slimy) represented boundary transgression and "chaos and devastation."[50] The demand for "order" and the normalization or elimination and expulsion of those imagined to pose a threat—invoking a "defense of society" against its internal enemies and "interior frontiers"—is a leitmotif of state racism, a key trope of its legitimating and policing apparatus. These are part of the architecture of racism, not explanations for it.

ON THE TACTICAL MOBILITY OF RACIAL DISCOURSE

Use of the term "discourse" here is not designed to signal a unity in the warped sense so often still attributed to Foucault. The pat gloss of "discourse" to designate a unified and coherent field of statements (as in "colonial discourse") ignores most of what Foucault had to say about discursive formations and is a fairly accurate description of what they are not. It is worth reviewing what he did write:

> [A discursive formation is marked by] the different possibilities that it opens of reanimating already existing themes, of arousing opposed strategies, of giving way to irreconcilable interests, of making it possible, with a particular set of concepts, to play different games. Rather than seeking the permanence of themes, images and opinions through time, rather than retracing the dialectic of their conflicts in order to individualize groups of statements, could one not rather mark out the dispersion of the points of choice, and define prior to any options, to any thematic preference, a field of strategic possibilities?[51]

Could the ubiquitous use of "discourse" be any further from this description? With respect to race, it reminds us of three crucial elements: its mobility, its dispersed political appearance, and its lack of thematic unity. Thinking with this "field of strategic possibilities," race work in late nineteenth-century colonial Java or of the National Front in contemporary France would not be expected to reveal a common set of intentions, consequences, or themes. A discourse is racial not because it always displays shared political interests but because it *delineates a field and set of conditions that make it impossible to talk about any range of domains—sexuality, class, moral values, sports, childcare,*

50. Bauman, *Modernity and Holocaust*, 39–40.
51. Michel Foucault, *The Archaeology of Knowledge* (1969) (New York: Pantheon, 1982), 36–37.

internet use without inscribing those relations of power with racialized distinctions and discriminations.[52]

The "polyvalent mobility" of race as a political concept opens to another seeming contradiction. Historiography has attended to how modern racisms build on, recruit, and take hold of old loyalties and pre-existing senses of commonality and difference in the service of new political projects. But racecraft does more: It recuperates and invents past legacies that provide utopian visions of the future. Both the social hygiene campaigns of the Nazi state in the 1930s and U.S. sterilization laws in the early twentieth century were forged in the spirit and language of a new and improved social order. Pat Robertson's "new world order" was a diagnostic of a political condition in the United States at the time and a blueprint for the future.[53] Jean-Marie Le Pen's National Front gained 30 percent of the votes in local elections in the late 1990s not only from closet reactionaries.[54] The National Front's platform was embraced precisely by those who saw themselves as anti-elitist, antistate, populist, and conservatively *progressive*, as is his daughter Marine Le Pen's National Front platform today, in which racism in the abstract is roundly condemned.[55]

The nationalist and patriotic appropriations of racial discourse have been explored, but one telling feature of colonial racial discourses has not.[56] Racism today is often considered distinct because it explicitly encourages those who adhere to its logic to see themselves *not* as racists but as protectors of the national patrimony, as "true" and patriotic citizens of the United States, England, Germany, Belgium, or France. Whether endorsing individual rights, "the right to difference," or Le Pen's "right to a national preference," a protection of (individual) rights, rational behavior, and racial

52. Foucault, *The Archaeology of Knowledge*, 144.

53. Pat Robertson, *The New World Order* (Dallas: Word, 1991).

54. For more on this issue, see chapter 8.

55. Pierre-André Taguieff, "The Doctrine of the National Front in France (1972–1989): A Revolutionary Programme? Ideological Aspects of a National-Populist Mobilization," *New Political Science* 8, 1–2 (September 1, 1989): 29–70. Pat Robertson's "populist" stance against class elites was insistent on this point. See also Lauren Joffrin, "Ce que les Lepenistes ont dans la tête," *Le Nouvel Observateur*, December 1995.

56. Among many others, see Étienne Balibar, *Masses, Classes, Ideas: Studies on Politics and Philosophy before and after Marx* (New York: Routledge, 1994), and the essays in Geoff Eley and Ronald Grigor Suny, *Becoming National: A Reader* (New York: Oxford University Press, 1996).

politics can easily go hand in hand.[57] In the "illiberal" politics of Dinesh D'Souza, twenty years ago, for whom racism was dead and the discourse about it should be, as well, his favored example—the "alleged racism" of a taxi driver who passes three men of color to pick up one who is white and is simply acting on reasoned, rational choice—rings as ever more delusional and specious in its reasoning today.[58]

The observation that racists in the postmodern era are encouraged not to see themselves as such may capture something significant about how racial discourses operate. But it does so by suggesting that earlier racial formations were broadly and candidly embraced by their advocates—a caricature of colonial racial sensibilities, not a description of them. Dutch colonials were not unique in declaring that they did not subscribe to racism and emphatically did hold to the equality of human rights.

When historical figures such as Arthur de Gobineau, Madison Grant, and Vacher de Lapouge are taken as exemplars, the wide band in which racial reasoning has operated is too easily narrowed, if not ignored. Focusing on such high profile figures dissuades questioning the blatant and nuanced ways in which *homo europeaus* was (and remains) practically secured in the gestural, spatial, and emotional economy of the everyday. Does the "new racism" really occupy a different and more intimate location, "above all, in family life" where "social processes" were turned into "natural, instinctive" processes, as Paul Gilroy argued for Britain in the 1980s?[59] Are subtle state interventions on the side of the postcolonial and Manichean, blunt racism really the signature of a colonial past? The assertion that "the new racism is primarily concerned with mechanisms of inclusion and exclusion" makes of colonial history a foreign country—as it does colonial presence today.[60] Colonial racism also was built on a politics of exclusion, making adults and children into racialized beings, educating their racially cued comportment, moral sentiments, and desires in ways that were invariably "about" civility and culture and less explicitly "about" race.

57. On racism and individual rights, see Stanley Fish, "How the Right Hijacked the Magic Words," *New York Times*, August 13, 1995, http://search.proquest.com.libproxy .newschool.edu/docview/430285946/50B352F33030476CPQ/1?accountid=12261.
58. Dinesh D'Souza, *The End of Racism: Principles for a Multiracial Society* (New York: Simon and Schuster, 1995), 250.
59. Gilroy, *"There Ain't No Black in the Union Jack,"* 43.
60. Gilroy, *"There Ain't No Black in the Union Jack,"* 43.

Not recognizing the cultural labor and affective policing that went into enabling those practices feeds off a prevailing myth about modern racism's origins—namely, that race was once a simpler affair, perceived as fixed and natural, "as fixed as a southern star." Fixity was both a signature of its emergence and an index of its proliferation. That view led the historian Michael Adas to argue that in the field of colonial technology and science, racism gained little purchase until the late nineteenth century, a case made on two grounds: that the "notion [that] biological factors were responsible for Europe's achievement and global dominance was not [yet] widely argued" and that European colonials shared a belief in the "improvability" of Asian and African populations. Such "proof" should command our attention: "the connections between innate physical characteristics and moral or intellectual capabilities *remained ill-defined* even in the most systematic of the racist tracts."[61] In such a model, racism's dominance emerges when the linkages between the physical and psychological are no longer "ill-defined."[62]

But racism not only thrives without such certainty; it does extremely well in its absence. Racial discourses mobilize new experts, new studies, and new technologies that keep alive and well the contests over *whether*—a "whether" that slides smoothly into a proliferating contest over *which of*—these linkages are "true" or "false." That the nineteenth century "science" of phrenology (the theory that a person's character and intelligence could be deduced from the shape of the skull) was quickly discredited as an accurate measure of racial endowment did nothing, as we know, to undermine the productive attention that continued to be placed on the relationship between physical measurements and mental aptitude. On the contrary, phrenology provided a placeholder where the search for a relationship between phenotype and genotype was not disqualified—only its specific coordinates. One might even argue that the search for a better measurement could remain an active subject, a reasonable quest in scientific and folk theories of race, as so much work on the "genetic reinscription" of race now attests.[63]

61. Michael Adas, *Machines as the Measure of Man: Science, Technology and Ideologies of Western Dominance* (Ithaca, NY: Cornell University Press, 1989), 274; emphasis added.

62. If Adas's account was sensitive to the fact that "race" had a wide range of ambiguous meanings, a fixed notion of what secures *racism* remains undisturbed by that observation.

63. Nadia Abu El-Haj, "The Genetic Reinscription of Race," *Annual Review of Anthropology* 36, 1 (2007): 283–300.

ON FIXITIES AND FLUIDITIES IN RACIAL DISCOURSE

Contra Winant's widely shared assumption that race was a fixed essence, I have argued here that in earlier colonial figurations it had more the consistency and constancy of the Milky Way—perceptible boundaries from a distance but made up of a moving constellation of parts of changing intensity—than the fixity of a southern star. A preeminent purveyor of anthropology's colonial history, George Stocking, held that Lamarck's contention that acquired traits could be inheritable and that human variation was responsive to environmental conditions were as much a part of nineteenth-century racial thinking and practice as those focused more squarely on the immutability and permanence of traits.[64]

In the Indies, it was not the assuredness of *homo europeaus* that was asserted but its tenuous certitude and fragility. Whether the "wavering classes" of indigent "mixed bloods" and impoverished Europeans should be considered properly white, and thereby entitled to state subsidies, well-funded schools, and privileges of those whose dispositions, comportment, and finances accorded with the European norm, took up thousands of pages of government commissions and confidential documents among those whose authority to make those distinctions had institutional support.[65] In a context in which "mixed-blooded" children of European fathers and Asian mothers occupied a thick corridor between colonizer and colonized, race could never be a matter of physiology alone. I have alluded to this issue often but note it here to underscore a crucial point: the porousness assigned to the contemporary concept of race is not a post–Second World War phenomenon, as Winant articulated and others have claimed. Fluidity was inherent in the concept itself, *not* a hallmark of a modernist much less postracial moment—and not necessarily a diagnostic of racism's demise. Histories of racism that narrate a shift from the fixed and biological to the cultural and fluid impose a progression that poorly characterizes what earlier racism looked like and weaken claims about what distinguishes and sustains it now. The argument that a "new" form of racial prejudice in the United States is less concerned with genes than with "moral character" could

---

64. George W. Stocking, *Race, Culture, and Evolution: Essays in the History of Anthropology* (Chicago: University of Chicago Press, 1968), 234–69.

65. For Dutch colonial debates over this "amalgama" of racialized groups, their political aspirations, and the political anxieties over how, with whom, and where those designated as European were supposed to live see Stoler, *Along the Archival Grain*, 141–78.

be claimed only by ignoring its history—and what now figures as some of the most contentious contemporary debates about what DNA says about race.[66] A racialized other "behaving badly," "undeserving" of poor relief, too indolent to work, and "spoiled" by state "charity" has a deep political genealogy. Even W. E. B. Du Bois repeated it in his Negro Academy Creed that "the first and greatest step toward the settlement of the present friction between the races lies in the correction of immorality, crime, and laziness among the Negroes themselves."[67]

Nineteenth-century racism was built not on the sure-footed classifications of science but on a potent set of cultural and affective criteria whose malleability was a key to the flexible scale along which economic privileges and social entitlements could be selectively accorded and, when necessary, reassigned. This is not to suggest that notions of "fixity" do not underwrite racial logics. My point is that the celebrated emphasis on fluidity may not be the trenchant postcolonial critique it has been taken to be. It may only signal a somewhat belated recognition that racisms gain force precisely through the double vision they foster and allow, in the fact that they combine notions of fixity and fluidity in ways that are basic to their grammar.[68] The "proof" that racial categories are fluid and not fixed confirms race as a fiction, but it does little else. It leaves untouched the infrastructures that make race an operative and commanding economic, political, and affective fact, very real in its effects, protracted in its imposed duress, and firmly in place.

Thus, even the fervent commentator on contemporary racism in France, Taguieff, takes the immutability of human kinds as a defining feature of racist thinking, both in its nineteenth-century biologized manifestation and in the context of the European Community's strong anti-immigrant stance

66. Donald R. Kinder and Lynn M. Sanders, *Divided by Color: Racial Politics and Democratic Ideals* (Chicago: University of Chicago Press, 1996). On the debates about DNA and race from a wide range of settings, see Kimberly TallBear, "DNA, Blood, and Racializing the Tribe," *Wicazo Sa Review* 18, 1 (2003): 81–107; Duana Fullwiley, "Can DNA 'Witness' Race? Forensic Uses of an Imperfect Ancestry Testing Technology," *Genewatch* 21, 3–4 (2008): 12–14; and the contributions in Keith Wailoo, Alondra Nelson, and Catherine Lee, eds., *Genetics and the Unsettled Past: The Collision of DNA, Race, and History* (New Brunswick, NJ: Rutgers University Press, 2012).

67. W. E. B. Du Bois, "The Conservation of Races" (1897), in *Theories of Race and Racism: A Reader*, ed. Les Back and John Solomos (New York: Routledge, 2000), 86.

68. My use of "double vision" here should not be confused with the sense in which Du Bois used that term at the turn of the century.

today. By his account, French antiracism's fierce defense of a "right to difference" was grounded in a cultural relativism derived from the very principles of the racism against which it was aimed. The critique is fair enough and is made by others.[69] But "immutability" as racism's defining feature is historically problematic because it never was—nor is it now—a necessary and sufficient condition to sustain a racist logic. Colonial authorities invested in fixing racial others with knowable traits and in securing their own racialized membership and privilege, but their doubts belie the success of that quest. As a political principle, race ironically accrues more force when the attributes designated as immutable are pliable and plastic to allow redefinitions at the boundaries of categories that remain resilient over time.[70]

The Euro-American racial discourse around "contamination" exemplifies the confused sensibilities and multiple ways of knowing on which folk and scientific theories of racial membership depend. Theories of racial contamination are asymmetric in how fixity is assigned. In popular and scholarly literatures, colonial contagions moved easily from native to European, but not, as the "one drop rule" in U.S. history so firmly insisted, the other way around. Racial contagion rested on two competing claims: on discrete categories of people and on the premise that those categories could be "sullied" through sexual contact, moral influence, and affective attachment—irrevocably tainted and transformed. Whether the category is fixed but not its membership or the category is altered by subtractions and supplements of members on its margins, "contamination" as a political concept does two kinds of work. It both confirms and calls into question the discreteness of human kinds.

This does not undermine the notion that essentialist thinking and practices are operative. Rather, it suggests that essentialisms are secured not by the rote rehearsal of fixed traits but by their substitutable and interchangeable instantiations. Colonial debates questioned where that immutable essence was located, unsure about its fixity and fragility but rarely forgoing the belief that there was no essence at all. *Essentialist thinking*

69. Cultural relativism has long been the culprit for conservatives such as D'Souza, as well, for whom liberal cultural relativism, not racism, is the cause of social tensions and inequities today. As Micaela di Leonardo has argued, "The diatribe against 'cultural relativism' is an extraordinary one-stop shop for a bricolage of New Right causes": Micaela di Leonardo, "Patterns of Culture Wars," *The Nation*, April 8, 1996, 26.

70. As Lawrence Hirschfeld notes, to say that "race is enduring" is *not* to say that "race is permanent" (or fixed): Hirschfeld, *Race in the Making*, 51–53.

may rest not on a psychological commitment to permanence but, rather, on the fact that its very attributes rest on moving and fungible parts.

RACIAL ESSENTIALISM: A MOVING TARGET

The changing topography of racialized ascriptions could be tracked through the charged contexts in which the dispositions of those assigned to racialized categories figure today. Anthropologists, sociologists, and those who read the fine print of racism are tracking as never before where and how these ascriptions appear—alternately sharp and blurred.[71] When the "preemptory challenges" to jurors were flagged in the press in the summer of 2015 as being used at least three times as often to rid juries of black potential jurors in Georgia, Louisiana, and North Carolina over the past decade, a contested term came up in the debate: Lawyers argued that their reasoning was "race-neutral."[72] Black jurors were eliminated for displaying the following: an "air of defiance," "arms folded," being "sullen," speaking in monosyllables, or showing "bad posture." These were considered "fair" reasons for removal because none of the reasons called on typical racial stereotypes or imputed race. But if prosecutors struck out a higher percentage of blacks in 93 percent of the trials, why did these descriptions work better to eliminate those who are black? What hidden dispositions were these descriptions supposed to signal? Or were these attributions meaningless in the abstract but significant in the case of someone who was black? If essentialism is at work here, it is doing complex work that is neither constant nor always the same.

The issue of ascription has had more lethal consequences in the barrage of killings of black men in 2012–15 plastered across the media and in outraged protests across the United States. Striking in nearly all of the cases is not only that nearly one hundred youths and adult men who were killed were identified as black. The violence perpetrated against them, multiple shootings, and the extreme force used were all based on *anticipatory re-*

---

71. See, e.g., John L. Jackson Jr., *Racial Paranoia: The Unintended Consequences of Political Correctness* (New York: Basic Civitas, 2008). Jackson sticks ethnographically close to the scrambled sensibilities in which racism endures, marking this moment in the United States as one drenched in "racial paranoia," in a story about "the historical and contemporary manifestations of racial distrust" and why that distrust is so tenacious: Jackson, *Racial Paranoia*, 8–9.

72. See Liptak, "Exclusion of Blacks from Juries Raises Renewed Scrutiny."

sponses to an *expectation* of behavior. It was not what these youths and men did that produced the conditions for the killings but what was imagined they could do, what a gesture meant, what demeanor was thought to indicate, how demeanor was assessed, and what they were imagined already to have done. These killings were based not only on essentialist construals but also on what was conceived as a prior knowledge of their dispositions, already cast in a ready set of frames.[73]

But more disturbing still is that Michael Brown, Trayvon Martin, Eric Garner, Dontre Hamilton—who was shot fourteen times by a police officer in a Milwaukee park—were all assigned a predictable, precarious unpredictability. They could not be trusted to be acting within some imaginary norm in which a toy gun is a toy gun and a request not to be shackled and beaten for driving with an outdated license or for standing on a corner is a reasonable response. At issue are the potent inferences about inner qualities that in a racist logic are considered warranted and can be reasonably made. In this deranged racial formation that is the United States, recursive history is at work. It has long been sensible to read a black man's body, gestures, silence, and speech differently from a white's. Such inferences render familiar actions threatening, signs of potential aggression that the racial inequalities of the United States inspire and condone. Some of these attributions and inferences are part of the deep history of racism, unflinchingly present, but some are not. How these dispositions are imagined, how they are assessed, revised, and inflicted course throughout the imperial landscapes of past and present, and as we know too well, they are not confined to the United States alone.

THE POLITICS OF RACIAL EPISTEMOLOGIES AGAIN

The relationship between knowledge production and racism is a densely occupied field of scholarship but less so in the narrow sense in which I suggest pursuing it further. If we know that racecraft has built on and engen-

73. Of the many efforts to understand, constrain, and change what continues to produce these conditions, see "Why Do U.S. Police Keep Killing Unarmed Black Men?" BBC News, May 26, 2015, http://www.bbc.com/news/world-us-canada-32740523; "Our Vision for a New America: Demands," Ferguson Action, n.d., http://fergusonaction .com/demands; "Issues," Million Hoodies Movement for Justice, n.d., http:// millionhoodies.net/issues, as well as the comprehensive platform for racial justice proposed by Campaign Zero.

dered a range of scientized research agendas—from Lamarckism to social Darwinism, eugenics, degeneracy theory, phrenology, anthropology, philology, and social psychology—I would contend that there is more work to do on the ways of knowing on which racisms build and the epistemological assumptions on which we, their critical witnesses who study them, rely.[74] To say that race bears "polyvalent mobility" does not mean that racism is infinitely adaptable. Instead, it points to a methodological portal: that racism takes on the form of other things, wraps itself around heated issues, descends on political pulse points, appears as reasoned judgments, beyond sentiment, as it takes over impassioned bodies.

A turn to inconsistencies and disparities in debates about subjects and social categories that ostensibly were and are not about race at all may better capture the specific ways in which that mobility was realized and its consequences.[75] Neither physiological characteristics nor essentialism gives racism its force; it is, rather, the elusive relationship between the two and the politics of the interpretive space that ambiguity affords. A notion of essence rests not necessarily on immovable parts but on the strategic inclusion of different attributes, of a changing constellation of features and a changing weighting of them. One way to bring racism's histories and current accounts of those histories into better line is to attend more closely to the disparities in both stories of origin and in the conflicting range of attributes by which racism gets dismissed or defined. Tension between the seen and the unseen, between the appearance of racism as always "new" and "renewed," of people being rendered invisible and too visible at the same time should be our subjects of inquiry, for these are part of racism's mobile apparatus and its operative signs. The race concept and the practices it sustains act on the

74. Ann Laura Stoler, "Epistemic Politics: Ontologies of Colonial Common Sense." *Folk Epistemology* 39, 3 (Fall 2008): 349–61. See also Nadia Abu El-Haj, *The Genealogical Science: The Search for Jewish Origins and the Politics of Epistemology* (Chicago: University of Chicago Press, 2012); Charles W. Mill, *The Racial Contract* (Ithaca, NY: Cornell University Press, 1997); Shannon Sullivan and Nancy Tuana, eds., *Race and the Epistemologies of Ignorance* (Albany: State University of New York Press, 2007). But if the edited volume *Race and Racism in Continental Philosophy* is at all indicative, the politics of racial epistemology remains marginal even to critical philosophy: Robert Bernasconi with Sybol Cook, eds., *Race and Racism in Continental Philosophy* (Bloomington: Indiana University Press, 2003).

75. Thus, see the treatment of surveillance through the lens of policing black lives in Simone Browne, *Dark Matters: On the Surveillance of Blackness* (Durham, NC: Duke University Press, 2015).

rules—not just on the particular strategies of power and politics. The point is not to find yet another site of origin but to understand the broad and contradictory investments that have tied, and continue to tie, distinctions of human quality to distinctions of—and violence against—those assumed to be of other human—and not-quite "properly" human—kinds.

III. "THE ROT REMAINS"

RACIST VISIONS AND THE COMMON SENSE OF FRANCE'S "EXTREME" RIGHT

It has been hard to keep up with Marine Le Pen and the barrage of daily head-lines she and the National Front (FN) command. She is ever on the move, with a glowing, soft smile, insistently disparaging racism and anti-Semitic and anti-Muslim pronouncements, "domesticating" the FN for popular consumption. She has been "distancing herself," as the press likes to re-peat, from the strident theatrics of her father, Jean-Marie Le Pen, the FN's founder, since she took over leadership from him in 2011. His high-drama "ouster" in 2015 from its rosters (long in the works) and the party's vote to sanction his speaking on its behalf might suggest that the FN under Ma-rine's leadership has simply learned to maneuver the affective registers of French politics with more finesse. But that would be to misconstrue the deeper history of her latest "magnificent" success, of which her promise to ban all legal and illegal immigration to France (if she is elected president in 2017) is only one manifestation.

French newspapers for the most part tell the same story. What was once a "fringe" party, a minor if boisterous voice, is now a key player in national politics. What in the 1990s and through the first decade of the twenty-first century, was still considered an extreme party with a small regional base in southern France and largely shunned or ignored by the right and the left is now at center stage. Marine's photo is plastered across the cover of every French newspaper and magazine. She is a guest on television and radio programs that never would have invited her father. She embodies the "new face" of the normalized, respectable FN, winning popular endorsement (if maybe hearts, as some would argue), with the FN garnering more votes across the country than was ever deemed possible twenty years ago. There will be an outpouring of analyses of her recent cascade of victories and their convergence with the increasingly right-wing parties in prominence across Europe. But as significant is how many of the "reforms" long proposed by the FN are now championed by centrist parties that have moved increasingly to the right (but not fast enough to garner the votes she can now command). Perhaps what is more striking is the increasing willingness of left-wing parties (most notably the Front de Gauche) that can now imagine an FN "alliance." Ever more adherents to the communist labor unions have given the FN their support. In December 2015, in the wake of the bombings in Paris the month before, the FN had overwhelming victory in six of the thirteen regional elections, catapulting her and the party to heights never before achieved.[1] She is expected to be one of the two contenders for the presidency in the 2017 national elections, and it is not only political pundits who think she can win.

This tidy description, rehearsed across the international media, is both accurate and misleading. It is true that the public face of the FN has radically changed. It is also true that its spokespeople have distanced themselves from the provocative racist speech of its founding leader and condemned him for a range of his notorious incendiary remarks, the most often cited being his description of the Jewish Holocaust as a historical "detail" (for which he was prosecuted and convicted). Le Pen senior now stands as a paragon of retrograde, defunct extremism that everyone can gleefully rally against and ignore.

But what is not true is more important—namely, the notion that the FN's xenophobic, anti-Arab, anti-immigrant sentiments; patriotic fervor; and the historical referents that it has long stood for and behind was ever fringe. On the contrary, not only did Jean-Marie Le Pen and the FN articulate a widespread set of fears, sympathies, and discontents in the 1990s—and political positions based on them—that were never on the outer margins of French society. They recruited political sensibilities and dispositions that were already there and that remain at the very core of France's once subjacent, and now openly embraced, political culture and affective economy.

1. As of December 7, 2015, Marine Le Pen was garnering nearly 30 percent of the national vote (and only 11% in 2010), with the largest percentage of 25 percent in the eighteen-to-twenty-four age group.

A "fringe" party should not be confused with "fringe" commitments, sentiments, and beliefs. As I argue in this chapter, much of what the FN pushed and harped on—albeit in what was then considered a repugnantly crass and excessively caricatured visual and verbal form—was never fringe at all. The posters have been toned down over the years but the underlying sympathies are in many ways unchanged. "No to Islam," "Immigration = Unemployment," "People of France, Rise Up"—the slogans in its public media—at once capture the explicitness of the message and the undeniable fact that they do not stand as uniquely FN positions; nor did they twenty-five years ago, when it was still a "fringe" party. The phrases that stood as testimony of FN "extremism" on the cusp of the twenty-first century when it still was considered the "far" right say a lot. Among those that caused the most clamor, such as a "national preference" and "France for the [really] French," were quietly embraced by many more. As one FN watcher put it, a vote for the "extreme right" was considered "morally forbidden," given the post-1945 zeitgeist.[2] "Let us produce what is French with Frenchmen," a favored slogan of the FN in the 1990s, played off a Communist Party slogan from the 1970s, "Produisons Français" The nationalist, xenophobic sentiment was there. Le Pen just added the explicit racist inflection "avec des Français." But it, too, was already there. Although few others were willing to voice it so blatantly, it would be hard to deny that these were already core features of a French racialized, and deeply historical, widely shared, if contested, common sense.

CRAFTING COMMON SENSE

The invocation of common sense has a long and well-documented history. The claim to speak for common sense can work in sundry ways. Common sense, as Clifford Geertz thought it, can be treated as a "relatively organized body of considered thought," a "down-to-earth, colloquial wisdom" made up of "judgments" and "assessments" that tell folks when that wisdom should be called on and by whom—and how it works.[3] By Geertz's account, common sense carries an "unspoken premise" from which it draws its

2. Daniel van Eeuwen and Jean Viard, *Main basse sur la Provence et la Côte d'Azur* (La Tour-d'Aigues, France: Aube, 2003), 15.

3. Clifford Geertz, "Common Sense as a Cultural System," in *Local Knowledge: Further Essays in Interpretive Anthropology* (New York: Basic, 1983), 75–76.

authority. It is both "historically constructed" and "subjected to historically defined standards of judgment." What philosophers sometimes call "untutored common sense" is, as Geertz put it, "what the plain man thinks when sheltered from the vain sophistications of schoolmen."[4] Common sense adjudicates normalities and enlists prescription to the salient borders it defines and polices. Jacques Rancière's assessment is harsher and closer to Antonio Gramsci's: Common sense celebrates the "simple wisdom of decent folk" while serving as the "master trope of modernity: exclusion by homage."[5] For Pierre Bourdieu, common sense (more often, "doxa") has an unmarked but remarkably powerful force to define and destabilize that which is tacitly and commonly accepted; it is a vehicle of domination in which a practice of self-censorship is honed and thrives.[6]

But common sense can do something more. It also can challenge existing authority. As Sophia Rosenfeld tracks its political history, common sense imposes "a minimal level of conformity . . . [necessary] for the existence of secure communities and a secure, delimited realm of truth."[7] Invoking common sense reminds us what we already know (with "intuitive" knowledge as our colloquial moral guide), what needs to be excluded "to secure communities," and what needs to be embraced, banished, or set aside. This valorization of what is already known but need not be said, on the one hand, and the challenge to the status quo, on the other, is key to both the force of common sense and an understanding of how it works. In the case of the FN, I would argue that this oscillation is the operative field in which the party performed, developed, and altered its platforms. One of these mise-en-scène was Vitrolles, where I worked in 1997–1998, a nondescript small town divided between its old center and low-income sprawl, squeezed between a strip of box stores that run from Aix-en-Provence to Marseille.[8]

4. Geertz, "Common Sense as a Cultural System," 77.

5. Andrew Parker, "Introduction," in Jacques Rancière, The Philosopher and His Poor, ed. Andrew Parker (Durham, NC: Duke University Press, 2004), xxvi.

6. On Bourdieu's capacious sense of common sense and the destabilizing and modifying forms it inherently takes, see Robert Holton, "Bourdieu and Common Sense," SubStance 26, 3 (January 1, 1997): 38–52.

7. Sophia A. Rosenfeld, Common Sense: A Political History (Cambridge, MA: Harvard University Press, 2011), 13, 15.

8. For an excellent but very different analysis of race and "common sense," see Deborah Posel's study of categories in which the apartheid state in South Africa adjudicated who belonged in what category and the "considerable latitude" that was given to those

This essay is about the idioms and practices of the French National Front today and in the late 1990s, the latter a key moment in the party's formulations. It was not a decisive moment so much as an emergent, experimental one in a transformation from the FN's early faltering efforts to its subsequent success in marshaling what many French thought in the privacy of their kitchen conversations but were less willing to profess in public. It is about how the FN, even in its failed moments, was in the process of shaping a platform and a vocabulary that tapped into and identified more general dispositions and racial sensibilities that were seemingly at odds with the principles of a democratic republic. There is too much evidence to rehearse that exclusionary principles have long flourished at the core of liberal (republican) polities, as they were and are today.

Vitrolles was celebrated and decried as an FN "laboratory" in the late 1990s for experimenting with how far it could go to recast social policy in explicitly racist ways; with which platforms would work to draw into its fold white working-class men and women in the provinces; and with what would be distinctly FN but broad enough to speak to the "real" French across the nation.

In a world in which racist perceptions and practices occupy global space and permeate private spheres, scholarly accountability has been sought in making sense of the tenacious resilience of race as a social, political, and psychological category that continues to define people and confine their options, to exclude and embrace, to grant and withhold entitlements. But scholars of racism in France have been far less ready, or willing, to ask why racist visions have such appeal to people who in good faith hold that they have no interest in race, but rather in defending their families and the nation. The narratives are now so common and familiar across contemporary Europe, they seem vacuous, generic, of rote quality. One hears from and about those who have nothing against those of "X" origin but don't want X's cultural priorities influencing "their" children in "their" schools. There is insistence that crime is the issue, not race. Their concern is for safe playgrounds, and only with "security."

---

local social engineers who were assigned to interpret it: Deborah Posel, "Race as Common Sense: Racial Classification in Twentieth-Century South Africa," *African Studies Review* 44, 2 (September 1, 2011): 87–113.

To observe that such talk is deeply racialized is hardly a provocative claim. The more important question is why the FN's programmatic statements have been so "easy to think" for a broad population who reject the idea that they are xenophobic, racist or politically "extreme" in any sense. That question was at the center of what I sought to understand better in Vitrolles in 1997–1998. It was the year after Jean-Marie Le Pen's right-hand man, Bruno Mégret, was disqualified from standing for local elections and maneuvered his wife, Catherine Mégret, to run in his stead for Vitrolle's mayor. She had no knowledge of or experience in politics. She won with 47 percent of the vote.

Vitrolles in 1998 provides not so much a snapshot of a relevant moment as the crystalline site of an ever more clearly articulated political project, silently endorsed by some, on the cusp of enunciation by others. Even those who voted for the FN at the time often refused to acknowledge their affiliation. They did not want to be associated with its name. Making sense of how racism figured on this politicized landscape posed challenges: how to write about what seemed abhorrent, to suspend prior judgments about what seemed still aberrant, and to reconsider the idioms of racial politics when race went unnamed. I wondered at the time what it would take to be analytically equipped to account for racialized platforms, practices, and sensibilities that moved between the crude and careful, the honed and ad hoc, the blunt and the subtle. As is likely clear from the preceding chapter, I still take it as an ongoing challenge and working project.

If much of my previous work had been on the colonial history of racial categories, it was contemporary debates on the "end of racism" in the United States and a "post-racial" Europe that pulled me away from the nearby colonial archives in Aix, where I had intended to spend my time. In Aix and its surroundings, talk of race produced a chillingly familiar and unfamiliar social world. While the FN and the racial slurs that went with it commanded presence, racialized inequities could be strikingly effaced—irrelevant—in a space in which nothing was really recognized to be changing at all.

By one reading, 1998 was a year in which extreme-right platforms and candidates moved from the menacing margins of French politics well into the center. It was the first time since the FN's founding in 1972 that a number of center-right candidates in regional campaigns accepted FN backing and acknowledged they needed that support to win. The left-wing press, invoking "Vichy," labeled them *collabo* (collaborators) for doing so. It was the year in which France's President Jacques Chirac made an unprecedented address on national television to say what many already thought: namely, that such compromises were endorsements of a "xenophobic" and "racist" France. It was a year in which media personalities who had long resisted interviewing FN leaders conceded that refusing to give them airtime would not make them disappear (even if their presence was still attributed to an unfortunate conjuncture). It was a year in which the progressive press printed headlines sounding the alarm that the "Front was everywhere" while a few months later a profusion of otherwise progressive public figures would applaud the World Cup victory of France's rainbow-colored soccer team as a "model of successful integration," a sign of the real France, and an antiracist victory.[9]

But there was also this strange phenomenon of "nothing happening." While the well-heeled environs of the tourist haven of Aix-en-Provence was neither obviously besieged by police nor silent on issues of race, it was still a place where talk of "racism" was confined to students and the press, not for polite company—where the word "race" was avoided as though a sullied four-letter word. If some university courses in Aix and Marseille were offered on issues related to immigration, none foregrounded or even broached the relationship between racism, immigration, and the history of France.[10] Acquaintances visibly squirmed when I brought up the "Front." Attempts to turn after-dinner conversations (that invariably touched on national and local politics) to the FN's increasing presence in May 1998, were met with impatience and awkward silence. When the FN began turning against itself and spiraled into what seemed to portend a decline in May 1999, there was smug satisfaction about its impending disappearance and an end to the need to talk about it at all.

This oscillating presence and absence marks something of the forcefield in which the FN was changing form. For it was also a moment in which both FN victories and anti-FN demonstrations were reported as front-page news—and as run-of-the-mill events. In towns and cities of Provence, FN elected officials had closed down local cultural centers, censored theater performances, banned "inappropriate" children's books (especially those with stories about "mixed" couples, or images of parents or children of color). Provence in 1997 is where, as in Vitrolles, FN elected city officials first installed new "security" measures, allocating municipal funds to hire

9. See Gérard Desportes, "Hommes, femmes, blancs, blacks, beurs . . . L'équipe finaliste du mondial, modèle d'intégration réussie," *Libération*, 1998.

10. Colonial history, by contrast, was suddenly becoming a new favorite subject in the popular and academic press, but with contemporary French racism displaced from those stories.

their own beefed-up squads of civil guards outfitted with motorcycle boots, truncheons, and black shirts, evoking memories of another era. The outfits were soon replaced, as one woman from Vitrolles put it, with "more respectable" and conventional blue uniforms, but its city hall and tiny central square remained wired with surveillance cameras aimed on the town's inhabitants for their "security."

What was striking in the aftermath of France's World Cup victory, then, was not only a euphoric gush of self-congratulatory sentiment in a depressed economy but how sure people seemed to be that France's multicultural soccer team and the widespread support and adoration for it symbolized a defeat of the extreme right. How could the evidence of two decades of increasing support for FN candidates (no French extreme-right party had ever survived as long) be annulled by a post-victory celebration of racial harmony?[11] Why was one player's popularity—that of Zinedane Zidane), the son of a "poor Algerian immigrant" (evinced in street chants of "Zidane for President")—interpreted as evidence of a meaningful multicultural romance rather than a one-night stand? How could the president of the French National Commission on the Rights of Man claim that the World Cup "inflicted a defeat for racism"?[12] On the streets and in the press, one could hear people say, "See, we've got them now," "The FN has been silenced by this outburst of racial goodwill," "The Marseillaise belongs to us again." Left-wing weeklies wrote about a "real national communion," a French antiracist "dream," a "plebiscite" for nationalism without exclusions. Intellectuals of diverse leanings hailed the unified, resounding celebration of Zidane (of "Zizous" as he was affectionately called in the press as if he was everyone's dear cousin, buddy, brother or best friend) as the expression of a "nationalism without chauvinism" that was truly French.

Similarly, what was commonly referred to as the FN's "implosion" in 1998 (as Le Pen and his former protégé, Bruno Mégret, battled for supremacy in a public standoff) was taken as further evidence that the popularity of

11. Lest one imagine that the surge in the FN's presence started in the 1990s, read Jane Kramer's prescient ethno-historical portrait of the face of race in the (very) provincial city of Dreux in the early 1980s, where the FN had already made its presence felt and where its housing projects were already seen as a breeding ground of Arab terrorists and those who "stole" jobs from the real French: Jane Kramer, "The Mayor of Dreux," New Yorker, February 17, 1986.

12. French National Commission on the Rights of Man, August 12, 1998 .at www .cncdh.fr.

the extreme right was a dead issue. In both cases, the confidence was myopic and misplaced. Press coverage continued in the months that followed, with sanguine predictions, reveling at the FN's acceleration into high gear "self-destruction" and an impending and much anticipated fall from grace. The sensationalism was a distraction and, symptomatic of a more general tendency in analyses of French social and political life: a refusal to confront what has encoded racialized sensibilities as common sense. It was the FN that was kept in the limelight not the recurrent exercise of racial distinctions, local and widespread, daily and incessant as the support and relay of exclusions, containments, and expulsions in France and across Europe then and today.

Optimism is one thing; political delusion is another. The reaction to Le Pen's victory over the socialist candidate Lionel Jospin in spring 2002, four years after Le Pen's supposed "demise," was dismay and "shock" in the national and international press. Political commentators referred to the "week of surprises" and a turn that "no one expected."[13] But one could argue that this dismay was more surprising than the victory—only understandable if one acknowledges a sustained aphasia about the colonial and racial history of France. A racial platform long relegated to the political extremes had shown itself as more widely embraced than virtually any commentator in the 1990s had been willing to see or suggest.

The responses to the FN's "civil war" in 1998 and to the 2002 election were indices of a deeper set of misconstruals about what has made up the force of the radical right, and what meaning the FN brand of racism has for its vocal and silent constituencies. That people *expected* the FN to be unsettled and irreparably damaged by the patriotic ecstasy around the World Cup and the internecine FN battles derives in part from caricaturing how racisms had manifested in the past and what, if anything, distinguishes their contemporary valence. It leaves little room to consider an affective response as a form of reflection or judgment on the part of those who support the FN. Not least, it misses both the multiple sites in which racial understandings of the social world are nurtured and the seemingly discrepant discourses that the FN has so successfully sustained. Taking the celebration

13. See "Chirac–Le Pen: La semaine de toutes les surprises," *Le Monde*, April 28, 2002; Suzanne Daley, "Extreme Right Eclipses Socialist to Qualify for Runoff in France," *New York Times*, April 22, 2002, http://www.nytimes.com/2002/04/22/international /europe/22FRAN.html.

of multiculturalism as fundamentally subversive of racial regimes ignores basic historical evidence. As we saw in the preceding chapter, cultural hybridities can be smoothly folded back within racial social formations that legislate disparities with or without the law.

TRACKING THE FN IN AN ETHNOGRAPHIC VEIN

"Fieldwork" in Vitrolles and its environs, from Aix to Marseille, was not of a genre I had done before. I did not know people in the way that comes from repeated, long, exhilarating, and exhausting day- and nighttime conversations with the same people by which "ethnography" garners its name. But if "immersion" is a criterion, as Marilyn Strathern holds, I was steeped deeply in a multimedia and multisensory barrage of encounters, words, gestures, and images that have come to be a common ethnographic vein. At the time, I thought to call my work "ethnography in the public sphere," but it was more an effort to capture the discord between what I saw, heard, and read, and an effort to identify the historical ontology of that dissonance and duress of the present.

I tracked the movements of people, publishing, and politics; discourses and differences that cut across local and national contexts—attentive to the verbal and visual presence that race and racism assumed in and out of the FN—in televised sound bites, websites, movies, radio, dinner parties, and graffiti. In the case of Vitrolles, the sensibilities about who was an outsider and who was not divided the town and was both tactile and present in the conversations with those with whom I talked at FN demonstrations in Marseille and counter-demonstrations confronting them; at court hearings in Aix, where the family of a *"beur"* (French Arab) girl denied access to a high school was pitted against her FN assailants. I tracked changes in the Front's websites and in newspapers that were overtly committed to its program as avidly as those set against it.

Women and men affiliated with the Front's parent-teacher organizations gave me their time. I followed FN candidates as they "worked" local markets in municipal elections and spoke with FN city officials, as well as with city workers who had lost their jobs when the Front moved in because their first or family names were North African. A friend who taught for years at Vitrolle's local *lycée* introduced me to her colleagues. I was glued to television interviews with FN leaders; tracked the new wave of documentaries about FN-occupied towns; spoke with journalists writing on the FN in Toulon and

Orange and with lawyers defending those subjected to FN aggression; visited the FN's national headquarters in St. Cloud, outside Paris; and sought out cafes known to be friendly to FN supporters. A new popular book on FN people and politics seemed to appear nearly every month. I neither "infiltrated" the Front nor hung out with its opponents; instead, I tried to understand how racism and fears of it affected people's movements by day and night, while tracking how race alternately remained unremarked and boldly articulated, in the public sphere.

If Provence's countryside is a favored destination for those seeking out the "real" and rural souls of France, the *département* in which Aix is located gives onto unseemly vistas and smells, as well. A huge Shell refinery takes up half of the polluted "lake" between Marseille and Aix, an elongated low end shopping mall extends between the two cities, and rows of grim subsidized housing are the norm in towns such as Vitrolles. Driving an hour and a half from Aix gets you to the towns of Toulon, Vitrolles, Marignane, and Orange—the infamous four sites of FN victories where as much as 45 percent of the population voted for platforms committed to "France for the French," "French first," expanded municipal police forces, exclusion of welfare for "immigrants," punitive measures for parents with "delinquent" children, and cash bonuses for couples who produce "French" babies.

This area has been the radical right's epicenter, and Vitrolles has been one of its prime locations, as both the Front and its opponents acknowledge. Vitrolles-en-Provence—as the new FN mayor, Catherine Mégret, renamed it to highlight its non-existent cultural attractions and potential tourist appeal—is where the FN's national programs were rehearsed; where experiments in vigilantism, cultural censorship, and selective access to schools depending on one's skin color have been implemented in part to gauge whether such measures might produce too much publicity (or not enough), whether they might scandalize too many people, or whether they might prove too tepid to mobilize greater support from those still on the fence about whether they would seek to become part of the FN's constituency.

The story told in this way is dramatic, but the protagonists are predictable and the plot is clichéd. The Front's politics often seem excessive, unreasoned, and extreme. There is even comfort in such an account. We know its elements; we can imagine its actors—men of repressed violence and a region beset by a population of uprooted, disenfranchised, former colonials (*pieds-noirs*) longing for a long-lost "French Algeria," people whose vision is narrow and desperate, whose employment opportunities are bleak, and who are too easily duped by simple answers to difficult questions.

But there was another side to the Front that is less easy to demonize, one less dissonant with mainstream public concerns. Its proponents have always spoken in the language of democracy and liberty. They condemned violence. This side of the Front was harder to distinguish from other positions; it was a side that those who assume they "know" the FN were less likely to see or hear. What is striking about the FN and those who make up its constituency is how unexceptional and commonplace they are. Take, for instance, the FN's platform and practices regarding increased urban security. Front watchers invariably characterized the party's program as committed to a heavy-handed crackdown on crime and juvenile delinquency. In Vitrolles in spring 1998, people talked in whispers about FN officials siphoning off municipal funds from cultural centers and reallocating them to pay for more police. FN town officials spoke unabashedly about the possible benefits of withholding state welfare payments to families who could not control their youth. To their mind, a critical problem in Vitrolles and elsewhere in France has been schools that are "too permissive," "too lax" (laxiste), and insufficiently "authoritarian." As Alain Cesari, Vitrolle's FN deputy mayor, explained, there were just too many families who do not know how to parent and high schools with too many left-leaning teachers catering to "problem kids," while those students with real potential and deserving attention are neglected and left on their own.

On the face of it, the position is quintessentially FN and racially marked: Juvenile delinquency disproportionately touches poor families, and poor families in urban France are disproportionately of North African origin. Withholding welfare payments for such families targets those most dependent on state resources, who live in badly maintained state-subsidized tenements, are often unemployed or working at impossibly low-paying jobs. It reads as a policy invested in buttressing a disciplinary, punitive exclusionary state, not an inclusive and liberal one.[14]

But this, too, is not exactly the case. Reportage that was not focused on the FN over those same years shows clearly that the Front was not alone

14. In April 2002, when Le Pen resumed his campaign, he did not bother to speak against immigration. As Le Figaro noted, "This time, it was enough to just speak of insecurity": "L'examen de conscience a commencé dans les cités où prospèrent les incivilités et sévit la violence: Le vote Le Pen vu des banlieues," Le Figaro, April 25, 2002.

in its preoccupation with these issues. A parliamentary report on juvenile delinquency, issued by the socialist government while Jospin was prime minister, also recommended imprisonment as punishment for parents who could not sufficiently monitor their young.[15] The proposal a month later of the right-wing mayor of Aix-les-Bains—a non–FN town of 28,000—to withhold state welfare from families with delinquent youths was no different than the policies advocated by the FN.[16]

FN rhetoric and the issues it addressed already slipped easily into concerns in a wider public sphere. In this chameleon-like form it was increasingly difficult to identify a purely FN position, partly because the Front was so effective at appropriating the rhetoric of the right, the left, the extremes, and, it seemed, everyone in between. As Jean-Marie Le Pen put it to Mayor Michael Bloomberg during a visit to New York, "I'm socially left, economically right, and more than ever and anything else, nationally for France."[17] It is not only, as Pierre-André Taguieff pointed out twenty-five years ago, that the radical right had appropriated the language of the French Revolution and patriotic nationalism.[18] Nor has it only played on anxieties over national identity, prompted by fears about a future with a borderless Europe and what was then the recent adoption of the euro.[19] Open discussions of immigration were disabled in part because raising the issue became synonymous with a racist position. Proprietary claims to the language of "democracy," "individual liberty," and "the public good" are belied by the fact that those terms appeared as often in FN speeches as in those of its opponents.

Even accusations of racism—so long directed at FN's leaders and their platforms—were no longer confined to anti–FN discourse. During 1998, the FN mounted a new campaign with a refurbished vocabulary, claiming that France's current problem was not its racist tendencies but, rather, the anti-patriotic, "anti-French racism" of its "assailants" who were the real

15. Hervé Vaudoit, "Mineurs délinquants: Pression sur les parents," La Provence, April 17, 1998.

16. Philippe Révil, "La croisade d'un élu contre la délinquance des mineurs," Le Monde, May 25, 1998, 9.

17. Quoted in Erwan Lecoeur, Un néo-populisme à la Française: Trente ans de Front National. Paris: La Découverte, 2003, 11.

18. See the sharp analysis of the multilayered mobilizing tactics of the Front in Pierre-André Taguieff, "The Doctrine of the National Front in France (1972–1989): A Revolutionary Programme? Ideological Aspects of a National-Populist Mobilization," New Political Science 8, 1–2 (September 1, 1989): 29–70.

19. Pierre-André Taguieff, Les fins de l'anti-racisme (Paris: Editions Michalon, 1995).

threat to national heritage and French identity. A distorting twist of the term "racism" was turned into its opposite. Rather than a relationship of power in which white Frenchmen come out on top, the FN's definition of "racism" targeted the country's leaders for being too swayed by a "cosmopolitan" intellectual left, more committed to globalization than to local French interests. Pat Robertson's concurrent injunctions against a conspiratorial "New World Order" spearheaded by a deracinated intellectual left was more than resonant.[20] In the FN scenario, such "anti-French racism" produced other victims—the old-stock of French citizens made vulnerable to encroachments on their jobs subjected to a denigrated cultural heritage, poor conditions in their schools, and infringements on their human rights. In a public colloquium in June 1998 on "anti-French racism" organized by the municipal library of the FN-run city Marignane, a favored example was the increasing prevalence of those who "spoke of" and "encouraged *métissage*" (mixing).[21]

The politics of appropriation cut both ways: As the FN talked about the defense of liberty, those opposed to xenophobia were appealing to categories that were not dissimilar to some of those of the FN. Broad-based public discussions described a deluge of immigrants, despite *decreased* immigration over the previous twenty years.[22] Politicians opposed to FN policies were pulled into debates over the evils or virtues of supporting the FN's platform for a "national preference." Whether or not they disagreed with its basic tenets, the *terms of the debate* were framed by the Front's demand for strict immigration quotas, a "return" of immigrants to their countries of origin (whether they had been born in France or not), and a war against a population for whom access to medical benefits, social assistance, and any political representation was on the line.

These are more than deft language games. They were part of a widely shared cultural repertoire of verbal and visual images that have had broad resonance and continuing appeal. Moreover, while FN tactics have been characterized as excessive and unprincipled, their positions have offered

20. See Pat Robertson, *The New World Order* (Dallas, TX: Word, 1991).

21. "Compte rendue d'un colloque publique à Marignane sur le theme: 'Le racisme anti-français,' " June 12, 1998.

22. The ambiguous use of "immigrant" to include "jeunes françaises d'origine immigrée" and "jeunes immigrés non français" is not fortuitous but instrumental in the racial politics of this discourse: see Yannick Lefranc, "Comment le parti de l'exclusion traité un mouvement pour l'intégration," *Mots* 58, 1 (1999): 60.

ready answers to hard questions. What the FN has conceived as "problems" and "solutions" often were more easily grasped than those of its socialist opponents. Front watchers have focused on the rhetoric of FN leaders for years, but something else was more disturbing and striking: the discursive space the Front provided both for its militant supporters and for its potential uncommitted sympathizers. Women and men I met in Vitrolles—some of whom avowed supporting the Front, although most did not—conveyed their fear and distaste in compellingly similar terms. Almost everyone expressed distrust of traditional politicians and politics.

Frontal attack on the Front's racism and xenophobia (in the profusion of books and newspaper articles in the late 1990s) enabled some discourses and closed off others. One could argue that it created an engaged and active public sphere in which racism's immorality was openly argued and multiculturalism was celebrated. But another case could be made: With so much attention focused on the evils of the FN and its rise and fall, less heed was paid elsewhere—to the sympathies of a broader French population whose visions and political principles were not incompatible with those of their more overtly xenophobic FN counterparts. Among those who distanced themselves from the FN was the common phrase, "I'm not a racist, but . . . ," followed by a narrative about why too many immigrants was France's most pressing problem. The FN did *not* hold a monopoly on racist visions and racist practices in 1999, and it certainly does not today.

THE FRONT'S COMMON SENSE:
ON BEING INDEPENDENT OF POLITICS

In Vitrolles, I posed two basic questions to those I met: What does it mean to be educated in France today, and what sorts of knowledge and know-how should go into that pursuit? To both, most people quickly responded that they were not interested in politics (although I rarely used the word "politics" or referred to party politics per se). They were tired of teachers' organizations, local interest groups, regional leaders, and national parties that were all *trop politisés* (too politicized). Women of the parent-student association APPEVE, supported by the FN, insisted that theirs was a strictly "independent" organization, unfettered by political affiliation. Their concern was pointed: for their children's education and safety and, unlike those associations backed by the socialist and centrist conservative parties, not political. No one with whom I spoke in APPEVE acknowledged its FN affiliation or connection. They were concerned instead with an educational system too subservient to politics, teachers who brought their (left-wing or liberal) politics to the classroom, and inadequate discipline in schools. "Laxity," "lack of discipline," "lack of limits," lack of restrictions on what teachers could encourage or say were the stressed and most frequent terms of those conversations. "Discipline" was a key word and lack of it a key concern. But this was at once distinctly FN and not. Mothers of the Front spoke forcefully about discipline, but so did those women with socialist and center-right affiliations. What differed was what they all meant by discipline and who was deemed to lack it.

BEYOND THE EXTREMES: ARE THESE REASONING WOMEN AND MEN?

Pierre-André Taguieff was lambasted in the 1980s by some on the left when he criticized France's vocal antiracist organizations for pathologizing extreme right adherents in ways that evoked the scapegoating central to racist discourse itself. FN militants and constituents, however, were pathologized in specific ways: as being outside reason, unduly impressionable, and morally weakened by disempowerment. This image of FN supporters as viscerally Other, delusional, and gullible had specific effects (as if one could almost smell their politics on their breath). Deemed outside the humanist tradition, they were in any context and all instances labeled irrational and unreasonable men (sic). It was their conjoined fears (of foreigners, of job loss, of change) that were taken as the FN's most powerful "common denominator."[23]

One could start from a less intuitive premise (at the time) but a more plausible one now: that the radical right has been populated not only by insecure and fearful malcontents on the margins of French society but also by reasoning women and men. One could set out with another supposition: Front adherents were not aberrant "monsters" but, instead, "rather likable" and "nice" (sympathetique). As one ardent FN watcher put it, theirs are "faces that might occupy the ranks of any political formation."[24] What if one starts not from the assumption that the FN's platforms have been

23. Michalina Vaughn, "The Extreme Right in France: 'Lepenisme' or the Politics of Fear," in The Far Right in Western and Eastern Europe, ed. Luciano Cheles, Ronnie Ferguson, and Michalina Vaughn (London: Longman, 1995), 215–33.

24. As Mark Hunter wrote, "There are, in reality, monsters in the Front; I have met several of them. But one equally finds people rather likable, attractive, which raises another question: what are they doing here among these monsters?": see Mark Hunter, Un Americain au Front: Enquête au sein du FN (Paris: Stock, 1998), 11. See also Jonathan Marcus,

based on ill will, small-mindedness, and sinister imaginings and not just that the FN's force derived from its trafficking in carefully crafted slogans and clever manipulations of signs. One could argue, rather, that the Front exercised a nuanced, if not subtle cultural politics. Racism as we know is not an excess and anomaly of modern states, bureaucratic machines gone out of whack, but fundamental to how the exercise of governance (as Foucault so famously suggested in 1976 to a then skeptical, unreceptive Collège de France audience).[25] This is a good starting point to understand the FN's appeal and the increased popularity of its claims.

"Subtlety" is not the first word that comes to mind to describe the extreme right in the United States or Canada, much less in Germany, Belgium, the Netherlands, England, or France. The term "extreme" or "radical" underscores a set of perceptions and practices deemed beyond the pale, violent, exaggerated, outside the norm. This may well describe some white-supremacist groups—the Canadian Western Guard, the Ku Klux Klan, and some FN adherents. But to stop there is to miss how such discourse operates. "Nuanced" may not capture what typified the FN's cultural know-how, but metaphors of excess coupled with descriptions of a flat-footed, crass, uninspired rhetoric do not do so either.

The point may seem obvious today but it was certainly not 15 years ago.. Many of those academics and intellectuals I knew in Aix and Marseille could not understand why I chose to study the FN. Jean-Marie Le Pen, I was told, was *nul* (a nothing), *pas la peine* (he was not worth the effort). I was wasting my time. These were not innocuous statements but tinged (from good friends) with annoyance, with impatient irritation that as an American I was misrecognizing and prejudging the issues at hand. More so, I did not know the political lay of the land. One could dismiss their criticisms (as when one acquaintance facetiously asked whether I was "going yet again to visit my FN buddies" (*copin[e]s*). There was a sense that I was already implicated, too close for comfort. Something was amiss and rubbing off, in even entertaining the possibility that they were not monsters, not wholly Other, like and not categorically different from "us."[26]

The National Front and French Politics: The Resistible Rise of Jean-Marie Le Pen (New York: New York University Press, 1995), 2.

25. Ann Laura Stoler, *Race and the Education of Desire: Foucault's History of Sexuality and the Colonial Order of Things* (Durham, NC: Duke University Press, 1995), 55–94.

26. George Marcus cast this very "complicity" as a way to access "the forms of anxiety that are generated by the awareness of being affected by what is elsewhere without

The FN's commitment to the trinity of *"Famille, Travail, Patrie"* (Family, Work, and Fatherland) has long had cross-cultural relevance and cross-class and nationalist appeal. Moral righteousness is at its center, much as it was in nineteenth- and early twentieth-century imperial formations where such invocations spoke to European colonial women as much as to men. As exclusionary invocations they do lots of work: they call up the coziness of belonging, speak in the language of the majority's protection, promise to "weed out" those racial and moral others who threaten the common good. A poster of the "Young People's FN" from 1997 urging a "de-pollution of the city" spoke explicitly to such concerns.

The FN's cultural politics are both well honed and in constant revision. Originary narratives on the real roots of France and on rightful member-ship in the national body have been rehearsed in countless publications. The FN already had its own small coterie of committed scholars billed as es-teemed scholars of the Sorbonne and devoted to producing publications on the true "origins of France."[27] These were not cheap political tracts. Printed with glossy covers on high-quality paper in paperback form, they were not easily distinguishable in content or form from the publication by a member of Chirac's centrist party titled *Insecurity: To Save the Republic* in 2001.[28]

The Front's poster art was pop and catchy, if misdirected, when it first came out. Some posters were clearly inspired by a combination of stark socialist realism and fascist populist imagery (bare-chested, glaringly white young men with short-cropped hair, toned and taut, working with tools in hand with eyes raised to the banner of France and the FN's eternal flame). Others made subtler commentaries. A poster I was proudly shown in the basement of the FN's national headquarters showed two cartoon-like figures—one a wasted, disheveled, drug-ridden student of left-wing vintage

---

knowing what the particular connections to that elsewhere might be": George E. Marcus, "The Uses of Complicity in the Changing Mise-en-Scène of Anthropological Fieldwork," *Representations* 59 (1997): 97.

27. Some of these are *Les origines de la France*, published "under the direction of Professor Jacques Robichez," among others, with Bruno Mégret and Jean-Marie Le Pen named as co-authors: Jacques Robichez, Yvan Blot, Jean Haudry, Pierre Vial, Jean-Marie Le Pen, and Bruno Mégret, *Les origines de la France* (Saint-Cloud: Éditions Nationales, 1996). The volume, published by the FN press, Éditions Nationales, was a product of its 12th Colloque du Conseil Scientifique du Front National: see Pierre Milloz, *L'immigration sans haine ni mépris: Les chiffres que l'on vous cache* (Saint-Cloud: Editions Nationales, 1997).

28. Christian Estrosi, *Insécurité, sauver le République* (Monaco: Rocher, 2001).

PRINTEMPS 98:
élections CROUS - élections RÉGIONALES

1968
1998

ETUDIANTS,
VOICI VOTRE BULLETIN DE VOTE !

RE RENOUVEAU ETUDIANT
4, rue Vauguyon - 92210 St-CLOUD
TEL. 01 41 12 50 99

with the year 1968 scrawled above his head, and the other, a well-groomed, bright-eyed, tousled blond-haired youth with the year 1998 over his.

These over-the-top references are no longer used today, but a theme and a phrase remain durable: the numerous invocations to rebel, to stand up (against the powers that be). The notion of the FN as a challenge to prevailing authority figures as the visual and verbal message of thousands of posters coming off the printing press in St. Cloud. One poster portrayed a young blond cartoon figure winking, with "Rebel! Join the Front!" in bold red type above his head and, to his right, a challenge to be "politically incorrect." What could better invoke the fight against the Parisian liberal and leftist status quo than an alignment with the rightist revolution on the FN's side and on the side of France's future leaders? As a retired schoolteacher from the south who was packaging posters at the FN headquarters reminded me, "See, we have our own intellectuals, too."

It is not just poster culture that was on the mark. The FN's cyberspace connections were informative, clear, and interactive for those who sought to join. Its website was updated regularly with statistics on local and national elections, new political tracts, online copies of FN books, and excerpts from the anti-FN popular press. In the tradition of the French Communist Party, whose famous annual festival combined family fun with cultural and political events, the FN hosted an array of summer universities, institutes for "cultural action," scientific meetings, colloquia for journalists, and educational workshops (such as one held in Toulon's Neptune Palace concert hall that took as its theme "Liberate the Republic"). These were vital and well-attended events, though the more recent ones have muted the blatantly racist images and are more inclusive.[29] In the late 1990s, FN national rallies had glitzy sound-and-light shows with singers of color blasting rap and reggae music. Radio Le Pen, which provided nonstop news for several years, stopped broadcasting as an independent station and joined the older, better-established station of right and far-right programming, Radio Courtoisie, which now showcases the FN.

In 1998, the FN press provided daily and weekly analyses of national events and incisive commentaries on articles from *Le Monde*, *Libération*, and the foreign press that accounted for how the FN was maligned. Attacks on

29. As Mabel Berezin noted, having attended the FN's annual Fete Bleu Blanc Rouge in 1998 and again in 2005: Mabel Berezin, "Revisiting the French National Front: The Ontology of a Political Mood," *Journal of Contemporary Ethnography* 36, 2 (2007): 139.

REBELLE-TOI
REJOINS LE
RE
POLITIQUEMENT INCORRECT!
RE
LES ETUDIANTS
FRANÇAIS D'ABORD !
4 rue Vauguyon - 92210 St Cloud
Tél : (1) 41 12 10 57

the FN were reported by its journalists as a badge of honor and were minutely tracked to add weight to their claim that FN supporters were the real ones who were being undemocratically harassed and subjected to violent aggression. *Canard Enchaîné*, a satirical weekly committed for years to goading the FN, was mocked in FN dailies, which scrupulously mimicked *Canard Enchaîné*'s black-and-red boldface type and layout form.[30] At a glance one could not distinguish the format and font of the FN press from that of its opponents.

Already in the late 1990s it was becoming difficult to isolate and specify what constituted the unique discourse of the extreme right in France. Mabel Berezin makes the case that "extremism does not win elections." And she is right. The usual narrative is that this "turn" to a more toned-down FN is recent, but what remains striking is that the emergent forms in which this recasting took place were not really a turn away from "the extreme" but, instead, a case of the mainstream, albeit in less crass styles, moving toward what the FN had long championed. Nor is the FN considered the party of the neglected little man any longer. As the collective authors of *Cette France-là* have so clearly argued, a "shameless right wing" in the halls of national governance has now fixated on "the immigrant question."[31] Its slogans, discourse, and policies melding with and confirming the validity and prescience of the FN's xenophobic directives and direction.

---

30. After the split between Mégret and Le Pen, the FN articles became noticeably more tepid, targeting safe and familiar targets—most notably, immigrants and those construed as such who were not.

31. *Cette France-là*, ed., *Xenophobie d'en haut: Le choix d'une droite ehontée* (Paris: La Découverte, 2012). The publications of the *Cette France-là* collective are by far the most sophisticated analyses of the language, policies, and practices that have surrounded the politics of immigration over the past ten years. Their impressive two volumes combine narratives of those who have lived the effects of France's immigration politics with documentation of the increasing severity of migration politics and treatment of those in refugee camps such as Sangatte, in the north of France. There is really nothing like these volumes with respect to the measured weight given to the range of actors implicated in, affected by, and reporting on and researching immigration politics: journalists, *sans-papiers* (immigrants without the requisite papers), prefects of police, civil servants charged with processing immigrants' applications for residence and citizenship, activists, and academics. Volume 1 alone provides eighty personal stories: see *Cette France-là Volume 1: 06 05 2007/30 06 2008*, and *Cette France-là Volume 2: 01 07 2008/ 30 06 2009* (Paris: La Découverte, 2009). Three more volumes are in preparation.

FIGURING THE FN: THE MAN, THE MOVEMENT, THE NATION

Problems in specifying what is specific to the FN are strongly reflected in changes in how journalists, scholars, and activists have profiled the extreme right and in the emphasis they place on its founder and leader. Between 1993 and 1998, there was a virtual explosion of literature on the "FN phenomenon," and a distinct set of registers in which that phenomenon was cast. Typologies rarely hold fast. Still, there was an identifiable shift in emphasis from a focus on the leader Le Pen to the FN as a fascist institution, to the radical right as a reflection of French society itself.

The first register conformed to a "big man theory of history" or the "cult of the man." Here the FN's power to persuade was framed as solely based on the debating skills and rhetorical flourish of the party's charismatic leader. According to this argument, people were pulled in inadvertently, almost accidentally, because of Le Pen's force as a leader. Ergo, if the FN was Le Pen, then it was only a short-lived, conjunctural phenomenon that would reasonably weaken with his fall (thus, titles such as In the Shadow of Le Pen, The Le Pen Effect, Le Pen: The Words and The Said and the Unstated of Le Pen).[32] The rise of Bruno Mégret in the late 1990s did not undermine that model. With focus on Mégret's more youthful, up-to-date style and (short-lived) panache, the "big men" were (possibly) changing, but not the premise of the analysis.

Journalists have a penchant for extravagantly newsworthy personalities, but eventually even they could no longer argue that the Front was only Le Pen. A second wave of books took up the conflict in successionary rights from Le Pen to Mégret and the growing tension between them. Those who once imagined that the FN would dissolve with Le Pen's demise now were predicting the opposite—that the FN was possibly taking on new force as the offensive brashness of Le Pen was replaced by a more muted, stately style. Cendrine Le Chevallier, a mayoral candidate in Toulon, was hard to bill as a populist candidate with her Hermès scarves, Chanel ensembles, and demeanor of a media star moving through an adoring crowd. The oppositional press lingered on her glittering jewels and the chime of her gold bracelets as she lightly (and just barely) brushed hands with would-be sup-

32. Examples might include Pascal Perrineau, Le symptôme Le Pen: Radiographie des électeurs du Front National (Paris: Fayard, 1997); Maryse Souchard, Stéphanie Wahnich, Isabelle Cuminal and Virginie Wathier, Le Pen, les mots: Analyse d'un discours d'extrême-droite (Paris: La Découverte, 1997); Lorrain de Saint Affrique and Jean-Gabriel Fredet, Dans l'ombre de Le Pen (Paris: Hachette Littératures, 1998). Jean-Gabriel Fredet is a former press officer for Le Pen.

porters in popular urban crowds. The flagship journal of Parisian intellectuals, *Le Nouvel Observateur*, opined that Le Chevallier had learned to "withdraw her claws" and mocked her passionate belief in "family values," while she insisted that she had nothing against immigrants and was not a racist.[33]

Being brash and outspoken were early FN hallmarks. The future, however, was invested with men and women literally of a different cloth. Mégret and his cohort wore expensively cut bankers' suits and preached alliances with the traditional right, not distance from it. While being outrageous and provocative was the strategy of an earlier moment, something else was now emerging. Confusing the camps, blurring the distinctions, tangling the terms of what was possible to discuss publicly all signaled appeal to a different set of sensibilities and strategies to win new support.

This second wave of analysis gave less emphasis to Le Pen than to the appeal of the Front as an organization, its recruitment strategies, its partisans, and its institutional frame. Demographic analyses of regional and national elections made efforts to identify the specific populations that "succumbed" to the FN, with focus on their idiosyncrasies and on the susceptibilities of those who might "fall" in the future. Starting more than two decades ago, with the first alarm at the FN's electoral success, the effort was to isolate those vulnerable to its appeals. This was a reasonable effort when the FN's numbers were still small and scattered unevenly throughout the population. In 1996, *Le Nouvel Observateur* could point to an FN constituency made up of "special" groups—for example, of *pieds-noirs* (repatriated Frenchmen born in Algeria), first-wave European immigrants from Italy and Portugal, and those described as dislocated, emasculated, unemployed young men.[34]

The 2002 elections suggested a broader constituency that had not been considered particularly vulnerable to FN claims: the rural and the elderly. In the south of France, deep resentment at the influx of *Nordistes* (those with advanced educational degrees from Paris and the north of France), well-paid engineers, and those with technological expertise in the "high-tech" industries created what in 1995 was called "a new poverty of an old-time people and the recent opulence of a new one"—and increasing support for the FN.[35]

33. Agathe Logeart, "Toulon: La droite en rade," *Nouvel Observateur*, 1998.

34. See also Pierre Tevanian and Sylvie Tissot, *Mots à maux: Dictionnaire de la lepénisation des esprits* (Paris: Dagorno, 1998).

35. Van Eeuwen and Viard, *Main basse sur la Provence et la Côte d'Azur*, 23.

This demographics of blame—the breakdown of which groups were considered susceptible to the FN's lure—had a lot of targets. Some studies optimistically asserted it was really only "the aged," hardline nostalgics for colonialism, or those most fearing change who were attracted. But that turned out to be an unsustainable analysis. The FN's closet constituency was far vaster. Others focused on its particular attraction to young men, either ignoring the numerous women won over or actually celebrating (incorrectly) that women were not falling into the FN trap. Political analysts addressed the regional clustering of FN support in the troubled working-class outskirts of Paris and southern France. In the latter case, the "cause" was found more specifically in a population known to have supported the Pétain/Vichy government during the wartime occupation, who then fled at the war's end to France's North African colonies, only to be grudgingly forced back to France in the early 1960s with Algeria's independence.

These studies certainly had something to say about the nature of FN support, but more to say about what researchers expected to find and how they framed their inquiries—namely, looking for evidence that the FN was a decidedly idiosyncratic and non-French phenomenon. Scholars shared this perspective with activists and the press. It was captured perhaps best in the favored derogatory slogan" "F is for Fascist, N is for Nazi," so often plastered across anti-FN posters and chanted (with patriotic confidence) at anti-FN rallies. It remained popular for some time, as though one had to look to the history of Italian and German political extremism for a source of sympathies that in fact were born and bred in France.

Much as it is no longer possible to maintain that the Vichy regime was only a foreign imposition on an unwilling and unknowing French population, so, too, did analyses of the FN in its third register turn away from this search for a foreign etymology and origin.[36] No longer seeking the anomalous nature of the FN within an otherwise republican French society, some analyses have sought other roots—that of a "Made in France" FN.[37] Vaguely concurrent with the FN's increasingly broad regional and class spread of constituencies, more emphasis was placed on it as a product of French nationalism gone awry, as an accurate mirror of the ills of French society

36. Among the first in this genre of Vichy exposé, see Henry Rousso, *Le Syndrome de Vichy: De 1944 à nos jours* (Paris: Seuil, 1990).

37. Hubert Huertas, *FN: Made in France* (Marseille: Autres Temps, 1997).

or, alternatively, as a distorted mirror of its malaise.[38] Here commentaries turned to the making of an endemically xenophobic movement that was neither foreign nor imposed but organically French.

Not surprisingly, these shifts in exposé style and scholarship were not dissimilar to the course of Holocaust studies over the past sixty years that also moved from studies of "the man" (Hitler/Le Pen) and then the party (National Socialist/National Front) to analyses more attentive to structural effects. These included economic depression, the anonymity of urban sprawl, and the party as a product of a technocratic state machine and a swollen and alienating bureaucracy.[39] But a glaring difference remained. In the German case, the relationship between racism and the (Nazi) state was fundamental to the analysis. Studies of the FN, on the contrary, systematically begged the statist question, in part because the starting premise was that the French republican state was the FN's nemesis and opposed to it.

But if one endorses Foucault's contention that racism is fundamental to the making of the modern state, other questions should now command our attention.[40] If state racism takes varied forms, can those forms be identified as firmly and explicitly entrenched both in the state's central institutions and in displaced sites of its shadow presence? What does the political presence of a vocal extreme right allow states to avoid? Does a Europe without borders call for more stringently defined and policed interior frontiers? Across Europe, political analysts have been documenting a rise in electoral support for overtly racist candidates for some twenty years in Austria, Denmark, Portugal, Switzerland, Italy, Belgium, and the Netherlands.[41]

But it may be these are not the wrong answers but the wrong questions. Assessing the force field of the FN may entail more than looking to its increased electoral successes, media presence, or organizational appeal. We should be looking at the political habitus it has helped to create to assess how much it governs a wide range of gestures, dictates the behavior and

38. Alain Bihr, *Le spectre de l'extrême droit: Les français dans le miroir du Front National*. Paris: De l'Atelier and Ouvrières, 1998).

39. On the Holocaust as "deeply rooted in the nature of modern society and in the central categories of modern social thought," see Zygmunt Bauman, *Modernity and the Holocaust* (Ithaca, NY: Cornell University Press, 2000).

40. Michel Foucault, *Society Must Be Defended: Lectures at the Collège de France, 1975–76* (New York: Picador, 2003).

41. See Julio Godoy, "Politics: The Right Is on the Rise across Europe," *The Monitor*, December 16, 2003, 1, http://www.monitor.net/monitor/0312a/copyright /europerightrise.html.

dispositions of those unsympathetic to it, and shapes the rules rather than the particular strategies of the game. We might ask not only about its aims, strategies, and tactics but also its practical effects on what has entered the range of the norm.

Take, for example, the "culture of fear" that was said to surround the FN in the 1990s. Was it produced by the FN or by those who opposed it? To what extent was it generated out of FN practices and or the result of the FN opposition creating the effect? And what was feared: FN supporters or the unacknowledged attraction that, the liberal left worried, the FN was already garnering? Reaction to my work on the FN during those years was to dissuade me from continuing. I was advised to get an unlisted phone number and a post office box rather than use my home address in Aix. Some suggested I refrain from talking to anyone at FN rallies and that I not carry a camera or even attend anti-FN demonstrations. Nearly everyone advised me to watch my back and to keep distance from the press. At one level, these were not unreasonable precautions: The FN was "known" to harass and threaten its opponents, and retain beefy bodyguards to protect their leaders in potentially hostile crowds. On a visit to the FN's St. Cloud headquarters, I deposited my ID at the door and tried not to cringe when my name was entered in the receptionist's computer. (I was later chided by friends for reckless bravado, for going there and relinquishing my ID.) These were not unusual "security" measures. Were these fears produced by the FN or by anti-FN caricatures?

But that is probably the wrong question. Fear of the Front permeates social relations in a wide political field. If credibility is defined by the capacity to impose both the categories of comprehension and common sense, then the FN has long been a strong player. It both reproduced a culture of fear and counted on that fear to reverberate and amplify in a range of public domains. This was more than evident in watching the effect of its victory in Vitrolles. With nearly 47 percent of the population having voted for the FN in the 1997 elections (and it did not seem to matter, as some residents claimed, that many in Vitrolles had registered only a "protest vote" against the preceding, supposedly spend-thrift, socialist mayor), people repeatedly talked about a tense atmosphere in town, expressed discomfort even greeting their neighbors. Some people named FN supporters in hushed voices. Others seemed not to want to know whom among their neighbors and friends had actually cast an FN vote. Some spoke about increased suspicion, distrust, and avoidance that was oppressive and not unlike a new brand of terror.

By 1999, two years after Catherine Mégret's victory, "security" was a prevailing trope that blanketed multiple sites and senses. Vitrolles's Mayor's Office, in its monthly magazine, boasted that "security in '98 was even better than '97," with the introduction of more police dogs, mounted police, surveillance cameras and a new "rapid intervention police brigade." In contrast, young women in subsidized public housing saw the issue of security otherwise: as a state of siege, a police presence so intense that they and their friends chose not to walk around at night. They said they felt the streets were safe and "secure" only in the *absence* of police in the light of day. If these fears that "security" engenders are now only part of a historical moment in Vitrolles's local politics, they have emerged as the very lineaments of mainstream politics and public life over the past two decades.

THE FAMILY FRONT AND GENDER POLITICS

The point of looking at scholarship on the FN is not to conclude that the analyses have all missed the mark. Rather it is to question both the certitudes and assumptions that organized the prevailing frames. At one of the first Front demonstrations I attended in fall 1997 on Marseille's waterfront, two angry and vocal elderly women stood in the midst of a large crowd, chiding "France" for not upholding its democratic principles. I assumed they were anti-FN demonstrators and were impressed by their brazen stance in a hostile crowd, only to realize that they were FN supporters and that the day's slogan, "We've had enough" (of liberalism, immigrants, anti–FN attacks), was on their lips, too. There was nothing out of the ordinary about the event—only my assumptions about who spoke the language of liberty, where, and in what way.

One issue consistently omitted from academic research and public commentary on the FN is the singular effacement of women and the party's gender politics. Coverage has focused on the FN and men—on the male elite who formulated its policies; on the young, male "immigrants" against whom its policies were and are aimed; and on the insecure and unemployed male population to which it supposedly has its greatest appeal. While men provided the majority of the FN's electoral support in the late 1990s, even then women made up about 25 percent of its support, a decisive percentage in the narrow margin by which the party often won local elections.

There is nothing to decipher in the FN posters from 1996 that called for *La famille* as a "national priority." "The family" is, as one would expect,

LA FAMILLE, PRIORITÉ NATIONALE

FRONT NATIONAL

4, rue Vauguyon 92210 Saint-Cloud - Tél : 41 12 50 00

FN

white, heterosexual, and nuclear. Not examining the appeal of the FN for a female constituency derived in part from an unstated assumption that women who cast their vote in its favor were simply following their fathers, brothers, sons—their men. But this misses a crucial node of what constituted its early appeal and what has emerged since then as a mainstream concern throughout the French electorate.

FN leaders knew there was a problem and sought to remedy it in specific ways. For one, it was in the late 1990s that women were increasingly planted—often unsuccessfully, as in the case of Catherine Mégret—in key leadership positions as substitutes for their husbands and, less often, as active agents in the Front's juggling of posts and people in local politics. As FN men such as Jean-Marie Le Pen, Bruno Mégret, and Jean-Marie de Chevallier were disqualified from elections on procedural grounds, their wives replaced them as candidates in mayoral and regional campaigns. Following the FN's split in fall 1998, Le Pen's daughter, Marie-Caroline, "defected" to Mégret's camp, highlighting a basic tension between loyalties to political kith versus intimate kin, especially charged because the FN's central platform has been so closely tied to "family values." The gender dynamics reflected in the fact that Mégret's wife, Catherine, could legitimately "stand in" for him as Vitrolles's mayor, despite her glaring inexperience, pushed on the relationship between family and politics yet again, snidely signaled in the anti-FN press reports via references to her husband, Bruno, as the "mayor consort"—a phrase that Jean-Marie Le Pen used repeatedly when Mégret broke with him in 1998 to create his own splinter party, the Mouvement National Républicain (MNR).

Catherine Mégret's installment was a disaster. She knew nothing about Vitrolles, lived elsewhere, and never set foot in town for the five months following her victory, confirming what everyone said they knew: Vitrolles was being run from elsewhere. Vitrolles became infamous for its violent tactics, for the numbers of city officials fired, for the closing of a cultural club considered anti-FN. Under the Mégrets' leadership, Vitrolles fell into more municipal debt than it had ever experienced before.

Family, gender, and politics emerged again with the surprise announcement by Le Pen that his wife, Janny, rather than Mégret, would stand in for him in the European parliamentary elections, a moment that, many argued, first publicly marked the severing of the FN into two camps.[42] The conflict

42. See, e.g., "FN: L'Histoire interdite," L'Evénement, 1999.

(and Janny Le Pen's unexpected and much publicized response to the press that she neither wanted to run nor knew anything about politics) brought the gender politics of substitutability to a new, heightened level. At stake were not only the new divisions within the FN but conflict over a safeguarding of its political credibility. Since its strong showing in the 2002 presidential elections, Marine, then referred to as Le Pen's "clone" daughter—a "broad-shouldered, blonde" thirty-five-year-old lawyer—became "the electable face of the extreme right" and her father's obvious successor. Le Pen himself already declared to *Le Monde* in 2003 that he was "transferring" to her the "hope of smashing the isolation of the FN."[43] In fear that she might realize that hope, the press in 2004 already considered her "more dangerous than her father."[44]

But affinal substitutes and parent-child betrayals are essentially titillations for the press and should not overshadow a more important feature of the FN's gender politics. Many of the major themes played out in public discourse targeted areas of life thought to be the domain of, and of special importance to, women: primary school education, day care, childrearing, family planning, and sexual morality. In the FN's favored slogan, "Family, Work, and Fatherland," it was "Family" that was first. Emphasis on the male contours of the Front failed to address critical arenas where it made its presence and power felt—all domains in which women have been actively called on to police the boundaries between the moral and the immoral, between what is considered public or private, between what should be handled at school and what has been and should remain affairs of parenting and the home. Not least, women were charged with the translation and micromanagement of "security" in the family domain.

These are issues that feminist scholars working in colonial situations and on the appeal of the conservative right in the United States and Britain have addressed for some time but for decidedly less time in France. If the issue of gender politics was examined at all, it focused on how extreme-right parties view women rather than *how women view those parties and their platforms.*[45] Seeking to learn something about how women of the Front pro-

43. Elie Barth, "M. Le Pen reporte sur sa fille l'espoir de briser l'isolement du FN," *Le Monde*, April 18, 2003, 8.

44. Jo Johnson, "Marine Le Pen in a Dawn Raid on French Voters," *Financial Times*, February 28, 2004.

45. See, e.g., Caludie Lesselier and Faimmetta Venner, eds., *L'extrême droite et les femmes: Enjeux and actualité* (Villeurbanne, France: Golias, 1997), one of the very few books on the subject.

cessed its programs and presented its appeal, I interviewed women who worked for Vitrolles's FN-run city government when I returned there in 1999. Many were well educated, well heeled, and politically learned mothers of school-age children. Unlike those in the FN backed teacher-student organizations whom I had sought out two years earlier, and who categorically refused any association or sympathy for its politics, these were women of the new Front—young Mégretistes who characterized Jean-Marie Le Pen as an outdated model for the FN and who were betting their political futures on Mégret.[46]

Schools were a problem for them, but they cast their concerns more widely. In an idiom that frequently invoked the problem of figurative and literal "thresholds," they feared the borders that were being crossed. Here it was the FN that cared to police the dangerous borders between France and its outside (with immigration quotas); the FN that understood the need to police school entrances; the FN that was vigilant about what belonged in school and what belonged at home. They were disconcerted by contemporary parenting styles and blamed "some" parents for neglecting the moral rearing of their young, for not instilling a sense of "good taste," for abandoning jobs to (socialist) teachers that they should have been attending to themselves. They blamed teachers for not leaving their politics outside the classroom. Mothers, they contended, should have the opportunity to stay at home. When I asked why so many FN women worked, one woman sighed and lamented that it was she who suffered, that she (and France) underwent a bit "too much feminism" when she was growing up. Work schedules were not designed with women in mind. Still, both she and her co-worker opposed propositions for gender parity. They called it an "aberration of the left."

How a new feminine, domestic face of the FN in the form of a young mother, Marine, would appeal to such sensibilities is a question to which FN analysts were not attending. And, as we know now and as evinced in Marine's profile today, these sentiments were widely shared. But the more important point is that below the radar of political commentary, the FN in the late 1990s was tapping into, experimenting with, and thinking through an intentionally amorphous and broad sense of "security" and

46. This was just a month before the court decision that the logo, name, and funds designated as those of the "FN" rightfully belonged to Le Pen and that Mégret could not use them without severe penalty.

"insecurity" that touched the intimate domains of family life that stretched beyond those who were FN supporters.

FUTURE DIRECTIONS AND OLD CONNECTIONS

What is striking about the Front's interventions in public education, welfare, immigration policy, library acquisitions, theater openings, and scholarship is the sort of racial thinking and racialized infrastructures it builds on and fashions for France and a wider European community for the twenty-first century. It is neither a new racism nor a replica of the old. France today harbors a racialized social ecology that is malleable, modernizing, and imbued with cultural currency.

The cultural ambiguities that characterized racism in colonial Indochina and the Dutch East Indies offer not historical contrasts so much as points of articulation in a recursive set of racialized forms of language, practices, and concerns. These were not considered "racial" issues, but, rather, questions of "security," as they are today. Tracking what designated "race" there and then should alert us to the fact that even those quintessential forms of racism on colonial terrain were built not on the truth claims of "qualified" scientific knowledge alone but, as discussed in chapter 6, on an affective logic of security. Here and there are a potent set of cultural and affective criteria whose malleability was a key to the sliding scale along which privilege was protected and privation was assigned. This ambiguity is not a hallmark of our postmodern critique—much less a postcolonial moment.

Still, what the face of racism looks like in this twenty-first century cannot be derived whole cloth from eighteenth-century and nineteenth-century templates. Nor can it be derived from the years of the FN's rapid ascension, followed by a succession of splits, failures, weakening, and resurgence. That two-thirds of France in a poll taken in summer 1998 could avow sympathy for at least some of the FN's platform was largely ignored at the time. Maybe now we can address the blunt ways in which xenophobic, racial polities produce such ample space for "solutions" to which not only FN adherents subscribe. Of far more concern is that these "solutions" are shared by a broad population for whom these are reasonable responses, "necessary," measured, and compassionate, if protective, common sense.

As I write in 2015, it is nearly two decades since the ethnographic work for this essay was first conceived and three decades since I began culling an FN archive, struck at the time by how resonant Le Pen's statements were with what I was reading in Aix's colonial archives next door. So much and so little has changed. One FN leader after another has been condemned by the French and European courts for siphoning funds out of public coffers and fired and sentenced to prison terms for an array of illegal acts. In 2014, *France Culture* aired a devastating report of the Mégret years in Vitrolles (which ended when Catherine Mégret was ousted in 2002). Those who lived in Vitrolles during those years describe it as a period of "municipal totalitarianism."[47]

Marine Le Pen, now presides over the FN, leads one of the largest parties in France. What were once seen as policies and perceptions peculiar to the extreme right are so widespread that phrases such as "French first" have virtually lost their FN signature. The "extreme" right is now the center. Marine Le Pen has fulfilled her promise to make the party more palatable and to provide a discourse and set of policies embraced and shared across more sites throughout Europe and on its margins. In 2002, Paul Gilroy astutely noted that racism was no longer a chic academic subject; it was worn-out, predictable, and passé—just as increasing support for racist parties was rising across Europe.

That insight should alert us even more than a decade later. The fantasy that the FN's rise was a conjunctural moment is over. The FN may disappear and Marine Le Pen may not win the 2017 Presidential election. But the fact that she will undoubtedly be a contender suggests that racialized entitlements, border closings, and celebratory insistence on protecting the "homeland" (that she and Donald Trump share with the reactionary and racist but *not extreme* supporters of Austria's Freedom party and the "Alternative for Germany") are deeply sedimented and resonant. The political landscape has changed, but the resilience of race as an organizing if unstated

47. See the detailed and excellent study by Gérard Perrier, a former *lycée* teacher in Vitrolles and close-up witness to the years before Catherine Mégret's election, the reactions to her "victory," and the reactions to the policies instituted during the Mégrets' five-year tenure in Vitrolles: Gérard Perrier, *Vitrolles, un laboratoire de l'extrême droite et de la crise de la gauche* (1983–2002) (Paris: Arcane 17, 2014).

principle of social practice and government policy underwrites more sites of contention in Europe (as it does in the United States) than ever before. An affective politics that targets immigrants, refugees, Roma, gays, and Muslims remains nestled in a conceptual vocabulary that still relies on "integration" of "foreigners," terms themselves that undo what "refuge" might mean and how much more radically it could and should be recast.

BODILY EXPOSURES

BEYOND SEX?

Are we really still in the same relationship of force, and does it allow us to exploit the knowledges we have dug out of the sand, to exploit them as they stand, without their becoming subjugated once more. . . . . . . isn't there a danger that they will be recoded, recolonized by these unitary discourses, which having first disqualified them and having then ignored them, when they reappeared, may now be ready to reannex them and include them in their own discourses and their own power-knowledge effects. . . . that is the trap.—Michel Foucault, "Society Must Be Defended" lecture, Collège de France, January 7, 1976

A striking feature marks the configuration of what (post)colonial studies looks like today: as this amorphous field has expanded to new parts of the global academy, it has contracted in others. Some of those who earlier claimed some affiliation now declare its demise, its conceptual frames obsolete and no longer salient to contemporary geopolitics. At the same time, new advocates have emerged among those seeking to rewrite effective histories of the present in political spaces and locales and in precarious conditions of life and labor where the concepts of empire and colonialism were contrived to have little purchase.

If (post)colonial studies gained its early foothold on the terrains of British Empire, the landscape has changed—as have the questions. Those working in, and on, the fractious colonial relations between France and Algeria, Israel and Palestine, Italy and Eritrea, Japan and Korea, the United States and Guam, or Guantánamo and Iraq, or on Native America's colonial and contemporary settler conditions, offer more than new entries to an old mix. They are redrawing imperial topographies and the political force fields in which colonial governance operates. They are identifying refurbished and new technologies of rule, the distribution of inequities instilled, and how colonial pasts figure in how sub-citizenships are conferred today. Not least, they are renaming and challenging the verbal tenses of inquiry, and asking what constitutes what was and is a colonial condition and an imperial situation.[1]

In the past decade, colonial scholars have ably demonstrated how and why sexuality has served as a key site of imperial control, of colonial anxieties, and as a dense transfer point of power. Its positioning as part of the "moral logic" of (post)colonial situations—and the "colonial present"—may be less clear now.[2] In this chapter, I ask how this may be so and why this moment invites renewed reflection. We now have a bulging archive to show that authorities in a range of colonial contexts endorsed a European-defined "respectability" as a norm to be sought and attained. Today it is "sexual freedom" and "liberation" from sexual oppression that has been appropriated as fundamental to what it is to be European and progressively modern. Sexual norms are said to mark specific (read, Muslim) minorities as "unassimilable" subjects, lacking the "cultural preconditions" that warrant full participation in their polities. Some would argue that sex is on the

1. Scott Lauria Morgensen, "Theorising Gender, Sexuality and Settler Colonialism" (2012); Elizabeth A. Povinelli, *Economies of Abandonment: Social Belonging and Endurance in Late Liberalism* (Durham, NC: Duke University Press, 2011); Noenoe K. Silva, *Aloha Betrayed: Native Hawaiian Resistance to American Colonialism* (Durham, NC: Duke University Press, 2014); Audra Simpson, *Mohawk Interruptus: Political Life across the Borders of Settler States* (Durham, NC: Duke University Press, 2014).

2. Derek Gregory, *The Colonial Present: Afghanistan, Palestine, Iraq* (Malden, MA: Blackwell, 2004). See Laura Briggs, *Reproducing Empire: Race, Sex, Science, and U.S. Imperialism in Puerto Rico.* Berkeley: University of California Press, 2002); Durba Ghosh, *Sex and the Family in Colonial India: The Making of Empire* (Cambridge: Cambridge University Press, 2006); Stephen Legg, *Prostitution and the Ends of Empire: Scale, Governmentalities, and Interwar India* (Durham, NC: Duke University Press, 2014); Philippa Levine, *Prostitution, Race and Politics: Policing Venereal Disease in the British Empire* (New York: Routledge, 2003); Philippa Levine, "Sexuality, Gender, and Empire," in *Gender and Empire*, ed. Philippa Levine (Oxford: Oxford University Press, 2010), 134–55; Anne McClintock, *Imperial Leather: Race, Gender, and Sexuality in the Colonial Contest* (New York: Routledge, 1995); Richard Phillips, *Sex, Politics and Empire: A Postcolonial Geography* (Manchester: Manchester University Press, 2006); Ann Laura Stoler, *Carnal Knowledge and Imperial Power: Race and the Intimate in Colonial Rule.* Berkeley: University of California Press, 2002); Ann Laura Stoler, *Race and the Education of Desire: Foucault's History of Sexuality and the Colonial Order of Things* (Durham, NC: Duke University Press, 1995).

political agenda to mark the borders of Europe as never before. Eric Fassin, for one, insists that in France the sexual politics of the headscarf and "gang rape" in the immigrant-populated, ghettoized urban outskirts (*banlieue*) provides the language of public discourse, and is positioned "at the heart of democratic self-definition."[3]

Now, it would seem, is the time to talk about sex and empire. When Gayle Rubin made the case in 1984 that "it's time to talk about sex," and I first argued in 1991 that sexuality was instrumental to the governing strategies of racialized colonial states, these were interventions about a politics of knowledge production that had restricted both the sites and the subjects in which politics was construed.[4] Today, when sexuality is at the spoken and ever present forefront of international humanitarian organizations, and of the triage apparatus mobilized to police who has rights to citizenship in European polities, it matters more than ever how these political issues are cast. Foucault's warning above is apt, for something seems askew in how the focus on sexuality has been animated and now framed. Sometimes colonial histories figure at dead center; sometimes they are detached as a non-contiguous political domain. Reaching a crescendo at precisely the same time that France's colonial past has been pried open for reassessment, debates about sexual politics and "sexual democracy" by and large are dislodged from the deep colonial history of France and the sexual politics of empire. Not least, those debates are aphasic with respect to colonial histories to which they are tied and often held apart from the genealogies

3. On LGBT issues as a litmus test for immigration, see Éric Fassin, "National Identities and Transnational Intimacies: Sexual Democracy and the Politics of Immigration in Europe," *Public Culture* 22, 3 (September 21, 2010): 507–29, and "The Rise and Fall of Sexual Politics in the Public Sphere: A Transatlantic Contrast," *Public Culture* 18, 1 (Winter 2006): 79–92. On the "refined" admission tests for immigrants to Britain, Germany, and the Netherlands that include questions about attitudes toward "forced marriages, homosexuality and women's rights," see Deanne Corbett, "Testing the Limits of Tolerance," DW.COM, March 16, 2006, http://dw.com/p/87cC; Human Rights Watch, "Netherlands: Discrimination in the Name of Integration," May 14, 2008, https://www.hrw.org/news/2008/05/14/netherlands-discrimination-name-integration.

4. Gayle Rubin, "Thinking Sex: Notes for a Radical Theory of the Politics of Sexuality," in *Pleasure and Danger: Exploring Female Sexuality*, 143–78, ed. Carole S. Vance (Boston: Routledge and Kegan Paul, 1984), Ann Laura Stoler, "Carnal Knowledge and Imperial Power: Gender, Race, and Morality in Colonial Asia," In *Gender at the Crossroads of Knowledge: Feminist Anthropology in the Postmodern Era*, ed. Micaela Di Leonardo (Berkeley: University of California Press, 1991), 51–100.

of "security" in which the disposability and policing of bodies exceeds the rubrics of sex.

The discrepancy raises hard questions. Have biopolitical technologies so substantially transformed in how they are understood to make their prior colonial coordinates no longer apposite? Are the management of sexuality and normative gendered distinctions now such a given in analyses of biopolitical governance that they need no longer be stressed? Or is it that understandings of what constitutes "the carnal"—with an emphasis more on the sexual than "on the flesh," as students of colonial histories have deployed them—are too constricted to account for the sorts of bodily intrusions and manipulations to which designated populations have been, and continue to be, exposed?

At a conference in Paris several years ago on "postcolonial situations and sexual regimes," both terms—and the attributes assigned to them— significantly were as varied as the analytic and political investments that animated their study.[5] The "postcolonial" as a political concept probably has had more than enough scrutiny, but what constitutes a "sexual regime" has not. Is a "regime of sex" a variant "regime of truth" in Foucault's sense— with discernible rules, possible discourses that are made to function as "true"; specific practices and regulations—or just like one? What might be understood by a "regime" in this context, and how fixed and commanding are such "regimes" imagined to be? Does a sexual regime govern all bodily intrusions that cannot be avoided, all unsolicited probings, the range of ambiguous handlings, and inadvertent touches that cannot be refused? Can it tell us when the accusations of sexual abuse will be requisitioned for right-wing political projects with racist design or for critical feminist ones?

Key to the sexual politics of colonial rule was never just sexual violations realized but the distribution of social and political vulnerabilities that nourished the *potential* for violation. Here I ask whether a privileging of sexual politics may not adequately capture the colonial and postcolonial forms of governance that manage the carnal, intimate, and affective relations to which people are subjected and by which they, in turn, reorder what most immediately presses on their movements, constrains their choices and manage the politics of their intimate lives. On colonial terrain,

5. See Anne Berger and Eleni Varikas, *Genres et postcolonialismes: Dialogues transcontinentaux* (Paris: Éditions des Archives Contemporaines, 2011). This essay is a much revised version of one that appeared in the Berger and Varikas volume, entitled "Beyond Sex: Bodily Exposures of the Colonial and Postcolonial Present."

this is not a new observation. Students of colonial history have asked how sexual morality, conduct, and coercion and sexual prescription and practice were perceived and enacted and repeatedly converged with the physical and psychological management of other domains.[6] Catharine MacKinnon once rightly claimed that state power hides sexual coercion behind consent, naturalizes dominance as difference, and conceals politics as morality.[7] But in the colonial regimes of French Indochina, the Netherlands Indies, and the United States, state-generated policy was only one element of a governing apparatus, supported by qualified expert knowledge and a crafted colonial common sense that did as much of that work. Debates over sexual morality and condoned sexual access calibrated the moral measure of social kinds and the broad spatial and social boundary-making projects of these racial formations. Imperial governance, as we know, cannot be reduced to workings of a state.

Sexuality was a preoccupation of colonial authorities, but never so in a constant or consistent manner. Sexual prescriptions were unevenly imposed and episodic in their application. Such prescriptions bore radically different weight as racial policies, definitions of security, and construed subversions changed.[8] Issues of sexual morality and its normative regulation vacillated between visible legal forms of control and others that were as imposing but went without saying—inscribed in the racial grammar of colonial common sense.

Nor was sexuality ever a *discrete* regime or an object of governance in its own right. The organization of domestic space in European and native households could index sexual degeneracy and racialized fears at some moments and remain unremarked at others. Underscoring the inextricable imbrication of race and sex, as does an analytics of "intersectionality," those working on the history of imperial formations too had been making that case for some time.[9] The racial coordinates of what constituted rape and

6. In addition to the references in footnote 1, see the contributions in Ann Laura Stoler, ed., *Haunted by Empire: Geographies of Intimacy in North American History* (Durham, NC: Duke University Press, 2006).

7. Catharine MacKinnon, "Mackinnon and Spivak on the Gendered State," *Feminist News* 25 (January 2007): 1.

8. See Stoler, *Carnal Knowledge and Imperial Power*, 41–78.

9. Kimberlé Crenshaw, "Demarginalizing the Intersection of Race and Sex: A Black Feminist Critique of Antidiscrimination Doctrine, Feminist Theory and Antiracist Politics," *University of Chicago Legal Forum*, 140 (1989): 139–67.

what did not, the rules and regulations around concubinage and prostitution between native women and European rank-and-file soldiers and between native women serving as the servants and sexual partners of colonial men in South Asia and Africa have been sustained subjects of inquiry for good reason. These forms of violation have been understood as never disentangled from what it meant to be white—and what it meant to be under the muted conditions of colonial duress. Sexual protocols were about sex, but they were as much about the racialized distributions of sentiment, about those inner states and affective dispositions they were imagined to index—and that so often eluded the state's control.

Rather than tease apart a distinct sexual politics to reflect on its (post)colonial inflections and colonial presence, we might do better to acknowledge the non-discrete forms in which governance operates. It is in the slippage between sexuality, intimacy, and bodily care where biopolitical interventions find their support and quotidian force. Numbers of historians have now made the case that sexuality was a "particularly dense *point de passage*" in the making of imperial power.[10] But we might remember Foucault's insistence in his treatment of the history of sexuality in Europe: This was neither the only *relais* through which power permeated the social field nor its only modality. What are the conditions that distinguish when sexual coercions and transgressions are pivotal to governance, or participate as a subjacent subscript to broader logics of intimidation, anticipatory violence, and control? As Didier and Éric Fassin have argued for contemporary France, the ambiguities of the racial and social/sexual questions are not obfuscations of reality or obstacles to understanding. That ambiguity faithfully registers how these issues are implicitly politicized in the public domain—and in the social reality of subordinations in which people live.[11]

Focus on the sexual politics in which imperial formations invest has the potential to lay out the logics of harm as much as it may distract from ongoing damages and displacements and the sorts of refusals they invoke. It is not sexual politics per se that opens to the decades in which former Algerian soldiers in the French colonial army (Harkis) and their families were segregated from French life in squalid encampments, to the continued decimation of young people's lives on Native American reservations, or to the

10. Michel Foucault, *La volonté de savoir* (Paris: Gallimard, 1997), 136.
11. Didier Fassin and Éric Fassin, *De la question sociale à la question raciale: Représenter la société française* (Paris: La Découverte, 2009).

enduring assault on Vietnamese who were and are exposed in a countryside polluted by Agent Orange.[12] Imperial governance makes itself felt less in the panoptic gaze of constant bodily surveillance than in the *arbitrary* means by which surveillance may quixotically shift into disregard and scrutiny is replaced by abandonment. As Achille Mbembe characterizes the violence of colonial management, it is the production of the *confused space* of the public and private that marks its force.[13]

What does that confused space look like today? Why, when understandings of the racial and sexual politics of empire generated such critical scholarship in preceding decades, did some of us who studied those interpellations take so long to respond to their current forms? It is significant that it was the "incidents" at Abu Ghraib that sounded the (post)colonial response and public alarm. Commentaries were not in short supply.[14] Sharp critics refused the facile convenience of moral outrage and instead sought to trace the photographed spectacles through a long history of Orientalist, homophobic fantasies about Arab men. Others insisted on the photographs' haunting familiarity, as did Hazel Carby, as part of the dark history of U.S. lynching "parties" and the glee of their audiences at the spectacle of close-up racial pornography.[15] Sexual manipulation, humiliation, and

12. The massacre of Harkis in Paris in October 1961 has been well documented, but the decades of their lives in isolated forest hamlets in the heartland of France has not. On the former, see Paulette Péju's *Ratonnades à Paris précédé de les harkis à Paris*, originally published and immediately banned in 1961 and republished, with an introduction by Pierre Vidal-Naquet, as Paulette Péju, *Ratonnades à Paris précédé de les harkis à Paris* (Paris: La Découverte, 2001). On the latter, see Tom Charbit, *Les harkis* (Paris: La Découverte, 2006); Vincent Crapanzano, *The Harkis: The Wound That Never Heals* (Chicago: University of Chicago Press, 2011).

13. Achille Mbembe, *On the Postcolony* (Berkeley: University of California Press, 2001), 28.

14. See, e.g., Nicholas Mirzoeff, "Invisible Empire: Visual Culture, Embodied Spectacle, and Abu Ghraib," *Radical History Review*, 95 (Spring 2006): 21–44; Jasbir K. Puar, "Abu Ghraib: Arguing against Exceptionalism," *Feminist Studies* 30, 2 (Summer 2004): 522–34; Jasbir K. Puar, *Terrorist Assemblages: Homonationalism in Queer Times* (Durham, NC: Duke University Press, 2007); Sherene H. Razack, "How Is White Supremacy Embodied? Sexualized Racial Violence at Abu Ghraib," *Canadian Journal of Women and the Law* 17, 2 (December 2005): 341–63; Mary Ann Tétreault, "The Sexual Politics of Abu Ghraib: Hegemony, Spectacle, and the Global War on Terror," *NWSA Journal* 18, 3 (Fall 2006): 33–50.

15. Hazel Carby, "A Strange and Bitter Crop: The Spectacle of Torture," OpenDemocracy, October 2004, https://www.opendemocracy.net/media-abu_ghraib/article_2149.jsp; Susan Sontag, "Regarding the Torture of Others," *New York Times Magazine*, May 23, 2004.

torture came into sensationalist play. Nor were colonial genealogies altogether missed. As Susan Sontag put it, "Belgians in the Congo and the French in Algeria too practiced torture and sexual humiliation on despised recalcitrant natives." These trophy pictures, as she and others insisted, were photographs of "us."[16]

As Frantz Fanon reminds us, the psychic distress and embodied duress of the Algerian War destroyed people's bodies and distorted their minds. These were not simply byproducts of the colonial order of things: Damaged personhood was central to that order and its making.[17] Jean Baudrillard called the Abu Ghraib photos "war porn," their "vileness . . . the ultimate symptom of a power that no longer knows what to do with itself."[18] Porn here speaks to more than sex: Obscenity is lodged in coerced exposure and the pleasures of eliciting shame and inflicting humiliation. How do we treat these acts of degradation as both sexual and not? Perhaps the task is not to write this into a sexual history of empire as once conceived but to ask how these events, at this time and this place, *at once reiterate and disrupt* as they refuse the ways these histories were written and their constitutive features have been displaced.

Or is Abu Ghraib as vile racial pornography a too easy target? As Anne McClintock astutely remarked, conflating torture with porn not only makes the torture seem banal. It averts the public gaze from race and imperialism and "from the calamitous scene of imperial misrule unfolding in Iraq."[19] Judith Butler's response too was not to abandon sexual politics but to focus attention elsewhere—on postcolonial Europe and the caricatures of Muslim morality that have informed citizenship requirements in a European Union anxiously vexed about its borders, on European liberal notions

---

16. Sontag, "Regarding the Torture of Others," 26. As Allen Feldman sharply put it, "Abu Ghraib is a photograph that Americans have taken of themselves—a self-portrait that refracts a collective identity whose spokespersons have conflated pre-emptive war and invasion with liberation": Allen Feldman, "Abu Ghraib: Ceremonies of Nostalgia," OpenDemocracy, October 18, 2004. https://www.opendemocracy.net/media-abu _ghraib/article_2163.jsp.

17. Frantz Fanon, *The Wretched of the Earth* (New York: Grove, 1963), 249.

18. Jean Baudrillard, "War Porn," *International Journal of Baudrillard Studies* 2, 1 (January 2005). The essay was originally published in *Libération* under the title as "Pornographie de la guerre."

19. Anne McClintock, "Paranoid Empire: Specters from Guantánamo and Abu Ghraib," *Small Axe* 13, 1 (March 2009): 61.

of sexual freedom being called on as instruments of coercion themselves.[20] Importantly, she looked less to sex than to the "generalized state of fragility and vulnerability in which some people are forced to live."[21] At issue is the uneven distribution of specific degradations and states of vulnerability, not a sexual regime per se. There is nothing abstract or generic about fragility. Certain people are rendered fragile, brought into vulnerable conditions, and have widely different recourse to ways to exit from them. If political passions are most profoundly centered on policing the borders of privilege, property, private and public space—and guarding against their permeability—as they have been in imperial formations, one might expect that security regimes and their biopolitical practices to fix on these, as well.

Security regimes do, as we know. They protect those spaces as they create them. But those who study the forms of biosecurity that have emerged since 9/11 point to increasingly indiscriminate violence that may "undo the rituals and rules that solidify hierarchies of social risk."[22] Laurent Bonelli argues that under cover of the war against insecurity, the French state has multiplied laws and decrees, generalizing social control to ever wider categories of the population. Duress multiplies in content and form. The coding of insecurity to broader spaces licenses police powers and missions of surveillance as it grants more social institutions the task and responsibility to define and then monitor security measures.[23] This is about bodily and psychic harm but not necessarily about sex.

SECURITY AND SEXUAL POLITICS IN THE UNITED STATES AND FRANCE

Anglophone and Francophone scholarship have differently approached—and elided—these subjects. In the former, three interpretive analytics came together inspired by Foucault, critical feminist theory, and an "historic turn" in the social sciences. We sought the making of racialized governance

20. Judith Butler, "Sexual Politics, Torture, and Secular Time," *British Journal of Sociology* 59, 1 (March 1, 2008): 1–23.

21. Judith Butler, "Vulnerability, Survivability: The Affective Politics of War." Lecture, March 27, 2008.

22. See Stefan Helmreich, "Biosecurity, a Response to Collier, Lakoff and Rabinow," *Anthropology Today* 21, 2 (April 2005): 21.

23. Laurent Bonelli, "Une vision policière de la société," *Le Monde Diplomatique*, February 2003, http://www.monde-diplomatique.fr/2003/02/BONELLI/9984.

not in policy pronouncements but in the details of the everyday—who bedded and wedded with whom, where, and when. But as important, being rendered a subject or citizen was tethered to sexual arrangements in ways that tied childrearing protocols and the recognition of paternity to the legal status of children as colonial subjects or citizens in their adult years. From governors-general down to local colonial doctors and schoolteachers, colonial archives were riddled with debates about family, "the necessary evil" of prostitution, and illicit unions. One need not look far. Concerns about racialized boundaries and the requirements of European membership rarely strayed far from enlisting moral arguments about sexual norms to do that work.

The contemporary landscape bears some features of that imprint but with a decidedly different valence. Significantly, in public and academic discussions of the imperial present after 9/11, the domestic, intimate, and sexual entailments of imperial pasts and presence were relegated to an increasingly marginal space.[24] Colonial intimacies—sexual or otherwise—somehow receded from view.[25] Those who first had something to say about the U.S. "macho security state" and a "hyper-masculine military" for the most part were not (post)colonial scholars.[26] It was Susan Faludi who identified a backlash against women in the United States in the wake of the Iraq war, in what she called a "sexualized struggle between depleted masculinity and overbearing womanhood."[27] But the United States as an imperial

24. Amy Kaplan wrote forcefully about "homeland insecurities," but not its sexual politics in "Homeland Insecurities: On Language and Space," *Radical History Review* 85 (Winter 2003): 82–93. Diane Nelson asked hard questions about gender and terror: see Diane Nelson, "Relating to Terror: Gender, Anthropology, Law, and Some September Elevenths." *Duke Journal of Gender Law and Policy* 9, 2 (July 1, 2002): 195–210. In reminding us that "empire is in the details," Catherine Lutz was among those who led the way to examine the "hypermasculinity" of military training: see Catherine Lutz, "Empire Is in the Details," *American Ethnologist* 33, 4 (November 1, 2006): 593–611.

25. See, e.g., Andrew J. Bacevich, *American Empire: The Realities and Consequences of U.S. Diplomacy* (Cambridge, MA: Harvard University Press, 2002); Linda Colley, *Captives: Britain, Empire, and the World, 1600–1850* (New York: Anchor Doubleday, 2004); Nicholas B. Dirks, *The Scandal of Empire: India and the Creation of Imperial Britain* (Cambridge, MA: Harvard University Press, 2008); Niall Ferguson, *Empire: The Rise and Demise of the British World Order and the Lessons for Global Power* (New York: Basic, 2004); Chalmers Johnson, *The Sorrows of Empire: Militarism, Secrecy, and the End of the Republic* (New York: Henry Holt, 2005).

26. See Frances Fox Piven, *The War at Home: The Domestic Costs of Bush's Militarism* (New York: New Press, 2004).

27. Susan Faludi, *The Terror Dream: Myth and Misogyny in an Insecure America* (New York: Picador, 2008). Identifying a veritable "purge" of women and feminist issues

formation was not part of her vocabulary, her archive, or her analysis. Zillah Eisenstein looked to the disciplining of women's bodies for khaki in "the rise of neoliberal empire" but not to the imperial histories of these relations.[28] Arundhati Roy's *An Ordinary Person's Guide to Empire* skewered the new workings of empire but with no mention of its sexual politics. Cynthia Enloe counts among the few who consistently placed sexuality at the center of her treatment of "a new age of empire" and women as a powerful source of counter-memory within it.[29]

In France, where (post)colonial studies has proceeded at a different pace and with decidedly different historical referents, the sexual politics of imperial France, until recently, had little place. If the early work of Catherine Coquery-Vidrovitch, Yvonne Knibiehler, and Régine Goutalier were about women and gender relations, it would be hard to make the case that their work addressed the management of sexuality to recast France's colonial history—or to rewrite its national one. Working in Paris libraries and the Aix colonial archives in the late 1980s on the racial politics of prostitution, illegitimate children, and venereal disease in the French colonies, it was hard to find a single dissertation on those subjects, or much more a decade later.

That is less the case today.[30] But even now, with the unprecedented turn to rethinking French national history through a colonial lens and with the avid tracing of the colonial templates of modern torture, confinement, and detention, the thick web of connections that join race, sex, and empire to the making and unraveling of Republican France still hover on the horizon. Elsa Dorlin's "sexual and colonial genealogy" of the French nation was a welcome entry, if coming a decade later than similar matrices were ex-

in the right-wing and progressive press, Faludi pointed to Bush's dismemberment of the Defense Advisory Committee on Women in the Services, arguing that the gender landscape of America has changed. To do so, she invoked the enduring myths of America and its captivity narratives of brave and resourceful pilgrims and pioneer women, a script inscribed in pop culture and in the racial politics of the United States.

28. Zillah Eisenstein, "Disciplining Female Bodies for Khaki: Title IX, Wars of Terror, and the Rise of Neoliberal Empire," keynote address to the North American Society for the Sociology of Sport, Montreal, October 2003.

29. Cynthia H. Enloe, *The Curious Feminist: Searching for Women in a New Age of Empire* (Berkeley: University of California Press, 2004).

30. See Emmanuelle Saada, *Empire's Children: Race, Filiation, and Citizenship in the French Colonies* (Chicago: University of Chicago Press, 2012); Christelle Taraud, *La prostitution colonial: Algérie, Tunisie, Maroc (1830–1962)* (Paris: Payot, 2003).

plored for colonialisms elsewhere.[31] There are critically ambitious histories that place sexual humiliation and torture at the center of French colonial policy. Raphaëlle Branche's *La torture et l'armée pendant la guerre d'Algérie* and Marnia Lazreg's *Torture in the Twilight of Empire* both focus on the period of Algerian War while Sylvie Thénault details the varied forms of unfreedom that internment instantiated as a practice of state agents in colonial Algeria.[32] Lazreg's book has not been published (and barely reviewed or flagged) in France.[33] Clearly, the "headscarf affair" has brought some features of its colonial etiology and nationalist discourse into conversation.[34] John Bowen, Mayanthi Fernando, and Joan Scott, among others, have identified the rationale for the new legislation and its Islamophobia as an effort to protect "French republican notions of sexuality."[35] Others have pointed to the targeted disciplining of women's bodies as it was emerging and spreading through Europe's public institutions.[36] But the racialized intimacies of an imperial biopolitics that sought to manage those relations are largely absent.[37] When Didier Fassin so pointedly reminded us that "history is not

31. See Elsa Dorlin, *La matrice de la race: Généalogie sexuelle et coloniale de la nation française* (Paris: La Découverte, 2009).

32. Sylvie Thénault, *Violence ordinaire dans l'Algerie colonial* (Paris: Odile Jacob, 2012).

33. Raphaëlle Branche, *La torture et l'armée pendant la guerre d'Algérie, 1954–1962* (Paris: Gallimard, 2001); Marnia Lazreg, *Torture and the Twilight of Empire: From Algiers to Baghdad* (Princeton, NJ: Princeton University Press, 2008).

34. John R. Bowen, *Why The French Don't Like Headscarves: Islam, the State, and Public Space* (Princeton, NJ: Princeton University Press, 2007); Mayanthi L. Fernando, *The Republic Unsettled: Muslim French and the Contradictions of Secularism* (Durham, NC: Duke University Press, 2014); Joan W. Scott, *The Politics of the Veil* (Princeton, NJ: Princeton University Press, 2007).

35. See Joan W. Scott, "Symptomatic Politics: The Banning of Islamic Head Scarves in French Public Schools," *French Politics, Culture and Society* 23, 3 (Winter 2005): 121.

36. See Gabrielle vom Bruck, "Naturalising, Neutralising Women's Bodies: The 'Headscarf Affair' and the Politics of Representation," *Identities* 15, 1 (January 22, 2008): 51–79.

37. In an otherwise important intervention, for example, Olivier Le Cour Grandmaison rehearsed a well-documented debate on "female emigration" with respect to white women in the making of French colonial morality, but with no entries for "rape," "sexual relations," or "concubinage" in the index: see Olivier Le Cour Grandmaison, *La république imperiale: Politique et racisme d'état* (Paris: Fayard, 2009). Among the edited volumes and special issues of journals to which I refer, see, among others, Pascal Blanchard, Nicolas Bancel, and Françoise Vergès, *La république coloniale: Essai sur une utopie* (Paris: A. Michel, 2003); Claude Liauzu and Leila Blili, eds., *Colonisation, droit d'inventaire* (Paris: Colin, 2004); "Qui a peur du postcolonial? Denis et controversies," *mouvements des*

merely a narrative" but "inscribed within our bodies and makes us think and act as we do," his context was the history of the past thirty years of what the lethal joining of AIDS and poverty produced in post-apartheid South Africa.[38] We might do well to apply his reminder that "bodies remember" to (post)colonial France.

Rape has increasingly been understood as a basic weapon of war and a violation for humanitarian intervention, but as Lazreg notes, the French outcry against torture in Algeria has never been accompanied by one against systematically condoned rape and sexual violation. Even Benjamin Stora, master of telling and retelling what has been "forgotten" about that war provides neither an account of nor references to the boundaries that were policed through sexual threat and violation. It has been neither part of his multiple accounts of historical erasure nor does it figure as the postcolonial and postcoital detritus of those relations.[39]

Attention to sexual violation has resurfaced elsewhere. The scandal of the tournantes (gang rapes) was the occasion for a media explosion between 2001 and 2003 in which racialized assumptions and accusations surfaced from left to right in the press and public imagination.[40] French feminists' outrage at the coverage of the tournantes was derided for their "racist benevolence" toward Arab women against Arab men.[41] The veil and violation (le

idees et des luttes, (septembre/octobre 2007); Yves Lacoste, "La question postcoloniale," Herodote 120, 1 (March 23, 2006): 5–27. In Le livre noir du colonialism (2006), a massive ledger of colonial crimes and recriminations, sexuality is paired with "women," cordoned off in a single chapter: see Marc Ferro, ed., Le livre noir du colonialisme, XVIe–XXIe siècle: De l'extermination à la repentance (Paris: Robert Laffont, 2003).

38. Didier Fassin, When Bodies Remember: Experiences and Politics of AIDS in South Africa (Berkeley: University of California Press, 2007), xix.

39. Benjamin Stora, La gangrène et l'oubli: La mémoire de la guerre d'Algérie (La Tour-d'Aigues, France: Aube, 1991), La guerre des mémoires: La France face à son passé colonial (La Tour-d'Aigues, France: 2001). This is not the case for his account of the "invisible war" in Algeria in the 1990s, in which he noted that the "particularity" of the war was the violence perpetrated against women, which was "among the most atrocious" in the form of rape, mutilation and decapitation: see Benjamin Stora, La guerre invisible: Algérie, années 90 (Paris: Presses de Sciences Po, 2001), 98–102.

40. See Laurent Mucchielli, Les scandales des "tournantes" (Paris: La Découverte, 2012), and numerous websites devoted to these gang rapes and the Islamophobia that often accompanies reporting on them.

41. Nacira Guénif-Souilamas and Éric Macé, Les féministes et le garçon arabe (La Tour-d'Aigues, France: Aube, 2004).

voile et le viol), as Éric Fassin wrote, were blurred into moral condemnation, made one and the same.[42]

Miriam Ticktin has questioned pointedly why this was so.[43] She has rightly asked why both a French public and the French state that had not been interested in rape or sexual violence suddenly became concerned about it. Her assessment makes troubling sense: Sexual violence has served as the language of French border control, anti-immigrant rhetoric, and what it means to be really French. She draws us to the topography of the uneven distribution of concern about sexuality—about those domains that figure as charged and central and those that do not. Moral outrage and moral panic about the treatment of white and brown women by brown men have deep imperial genealogies and a strategic politics of their own.

But heightened moral outrage is not necessarily about changing the critical conditions of risk to which the purported subjects of concern are exposed. We may have something to learn from the turn to sexual violence and rape as the ultimate form of human violation by international humanitarian organizations and their advocates. Alice Miller warns that the current focus on sexual harm in human rights discourse and a concomitant use of "intimate storytelling by individual women" of rape experiences "too horrendous to ignore" serve to locate a woman's chastity as "the most important thing to know about [her]," without addressing the broader precarious conditions of her life.[44]

To reiterate: A turn to sex and the workings of imperial authority was an intervention at a particular moment, a critique of disembodied histories of racial discourse and of what constituted the political in imperial politics. It was a call to attend to how and why that history was effaced. But in a public sphere in which in 2003 George Bush Jr. could call for an end to the "sexual slavery of girls and women" as part of the "war against terror" and, in the same year, the French press remained riveted on the *tournantes* in the "sensitive" urban quartiers, it bears asking: What work a focus on the fear of

42. Éric Fassin, "Pourquoi et comment notre vision du monde se 'racialisé,'" April 17, 2007, 15, http://www.lemonde.fr/societe/article/2007/04/17/pourquoi-et -comment-notre-vision-du-monde-se-racialise_878567_3224.html.

43. Miriam Iris Ticktin, "Sexual Violence as the Language of Border Control: Where French Feminist and Anti-Immigrant Rhetoric Meet," *Signs* 33, 4 (Summer 2008): 863–89.

44. Alice Miller, "Sexuality, Violence against Women, and Human Rights: Women Make Demands and Ladies Get Protection," *Health and Human Rights* 7, 2 (2004): 17–47.

brown-skinned men as sexual predators, "disrespectful" of white women, and roaming the streets of Europe (as the new year's eve 2016 events in Cologne Germany were portrayed in the international press) is doing now?

A dispositif, we might remember, is not a "technology" of a fixed machinery but, rather, a réseau—a network established between elements, "a . . . formation whose major function is to respond to an urgency."[45] The activation of a dispositif occurs at specific, pressing moments. Treating sexual protocols and prescriptions as a mobile dispositif requires accounting for both their presence *and* their absence and when they are revoked and invoked. Attending to such movement may offer more than the notion of a sexual regime of a fixed set of attributes already in place. A réseau can be entered at many points and used to contrary and subversive ends. Subjugated knowledges course through them. Circuits can be clogged, disrupted by differential knowledge, redirected and differently engaged.

What sorts of carnal knowledge figure in the interstices of (post)colonial conditions and colonial presence today? Addressing that question calls for some rethinkings: one, about the politics of comparison; two, about what counts as the intimate; and three, how the inflation and expansion of "security" as a dispositif presses closer to some bodies as the circumferences of fear are being redrawn around others.

THE POLITICS OF COMPARISONS

Comparison is at the center of current debates about what empires did and do and what can be claimed about their common properties.[46] What gets

45. Michel Foucault, Dits et écrits: 1954–1988, Volume 3: 1976–1979, ed. Daniel Defert (Paris: Gallimard, 2000), 299. See also Giorgio Agamben, Qu'est-ce qu'un dispositif? trans. Martin Rueff (Paris: Payot and Rivages, 2014), 9–10.

46. This section of the chapter draws on Ann Laura Stoler, "Zones of the Intimate in Imperial Formations," in Carnal Knowledge and Imperial Power: Race and the Intimate in Colonial Rule (Berkeley: University of California Press, 2002), ix–xxxiv. The impetus to consider the political effects of comparison is evident in many quarters. On the comparative study of cultural formations, see Pheng Cheah and Jonathan D. Culler, eds., Grounds of Comparison: Around the Work of Benedict Anderson (New York: Routledge, 2003); Benedict R. O'G. Anderson, The Spectre of Comparisons: Nationalism, Southeast Asia, and the World (London: Verso, 1998). A new generation of students of Japanese, Chinese, Russian, Italian, and Ottoman imperial expansion draw on the insights of critical colonial studies without assuming that the defining features of empire across time and space are everywhere the same: see, e.g., Barbara Brooks, "Reading the Japanese Colonial Archive: Gender and Bourgeois Civility in Korea and Manchuria before 1932," in Gendering

to be named and to count as a "colonial situation" remains as contested as does the question of what structured inequities are inscribed in the "post-colony" today.[47] The *politics of comparison* points to comparing as an "active political verb," called on by colonial governing strategies themselves.[48] Choices of comparison were consequential to the strategies of governance and remain equally so to the implicit conceptual arguments and the kinds of questions raised or dismissed by those who study them. Such choices are not benign. Here, alternative "counter-comparisons"—those that confront the comparative choices of colonial regimes and imperial formations today—bear critical weight.

In the challenge to what has been excluded from the national histories of France, Israel, Belgium, Germany, Japan, China, and the United States, and what has *no choice but to be included* in the histories of Algeria, Palestine, Jordan, the former Belgian Congo, Korea, Puerto Rico, Martinique, and Tibet, is a basic asymmetry and shared effect. At issue is recognition that specific colonial histories have shaped who now makes up their populations; who has been disappeared from them; and who has been dispersed, dislocated, disposed of, made vulnerable, and segregated within and outside their borders.

Foucault's challenge "to think the unthought" directs us to the "landscape of shadow" in which our thinking is situated and by which it is framed.[49] That "shadowed landscape" came to the center of an emergent conversation in 2000 with U.S. historians about the intimate sites of U.S empire. We asked how much the histories of sexually inflicted racism, miscegenation laws, and the "problem of poor whites," were also histories of the U.S. as an imperial formation. Said's attention to U.S. imperial pursuits

---

Modern Japanese History, ed. Barbara Molony and Kathleen Uno (Cambridge, MA: Harvard University Press, 2008); Todd A. Henry, "Sanitizing Empire: Japanese Articulations of Korean Otherness and the Construction of Early Colonial Seoul, 1905–1919," *Journal of Asian Studies* 64, 3 (August 1, 2005): 639–75; Fouad Makki, "Imperial Fantasies, Colonial Realities: Contesting Power and Culture in Italian Eritrea," *South Atlantic Quarterly* 107, 4 (Fall 2008): 735–54.

47. See Mbembe, *On the Postcolony*.

48. On the "politics of comparison," see Ann Laura Stoler and Carole McGranahan, "Introduction: Refiguring Imperial Terrains, in *Imperial Formations*, ed. Ann Laura Stoler, Carole McGranahan, and Peter C. Perdue (Santa Fe, NM: School for Advanced Research Press, 2007), 15.

49. Foucault discusses "thinking the unthought" (*penser l'impenser*) in his most precise way in Michel Foucault, *The Order of Things: An Archaeology of the Human Sciences* (1966) (New York: Vintage, 1994), 326–27.

rather than British and French Orientalist variants, garnered our renewed attention.[50]

The product of those conversations was *Haunted by Empire: Geographies of the Intimate in North American History*. There we collectively asked what constituted a viable comparison between U.S. empire and other imperial forms; why certain comparisons seem appropriate and some more "counterintuitive" than others? Some contributors trained their sights on contexts in which the intimate coordinates of empire were obvious and easily accessible in documents. Some looked to contexts in which imperial imperatives had been framed by scholars—or, in vernacular terms, by historical actors—that rendered their effects hard to track. Bent on making more accessible the circuits of empire and the intimate lives of those who lived in and off them, we turned to practices rather than rubrics, to the effects of policies rather than how they were named. Our comparisons were rooted in both the local analytics of race making and the moral imaginaries of colonial policies themselves. Children mattered—how they were fed, schooled and raised. Heterosexual and homosexual alliances mattered: who slept with whom and who was condemned or licensed to do so, where, and when. Governing agents targeted the cultural, domestic, and sexual proximities that they imagined as reliable indices of personhood and political inclinations—still knowing that they did not really know about what they sought to verify—people's sentiments and moral states.

Unable to measure what they wanted to know, they sought instead to calculate the quantity and quality of food and clothing they would allot; the work children would perform; the physical contact that would be prohibited; the small exchanges of food, objects, and information that made up the minutiae of cordoned lives.[51] These practices of proscription and prescription spoke to carnal concerns, security fears, and carceral goals. Designed to temper dispositions, these choreographies of time and physi-

50. I was taken first by Edmund Morgan's insight that the inclusive principles of the American republic were developed through and dependent on racial exclusions. But it was the history of the U.S. slave plantation economy and the sexual license and prohibitions it conferred that seemed even more relevant and resonant with colonial histories elsewhere: see Edmund S. Morgan, *American Slavery, American Freedom: The Ordeal of Colonial Virginia* (New York: W. W. Norton, 1975). For a fuller account of this project and the initiatives that brought it about, see my preface and acknowledgments in Stoler, *Haunted by Empire*, x–xvii.

51. See Ann Laura Stoler, *Along the Archival Grain: Epistemic Anxieties and Colonial Common Sense* (Princeton, NJ: Princeton University Press, 2009), 105–39.

cal proximities were poor substitutes for monitoring the dispositions and intentions they could neither see nor control.

Such practices do more than "haunt" the landscapes of formerly colonized regions and the histories written about them. The French internment centers of Larzac and Aveyron established in the name of security during the Algerian War, not unlike the Harki encampments, maintained thousands in disjointed time and place, suspended from civil society and (unsuccessfully) from politics.[52] These forms of violence relocate the intimacies of empire in nondomestic space as they open to an emotional economy of intimate injuries that re-member bodily harm in residual humiliations and emergent indignant acts. Shattered possibilities to bear a child, a weakened constitution, enforced immobility, and "formless threats" render intimate violence as something else.[53] Such a reorientation does not make intimate intrusions less relevant; rather, it expands what dwelling in such spaces entails, a dwelling that can be suddenly invaded, accessed to monitor "contagions," and scrutinized for security measures. It resituates the intimate as a zone that is vulnerable to crushing nearness and *arbitrary* intrusion in the "lower frequencies" of the everyday.

Within a broader arc of biopolitical governing strategies, colonial governance was ordered, but its logic was contingent on irregular assaults on time and space. As Achille Mbembe also underscores, "What marked violence in the colony was . . . its miniaturization; it occurred in what might be called the details. It tended to erupt at any time, on whatever pretext and anywhere."[54] Sylvie Thénault makes just this point about the arbitrary nature of French violence in colonial Algeria, tracking the long history of internment and the ordinary violence that accompanied the conquest of Algeria in the 1830s and lasted well beyond the Algerian War.[55]

Such violence does more than "confuse the public and private."[56] It depends on and reproduces that confused space. As Ariella Azoulay has argued in the case of Palestinians whose homes are subject to night raids and

52. See Stéphanie Abrial, *Les enfants de Harkis* (Paris: L'Harmattan, 2001); Crapanzano, *Les Harkis*.

53. Rob Nixon, "Slow Violence, Gender, and the Environmentalism of the Poor," *Postcolonial Studies and Ecocriticism* 13, 1 (Fall 2006): 14.

54. Mbembe, *On the Postcolony*, 28.

55. Sylvie Thénault, *Violence ordinaire dans l'Algerie colonial: Camps, internements, assignations à résidence* (Paris: Jacob, 2012).

56. Mbembe, *On the Postcolony*, 28.

ransacked for purportedly harboring "terrorists," there is no private at all.[57] Any accounting for the visceral injuries of empire and how duress is lived must reckon with this range of intrusions, both the residual forms they reanimate and the emergent forms they take.

The enclosures and border regimes of colonial confinement are not limited to those sealed with barbed wire. Families and friendships, mobility and bodily health, childbirth, life and death—as Nadera Shalhoub-Kevorkian describes in an unprecedented study of what she calls "security theology" with respect to Palestinian surveillance by the Israeli state—remain precariously shaped by where people are located in the liminal zones among subject, citizen, and statelessness and how those caught in these ambiguous corridors have succumbed to and circumvented surveillance and control.[58]

It is hard not to come back to the Harkis when one writes about exposure and duress. When the sixty thousand-odd Algerians who served as French auxiliaries in the Algerian War of Independence (1954–62) made their way to France in the 1960s (after some 80,000–150,000 were abandoned by French authorities and slaughtered in Algeria), transition camps in southern France were only one of the many spaces of containment to which they were moved.[59] Closed in 1975, these camps were replaced by isolated forestry hamlets under military administration that for fourteen thousand Harkis became their permanent homes. In the 1990s, Harki families were still living sequestered, squalid lives with the lowliest of jobs, unseen on the dark edges of southern French small towns and villages.[60]

While these hamlets were rendered invisible to the French "proper" and abandoned by the French state, the histories that produced these conditions remain furtively unspoken to the Harki children who bear their weight.[61] These are not the "intimate frontiers of empire" evident in the taut relations between those abandoned mixed-blood children who were unrecognized

57. Ariella Azoulay, "When a Demolished House Becomes a Public Square," in Imperial Debris: On Ruins and Ruination, ed. Ann Laura Stoler (Durham, NC: Duke University Press, 2013), 194–224.

58. Nadera Shalhoub-Kevorkian, Security Theology, Surveillance and the Politics of Fear (New York: Cambridge University Press, 2015).

59. See Vincent Crapanzano, "From Anger to Outrage: The Harki Case," Anthropologie et Sociétés 32, 3 (2008): 121–38. See also Charbit, Les harkis.

60. See "Le Logis d'Anne, une honte pour la France," March 1995, http://alger-roi.fr /Alger/mon_algerie/harkis/pages_liees/logis_danne_pn55.htm.

61. The first studies carried out with Harkis were in the field of psychiatric medicine on the pathologies produced by their suffering: Charbit, Les harkis, 64–67.

by their European fathers, between Dutch men who left behind the Java-nese women who bore their children. There were no "custody battles" in the courts or custody scandals in the colonial press. In the Dutch East Indies, Dutch citizenship was conferred by acknowledgment of Dutch paternity. Subject status was conferred when Dutch fathers decided these were not children they were willing to raise. But not unlike the "intimate frontiers" of the colonial Indies that were always imagined to harbor "fraudulent" Dutchmen and unworthy mixed-bloods making claims to European status by dint of their manner or dress, physical and invisible borders marked the "interior frontiers" by which Harkis were sequestered.[62] They, too, have been subject to perceptions and policies geared to distinguish who is really French or only so in name. They make up a telling part of what some have come to now call France's *République coloniale*.[63]

Tacking between colonial pasts and presents has productive and unset-tling consequences that challenge, as I have argued throughout this book, cherished concepts and the attributes assigned to them. In 2003, with the U.S. invasion of Iraq and the crescendo of empire talk that followed, it was hard not to ask how policy makers, journalists, and conservative schol-ars could talk about a new imperial mission when the United States had such a well-documented history for so long. Why did the situation in Iraq only garner the attention of feminist scholars when the situation at Guan-tánamo and the torture tactics of Abu Ghraib receded as abruptly as they appeared? And who was doing the talking? Some answers may be sought in the authority that neoconservative commentators commanded with re-spect to "international studies and foreign affairs" and in the disciplinary strictures that make those in political science more audible voices in the mainstream press.

But other reasons seemed equally rooted in (post)colonial studies itself and in its prevailing conceptual frames. As I argued in chapter 5, blurred genres of rule were not marginal manifestations of imperial authority; nor were they signs of states in distress. They were the artifices that installed precarious conditions for peoples subject to them. Ben Anderson once wrote about Southeast Asia as a region characterized by "a strange history

62. For the perspective of a psychoanalyst on the impossibility of forgetting and the impossibility of verbalizing colonial violence in the present, see Alice Cherki, *La frontière invisible: Violences de l'immigration* (Paris: Elema, 2006).

63. Blanchard et al., *La république coloniale*.

of a mottled imperialism," but we might better think of mottled imperial forms as their common lot.[64] *Partial and ambiguous sovereignties* over land, labor, and "regimes of living" characterized imperial polities, cross-hatched with competing interests, multiple nationals, and competing economic and ethical claims.[65] Understanding the nature of U.S. imperial relations in Latin America or Iraq, or the technologies of Israeli colonization and surveillance, entails appreciating them as part of colonialism's foundational repertoire. The temporal dimension is key: As *states of postponement and deferral*, imperial formations thrive, I repeat, on promissory notes for sovereignty, autonomy, and services that are issued, suspended, conferred, or curtailed and reissued again. International development programs and humanitarian refugee camps rehearse that political deferral again and again.[66]

INTIMACIES OF OTHER ZONES AND OTHER REGISTERS

These reformulations bring a prominent condition of colonial rule into sharper relief as it circles us back to the issue of bodily exposures. Uncertain domains of jurisdiction produce thick corridors of ambiguous political status. Struggles over who is a citizen or subject, who is exempt from marriage laws, to whom pass laws apply, who can live where, who can travel and be issued a passport, whose children have access to which schools, who is incarcerated (where, in what conditions, and for how long) make up the micro-nodes of governance that impinge on and give distinct shape to the duress of people's personal and family lives. If the intimate does not inhabit "the outskirts of the social" but designates a site that can be "protected, manipulated, or besieged by the state," as Svetlana Boym held, there should be no surprise that what constitutes the "innermost" and assaults on it would be an embattled space.[67] Interior physical and mental space may be sites to fortify, a refuge from colonial intrusions, but there is more evidence that

64. Anderson, *The Spectre of Comparison*, 4–5.

65. See Stephen J. Collier and Andrew Lakoff, "On Regimes of Living," in *Global Assemblages: Technology, Politics, and Ethics as Anthropological Problems*, ed. Aihwa Ong and Stephen J. Collier (Malden, MA: Blackwell, 2005), 22–39.

66. Michel Agier, *Gérer les indésirables: Des camps de réfugiés au gouvernement humanitaire* (Paris: Flammarion, 2008); Didier Fassin and Patrice Bourdelais, eds., *Les constructions de l'intolérable: Etudes d'anthropologie et d'histoire sur les frontières de l'espace moral* (Paris: La Découverte, 2005).

67. See Svetlana Boym, *The Future of Nostalgia* (New York: Basic, 2001), 253, and her brief but poignant discussion of "diasporic intimacy" on pages 251–58.

they have been and continue to be privileged quarters for punctuated and patterned interventions.

In earlier work I treated intimacy more as a descriptive marker of the familiar and close at hand. Intimacy spoke to relations that were affectively charged, both tender and taut, of certain kinds of proximities grounded in uneasy attachments, encumbering affections, and abrupt departures. Such relations extended, as argued here, beyond those grounded in sex. Close attachments of other kinds drew political attention: between European fathers and their children of a different hue, between native housemaids who served as interim lovers, of children too close to their native caretakers—who could also be their mothers. But it was those affections at odds with prevailing colonial narratives that stopped me short: of a French naval employee for his mixed-blood son, a love seen as impossible in the late nineteenth-century by Indochina's colonial court; of the Javanese mother for the daughter she was said to "give up" but for whom she pined when taken from her; of an "Indo" boy of mixed parentage who ran away from a settlement house to be with his Javanese father, whom Dutch social workers were convinced cared nothing for him.[68] In each of these instances, colonial narratives followed a storyline that contradicted the sentiments expressed. Violence was acute and subcutaneous, not sexual; it cut into the intimate and into the flesh.

Haunted by Empire stayed this course but with more focus on the taut nature of those relations. It held closer to "tense and tender ties" within and outside what people at particular times considered private or called "home." Here the "intimate" expanded in breadth to "precarious affections, awkward familiarities, unsolicited attentions, uninvited caresses, probings that could not be easily refused."[69] Working off disparate senses of the intimate provided an untidy and productive mix of proximities refashioned in specific contexts for and by specific populations. Violation and violence hovered on the edges of those pages as revelations about Abu Ghraib and Guantánamo Bay saturated the press. Still, (as noted at the time) domestic space, schooling, child-care prescriptions, and public hygiene figured more prominently than the pungent, violent intimacy of prisons, barracks, and detention centers.

68. Stoler, "Sexual Affronts and Racial Frontiers" in *Carnal Knowledge and Imperial Power*, 79–111.

69. Stoler, *Haunted by Empire*, 15.

A constrained notion of domesticity and a circumscribed sense of the colonial conditions still crowded out sites and situations in which colonial intimacies took on more directly destructive and ruinous forms: sexual violations that accompanied surveillance; family ties warped by resettlement; parent-child bonds strained by dislocation; domestic spaces eviscerated by scorched-earth policies; foodstuffs that never got cooked because electricity was cut; Algerian sons and daughters rounded up at dusk; those Palestinian youth, cut off from their villages by impromptu Israeli barricades, who disappeared and never made it to the dinner table. Sensory assaults and deprivations of prolonged detention alter bodily integrity and function. Such reordering of the intimate may ensure that no place is safe; the familiar is treacherous; and no place is home.

To push out from domesticated sites of the intimate to other domains demands other points of entry: not the policed scene of the white child and Javanese nursemaid or even of the pursued housekeeper forced to accept entry into the master's bed. We might start instead with the sort of intimacy described by the philosopher Adi Ophir in his essay "There Are No Tortures in Gaza." Of torture, he writes:

> It is closeness that is intolerable, its immediate presence, which soon becomes all too familiar. There is hardly any situation of torture without the propinquity of something very familiar, with the intimacy of a room, a neighbor, a friend, or a lover. The torturers care for details. Torture is not only a moment of proximity to the other but a form of care for the other. The torturer comes very close, scraping or penetrating the surface of the victim's body, peering through the halls of his or her soul. Sometimes he is all over, sometimes he is inside, informing and de-forming, and even when he leaves something of him refuses to go away.[70]

Intimacy here is a matter of that which is immediate violation and crushingly close. Ophir's choice of language is chilling, in part because the very terms he calls on ("care," the "familiar," a "friend" or "lover") evoke associations of the intimate that promise other sorts of affective ties and a safe space. The juxtapositions should do more than jolt the senses. They are forceful reminders of the wider berth of intimate encounters predicated

70. Adi Ophir, "There Are No Tortures in Gaza," *South Central Review* 24, 1 (April 1, 2007): 27–36.

on humiliation, trespass, and intrusions—the sort that checkpoints, strip searches, interrogations, and midnight raids on homes foist on those subject to them.[71] These are part of the modern apparatus of colonial governance, but they are not new. As Marnia Lazreg writes, "rape, beatings with a *matraque* [truncheon], exposure of naked bodies and starvation" were used in the aftermath of the invasion of Algeria in 1830 and long after.[72] Simone de Beauvoir and Gisèle Halimi's account of the torture and rape of Djamila Boupacha during the French Algerian War in 1962 made public what Algerian women knew were far more common than in the war years alone: threats to bodily integrity that one could neither escape nor refuse.[73] If torture is at once about the relentless assault on personhood, the crushing of will, and the fissures produced by humiliations, how intimacies matter to imperial pursuits cannot but be about psychic and physical exposure.[74]

These intimacies come in forms that cut across the different moments of conquest and colonization. Eyal Weizman's accounts of the "micro-tactical actions" of Israeli assault on Palestinian domestic space as actions that literally wreak havoc with what is inside and out of the home by "punching holes through party walls, ceilings and floors, and moving across them through one hundred meter-long pathways of domestic interior hollowed out of the dense and contiguous city fabric" reorders the intimate yet again.[75] This is what the Israeli military calls a strategy of "walking through walls." Nuba Khoury describes her experience of it:

"Go inside, he ordered in hysterical broken English. Inside!—I am already inside! It took me a few seconds to understand that this young soldier was redefining inside to mean anything that is not

71. Béchir Boumaza and Jérôme Lindon, *La gangrène* (Paris: Minuit, 1959), seized and banned in France, was then published in English as Béchir Boumaza and Jérôme Lindon, *The Gangrene*, trans. Robert Silvers (New York: Lyle Stuart, 1960).

72. See Lazreg, *Torture and the Twilight of Empire*, 3.

73. See Simone de Beauvoir and Gisèle Halimi, *Djamila Boupacha* (Paris: Gallimard, 1962).

74. The impact of such intimate violations were rarely private. As Crapanzano insists, Algerian neighbors and kin knew well that torture was going on. Even if it was not seen, the screams were heard and meant to be heard behind closed doors: Vincent Crapanzano, personal communication, March 2010.

75. Eyal Weizman, *Hollow Land: Israel's Architecture of Occupation* (London: Verso, 2007), 185.

visible, to him at least. My being 'outside' within the 'inside' was bothering him."[76]

The assault on the "inside" relocates governance within half-demolished living rooms, on apartment balconies, on doorsteps, in bedrooms and hallways. At the Aida refugee camp in the cordoned Palestinian quarter of Bethlehem, there is little protected interior space. Gashes are evident on nearly every house, whitewashed and re-plastered outer walls bear the recessed imprints of mortar fire. The twenty-eight-foot-high slabs of concrete that make up the Israeli "security" wall around Palestinian territories splice through villages and house compounds as they separate olive-laden trees from homes. Colonial occupation makes front stoops in Hebron legally off-limits and not one's own.[77]

The interior frontiers designated by Israeli authorities may call on new tools, but like earlier techniques of colonial surveillance, those markings shuffle the relationship between public and private, between acts and intentions, between the actual and the expectant. Nowhere is the personal more political than in the security regimes of imperial formations that anticipate which interior states need to be controlled. The methods may be new in the colonial present, but they are not unrelated to well-honed notions of intelligence that operate, as we have seen, in the future conditional tense.

SOCIETIES OF SECURITY AND BODILY EXPOSURE

Biosecurity is not a new term, but it has expanded in use and breadth since 9/11. It is a concept with several definitions.[78] One refers to nonindigenous species (e.g., plants and animals) that adversely affect the habitats they invade economically, environmentally, or ecologically. The concept has been used in this sense by government organizations, as well as by conservation groups. A second definition broadens the boundaries to include both native and non-native species that heavily colonize a particular habitat. Its predicates are plants and animals, but the discursive space and practices it calls on are forms of surveillance of human bodies, not only as potential

76. Weizman, Hollow Land, 185.

77. See Ofir Feuerstein, Ghost Town: Israel's Separation Policy and Forced Eviction of Palestinians from the Center of Hebron (Jerusalem: B'Tselem, 2007).

78. See Wikipedia, "Biosecurity," http://en.wikipedia.org.wiki/Biosecurity.

victims of bioterrorism, but also as carriers of social harm. Biosecurity is also defined as "the policies and measures taken to protect from [biological] harm" by "an invasive species."

The concept's potential analytical purchase has not been missed. In a collaborative project, Paul Rabinow, Stephen Collier, and Andrew Lakoff define "biosecurity" as a term developed to think about "the genealogies, imaginaries and emergent articulations of biodefense."[79] While their incisive work has focused on global health and security, to my mind it invokes something else, something that Foucault could have coined. Biosecurity could be another name for a strategic *dispositif*. It calls up strategies of governance mobilized to protect society from the contaminations of its external enemies and to produce and identify those enemies within.[80] In this frame, biosecurity conjures new and renewed social and sexual objects: technologies designed to secure borders from "penetration," to police populations from infiltration, and to prepare national and transnational macropolitical territories for defense. At issue would be those features of "bios" in jeopardy, whose "bios" is at issue, and the sexual politics by which security is assured and by which the "bios" is framed.

The quest for biosecurity by the U.S. Department of Homeland Security (DHS), so deeply tied to the biopolitics of earlier imperial states, has as its goal "emergency preparedness" against potential enemies in the making.[81] "Home" and "homeland" take on a different sense in the hands of U.S. intelligence experts for whom a need for "intimate knowledge"—their term—requires accessing the recesses of people's friendships, hangouts, and earlier lives. Counterinsurgency operates in this active expectant temporal mode as with the "Violent Intent" program of the DHS discussed

79. See Stephen J. Collier, Andrew Lakoff, and Paul Rabinow, "Biosecurity: Towards an Anthropology of the Contemporary," *Anthropology Today* 20, 5 (October 2004): 3–7; Andrew Lakoff and Stephen J. Collier, eds., *Biosecurity Interventions: Global Health and Security in Question* (New York: Columbia University Press, 2008).

80. Michel Foucault, *Il faut défendre la société: Cours au Collège de France, 1975–1976* (Paris: Gallimard and Seuil, 1997).

81. On the "Emergency Preparedness Guide," see Ann Laura Stoler with David Bond, "Refractions Off Empire: Untimely Comparisons in Harsh Times," *Radical History Review* 95 (Spring 2006): 102. For a much fuller treatment, see Stephen J. Collier and Andrew Lakoff, "Distributed Preparedness: The Spatial Logic of Domestic Security in the United States," *Environment and Planning D: Society and Space* 26, 1 (2007): 7–28.

in chapter 6.[82] Netherlands Indies authorities did much the same with less refined tools but with similar goals—namely with efforts designed to intercept attachments, and familiarities they could not control. Unlike disciplinary regimes, those of security work on the future conditional, on what the DHS calls "pre-violent" detection, on what could happen, on "possible events" (as Foucault put it, "tenir compte de ce qui peut se passer").[83]

Project Hostile Intent as we might remember harbors one of the new forms of intimate intrusions. Designed "to build devices that can pick up telltale signs of hostile intent or deception from people's heart rates, perspiration and tiny shifts in facial expressions," its technologies are based on imaginary rather than substantiated connections between somatic variations and interior states.[84] Collier and Lakoff consider it a virtual rather than actual "biosecurity apparatus," with "no reliable means of evaluating the adequacy of these measures." The apparatus may be virtual, but the effects are not. As its architects describe it, Project Malintent (the program's alternate name) incorporated "cultural knowledge in the analytical process . . . ideally [to] deter . . . terrorist attacks *before* they occur, spotting an emerging attack before it can be executed." It is a "visual analytics," but its targets are the dispositions and sentiments that are hidden in people's psyches and inner states. How this will be assessed and who is a potential threat, as defined by linguistic cue, dress, blood pressure, and comportment, depends on politically defined corporeal translations of the moral logic of defense and the arbitrary designation of dangerous outsiders.[85]

In his essay, "The Rush to the Intimate," Derek Gregory underscores an "intrusive *intimacy* of the biometric systems used by the U.S. military to individualize the Iraqi population."[86] Military attraction to domains of the

82. See A. P. Sanfilippo and F. G. Nibbs, "Violent Intent Modeling: Incorporating Cultural Knowledge into the Analytical Procedure," Pacific Northwest National Laboratory, U.S. Department of Energy, August 2007. For more sources on the topic of "Violent Intent Modeling and Simulations" (VIMS/Malintent), see chapter 6, note 85.

83. Michel Foucault, *Securité, territoire, population: Cours au Collège de France, 1977–1978* (Paris: Seuil and Gallimard, 2004), 4–89.

84. See U.S. Department of Homeland Security, "Privacy Impact Assessment for the Experimental Testing of Project Hostile Intent Technology," February 25, 2008, http://www.dhs.gov/xlibrary/assets/privacy/privacy_pia_st_phi.pdf.

85. Didier Bigo, "The Globalisation of Counter-Terror," *Le Monde Diplomatique*, January 2009, 11.

86. Derek Gregory, "The Rush to the Intimate: Counterinsurgency and the Cultural Turn," *Radical Philosophy* 150 (July–August 2008), http://www.radicalphilosophy.com .libproxy.newschool.edu/article/%e2%80%98the-rush-to-the-intimate%e2%80%99.

"intimate" has made what are deemed to be ethnographic methods into strategic military ones.[87] These liminal thresholds of "inside" and "out" may sometimes be geographically secured, as with the cauterized "sterile zones" through which no Palestinian may pass, or as wide as the desert between the United States and Mexico, or as "invisible" as the cordoned-off space of the Larzac internment camp or the former Harki hamlet of Logis d'Anne in the Lubéron.[88] "Security" regimes and "empires of intelligence," designed to track, measure, and heighten fear of the unseen and unknowable, do more. They concentrate the imaginaries of threat, manage disorder, and put into interactive motion multiple vectors of violence.

Some of these sites of intrusion may be new to the post-9/11 world but not to the zones of suspended rights that are part of the sexual history of empire. Reemergence of discourses about the "white slave trade" with respect to the trafficking of Eastern European women who transgress the borders of the European Commnity; the sexual violence against "enemy combatants" in detention centers such as Abu Ghraib; the strip searches at "vulnerable borders"; and the sexual abuse of refugee women, men, and children in detention centers for undocumented immigrants in the United States are points of blockage and intimate contact, violence, and penetration. In each of these sites, the practices called up are not new in the biopolitics of moral and political defense. Some are blatantly sanctioned as demanded for defense against perceived threats. Some, coded more obliquely, enlist a fear of transgressions of external borders and moral frontiers. Many are "preventive" measures—and this issue of preemptiveness is key—in which bodily scrutiny is deemed necessary, assaults on bodily integrity heightened in the name of warding off danger and protecting the moral order in the name of peace.

Among the DHS's expanded domains for surveillance, as studied by the anthropologist Greta Uehling, is the international smuggling of children.[89] The Homeland Security Act of 2002 transferred the care of unaccompanied alien children who were apprehended for immigration violations to the Office of Refugee Resettlement. Children are perceived as both at risk and as risks in themselves. In that delicate balance, the "politics of compassion"

87. Stoler with Bond, "Refractions Off Empire."
88. See Jackie Orr, "The Militarization of Inner Space," Critical Sociology 30, 2 (July 2004): 451–81.
89. Greta Lynn Uehling, "The International Smuggling of Children: Coyotes, Snakeheads, and the Politics of Compassion," Anthropological Quarterly 81, 4 (Fall 2008): 833–71.

stops at adolescence: Children elicit it; teenagers decidedly do not. Teenagers are considered a physical and political threat, and those who care for children are potential dangers, as they have long been in colonial situations. At one facility where small children are housed, a wall poster reads, "The hand that rocks the cradle controls the nation." It is a message that Dutch authorities in colonial Indonesia took as a credo for their expansive understanding of "security," as well.

DOUBLE EXPOSURE

Defining commensurabilities and making comparisons are historical, political acts—and ethical ones. The recent outrage, particularly among feminist activists who refer to the white slave trade to describe contemporary practices of trafficking of Eastern European women for prostitution rings, is a case in point. The historical reference is clear. International crusades against the white slave trade were a staple of imperial moralizing missions in the early twentieth century. But as Edward Bristow has argued, "Purity and preparedness were not the whole story."[90] The term developed with the effort to ban what was described as the abduction of European women for prostitution in South America, Africa, and "the Orient" by Asian and, especially, Arab men. Jews were cast as the conduits. Active websites of anti-Semitic white supremacists replay these narratives in Technicolor today.

But once again, the sexual regime that this form of "captivity" substantiates is less than clear. Linda Colley argues that the captivity of subaltern whites was the rule in Britain's always underpopulated imperial expansion.[91] In Colley's narrative, captivity is the underbelly of empire, but her story assiduously circumvents sex, forced prostitution, and rape. What some refer to as the "myth of 'white slavery' " and the moral panic it now activates draw on a deep imperial logic, but the boundaries are being redrawn.[92] To what

90. Edward J. Bristow, "The International Crusade against the White-Slave Traffic," in *Vice and Vigilance: Purity Movements in Britain since 1700* (Dublin: Gill and Macmillan, 1977), 175–99. Also see Petra de Vries, "White Slaves in a Colonial Nation: The Dutch Campaign against the Traffic in Women in the Early Twentieth Century," *Social and Legal Studies* 14, 1 (March 1, 2005): 39–60.

91. Colley, *Captives.*

92. For a comprehensive discussion of the debate (and an extensive bibliography therein), see Jo Doezema, "Loose Women or Lost Women? The Re-emergence of the Myth of White Slavery in Contemporary Discourses of Trafficking in Women," *Gender Issues* 18, 1 (Winter 2000): 1–24, 23.

anxiety does this invocation of a white slave trade respond? And who and what is the subject of protection?

The anthropologist Karolina Szmagalska-Follis, working on the contemporary border between Ukraine and Poland, documents sexual violence as part of the language and practice of border regimes that increasingly invades women's bodies to secure the ever muddier boundaries of what is Europe proper and the European Union.[93] Miriam Ticktin similarly argues that sexual violence ensures what French authorities call "public order" by policing and deporting Eastern European and sub-Saharan African women through exceptional, discretionary measures.[94] Surveillance is done in the name of protection against the "global traffic in women." Here is a site where a familiar sexual politics of empire and border control works with and against humanitarian efforts, calls into question the moral righteousness of authorities, and dismantles the enduring pretense of protection in the name of a security measure. Here the management of sex is about constricting the movement of people, about the boundaries of what constitutes Europe. As welfare rolls expanded under the worldwide recession and plans for a broadened European Union were strained, the "bio" in biosecurity identified more bodies to be relegated to the outside, thicker surveillance of interior frontiers, and, as Bonelli predicted, with increasing fears of "insecurity," more social institutions assigned to participate in strategies of control.[95]

Whether these sites are part of the new "intimate frontiers of empire" or represent merely homonyms for very different phenomena and therefore spurious connections depends largely on what questions we think it matters to ask. Perhaps carnal knowledge needs to be rethought as knowledge that mutates, as does its etymology; as that which is never only of the sexual as it is never only of the flesh. And as with the intimate, it might be worth halting in those spaces where things are not located where convention assigns them. The familiar may not be what it just was; nor is the intimate what it seemed to be: where what was "inside" has shifted; where the boundaries

93. Karolina Szmagalska-Follis, "Counter-Trafficking as Complicity and Subversion: The Politics of Rescue in the Polish-Ukrainian Borderland." Paper presented at the 105th Annual Meeting of the American Anthropological Association, San Jose, CA, November, 15–19, 2006.

94. Ticktin, "Sexual Violence as the Language of Border Control."

95. Stephen Erlanger and Stephen Castle, "Dire Economy Threatens Idea of One Europe," New York Times, March 2, 2009, 1; Bonelli, "Une vision policière de la société."

of surveillance have realigned or been abandoned; where what was once assuredly the signature of the colonial order of things is now something else. If a defining feature of imperial formations is in the *evasive quality* of their nomenclatures, the arbitrariness of their rules, their capacity to call things by other names, it is precisely this corporeal space that smudges distinctions between the public and the private, the carceral and the carnal—here guarded, there unintended; here besieged, there abandoned; here desired, there rendered disgusting, and repulsed. The arts of governance may be most intrusively honed as they retreat from direct contact, as sources of duress appear unhinged from corporeal assaults, and as that which constitutes protection and exposure are dangerously scrambled as the targets of "security" change.

IMPERIAL DEBRIS AND RUINATION

Debris and duress wrap around each other in this final chapter, extending and intensifying their convergent effects. But imperial debris also calls forth the endurance that duress demands, dissent from the damage that both debris and duress impose. Since the first rendition of this essay in 2008, and then again in expanded form introducing an edited volume in 2013, I have been struck by its resonance with the ongoing work of others whose subjects are not focused on imperial projects, but whose concerns are nevertheless contiguous with my own. Studies of waste, trash, rubble, decaying matter, and the infrastructures—deteriorated or still not in place to deal with these multiple forms of debris—are concerns of inquiry among those who work in the fields of political ecology, geography, urban infrastructure, history, architecture, and design. Literary critics, artists, and ethnographers have furnished an expanding corpus of startling visual forms and vernacular idioms culled from those for whom duress and debris are joined.

To some extent these initiatives have assuaged my reticence to call on such a loaded and negative image as "debris" to refer to what people are left with and the ways they seek to confront the durability of what is not easily disposable or possible to set aside. From the studies of trash in urban Dakar, degraded land in Southeast Asia, colonial and postcolonial water management in Jakarta, the "historically rooted" effects of "international ecological depredation" in Guyana that implicates "local profiteers" in a "neocolonialist paradigm," these projects are tracking how history and the temporalities of decomposition matter to citizenship, susceptibilities to disease, residence, and, more generally, people's lives.[1] Thinking with this work alters the scope and breadth of ruination, sometimes in forms similar to what I too had sought to identify, sometimes in the harsh details of ruination I did not know or did not yet know how to see.

Still, it is the occluded histories of "imperial debris" as active agents that command my ongoing attention precisely because these ubiquitous forms of cumulative damage are too easily transposed into processes that so readily get identified by other names. Displaced people have become the "toxic" refuse of our contemporary world, while the deceptive appellate "environmental refugees" deflects from the historical and political conditions that have produced these effects. Fear of their unmanageable temporary habitations raises biosecurity alarms. By most accounts, these dislocations are a result of "ethnic strife," "corrupt state officials," rapacious investors, both domestic and foreign. Indeed, some may be. But it would be more than shortsighted to ignore their colonial etiologies. This essay stands as a challenge to that historically truncated optic by offering a vocabulary that makes it harder to settle for a constricted temporality and geopolitical range. Its revisions speak to the insights of this adjacent work, but it remains fixed on the durable damages of imperial relations on newly configured imperial and (post)colonial terrains.

RUINS OF A GREAT HOUSE

A green lawn, broken by low walls of stone,
Dipped to the rivulet, and pacing, I thought next
Of men like Hawkins, Walter Raleigh, Drake,
Ancestral murderers and poets, more perplexed

---

1. See William Viney, *Waste: A Philosophy of Things* (London: Bloomsbury Academic, 2014), esp. 127–76; Michelle Kooy and Karen Bakker, "Technologies of Government: Constituting Subjectivities, Spaces, and Infrastructures in Colonial and Contemporary Jakarta," *International Journal of Urban and Regional Research* 32, 2 (June 1, 2008): 375–91; Aaron Eastley, "Exploiting El Dorado: Subalternity and the Environment," *Postcolonial Studies and Ecocriticism* 13, 1 (October 15, 2006): 38–58; Rosalind Fredericks, "Vital Infrastructures of Trash in Dakar," *Comparative Studies of South Asia, Africa and the Middle East* 34, 3 (2014): 532–48; Sterling Johnson, "Extreme Events and Haitian Environmental Refugees," *ICE Case Studies* 209 (May 2007), http://www1.american.edu/ted/ice/haiti -hurricane.htm (see in particular a short section on the "French Link to Deforestation"); Hilton Als, "Exiles: The Maroons of Suriname and French Guiana," *New Yorker*, June 8, 2015, http://www.newyorker.com/magazine/2015/06/08/exiles-portfolio-lo-calzo. See also Elizabeth M. DeLoughrey and George B. Handley, eds., *Postcolonial Ecologies: Literatures of the Environment* (New York: Oxford University Press, 2011).

In memory now by every ulcerous crime.
The world's green age then was a rotting lime
Whose stench became the charnel galleon's text.
The rot remains with us, the men are gone.
But, as dead ash is lifted in a wind
That fans the blackening ember of the mind,
My eyes burned from the ashen prose of Donne.[2]

Derek Walcott's searing eulogy to empire and its aftermath as an "ulcer-ous crime" captures something that seems to elude colonial histories of the present again and again. His verbs shift among multiple tenses. If the insistence is on a set of brutal finite acts in the distant slave-trading past, the process of decay is ongoing: Acts of the past blacken the senses, their effects without clear termination. These crimes have been named and in-dicted across the globe, but the eating away of less visible elements of soil and soul more often has not. Walcott's caustic metaphors slip and mix, juxtaposing the corrosive degrading of matter and mind. Most critically, Walcott sounds a warning to the distracted reader too easily lost in a receding past. Proceed with caution, stay alert: The "rot remains" long after murderous men like Drake have perished; rapacious planters have turned to ash; colonial officials have returned "home"; and anxious white settlers have long gone. His cadence joins the acidic stench of "rotting lime" with an "ulcerous crime," a sensory regime embodied, gouged deep in sensibili-ties of the present.

One could read Walcott's fierce phrasing as the hyperbolic, enraged words of a gifted poet in a "quarrel with history," whose metaphoric might weighs heavily against the sixteenth-century slave trade—its lucrative spoils and ru-inous effects.[3] One could lament the verbosity of scholarly depictions, pale and placid next to Walcott's spare and piercing prose. But in first reading his poem a decade ago, I fastened to his choice of language as something more, as a harsh clarion call and a provocative challenge to name the toxic

2. Derek Walcott, "Ruins of a Great House," in *Collected Poems: 1948–1984* (New York: Noonday, 1990), 20.

3. Patricia Ismond, *Abandoning Dead Metaphors: The Caribbean Phase of Derek Walcott's Poetry* (Kingston, Jamaica: University of the West Indies Press, 2001), 40. As the book title implies, Ismond takes Walcott's use of metaphor to be at the center of his political, anticolonial project, with metaphor as a "major term of reference": Ismond, *Abandoning Dead Metaphors*, 2–3. This relationship between metaphor in language and metamorpho-sis of life runs throughout commentaries on Walcott's corpus.

corrosions and violent accruals of colonial aftermaths, the durable forms in which they bear on the material environment and on people's minds. Riveted on the "rot" that remains, Walcott refuses a time frame bounded by the formal legalities of imperial sovereignty over persons, places, and things. His positioning struck me as both summons and invitation to pursue that which poems ordinarily cannot, disrupting facile distinction between political history and poetic form, urging us to think differently about both the language that might be sought to capture the tenacious hold of imperial effects and their tangible if elusive forms.

Walcott does more than alert us to how much language choice is key. His prose can serve to humble those of us grappling with analytic vocabularies that are inadequate to their task. Nietzsche may have been right that concepts are dead metaphors, but they can also be generative sites for concept formation. In the absence of ready concepts, metaphors speak to the non-spoken and to sensibilities that escape consolidated conceptualized forms. Metaphors are anything but seamless versions of that which they represent. They are "disturbances"—as Hans Blumenberg once put it—that are and must be discrepant, askew, and suggestive of something more than, different from, that to which they refer.[4] It is here that new political critique becomes more available, as new analytic space and the associations they afford are differently opened.

If concepts always leave a remainder, as Theodor Adorno insisted, metaphors gain their traction precisely from their suggestive imprecision.[5] In the case of Walcott's "rot" that "remains," his metaphors take on a living valence. "Rot" contains an active substance. It is not a steady state, and it is hard to wipe out. It does not stay the same. Such references have more than poetic purchase: They hold tight to the ongoing work of debris-making that we should retain.

This chapter pursues imperial duress in ways that have been alluded to throughout this book. It invites us to ask how empire's ruins contour and carve through the psychic and material space in which people live and what compounded layers of imperial debris do to them. It, too, sounds an alert: to the uneven temporal sedimentations in which imperial formations leave their

4. Hans Blumenberg, *Shipwreck with Spectator: Paradigm of a Metaphor for Existence* (Cambridge, MA: MIT Press, 1997), 82.

5. Adorno, *Negative Dialectics* (London: Routledge, 1973), 5. Or, as he put it more bluntly, "The concept does not exhaust the thing conceived."

marks. There is nothing uniform in how one might broach the relationship between ruin and ruination—either the opacities in which these histories reside or the visceral reckoning with landscapes and lives in which they may be traced. Sensory regimes might be called on to do the work that concepts cannot. I think here of the historian Nancy Hunt, who in her efforts to convey the durability of the Belgian Congo's rubber regime, rejects "mutilation photographs," explicitly turning away from the visual field toward those of hearing and sound.[6] Or we might look to the art curator and incisive student of visual culture Ariella Azoulay, who fiercely embraces the visual as she attends to the concerted work of the Israeli state to create invisibilities in the visual field of Palestinian dispossession. Her analysis wrestles with the task of seeing acts of violation for which there are no photographs able to document bodily exposures and intrusions of space.[7] Here, debris is the built environment of Palestinian habitation, shorn of the private, as Azoulay argues, and unprotected by the boundaries of what the privileged get to call home. Each responds differently to the call to develop tactical methodologies that are keenly attentive to the occluded, unexpected sites in which earlier imperial formations carve their embedded marks and in which contemporary inequities work their way through them.

EMERGENCY'S COUNTERPOINT AND OTHER URGENCIES

Scholarship is produced in uneven waves of reaction and anticipation, sometimes prescient about what has not yet entered the public domain; at other times struggling to keep up with seismic shifts and unanticipated events that render our observations belabored and late. Studies of empire share something of both. As we saw in chapter 5, reactions in the United States to 9/11, the invasion of Iraq, and public revelations about the treatment of detainees at Guantánamo and Abu Ghraib moved students of colonial and imperial history to counter with unusual urgency the resurgent assertions of imperial priorities and the sorts of comparisons to earlier imperial formations then being made.

6. Nancy Rose Hunt, "An Acoustic Register," in *Imperial Debris: On Ruins and Ruination*, ed. Ann Laura Stoler (Durham, NC: Duke University Press, 2013), 39–66.

7. Ariella Azoulay, "*When a Demolished House becomes a Public Square*," in Imperial Debris: On Ruins and Ruination, ed. Ann Laura Stoler (Durham, NC: Duke University Press, 2013), 194–224.

Empires past have long served arguments about how Euro-American geopolitics could and should comport themselves in contemporary political predicaments.[8] But recent writing on empire did more than treat colonial history as a lesson plan in an analogic mode. What has been striking about the past decade of scholarship is how swiftly it has produced provocative and deep imperial genealogies of the present, pointed assaults on the common keywords and political concepts that surfaced as the "war on terror" took hold: torture in the name of truth, displacement of targeted populations in the name of security, states of emergency to sanction violent intervention, and states of exception that justified the suspension of legal constraints and the expansion of new imperial sovereignties.

Such counter-histories have withered the conceit that the politics of compassion and humanitarianism makes for "empire lite." They have tracked the emergence of the U.S. "surveillance state" as one forged on the experimental terrain of counterinsurgency projects in the colonial Philippines of the early twentieth century; they have demonstrated that "empires of intelligence" have provided the architecture of British imperial pursuits throughout the Middle East and of the French empire's "structural imperative" for militarized terror in North Africa.[9] These revisions have been predicated in part on reassessing what constitutes contemporary colonial relations,

8. Edward Gibbon's The History of the Decline and Fall of the Roman Empire, written in six volumes between 1776 and 1788, was among the earliest and best regarded of this genre: Edward Gibbon, Decline and Fall of the Roman Empire, 6 vols. (London: Everymans Library, 2010). For recent analogies, see Cullen Murphy, Are We Rome? The Fall of an Empire and the Fate of America (Boston: Houghton Mifflin, 2008). For a pointed review of Murphy's "simplistic historical analogies," see Walter Isaacson, "The Empire in the Mirror," New York Times, May 13, 2007, http://www.nytimes.com/2007/05/13/books/review/Isaacson-t.html. See also Peter Heather, Empires and Barbarians: The Fall of Rome and the Birth of Europe (New York: Oxford University Press, 2010). For a critique of contemporary U.S. foreign policy analysts who call on parallels with the Roman empire, see Chalmers Johnson, The Sorrows of Empire: Militarism, Secrecy, and the End of the Republic (New York: Henry Holt, 2005).

9. Among those, see Terry Eagleton, Holy Terror (Oxford: Oxford University Press, 2005); Paul W. Kahn, Sacred Violence: Torture, Terror, and Sovereignty (Ann Arbor: University of Michigan Press, 2008); Rashid Khalidi, Resurrecting Empire: Western Footprints and America's Perilous Path in the Middle East (Boston: Beacon, 2004); Marnia Lazreg, Torture and the Twilight of Empire: From Algiers to Baghdad (Princeton, NJ: Princeton University Press, 2008); Olivier Le Cour Grandmaison, La république impériale: Politique et racisme d'état (Paris: Fayard, 2009); Alfred W. McCoy, Policing America's Empire: The United States, the Philippines, and the Rise of the Surveillance State (Madison: University of Wisconsin Press, 2009); Martin Thomas, Empires of Intelligence: Security Services and Colonial Disorder after 1914 (Berkeley: University of California Press, 2008).

what counts as an imperial pursuit, and which geopolities rest on residual or reactivated imperial practices—or have abandoned their imperious ambitions all together. Seasoned students of colonial history have been joined by a new cohort of commentators and scholars from a range of disciplines who are asking about the lessons of empire and what should be garnered from them.[10]

Obviously, not all colonial and (post)colonial scholarship works in such a pressing mode. Some turned to the current immediacies of empire, but as much labors to revise what constitutes the archives of imperial pursuit, to reanimate "arrested histories," to rethink the domains of imperial governance and the forms of knowledge that evaded and refused colonial mandates to succumb, "civilize," and serve.[11]

Still, academic debates about the lessons of empire—which first came to a crescendo and then diminished as the war on Iraq intensified and was then rendered a norm—have taken a very particular direction. In the rush to account for the violence that U.S. policy has produced and its similarities or differences from earlier European and U.S. imperial interventions, a restrictive conceptual apparatus came to occupy dominant analytic space. Its vocabulary has been pointed and critical, bound by the political idioms of our moment and the urgent themes to which they speak: security, disaster, defense, preparedness, states of emergency, and exception.

This chapter, as with earlier ones, does not so much turn away from these concerns as seek to work through the less perceptible effects of imperial interventions that settle into the social and material ecologies in which people dwell, and survive. Those interventions are rarely, as Achille Mbembe has insisted, a matter of wholesale adaptations of colonial technologies. They are instead about reformulations and deformations of the

10. Craig Calhoun, Frederick Cooper, Kevin W. Moore, and Social Science Research Council, eds., *Lessons of Empire: Imperial Histories and American Power* (New York: New Press, 2006).

11. See, e.g., Laurent Dubois, *A Colony of Citizens: Revolution and Slave Emancipation in the French Caribbean, 1787–1804* (Chapel Hill: University of North Carolina Press, 2004), and *Haiti: The Aftershocks of History* (New York: Picador and Metropolitan, 2013); Ilana Feldman, *Governing Gaza: Bureaucracy, Authority, and the Work of Rule, 1917–1967* (Durham, NC: Duke University Press, 2009); Carole McGranahan, *Arrested Histories: Tibet, the CIA, and Memories of a Forgotten War* (Durham, NC: Duke University Press, 2010); David Scott, *Conscripts of Modernity: The Tragedy of Colonial Enlightenment* (Durham, NC: Duke University Press, 2004), and *Omens of Adversity: Tragedy, Time, Memory, Justice* (Durham, NC: Duke University Press, 2014).

crafts of governance in the management of people's lives.[12] Perhaps even more so than in earlier chapters, the focus here is on the less dramatic durabilities of duress that imperial formations produce as ongoing, persistent features of their ontologies—those set aside as if less pressing, and less relevant to current global priorities and political situations than their more attention-grabbing counterparts.

Such a perspective raises a set of questions not often addressed: What conditions the possibilities of some features of colonial relations to remain more resilient, persistent, and visible than others? If "violent environments" are not made so by a scarcity of resources but by grossly uneven reallocation of access to them, the dispossessions and dislocations that accompany that violence takes place not always in obvious and abrupt acts of assault and seizure but also in more drawn-out, less eventful, and occluded ways.[13] The focus is on these more protracted imperial processes that saturate the subsoil of people's lives and persist, sometimes subjacently, over a longer durée.

But the challenge is directed more broadly at a deeper set of assumptions about the relationship between colonial pasts and colonial presents, the residues that abide and are revitalized—if in different working order today. Thus, to return to the question raised in this book's opening chapter: whether postcolonial studies has too readily assumed knowledge of the multiple forms in which colonial pasts bear on the present and has been too quick to assert what is actually postcolonial in current situations. Here I take this query as an opportunity to consider more carefully the physical structures, objects, and dispositions in which those histories are conveyed; and, not least, to attend, as Daniel Miller more generally advocates, to the "unexpected capacity of objects to fade out of focus" as they "remain peripheral to our vision" and yet potent in marking partitioned lives.[14] Rethinking and expanding how to approach the "tangible" effects of ruination is key. While the "tangible" most commonly refers to

12. See Achille Mbembe, *On the Postcolony* (Berkeley: University of California Press, 2001), a compelling effort to address how colonial logics, imaginaries, and violence are reworked and mutate in Africa's postcolonial present. See also Achille Mbembe, *Sortir de la grande nuit: Essai sur l'Afrique décolonisée* (Paris: La Découverte, 2013).

13. See Nancy Lee Peluso and Michael Watts, *Violent Environments* (Ithaca, NY: Cornell University Press, 2001).

14. Daniel Miller, "Introduction," in *Materiality*, ed. Daniel Miller, 1–50 (Durham, NC: Duke University Press, 2005), 5.

that which is "capable of being touched," it equally refers to that which is substantial and capable of being perceived. Such ambiguities locate this venture's effort to identify new ways to discern what constitute those tangibilities.

IMPERIAL (IN)TANGIBILITIES

At issue is more than that long-contested term "(post)colonialism," which may be employed "thinly" to mark a sequential moment or to indicate people and places once and no longer colonized, or to reflect "thickly" and critically on when a present political reality, a set of social represen-tations, a physical or psychological environment is regarded as shaped directly by a prior set of colonial relations. How those relations bear on the present is sometimes precisely specified, though (post)colonial stud-ies' critics contend that the age of empire is over, imperial regimes are defunct, colonialism has been long abandoned, and political analysis and scholarship should move on, as well. We should now be familiar with some of these testy critiques: that an analytics committed to searching for colonial effects has dulled what once appeared as (post)colonial studies' critical edge, that its accounts of the present are inadequate and partial; its agents and subjects, long dead; and its political charge, increasingly irrelevant.[15] A more pointed critique prevails: namely, that its consolida-tion as an academic specialization decidedly removed from the analysis of imperialism ensured that it "had always already lost the plot."[16] Mean-while, conservative constituencies in Canada, France, Australia, and the United States often take the issue elsewhere, insisting that colonial his-tories matter far less than they are contrived to do; that they are deployed strategically by specific disenfranchised populations to register (unrea-sonable) political demands. In this view, the recourse to colonial gene-

15. Arif Dirlik, "Historical Colonialism in Contemporary Perspective," Public Culture 14, 3 (2002): 611–15, is exemplary in this regard. Dirlik argues that "it is no longer very plausible to offer colonialism as an explanation of [the] condition" in which the "vast majority of the populations of formerly colonized society live in conditions of despair": Dirlik, "Historical Colonialism in Contemporary Perspective," 611.

16. Neil Lazarus, "Postcolonial Studies after the Invasion of Iraq," New Formations 59 (September 22, 2006): 16. This is developed further in Neil Lazarus, The Postcolonial Unconscious (Cambridge: Cambridge University Press, 2011).

alogies serves to foster unfounded claims for redemption, apology, and retribution.[17]

As is clear from each of the preceding chapters, I defer from these latter assessments. Far more has emerged in the call to rewrite colonial genealogies, in debates over old and new forms of imperial venture, and in the acrimonious exchanges over what counts as a colonial "legacy" and what does not. The fact that imperial forms have changed should provide a challenge, not render study of their obscured entailments obsolete. It is these entailments and subjacent durabilities that should be our objects of inquiry, as insisted throughout this book. They are far from given effects or fully understood facts. Some of these issues and contexts were raised in earlier chapters. But there are others: while students of Korean history are rewriting colonial accounts of the Japanese imperium and Korea's subjugation, increasing references to "(post)colonial" Poland or to the "postcolonies of communism" incite conceptual contestation and ongoing deliberation. Still, the "domestic" history of the U.S., has been exploded over the past decade by a new generation tracing policies of containment, enclosure, and segregation that inextricably link the internal and external techniques of governance to imperial patterns across the globe. And all of these are proliferating when in other quarters something called (post)colonial studies is deemed poorly equipped to speak to the present.

The uncomfortable tenor of such discrepancies might be broached more productively as the diagnostic of a contemporary mal-aise—in its literal sense of embodied disquiet, a lethargy borne of vague ill ease. To posit a colonial presence, as I have done, is not to suggest that the contemporary world can be accounted for by colonial histories alone. It is rather to understand how that presence—especially when effaced—yields new damages and renewed disparities.

Some sources of this malaise should now be clear, evinced in models of empire that distract from gradated forms of imperial sovereignty with dif-

---

17. In France, it is a debate that reflects equally strong political investments: see Pascal Bruckner, *La tyrannie de la pénitence essai sur le masochisme occidental*. Paris: Librairie Générale Française, 2008); Daniel Lefeuvre, *Pour en finir avec la repentance colonial* (Paris: Flammarion, 2008). See also Jean-François Bayart, *Les études postcoloniales: Un carnaval académique*. Paris: Karthala, 2010); his response to his critics in Jean-François Bayart, "Les très fâché(e)s des études postcoloniales," *Sociétés Politiques Comparées* 23 (March 2010): 1–12; "Racial France," special issue of *Public Culture* 23, 1 ([Winter 2011]), guest edited by Janet L. Roitman.

ferential breadth. Other sources too have been addressed: not least an overly expansive sense of what we imagine to know about the tenacious qualities of empire and the tangibilities they inhabit. The subject of colonial ruins crystallizes where attention still inordinately rests. Colonial memorials and *recognized* ruins may offer less purchase on where these histories lodge and what they eat through than does a tracking of cumulative debris less available to scrutiny and less accessible to chart. In that pursuit, focus here is less on the noun "ruin" than on "ruination" as an active, ongoing process that disperses imperial debris differentially and "to ruin" as a violent verb that unites apparently disparate moments, places, people, and objects.

Ironically, in a field charged with discerning how history matters, we have not always done so. The literary critic Tony Eagleton also suggests that (post)colonial studies has suffered from an "increasingly blunted" historical sense.[18] Frederick Cooper has charged that a flattening of time has "unmoored" analyses from specific relations between colonial policy and (post)colonial political structures.[19] What precipitates and sustains such historical "blunting" is worth pursuing further.

The charge is a serious one that deserves a concerted response: to refocus on the *connective tissue* that continues to bind human potential to degraded environments and degraded personhoods to the material refuse of imperial projects—to the spaces redefined, to the soils turned toxic, to the relations severed between people and between people and things. At issue is at once the uneven sedimentation of debris and the uneven pace at which people can extricate themselves from the structures and signs by which remains take hold. Rubrics such as "colonial legacy" offer little help. They fail to capture how people choose—and are forced—to reckon with features of those formations in which they remain vividly bound. They also gloss over the creative and critical—and sometimes costly—measures people take to defy those constraints, to name that damage, or to become less entangled.

TO RUIN: A VIRULENT VERB

We might return once again to the concept of "imperial formations" to register the ongoing quality of processes of decimation, displacement, and

18. Terry Eagleton, *After Theory* (New York: Basic, 2003), 7.

19. Frederick Cooper, "Decolonizing Situations: The Rise, Fall, and Rise of Colonial Studies, 1951–2001," *French Politics, Culture and Society* 20, 2 (July 1, 2002): 47–76.

reclamation. Imperial formations are relations of force. They harbor those mutant, rather than simply hybrid, political forms that endure beyond the formal exclusions that legislate against equal opportunity, commensurate dignities, and equal rights. Imperial formations, as I have defined them, are racialized relations of allocation and appropriation. Unlike empires, they are processes of becoming, not fixed things.

Edouard Glissant captured a critical feature: A population "whose domination by an Other is concealed . . . must search elsewhere for the principle of domination . . . because the system of domination . . . is not directly tangible."[20] Such opacities obscure the vectors of accountability and the lasting conceptual and concrete forms in which ruination operates—and on which such formations thrive. It is at the nexus of the tangible and opaque where the political force of these histories lie.

In its common usage, "ruins" are privileged sites of reflection—of pensive rumination. Portrayed as enchanted, desolate spaces, large-scale monumental structures abandoned and grown over, ruins provide a favored image of a vanished past, what is beyond repair and in decay, thrown into aesthetic relief by nature's tangled growth. Such sites come easily to mind: Cambodia's Angkor Wat, the Acropolis, the Roman Coliseum, icons of a romantic loss and longing that inspired the melancholic prose of generations of European poets and historians who devotedly chronicled pilgrimages and coming of age narratives to them.[21] Perhaps this is one reason why transnational institutions like UNESCO work so hard at their "preservation."

Thinking here about "ruins of empire" is to work explicitly against that melancholic gaze, repositioning the present in the wider structures of vulnerability, damage, and refusal that imperial formations sustain. Nor is it the wistful gaze of imperial nostalgia to which we should turn. Walter Benjamin provides the canonical text for thinking about ruins as "petrified life," as traces that mark the fragility of power and the force of destruction. But ruins do more: They are also sites that condense alternative senses of history that weigh on the future. Unlike Benjamin, a focus on imperial debris

20. Edouard Glissant, *Collected Essays* (Charlottesville: University of Virginia Press, 1989), 20.

21. For one good example of the continuing pleasures yielded by this laconic mood, see Christopher Woodward, *In Ruins: A Journey through History, Art, and Literature* (New York: Vintage, 2003).

seeks to mark the "trail of the psyche"—a venture he rejected—as much as it seeks to follow his acute alertness to the "track of things."[22]

"To ruin," according to the OED, is "to inflict or bring great and irretrievable disaster upon, to destroy agency, to reduce to a state of poverty, to demoralize completely."[23] "To ruin" is an active process and a vibrantly violent verb. In turning with intention not to the immediate violence of Iraq, Afghanistan, and recognized zones of active war but to the enduring quality of imperial remains, we need to ask what they impinge on and how their accrual distributes unevenly impaired states.

Let me be clear: This is not a turn to ruins as memorialized monumental "leftovers" or relics. The political issue is only in part what is left, the state it is in, and why it is left and not something else (suggesting, of course, that little is ever just "left"; it is "left" to be cared for). But equally and more important with respect "to ruin" is not what is "left" but what people are "left *with*": what remains that blocks livelihoods and health; the aftershocks of imperial assault; the social afterlife of degraded infrastructures; distressed sensibilities; and the things by which one is assailed and assaulted by their very presence.[24] Such effects reside in the corroded hollows of landscapes, in the gutted infrastructures of segregated cityscapes, and in the micro-ecologies of matter and mind. The focus, then, is not on inert remains but on the histories they recruit and on their vital refigurations.

Imperial effects occupy multiple historical tenses. They are at once products of the past imperfect that selectively permeate the present as they shape the conditional subjunctive and uncertain futures. Such effects are never done with, as Walcott reminds us, in the definitely closed-off *passé composé*. Frantz Fanon identified the extensive mental disorders that followed French rule in Algeria as the "tinge of decay"—the indelible smack of degraded personhoods, occupied spaces, and limited possibilities—that were (and remain) resistant to discern or erase.[25] They are also the hardest to critically locate.

22. Walter Benjamin, *The Arcades Project* (Cambridge, MA: Harvard University Press, 2002), 212.

23. H. W. Fowler, F. G. Fowler, and James A. H. Murray, *The Concise Oxford Dictionary of Current English* (Oxford: Clarendon, 1964), 1095.

24. I think here with Heidegger's understanding of "mood" as that which "assails" us: Martin Heidegger, *Being and Time*, trans. John Macquarrie and Edward Robinson (New York: Harper and Row, 1962), 176.

25. Frantz Fanon, *The Wretched of the Earth* (New York: Grove, 1963), 249. The full quote, opening the chapter on "Colonial War and Mental Disorder," reads, "That imperialism which today is fighting against a true liberation of mankind leaves in its wake

Fanon worked between two poles of decay. At one pole was an evocative figurative sense that situated the breakdown of persons, their pathologies and mental disabilities, as the disturbed temperaments of imperial effects. For Fanon, the future of such patients was already "mortgaged" by the "malignancy" of their psychological states. Subject to what he called "a generalized homicide," a whole generation of Algerians would be "the human legacy of France in Algeria."[26] In 1955, Aimé Césaire called that affliction a "gangrene . . . distilled into the veins of Europe" in the racialized rule of domestic France.[27]

Such images could be construed as "mere" metaphor, but the ruinous "tinge of decay" for Fanon was never figurative alone. At the other pole lay the material, tangible, and physical destruction of Algerian landscapes— drained swamps, charred homes, and gutted infrastructures of more than a century of French rule and nearly a decade of colonial war. To work between these poles is to acknowledge both the potential and the problems in sustaining a balance between the analytic power that "to ruin" carries as an evocative metaphor and the critical purchase it offers for grounding processes of actual decomposition, recomposition, and renewed neglect. The latter processes are of our time as they build on and reactivate the effects of another. Such detritus impinges on the allocation of space and resources and on embodied conditions of material life. The challenge is political and analytic: to work productively, if uneasily, with and across this tension. In so doing, the aim is not to fashion a genealogy of catastrophe or redemption. Making connections where they are hard to trace is not designed to settle scores or, as Wendy Brown warns, to nurture undurable *ressentiments* and "wounded attachments."[28] It is instead to recognize that these are not finished histories of a victimized past but *consequential livid histories of differential futures.*

"Ruin" is both the claim about the state of a thing and a process affecting it. It serves as both noun and verb. To turn to its verbal, active sense is to begin from a location that the noun, "ruin," too easily freezes into stasis,

---

here and there tinctures of decay which we must search out and mercilessly expel from our land and our spirits."

26. Fanon, *The Wretched of the Earth*, 251–52.

27. Aimé Césaire, *Discourse on Colonialism*, trans. Robin D. G. Kelley (New York: Monthly Review, 2000), 35–36.

28. Wendy Brown, "Wounded Attachments," *Political Theory* 21, 3 (August 1, 1993): 390–410.

into inert object, passive form. Imperial projects are themselves processes of ongoing ruination, processes that "bring ruin upon," exerting material and social force in the present and through their presence.

By definition ruination is an ambiguous term; both an act of ruining, a condition of being ruined, and a precipitant of it. Ruination is an *act* perpetrated, a *condition* to which one is subject, and a *cause* of loss. These three senses may overlap in effect, but they are not the same. Each has its own temporality. Each identifies different durations and moments of exposure to a range of violences and degradations that may be immediate or delayed, subcutaneous or visible, prolonged or instant, diffuse or direct.

By the OED again, ruination is a process that brings about "severe impairment, as of one's health, fortune, honor, or hopes"—again a defining feature being its material and affective registers. Conceptually, ruination may condense those impairments or sunder them apart. To speak of colonial ruination is to trace the fragile and durable substance of signs, the visible and visceral senses in which the effects of empire are reactivated and remain. But ruination is more than a process that sloughs off debris as a byproduct. It is also a *political project* that lays waste to certain people, relations, and things that accumulate in specific places. To think with ruins of empire as ruination is to emphasize less the artifacts of empire as dead matter or remnants of a defunct regime than to attend to their reappropriations, strategic neglect, and active positioning within the politics of the present.

To focus on ruins is to broach the protracted quality of decimation in people's lives, to track the production of new exposures and enduring accrued damage.[29] Elements of this concern have been the subject of critical geography and environmental historians for some time.[30] Campaigns

29. Not all ruins located in empire are imperial ones. For a nuanced study of Malagasy relics, see, e.g., Michael Lambek, *The Weight of the Past: Living with History in Mahajanga, Madagascar* (New York: Palgrave Macmillan, 2002).

30. For foundational works that do this work on different spatial and temporal scales, see Alfred W. Crosby, *Ecological Imperialism: The Biological Expansion of Europe, 900–1900* (Cambridge: Cambridge University Press, 1986); Richard H. Grove, *Green Imperialism: Colonial Expansion, Tropical Island Edens and the Origins of Environmentalism, 1600–1860* (Cambridge: Cambridge University Press, 1995); Michael Watts, *Silent Violence: Food, Famine, and Peasantry in Northern Nigeria* (Athens: University of Georgia Press, 2013). Peluso and Watts, *Violent Environments*, focuses pointedly on how environmental degradation has been made into a political issue and posed as a threat to national security. On state violence, nature preservation, and forced relocation in Tanzania, see Roderick P. Neumann, *Imposing Wilderness: Struggles over Livelihood and Nature Preservation in Africa* (Berkeley: University of California Press, 1998).

against what is now commonly referred to as "environmental racism" have been instrumental and effective in the public domain in documenting the grossly disproportional distribution of pollution, waste disposal, and bio-waste among impoverished populations in the United States and worldwide.[31] Much of this critical work targets the long-term practices of multinationals, mining conglomerates, and successive U.S. administrations and Departments of Defense, Agriculture, and, more recently, Homeland Security, that have laid to waste and continue to destroy micro-ecologies and the livelihoods of populations who live off and in them.[32]

Critical geographers, environmental historians, and historically inclined anthropologists have taken the relationship between colonial rule and degraded environments as their subject, yet it is striking how little of this work has made its way back to the analytic center of (post)colonial scholarship or has been taken as the critical archival labor demanded by (post)colonial situations.[33] The American studies scholar Valerie Kuletz has seen it

31. See, e.g., Daniel Brook, "Environmental Genocide: Native Americans and Toxic Waste," *American Journal of Economics and Sociology* 57, 1 (January 1998), 105–13; David V. Carruthers, ed., *Environmental Justice in Latin America: Problems, Promise, and Practice* (Cambridge, MA: MIT Press, 2008); Donald A. Grinde and Bruce E. Johansen, *Ecocide of Native America: Environmental Destruction of Indian Lands and Peoples* (Santa Fe, NM: Clear Light, 1995); Jake Kosek, *Understories: The Political Life of Forests in Northern New Mexico* (Durham, NC: Duke University Press, 2006). Gregory Hooks and Chad Smith argue that capitalism alone does not explain the distribution of toxic waste on Native American reservations: Gregory Hooks and Chad L. Smith, "The Treadmill of Destruction: National Sacrifice Areas and Native Americans," *American Sociological Review* 69, 4 (August 1, 2004): 558–75. See also Dan McGovern, *The Campo Indian Landfill War: The Fight for Gold in California's Garbage* (Norman: University of Oklahoma Press, 1995); Wendy Nelson Espeland, *The Struggle for Water: Politics, Rationality, and Identity in the American Southwest* (Chicago: University of Chicago Press, 1998), esp. 183–222. On biowaste, see esp. Sarah Hodges, "Chennai's Biotrash Chronicles: Chasing the Neo-Liberal Syringe," *Garnet Working Paper* 44/08 (May 2008), http://www2.warwick.ac.uk/fac/soc/garnet/workingpapers/4408.pdf.

32. See, e.g., Katherine T. McCaffrey, "The Struggle for Environmental Justice in Vieques, Puerto Rico," in *Environmental Justice in Latin America: Problems, Promise, and Practice*, ed. David V. Carruthers (Cambridge, MA: MIT Press, 2008), 263–86; Steven L. Simon, André Bouville, Charles E. Land, and Harold L. Beck., "Radiation Doses and Cancer Risks in the Marshall Islands Associated with Exposure to Radioactive Fallout from Bikini and Enewetak Nuclear Weapons Tests: Summary," *Health Physics* 99, 2 (August 2010), 105–23.

33. See, e.g., Kate B. Showers, *Imperial Gullies: Soil Erosion and Conservation in Lesotho* (Athens: Ohio University Press, 2005). William Beinart and Lotte Hughes seek to "compare the impact of different commodity frontiers on colonized people": William Beinart and Lotte Hughes, *Environment and Empire* (Oxford: Oxford University Press, 2007), vi. A strong tradition of such work has developed for Madagascar: see, e.g., Lucy Jarosz,

as appropriate to identify the abuse of the land of indigenous peoples in the United States, Micronesia, and Polynesia as "nuclear colonialism" and as acts of "social ruin," a fact that people in those places, as she notes, recognize and have long articulated. Such work has rested on the margins of the conceptual reformulations in (post)colonial studies, but it will not stay there for long.[34] As the politics of colonial conditions are being taken up by new interlocutors, these issues—in Palestine, Australia, and with respect to Native American lands, most notably—are surfacing as colonial debris with disposal of toxicities and people rendered disposable tethered in ways long expressly denounced, but less audible before.[35]

If the multiple "legacies" of empire are what (post)colonial scholarship has long imagined itself to arise from and account for, if not explain, one crucial task is to bring these fields of inquiry into more organic conversation. Disciplinary protocols of presentation, venues of publication, and concepts that translate poorly can impede the task. Such work needs to traverse a heteroclite set of fields. Imperialism is as much part of these accounts as imperial logics and colonial cultures.

Thus, a founding premise: What is most significantly left may not be blatantly evident, easy to document, or easy to see.[36] The concepts conventionally used to reference colonial histories are symptomatic of the lack of clarity. Pervasive ones such as "colonial legacy" and "colonial vestige" are deceptive terms, deflecting analysis more than they clear the way. In the case of imperial formations, a "legacy" makes no distinctions between

---

"Defining and Explaining Tropical Deforestation: Shifting Cultivation and Population Growth in Colonial Madagascar (1896–1940)," *Economic Geography* 69, 4 (October 1993), 366–79; Christian A. Kull, *Isle of Fire: The Political Ecology of Landscape Burning in Madagascar* (Chicago: University of Chicago Press, 2004); Genese Sodikoff, "Forced and Forest Labor in Colonial Madagascar, 1926–1936." *Ethnohistory* 52, 2 (March 2005), 407–35.

34. See Valerie Kuletz, *The Tainted Desert: Environmental Ruin in the American West* (New York: Routledge, 1998); Nancy Lee Peluso and Micheal Watts, eds., *Violent Environments*, (Ithaca: Cornel University Press, 2001). See also David Vine, *Island of Shame: The Secret History of the U.S. Military Base on Diego Garcia* (Princeton, NJ: Princeton University Press, 2009).

35. See, e.g., Amira Hass, "The Israeli 'Watergate' Scandal: The Facts about Palestinian Water," February 16, 2014, http://www.haaretz.com/middle-east-news/1.574554.

36. In this, one can appreciate and share the dilemma of the ambitious volume *Postcolonial Disorders*, whose contributors tack between the unspoken and the everyday, the unspeakable and the hidden, and place both the political and the psychological at the center of what constitutes "postcolonial disorders": Mary-Jo DelVecchio Good, Sarah Pinto, Sandra Teresa Hyde, and Byron J. Good, eds., *Postcolonial Disorders* (Berkeley: University of California Press, 2008).

what holds and what lies dormant, between residue and recomposition, between what is a hold over and what is reinvested, between a weak and a tenacious "trace." Such rubrics instill overconfidence in the knowledge that colonial histories matter—far more than they animate an analytic vocabulary for deciphering how they do so. Such terms do little to account for what people themselves count as colonial effects and, as importantly, what they do about what they are left with.

With this in mind, a focus on "ruins of empire" is not about a gaze but a critical vantage point on one. Asking how people live with and in ruins and articulate those conditions redirects the engagement elsewhere: to the politics animated, to the common sense such habitations disturb, to the critiques condensed or disallowed, and to the social relations avidly coalesced or shattered around them. What material form do ruins of empire take when we turn to shattered infrastructures, polluted places, dispersed families rather than to the leisure of evocations? Situations of disparate time and place come into renewed view. Sequestered and displaced histories do, as well. Imperial ruins are, not least, *racialized markers on a global scale* that leave their deposits in the Agent Orange–infested landscapes of Vietnam, the hazardous wastes in former nuclear test sites of the Bikini Atoll, the continually battered compounds of dispossessed Palestinians—flooded with raw sewage from adjacent Israeli settlements—in which they do not have a choice not to live.[37] Imperial ruins may include the defunct sugar mills of central Java, as well as the decrepit barracks of India's railway communities, where many Anglo-Indians still dwell uneasily while others refuse to recognize that these are feasible places to live.[38]

These processes of ruination bear on material and social micro-ecologies in different ways. How conditions of ruin as well as ruins are maintained open to the political investments that surround them; some are left to decompose, and some are remanded; others are reconsigned or disregarded. Some remains are ignored as innocuous leftovers, others petrify; some hold and spread their toxicities and become poisonous debris. Others are stubbornly inhabited by those who have been displaced to make a political

37. Mel Frykberg, "Villages Contaminated by Settlement Sewage," Electronic Intifada, April 29, 2010, https://electronicintifada.net/content/villages-contaminated -settlement-sewage/8804.

38. On the Indian railway communities, see Laura Bear, "Ruins and Ghosts," in *Lines of the Nation: Indian Railway Workers, Bureaucracy, and the Intimate Historical Self* (New York: Columbia University Press, 2007), 257–84.

claim, requisitioned for a newly refurbished commodity life for tourist consumption, or occupied by those left with nowhere else to turn.

How to reckon with those sites of decomposition that fall outside historical interest and preservation, places not honored or graced as ruins of empire proper and that go by other names? Some remains are rejected as ruins all together. Much depends, as Derek Walcott again reminds us, on who is doing the labeling. As he noted in his Nobel lecture of 1992, the *tristes tropiques* that Claude Lévi-Strauss so lamented in elegy to "the already decrepit suburbs" of Lahore may have been a pathos of empire felt more by nineteenth-century European transients—anthropologists and the like—than by those who actually lived there.[39] Walcott observes that "the sigh of History rises over ruins, not landscapes," but in the Antilles the only ruins were those of "sugar estates and abandoned forts," and there "the sigh of history dissolves."

But does it? The "sigh of history" can manifest in the sensibilities and materialities that surround them—severed tree stumps, the shard of a floor tile, or scattered stones from the wall of a house—re-membering what was once there. Nature rots quickly in the colonial tropics. In the Netherlands Indies, railway tracks for hauling rubber were rapidly overgrown; tobacco sheds made of plaited bamboo and wood were eaten through by termites, leaving no structural fragments of iron or stone. But a lot more than a trace remains of how the land was used and what connects colonial rubber production in Sumatra to Indonesia's Reebok and Adidas factories, what land has been made available and converted for new kinds of export production and who profits from them. The peat fires (almost ten thousand fires across Kalimantan this year) that produced what some have called a "carbon bomb" across the archipelago and into Malaysia) have a specific source: They are concentrated consequences of land managed by palm oil, pulpwood, and logging concessions that have mushroomed in the past decade. This is not a colonial vestige (although palm oil was introduced by multinationals in Sumatra in the early twentieth century) but the consequences of a multinational capitalist rampage built on an earlier colonial introduction (devastating in itself at the time) that the archipelago cannot contain.[40] The colonial imprint is deep in Indonesia and elsewhere.

39. Claude Lévi-Strauss, *Tristes tropiques* (New York: Atheneum, 1955), 44.
40. See, e.g., Damian Carrington, "Indonesian Forest Fires on Track to Emit More CO2 than UK," *The Guardian*, October 7, 2015, http://www.theguardian.com

Much depends on where we look for detritus, what we expect it to look like, and what we expect to see. That the "absence of ruins" in the Caribbean equals an absence of living history is not an assessment with which all agree. Richard Price instructs us to seek evidentiary truths elsewhere, in the "semi-parodic artworks" of the iconic Martiniquan figure of Médard, a man who in the 1950s and 1960s "made from the detritus of industrial society (cellophane from cigarette packages, silver paper from gum wrappers, bentwood from boxes of Camembert)"—objects that retold stories of colonial products and profits as he rewrote their plots.[41]

Walcott, too, was impatient with the "consoling pity" of travelers who "carried with them the infection of their own malaise," those consumed with sadness because they "misunderstood the light and the people on whom the light falls."[42] Rejecting the pathos of ruins, he opted for a celebration of survival. But his vision was hardly romantic. It was full of rage. His descriptions of the sewers that spew into white sand beaches and "polluted marinas" call attention to ruined ecologies as the profit of some and the ruination of others. "Proceed with caution," Doris Sommer warns. Better to resist "the rush of sentimental identification that lasts barely as long as the read" or the mournful regard.[43] Melancholy, compassion, and pity nourish imperial sensibilities of destruction and the redemptive satisfaction of chronicling loss. We are schooled to be alert to the fact that ruins hold histories, that ruins are the ground on which histories are contested and remade.[44] Still, the nominative form of a "ruin" does less work than "to ruin" as an ongoing process. Ruins can represent both something more and something less than the sum of the sensibilities of people who live in them. Instead, we might turn to ruins as epicenters of renewed collective claims, as history in a spirited voice, as sites that animate both despair and new

---

/environnment/2015/oct/07/Indonesian-forest-forest-fires-on-track-to–emit-more-co2 -than-uk.

41. Richard Price, *The Convict and The Colonel* (Boston: Beacon, 1998).

42. Derek Walcott, "The Antilles: Fragments of Epic Memory," in *Nobel Lectures in Literature: 1991–1995*, ed. Sture Allen (Amsterdam: Elsevier, 1997), 25–40.

43. Doris Sommer, *Proceed with Caution, When Engaged with Minority Writing in the Americas* (Cambridge, MA: Harvard University Press, 1998), 15.

44. This point is made lucidly in Nadia Abu El-Haj, *Facts on the Ground: Archaeological Practice and Territorial Self-Fashioning in Israeli Society* (Chicago: University of Chicago Press, 2001); Robert Ginsberg, *The Aesthetics of Ruins* (Amsterdam: Rodopi, 2004); and many of the contributions in Michael J. Lazzara and Vicky Unruh, eds., *Telling Ruins in Latin America* (New York: Palgrave Macmillan, 2009).

possibilities, bids for entitlement, and unexpected collaborative political projects.[45]

Some kinds of imperial ruin are easier to identify than others. Projects of cultural salvage—whether of monuments, artifacts, or customs and peoples—are available for scrutiny in the way others are not. There are resurrected ruins, such those studied by John Collins, part of the World Bank/ UNESCO cultural heritage projects designed to "harvest the economic value" and capitalize on the allure of partially restored people and things and their ostensibly uniting essences. Yet such restorations disperse and redistribute people, making their ways of being vital to national development as productive of new inequalities.[46] Then there are those ruins that stirred Jamaica Kincaid's derisive and angry view of Antigua, marked with buildings whose faded placards note "repairs pending" for decades while damaged but "splendid old buildings from colonial times" are well maintained in carefully tended disrepair.[47]

Some imperial ruins can be distinguished by where they are located: in metropole or colony—or on faded imperial maps. Others cannot. Strewn throughout the Caribbean, Africa, and Asia are the enticements of enjoying "Ruins by Day, Luxury by Night," as eager travelers "balance the indolence of a colonial-era luxury hotel with the more demanding task of exploring centuries-old Khmer ruins from dawn 'til dusk."[48] These are more than leisurely distractions for the history-minded, knowledge-seeking traveler. Edification here, like the Grand Tour of the European bourgeoisie in earlier centuries, not only distinguishes Culture from cultures. It replays the "salvage" rescue operation that European empires claimed as their expert knowledge and benevolent task. Napoleon took more archaeologists and "rubble seek-

45. See Éric Soriano's powerful history of how the French colonial category of *indigène* was reappropriated in the politics of New Caledonia to assert "Kanak" sovereignty in a charged situation in which the Kanak were "colonized" but "French citizens" who were "eligible but not whites, French but black, and attached to something obscure called 'custom' ": Éric Soriano, *La fin des indigènes en Nouvelle-Calédonie: Le colonial à l'épreuve du politique, 1946–1976* (Paris: Karthala, 2014), 12.

46. See John F. Collins, *Revolt of the Saints: Memory and Redemption in the Twilight of Brazilian Racial Democracy* (Durham, NC: Duke University Press, 2015), and "Ruins, Redemption, and Brazil's Imperial Exception," in *Imperial Debris: On Ruins and Ruination*, ed. Ann Laura Stoler (Durham, NC: Duke University Press, 2013), 162–93.

47. Jamaica Kincaid, *A Small Place* (New York: Farrar, Straus and Giroux, 1988), 9.

48. Mark Landler, "Ruins by Day, Luxury by Night," *New York Times*, November 26, 2000, http://www.nytimes.com/2000/11/26/travel/ruins-by-day-luxury-by-night.html.

ers" with him to Egypt than surgeons and surveyors. Nineteenth-century colonials in the Netherlands Indies participated in Europe's obsession with visiting Hindu ruins, accruing cultural capital on their days off.

Colonialism has been predicated on guarding natural and cultural patrimonies for populations assumed to need guidance in how to value and preserve them.[49] This sort of attention to ruins chronicles a present landscape and people already found wanting. But this heartfelt gaze on the ruin, so much a part of the contemporary analysis of the ruins of modernity—a gaze that echoed Diderot's sense that he felt "freer" in the presence of ruins—is not my interest here.[50] Rather than the introspective gaze of Europeans on ruins, we need to look to the lives of those living in them. That is precisely what the anthropologist Janet Finn has done in tracing the dried-up veins of Anaconda's copper mines that joined Butte, Montana, and Chuquicamata, Chile, and brought privation to the lives and bodies of their sequestered laboring populations.[51]

Imperial nostalgia plays through and sells sojourns among colonial ruins in other, predictable ways. There is the "find" of worthy voyagers, the "ruins of Popokvil atop Bokor Mountain in Cambodia. . . . There, you'll find the remains of a French colonial-era town—a crumbling post office, an empty Catholic church."[52] At the Mbweni Ruins Hotel in Zanzibar, guests can sleep in what was once a school for "freed slave girls," the first Anglican Christian missionary settlement in East Africa made into a domesticated "colony." Arranged in 1871 in clusters of small neat houses and garden plots, this was precisely the bucolic vision that imperial architects harbored to domesticate their recalcitrant, racially ambiguous, and destitute populations throughout

49. See, e.g., the discussion of "colonial conservation" and national parks in Beinart and Hughes, *Environment and Empire*, 1–21.

50. For a pointed critique of the "imperial ruin gazer" and the new ruins that have become part of it, see Julia Hell and Andreas Schönle, eds., *Ruins of Modernity* (Durham, NC: Duke University Press, 2010).

51. On these industrial ruins of U.S. empire, see Janet L. Finn, *Tracing the Veins of Copper, Culture, and Community from Butte to Chuquicamata* (Berkeley: University of California Press, 1998).

52. "The Follow-Your-Bliss List," *New York Magazine*, Winter 2005, http://nymag.com/nymetro/travel/features/winter/2005/14792; "Ruins of a French Colonial Ghost Town," Messynessychic.com, December 12, 2012, http://www.messynessychic.com/2012/12/12/ruins-of-a-french-colonialist-ghost-town/. But also see Seth Meixner, "Cambodia: Ghosts and Grandeur." iAfrica.com, March 8, 2007, http://travel.iafrica.com/destin/asia/655247.htm.

the colonial world.[53] Guests can learn the history of philanthropic imperial projects *and* take solace in the multiple times that the buildings were abandoned and restored with the intervention of European good works, at the height of imperial expansion and after.[54] Renato Rosaldo's astute observation comes to mind: Imperialist nostalgia is not a (post)colonial pleasure but a concerted colonial one, a mourning contingent on and concomitant with what colonialisms destroy.[55] Such ruins might be read as vestige and remnant, but they are neither history's refuse nor its unclaimed debris.[56] Sometimes colonial nostalgia is not the issue at all. The Grande Hotel in Beira, Mozambique, built in the 1960s under Portuguese rule, is now a modernist ruin inhabited by more than 2500 squatters.[57]

Imperial ruins can also mark the contest for originary racialist claims. Zanzibar's tourists may be unknowing participants in the celebration of empire in the Mbweni Ruins Hotel, but often the political life of ruins are more explicit for all to contest and see. In Zimbabwe, it was from the sixty acres of stone ruins, "the Great Zimbabwe," that Cecil Rhodes pilfered the prized soapstone bird with which he adorned his house in Cape Town in 1889, the year before he established a Royal Charter for the British South Africa Company. The stone birds and the ruins that housed them were confiscated by Rhodes, but it was successive states controlled by white

53. On the scale and scope of this imperial imagery—namely, the depoliticized small-scale farmer ensconced in his self-contained space—see Ann Laura Stoler, *Along the Archival Grain: Epistemic Anxieties and Colonial Common Sense* (Princeton, NJ: Princeton University Press, 2009).

54. See http://www.mbweni.com/bweniruins.htm and numerous other sites with visitors' comments. See also Edward M. Bruner, *Culture on Tour: Ethnographies of Travel* (Chicago: University of Chicago Press, 2005). Bruner's is one of many studies that refers to African American heritage tourists' visits to the dungeons from which slaves were sent from West Africa to the Americas.

55. Renato Rosaldo, "Imperialist Nostalgia," in *Culture and Truth: The Remaking of Social Analysis* (Boston: Beacon, 1989), 68–87.

56. Tom Edensor conceives of exploring a ruin as a "kind of anti-tourism" because "movement is rough, disrupted and potentially perilous, replete with sensations other than the distanced gaze": Tom Edensor, in *Industrial Ruins: Spaces, Aesthetics, and Materiality*. Oxford: Berg, 2005), 95. But this is precisely the allure of the ruins of Detroit and the ones mentioned here, suggesting not "anti-tourism" but tourists' delight, orchestrated participation in the adventure of imagining another time without having to imagine what political processes displaced those who lived in them.

57. See http://www.failedarchitecture.com/once-a-colonial-hotel-now-an-inhabited-ruin. Also see photographer Guy Tillim's *Avenue Patrice Lumumba* (Cambridge, MA: Prestel, 2009).

settlers and, later, by African nationalists who each made the ruins their own. White racial supremacy and refusal of it, as the late Henrietta Kuklick so eloquently wrote, were fought on the terrain of these ruins. The Great Zimbabwe was requisitioned as "proof" of racialized progenitors in the nineteenth century and reemerged at the center of heated political contest a century later.[58] Clearly, these are not all imperial "ruins" of common vintage; nor are their political entailments the same. What they might share is what the Afghan photographer and performance artist Lida Abdul has called sites and structures "around which stories are wrapped to hide the sounds and images that roam" through them.[59]

Imperial debris deposits in the disabled, racialized spaces of colonial histories past and present. It is gendered as well—in how it is embodied, where it is lodged, and how it is expressed. It is particular women who voice the injuries to which this debris gives rise, as in John Collins's call on the critical repartee of Topa, a woman whose body was as marked as was her bearing and her history by precarious poverty and the assumptions of those who would claim to alleviate it.[60] In his work on apartheid's remains, Sharad Chari turns to the demand of Jane Clover for her own "piece of oxygen" to describe the atmospheric pressure in which people live close to oil refineries of post-apartheid Durban. Vyjayanthi Rao provides the songs of lament that female farmers chant in their displaced fields and about their submerged South Indian village in the wake of the making of the Srisailam mega-dam.[61] Over and again, it is women who seem to loudly attest.

Gender may inflect how ruination is embodied and who bears the debris. Nancy Hunt rivets on "the sound of twisted and anguished laughter collected, convulsed, and retracted around the forms of sexual violence that

58. Henrietta Kuklick, "Contested Monuments: The Politics of Archaeology in Southern Africa," in Colonial Situations: Essays on the Contextualization of Ethnographic Knowledge, ed. George W. Stocking (Madison: University of Wisconsin Press, 1991), 135–69. See also Joost Fontein, The Silence of Great Zimbabwe: Contested Landscapes and the Power of Heritage (Harare, Zimbabwe: Weaver, 2006). On another sort of contested colonial monument, the war memorial, see Gregory Mann, "Locating Colonial Histories: Between France and West Africa," American Historical Review 110, 2 (April 2005), 409–34.

59. This quote appears on a postcard in a photography series entitled "A History of the World through Ruins, 2005–2007," by Lida Abdul. It was part of the "Memorial to the Iraq War" exhibition, Institute of Contemporary Art, London, May 23–June 27, 2007. I thank Hugh Raffles for giving me the postcards.

60. See Collins, "Ruins, Redemption, and Brazil's Imperial Exception," in Stoler, Imperial Debris, 162–93.

61. See Vyjayanthi Rao, "The Future in Ruins," in Stoler, Imperial Debris, 287–321.

were basic to, indeed constitutive of, the reproductive ruination of the rubber regimes in Leopold's Congo."[62]

But while each of these authors is keenly attuned to the gender dispositions that mark recollection, none seizes on those distinctions to frame her or his arguments. Ariella Azoulay, who otherwise speaks so directly to how gender inequalities are "lauded and glorified" in the history of the visual fields in which she works, chooses not to do so.[63] In the photograph from 2009 that she points to of sleeping Israeli soldiers wrapped in colorful blankets in what we quickly learn is a Palestinian home (available at Israelforever .org), positions are staked out by male soldiers. But Azoulay's examination of the celebration of the "ruination of a Palestinian house as a private space" is not confined to men. On the contrary, in the stream of photo images on the Internet during the last attack on Gaza in 2014, Israeli women and men stand together on a hilltop "to show their children both the symmetry that justifies Israel's devastation of Gaza, and Israel's spectacular show of force."[64] Her point is mutely expressed but explicit: Imperial debris accrues with different gendered effects. But this is not what she chooses to underscore or where she chooses to pull our attention. When she describes the applause at the sight of the smoking ruins of Palestinian homes, the exuberant shouts of "We've done it!" are raised voices of Israeli women and men. Nancy Hunt's treatment of the rapes committed in the Congo under King Leopold is not insensible to what was done to young women in particular. She is direct in arguing that cannibalism and mutilation were able to enter Roger Casement's humanitarian narrative in ways that rape could not.

Even in the extraordinary work done by the feminist geographer Juanita Sundberg on the geopolitics of trash in the U.S.-Mexican borderlands, so attentive to the intimate, "close encounters" between bodies, comportments, and objects, it is not gender differences that she underscores to track what undocumented immigrants leave behind but, rather, how a discourse about dirt and trash adheres to the kinds of people that those attempting to cross are imagined to be.[65] Imperial debris here is conveyed as a sensory racial

62. Hunt, "An Acoustic Register."

63. See Ariella Azoulay, "Has Anyone Ever Seen a Photograph of a Rape?" in the *Civil Contract of Photography* (New York: Zone, 2008).

64. Azoulay, "When a Demolished House Becomes a Public Square," in Stoler, *Imperial Debris*, 194–224.

65. Juanita Sundberg, " 'Trash-Talk' and the Production of Quotidian Geopolitical Boundaries in the USA-Mexico Borderlands," *Social and Cultural Geography* 9, 8 (Decem-

overload. Sundberg writes about "unsightly" and "smelly" garbage transfigured into the very bodily, environmental, and hygienic boundaries between those who belong and those who should be kept out. Each of these works suggest that how gendered dispositions matter to living in imperial debris, to reckoning with it, and to subverting its effects are still left to specify— their corporeal, political, and affective registers.

IMPERIAL DEBRIS BY OTHER NAMES

Perhaps the most critical task to address, if not answer, is the question prompted by Derek Walcott in "Ruins of a Great House": What is the rot that remains when the men are gone? What forms does rot take? What does it corrode; what interior spaces does it touch; and how does it seep through the social and material fabric where it remains? Walcott's language is poetic, but the dispersed ruination he looks to is not. There may be remnants that slip from immediate vision, detritus that is harder to grasp—intimate injuries that appear as only faint indentations of time or deep deformations and differentiations of social geography that go by other names.

There are social dislocations whose etiologies are found in labels that lead away from imperial effects and push analysis far from colonial histories, cutting off those connections. The terms substituted are familiar—"urban decay," "the perils of progress," "environmental degradation," "industrial pollution," "racialized unemployment"—in analyses of contexts "unmoored" from their histories. In these endorsed mainstream narratives, these processes happen in places swept up by modernization and to those swept aside as the refuse of capitalist markets that have since moved on.

What work does it do to identify these as ruins of empire and acts of ruination? What insights does it offer to recast these generic labels and processes as patterned imperial effects that produce subjects with more limited possibilities and who are hampered differently by those effects? One argument might be that such a critical move makes connections that are not otherwise readily visible. Such renaming relocates processes dislodged from their specific histories, disjointed from the connections that made

---

ber 2008), 871–90. See also Juanita Sundberg and Bonnie Kaserman, "Cactus Carvings and Desert Defecations: Embodying Representations of Border Crossings in Protected Areas on the Mexico-U.S. Border." *Environment and Planning D: Society and Space* 25, 4 (2007), 727–44.

some people and places susceptible to ruin or abandonment. These are not ruins of empire in any figurative sense. These are zones of vulnerability that the living inhabit and in which they are forced to dwell. Their genealogies demand a sharply formulated forensics of occlusions and a challenge to stay within them and not move on.

Greg Grandin's riveting account of Fordlandia, Henry Ford's vision of a bucolic American settlement and way of life in the Amazonian jungle in the early twentieth century, does more than remind us that Ford's success was contingent on the production of rubber in colonial possessions through Southeast Asia.[66] He underscores that "Detroit not only supplied a continual stream of symbols of America's cultural power but offered the organizational know-how necessary to run a vast industrial enterprise like a car company—or an empire."[67] Treating Detroit as an imperial nexus imbricated in and dependent on colonial labor regimes throughout the world rejects the American "exception," as it resituates the fulcrum of Detroit's demise. By placing it in the balance of a broader sweep of imperial debris, Detroit is repositioned not on the outer fringes of the "Rust Belt," but as one of the corrosive centers of one disabled form of U.S. imperial vision and failed pursuit.[68] The current caché of what some critics call "ruin porn" with respect to the guided tours of Detroit's "splendid ruins" pushes those connections even further away.[69]

One impulse in addressing the admittedly broad sense of imperial ruin embraced here might be to distinguish between those processes played out in imperial centers and those situations and sites that appear in formerly colonized regions. But more might be gained by suspending that impulse and not making such distinctions too readily. The "interior" and "exterior" spaces of imperial formations correspond only to the common geopolitical designations that imperial architects scripted themselves. Terms such as "metropole" and "colony," "core" and "periphery" presume to make clear

66. Greg Grandin, *Fordlandia: The Rise and Fall of Henry Ford's Forgotten Jungle City* (New York: Picador, 2009).

67. Greg Grandin, "Touring Empire's Ruin: From Detroit to the Amazon," *The Nation*, June 23, 2009, http://www.thenation.com/article/touring-empires-ruins-detroit -amazon/.

68. This is not a focus of the current fascination with "The Fabulous Ruins of Detroit" ("Welcome to the 'The Fabulous Ruins of Detroit Tour,'" *Detroit Yes!*, http://www .detroityes.com/fabulous-ruins-of-detroit) or Witold Rybczynski's "Incredible Hulks," *Slate*, March 18, 2009.

69. See Michael Hodges, "Opportunistic Art," *Detroit News*, July 1, 2010.

what is not. We might instead think of other criteria to distinguish the contemporary zones of imperial duress that are more mutable and as mutable as imperial formations themselves: the narrowing breadth of corridors in which people can move, the virtual barriers by which they are cordoned off, the kinds of infrastructure to which they have access or are prohibited entry, the skewed geographies of waste dumping, accumulation, and removal, the preemptive racialized exclusions and exemptions that "security" measures animate for the greater good of all.

In an article for an American audience, the Israeli novelist David Grossman described the apathy and studied indifference that ongoing political, military, and religious conflict imposes on those living in Israel, Palestine, Iraq, Afghanistan, and elsewhere in war-torn places of the world. The image he conjures is of people whose moral compasses are narrowed, whose feelings are numbed, whose language is rendered shallower, thinned by the onslaught on their everyday. As he put it, there is a "*shrinking of the 'surface area' of the soul* that comes in contact with the bloody and menacing world out there." Destruction for Grossman is inside people and out—coating their outer skin, pressed through their micro- and immediate environments.[70] The resonance—and sharp contrast—with Walcott's "rot that remains" and Fanon's "tinge of decay" is striking. In the protracted, extended conditions of the latter, numbness can give way to critique and language can become sharpened and thickened—rather than thinned—with double-entendres that mock the security measures that terrorize and destroy rather than protect.

Stories congeal around imperial debris, as do critiques. So do disqualified knowledge and subjugated genealogies decoupled from the processes of which they were a part. The overgrown ruins of Sans-Souci Palace in Haiti's northern mountains (built by its first black king after the defeat of the French in 1804), which Michel-Rolph Trouillot so powerfully described, harbors a suspended, (dis)quieted history of the Haitian Revolution and the differential histories of colonial relations wedged between mortar and

70. On the relationship between people and debris, on the affective space produced by living in piles of rubbish and ruined environments, see the analysis of Lefkosha/ Lefkosa, a city divided since the Turkish invasion of Northern Cyprus in 1974, in Yael Navaro-Yashin, *The Make-Believe Space: Affective Geography in a Postwar Polity* (Durham, NC: Duke University Press, 2012).

crumbling stone.[71] Michelle Cliff framed her novel No Telephone to Heaven around the Jamaican term "ruinate" that as a noun subsumes within it "to ruin" as a verb. She described it as cultivated land left to lapse into overgrown vegetation. "Ruinate" in its use is steeped in colonial history and marks its durability. But it seems to be as mobile as the people who attempt to escape it, as they move to and return from the New York City boroughs of the Bronx and Queens. It carries both the palpable colonial history of abandoned European plantations, living waste, and as yet un-reclaimed futures.[72]

Ruins, as Kuklick found in Zimbabwe, can take on a political life of their own. As Nadia Abu El-Haj writes, in Jerusalem "partly destroyed buildings were partially restored and reconstructed as ruins in order to memorialize more recent histories of destruction, and older stones were integrated into modern architectural forms in order to embody temporal depth."[73] Her point is now commonly shared: Ruins are not just found; they are made. They become repositories of public knowledge and new concentrations of public declaration.

We need little more evidence that the public or state recognition of something as a ruin, as well as the claims made for it, is in itself a charged political act. Such recognized ruins are politicized, but the most enduring ruins in Israel are recognized neither as ruins nor as ruination wrought by colonial policies. For many non-Palestinians, these ruins are not acknowledged to be there at all: They are the literal ruins of Palestinian villages razed, bulldozed, and buried by the Israeli military and a state-endorsed Israeli Afforestation Project. This intensive planting campaign (for which children attending Hebrew school in Europe and the United States have been avidly encouraged to contribute their pennies "to plant a tree for Israel") have literally obliterated the very presence of Palestinian villages and farmsteads on Jerusalem's periphery for more than sixty years.[74] If planting

71. Michel-Rolph Trouillot, Silencing the Past: Power and the Production of History (Boston: Beacon, 1995).

72. Michelle Cliff, No Telephone to Heaven (New York: Vintage, 1987), 1. I thank Meredith Edwards of Furman University for alerting me to Cliff's use of "ruinate" when I delivered a version of this essay in February 2011.

73. El-Haj, Facts on the Ground, 164.

74. See Shaul Ephraim Cohen, The Politics of Planting: Israeli-Palestinian Competition for Control of Land in the Jerusalem Periphery (Chicago: University of Chicago Press, 1993); Walid Khalidi, ed., All That Remains: The Palestinian Villages Occupied and Depopulated by Israel in

is a key technology in Israeli politics, inciting notions of fecund futures, here ruination has a perverse, protracted, and violent colonial history. "Security groves" have replaced Palestinian olive orchards with cypress and pines; recreational parks dense with eucalyptus trees smooth over Palestinian cemeteries. Remains of Arab villages have been effaced—as are the claims of their former inhabitants that these were never "abandoned" fields but ones they owned, lived off, and long cultivated.

In Bethlehem's Aida refugee camp, such fields "abandoned" to Israeli occupation are called by other names. There, children are armed at the Lajee Children's Center with computers and cameras, taught how to collect the stories of their grandparents whose land was seized, to locate the trees they harvested, to smell the herbs their grandparents remember, to scavenge the hilltops where their houses were destroyed to make way for Israeli settlements. Sometimes there are no ruins at all. Asked by their elders to collect thyme and sage from the fields, these grandchildren often brought back stones and soil instead.[75] Some found old olive trees among the new pines. In Beit Jibreen, twelve-year-old Suhaib photographed the ruins of an old house on the hill, only imagining that it might have been his grandmother's.[76]

Ruins are made, but not just by anyone, anytime, anywhere. Large-scale ruin making takes resources and planning that may involve forced removal of populations and new zones of uninhabitable space, reassigning inhabitable space, and dictating how people are supposed to live in them. As such, these ruin-making endeavors are typically state projects that are often strategic, nation-building, and politically charged.[77] The fabrication of nuclear ruins, for instance, was critical in the construction of Cold War national defense policies and in shaping a U.S. public prompted to be fascinated and traumatized by the specter of nuclear war.[78] As Joe Masco has argued, nuclear ruins remain central to the political imaginary of the U.S. security state today. Cold War planners took their task to be one of molding and emotionally managing an American public. They did so with simulated

---

1948 (Washington, DC: Institute for Palestine Studies, 2006). I thank Jennifer Lynn Kelly for first pointing me to the Afforestation Project and for sharing her research with me.

75. "Dreams of Home," created by the children of Lajee Center with Rich Wiles.

76. I thank members of the Lajee Center for sharing their publications, the photographs that children took, and the stories they collected when I visited in 2008.

77. This point is illustrated in detail in El-Haj, *Facts on the Ground*.

78. See Joe Masco, "Engineering the Future," in Stoler, *Imperial Debris*, 252–286.

bomb threats and theatrical evacuations in cities and towns across the country. Strategic public operations imagined ruins, televised ruins, and simulated ruins, all with attention to particular domestic objects, pointedly anticipating the decimation of what touched Americans most closely, the hard-won household technology and material comforts of postwar quotidian life.

Ruins draw on residual pasts to make claims on futures. But they can also create a sense of irretrievability or of futures lost. The Ochagavía hospital in Santiago's suburbs, built as a "spectacular showcase" to Pinochet's vision of Chile's modernity and progressivism, showcases something else: With what Jon Beasley describes as "the beached whale of a monument whose presence has been repressed and ignored," the half-built hospital recollects what could have been rather than what was.[79] How such modernist ruins differ from imperial ones would be suggested not only by the different histories they unsettle and differently call on, but also by the specific people dispossessed or otherwise laid to waste by them.

This sense of arrested rather than possible futures and the ruins they produce is one way to convey the problematic processes of development policies. Vyjayanthi Rao's ethnographic account of the building of the Srisailam mega-dam in southern India inspires such a perspective. Begun in 1981, the mega-dam displaced more than 150,000 people and submerged more than one hundred villages. During the dry season every year, these submerged villages reappear to haunt those who once lived there, and then disappear, as both sign and substance for those same people of their precarious futures and of national development's unfulfilled promise. The village ruins contrast the archaeological salvage project of valued and valorized Hindu temples enacted in the same space. The critique of development is laid bare in a landscape scarred with ruined villages, laid to waste alongside the transplanted temple ruins, preened for historical tourism and preserved as part of India's national heritage.[80]

79. Jon Bearsley-Murray, "Vilcashuaan: Telling Stories in Ruins," in *Ruins of Modernity*, ed. Julia Hell and Andreas Schönle (Durham, NC: Duke University Press, 2010), 212–31. See also Beatriz Jaguaribe, "Modernist Ruins: National Narratives and Architectural Forms," *Public Culture* 11, 1 (January 1999): 295–312. William Bissell looks at the critical purchase that colonial nostalgia can afford in the face of devastated landscapes and "dimming memories of modernity": Swarms, quoted in William Cunningham Bissell, "Engaging Colonial Nostalgia," *Cultural Anthropology* 20, 2 (May 2005): 21.

80. Rao, "The Future in Ruins." in Stoler, *Imperial Debris*, 287–321.

Looking to imperial ruins not necessarily as monuments but as ecologies of remains opens to wider social topographies. The ruins of Native American burial sites mark only one site in a more broadly contested ground of new land claims and entitlements.[81] But we might also think of the carceral archipelago of empire described in chapter 3 that distributed convict islands, detention centers, pauper and children's and penal colonies across the globe—gradated zones of containment that mixed and matched "security" and defense with confinement, abuse, "education," and abandonment. Such infrastructures of large and small scale bear what captivated Walter Benjamin: the "marks and wounds of the history of human violence."[82] It is these spatially assigned "traces of violence," more than the "deadening of affects," to which such forms of imperial debris compel us to turn.[83]

Focusing on the materiality of debris is what Nancy Hunt did with consummate care in A Colonial Lexicon, where she urged us to stay in the "logic of the concrete," invoking Lévi-Strauss's term.[84] Ruins can be marginalized structures that continue to shape and sever socialities that cease to function as they once did. What happens at the threshold of transformation when unfinished development projects are put to other use, when test sites are grown over, when Soviet military camps are abandoned and remade as in the Ukrainian-Polish borderlands?[85] What happens when island enclaves, no longer a declared nuclear zone, as in the Bikini Atoll, become repositories of vulnerabilities that last so much longer than the political structures that produced them? Each of these points not to ruins set off from people's lives but to what it takes to live both with their consequences and with a modicum of dignity that affirms that one is not wholly entrapped by them.

In thinking about imperial debris and ruin, one is struck by how intuitively evocative and elusive such effects are, how easy it is to slip between

81. On the history and contemporary battles over the theft, protection, and repatriation of American Indian remains and objects, see Kathleen S. Fine-Dare, Grave Injustice: The American Indian Repatriation Movement and NAGPRA (Lincoln: University of Nebraska Press, 2002).

82. Susan Buck-Morss, The Dialectics of Seeing: Walter Benjamin and the Arcades Project (Cambridge, MA: MIT Press, 1989), 163.

83. Buck-Morss, The Dialectics of Seeing, 170, 182.

84. Nancy Rose Hunt, A Colonial Lexicon of Birth Ritual, Medicalization, and Mobility in the Congo (Durham, NC: Duke University Press, 1999).

85. See Karolina Szmagalska-Follis, "Repossession: Notes on Restoration and Redemption in Ukraine's Western Borderland." Cultural Anthropology 23, 2 (November 2012), 329–60.

metaphor and material object, between infrastructure and imagery, between remnants of matter and mind. The point is not to look "underneath" or "beyond" that slippage but to understand the work that slippage does and the political sensibilities it harbors. Reading W. G. Sebald's *On the Natural History of Destruction*, a meditation on Germany during and just after the Second World War, the numbness of living in the still smoldering ruins, the sheer mass of debris, the (deceptive) "silence above the ruins" contrasts and converges with the sorts of remains referenced here—in and out of focus, in and out of speakable bounds.[86]

These diverse sites of imperial presence open to what Rob Nixon calls the "slow violence" and "long dyings" that mark zones of neglect, attenuated possibilities, and abandonment.[87] If Giorgio Agamben developed the concept of social abandonment; it is in João Biehl's fine-grained ethnography *Vita: Life in a Zone of Social Abandonment* where it is given flesh. For Biehl that zone produces persons who become "a human ruin," "leftover" in their unexceptional, patterned subjection "to the typically uncertain and dangerous mental health treatment reserved for the urban working poor" in Brazil.[88] The social abandonments under scrutiny in these pages are ruinations of a different sort: sites of diminished or degraded resources proportioned by imperial effects.

Thus, a critical question: How to track the "concrete trajectory" of colonial exclusions and derailments that carve out the structures of privilege, profit, and destruction today? Naomi Klein's *The Shock Doctrine* could help lead back in that direction. There are no index entries for "empire" or "imperialism" in her scathing account of what she calls "the disaster capitalism complex," but the psychic and material connections are threaded through every chapter, from the two hundred billion dollar "homeland security industry" back to U.S. support for military governments that eviscerated the subsistence of peoples in Argentina, Chile, Uruguay, and Brazil.[89]

86. Winfried Georg Sebald, *On the Natural History of Destruction*, trans. Anthea Bell (New York: Modern Library, 2004), 67.

87. Giorgio Agamben, *Homo Sacer: Sovereign Power and Bare Life*, trans. Daniel Heller-Roazen (Stanford, CA: Stanford University Press, 1998), 27–28; João Biehl, *Vita: Life in a Zone of Social Abandonment* (Berkeley: University of California Press, 2005); Rob Nixon, *Slow Violence and the Environmentalism of the Poor* (Cambridge, MA: Harvard University Press, 2011).

88. Biehl, *Vita*, 18.

89. Naomi Klein, *The Shock Doctrine: The Rise of Disaster Capitalism* (New York: Picador, 2008).

This is not to suggest that complex histories of capitalism and empire should all be folded into an imperial genealogy. But it is an historical distortion to imagine that "neoliberalism" invented these effects. It is, rather, to attend to the *evasive* history of empire that disappears so easily into other appellations and other, more available, contemporary terms. It is to recognize that the "bio" in biopolitical degradations is not haphazardly joined with histories of empire. The social terrain on which colonial processes of ruination leave their material and mental marks are patterned by the social kinds those political systems produced, by the racial ontologies they called into being, and by the cumulative historical deficiencies certain populations are seen to embody—and the ongoing threats to the body politic associated with them. Expulsion as in the case of Palestinians is posited as the defense of society against its internal enemies; partition and arbitrary violence are the results. As David Lloyd argues for the history of British state policies in Northern Ireland, "partition, which is the foundation of the state, is also its ruination."[90]

Zygmunt Bauman identifies the production of waste and "wasted lives" as the required, intended, and inevitable debris of the modern.[91] Bauman may be partially right, but such a frame can only account for the fact of accumulated leftovers, of superfluous, obsolete, and bypassed people and things. It *cannot, however, account for their densities and distribution.* Modernity and capitalism can account only partly for the left aside; it cannot account for where people are left, what they are left with, and what means they have to deal with what remains. Globalization may account for the dumping of toxic waste on the Ivory Coast but not for the trajectory of its movement and the history that made West Africa a suitable and available site. In 1992, Jim Puckett of Greenpeace was already calling this "toxic colonialism."[92] Capitalism can account for the oil spills in the Gulf of Mexico by BP in 2010 and by Texaco later, as well as Chevron's three decades of toxic contamination

90. David Lloyd, "Ruination: Partition and the Expectation of Violence (on Allan deSouza's Irish Photography)," *Social Identities* 9, 4 (December 2003): 487.

91. Zygmunt Bauman, *Wasted Lives: Modernity and Its Outcasts* (Cambridge: Polity, 2004).

92. Laura Pratt, "Decreasing Dirty Dumping? A Reevaluation of Toxic Waste Colonialism and the Global Management of Transboundary Hazardous Waste," *William and Mary Environmental Law and Policy Review* 35, 2 (February 2011): 581–623. Pratt, a lawyer, makes the strong case that although the term is no longer in use, the issues it addressed are alive and well.

and the decimated livelihoods of residents of the Amazon rain forest, but not for the worldwide coverage of, and outrage over, the former and the sparse note of the latter.[93]

Again, there are ruins of empire that are called "ruins" and those that are not. The political economy of nuclear testing can account for the proliferation of waste dumps but not for the campaign in 1996 to locate the Ward Valley nuclear waste dump in the heart of the Mojave Desert National Preserve and on land that Native American nations held sacred.[94] After thirty years of uranium mining, carried out from the late 1940s through the 1960s across Navajo lands in Arizona and New Mexico, native populations still refer to their late-onset cancers as a "legacy of tears."[95] The social and physical effects of uranium mining on Aboriginal populations in Australia for the past three decades is a colonial story—of state commissions mounted and ignored, of "spillages and silences," of cancer rates massively increasing among Aboriginal populations near these sites of regard and disregard—of its own.[96] At issue is whether recognition produces more effective histories, "relational histories" that "connect fragments to wholes" of the imperial present.[97] Rethinking imperial formations as polities of dislocation and de-

93. On oil spills that have mattered less, see John Vidal, "Nigeria's Agony Dwarfs the Gulf Oil Spill: The U.S. and Europe Ignore It," The Guardian, May 29, 2010, http://www.theguardian.com/world/2010/may/30/oil-spills-nigeria-niger-delta-shell.

94. On the Ward Valley Nuclear Waste Dump proposals of 1996 and the successful campaign that suspended its construction in 1999, see www.alpinistas.org/env/ward.ward.html. For a synthesis of the legal debates about the spoilage of "Indian Country" (the term used in legal documents) that takes tribal sovereignty to be central to the issue, see Robert Sitkowski, "Commercial Hazardous Waste Projects in Indian Country: An Opportunity for Tribal Economic Development through Land Use Planning," Journal of Land Use and Environmental Law 10, 2 (April 1, 1995): 239–72. On broken treatises with respect to the storage of radioactive and other hazardous waste, and dissension within tribes on the issue, see "Reservations about Toxic Waste: Native American Tribes Encouraged to Turn Down Lucrative Hazardous Disposal Deals," March 31, 2010, http://www.scientificamerican.com/article/earth-talk-reservations-about-toxic-waste.

95. Colin Tatz, Alan Cass, John Condon, and George Tippet, "Aborigines and Uranium: Monitoring the Health Hazards," Australian Institute of Aboriginal and Torres Islander Studies discussion paper 20, December 2006, http://aiatsis.gov.au/publications/products/aborigines-and-uranium-monitoring-health-hazards.

96. Tatz et al., "Aborigines and Uranium."

97. Sunil Agnani et al., "Editor's Column: The End of Postcolonial Theory? A Round-table with Sunil Agnani, Fernando Coronil, Gaurav Desai, Mamadou Diouf, Simon Gikandi, Susie Tharu, and Jennifer Wenzel," PMLA 122, 3 (May 2007): 633–51.

ferral, which cut through the nation-state by delimiting interior frontiers as well as exterior ones, is one step in reordering our attention.[98]

RACE AND IMPERIAL DEBRIS

Might we turn back to James Agee and Walker Evan's *Let Us Now Praise Famous Men*, not to mark the universal dignity and damage that dire poverty bestows, but as specific places and specific sorts of people abandoned by specific state policies and historical acts, as the embodied ruins of a racialized American empire?[99] Why does it seem at once forced and counterintuitive to do so?

Kathleen Stewart makes it seem less so in her ethnography of those people who live among the detritus of West Virginia's coal-mining industry today. She excavates "the ruined and trashed" economy of the American South, whose historical veins are coursed through with the U.S. Coal and Oil Company's land buyouts at the turn of the twentieth century, with hills that "became a wasteland of the unemployed" during the Depression of the 1930s, and with "over 100,000 dead in the mines since 1906."[100] Resisting a seamless narrative, she turns instead to the "trash that collects around people's places, like the ruins that collect in the hills" to track the composition and decomposition of people's lives, their movement through decay, melancholy, and engagement.[101] As she writes, "Things do not simply fall into ruin or dissipate. . . . [They] fashion themselves into powerful effects that remember things in such a way that 'history' digs itself into the present and people cain't [*sic*] help but recall it."[102]

Agee's story too might be rewritten in another vein, not as the iconic story of the dignity that emerges from the indignities of being poor white (and black) in the rural South or only as a national, domestic racial story of industrializing America. One could imagine a reframing of this form of ru-

98. See Nicolas de Genova, "The Stakes of an Anthropology of the United States," *New Centennial Review* 7, 2 (2007): 231–77; Ann Laura Stoler, ed., *Haunted by Empire: Geographies of Intimacy in North American History* (Durham, NC: Duke University Press, 2006).

99. James Agee and Walker Evans, *Let Us Now Praise Famous Men* (1939) (Boston: Houghton Mifflin, 1988).

100. Kathleen Stewart, *A Place on the Side of the Road: Cultural Poetics in an "Other" America* (Princeton, NJ: Princeton University Press, 1996), 90–112.

101. Stewart, *A Place on the Side of the Road*, 96.

102. Stewart, *A Place on the Side of the Road*, 111.

ination as one moment in a broader history of U.S. empire that would track cotton production and the creation of expert knowledge of eugenics that authorized institutionalized neglect both of newly freed blacks and "poor whites." These are not untold stories. They have been told as racialized histories, but not as racialized histories of the United States as an imperial formation.[103] When Agee wrote of those "acclimatized to insult," of those whose lives are marked by "a slendering of forms of unfreedom" one could take those words as one piercing definition of ruination.[104]

Moving between ruins and ruination, between material objects and processes of accrued damage is sometimes easier said than done. Sometimes the ruins are claimed to retain ghosts in vivid form: Some such phantoms haunt central Java's sugar factories, described by John Pemberton as "forces moving on their own, operating by uncertain contracts and demanding untoward sacrificial exchange."[105] But in fact, in much of the colonial tropics, one is struck by the absence of colonial ruins, as in vast tracts of Vietnam once overrun by a multinational plantation industry. In some places, as Walcott claims, there is hardly a trace of a colonial ruin at all. There are no petrified dwellings, as in Dresden, partially burned to the ground; no open sewers clogging the senses; no rampage of rats claiming new quarters; none of the zoos Sebald so horrifically described full of mangled animals, no crushed watches that stopped ticking, no dolls with severed heads. Here we are not talking about an event of bombardment and the fast-acting decomposition that follows. The ruins of empire may have none of that sort of immediacy.

But they can be as close at hand with an immediacy of another kind. Valentine Daniel's poem "The Coolie," on Sri Lanka's tortured colonial history, provides a counterpoint to the master's ruinous tale.[106] As he writes:

103. Sven Beckert's award-winning *Empire of Cotton* provides a breathtaking account of the history and growth of a trans-imperial matrix of cotton production, consumption, and the super-exploitation of workers on which it depended across the globe. The "ruins of empire" that he tracks are Catalonia's eighteen now abandoned cotton factories that hug the Llabregat River, not the racial politics of those ruins in the United States. See Sven Beckert, *Empire of Cotton: A Global History* (New York: Alfred A. Knopf, 2014), 427.

104. James Agee and Walker Evans, *Let Us Now Praise Famous Men* (Boston: Houghton Mifflin, 1988 [1939], 109.

105. John Pemberton, "The Specter of Coincidence," in *Southeast Asia over Three Generations: Essays Presented to Benedict R. O'G. Anderson*, ed. Benedict R. O'G. Anderson, James T. Siegel, and Audrey Kahin (Ithaca, NY: Southeast Asia Program Publications, Southeast Asia Program, Cornell University, 2003), 75–90.

106. E. Valentine Daniel, "The Coolie," *Cultural Anthropology* 23, 2 (May 2008), 257–78, 267.

The sole witness
to bloodshed? The land, of course, with its wounds unfurled:
gouged here, leveled there, with rivers dry-bedded
run, flooding pits, filling dams, in this redeemed world.

And if hunting down the rusted guns in the Congo, as Hunt has argued, does not access the "real" remains of the violence of rubber extraction, or really what is left, sometimes—as in Vietnam today—live ammunition is the political point.[107]

Vietnam challenges us to reject the stable noun form in which "ruins" tends to rest, to make room for ruins' livid morphing, their spread—like rot—in fungible forms. These are not "ruins" per se, although we might reconsider them just that, the more than eight million tons of bombs dropped in Vietnam thirty years ago, with the active remains of more than 300,000 tons of unexploded ordnance (UXOs) that includes what the Vietnamese government estimates are 800,000 cluster bombs, M79 grenade bombs, and flechette bombs still in the soil.[108] Limbs and lives are still being lost.

Agent Orange, the military colloquialism for the twenty million gallons of deadly herbicides sprayed across Vietnam for ten years between 1961 and 1971 by U.S. forces has potent presence still. Its purpose was described as twofold: to lay bare the jungles and the cover under which Viet Cong soldiers could potentially hide and to destroy their food supplies. It defoliated more than five million acres of land.[109] Five hundred thousand acres

107. Hunt, "An Acoustic Register." in Stoler, Imperial Debris, 39–66.

108. It is estimated that eighty-two million "bomblets" were dropped in Vietnam between 1961 and 1973. Duds continue to be found in forty-three of the sixty-five provinces in Vietnam thirty years later. Similar cluster bombs were used by the United States in Kuwait in 1991 and in Afghanistan in 2001: see Ellen Massey, "Disarmament: Will the U.S. Finally End Cluster Bomb Imports?" Anti War, http://www.antiwar.com/orig/browne.php?articleid=11328http://www.antiwar.com/orig/browne.php?articleid=11328. The estimates of unexploded ordnance range between 300,000 tons and as much as 800,000 tons. I have taken the more conservative estimate.

109. Monica J. Casper and Diane Fox, eds., "Chemical Politics and the Hazards of Modern Warfare: Agent Orange," in Synthetic Planet: Chemical Politics and the Hazards of Modern Life, ed. Monica J. Casper (New York: Routledge, 2003), 73–89. See also Diane Fox, "One Significant Ghost: Agent Orange: Narratives of Trauma, Survival, and Responsibility," Ph.D. diss., University of Washington, Seattle, 2007. See also Frank Browning and Dorothy Forman, The Wasted Nations: Report of the International Commission of Enquiry into United States Crimes in Indochina, June 20–25, 1971 (New York: Harper and Row, 1972); Peter H. Schuck, Agent Orange on Trial: Mass Toxic Disasters in the Courts (Cambridge, MA: Harvard University Press, 1986); Barry Weisberg, Ecocide in Indochina: The Ecology of

of crops were destroyed. Toxic residues remain in soils, riverbeds, and the food chain. But the witnesses were also bodies themselves. Ten diseases are now linked to exposure at the lethal levels used in Vietnam, including cancers, respiratory disorders, severe mental retardation, and muscular-skeletal, organic, and developmental birth defects.[110]

There is nothing "over" about this form of ruination. It remains in bodies, in the poisoned soil, in water on a massive and enduring scale. In 1984, veterans of the Vietnam War filed a class-action lawsuit against Dow Chemicals, Monsanto, and five other companies. They were accorded an out-of-court settlement of $180 million. No compensation has been ever made to Vietnamese civilians.[111] Their appeals over the past decade have been repeatedly dismissed on the grounds that although dioxin is a poison, it was never intended to be used on humans and therefore constitutes neither a "chemical" weapon nor a violation of international law. This particular "imperial debris" rests in the deformed bodies of children whose grandparents were exposed and a U.S. empire that protects its own citizens maimed and killed in the name of a failed imperial project. New development projects are coming with new risks: As new land is being cultivated, bombs buried for decades are now exploding.[112] In the meantime, beds and

War (San Francisco: Canfield, 2007); Thomas Whiteside, The Withering Rain: America's Herbicidal Folly (New York: E. P. Dutton, 1971).

110. In a recent study of dioxin use by U.S. troops in Vietnam, the epidemiologist Jean Stellman at Columbia University estimates, on the basis of detailed lists of more than nine thousand herbicide spray missions, that far more dioxin was sprayed than any government study has ever acknowledged: see "Columbia University Study of Agent Orange and Vietnam Veterans," New York-Presbyterian Hospital website, http://www .nypcancer.org/prevention/issue6/sop_age_ora.html. See also the photographs by the Welsh photojournalist Philip Jones Griffiths in Philip Jones Griffiths, Agent Orange: "Collateral Damage" in Viet Nam (London: Trolley, 2003).

111. In May 2005, a lawsuit filed by Vietnamese victims of Agent Orange against the chemical companies was dismissed. In July 2005, a program to investigate the health and environmental damage caused by the defoliant was canceled before it began: see Declan Butler, "U.S. Abandon Health Study on Agent Orange," Nature 434, 7034 (April 2005): 687. The case was appealed and heard by Manhattan's Second Circuit Court of Appeals in June 2007, when the court ruled again that the chemical companies were acting as contractors for the U.S. government and therefore shared its immunity. In the most recent round, in March 2009, the Supreme Court refused to reconsider the ruling of the lower court.

112. Aaron Glantz and Ngoc Nguyen, "Villagers Build Lives out of Unexploded Bombs," November 26, 2003, http://www.ipsnews.net/2003/11/vietnam-villagers-build -lives-out-of-unexploded-bombs.

table legs are being made of the steel from recycled unexploded bombs. As the journalists Aaron Glantz and Ngoc Nguyen note, industrialists are not worried about their supplies running out.

The story does not end here. It circles back to the imperial domestic heartland, to Gagetown, New Brunswick, in Canada, where the Tripartite Technical Cooperation Program, initiated in 1957 by the United States, Canada, and the United Kingdom, carried out the first research with Agent Orange, spraying nearly 200,000 gallons in the surrounding forests. While giving a talk based on this essay in Vancouver several years ago, I was approached by a woman from Gagetown who still suffers from its effects. "Everyone knows," she insisted, that the damage was far more extensive than any of the official calculations suggest. According to "Orange Witness," a platform for those exposed to Agent Orange, $250,000 was allocated to local farmers whose crops were destroyed.[113]

"GROANING AMONG THE SHADOWS"—OR RESENTMENT IN THEM

In 1964, Derek Walcott warned that "decadence begins when a civilization falls in love with its ruins."[114] By Walcott's account, England is doomed, as are those transposed former colonial subjects such as V. S. Naipaul who pined for the grandeur of empire (as much as, or more than, some British nostalgics themselves). Some ruins are loved more than others. One set of "nobly built but crumbling spaces" in the English "cult of ruin" enjoys particular and current favor. Ian Baucom refers to them as part of "country-house England," an "ordered and disciplinary England that at once is financed by the economics of empire and marks, in dazzling expanses of Italian marble and filigreed iron, the dominion of the metropolis over domestic and colonial countrysides—for which a current generation of English nostalgics yearns."[115]

Nostalgia is often about that which one has never known or ever seen. It also carries a sense that one is already always too late. As Naipaul lamented in The Enigma of Arrival, "I had come to England at the wrong time. . . . I

113. Andrew Nisker, dir, Orange Witness, Green Planet Films, 2012; Kelly Porter-Franklin, "Fifty Years of Silence: Agent Orange in Canada," Dialogue, July 2007, 4–5.

114. Quoted in Derek Walcott, "A Dilemma Faces W[est] I[ndian] Artists," Sunday Guardian, January 12, 1964.

115. Ian Baucom, Out of Place: Englishness, Empire, and the Locations of Identity (Princeton, NJ: Princeton University Press, 1999), 172.

had come too late to find the England, the heart of empire, which (like a provincial, from a far corner of the empire) I had created in my fantasy."[116] Lévi-Strauss shared the same sense of "missing out," of belatedness in his first ethnographic travels. Disappointed by the "already decrepit suburbia" of Lahore,[117] annoyed by the

> huge avenues sketched out among the ruins (due, these, to the riots of the recent years) of houses five hundred years old. . . . When was the right moment to see India? At what period would the study of the Brazilian savage have yielded the purest satisfaction, the savage himself been at his peak? . . . Either I am a traveler of ancient times . . . or I am a traveler of our own day. . . . In either case I am the loser, . . . for today, as I go groaning among the shadows, I miss, inevitably, the spectacle that is now taking shape. . . . What I see is an affliction to me; and what I do not see, a reproach.[118]

Lévi-Strauss cringed with self-mockery at his disdain for the now. Naipaul does not bother. Though both are all too aware of having been duped by a fantasy of the ruin, they still crave what they imagine to be authentic, the Real. Naipaul wants more than the ruins of empire. Like Lévi-Strauss, his nostalgia is for what he can never know and has never seen. For Lévi-Strauss, it is a primitive in his untouched prime, for Naipaul, the evidence that empire was (and always will be) in opulent and working order. Both desire a state before the fall. Ian Baucom pinpoints when "things went wrong" for Naipaul: just when his England was sullied by large-scale migration of former colonial subjects.[119] But maybe things went really wrong when those subjects more loudly refused colonialism's terms of privilege, voided the imperial contract, and had no regard for Naipaul's ruins at all.

DOCUMENTS TO DAMAGE

Imperial ruins are less sites of love and lament for the bygone than vortexes of implacable resentment, disregard, and abandonment. Faisal Devji calls them the "scene of a crime," but they are also an ungraspable moment, a

116. Baucom, Out of Place, 199.
117. I thank Trisha Gupta for pointing me to this passage on Lahore.
118. Lévi-Strauss, Tristes tropiques, 44–45.
119. Baucom, Out of Place, 186–87.

vanishing point that can never come into clear view.[120] As documents to damage, they can never be used to condemn the colonial alone. Nor should this be the point.[121] To call the low-income high rises that hover on the periphery of Paris, where most of the riots took place in fall 2005, "ruins of French empire" is a metaphoric, political, and material claim. It makes pointed *material and affective* connections that public commentators have made only as a generic indictment of a colonial history that is now of the past. It reconnects the timing of their construction (beginning in 1950) with the material cement blocks that were used, with the former colonial North African people housed in them (they replaced the segregated shantytowns of immigrant men working for Peugeot), with the political and economic barriers erected to keep them in place.[122] As we saw in chapter 4 on colonial aphasia, it connects state racism with its colonial coordinates and with the 40 percent unemployment of those who live on the outskirts of France's political and economic life.

The geographies of the revolts were colonial through and through.[123] More important, understanding them as sites of colonial ruination registers the claims that young people in Clichy-sous-Bois and elsewhere in France are making when they proclaim themselves "*indigènes de la république*" and demand, as Hannah Arendt so famously put it, "the right to have rights." As reported in the press, Clichy-sous-Bois has no local police station, no movie theater, no swimming pool, no unemployment office, no child welfare agency, and no subway or interurban train into the city. Cordoned off and excised from the polity, those living those privations are refusing those conditions and terms. As Fanon predicted, French rule would not only wreak havoc on the futures of the colonized. Those relations would

120. Faisal Devji's comments were made at the Scarred Landscapes/Imperial Debris conference, New School for Social Research, New York, October 2006.

121. Jane Burbank and Frederick Cooper make the important point that the "prosecutorial stance" and the currency of indicting the colonial in France today and equating it with totalitarianism misses "the limits of power as actually exercised, the constraints on colonial regimes' ability to transform or to exploit . . . their frequent dependence on indigenous economic and political actors whom they could not fully control": Jane Burbank and Frederick Cooper, "Review of *Le livre noir du colonialisme,*" *Cahiers d'études africaines* 44 (January 2004): 455–63.

122. On the history of immigrant housing in France, see Marc Bernardot, *Loger les immigrés: La Sonacotra 1956–2006* (Bellecombe-en-Bauges, France: Croquant, 2008).

123. Étienne Balibar made the point with force in "Uprisings in the 'Banlieues,'" *Constellations* 14, 1 (March 2007): 47–71—as have some others—but with little historical analysis.

"haunt French believers in democracy."[124] And it does. It took fifty years for the French government to officially acknowledge the use of the term "Algerian War"—the same amount of time it took some French scholars to acknowledge that the French Republic was from its start a racialized colonial formation.[125]

Sebald remarks that Jean Amery saw resentment as essential to a critical view of the past. As Amery put it, "Resentment nails every one of us onto the cross of this ruined past. Absurdly, it demands that the irreversible be turned around, that the event be undone."[126] Resentment is an active, critical force in the present. It is about the possibility of naming injuries for what they are, a demand that the conditions of constraint and injury be reckoned with and acknowledged. The state of emergency that the French state imposed across a quarter of its national territory during the riots of 2005 was a response to the riots but also to decades of a systematic project to disregard and destroy the health, livelihood, and psychic endurance of a very particular population. This form of ruination defines both a process and a sustained political project on which imperial states did, and continue to, deeply depend. It does not produce passive or docile subjects but political and affective states of sustained resentment and duress that redirect what will be in ruins and who will be living in them.

For students of (post)colonial studies, this should sound an alarm. The point would not be, as some French scholars have imagined, to mount a charge that every injustice of the contemporary world has colonial roots—or to emphatically insist on none at all—but, rather, to delineate the specific ways in which peoples and places are laid to waste, around whose lives debris accumulates, where it falls, and what constitutes "the rot that remains." One task of a renewed (post)colonial studies would be to sharpen our senses and sense of how to track the tangibilities of empire as effective histories of the present. This would not be to settle scores, to dredge up what is long gone, but to refocus a sharper and finer historical lens on distinctions between what is residual and tenacious, what is dominant but hard to see, and, not least, what is emergent in today's imperial formations—and critically resurgent in responses to them. At least one challenge is not to

124. Fanon, The Wretched of the Earth, 249.

125. Benjamin Stora, Le transfert d'une mémoire: De l' "Algérie française" au racisme anti-arabe (Paris: Découverte, 1999).

126. Amery, quoted in Sebald, A Natural History of Destruction, 156.

imagine either "the postcolony" or the (post)colonial imperium as a replica of earlier degradations or as the inadvertent, inactive leftover of once more violent colonial relations. The challenge instead is to track how new deformations in our social fabric and new forms of debris work on matter and mind to eat through people's resources and resiliencies as they embolden new political actors with indignant refusal, forging insurgent vocabularies and unanticipated, entangled, and empowered alliances.

BIBLIOGRAPHY

Abonnenc, E., and M. Abonnenc, "Le bagne de la Guyane française durant les années 1856 à 1872." *Bulletin de La Société de Pathologie Exotique* 74, 2 (1981): 235–52.

Abrial, Stéphanie. *Les enfants de Harkis: De la révolte à l'intégration.* Paris: L'Harmattan, 2001.

Abu-Lughod, Ibrahim A., ed. *The Transformation of Palestine: Essays on the Origin and Development of the Arab-Israeli Conflict.* Evanston, IL: Northwestern University Press, 1971.

Abu-Lughod, Ibrahim A., and Baha Abu-Laban, eds. *Settler Regimes in Africa and the Arab World: The Illusion of Endurance.* Wilmette, IL: Medina University Press International, 1974.

Abu-Manneh, Bashir. "Israel in the U.S. Empire." *Monthly Review* 58, 10 (2007). http://monthlyreview.org/2007/03/01/israel-in-the-u-s-empire.

Adas, Michael. *Machines as the Measure of Men: Science, Technology and Ideologies of Western Dominance.* Ithaca, NY: Cornell University Press, 1989.

Adler, Laure. *Marguerite Duras: Folio.* (French Edition) Paris: Gallimard, 2014.

Adorno, Theodor W. *Negative Dialectics.* London: Routledge, 1973.

Adorno, Theodor W., Else Frenkel-Brunswick, Daniel Levinson, and R. Nevitt Sanford, eds. *The Authoritarian Personality.* New York: W. W. Norton, 1982 [1950].

Afzal-Khan, Fawzia, and Kalpana Seshadri-Crooks, eds. *The Pre-Occupation of Postcolonial Studies.* Durham, NC: Duke University Press, 2000.

Agamben, Giorgio. *Homo Sacer: Sovereign Power and Bare Life,* trans. Daniel Heller-Roazen. Stanford, CA: Stanford University Press, 1998.

———. *Means without End: Notes on Politics.* Minneapolis: University of Minnesota Press, 2000.

———. *Qu'est-ce qu'un dispositif?* trans. Martin Rueff. Paris: Payot and Rivages, 2014.

———. *State of Exception.* Chicago: University of Chicago Press, 2005.

———. "What Is a Paradigm?" In *The Signature of All Things: On Method.* Trans. Luca D'Isanto and Kevin Attell, 9–32. New York : Cambridge, Mass: Zone Books, 2009.

———. "What Is a Paradigm?" *Filozofski Vestnik* 30, 1 (2009): 107–25.

Agee, James, and Walker Evans. *Let Us Now Praise Famous Men* (1939). Boston: Houghton Mifflin, 1988.

Agier, Michel. *Gérer les indésirables: Des camps de réfugiés au gouvernement humanitaire*. Paris: Flammarion, 2008.

———. *Le couloir des exilés: Être étranger dans un monde commun*. Bellecombe-en-Bauges, France: Croquant, 2011.

Agnani, Sunil, et al. "Editor's Column: The End of Postcolonial Theory? A Roundtable with Sunil Agnani, Fernando Coronil, Gaurav Desai, Mamadou Diouf, Simon Gikandi, Susie Tharu, and Jennifer Wenzel." *PMLA* 122, 3 (May 1, 2007): 633–51.

Ahmad, Aijaz. *In Theory: Classes, Nations, Literatures*, repr. ed. London: Verso, 2000.

Ahmad, Eqbal. *Confronting Empire: Interviews with David Barsamian*. Cambridge, MA: South End, 2000.

Aldrich, Robert. "Colonial Past, Post-Colonial Present: History Wars French-Style." *History Australia* 3, 1 (2006): 14.1–14.10.

Aleinikoff, Thomas Alexander. *Semblances of Sovereignty: The Constitution, the State, and American Citizenship*. Cambridge, MA: Harvard University Press, 2002.

Alleg, Henri. *La Question*. Paris: Minuit, 1961.

Al-Saji, Alia. "'A Past Which Has Never Been Present': Bergsonian Dimensions in Merleau-Ponty's Theory of the Prepersonal." *Research in Phenomenology* 38, 1 (September 2008): 41–71.

———. "The Past." *Political Concepts: A Critical Lexicon*. Forthcoming online.

Al-Shaikh, Abdul-Rahim. "Palestine: The Tunnel Condition." *Contemporary Arab Affairs* 3, 4 (October 1, 2010): 480–94.

Alvarez, Josefina Echavarría. "Re-Thinking (In)security Discourses from a Critical Perspective." *Asteriskos* 1–2 (2006): 61–82.

Anderson, Benedict R. O'G. "The Languages of Indonesian Politics." *Indonesia* 1 (April 1966): 89–116.

———. "The Languages of Indonesian Politics." In *Language and Power: Exploring Political Cultures in Indonesia*, 123–51. Ithaca, NY: Cornell University Press, 1990.

———. *The Spectre of Comparisons: Nationalism, Southeast Asia, and the World*. London: Verso, 1998.

Anderson, David M. *Histories of the Hanged: Britain's Dirty War in Kenya and the End of Empire*. New York: W. W. Norton, 2005.

Anderson, Warwick. *Colonial Pathologies: American Tropical Medicine, Race, and Hygiene in the Philippines*. Durham, NC: Duke University Press, 2006.

Anghie, Antony. *Imperialism, Sovereignty, and the Making of International Law*. Cambridge: Cambridge University Press, 2007.

Appiah, Kwame Anthony. *In My Father's House: Africa in the Philosophy of Culture*. New York: Oxford University Press, 1993.

Apter, Emily S. "Out of Character: Camus's French Algerian Subjects." *MLN* 112, 4 (1997): 499–516.

Aradau, Claudia. "Law Transformed: Guantánamo and the 'Other' Exception." *Third World Quarterly* 28, 3 (January 1, 2007): 489–501.

Arendt, Hannah. *On Revolution* (1963). New York: Penguin, 2006.

———. *The Origins of Totalitarianism* (1951). New York: Harcourt Brace, 1979.

Armitage, David. *The Ideological Origins of the British Empire.* Cambridge: Cambridge University Press, 2000.

Arneil, Barbara. "Liberal Colonialism, Domestic Colonies and Citizenship." *History of Political Thought* 33, 3 (2012): 491–523.

Arnold, David. "White Colonization and Labour in Nineteenth-Century India." *Journal of Imperial and Commonwealth History* 11, 2 (January 1, 1983): 133–58.

Artières, Philippe, and Mathieu Potte-Bonneville. *D'après Foucault: Gestes, luttes, programmes.* Paris: Contemporary French Fiction, 2012.

Asad, Talal, ed. *Anthropology and the Colonial Encounter,* repr. ed. Amherst, NY: Ithaca Press, 1973.

———. *Genealogies of Religion: Discipline and Reasons of Power in Christianity and Islam.* Baltimore: Johns Hopkins University Press, 1993.

Atran, Scott. "The Surrogate Colonization of Palestine, 1917–1939." *American Ethnologist* 16, 4 (November 1, 1989): 719–44.

Austin, J. L. "A Plea for Excuses: The Presidential Address." *Proceedings of the Aristotelian Society* 57, new series (January 1, 1956): 1–30.

Azoulay, Ariella. *The Civil Contract of Photography.* New York: Zone, 2008.

———. "When a Demolished House Becomes a Public Square." In *Imperial Debris: On Ruins and Ruination,* ed. Ann Laura Stoler, 194–224. Durham, NC: Duke University Press, 2013.

Bacevich, Andrew J. *American Empire: The Realities and Consequences of U.S. Diplomacy.* Cambridge, MA: Harvard University Press, 2002.

Bachelard, Gaston. *La philosophie du non: Essai d'une philosophie du nouvel esprit scientifique.* Paris: Presses Universitaires de France, 1940.

Badiou, Alain, and Slavoj Žižek. *Philosophy in the Present.* Cambridge: Polity, 2009.

Balandier, Georges. *Une anthropologie des moments critiques: Entretien avec Georges Balandier.* Paris: Maison des Sciences de l'Homme, 1996.

———. "The Colonial Situation: A Theoretical Approach." In *Social Change: The Colonial Situation,* ed. Immanuel Maurice Wallerstein, 34–61. New York: John Wiley & Sons Inc., 1966.

Balibar, Étienne. *Le droit de cité: Culture et politique en démocratie?* La Tour-d'Aigues, France: Aube, 1998.

———. "Le droit de cité or apartheid." In *Sans-papiers: L'archaïsme fatal,* ed. Étienne Balibar, 68–92. Paris: La Découverte, 1999.

———. *Les frontières de la démocratie.* Paris: La Découverte, 1992.

———. *Masses, Classes, Ideas: Studies on Politics and Philosophy before and after Marx.* New York: Routledge, 1994.

———. "Racism as Universalism." *New Political Science* 8, 1–2 (September 1989): 9–22.

———. "Uprisings in the 'Banlieues.'" *Constellations* 14, 1 (March 1, 2007): 47–71.

———. "Y a-t-il un neo-racisme?" In *Race, nation, classe: Les identités ambiguës,* eds. Etienne Balibar and Immanuel Wallerstein, 27–41. Paris: La Découverte, 1988.

Ballhatchet, Kenneth. *Race, Sex, and Class under the Raj: Imperial Attitudes and Policies and Their Critics, 1793–1905.* London: Weidenfeld and Nicolson, 1980.

Bancel, Nicolas, et al., eds. *Ruptures postcoloniales : Les nouveaux visages de la societe francaise.* Paris: La Découverte, 2010.

Banton, Michael. *The Idea of Race.* London: Tavistock, 1977.

Baring, Edward. "Liberalism and the Algerian War: The Case of Jacques Derrida." *Critical Inquiry* 36, 2 (January 1, 2010): 239–61.

Barth, Elie. "M. Le Pen reporte sur sa fille l'espoir de briser l'isolement du FN," *Le Monde,* April 18, 2003.

Baucom, Ian. *Out of Place: Englishness, Empire, and the Locations of Identity.* Princeton, NJ: Princeton University Press, 1999.

Baudrillard, Jean. "War Porn." *International Journal of Baudrillard Studies* 2, 1 (January 2005). http://www2.ubishops.ca/baudrillardstudies/vol2_1/taylor.htm.

Bauman, Zygmunt. *Modernity and the Holocaust.* Ithaca, NY: Cornell University Press, 2000.

———. "Wars of the Globalization Era." *European Journal of Social Theory* 4, 1 (February 1, 2001): 11–28.

———. *Wasted Lives: Modernity and Its Outcasts.* Cambridge: Polity, 2004.

Bayart, Jean-François. *Les études postcoloniales: Un carnaval académique.* Paris: Karthala, 2010.

———. "Les études postcoloniales, une invention politique de la tradition?" *Sociétés Politiques Comparées* 14 (April 2009): 1–46.

———. "Les très faché(e)s des études postcoloniales." *Sociétés Politiques Comparées,* 23 (March 2010): 1–12.

Bayly, Christopher Alan. *Empire and Information: Intelligence Gathering and Social Communication in India, 1780–1870.* Cambridge: Cambridge University Press, 1996.

Bear, Laura. "Ruins and Ghosts." In *Lines of the Nation: Indian Railway Workers, Bureaucracy, and the Intimate Historical Self,* 257–84. New York: Columbia University Press, 2007.

Bearsley-Murray, Jon. "Vilcashuaan: Telling Stories in Ruins." In *Ruins of Modernity,* ed. Julia Hell and Andreas Schönle, 212–31. Durham, NC: Duke University Press, 2010.

Beaumont de la Bonninière, Gustave Auguste de, and Alexis de Tocqueville. *On the Penitentiary System in the United States and Its Application in France, with an Appendix on Penal Colonies and also Statistical Notes.* Philadelphia: Carey, Lea and Blanchard, 1833.

Beckert, Sven. *Empire of Cotton: A Global History.* New York: Alfred A. Knopf, 2014.

Beinart, William, and Lotte Hughes. *Environment and Empire.* Oxford: Oxford University Press, 2007.

Beinin, Joel, and Rebecca Stein, eds. *The Struggle for Sovereignty: Palestine and Israel, 1993 2005.* Stanford, CA: Stanford University Press, 2006.

Bel, Maurice. *Les colonies agricoles de 1848.* Nice: Maurice Bel, 1997.

Belvaude, Catherine. *L'Algérie.* Paris: Karthala, 1991.

Bendhif-Syllas, Myriam. "Les 'corps perdus' de Mettray." *Revue d'Histoire de l'Enfance "Irrégulière,"* 8 (November 15, 2006): 133–48.

Benjamin, Walter. *The Arcades Project.* Cambridge, MA: Harvard University Press, 2002.

Ben Jelloun, Tahar. *La plus haute des solitudes: Misère affective et sexuelle d'émigrés nord-africains.* Paris: Seuil, 2003.

Benton, Lauren A. *A Search for Sovereignty: Law and Geography in European Empires, 1400–1900.* Cambridge: Cambridge University Press, 2010.

Berezin, Mabel. "Revisiting the French National Front: The Ontology of a Political Mood." *Journal of Contemporary Ethnography* 36, 2 (2007): 129–46.

Berger, Anne, and Eleni Varikas, eds. *Genre et postcolonialismes: Dialogues transcontinentaux.* Paris: Éditions des Archives Contemporaines, 2011.

Bergson, Henri. *Matter and Memory* (1896), trans. N. M. Paul and W. S. Palmer. New York: Zone, 1991.

Berman, Russell A. *Enlightenment or Empire: Colonial Discourse in German Culture.* Lincoln: University of Nebraska Press, 1998.

Bernardot, Marc. *Camps d'étrangers.* Bellecombe-en-Bauges, France: Croquant, 2008.

———. "Les camps d'étrangers, dispositif colonial au service des sociétés de contrôle." *Revue Projet* 308, 1 (January 1, 2009): 41–50.

———. *Captures.* Bellecombe-en-Bauges, France: Croquant, 2012.

———. "Les mutations de la figure du camp." In *Le retour des camps: Sangatte, Lampedusa, Guantanamo,* ed. Olivier Le Cour Grandmaison, Gilles Lhuilier, and Jérôme Valluy, 42–57. Paris: Autrement, 2007.

———. *Loger les immigrés: La Sonacotra 1956–2006.* Bellecombe-en-Bauges, France: Croquant, 2008.

Bernasconi, Robert, with Sybol Cook, eds. *Race and Racism in Continental Philosophy.* Bloomington: Indiana University Press, 2003.

Bertrand, Romain. *Mémoires d'empire: La controverse autour du fait colonial.* Bellecombe-en-Bauge, France: Croquant, 2006.

Bessire, Lucas, and David Bond. "Ontological Anthropology and the Deferral of Critique." *American Ethnologist* 41, 3 (2014): 440–56.

Biehl, João, and Torben Eskerod. *Vita: Life in a Zone of Social Abandonment.* Berkeley: University of California Press, 2005.

Bihr, Alain. *Le spectre de l'extrême droite: Les français dans le miroir du Front National.* Paris: De l'Atelier and Ouvrières, 1998.

Bilgrami, Akeel. "Occidentalism, the Very Idea: An Essay on Enlightenment and Enchantment." *Critical Inquiry* 32, 3 (2006): 381–411.

Biondi, Jean-Pierre, and Gilles Morin. *Les anticolonialistes, 1881–1962.* Paris: R. Laffont, 1992.

Bissell, William Cunningham. "Engaging Colonial Nostalgia." *Cultural Anthropology* 20, 2 (May 1, 2005): 215–48.

Bjørgo, Tore, and Rob Witte. *Racist Violence in Europe.* Basingstoke: Macmillan, 1993.

Blanchard, Pascal, and Nicolas Bancel eds. *Culture Post-Coloniale 1961–2006: Traces et Mémoires Coloniales en France.* Paris: Autrement, 2005.

Blanchard, Pascal, and Sandrine Lemaire, eds. *Culture coloniale 1871–1931.* Paris: Autrement, 2003.

———. *Culture impériale: Les colonies au coeur de la République, 1931–1961.* Paris: Autrement, 2004.

Blanchard, Pascal, Nicolas Bancel, and Françoise Vergès. *La république coloniale: Essai sur une utopie.* Paris: A. Michel, 2003.

Blanchard, Pascal, Nicolas Bancel, and Sandrine Lemaire eds. *La fracture coloniale : La société française au prisme de l'héritage colonial.* Paris: Cahiers Libres, 2005.

Blanchard, Pascal, Sandrine Lemaire, and Nicolas Bancel, eds. *Culture coloniale en France: De la Révolution française à nos jours.* Paris: Autrement, 2008.

Bloch, Maurice. *Marxism and Anthropology: The History of a Relationship.* New York: Oxford University Press, 1983.

Blumenberg, Hans. *Shipwreck with Spectator: Paradigm of a Metaphor for Existence.* Cambridge, MA: MIT Press, 1997.

Boltanski, Luc. *Distant Suffering: Morality, Media, and Politics.* Cambridge: Cambridge University Press, 1999.

Bonelli, Laurent. *La France a peur: Une histoire sociale de "l'insécurité."* Paris: La Découverte, 2010.

Bonilla-Silva, Eduardo. *Racism without Racists: Color-Blind Racism and the Persistence of Racial Inequality in the United States.* Lanham, MD: Rowman and Littlefield, 2006.

Boucher, Ellen. "The Limits of Potential: Race, Welfare, and the Interwar Extension of Child Emigration to Southern Rhodesia." *Journal of British Studies* 48, 04 (October 2009): 914–34.

Boulbina, Seloua Luste. *Le singe de Kafka: Et autres propos sur la colonie.* Lyon: Parangon, 2008.

Boumaza, Béchir, and Jérôme Lindon. *La gangrène.* Paris: Minuit, 1959.

——. *The Gangrene,* trans. Robert Silvers. New York: Lyle Stuart, 1960.

Bourdieu, Pierre. *Distinction: A Social Critique of the Judgement of Taste.* London: Routledge and Kegan Paul, 1986.

——. "Guerre et mutation sociale en Algérie." *Études Méditerranéennes* 7 (1960): 25–37.

——. *Images d'Algérie: Une affinité élective.* Archives Privées. Arles: Actes Sud, 2003.

——. *La distinction: Critique sociale du jugement.* Paris: Minuit, 1979.

——. "Les sous-prolétaires algériens." *Les Temps Modernes* 199 (December 1962): 1030–51.

Bourgeault, Ron. "Canada/Indians: The South African Connection." *Canadian Dimensions* 21, 8 (January 1988): 6–10.

Bouteldja, Houria, Sadri Khiari, and Félix Boggio Évanjé-Épée. *Nous sommes les indigènes de la République.* Paris: Amsterdam, 2012.

Bowen, John R. *Why the French Don't Like Headscarves: Islam, the State, and Public Space.* Princeton, NJ: Princeton University Press, 2007.

Boym, Svetlana. *The Future of Nostalgia.* New York: Basic, 2001.

Bracken, H. M. "Essence, Accident and Race." *Hermathena,* 116 (December 1, 1973): 81–96.

Branche, Raphaëlle. "La torture dans *Muriel* d'Alain Resnais, une réflexion cinématographique sur l'indicible et l'inmontrable." *L'Autre* 3, 1 (2002): 67–76.

——. *La torture et l'armée pendant la guerre d'Algérie, 1954–1962.* Paris: Gallimard, 2001.

Briggs, Laura. *Reproducing Empire: Race, Sex, Science, and U.S. Imperialism in Puerto Rico.* Berkeley: University of California Press, 2002.

Bristow, Edward J. "The International Crusade against the White-Slave Traffic." In *Vice and Vigilance: Purity Movements in Britain since 1700,* 175–99. Dublin: Gill and Macmillan, 1977.

Brook, Daniel. "Environmental Genocide: Native Americans and Toxic Waste." *American Journal of Economics and Sociology* 57, 1 (January 1, 1998): 105–13.

Brooks, Barbara. "Reading the Japanese Colonial Archive: Gender and Bourgeois Civility in Korea and Manchuria before 1932." In *Gendering Modern Japanese History*, ed. Barbara Molony and Kathleen Uno, 295–317. Cambridge, MA: Harvard University Press, 2008.

Brown, Cameron S. "Answering Edward Said's *The Question of Palestine*." *Israel Affairs* 13, 1 (January 2007): 55–79.

Brown, Wendy. *Politics out of History*. Princeton, NJ: Princeton University Press, 2001.

———. "Wounded Attachments." *Political Theory* 21, 3 (August 1, 1993): 390–410.

Browne, Simone. *Dark Matters: On the Surveillance of Blackness*. Durham, NC: Duke University Press, 2015.

Browning, Frank, and Dorothy Forman, eds. *The Wasted Nations: Report of the International Commission of Enquiry into United States Crimes in Indochina, June 20–25, 1971*. New York: Harper and Row, 1972.

Broyard, Bliss. *One Drop: My Father's Hidden Life*. New York: Back Bay, 2007.

Bruck, Gabriele vom. "Naturalising, Neutralising Women's Bodies: The 'Headscarf Affair' and the Politics of Representation." *Identities* 15, 1 (January 22, 2008): 51–79.

Bruckner, Pascal. *La tyrannie de la pénitence essai sur le masochisme occidental*. Paris: Librairie Générale Française, 2008.

Brudholm, Thomas. *Resentment's Virtue: Jean Améry and the Refusal to Forgive*. Philadelphia: Temple University Press, 2008.

Bruner, Edward M. *Culture on Tour: Ethnographies of Travel*. Chicago: University of Chicago Press, 2005.

Buck-Morss, Susan. *The Dialectics of Seeing: Walter Benjamin and the Arcades Project*. Cambridge, MA: MIT Press, 1989.

Bullard, Alice. *Exile to Paradise: Savagery and Civilization in Paris and the South Pacific, 1790–1900*. Stanford, CA: Stanford University Press, 2000.

Burbank, Jane, and Frederick Cooper. *Empires in World History: Power and the Politics of Difference*. Princeton, NJ: Princeton University Press, 2010.

———. "Review of *Le livre noir du colonialisme*." *Cahiers d'Études Africaines* 44, 173–74 (January 1, 2004): 455–63.

Bury, J. P. T. *France, 1814–1940*. London: Routledge, 2003.

Butler, Declan. "U.S. Abandons Health Study on Agent Orange." *Nature* 434, 7034 (April 7, 2005): 687.

Butler, Judith. *Giving an Account of Oneself*. New York: Fordham University Press, 2005.

———. "Sexual Politics, Torture, and Secular Time." *British Journal of Sociology* 59, 1 (March 1, 2008): 1–23.

———. "What Is Critique? An Essay on Foucault's Virtue." In *The Political: Readings in Continental Philosophy*, ed. David Ingram, 212–28. Malden, MA: Blackwell, 2002.

Calhoun, Craig, Frederick Cooper, Kevin W. Moore, and Social Science Research Council, eds. *Lessons of Empire: Imperial Histories and American Power*. New York: New Press, 2006.

Campomanes, Oscar V. "1898 and the Nature of the New Empire." *Radical History Review*, 73 (Winter 1999): 130–46.

Camus, Albert. *Chroniques algériennes, 1939–1958*. Paris: Gallimard, 1958.

Cantagrel, François. *Mettray et Ostwald: Étude sur ces deux colonies agricoles.* Paris: Librairie de l'École Sociétaire, 1842.

Carey, Susan. *The Origin of Concepts.* Oxford: Oxford University Press, 2011.

Carlier, Christian. *La prison aux champs: Les colonies d'enfants délinquants au Nord de la France au xixe siècle.* Paris: Éditions de l'Atelier and Éditions Ouvrières, 1994.

Carmi, Shulamit, and Henry Rosenfeld. "The Origins of the Process of Proletarianization and Urbanization of Arab Peasants in Palestine." *Annals of the New York Academy of Sciences* 220, 6 (March 1, 1973): 470–85.

Carruthers, David V., ed. *Environmental Justice in Latin America: Problems, Promise, and Practice.* Cambridge, MA: MIT Press, 2008.

Casper, Monica J., and Diane Fox, eds. "Chemical Politics and the Hazards of Modern Warfare: Agent Orange." In *Synthetic Planet: Chemical Politics and the Hazards of Modern Life,* ed. Monica J. Casper, 73–89. New York: Routledge, 2003.

Césaire, Aimé. *Discourse on Colonialism,* trans. Robin D. G. Kelley. New York: Monthly Review, 2000.

———. *Toussaint L'Ouverture: La révolution française et le problème colonial.* Paris: Présence Africaine, 1961.

Cette France-là. *Cette France-là Volume 1: 06 05 2007/30 06 2008.* Paris: Découverte, 2009.

———. *Cette France-là Volume 2: 01 07 2008/30 06 2009.* Paris: La Découverte, 2009.

———, ed. *Xénophobie d'en haut: Le choix d'une droite éhontée.* Paris: La Découverte, 2012.

Chakrabarty, Dipesh. *Provincializing Europe: Postcolonial Thought and Historical Difference.* Princeton, NJ: Princeton University Press, 2000.

Chamayou, Grégoire. *Les chasses à l'homme: Histoire et philosophie du pouvoir cynégétique.* Paris: Fabrique, 2010.

———. *Manhunts: A Philosophical History.* Princeton, NJ: Princeton University Press, 2012.

Champagne, Helene. "Breaking the Ice: A Burgeoning Post-Colonial Debate on France's Historical Amnesia and Contemporary 'Soul Searching.'" *Modern and Contemporary France* 16, 1 (February 1, 2008): 67–72.

Charbit, Tom. *Les harkis.* Paris: La Découverte, 2006.

Chatterjee, Partha. *Nationalist Thought and the Colonial World: A Derivative Discourse.* Minneapolis: University of Minnesota Press, 1993.

———, ed. *Texts of Power: Emerging Disciplines in Colonial Bengal.* Minneapolis: University of Minnesota Press, 1995.

Cheah, Pheng, and Jonathan D. Culler, eds. *Grounds of Comparison: Around the Work of Benedict Anderson.* New York: Routledge, 2003.

Cherki, Alice. *La frontière invisible: Violences de l'immigration.* Paris: Elema, 2006.

Chow, Y. W., R. Pietranico, and A. Mukerji. "Studies of Oxygen Binding Energy to Hemoglobin Molecule." *Biochemical and Biophysical Research Communications* 66, 4 (October 27, 1975): 1424–31.

Christofferson, Michael Scott. *French Intellectuals against the Left: The Antitotalitarian Moment of the 1970s.* New York: Berghahn, 2004.

Cixous, Hélène. "My Algeriance: In Other Words, to Depart Not to Arrive from Algeria." *TriQuarterly,* 100 (1997): 259–79.

Cliff, Michelle. *No Telephone to Heaven*. New York: Vintage, 1987.

Coates, Timothy J. *Convicts and Orphans: Forced and State-Sponsored Colonizers in the Portuguese Empire, 1550–1755*. Stanford, CA: Stanford University Press, 2001.

———. "Preliminary Considerations on European Forced Labor in Angola, 1880–1930." *Portuguese Literary and Cultural Studies* 14–15 (2010): 79–105.

———. "Social Exclusion: Practice and Fear of Exile (*Degredo*) in Portuguese History." *Edições* 2 (2005): 122–24.

Cohen, Jean L. *Globalization and Sovereignty: Rethinking Legality, Legitimacy and Constitutionalism*. Cambridge: Cambridge University Press, 2012.

———. "Sovereign Equality versus Imperial Right: The Battle over the 'New World Order.'" *Constellations* 13, 4 (December 1, 2006): 485–505.

———. "Whose Sovereignty? Empire versus International Law." *Ethics and International Affairs* 18, 3 (December 2004): 1–24.

Cohen, Roger. "The World: The Ends of Empire." *New York Times*, July 4, 2004, Week in Review. http://www.nytimes.com/2004/07/04/weekinreview/world-ends-empire-strange-bedfellows-imperial-america-retreats-iraq.html.

Cohen, Shaul Ephraim. *The Politics of Planting: Israeli-Palestinian Competition for Control of Land in the Jerusalem Periphery*. Chicago: University of Chicago Press, 1993.

Cohen, Stu, and Beshara Doumani. "Contesting Zionism: Two Views of the Question of Palestine." *MERIP Reports*, 100–101 (October 1, 1981): 44–48.

Cole, Jennifer. *Forget Colonialism? Sacrifice and the Art of Memory in Madagascar*. Berkeley: University of California Press, 2001.

Colley, Linda. *Captives: Britain, Empire, and the World, 1600–1850*. New York: Anchor Doubleday, 2004.

Collier, Stephen J. "Topologies of Power: Foucault's Analysis of Political Government beyond 'Governmentality.'" *Theory, Culture and Society* 26, 6 (November 1, 2009): 78–108.

Collier, Stephen J., and Andrew Lakoff. "Distributed Preparedness: The Spatial Logic of Domestic Security in the United States." *Environment and Planning D: Society and Space* 26, 1 (2007): 7–28.

———. "On Regimes of Living." In *Global Assemblages: Technology, Politics, and Ethics as Anthropological Problems*, ed. Aihwa Ong and Stephen J. Collier, 22–39. Malden, MA: Blackwell, 2005.

Collier, Stephen J., Andrew Lakoff, and Paul Rabinow. "Biosecurity: Towards an Anthropology of the Contemporary." *Anthropology Today* 20, 5 (October 2004): 3–7.

Collins, John F. *Revolt of the Saints: Memory and Redemption in the Twilight of Brazilian Racial Democracy*. Durham, NC: Duke University Press, 2015.

———. "Ruins, Redemption, and Brazil's Imperial Exception." In *Imperial Debris: On Ruins and Ruination*, ed. Ann Laura Stoler, 162–93. Durham, NC: Duke University Press, 2013.

La Commission nationale consultative des droits de l'homme. *1994: La lutte contre le racisme et la xénophobie*. Paris: La documentation Française, 1995.

The Compact Edition of the Oxford English Dictionary: Complete Text Reproduced Micrographically. Oxford: Clarendon, 1971.

Condette, Jean-François. "Entre enfermement et culture des champs, les vertus éducatives supposées du travail de la terre et de l'atelier. Les enfants de Clairvaux (1850–1864)." *Le Temps de l'Histoire*, 7 (November 15, 2005): 41–75.

Conrad, Sebastian. "Enlightenment in Global History: A Historiographical Critique." *American Historical Review* 117, 4 (October 1, 2012): 999–1027.

———. *Globalisation and the Nation in Imperial Germany*. Cambridge: Cambridge University Press, 2010.

Cooper, Frederick. *Decolonization and African Society: The Labor Question in French and British Africa*. Cambridge: Cambridge University Press, 1996.

———. "Decolonizing Situations: The Rise, Fall, and Rise of Colonial Studies, 1951–2001." *French Politics, Culture and Society* 20, 2 (July 1, 2002): 47–76.

Cooper, Frederick, and Ann Laura Stoler. "Between Metropole and Colony." In *Tensions of Empire: Colonial Cultures in a Bourgeois World*, ed. Frederick Cooper and Ann Laura Stoler, 1–56. Berkeley: University of California Press, 1997.

Coquery-Vidrovitch, Catherine. *Enjeux politiques de l'histoire coloniale*. Marseille: Agone, 2009.

Coronil, Fernando. "After Empire: Reflections on Imperialism from the Americas." In *Imperial Formations*, ed. Ann Laura Stoler, Carole McGranahan, and Peter C. Perdue, 241–73. Santa Fe, NM: School for Advanced Research Press, 2007.

———. "Latin American Postcolonial Studies and Global Decolonization." In *The Cambridge Companion to Postcolonial Literary Studies*, ed. Neil Lazarus, 221–40. New York: Cambridge University Press, 2004.

Crapanzano, Vincent. "From Anger to Outrage: The Harki Case." *Anthropologie et Sociétés* 32, 3 (2008): 121–38.

———. *The Harkis: The Wound That Never Heals*. Chicago: University of Chicago Press, 2011.

Crenshaw, Kimberlé. "Demarginalizing the Intersection of Race and Sex: A Black Feminist Critique of Antidiscrimination Doctrine, Feminist Theory and Antiracist Politics." *University of Chicago Legal Forum* 140 (1989): 139–67.

Crosby, Alfred W. *Ecological Imperialism: The Biological Expansion of Europe, 900–1900*. Cambridge: Cambridge University Press, 1986.

Crossley, Ceri. "Using and Transforming the French Countryside: The 'Colonies Agricoles' (1820–1850)." *French Studies* 45, 1 (1991): 36–54.

Curtin, Philip D. *The Image of Africa: British Ideas and Action, 1780–1850*. Madison: University of Wisconsin Press, 1973.

Cusset, François. *La décennie: Le grand cauchemar des années 1980*. Paris: La Découverte and Poche, 2008.

Dalrymple, Theodore. "The Barbarians at the Gates of Paris." *City Journal* 12 (Autumn 2002). http://www.city-journal.org/html/12_4_the_barbarians.html.

Daniel, E. Valentine. "Ann Laura Stoler Interviewed by E. Valentine Daniel." *Public Culture* 24, 3 (2012): 487–508.

———. "The Coolie: An Unfinished Epic." In *Imperial Debris: On Ruins and Ruination*, ed. Ann Laura Stoler, 67–114. Durham, NC: Duke University Press, 2013.

Daniel, Jean. "Une terre à tous promise." In *L'ère des ruptures*. Paris: Grasset and Fasquelle, 1979.

Daoud, Kamel. *Meursault, contre-enquête*. Arles: Actes Sud, 2014.

———. *The Meursault Investigation*, trans. John Cullen. New York: Other Press, 2015.

Darwish, Maḥmud. *In the Presence of Absence*, trans. Sinan Antoon. Brooklyn, NY: Archipelago, 2011.

Dasgupta, Sudeep. "Art Is Going Elsewhere and Politics Has to Catch It: An Interview with Jacques Rancière." *Krisis* 9 (2008): 70–76.

Davis, Diane E., ed. *Political Power and Social Theory*, 11. Greenwich, UK: Emerald Group, 1997.

Davis, Stacey Renee. "Turning French Convicts into Colonists: The Second Empire's Political Prisoners in Algeria, 1852–1858." *French Colonial History* 2, 1 (2002): 93–113.

De Beauvoir, Simone, and Gisèle Ḥalimi. *Djamila Boupacha*. Paris: Gallimard, 1962.

De Certeau, Michel. *Heterologies: Discourse on the Other*. Minneapolis: University of Minnesota Press, 1986.

Deeb, Lara, and Jessica Winegar. *Anthropology's Politics: Disciplining the Middle East*. Stanford, CA: Stanford University Press, 2015.

De Genova, Nicholas. "The Stakes of an Anthropology of the United States." *New Centennial Review* 7, 2 (2007): 231–77.

De Gérando, Joseph Marie. *De la bienfaisance publique*. Paris: Jules Renouard et cie, Libraries, 1839.

Dekker, Jeroen J. H. "Punir, sauver et éduquer: La colonie agricole 'Nederlandsch Mettray' et la rééducation résidentielle aux Pays-Bas, en France, en Allemagne et en Angleterre entre 1814 et 1914." *Le Mouvement Social* 153, 3 (September 1, 1990): 63–90.

De l'Estoile, Benoît. "L'oubli de l'héritage colonial." *Le Débat* 147, 5 (2007): 91–99.

Deleuze, Gilles. *Foucault*, repr. ed. London: Continuum, 2012.

———. "What Is a Dispositif?" In *Michel Foucault, Philosopher: Essays*, trans. Timothy J. Armstrong, 159–68. New York: Harvester Wheatsheaf, 1992.

———. *What Is Philosophy?* New York: Columbia University Press, 1994.

Deleuze, Gilles, and Félix Guattari. "What Is a Concept?" In *What Is Philosophy?* 15–34. New York: Columbia University Press, 1994.

———. *What Is Philosophy?* New York: Columbia University Press, 1994.

DeLoughrey, Elizabeth M., and George B. Handley, eds. *Postcolonial Ecologies: Literatures of the Environment*. New York: Oxford University Press, 2011.

De Lurieu, Gabriel, and Hippolyte Françoise Marie Romand. *Etudes sur les colonies agricoles de mendiants, jeunes detenus, orphelins et enfants trouves: Hollande, Suisse, Belgique, France*. Paris: General Books, 2012.

Demetz, Frédéric-Auguste. "Société d'économie charitable." *Revue d'Économie Chrétienne*, Tome 7. Paris: Adrien Le Clerc, 1864.

De Pommeuse, Heurne. *Des colonies agricoles et leurs avantages*. Paris: Huzard, 1832.

Derrida, Jacques. *Margins of a Philosophy*, trans. Alan Bass. Chicago: University of Chicago Press, 1997.

———. *Rogues: Two Essays on Reason*. Stanford, CA: Stanford University Press, 2005.

———. "White Mythology: Metaphor in the Text of Philosophy," trans. F. C. T. Moore. *New Literary History* 6, 1 (October 1, 1974): 5–74.

De Tocqueville, Alexis. *Writings on Empire and Slavery*, ed. Jennifer Pitts. Baltimore: Johns Hopkins University Press, 2001.

De Tourdonnet, A. Comte. *Essais sur l'éducation des enfants pauvres: Des colonies agricoles d'education*, Tome I: Principes fondamentaux. Paris: P. Brunet, 1862.

Diagne, Souleymane Bachir. "Bergson in the Colony: Intuition and Duration in the Thought of Senghor and Iqbal." *Qui Parle* 17, 1 (October 1, 2008): 125–45.

Dillon, Michael. *Politics of Security: Towards a Political Philosophy of Continental Thought*. London: Routledge, 1996.

———. "The Sovereign and the Stranger." In *Sovereignty and Subjectivity*, ed. Jenny Edkins, Nalini Persram, and Véronique Pin-Fat, 117–40. Boulder, CO: Lynne Rienner, 1999.

Dillon, Michael, and Andrew W. Neal, eds. *Foucault on Politics, Security and War*. Basingstoke, UK: Palgrave Macmillan, 2011.

Dirks, Nicholas B., ed. *Colonialism and Culture*. Ann Arbor: University of Michigan Press, 1992.

———. *The Scandal of Empire: India and the Creation of Imperial Britain*. Cambridge, MA: Harvard University Press, 2008.

Dirlik, Arif. "Historical Colonialism in Contemporary Perspective." *Public Culture* 14, 3 (2002): 611–15.

———. "The Postcolonial Aura: Third World Criticism in the Age of Global Capitalism." *Critical Inquiry* 20, 2 (January 1, 1994): 328–56.

Djebar, Assia. *Algerian White: A Narrative*. New York: Seven Stories, 2000.

Doane, Ashley W., and Eduardo Bonilla-Silva, eds. *White Out: The Continuing Significance of Racism*. New York: Routledge, 2003.

Doezema, Jo. "Loose Women or Lost Women? The Re-emergence of the Myth of White Slavery in Contemporary Discourses of Trafficking in Women." *Gender Issues* 18, 1 (Winter 2000): 23 -50.

Donadey, Anne. "Between Amnesia and Anamnesis: Re-membering the Fractures of Colonial History." *Studies in 20th and 21st Century Literature* 23, 1 (January 1, 1999): 111–16.

Dorlin, Elsa. *La matrice de la race: Généalogie sexuelle et coloniale de la nation française*. Paris: La Découverte, 2009.

Doumani, Beshara. "Palestine versus the Palestinians? The Iron Laws and Ironies of a People Denied." *Journal of Palestine Studies* 36, 4 (July 1, 2007): 49–64.

D'Souza, Dinesh. *The End of Racism: Principles for a Multiracial Society*. New York: Simon and Schuster, 1995.

Dubois, Laurent. *A Colony of Citizens: Revolution and Slave Emancipation in the French Caribbean, 1787–1804*. Chapel Hill: University of North Carolina Press, 2004.

———. *Haiti: The Aftershocks of History*. New York: Picador and Metropolitan, 2013.

Du Bois, W. E. B. "The African Roots of War." *The Atlantic*, May 1915, 707–14.

———. "The Conservation of Races" (1897). In *Theories of Race and Racism: A Reader*, ed. Les Back and John Solomos, 79–86. New York: Routledge, 2000.

———. *Darkwater: Voices from within the Veil* (1920). Mineola, NY: Dover, 1999.

Duras, Marguerite. *Cahiers de la guerre et autres textes*. Paris: Paul Otchakovsky-Laurens and Institut mémoires de l'édition contemporaine, 2006.

———. *The Sea Wall*. New York: Perennial Library, 1986.

Eagleton, Terry. *After Theory*. New York: Basic, 2003.

———. *Holy Terror*. Oxford: Oxford University Press, 2005.

Easterling, Keller. *Enduring Innocence: Global Architecture and Its Political Masquerades*. Cambridge, MA: MIT Press, 2005.

———. *Extrastatecraft: The Power of Infrastructure Space*. London: Verso, 2014.

Eastley, Aaron. "Exploiting El Dorado: Subalternity and the Environment." *Postcolonial Studies and Ecocriticism* 13, 1 (October 15, 2006): 38–58.

Edensor, Tim. *Industrial Ruins: Spaces, Aesthetics, and Materiality*. Oxford: Berg, 2005.

Edkins, Jenny, Nalini Persram, and Véronique Pin-Fat, eds. *Sovereignty and Subjectivity*. Boulder, CO: Lynne Rienner, 1999.

Eeuwen, Daniel van, and Jean Viard. *Main basse sur la Provence et la Côte d'Azur*. La Tour-d'Aigues, France: Aube, 2003.

Egron, Adrien. *Le livre du pauvre*. Paris Librairie des Livres Liturgiques Illustrés, 1847.

Eley, Geoff, and Ronald Grigor Suny, eds. *Becoming National: A Reader*. New York: Oxford University Press, 1996.

El-Haj, Nadia Abu. "Edward Said and the Political Present." *American Ethnologist* 32, 4 (November 1, 2005): 538–55.

———. *Facts on the Ground: Archaeological Practice and Territorial Self-Fashioning in Israeli Society*. Chicago: University of Chicago Press, 2001.

———. *The Genealogical Science: The Search for Jewish Origins and the Politics of Epistemology*. Chicago: University of Chicago Press, 2012.

———. "The Genetic Reinscription of Race." *Annual Review of Anthropology* 36, 1 (2007): 283–300.

Elkins, Caroline. *Imperial Reckoning: The Untold Story of Britain's Gulag in Kenya*. New York: Henry Holt, 2006.

Ellison, Julie. "A Short History of Liberal Guilt." *Critical Inquiry* 22, 2 (January 1, 1996): 344–71.

Ellison, Ralph. *Invisible Man*. New York: Random House, 1952.

Emmanuel, Arghiri. "Le colonialisme ces 'poor-whites' et le mythe de l'impérialisme d'investissement?" *L'Homme et la Société* 22, 1 (1971): 67–96.

———. "White-Settler Colonialism and the Myth of Investment Imperialism." *New Left Review* 1, 73 (June 1972): 35–57.

Enfantin, Prosper. *Colonisation de l'Algérie*. Paris: P. Bertrand, 1843.

Enloe, Cynthia H. *The Curious Feminist: Searching for Women in a New Age of Empire*. Berkeley: University of California Press, 2004.

———. *The Morning After: Sexual Politics at the End of the Cold War*. Berkeley: University of California Press, 1993.

Espeland, Wendy Nelson. *The Struggle for Water: Politics, Rationality, and Identity in the American Southwest*. Chicago: University of Chicago Press, 1998.

Estrosi, Christian. *Insécurité, sauver la République*. Monaco: Rocher, 2001.

Ezekiel, Raphael S. *The Racist Mind: Portraits of Neo-Nazis and Klansmen*. New York: Penguin, 1996.

Fabian, Johannes. *Out of Our Minds: Reason and Madness in the Exploration of Central Africa*. Berkeley: University of California Press, 2000.

Faludi, Susan. *The Terror Dream: Myth and Misogyny in an Insecure America*. New York: Picador, 2008.

Fanon, Frantz. *Peau noire, masques blancs*. Paris: Seuil, 1952.

———. *The Wretched of the Earth*. New York: Grove, 1963.

Fassin, Didier. "Compassion and Repression: The Moral Economy of Immigration Policies in France." *Cultural Anthropology* 20, 3 (August 1, 2005): 362–87.

———. "Du déni à la dénégation: Psychologie politique de la représentation des discriminations." In *De la question sociale à la question raciale: Représenter la société française*, ed. Didier Fassin and Eric Fassin, 133–57. Paris: Découverte, 2009.

———. "Riots in France and Silent Anthropologists." *Anthropology Today* 22, 1 (February 1, 2006): 1–3.

———. *When Bodies Remember: Experiences and Politics of AIDS in South Africa*. Berkeley: University of California Press, 2007.

Fassin, Didier, and Patrice Bourdelais, eds. *Les constructions de l'intolérable: Etudes d'anthropologie et d'histoire sur les frontières de l'espace moral*. Paris: Découverte, 2005.

Fassin, Didier, and Éric Fassin, eds. *De la question sociale à la question raciale: Représenter la société française*. Paris: Découverte, 2009.

Fassin, Éric. "National Identities and Transnational Intimacies: Sexual Democracy and the Politics of Immigration in Europe." *Public Culture* 22, 3 (September 21, 2010): 507–29.

———. "The Rise and Fall of Sexual Politics in the Public Sphere: A Transatlantic Contrast." *Public Culture* 18, 1 (Winter 2006): 79–92.

Fassin, Éric, Carine Fouteau, Serge Guichard, and Aurélie Windels. *Roms et riverains: Une politique municipale de la race*. Paris: Fabrique, 2014.

Faubion, James, ed. *Foucault Now: Current Perspectives in Foucault Studies*. Cambridge: Polity, 2014.

Feagin, Joe R., Hernan Vera, and Pinar Batur. *White Racism: The Basics*. New York: Routledge, 2001.

Feldman, Ilana. *Governing Gaza: Bureaucracy, Authority, and the Work of Rule, 1917–1967*. Durham, NC: Duke University Press, 2008.

Ferguson, Niall. *Empire: The Rise and Demise of the British World Order and the Lessons for Global Power*. New York: Basic, 2004.

Fernando, Mayanthi L. *The Republic Unsettled: Muslim French and the Contradictions of Secularism*. Durham, NC: Duke University Press, 2014.

Ferro, Marc, ed. *Le livre noir du colonialisme, XVIe–XXIe siècle: De l'extermination à la repentance*. Paris: Robert Laffont, 2003.

Feuerstein, Ofir. *Ghost Town: Israel's Separation Policy and Forced Eviction of Palestinians from the Center of Hebron*. Jerusalem: B'Tselem, 2007.

Fields, Barbara J. "Ideology and Race in American History." In *Region, Race, and Reconstruction: Essays in Honor of C. Vann Woodward*, ed. J. Morgan Kousser and James M. McPherson, 143–77. New York: Oxford University Press, 1982.

Fields, Karen E., and Barbara J. Fields. *Racecraft: The Soul of Inequality in American Life*. London: Verso, 2014.

Fine-Dare, Kathleen S. *Grave Injustice: The American Indian Repatriation Movement and NAGPRA*. Lincoln: University of Nebraska Press, 2002.

Finn, Janet L. *Tracing the Veins of Copper, Culture, and Community from Butte to Chuquicamata*. Berkeley: University of California Press, 1998.

Foerster, Heinz von. "For Niklas Luhmann: How Recursive Is Communication?" trans. Richard Howe. In *Understanding Understanding*, 305–23. New York: Springer, 2003.

———. "Für Niklas Luhmann: Wie rekursiv ist die Kommunikation?" In *Teoria Soziobiologica* 1, 2:61–88. Milan: Franco Angeli, 1993.

Fontein, Joost. *The Silence of Great Zimbabwe: Contested Landscapes and the Power of Heritage*. Harare, Zimbabwe: Weaver, 2006.

Forensic Architecture, ed. *Forensis: The Architecture of Public Truth*. Berlin: Sternberg, 2014.

Forlivesi, Luc, Georges-François Pottier, and Sophie Chassat eds., *Eduquer et punir: La colonie agricole et pénitentiaire de Mettray (1839–1937)*. Rennes: Presses Universitaires de Rennes, 2005.

Forster, Colin. *France and Botany Bay: The Lure of a Penal Colony*. Carlton South, Australia: Melbourne University Press, 1996.

"Forum: The German Colonial Imagination." *German History* 26, 2 (April 1, 2008): 251–71.

Foster, Anne L. *Projections of Power: The United States and Europe in Colonial Southeast Asia, 1919–1941*. Durham, NC: Duke University Press, 2010.

Foucault, Michel. *The Archaeology of Knowledge* (1969). New York: Pantheon, 1982.

———. "The Confession of the Flesh." In *Power/Knowledge: Selected Interviews and Other Writings, 1972–1977*, ed. Colin Gordon, 194–228. New York: Pantheon, 1980.

———. *Discipline and Punish: The Birth of the Prison*. New York: Random House, 1977.

———. *Dits et écrits: 1954–1988, Volume 3: 1976–1979*, ed. Daniel Defert. Paris: Gallimard, 2000.

———. *Essential Works of Foucault, 1954–1988*, ed. Paul Rabinow. New York: New Press, 1997.

———. "Faire vivre et laisser mourir: La naissance du racisme." *Les Temps Modernes*, 535 (February 1991): 37–61.

———. *Il faut défendre la société: Cours au Collège de France, 1975–1976*. Paris: Gallimard and Seuil, 1997.

———. *The Foucault Effect: Studies in Governmentality, with Two Lectures by and an Interview with Michel Foucault*, ed. Graham Burchell, Colin Gordon, and Peter Miller. Chicago: University of Chicago Press, 1991.

———. *History of Madness*. New York: Routledge, 2006.

———. *The History of Sexuality, Volume 1: An Introduction*, trans. Robert Hurley. New York: Vintage, 1990.

———. *Les mots et les choses: Une archéologie des sciences humaines*. Paris: Gallimard, 1966.

———. "Nietzsche, Genealogy, History." In *The Foucault Reader*, ed. Paul Rabinow, 76–100. New York: Pantheon, 1984.

———. "Omnes et singularum." In *The Tanner Lectures on Human Values*, ed. Sterling M. McMurrin, 223–54. Salt Lake City: University of Utah Press, 1981.

———. *The Order of Things: An Archaeology of the Human Sciences* (1966). New York: Vintage, 1994.

———. *The Politics of Truth*. New York: Semiotext(e), 1997.

———. "Questions on Geography." In *Power/Knowledge: Selected Interviews and Other Writings, 1972–1977*, ed. Colin Gordon, 63–77. New York: Pantheon, 1980.

———. *Sécurité, territoire, population: Cours au Collège de France, 1977–1978*. Paris: Seuil and Gallimard, 2004.

———. *Society Must Be Defended: Lectures at the Collège de France, 1975–76*. New York: Picador, 2003.

———. *Surveiller et punir: Naissance de la prison*. Paris: Gallimard, 1975.

———. "Table Ronde du 20 mai 1978." In Dits et écrits: 1954–1988, Volume 4: 1980–1988, ed. Daniel Defert, 20–35. Paris: Gallimard, 1984.

———. "Two Lectures." In *Power/Knowledge: Selected Interviews and Other Writings, 1972–1977*, ed. Colin Gordon, 78–108. New York: Pantheon, 1980.

———. *La volonté de savoir*. Paris: Gallimard, 1976.

———. *La volonté de savoir*. Paris: Gallimard, 1997.

Fowler, Henry Watson, Francis George Fowler, and James Augustus Henry Murray, eds. *The Concise Oxford Dictionary of Current English*. Oxford: Clarendon, 1964.

Fox, Diane. "One Significant Ghost: Agent Orange: Narratives of Trauma, Survival, and Responsibility." Ph.D. diss., University of Washington, Seattle, 2007.

Fredericks, Rosalind. "Vital Infrastructures of Trash in Dakar." *Comparative Studies of South Asia, Africa and the Middle East* 34, 3 (2014): 532–48.

Fredrickson, George Marsh. *Racism: A Short History*. Princeton, NJ: Princeton University Press, 2003.

Freud, Sigmund. *Contribution à la conception des aphasies une étude critique* (1891). Paris: Presses Universitaires de France, 1983.

Frow, John. "In the Penal Colony." *Journal of Australian Studies* 24, 64 (January 1, 2000): 1–13.

Fullwiley, Duana. "Can DNA 'Witness' Race? Forensic Uses of an Imperfect Ancestry Testing Technology." *Genewatch* 21, 3–4 (2008): 12–14.

Furani, Khaled, and Dan Rabinowitz. "The Ethnographic Arriving of Palestine." *Annual Review of Anthropology* 40, 1 (2011): 475–91.

Gay, Peter. *The Enlightenment: An Interpretation*. New York: W. W. Norton, 1977.

Geertz, Clifford. "Common Sense as a Cultural System." In *Local Knowledge: Further Essays in Interpretive Anthropology*, 73–93. New York: Basic, 1983.

———. "Thinking as a Moral Act: Ethical Dimensions of Anthropological Fieldwork in the New States." *Antioch Review* 28, 2 (July 1, 1968): 139–58.

Gelman, Susan A., and Cristine H. Legare. "Concepts and Folk Theories." *Annual Review of Anthropology* 40, 1 (2011): 379–98.

Ghosh, Durba. *Sex and the Family in Colonial India: The Making of Empire*. Cambridge: Cambridge University Press, 2006.

Ghosh, Ranjan, and Ethan Kleinberg, eds. *Presence: Philosophy, History and Cultural Theory for the Twenty-First Century*. Ithaca, NY: Cornell University Press, 2013.

Gibbon, Edward. *The Decline and Fall of the Roman Empire, Vol. 1–6*. London: Everyman's Library, 2010.

Gide, André. *Voyage au Congo suivi de le retour du Tchad. Carnets de route*. Paris: Gallimard, 2004.

Gilroy, Paul. "There Ain't No Black in the Union Jack": The Cultural Politics of Race and Nation. Chicago: University of Chicago Press, 1991.

Ginsberg, Robert. The Aesthetics of Ruins. Amsterdam: Rodopi, 2004.

Glissant, Edouard. Collected Essays. Charlottesville: University of Virginia Press, 1989.

Godelier, Maurice. Horizon, trajets marxistes en anthropologie. Paris: Maspéro, 1973.

Goldberg, David Theo. Are We All Postracial Yet? Malden, MA: Polity, 2015.

———. Racist Culture: Philosophy and the Politics of Meaning. Cambridge, MA: Blackwell, 1993.

Goldberg, Jonathan. Sodometries: Renaissance Texts, Modern Sexualities. New York: Fordham University Press, 2010.

Goldstein, Daniel M. "Toward a Critical Anthropology of Security." Current Anthropology 51, 4 (August 1, 2010): 487–517.

Goodglass, Harold. Understanding Aphasia. San Diego: Academic Press, 1993.

Goodman, Jane E., and Paul A. Silverstein, eds. Bourdieu in Algeria: Colonial Politics, Ethnographic Practices, Theoretical Developments. Lincoln: University of Nebraska Press, 2009.

Good, Mary-Jo DelVecchio, Sarah Pinto, Sandra Teresa Hyde, and Byron J. Good, eds. Postcolonial Disorders. Berkeley: University of California Press, 2008.

Goss, Andrew. The Floracrats: State-Sponsored Science and the Failure of the Enlightenment in Indonesia. Madison: University of Wisconsin Press, 2011.

Gough, Kathleen. "Anthropology and Imperialism." Monthly Review 19, 11 (April 2, 1968): 12–27.

Grandin, Greg. Fordlandia: The Rise and Fall of Henry Ford's Forgotten Jungle City. New York: Picador, 2009.

Granjon, Marie-Christine, ed. Penser avec Michel Foucault: Théorie critique et pratiques politiques. Paris: Karthala, 2005.

Green, Nancy L. "Le Melting-Pot: Made in America, Produced in France." Journal of American History 86, 3 (December 1, 1999): 1188–208.

Gregory, Derek. The Colonial Present: Afghanistan, Palestine, Iraq. Malden, MA: Blackwell, 2004.

———. "The Rush to the Intimate: Counterinsurgency and the Cultural Turn." Radical Philosophy 150 (July–August 2008), http://www.radicalphilosophy.com.libproxy.newschool.edu/article/%e2%80%98the-rush-to-the-intimate%e2%80%99.

Griffiths, Philip Jones. Agent Orange: "Collateral Damage" in Viet Nam. London: Trolley, 2003.

Grinde, Donald A., and Bruce E. Johansen. Ecocide of Native America: Environmental Destruction of Indian Lands and Peoples. Santa Fe, NM: Clear Light, 1995.

Grove, Richard H. Green Imperialism: Colonial Expansion, Tropical Island Edens and the Origins of Environmentalism, 1600–1860. Cambridge: Cambridge University Press, 1995.

Guénif-Souilamas, Nacira, and Éric Macé. Les féministes et le garçon arabe. La Tour-d'Aigues, France: Aube, 2004.

Guillaumin, Colette. "The Idea of Race and Its Elevation to Autonomous, Scientific and Legal Status." In Racism, Sexism, Power, and Ideology, 61–98. London: Routledge, 1995.

Hacker, Andrew. Two Nations: Black and White, Separate, Hostile, Unequal. New York: Charles Scribner's Sons, 1992.

Hacking, Ian. "Déraison." Paper presented at Foucault across the Disciplines conference, University of California, Santa Cruz, March 2, 2008.

———. "Foreword." In Michel Foucault, History of Madness, ed. Jean Khalfa, ix–xii. New York: Routledge, 2006.

———. Historical Ontology. Cambridge, MA: Harvard University Press, 2002.

———. "Making Up People." In Historical Ontology, 99–114. Cambridge, MA: Harvard University Press, 2004.

———. The Taming of Chance. Cambridge: Cambridge University Press, 1990.

Hage, Ghassan. Alter-Politics: Critical Anthropology and the Radical Imagination. Australia: Melbourne University Press, 2015.

Hall, Anthony J. The American Empire and the Fourth World. Montreal: McGill-Queen's University Press, 2003.

Hamilton, John T. Security: Politics, Humanity, and the Philology of Care. Princeton, NJ: Princeton University Press, 2013.

Hannoum, Abdelmajid. "The Historiographic State: How Algeria Once Became French." History and Anthropology 19, 2 (June 1, 2008): 91–114.

Hardt, Michael, and Antonio Negri. Empire. Cambridge, MA: Harvard University Press, 2000.

Harootunian, Harry D. The Empire's New Clothes: Paradigm Lost, and Regained. Chicago: Prickly Paradigm, 2004.

Harvey, David. The New Imperialism. Oxford: Oxford University Press, 2005.

Heather, Peter. Empires and Barbarians: The Fall of Rome and the Birth of Europe. New York: Oxford University Press, 2010.

Heffernan, Michael J. "The Parisian Poor and the Colonization of Algeria during the Second Republic." French History 3, 4 (December 1, 1989): 377–403.

Heidegger, Martin. Being and Time, trans. John Macquarrie and Edward Robinson, New York: Harper and Row, 1962.

———. "Heidegger on the Art of Teaching." In Heidegger, Education, and Modernity, ed. Michael Peters, trans. Valerie Allen and Ares Axiotis, 27–46. Lanham, MD: Rowman and Littlefield, 2002.

Hell, Julia, and Andreas Schönle, eds. Ruins of Modernity. Durham, NC: Duke University Press, 2010.

Helmreich, Stefan. "Biosecurity, a Response to Collier, Lakoff and Rabinow." Anthropology Today 21, 2 (April 2005): 21.

Helsloot, John. "Zwarte Piet and Cultural Aphasia in the Netherlands." Quotidian 3, 1 (February 2012), http://www.quotidian.nl/vo103/nr01/a01.

Henry, Todd A. "Sanitizing Empire: Japanese Articulations of Korean Otherness and the Construction of Early Colonial Seoul, 1905–1919." Journal of Asian Studies 64, 3 (August 1, 2005): 639–75.

Hernon, Ian. Massacre and Retribution: Forgotten Wars of the Nineteenth Century. Stroud, UK: Sutton, 1998.

Herrera, Rémy. "Three Moments of the French Revolt." Monthly Review 58 (2006). https://monthlyreview.org/2006/06/01/three-moments-of-the-french-revolt.

Himmelfarb, Gertrude. The Roads to Modernity: The British, French, and American Enlightenments. New York: Vintage, 2005.

Hirschfeld, Lawrence A. "Art in Cunaland: Ideology and Cultural Adaption." *Man*, new series, 12, 1 (April 1, 1977): 104–23.

———. "The Conceptual Politics of Race: Lessons from Our Children." *Ethos* 25, 1 (March 1, 1997): 63–92.

———. *Race in the Making: Cognition, Culture, and the Child's Construction of Human Kinds*. Cambridge, MA: MIT Press, 1998.

Hirschman, Albert O. *The Passions and the Interests: Political Arguments for Capitalism before Its Triumph*. Princeton, NJ: Princeton University Press, 1977.

Hofschneider, Penelope Bordallo. *A Campaign for Political Rights in the Island of Guam, 1899 to 1950*. Saipan: Commonwealth of the Northern Mariana Islands, Division of Historic Preservation, 2001.

Holbraad, Martin. *Truth in Motion: The Recursive Anthropology of Cuban Divination*. Chicago: University of Chicago Press, 2012.

Holt, Thomas C. *The Problem of Freedom: Race, Labor, and Politics in Jamaica and Britain, 1832–1938*. Baltimore: Johns Hopkins University Press, 1992.

Holton, Robert. "Bourdieu and Common Sense." *SubStance* 26, 3 (January 1, 1997): 38–52.

Hooks, Gregory, and Chad L. Smith. "The Treadmill of Destruction: National Sacrifice Areas and Native Americans." *American Sociological Review* 69, 4 (August 1, 2004): 558–75.

Horowitz, Irving Louis. *The Rise and Fall of Project Camelot: Studies in the Relationship between Social Science and Practical Politics*. Cambridge, MA: MIT Press, 1967.

Huertas, Hubert. *FN: Made in France*. Marseille: Autres Temps, 1997.

Hull, Isabel V. *Absolute Destruction: Military Culture and the Practices of War in Imperial Germany*. Ithaca, NY: Cornell University Press, 2006.

Hunter, Mark. *Un Américain au Front: Enquête au sein du FN*. Paris: Stock, 1998.

———. "An Acoustic Register." In *Imperial Debris: On Ruins and Ruination*, ed. Ann Laura Stoler, 39–66. Durham, NC: Duke University Press, 2013.

Hunt, Nancy Rose. *A Colonial Lexicon of Birth Ritual, Medicalization, and Mobility in the Congo*. Durham, NC: Duke University Press, 1999.

Ignatieff, Michael. *Empire Lite: Nation-Building in Bosnia, Kosovo and Afghanistan*. London: Vintage, 2003.

Ismond, Patricia. *Abandoning Dead Metaphors: The Caribbean Phase of Derek Walcott's Poetry*. Kingston, Jamaica: University of the West Indies Press, 2001.

Israel, Jonathan Irvine. *The Dutch Republic: Its Rise, Greatness, and Fall, 1477–1806*. Oxford: Clarendon, 1995.

———. *Enlightenment Contested: Philosophy, Modernity, and the Emancipation of Man, 1670–1752*. Oxford: Oxford University Press, 2008.

———. "Enlightenment! Which Enlightenment?" *Journal of the History of Ideas* 67, no. 3 (2006): 523–45.

Ivekovic, Rada. "Langue coloniale, langue globale, langue locale." *Rue Descartes* 58, 4 (2007): 26 -36.

Jackson, John L. *Racial Paranoia: The Unintended Consequences of Political Correctness*. New York: Basic Civitas, 2008.

Jaguaribe, Beatriz. "Modernist Ruins: National Narratives and Architectural Forms." *Public Culture* 11, 1 (January 1999): 295–312.

Jakobson, Roman. *Studies in Child Language and Aphasia*. The Hague: Mouton De Gruyter, 1971.

James, C. L. R. *The Black Jacobins: Toussaint L'Ouverture and the San Domingo Revolution*. New York: Vintage, 1989.

James, Susan. *Passion and Action: The Emotions in Seventeenth-Century Philosophy*. Oxford: Clarendon, 1997.

Jarosz, Lucy. "Defining and Explaining Tropical Deforestation: Shifting Cultivation and Population Growth in Colonial Madagascar (1896–1940)." *Economic Geography* 69, 4 (October 1, 1993): 366–79.

Jay, Martin. *Downcast Eyes: The Denigration of Vision in Twentieth-Century French Thought*. Berkeley: University of California Press, 1993.

Jennings, Eric T. *Vichy in the Tropics: Petain's National Revolution in Madagascar, Guadeloupe, and Indochina, 1940–44*. Stanford, CA: Stanford University Press, 2001.

Johnson, Chalmers. *Blowback: The Costs and Consequences of American Empire*. New York: Henry Holt, 2004.

———. *The Sorrows of Empire: Militarism, Secrecy, and the End of the Republic*. New York: Henry Holt, 2005.

Johnson, Walter. "Time and Revolution in African America: Temporality and the History of Atlantic Slavery." In *A New Imperial History: Culture, Identity, and Modernity in Britain and the Empire, 1660–1840*, ed. Kathleen Wilson, 197–215. Cambridge: Cambridge University Press, 2004.

Jones, Craig A. "Frames of Law: Targeting Advice and Operational Law in the Israeli Military." *Environment and Planning D: Society and Space* 33.4 (2015): 676–96.

Jordan, James. "Review of *The Question of Palestine*." *Antioch Review* 38, 2 (April 1, 1980): 257.

Jordan, Winthrop D. *White over Black: American Attitudes toward the Negro, 1550–1812*. Chapel Hill: University of North Carolina Press, 1968.

Judt, Tony. *Past Imperfect: French Intellectuals, 1944–1956*. Oakland: University of California Press, 1992.

Julliard, Jacques, and Michel Winock, eds. *L'impossible prison: Recherches sur le système pénitentiaire au xixe siècle*. Paris: Seuil, 1980.

Kafka, Franz. *In the Penal Colony*. Leipzig: Kurt Wolff, 1919.

Kagan, Robert. "The Benevolent Empire." *Foreign Policy*, 111 (July 1, 1998): 24–35.

Kahn, Paul W. *Sacred Violence: Torture, Terror, and Sovereignty*. Ann Arbor: University of Michigan Press, 2008.

Kalifa, Dominique. *Biribi: Les bagnes coloniaux de l'armée française*. Paris: Grand Livre du Mois, 2009.

Kaplan, Amy. *The Anarchy of Empire in the Making of U.S. Culture*. Cambridge, MA: Harvard University Press, 2005.

Kaplan, Amy, and Donald E. Pease, eds. *Cultures of United States Imperialism*. Durham, NC: Duke University Press, 1993.

Kauanui, J. Kehaulani. *Hawaiian Blood: Colonialism and the Politics of Sovereignty and Indigeneity*. Durham, NC: Duke University Press, 2008.

Kelly, John D., Beatrice Jauregui, Sean T. Mitchell, and Jeremy Walton, eds. *Anthropology and Global Counterinsurgency*. Chicago: University of Chicago Press, 2010.

Khalidi, Rashid. *Brokers of Deceit: How the U.S. Has Undermined Peace in the Middle East.* Boston, MA: Beacon Press, 2013.

———. *Resurrecting Empire: Western Footprints and America's Perilous Path in the Middle East.* Boston: Beacon, 2004.

Khalidi, Walid, ed. *All That Remains: The Palestinian Villages Occupied and Depopulated by Israel in 1948.* Washington, D.C.: Institute for Palestine Studies, 2006.

Khiari, Sadri. *Pour une politique de la racaille: Immigré-E-S, indigènes et jeunes de banlieues.* Paris: Textuel, 2006.

Killian, Caitlin. "The Other Side of the Veil: North African Women in France Respond to the Headscarf Affair." *Gender and Society* 17, 4 (August 1, 2003): 567–90.

Kincaid, Jamaica. *A Small Place.* New York: Farrar, Straus and Giroux, 1988.

Kinder, Donald R., and Lynn M. Sanders. *Divided by Color: Racial Politics and Democratic Ideals.* Chicago: University of Chicago Press, 1996.

King, C. Richard, ed. *Postcolonial America.* Urbana: University of Illinois Press, 2000.

Klein, Naomi. *The Shock Doctrine: The Rise of Disaster Capitalism.* New York: Picador, 2008.

Ko, Hee Jung. "Nazis in the French-Indochina War: The Vichy Syndrome and the Politics of Memory." Paper presented at the Mass Political Violence in Twentieth-Century Southeast Asia conference, University of California, Berkeley, 2001.

Kohn, Margaret. "Kafka's Critique of Colonialism." *Theory and Event* 8, 3 (2005), https://muse.jhu.edu/journals/theory_and_event/v008/8.3kohn.html.

Kooy, Michelle, and Karen Bakker. "Technologies of Government: Constituting Subjectivities, Spaces, and Infrastructures in Colonial and Contemporary Jakarta." *International Journal of Urban and Regional Research* 32, 2 (June 1, 2008): 375–91.

Kosek, Jake. *Understories: The Political Life of Forests in Northern New Mexico.* Durham, NC: Duke University Press, 2006.

Kotef, Hagar. *Movement and the Ordering of Freedom: On Liberal Governances of Mobility.* Durham, NC: Duke University Press, 2015.

Kramer, Paul A. "Empires, Exceptions, and Anglo-Saxons: Race and Rule between the British and United States Empires, 1880–1910." *Journal of American History* 88, 4 (March 2002): 1315–53.

Kristeva, Julia. *Black Sun: Depression and Melancholia.* New York: Columbia University Press, 1989.

Kuklick, Henrietta. "Contested Monuments: The Politics of Archaeology in Southern Africa." In *Colonial Situations: Essays on the Contextualization of Ethnographic Knowledge*, ed. George W. Stocking, 135–69. Madison: University of Wisconsin Press, 1991.

Kuletz, Valerie. *The Tainted Desert: Environmental Ruin in the American West.* New York: Routledge, 1998.

Kull, Christian A. *Isle of Fire: The Political Ecology of Landscape Burning in Madagascar.* Chicago: University of Chicago Press, 2004.

Kurtz, Matthew. "Ruptures and Recuperations of a Language of Racism in Alaska's Rural/Urban Divide." *Annals of the Association of American Geographers* 96, 3 (September 2006): 601–21.

Kwarteng, Kwasi. *The Ghosts of Empire: Britain's Legacies in the Modern World.* London: Bloomsbury, 2011.

Kwon, Heonik. *Ghosts of War in Vietnam*. Cambridge: Cambridge University Press, 2008.

Labanca, Nicola. "Italian Colonial Internment." In *Italian Colonialism*, ed. Ruth Ben-Ghiat and Mia Fuller, 27–36. Basingstoke, UK: Palgrave Macmillan, 2008.

Lacoste, Yves. "La question postcoloniale." *Hérodote* 120, 1 (March 23, 2006): 5–27.

Lakoff, Andrew, and Stephen J. Collier, eds. *Biosecurity Interventions: Global Health and Security in Question*. New York: Columbia University Press, 2008.

Lambek, Michael. *The Weight of the Past: Living with History in Mahajanga, Madagascar*. New York: Palgrave Macmillan, 2002.

Lawlor, Leonard. *Thinking through French Philosophy: The Being of the Question*. Bloomington: Indiana University Press, 2003.

Lazarus, Neil. "Postcolonial Studies after the Invasion of Iraq." *New Formations*, 59 (September 22, 2006): 10.

———. *The Postcolonial Unconscious*. Cambridge: Cambridge University Press, 2011.

Lazreg, Marnia. *Torture and the Twilight of Empire: From Algiers to Baghdad*. Princeton, NJ: Princeton University Press, 2008.

Lazzara, Michael J., and Vicky Unruh, eds. *Telling Ruins in Latin America*. New York: Palgrave Macmillan, 2009.

Lebovics, Herman. *True France: The Wars over Cultural Identity, 1900–1945*. Ithaca, NY: Cornell University Press, 1994.

Le Bras, Hervé. *Le démon des origines: démographie et extrême droite*. Paris: L'aube, 1998.

Lecoeur, Erwan. *Un néo-populisme à la française: Trente ans de Front National*. Paris: La Découverte, 2003.

Le Cour Grandmaison, Olivier. *Coloniser/exterminer: Sur la guerre et l'état colonial*, Paris: Fayard, 2005.

———. *La république impériale: Politique et racisme d'état*. Paris: Fayard, 2009.

Lefeuvre, Daniel. *Pour en finir avec la repentance coloniale*. Paris: Flammarion, 2008.

Lefranc, Yannick. "Comment le parti de l'exclusion traite un mouvement pour l'intégration." *Mots* 58, 1 (1999): 57–77.

Legg, Stephen. *Prostitution and the Ends of Empire: Scale, Governmentalities, and Interwar India*. Durham, NC: Duke University Press, 2014.

Leiris, Michel. *Cinq études d'ethnologie*. Paris: Gallimard, 1968.

———. "L'ethnographie devant le colonialisme." *Les Temps Modernes*, 58 (1950).

Lemov, Rebecca. "On Being Psychotic in the South Seas, circa 1947: Making a Science of the Human." Presentation at the *Colloquium at Max-Planck-Institut für Wissenschaftsgeschichte*, Berlin, 2010.

Lesselier, Claudie, and Fiammetta Venner, eds. *L'extrême droite et les femmes: Enjeux and actualité*. Villeurbanne, France: Golias, 1997.

L'Estoile, Benoît de. "L'oubli de l'héritage colonial." *Le Débat* 147, 5 (November 1, 2007): 91–99.

Levine, Philippa. *Prostitution, Race, and Politics: Policing Venereal Disease in the British Empire*. New York: Routledge, 2003.

———. "Sexuality, Gender, and Empire." In *Gender and Empire*, ed. Philippa Levine, 134–55. Oxford: Oxford University Press, 2010.

Lévi-Strauss, Claude. *Tristes Tropiques*. New York: Atheneum, 1955.

Liauzu, Claude, ed. *Colonisation, droit d'inventaire.* Paris: Colin, 2004.

Lindqvist, Sven. *"Exterminate All the Brutes": One Man's Odyssey into the Heart of Darkness and the Origins of European Genocide,* trans. Joan Tate. New York: New Press, 1997.

Little, Douglas. *American Orientalism: The United States and the Middle East since 1945.* Chapel Hill: University of North Carolina Press, 2002.

Lloyd, David. *Ireland after History.* Notre Dame, IN: University of Notre Dame Press and Field Day, 1999.

———. *Irish Times: Temporalities of Modernity.* Dublin: Field Day and Keough-Naughton Institute for Irish Studies, University of Notre Dame, 2008.

———. "Ruination: Partition and the Expectation of Violence (on Allan deSouza's Irish Photography)." *Social Identities* 9, 4 (December 1, 2003): 475–509.

Lockman, Zachary. "Exclusion and Solidarity: Labor Zionism and Arab Workers in Palestine, 1897–1929." In *After Colonialism: Imperial Histories and Postcolonial Displacements,* ed. Gyan Prakash, 211–40. Princeton, NJ: Princeton University Press, 1995.

Luhmann, Niklas. *Theories of Distinction: Redescribing the Descriptions of Modernity.* Stanford, CA: Stanford University Press, 2002.

Lustick, Ian. *Arabs in the Jewish State: Israel's Control of a National Minority.* Austin: University of Texas Press, 1982.

———. *For the Land and the Lord: Jewish Fundamentalism in Israel.* New York: Council on Foreign Relations, 1988.

Lutz, Catherine. "Empire Is in the Details." *American Ethnologist* 33, 4 (November 1, 2006): 593–611.

MacIntyre, Alasdair C. *After Virtue: A Study in Moral Theory.* Notre Dame, IN: University of Notre Dame Press, 1981.

MacKinnon, Catharine. "Mackinnon and Spivak on the Gendered State." *Feminist News* 25 (January 2007): 1; 10.

Madley, Benjamin. "From Africa to Auschwitz: How German South West Africa Incubated Ideas and Methods Adopted and Developed by the Nazis in Eastern Europe." *European History Quarterly* 35, 3 (July 1, 2005): 429–64.

———. "From Terror to Genocide: Britain's Tasmanian Penal Colony and Australia's History Wars." *Journal of British Studies* 47, 1 (January 2008): 77–106.

Makki, Fouad. "Imperial Fantasies, Colonial Realities: Contesting Power and Culture in Italian Eritrea." *South Atlantic Quarterly* 107, 4 (Fall 2008): 735–54.

Malinowski, Bronislaw. "Dynamics of Culture Change." In *Social Change: The Colonial Situation,* ed. Immanuel M. Wallerstein, 11–24. New York: John Wiley, 1966.

Mann, Gregory. "Locating Colonial Histories: Between France and West Africa." *American Historical Review* 110, 2 (April 1, 2005): 409–34.

Mann, Michael. *The Incoherent Empire.* London: Verso, 2005.

Marcus, George E. "The Uses of Complicity in the Changing Mise-en-Scène of Anthropological Fieldwork." *Representations,* 59 (1997): 85–108.

Marcus, Jonathan. *The National Front and French Politics: The Resistible Rise of Jean-Marie Le Pen.* New York: New York University Press, 1995.

Marrus, Michael Robert, and Robert O. Paxton. *Vichy France and the Jews.* Stanford, CA: Stanford University Press, 1995.

Martín-Criado, Enrique. *Les deux Algéries de Pierre Bourdieu*. Broissieux, France: Croquant, 2008.

Masco, Joseph. "Engineering the Future," In *Imperial Debris: On Ruins and Ruination*, ed. Ann Laura Stoler, 252–86. Durham, NC: Duke University Press, 2013.

Massad, Joseph Andoni. *The Persistence of the Palestinian Question: Essays on Zionism and the Palestinians*. New York: Routledge, 2006.

———. "The 'Post-Colony' Colony: Time, Space, and Bodies in Palestine/Israel." In *The Persistence of the Palestinian Question: Essays on Zionism and the Palestinians*, 13–40. New York: Routledge, 2006.

Maurin, Eric. *Le ghetto français: Enquête sur le séparatisme social*. Paris: Seuil, 2004.

Mbembe, Achille. "Décoloniser les structures psychiques du pouvoir." *Mouvements* 51 (October 2007): 142–55.

———. *On the Postcolony*. Berkeley: University of California Press, 2001.

———. *Sortir de la grande nuit: Essai sur l'Afrique décolonisée*. Paris: La Découverte, 2013.

McCaffrey, Katherine T. "The Struggle for Environmental Justice in Vieques, Puerto Rico." In *Environmental Justice in Latin America: Problems, Promise, and Practice*, ed. David V. Carruthers, 263–86. Cambridge, MA: MIT Press, 2008.

McClintock, Anne. *Imperial Leather: Race, Gender, and Sexuality in the Colonial Contest*. New York: Routledge, 1995.

———. "Paranoid Empire: Specters from Guantánamo and Abu Ghraib." *Small Axe* 13, 1 (March 2009): 50–74.

McCoy, Alfred W. *Policing America's Empire: The United States, the Philippines, and the Rise of the Surveillance State*. Madison: University of Wisconsin Press, 2009.

McGovern, Dan. *The Campo Indian Landfill War: The Fight for Gold in California's Garbage*. Norman: University of Oklahoma Press, 1995.

McGranahan, Carole. *Arrested Histories: Tibet, the CIA, and Memories of a Forgotten War*. Durham, NC: Duke University Press, 2010.

———. "Empire Out of Bounds: Tibet in the Era of Decolonization." In *Imperial Formations*, ed. Ann Laura Stoler, Carole McGranahan, and Peter C. Perdue, 173–209. Santa Fe, NM: School for Advanced Research Press, 2007.

Mehozay, Yoav. "The Fluid Jurisprudence of Israel's Emergency Powers: Legal Patchwork as a Governing Norm." *Law and Society Review* 46, 1 (March 2012): 137–66.

Mehta, Uday S. *The Anxiety of Freedom: Imagination and Individuality in Locke's Political Thought*. Ithaca, NY: Cornell University Press, 1992.

———. *Liberalism and Empire: A Study in Nineteenth-Century British Liberal Thought*. Chicago: University of Chicago Press, 1999.

———. "The Liberal Strategies of Exclusion." *Politics and Society* 18, 4 (December 1, 1990): 427–54.

Meillassoux, Claude. *Anthropologie économique des Gouro de Côte d'Ivoire: De l'économie de subsistance à l'agriculture commerciale*. Paris: Mouton, 1964.

Memmi, Albert. *The Colonizer and the Colonized* (1957). Boston: Beacon, 1991.

Merien, Gilles. "La colonisation de l'Algérie ou le Pied Noir sans foi." *Histoire, Économie et Société* 6, 3 (1987): 427–32.

Merleau-Ponty, Maurice. *Phenomenology of Perception*. New York: Routledge, 2013.

————. *Signs*. Evanston, IL: Northwestern University Press, 1964.

————. *The Visible and the Invisible*. Evanston, IL: Northwestern University Press, 1968.

Métraux, Alfred. "Race and Civilization." *UNESCO Courier* 3, 6–7 (August 1950): 8.

Migdal, Joel S. "The Question of Palestine." *Political Science Quarterly* 95, 4 (December 1, 1980): 726–27.

Mignolo, Walter. *Local Histories/Global Designs: Coloniality, Subaltern Knowledges, and Border Thinking*. Princeton, NJ: Princeton University Press, 2012.

Miller, Alice. "Sexuality, Violence against Women, and Human Rights: Women Make Demands and Ladies Get Protection." *Health and Human Rights* 7, 2 (2004): 17–47.

Miller, Daniel. "Introduction." In *Materiality*, ed. Daniel Miller, 1–50. Durham, NC: Duke University Press, 2005.

Milloz, Pierre. *L'immigration sans haine ni mepris: Les chiffres que l'on vous cache*. Saint-Cloud: Paris: Editions Nationales, 1997.

Mills, Charles W. *The Racial Contract*. Ithaca, NY: Cornell University Press, 1997.

Ming, Hanneke. "Barracks-Concubinage in the Indies, 1887–1920." *Indonesia*, 35 (April 1, 1983): 65–94.

Ministère de l'Intérieur. *Enfants assistés. Enquête générale ouverte en 1860 dans les 86 départements de l'empire. Rapport de la Commission instituée le 10 Octobre 1861*. Paris: Imprimerie Impérial, 1862.

Mirzoeff, Nicholas. "Invisible Empire: Visual Culture, Embodied Spectacle, and Abu Ghraib." *Radical History Review*, 95 (Spring 2006): 21–44.

Mitchell, Timothy. "The Middle East in the Past and Future of Social Science." In *The Politics of Knowledge: Area Studies and the Disciplines*, ed. David L. Szanton, 74–118. Berkeley: University of California Press, 2004.

Mitchell, W. J. T. *Seeing through Race*. Cambridge, MA: Harvard University Press, 2012.

Montag, Warren. "Pierre Macherey: Between the Quotidian and Utopia." *Décalages* 1, 3 (January 1, 2013). http://scholar.oxy.edu/decalages/vol1/iss3/10.

Morgan, Edmund S. *American Slavery, American Freedom: The Ordeal of Colonial Virginia*. New York: W. W. Norton, 1975.

Morrissey, Lee. "Derrida, Algeria, and 'Structure, Sign, and Play.'" *Postmodern Culture* 9, 2 (1999): 1–22.

Morgensen, Scott Lauria. "Theorising Gender, Sexuality and Settler Colonialism: An Introduction." *Settler Colonial Studies* 2, 2 (2012): 2–22.

Morsberger, Katharine M. "John Locke's 'An Essay Concerning Human Understanding': The 'Bible' of the Enlightenment." *Studies in Eighteenth-Century Culture* 25, 1 (1996): 1–19.

Mosse, George L. *Nationalism and Sexuality: Respectability and Abnormal Sexuality in Modern Europe*. New York: H. Fertig, 1997.

————. *Toward the Final Solution: A History of European Racism*. New York: H. Fertig, 1985.

Motha, Stewart. "Veiled Women and the Affect of Religion in Democracy." *Journal of Law and Society* 34, 1 (March 1, 2007): 139–62.

Mucchielli, Laurent. *Le scandale des "tournantes."* Paris: La Découverte, 2012.

Mufti, Aamir. *Enlightenment in the Colony: The Jewish Question and the Crisis of Postcolonial Culture*. Princeton, NJ: Princeton University Press, 2007.

Murphy, Cullen. *Are We Rome? The Fall of an Empire and the Fate of America.* Boston: Houghton Mifflin, 2008.

Muthu, Sankar. *Enlightenment against Empire.* Princeton, NJ: Princeton University Press, 2003.

Navaro-Yashin, Yael. *The Make-Believe Space: Affective Geography in a Postwar Polity.* Durham, NC: Duke University Press, 2012.

Nelson, Diane. "Relating to Terror: Gender, Anthropology, Law, and Some September Elevenths." *Duke Journal of Gender Law and Policy* 9, 2 (July 1, 2002): 195–210.

Neumann, Roderick P. *Imposing Wilderness: Struggles over Livelihood and Nature Preservation in Africa.* Berkeley: University of California Press, 1998.

Newman, Karen. "'And Wash the Ethiop White': Femininity and the Monstrous in Othello." In *Shakespeare Reproduced: The Text in History and Ideology,* ed. Jean Elizabeth Howard and Marion F. O'Connor, 143–62. New York: Routledge, 1990.

Nietzsche, Friedrich. *On Truth and Lies in a Nonmoral Sense.* 1873.

———. *Untimely Meditations,* trans. R. J. Hollingdale. Cambridge: Cambridge University Press, 1997.

Nixon, Rob. *Slow Violence and the Environmentalism of the Poor.* Cambridge, MA: Harvard University Press, 2011.

———. "Slow Violence, Gender, and the Environmentalism of the Poor." *Postcolonial Studies and Ecocriticism* 13, 1 (Fall 2006): 14–37.

Noiriel, Gérard. *Le creuset français: Histoire de l'immigration XIXe–XXe siècle.* Paris: Seuil, 1988.

———. "Français et étrangers." In *Les lieux de mémoire,* ed. Pierre Nora, 2433–65. Paris: Gallimard, 1997.

———. *The French Melting Pot: Immigration, Citizenship, and National Identity.* Minneapolis: University of Minnesota Press, 1996.

———. *Immigration, antisémitisme et racisme en France, XIXe–XXe siècle: Discours publics, humiliations privées.* Paris: Hachette Littératures, 2009.

Nora, Pierre. *Les français d'Algérie.* Paris: Julliard, 1961.

———. *Les français d'Algérie.* Paris: Bourgois, 2012.

———, ed. *Les lieux de mémoire.* 3 vols. Paris: Gallimard, 1984–1992.

Nora, Pierre, and Lawrence D. Kritzman, eds. *Realms of Memory: Rethinking the French Past.* New York: Columbia University Press, 1996.

Nordmann, Charlotte, and Étienne Balibar, eds. *Le foulard islamique en questions.* Paris: Amsterdam, 2004.

Norindr, Panivong. *Phantasmatic Indochina: French Colonial Ideology in Architecture, Film, and Literature.* Durham, NC: Duke University Press, 1996.

Norton, Anne. "The Red Shoes: Islam and the Limits of Solidarity in Cixous's Mon Algériance." *Theory and Event* 14, 1 (2011), doi:10.1353/tae.2011.0013.

Obenziner, Hilton. "The Heart of the Matter." *Journal of Palestine Studies* 9, 3 (Spring 1980): 137–42.

O'Brien, Conor Cruise. *Albert Camus.* New York: Viking, 1970.

Omi, Michael, and Howard Winant. "On the Theoretical Status of the Concept of Race." In *Race, Identity, and Representation in Education,* ed. Cameron McCarthy and Warren Crichlow, 3–10. New York: Routledge, 1993.

———. *Racial Formation in the United States: From the 1960s to the 1980s*. New York: Routledge and Kegan Paul, 1986.

Ong, Aihwa. "Graduated Sovereignty in South-East Asia." *Theory, Culture and Society* 17, 4 (August 1, 2000): 55–75.

Ophir, Adi. "There Are No Tortures in Gaza." *South Central Review* 24, 1 (April 1, 2007): 27–36.

Ophir, Adi, Michal Givoni, and Sari Ḥanafi, eds. *The Power of Inclusive Exclusion: Anatomy of Israeli Rule in the Occupied Palestinian Territories*. New York: Zone, 2009.

Orr, Jackie. "The Militarization of Inner Space." *Critical Sociology* 30, 2 (July 2004): 451–81.

Osborne, Thomas J. *"Empire Can Wait": American Opposition to Hawaiian Annexation, 1893–1898*. Kent, OH: Kent State University Press, 1981.

Ouennoughi, Mélica. *Algériens et maghrébins en Nouvelle-Calédonie: Anthropologie historique de la communauté arabo-berbère de 1864 à nos jours*. Algiers: Casbah, 2008.

Oushakine, Serguei. "In the State of Post-Soviet Aphasia: Symbolic Development in Contemporary Russia." *Europe-Asia Studies* 52 (2000): 991–1016.

Outram, Dorinda. *The Enlightenment*. Cambridge: Cambridge University Press, 2005.

Pappé, Ilan. *The Ethnic Cleansing of Palestine*. Oxford: Oneworld, 2007.

Paxton, Robert O. *Vichy France: Old Guard and New Order, 1940–1944*. New York: Columbia University Press, 2001.

Peabody, Sue, and Tyler Edward Stovall, eds. *The Color of Liberty: Histories of Race in France*. Durham, NC: Duke University Press, 2003.

Péju, Paulette. *Ratonnades à Paris précédé de les harkis à Paris*. Paris: La Découverte, 2001.

Peluso, Nancy Lee, and Michael Watts, eds. *Violent Environments*. Ithaca, NY: Cornell University Press, 2001.

Pemberton, John. "The Specter of Coincidence." In *Southeast Asia over Three Generations: Essays Presented to Benedict R. O'G. Anderson*, ed. Benedict R. O'G. Anderson, James T. Siegel, and Audrey Kahin, 75–90. Ithaca, NY: Southeast Asia Program Publications, Southeast Asia Program, Cornell University, 2003.

Penrod, Lynn. "Algeriance, Exile, and Hélène Cixous." *College Literature* 30, 1 (Winter 2003): 135–45.

Perkinson, Robert. *Texas Tough: The Rise of America's Prison Empire*. New York: Metropolitan, 2010.

Perrier, Gérard. *Vitrolles: Un laboratoire de l'extrême droite et de la crise de la gauche (1983–2002)*. Paris: Arcane 17, 2014.

Perrineau, Pascal. *Le symptôme Le Pen: Radiographie des électeurs du Front National*. Paris: Fayard, 1997.

Phillips, Richard. *Sex, Politics, and Empire: A Postcolonial Geography*. Manchester: Manchester University Press, 2006.

Pinch, Adela. *Strange Fits of Passion: Epistemologies of Emotion, Hume to Austen*. Stanford, CA: Stanford University Press, 1999.

Pirey, Philippe Arnoulx de. "Operation-Gachis." *Les Temps Modernes* 92 (July 1953): 100.

Piven, Frances Fox. *The War at Home: The Domestic Costs of Bush's Militarism*. New York: New Press, 2004.

Plamper, Jan. "Foucault's Gulag." *Kritika* 3, 2 (2002): 255–80.

Posel, Deborah. "Race as Common Sense: Racial Classification in Twentieth-Century South Africa." *African Studies Review* 44, 2 (September 1, 2001): 87–113.

Povinelli, Elizabeth A. *Economies of Abandonment: Social Belonging and Endurance in Late Liberalism.* Durham, NC: Duke University Press, 2011.

Prakash, Gyan, ed. *After Colonialism: Imperial Histories and Postcolonial Displacements.* Princeton, NJ: Princeton University Press, 1995.

———. *Another Reason: Science and the Imagination of Modern India.* Princeton, NJ: Princeton University Press, 1999.

Pratt, Laura. "Decreasing Dirty Dumping? A Reevaluation of Toxic Waste Colonialism and the Global Management of Transboundary Hazardous Waste." *William and Mary Environmental Law and Policy Review* 35, 2 (February 1, 2011): 581–623.

Pratt, Mary Louise. "Mapping Ideology: Gide, Camus, and Algeria." *College Literature* 8, 2 (April 1, 1981): 158–74.

Price, Richard. *The Convict and the Colonel.* Boston: Beacon, 1998.

Puar, Jasbir K. "Abu Ghraib: Arguing against Exceptionalism." *Feminist Studies* 30, 2 (Summer 2004): 522–34.

———. *Terrorist Assemblages: Homonationalism in Queer Times.* Durham, NC: Duke University Press, 2007.

Puwar, Nirmal. "Sensing a Post-Colonial Bourdieu: An Introduction." *Sociological Review* 57, 3 (August 1, 2009): 371–84.

Pyenson, Lewis. *Empire of Reason: Exact Sciences in Indonesia, 1840–1940.* Leiden: E. J. Brill, 1989.

Rabinow, Paul. *Anthropos Today: Reflections on Modern Equipment.* Princeton, NJ: Princeton University Press, 2003.

———. *French Modern: Norms and Forms of the Social Environment.* Chicago: University of Chicago Press, 1989.

Rabinow, Paul, and Nikolas S. Rose. "Foucault Today." In *The Essential Foucault: Selections from Essential Works of Foucault, 1954–1984,* ed. Paul Rabinow and Nikolas S. Rose, vii–xxxv. New York: New Press, 2003.

Rabinowitz, Dan. "Oriental Othering and National Identity: A Review of Early Israeli Anthropological Studies of Palestinians." *Identities* 9, 3 (July 1, 2002): 305–25.

Rai, Amit. *The Rule of Sympathy: Sentiment, Race, and Power, 1750–1850.* New York: Palgrave, 2002.

Rancière, Jacques. *Dissensus: On Politics and Aesthetics,* ed. Steve Corcoran. London: Continuum, 2010.

———. *The Philosopher and His Poor,* ed. Andrew Parker. Durham, NC: Duke University Press, 2004.

Rao, Vyjayanthi. "The Future in Ruins." In *Imperial Debris: On Ruins and Ruination,* ed. Ann Laura Stoler, 287–321. Durham, NC: Duke University Press, 2013.

Razack, Sherene H. "How Is White Supremacy Embodied? Sexualized Racial Violence at Abu Ghraib." *Canadian Journal of Women and the Law* 17, 2 (December 2005): 341–63.

Redfield, Peter. *Space in the Tropics: From Convicts to Rockets in French Guiana.* Berkeley: University of California Press, 2000.

Revel, Judith. *Foucault, une pensée du discontinu*. Paris: Mille et Une Nuits, 2010.

Rex, John. "The Theory of Race Relations: A Weberian Approach." In *Sociological Theories: Race and Colonialism*, ed. UNESCO, 117–42. Paris: UNESCO, 1980.

Rheinberger, Hans-Jörg. *Toward a History of Epistemic Things: Synthesizing Proteins in the Test Tube*. Stanford, CA: Stanford University Press, 1997.

Richards, Thomas. *The Imperial Archive: Knowledge and the Fantasy of Empire*. London: Verso, 1993.

Richardson, Louise. *When Allies Differ: Anglo-American Relations during the Suez and Falklands Crises*. New York: St. Martin's Press, 1996.

Richter, Melvin. "Tocqueville on Algeria." *Review of Politics* 25, 3 (July 1, 1963): 362–98.

Robertson, Pat. *The New World Order*. Dallas: Word, 1991.

Robichez, Jacques, Yvan Blot, Jean Haudry, Pierre Vial, Jean-Marie Le Pen, and Bruno Mégret. *Les origines de la France*. Paris: Éditions Nationales, 1996.

Rodinson, Maxime. *Israel: A Colonial-Settler State?* trans. David Thorstad. New York: Pathfinder, 1973.

Roediger, David R. *The Wages of Whiteness: Race and the Making of the American Working Class*. London: Verso, 1991.

Rogers, Robert F. *Destiny's Landfall: A History of Guam*. Honolulu: University of Hawai'i Press, 1995.

Rohde, Joy. *Armed with Expertise: The Militarization of American Social Research during the Cold War*. Ithaca, NY: Cornell University Press, 2013.

Rohrer, Jonathan D., William D. Knight, Jane E. Warren, Nick C. Fox, Martin N. Rossor, and Jason D. Warren. "Word-Finding Difficulty: A Clinical Analysis of the Progressive Aphasias." *Brain* 131, 1 (January 1, 2008): 8–38.

Roitman, Janet L. *Anti-Crisis*. Durham, NC: Duke University Press, 2013.

Ronell, Avital. *Stupidity*. Urbana: University of Illinois Press, 2003.

Rosaldo, Renato. "Imperialist Nostalgia." In *Culture and Truth: The Remaking of Social Analysis*, 68–87. Boston: Beacon, 1989.

Rosenfeld, Sophia A. *Common Sense: A Political History*. Cambridge, MA: Harvard University Press, 2011.

Ross, Kristin. *Fast Cars, Clean Bodies: Decolonization and the Reordering of French Culture*. Cambridge, MA: MIT Press, 1996.

Roudinesco, Elisabeth. *Philosophy in Turbulent Times: Canguilhem, Sartre, Foucault, Althusser, Deleuze, Derrida*. New York: Columbia University Press, 2008.

Rousso, Henry. *Le syndrome de Vichy: De 1944 à nos jours*. Paris: Seuil, 1990.

Rubin, Gayle. "Thinking Sex: Notes for a Radical Theory of the Politics of Sexuality." In *Pleasure and Danger: Exploring Female Sexuality*, ed. Carole S. Vance, 143–78. Boston: Routledge and Kegan Paul, 1984.

Rude, Fernand. *Bagnes d'Afrique: Trois transportés en Algérie après le coup d'état du 2 décembre 1851*. Paris: Maspero, 1981.

Ruscio, Alain. *Y'a bon les colonies? La France Sarkozyste face à l'histoire coloniale, à l'identité nationale et à l'immigration*. Paris: Le Temps des Cerises, 2011.

Saada, Emmanuelle. "Abdelmalek Sayad and the Double Absence: Toward a Total Sociology of Immigration." *French Politics, Culture and Society* 18, 1 (April 1, 2000): 28–47.

—————. *Empire's Children: Race, Filiation, and Citizenship in the French Colonies*. Chicago: University of Chicago Press, 2012.

Saar, Martin. "Understanding Genealogy: History, Power, and the Self." *Journal of the Philosophy of History* 2, 3 (September 2008): 295–314.

Sacks, Oliver W. *The Man Who Mistook His Wife for a Hat and Other Clinical Tales*. New York: Simon and Schuster, 1998.

Sa'di, Ahmad H. *Thorough Surveillance: The Genesis of Israeli Policies of Population Management, Surveillance and Political Control towards the Palestinian Minority*. Manchester: Manchester University Press, 2014.

Sa'di, Ahmad H., and Lila Abu-Lughod, eds. *Nakba: Palestine, 1948, and the Claims of Memory*. New York: Columbia University Press, 2007.

Said, Edward W. *Joseph Conrad and the Fiction of Autobiography*. New York: Columbia University Press, 2008.

—————. *Orientalism*. New York: Vintage, 1979.

—————. "Orientalism Once More." *Development and Change* 35, 5 (November 2004): 869–79.

—————. *The Question of Palestine*. New York: Vintage, 1979.

—————. *Reflections on Exile and Other Essays*. Cambridge, MA: Harvard University Press, 2002.

Saint Affrique, Lorrain de, and Jean-Gabriel Fredet. *Dans l'ombre de Le Pen*. Paris: Hachette Littératures, 1998.

Salzman, Philip Carl. *Culture and Conflict in the Middle East*. Amherst, NY: Humanity, 2008.

Salzman, Philip Carl, and Donna Robinson Divine, eds. *Postcolonial Theory and the Arab-Israel Conflict*. New York: Routledge, 2008.

Sandars, C. T. *America's Overseas Garrisons: The Leasehold Empire*. Oxford: Oxford University Press, 2000.

Santiago-Valles, Kelvin. " 'Bloody Legislations,' 'Entombment,' and Race Making in the Spanish Atlantic: Differentiated Spaces of General(ized) Confinement in Spain and Puerto Rico, 1750–1840." *Radical History Review* 2006, 96 (September 21, 2006): 33–57.

Sartre, Jean-Paul. "Et bourreaux et victimes." *Les Temps Modernes* 15 (December 1946).

—————. "Nous sommes tous des assassins." *Les Temps Modernes* 145 (March 1958): 1574–76.

—————. "Vous êtes formidables." *Les Temps Modernes* 135 (May 1957): 1641–47.

Satia, Priya. *Spies in Arabia: The Great War and the Cultural Foundations of Britain's Covert Empire in the Middle East*. Oxford: Oxford University Press, 2010.

Saul, John S. "Two Fronts of Anti-Apartheid Struggle: South Africa and Canada." *Transformation: Critical Perspectives on Southern Africa* 74, 1 (2010): 135–51.

Sayad, Abdelmalek. *La double absence des illusions de l'émigré aux souffrances de l'immigré*. Paris: Seuil, 1999.

Sayegh, Fayez A. *Zionist Colonialism in Palestine*. Beirut: Research Center, Palestine Liberation Organization, 1965.

—————. "Zionist Colonialism in Palestine (1965)." *Settler Colonial Studies* 2, 1 (January 1, 2012): 206–25.

Schmitt, Carl. *The Concept of the Political* (1927). Chicago: University of Chicago Press, 2007.

—————. *The Nomos of the Earth in the International Law of the Jus Publicum Europaeum* (1950), trans. G. L Ulmen. New York: Telos, 2003.

Schrauwers, Albert. "The 'Benevolent' Colonies of Johannes van den Bosch: Continuities in the Administration of Poverty in the Netherlands and Indonesia." *Comparative Studies in Society and History* 43, 2 (April 2001): 298–328.

Schuck, Peter H. *Agent Orange on Trial: Mass Toxic Disasters in the Courts.* Cambridge, MA: Harvard University Press, 1986.

Scott, David. *Conscripts of Modernity: The Tragedy of Colonial Enlightenment.* Durham, NC: Duke University Press, 2004.

———. *Omens of Adversity: Tragedy, Time, Memory, Justice.* Durham, NC: Duke University Press, 2014.

Scott, Joan W. *The Politics of the Veil.* Princeton, NJ: Princeton University Press, 2007.

———. "Symptomatic Politics: The Banning of Islamic Head Scarves in French Public Schools." *French Politics, Culture and Society* 23, 3 (Winter 2005): 106–27.

Scullion, Rosemarie. "Unforgettable: History, Memory, and the Vichy Syndrome." *Studies in 20th and 21st Century Literature* 23, 1 (January 1, 1999): 11–26.

Sebald, Winfried Georg. *On the Natural History of Destruction,* trans. Anthea Bell. New York: Modern Library, 2004.

Seddon, David, ed. *Relations of Production: Marxist Approaches to Economic Anthropology.* London: Frank Cass, 1978.

Serres, Michel. "The Geometry of the Incommensurable." In *Foucault and His Interlocutors,* ed. Arnold I. Davidson, 36–56. Chicago: University of Chicago Press, 1997.

Shalhoub-Kevorkian, Nadera. *Militarization and Violence against Women in Conflict Zones in the Middle East: A Palestinian Case-Study.* Cambridge: Cambridge University Press, 2009.

———. *Security Theology, Surveillance and the Politics of Fear.* New York: Cambridge University Press, 2015.

Shaw, Martin. "Post-Imperial and Quasi-Imperial: State and Empire in the Global Era." *Millennium* 31, 2 (March 1, 2002): 327–36.

Shehadeh, Raja. *A Rift in Time: Travels with My Ottoman Uncle.* London: Profile, 2010.

Shenhav, Yehouda A. *The Arab Jews: A Postcolonial Reading of Nationalism, Religion, and Ethnicity.* Stanford, CA: Stanford University Press, 2006.

———. *Beyond the Two-State Solution: A Jewish Political Essay.* Cambridge: Polity, 2012.

Shepard, Todd. *The Invention of Decolonization: The Algerian War and the Remaking of France.* Ithaca, NY: Cornell University Press, 2008.

Shohat, Ella. "Notes on the 'Post-Colonial.'" *Social Text,* 31–32 (January 1, 1992): 99–113.

———. *Taboo Memories, Diasporic Voices.* Durham, NC: Duke University Press, 2006.

Showers, Kate B. *Imperial Gullies: Soil Erosion and Conservation in Lesotho.* Athens: Ohio University Press, 2005.

Shweder, Richard A. "Anthropology's Romantic Rebellion against the Enlightenment, or There's More to Thinking than Reason and Evidence." In *Culture Theory: Essays on Mind, Self, and Emotion,* ed. Richard A. Shweder and Robert Alan LeVine, 7–66. Cambridge: Cambridge University Press, 1984.

Sica, Alan. *Weber, Irrationality, and Social Order.* Berkeley: University of California Press, 1988.

Silva, Noenoe K. *Aloha Betrayed: Native Hawaiian Resistance to American Colonialism.* Durham, NC: Duke University Press, 2004.

Silverblatt, Irene Marsha. *Modern Inquisitions: Peru and the Colonial Origins of the Civilized World*. Durham, NC: Duke University Press, 2004.

Simon, Jonathan. "Rise of the Carceral State." *Social Research* 74, 2 (July 1, 2007): 471–508.

Simon, Steven L., André Bouville, Charles E. Land, and Harold L. Beck. "Radiation Doses and Cancer Risks in the Marshall Islands Associated with Exposure to Radioactive Fallout from Bikini and Enewetak Nuclear Weapons Tests: Summary." *Health Physics* 99, 2 (August 2010): 105–23.

Simpson, Audra. *Mohawk Interruptus: Political Life across the Borders of Settler States*. Durham, NC: Duke University Press, 2014.

Simpson, Audra, and Andrea Smith, eds. *Theorizing Native Studies*. Durham, NC: Duke University Press, 2014.

Sitkowski, Robert. "Commercial Hazardous Waste Projects in Indian Country: An Opportunity for Tribal Economic Development through Land Use Planning." *Journal of Land Use and Environmental Law* 10, 2 (April 1, 1995): 239–72.

Smith, Edward E., and Douglas L. Medin. *Categories and Concepts*. Cambridge, MA: Harvard University Press, 1981.

Smith, Neil. *American Empire: Roosevelt's Geographer and the Prelude to Globalization*. Berkeley: University of California Press, 2004.

Smith, Tony. "Idealism and People's War: Sartre on Algeria." *Political Theory* 1, 4 (November 1, 1973): 426–49.

Smouts, Marie-Claude, ed. *La situation postcoloniale: Les postcolonial studies dans le débat français*. Paris: Fondation Nationale des Sciences Politiques, 2007.

Sodikoff, Genese. "Forced and Forest Labor Regimes in Colonial Madagascar, 1926–1936." *Ethnohistory* 52, 2 (March 20, 2005): 407–35.

Solomon, Robert C. "On Emotions as Judgments." *American Philosophical Quarterly* 25.2 (1988): 183–91.

Solzhenitsyn, Aleksandr Isaevich. *The Gulag Archipelago, 1918–1956: An Experiment in Literary Investigation*. New York: Harper and Row, 1974.

Sommer, Doris. *Proceed with Caution, When Engaged by Minority Writing in the Americas*. Cambridge, MA: Harvard University Press, 1999.

Sontag, Susan. "Review: Muriel: Ou Le Temps d'un Retour by Alain Resnais." *Film Quarterly* 17, 2 (December 1, 1963): 23–27.

Soriano, Éric. *La fin des indigènes en Nouvelle-Calédonie: Le colonial à l'épreuve du politique, 1946–1976*. Paris: Karthala, 2014.

Souchard, Maryse, Stéphanie Wahnich, Isabelle Cuminal, and Virginie Wathier, eds. *Le Pen, les mots: Analyse d'un discours d'extrême-droite*. Paris: La Découverte, 1997.

Sperber, Dan, and Deirdre Wilson. *Relevance: Communication and Cognition*. Oxford: Blackwell, 1988.

Spieler, Miranda Frances. *Empire and Underworld: Captivity in French Guiana*. Cambridge, MA: Harvard University Press, 2011.

Stein, Rebecca L., and Ted Swedenburg, eds. *Palestine, Israel, and the Politics of Popular Culture*. Durham, NC: Duke University Press Books, 2005.

Steinmetz, George. "Return to Empire: The New U.S. Imperialism in Comparative Historical Perspective." *Sociological Theory* 23, 4 (December 1, 2005): 339–67.

———. "The State of Emergency and the Revival of American Imperialism: Toward an Authoritarian Post-Fordism." *Public Culture* 15, 2 (2003): 323–45.

Stewart, Kathleen. *A Space on the Side of the Road: Cultural Poetics in an "Other" America.* Princeton, NJ: Princeton University Press, 1996.

Stocking, George W. *Race, Culture, and Evolution: Essays in the History of Anthropology.* Chicago: University of Chicago Press, 1968.

Stoler, Ann Laura. *Along the Archival Grain: Epistemic Anxieties and Colonial Common Sense.* Princeton, NJ: Princeton University Press, 2009.

———. "Carnal Knowledge and Imperial Power: Gender, Race, and Morality in Colonial Asia." In *Gender at the Crossroads of Knowledge: Feminist Anthropology in the Postmodern Era,* ed. Micaela Di Leonardo, 51–100. Berkeley: University of California Press, 1991.

———. *Carnal Knowledge and Imperial Power: Race and the Intimate in Colonial Rule.* Berkeley: University of California Press, 2002.

———. "Considerations on Imperial Comparisons." In *Empire Speaks Out Languages of Rationalization and Self-Description in the Russian Empire,* ed. Ilyā Gerasimov, Jan Kusber, and Alexander Semyonov, 33–57. Leiden: E. J. Brill, 2009.

———. "Developing Historical Negatives." In *Along the Archival Grain: Epistemic Anxieties and Colonial Common Sense,* 105–40. Princeton, NJ: Princeton University Press, 2009.

———. "Epistemic Politics: Ontologies of Colonial Common Sense." *Folk Epistemology* 39, 3 (Fall 2008): 349–61.

———. "Fieldwork in Philosophy: Refiguring Social Inquiry's Conceptual Labor." Jensen Memorial Lectures delivered at the Frobenius Institute, Johann Wolfgang Goethe University, Frankfurt, Germany, May–June 2014.

———, ed. *Haunted by Empire: Geographies of Intimacy in North American History.* Durham, NC: Duke University Press, 2006.

———. "Imperial Dispositions of Disregard." In *Along the Archival Grain: Epistemic Anxieties and Colonial Common Sense,* 237–78. Princeton, NJ: Princeton University Press, 2009.

———. "On Archival Labor: Recrafting Colonial History." *Diálogo Andino,* 46 (March 2015): 153–65.

———. "On Degrees of Imperial Sovereignty." *Public Culture* 18, 1 (Winter 2006): 125–46.

———. *Race and the Education of Desire: Foucault's History of Sexuality and the Colonial Order of Things.* Durham, NC: Duke University Press, 1995.

———. "Sexual Affronts and Racial Frontiers." In *Carnal Knowledge and Imperial Power: Race and the Intimate in Colonial Rule,* 79–111. Berkeley: University of California Press, 2002.

———. "Tense and Tender Ties: The Politics of Comparison in North American History and (Post)Colonial Studies." *Journal of American History* 88, 3 (December 2001): 829–65.

Stoler, Ann Laura, and David Bond. "Refractions Off Empire: Untimely Comparisons in Harsh Times." *Radical History Review,* 95 (Spring 2006): 93–107.

Stoler, Ann Laura, and Frederick Cooper. *Repenser le colonialisme.* Paris: Payot, 2013.

Stoler, Ann Laura, and Carole McGranahan. "Introduction: Refiguring Imperial Terrains." In *Imperial Formations,* ed. Ann Laura Stoler, Carole McGranahan, and Peter C. Perdue, 3–44. Santa Fe, NM: School for Advanced Research Press, 2007.

Stoler, Ann Laura, Carole McGranahan, and Peter C. Perdue, eds. *Imperial Formations.* Santa Fe, NM: School for Advanced Research Press, 2007.

Stora, Benjamin. *La gangrène et l'oubli: La mémoire de la guerre d'Algérie*. La Tour-d'Aigues, France: Aube, 1991.

———. *La guerre des mémoires: La France face à son passé colonial*. La Tour-d'Aigues, France: Aube, 2007.

———. *La guerre invisible: Algérie, années 90*. Paris: Presses de Sciences Po, 2001.

———. *Le transfert d'une mémoire: De l "Algérie française" au racisme anti-arabe*. Paris: Découverte, 1999.

Sullivan, Shannon, and Nancy Tuana, eds. *Race and Epistemologies of Ignorance*. Albany: State University of New York Press, 2007.

Sundberg, Juanita. " 'Trash-Talk' and the Production of Quotidian Geopolitical Boundaries in the USA-Mexico Borderlands." *Social and Cultural Geography* 9, 8 (December 1, 2008): 871–90.

Sundberg, Juanita, and Bonnie Kaserman. "Cactus Carvings and Desert Defecations: Embodying Representations of Border Crossings in Protected Areas on the Mexico-- U.S. Border." *Environment and Planning D: Society and Space* 25, 4 (2007): 727–44.

Sunderland, Willard. *Taming the Wild Field: Colonization and Empire on the Russian Steppe*. Ithaca, NY: Cornell University Press, 2006.

Swinney, David. "Aphasia." In *The MIT Encyclopedia of the Cognitive Sciences*, ed. Robert Andrew Wilson and Frank C. Keil, Cambridge, MA: MIT Press, 2001.

Szmagalska-Follis, Karolina. "Repossession: Notes on Restoration and Redemption in Ukraine's Western Borderland." *Cultural Anthropology* 23, 2 (November 2, 2012): 329–60.

———. "Counter-Trafficking as Complicity and Subversion: The Politics of Rescue in the Polish-Ukrainian Borderland." Paper presented at the 105th Annual Meeting of the American Anthropological Association, San Jose, CA, November 15–19, 2006.

Taguieff, Pierre-André. "The Doctrine of the National Front in France (1972–1989): A Revolutionary Programme? Ideological Aspects of a National-Populist Mobilization." *New Political Science* 8, 1–2 (September 1, 1989): 29–70.

———. *Face au racisme, Tome 1: Les moyens d'agir*. Paris: La Découverte, 1991.

———. *Face au racisme, Tome 2: Analyses, hypothèses, perspectives*. Paris: La Découverte, 1991.

———. *Les fins de l'antiracisme*. Paris: Editions Michalon, 1995.

———. *La force du préjugé: Essai sur le racisme et ses doubles*. Paris: La Découverte, 1988.

TallBear, Kimberly. "DNA, Blood, and Racializing the Tribe." *Wicazo Sa Review* 18, 1 (2003): 81–107.

Taraud, Christelle. *La prostitution coloniale: Algérie, Tunisie, Maroc (1830–1962)*. Paris: Payot, 2003.

Taussig, Michael. "Culture of Terror—Space of Death: Roger Casement's Putumayo Report and the Explanation of Torture." *Comparative Studies in Society and History* 26, 3 (July 1, 1984): 467–97.

Taylor, Jean Gelman. *The Social World of Batavia: Europeans and Eurasians in Colonial Indonesia*. Madison: University of Wisconsin Press, 1983.

Terray, Emmanuel. *Face aux abus de mémoire*. Arles: Actes Sud, 2006.

———. *Marxism and "Primitive" Societies: Two Studies*. New York: Monthly Review, 1972.

Tétreault, Mary Ann. "The Sexual Politics of Abu Ghraib: Hegemony, Spectacle, and the Global War on Terror." *NWSA Journal* 18, 3 (Fall 2006): 33–50.

Tevanian, Pierre, and Sylvie Tissot. *Mots à maux: Dictionnaire de la lepénisation des esprits.* Paris: Dagorno, 1998.

Thénault, Sylvie. *Violence ordinaire dans l'Algérie coloniale: Camps, internements, assignations à résidence.* Paris: Jacob, 2012.

Thomas, Martin. *Empires of Intelligence: Security Services and Colonial Disorder after 1914.* Berkeley: University of California Press, 2008.

Ticktin, Miriam Iris. *Casualties of Care: Immigration and the Politics of Humanitarianism in France.* Berkeley: University of California Press, 2011.

———. "Sexual Violence as the Language of Border Control: Where French Feminist and Anti-Immigrant Rhetoric Meet." *Signs* 33, 4 (Summer 2008): 863–89.

Todd, Emmanuel. *Le destin des immigrés: Assimilation et ségrégation dans les démocraties occidentales.* Paris: Seuil, 1994.

Todorov, Tvetan. *Nous et les autres.* Paris: Seuil, 1989.

———. "Tocqueville et la doctrine coloniale." In *De la colonie en Algerie,* 9–36. Paris: Complexe, 1988.

Tomich, Dale. "Thinking the 'Unthinkable': Victor Schoelcher and Haiti." *Review* 31, 3 (January 1, 2008): 401–31.

Toth, Stephen A. *Beyond Papillon: The French Overseas Penal Colonies, 1854–1952.* Lincoln: University of Nebraska Press, 2008.

Touhouliotis, Vasiliki. "Weapons between Wars: Cluster Bombs, Technological Failure and the Durability of War in South Lebanon." Ph.D. diss., New School for Social Research, New York, 2015.

Tourdonnet, A. de. *Essais sur l'education des enfants pauvres: Des colonies agricoles d'education.* Paris: Brunet, 1863.

Trouillot, Michel-Rolph. "Port-au-Prince, Haiti, l'état d'un siège." *Lire Haiti* 1, 1 (December 2000): 5–13.

———. *Silencing the Past: Power and the Production of History.* Boston: Beacon, 1995.

Truffaut, François. *The Films in My Life.* New York: Da Capo, 1994.

Tyrrell, Ian. "American Exceptionalism in an Age of International History." *American Historical Review* 96, 4 (October 1, 1991): 1031–55.

Uehling, Greta Lynn. "The International Smuggling of Children: Coyotes, Snakeheads, and the Politics of Compassion." *Anthropological Quarterly* 81, 4 (Fall 2008): 833–71.

Vattimo, Gianni, and Michael Marder, eds. *Deconstructing Zionism: A Critique of Political Metaphysics.* New York: Bloomsbury, 2014.

Vaughn, Michalina. "The Extreme Right in France: 'Lepenisme' or the Politics of Fear." In *The Far Right in Western and Eastern Europe,* ed. Luciano Cheles, Ronnie Ferguson, and Michalina Vaughan, 215–33. London: Longman, 1995.

Verdès-Leroux, Jeannine. *Les français d'Algérie de 1830 à aujourd'hui: Une page d'histoire déchirée.* Paris: Fayard, 2001.

Vidal-Naquet, Pierre. *La torture dans la république: essai d'histoire et de politique contemporaine (1954–1962),* Minuit, [1972] 2000.

Vine, David. *Island of Shame: The Secret History of the U.S. Military Base on Diego Garcia.* Princeton, NJ: Princeton University Press, 2009.

Viney, William. *Waste: A Philosophy of Things.* London: Bloomsbury Academic, 2014.

Vries, Petra de. "'White Slaves' in a Colonial Nation: The Dutch Campaign against the Traffic in Women in the Early Twentieth Century." *Social and Legal Studies* 14, 1 (March 1, 2005): 39–60.

Wailoo, Keith, Alondra Nelson, and Catherine Lee, eds. *Genetics and the Unsettled Past: The Collision of DNA, Race, and History.* New Brunswick, NJ: Rutgers University Press, 2012.

Wakin, Eric. *Anthropology Goes to War: Professional Ethics and Counterinsurgency in Thailand.* Madison: University of Wisconsin, Center for Southeast Asian Studies, 1992.

Walcott, Derek. "The Antilles: Fragments of Epic Memory." In *Nobel Lectures in Literature: 1991–1995,* ed. Sture Allen, 25–40. Amsterdam: Elsevier, 1997.

———. *Collected Poems: 1948–1984.* New York: Noonday, 1990.

Walston, James. "History and Memory of the Italian Concentration Camps." *Historical Journal* 40, 1 (March 1997): 169–83.

Ward, Kerry. *Networks of Empire: Forced Migration in the Dutch East India Company.* Cambridge: Cambridge University Press, 2011.

Watts, Michael. *Silent Violence: Food, Famine, and Peasantry in Northern Nigeria.* Athens: University of Georgia Press, 2013.

Weber, Max. *Economy and Society: An Outline of Interpretive Sociology,* trans. Guenther Roth and Claus Wittich. Los Angeles, CA: University of California Press, 2013.

———. "Legitimate Authority and Bureaucracy." In *Organization Theory Selected Classic Readings,* ed. Derek Salman Pugh, 3–15. London: Penguin, 2007.

Weil, Patrick. *La France et ses étrangers.* Paris: Gallimard, 1991.

———. *Liberté, égalité, discriminations: L'identité nationale au regard de l'histoire.* Paris: Grasset, 2008.

Weil, Simone. *Simone Weil on Colonialism: An Ethic of the Other,* ed. J. P. Little. Lanham, MD: Rowman and Littlefield, 2003.

Weisberg, Barry. *Ecocide in Indochina: The Ecology of War.* San Francisco: Canfield, 1970.

Weizman, Eyal. *Hollow Land: Israel's Architecture of Occupation.* London: Verso, 2007.

West, Cornel. *Prophesy Deliverance! An Afro-American Revolutionary Christianity.* Louisville, KY: Westminster John Knox Press, 1982.

Whiteside, Thomas. *The Withering Rain: America's Herbicidal Folly.* New York: E. P. Dutton, 1971.

Wierviorka, Michel ed. *La France Raciste.* Paris: Seuil, 1992.

Wilder, Gary. *Freedom Time: Negritude, Decolonization, and the Future of the World.* Durham, NC: Duke University Press, 2015.

Williams, Patrick, and Laura Chrisman, eds. *Colonial Discourse and Post-Colonial Theory: A Reader.* New York: Columbia University Press, 1994.

Williams, William Appleman. *Empire as a Way of Life: An Essay on the Causes and Character of America's Present Predicament, along with a Few Thoughts about an Alternative.* London: Oxford University Press, 1982.

Wilson, Kathleen, ed. *A New Imperial History: Culture, Identity, and Modernity in Britain and the Empire, 1660–1840.* Cambridge: Cambridge University Press, 2004.

Winichakul, Thongchai. *Siam Mapped: A History of the Geo-Body of a Nation.* Honolulu: University of Hawai'i Press, 1997.

Winock. Michel. *Nationalisme, antisémitisme et fascisme en France.* Paris: Seuil, 1982.

Wittgenstein, Ludwig. *Philosophical Investigations* (1953), trans. G. E. M. Anscombe, 3rd ed. Englewood Cliffs, NJ: Prentice Hall, 2000.

Wolfe, Patrick. "Settler Colonialism and the Elimination of the Native." *Journal of Genocide Research* 8, 4 (December 2006): 387–409.

———. *Settler Colonialism and the Transformation of Anthropology: The Politics and Poetics of an Ethnographic Event.* London: Cassell, 1999.

Woodward, Christopher. *In Ruins: A Journey through History, Art, and Literature.* New York: Vintage, 2003.

Wright, Gwendolyn. "Tradition in the Service of Modernity: Architecture and Urbanism in French Colonial Policy, 1900–1930." *The Journal of Modern History* 59, 2 (1987): 291–316.

Yacine, Tassadit, Loïc Wacquant, and James Ingram. "Pierre Bourdieu in Algeria at War: Notes on the Birth of an Engaged Ethnosociology." *Ethnography* 5, 4 (December 1, 2004): 487–510.

Young, Robert J. C. "Edward Said: Opponent of Postcolonial Theory." In *Edward Said's Translocations: Essays in Secular Criticism,* ed. Tobias Döring and Mark Stein, 23–43. New York: Routledge, 2012.

———. "Postcolonial Remains." *New Literary History* 43, 1 (2012): 19–42.

———. *White Mythologies: Writing History and the West.* London: Routledge, 1990.

Zarka, Yves Charles, ed. "Michel Foucault: De la guerre des races au biopouvoir." *Cités: Philosophe, Politique, Histoire* 2 (2000).

Zimmerer, Jürgen. "The Birth of the *Ostland* out of the Spirit of Colonialism: A Postcolonial Perspective on the Nazi Policy of Conquest and Extermination." *Patterns of Prejudice* 39, 2 (June 1, 2005): 197–219.

Zobel, Clemens. "The 'Indigènes de la République' and Political Mobilization Strategies in Postcolonial France." *E-Cadernos Ces,* 7 (March 1, 2010): 52–67.

Zwick, Jim. *Confronting Imperialism: Essays on Mark Twain and the Anti-Imperialist League.* West Conshohocken, PA: Infinity, 2007.

INDEX

Aboriginal peoples, 104, 370. *See also* Indigenous peoples

Abu El-Haj, Nadia, 42n6, 55n37, 364

Abu Ghraib, 311, 332, 340; photographs at, 153, 185n29, 312; torture at, 324, 326. *See also* Guantánamo Bay; torture

Abu-Lughod, Ibrahim, 48

administration: of colonies, 212; of military, 323; of Netherlands Indies, 214n24, 219, 225; of U.S. government, 173, 181, 351

Adorno, Theodor, 339

affect, 5, 47, 225, 229–30, 260, 278, 308, 326, 367

affective: analytics of, 302; attachments, 219, 261, 327, 377; contamination, 250; distributions, 239, 310; economy, 188, 216, 270; genealogy, 205; history, 135; injury, 16; knowledge, 167, 209, 227; policing of, 258; practice, 34, 123; registers, 226, 269, 350, 361; sensibility, 151, 208; space, ix, 147, 201, 231, 236, 363n70; states, 170, 224, 228, 378

Afghanistan, 47n17, 181–82, 184, 348, 363, 373n108

Africa, 65, 67n67, 73, 103, 105, 109, 137, 141, 148, 179–80, 193, 251n37, 310, 333, 356, 359; East, 103, 357; pollution of, 3; Sub-Saharan, 334; West, 369. *See also* North Africa; South Africa

Agamben, Giorgio, 22, 36, 77, 105–6, 196n69, 202, 223, 368

Agee, James, *Let Us Now Praise Famous Men* (with Walker Evans), 371–72

Agent Orange (Herbicide Orange), 17, 311, 353, 373, 374n110, 375

agricultural colony. *See colonies agricoles, les*

Aix-en-Provence, 273–76, 279–80, 286, 296, 315

Al-Saji, Alia, 34–35

Aleinikoff, Alexander, *Semblances of Sovereignty*, 194. *See also* sovereignty

Algeria, 90–92, 99–101, 112–14, 120, 123–24, 127, 136–38, 145, 147, 152, 155, 156n109, 157, 160, 170, 305, 317, 320, 348; Algerian War, 48, 109, 125, 131, 135, 144, 148–49, 154, 161, 183–84, 310, 312, 316, 322, 323, 378; camps in, 73, 75, 81, 88, 103, 115, 126; colonial Algeria, 34, 64n58, 94–97, 108, 118, 130n20, 140, 180, 185, 197, 221, 280, 349; independence of, 294; invasion of, 328; labor in, 150n90; torture in, 143n64, 153

Algerian National Front (FLN), 153.
  See also Algeria
Alleg, Henri, 126
alterity: philosophies of, 133
Amery, Jean, 378
amnesia. See colonial aphasia
Anderson, Benedict, 230, 324
Anderson, Warwick, 104
Anghie, Antony, 176–77
anthropology, 43, 49, 212, 234n81; colony
  as field site, 71; critique of, 141, 259,
  264; in France, 134, 140; Marxism in,
  142n60; of empire, 51, 186; of Israel,
  40, 58; of security, 236n87, ontology in,
  16; recursive method in, 27n34. See also
  ethnography
Antilles, 354; French, 81; Spanish, 105n93
anti-Muslim, 185n26, 269–70. See also
  Orientalism
anti-Semitism, 30, 59, 66, 151–52, 160,
  165, 269, 333
apartheid, 58, 133; European, 166; in
  South Africa, 65, 104n89, 273n8, 317,
  359
aphasia. See colonial aphasia
Arab-Israeli War, 18, 43; Arab-Israeli
  conflict, 49
Arabs, 90n49, 92, 140, 160, 183, 311, 317,
  333, 365; as disappeared, 124; portrayal
  of, 45, 48, 123, 204; terrorism, 277. See
  also Orientalism; anti-Muslim
Archaeology of Knowledge (Michel Foucault),
  19, 28–29
archive, 56, 81–83, 93, 178, 199, 209, 228;
  archival field, 39; archival labor, 21, 351;
  archival turn, 21, 137; colonial archives,
  5, 11, 14–15, 47, 53, 72–75, 109, 117, 147,
  193, 202, 212–16, 219, 222, 233, 237, 240,
  275, 303, 314–15, 342; of security, 220;
  protean archive, 80; virtual archive, 82,
  118, 120
Arendt, Hannah, 71, 93, 189–90, 195,
  198–99, 226, 254, 377
Aristotle, 222

Arnold, David, 60
Asad, Talal, 49, 214n27
(APPEVE) Association des Parents et
  Personnes ayant une Exstrophie Vési-
  cale et/ou un Epispadias, 284
Atlas, James, 181
Augé, Marc, 142
Austin, John, 12, 79, 230. See also fieldwork
  in philosophy
Australia, ix, 59, 60, 83, 94–95, 103–4, 344,
  352, 370. See also Aboriginal peoples;
  penal colony
Austria, 295
Azoulay, Ariella, 322, 340, 360

Bachelard, Gaston, 215
Bacon, Francis, 211
Badiou, Alain, 139
bagnes (penal colonies), 81, 93–94, 109
Balandier, Georges, 125, 140–44, 151
Balibar, Étienne, 132, 158, 166, 246
Bancel, Nicolas, 129
banlieue, 131, 149, 307; as zone of abandon-
  ment, 134
Bantustans, 17, 104
bare life, 116
Battle of Algiers, The (1965), 183–85. See also
  Algeria
Bauman, Zygmunt, 246, 254, 369
Bayart, Jean-François, 146–47, 163
Belgium, 71, 83, 86, 91, 187, 190, 256, 286,
  295, 320
Bergson, Henri, 34, 156,
Biehl, João, Vita: Life in a Zone of Social
  Abandonment, 368
Bikini Atoll (Islands), 194, 353, 367
biopolitics, 29, 31, 69, 78, 116, 195n61,
  308, 313, 322, 330, 332, 369; and camps,
  105; race and, 28, 163, 316
biopower, 164
biosecurity, 330–31, 334, 337; since 9/11,
  313, 329
Black Pete, 12
Blair, Tony, 181

Blanchard, Pascal, 129

blood: fictions of, 244; fraudulence of, 203; symbolics of, 27–28. *See also* mixed-blood

Boer War, 64n58, 104–5

bombs: unexploded ordinance (UXO), 17, 373–75

Bonelli, Laurent, 313, 334

borders, 3, 6, 59, 65, 105, 193, 273, 301, 320, 324; and biosecurity, 330; and boundaries, 82; imperial borderlands, 108, 111; of disciplinary expertise, 142; of empire, 21, 186, 196; of Europe, 156, 164, 295, 307, 312, 332; of Israel/Palestine, 120, 194; of sovereignty, 177, 194; of the social, 309; refugee camps, 24, 37; transgression of, 124, 255. *See also* frontiers; sovereignty

Bourdieu, Pierre, 79, 126, 136–38, 144, 273

Botany Bay, 94

Boycott, Divestment, and Sanctions movement (BDS), 58, 67n567

BP (f.k.a. British Petroleum), 369. *See also* environment

Branche, Raphaëlle, 34, 316

Brazil, 368

breach: of law, 58; of security, 118, 229, 234, 236; of self evidence (event), 22, 45, 75, 109, 216. *See also* epistemology; event; genealogy

Britain, 81n28, 86, 115, 119, 181, 190, 195, 220, 257, 300, 307n3, 333; United Kingdom, 375 *See also* England

British South Africa Company, 358

Brown, Michael, 263

Brown, Wendy, 23, 349

Bugeaud, Thomas, 99

Bush, George Herbert Walker, 226

Bush, George Walker, 173, 315n27; Bush administration, 181

Butler, Judith, 14, 143, 312

Caché (2006), 157–58

Calhoun, Craig, 180

camp, 77, 81, 102, 106, 109–10, 125, 310; colony and, 12, 19, 24, 75–79, 93, 95, 101, 103, 105, 113, 115, 119, 193; concentration, 64n58; internment/detention, 73–75, 81, 126, 332; labor/work, 88, 90, 93–94, 108; military, 24, 100, 118; refugee/transition, 37, 57, 81, 116, 323, 325, 329, 365; resettlement/relocation, 65, 78; Soviet, 106–7, 367. *See also* colony; Harki; reservation

Camus, Albert: *The Stranger*, 123–24, 139–40; *Chroniques algériennes*, 143–44

Canada, 17, 60, 81n28, 344, 275. *See also* reservation (reserve)

Canadian Western Guard, 286

carceral archipelago, 75–78, 87–88, 95, 104–9, 111–15, 125, 209n10, 367

carceral institutions, 82, 90, 102. *See also colonies agricoles, les*

Caribbean, 195, 356

carnal, 321, and carceral 335; knowledge, 319, 334; management of, 308

categories, 9–10, 82, 113, 160–61, 163, 167–68, 173, 187, 193, 201, 217–18, 224, 240, 283; analytic categories, 66, 132; and ontology, 16; of colonial archives, 72, 80; of colonial narratives, 15, 178; of empire, 145; of people/race, 35, 73, 83, 96, 135, 141, 177, 186, 192, 196, 207, 216, 219, 228, 231, 237–38, 244, 249, 251, 260–62, 175, 286, 313; of the social, 209, 223, 264, 274; rationality of, 221, 296. *See also* Hacking, Ian

Catherine the Great, 111

Césaire, Aimé, 127, 131–32, 151, 161, 349

Central Intelligence Agency (CIA), 43, 51

Chakrabarty, Dipesh, 211, 215–16; *Provincializing Europe*, 53

Chatterjee, Partha, 210–11, 226

chemical weapons, 373–74. *See also* Agent Orange

Chevron, 369

China, 103, 113, 320

Chirac, Jacques, 153, 275, 287

essentialisms, 222, 261, mobile essentialisms, 16, 240; of race, 239, 262, 264

ethics of discomfort, 18, 143

ethnography, 36n58, 90, 92, 136, 141, 183,
226, 262n71, 279, 303, 332, 336, 366, 368,
371, 376; and the U.S. military, 178n8,
179; as fieldwork in philosophy, 79;
of Israel, 49; ontological turn in, 16;
Marxism in, 142n68

Europe, 48, 74, 81, 86, 88–92, 104, 116,
119, 127, 131, 159–60, 164, 166, 176, 179,
216, 225, 258, 270, 274, 278, 282, 295,
303–4, 307, 312, 316, 319, 334, 349, 364;
and ruins, 357; history of sexuality in,
310; Islam in, 57, 200; race in, 16, 156,
275; social reform in, 11, 82, 84

European Union (EU), 312, 334

event, 22, 45, 70, 75, 109, 118, 222–23, 297,
378. See also breach; genealogy

exceptionalism, 54–56, 175n4, 177, 179,
197; exceptional status, 40, 47

exclusion, 178, 228, 273; inclusion and,
257; of race, 165, 250; of welfare, 280;
politics of, 67; separation and, 134;
sites of, 93, 109; zones of, 75

Fabian, Johannes, *Out of Our Minds*, 226

Famille, Travail, Patrie (Family, Work, and
Fatherland), 287

family values, 293, 299

Fanon, Frantz, 8, 45, 47, 127, 132, 150, 235,
312, 348–49, 377

fascism, 30, 164–65, 287, 292, 294

Fassin, Eric, 20n28, 165, 307, 310, 318,

Fassin, Didier, 67, 116, 134, 155, 165, 168,
310, 316

feminist scholarship, 146, 300–301, 313,
317, 324, 333

Ferro, Marc, 128

fieldwork, 279; ethic of, 50n24

fieldwork in philosophy, 79–80

Fordlandia (Henry Ford), 362

France, 12, 16, 48, 49n22, 67n67, 71–75,
81–85, 91–94, 97–103, 115, 109, 111,
119, 122–70, 185–86, 190, 194–95, 197,
237, 255–56, 269–71, 275–303, 305, 310,
311n12, 313–24, 344, 345n17; genocidal
policies of, 73; immigrants in 131, 151,
156–58, 270, 280, 283–84, 291, 293,
297, 307; Islam and, 165; pauperism
in, 83, 101; race in, 74, 122–25, 133, 139,
157, 163–64, 170, 187, 260, 274–78, 282,
349, 377. *See also colonies agricoles; Front
National*

freedom, 98, 124, 252; degrees of unfreedom, 102, 120, 316, 372; of movement,
118; of speech, 59; sexual, 306, 313

French Foreign Legion, 149, 162

French Indochina, 60, 81, 88, 125, 144,
161, 197, 227–28, 250, 302, 309, 326; war
in, 162

French Indochina War, 162

French Revolution, 84, 92, 112n114, 152,
282

Freund, Julien, 229

Front National (FN), 150, 165, 269–303. *See
also* Le Pen, Jean-Marie

frontiers, 87, 95, 108, 110; interior frontiers, 52, 76, 111, 120, 202, 255, 295,
324, 329, 334, 371; intimate frontiers,
323–24, 334; moral frontiers, 332

Foucault, Michel, 9–11, 14n12, 18–19,
21–22, 24, 26–32, 45, 66, 75, 77–80,
82, 87–88, 95–97, 105–20, 143, 163–69,
200, 209n10, 210–11, 223, 232–33, 239,
245, 247, 250–52, 255, 295, 305–10, 320,
330–31; methodology, 23, 31, 35. *See
also* biopower; *déraison; dispositif;* ethics
of discomfort; geneaology; *individual
publications*

Garner, Eric, 263

Gay, Peter, 211, 218

Gaza, 57, 327, 360; *See also* Palestine

Geertz, Clifford, 50n24, 221, 271, 273

genealogy, 6, 9, 11, 14, 22, 61, 82, 88–89,
96–97, 105, 119, 147, 151–52, 155, 195,
208–11, 225, 238, 251, 260, 307, 262–63;

Hitchens, Christopher, 185
Hobsbawm, Eric, 181
Holland. *See* Netherlands, The
Hollande, François, 154–55
Holocaust, 35, 52, 73, 270, 295
Holt, Thomas, 248
home, 100, 124, 150, 199, 203, 300, 326–27, 349; at home, 228, 231, 301, 322; colonial home, 5, 109, 121, 149, 158, 323, 338; homeland, 303, 330; in Palestine/Israel, 37, 40, 55, 235, 329, 340
homo europeaus, 257, 259
Hopkins, Antony Gerald, 181
human kinds, 117, 243, 260–61, 265
humanitarianism, 3, 186, 188–89, 194, 201, 307, 317–18, 325, 334, 341, 360; imperialism, 181–82
Hume, David, 208
humiliation, 16, 134, 147, 203, 311, 322, 328; economies of, 4; sexual, 312, 316. *See also* affect
Hunt, Nancy, 340, 359–60, 367, 373
Huntington, Samuel, 200

immigration, 16, 127, 129, 165, 269, 271, 276, 282, 301–2, 332; anti-immigrant sentiment, 151, 260, 270, 284, 304, 318; immigrants, 111, 131, 156–57, 160, 196, 200, 277, 280, 283, 291, 293, 297, 307, 332, 360, 377
imperial archives, 202; as virtual, 109. *See also* archives
imperial borderlands, 108, 111. *See also* borders
imperial debris, 17, 22, 32, 336, 339, 346–47, 359–60, 363, 367, 371, 374; occluded histories of, 337; toxins of, 5
imperial dispositions, 4, 209, 233; of disregard, 9
imperial duress, 7–8, 36–37, 106, 339, 363. *See also* duress
imperial effects, 3, 349
imperial formation, 3, 6–10, 17–20, 31, 35, 41, 54–56, 69–74, 83, 93, 106, 113, 152,

163, 168–69, 175n3, 177–78, 186–90, 194–95, 198–99, 205, 207, 216, 225, 227n62, 287, 309–10, 313, 320, 325, 329, 335, 339–40, 343, 346–47, 352, 362–63, 370–72, 378. *See also* empire
imperial governance, 14–15, 17, 22, 31, 77, 80, 82, 112, 175–78, 195, 206, 216, 220, 231, 309, 311, 342
imperial histories, 234, 315. *See also* histories
imperial knowledge, 46, 113, 211, 231
imperial logic, 21, 62, 72, 82, 333, 352
imperial sovereignty, 14, 21, 175, 339, 345; on degrees of, 22, 41, 54, 177. *See also* sovereignty
imperialism, 45, 173, 344, 352, 368; continental, 190; Enlightenment as, 207; epistemology of, 55; humanitarian, 181–82, 188; mottled; new, 111, 183; race and, 312; U.S., 45–47, 51. *See also* empire; colonialism
imperialist nostalgia, 149, 347, 357–58, 366n79, 375–76
India, 14, 56, 60, 210–12, 213n25, 219, 251n37, 353, 359, 366, 376
Indies. *See* Netherlands Indies
indigeneity movements, 60
Indigènes de Rèpublique, 134, 144, 145n72, 377
Indigenous peoples: and land, 352; in the Declaration of Independence, 199. *See also* Native America; reservation
individual rights, 252, 256. *See also* equality; liberalism
inlandsche kinderen, 223, 249
insecurity (*onveiligheid*), 20n28, 121, 231, 233–34, 236, 287, 302, 313, 334. *See also* security
intelligence; 41, 61, 64n58, 90, 116, 220, 230, 236, 329; empires of, 332, 341; human, 183; imperial, 191, 203, 222; political, 219, race and, 239, 258; U.S. intelligence. *See also* Central Intelligence Agency

International High Court in The Hague (The Hague), 38n2, 58

intersectionality, 309

intimacy, 14, 24, 203, 220, 299, 308, 310, 318–19, 321, 325, 328, 332, 360; colonial intimacies, 21, 314, 316, 320, 327; of empire, 204, frontiers, 323–24, 334; space, 176, 204, 257, 302, violence, 16, 126, 322, 326, 331, 361; technologies of, 126

Invisible Man (Ralph Ellison), 7, 124

Iraq, 20n29, 33, 181–82, 184–85, 235, 305, 312, 325; population of, 331, 363; war in, 37, 174, 314, 324, 340, 342, 348. *See also* Abu Ghraib

irretrievability, 12, 157, 366

Islam, 44, 58, 132, 200, 222, 271; and fundamentalism, 165; and Orientalism, 47n18, 57; and terrorism, 184, 235

Islamophobia, 165, 271, 316. *See also* anti-Muslim

Israel, 128, 154, 170, 176, 305, 320, 323, 363; and Lebanon, 17; as a colonial state, 11–12, 235, 325, 327–29, 340, 360, 365; borders of, 194; cordon sanitaire, 52; in (post)colonial studies, 37–67; ruins in, 364

Israel, Jonathan, 206, 209n10

Israeli Afforestation Project, 364–65

Israeli military operations: Operation Cast Lead, 59; Operation Pillar of Defense, 59; Operation Protective Edge, 59

Italy, 101, 293, 295

James, Susan, 208, 222, 225

Japan, 128, 162, 305, 320, 345

Java, 82, 91–92, 112, 114, 213n24–25, 215, 218–19, 250, 255, 324–27, 353

Jennings, Eric, 161

Johnson, Chalmers, 51–52, 187

Jordan, 320

Jordan, Winthrop, 249, 254

Julien, Charles-André, 159, 161

Judt, Tony, 130

Kagan, Robert, 181

Kant, Immanuel, 206n2, 217

Kaplan, Amy, 50, 314n24

Ko, Jung, 162

Korea, 128, 305, 320, 345

Kristeva, Julia, 139

Kristol, William, 182

Ku Klux Klan, 286

Kurth, James, 186, 200

Lakoff, Andrew, 330–31

Lambesc, 101

Latin America, 43n49, 51n27, 179, 190n47, 200, 211, 325. *See also* South America

Lazreg, Marnia, 152, 317, 328

Le Bras, Hervé, 165

Le Chevallier, Cendrine, 292–93, 299

Le Pen, Janny, 299–300

Le Pen, Jean-Marie, 150, 256, 269, 270–71, 275, 277–78, 281n14, 282, 286, 292–93, 295, 299, 300–301, 303

Le Pen, Marie-Caroline, 299

Le Pen, Marine, 12, 150, 256, 269, 270n1, 300, 303

Le Cour Grandmaison, Olivier, *Coloniser/ exterminer*, 59, 64n58, 102, 129, 147, 316n37

Lebanon, 17; bombing of, 59, Civil War, 42

Lebovics, Herman, 151

legacies, 18, 21, 345–46, 349, 352, 370; inadequacy of the concept of, 25, 33, 352; of the Enlightenment, 215, 217, 226; of racecraft, 256. *See also* continuity

Leiris, Michel, 141

Lemaire, Sandrine, 129

Leopold II, 179, 360

Let Us Now Praise Famous Men (James Agee), 371–72

Lévi-Strauss, Claude, 354, 367, 376

liberalism, 67n67, 242, 246, 297; and racism, 141, 225, 239, 247, 253; and rationality, 210; exclusionary practices

of, 73; modernity and, 248; neoliberal-
ism, 69, 236n87, 254, 369
Libération, 289
lieux de mémoire (memory sites), 158–59, 161
Lionel, Jospin, 152, 278, 282
Locke, John, 208
longue durée, 112, 164, 203, 343
Luhmann, Niklas, 10, 26n34, 33

Machery, Pierre, 69, 120
MacIntyre, Alasdair, 205
Madagascar, 161, 351n33; Madagascar
Plan, 104. *See also* Third Reich
Making Up People (Ian Hacking), 228
Malinowski, Bronislaw, 141
Malintent, Project (Violent Intent), 235,
330–31
Malta, 101
Mann, Michael, 182
Mariana Islands, 15, 195
Marseille, 273, 276, 279–80, 286
Martin, Thomas, 63n57, 191
Martinique, 63, 115, 320
Marx, Karl, 32, 166n145
Marxism, 45, 142n60
Masco, Joe, 365
Massad, Joseph, 34, 62
Maylaya, 197
Mbembe, Achille, 134, 152; *On the Post-
colony*, 192, 311, 322, 343
McClintock, Ann, 50, 312
Médard, 115, 355
Mégret, Bruno, 275, 291n30, 292–93, 299,
301, 303
Mégret, Catherine, 275, 280, 299, 303
Mehta, Uday, 210, 246
Memmi, Albert, 121, 127, 132, 233
memory, 21, 35, 125, 143, 146, 152–61,
185n26, 315, 338. *See also* colonial
aphasia
Merleau-Ponty, Maurice, 34; *The Phenom-
enology of Perception*, 35
methodology, 6, 15, 18, 31, 39, 74–75, 168,
264, 340; as attention to doubt, 22;

concept-work as, 17, 19, 79; *déraison* as,
232; expectations of, 28; genealogy as,
23, 35, 76, 96; *Orientalism* as methodological guide, 57. *See also* concept-
work; genealogy
Métraux, Alfred, 141
metropole, 71, 74, 91, 108–9, 118, 141–42,
356, 362. *See also* colony
Mettray, le colonie de, 85n33, 86–92, 97, 107,
109, 114. *See also* colonies agricoles, les;
Demetz, Frédéric-Auguste
mestizo, 244, 249. *See also* mixed-blood
metaphor, 25, 34, 111, 146, 201, 286, 349,
368; and concepts, 78, 115, 167, 339; and
empire, 179, 183, 338, 377; of geography, 107. *See also* concept-work
métis, 228, 250. *See also* mixed-blood
métissage (mixing) 144, 283. *See also*
mixed-blood
Mexico, 200, 332
Middle East, 38, 43–44, 46, 55–56, 65, 179,
191, 195, 220
Mignolo, Walter, 210
military colonies (*colonies militaries*), 71, 85,
88, 92–93, 95, 101, 112
military installations, 12, 51; bases, 15, 51,
78, 136n31, 187
mining, 351; coal and iron, 108, 371;
uranium, 370
misrecognition, 8, 15, 19, 157, 163, 248.
See also recognition
mixed-blood, 81, 114, 198, 224, 231, 249,
259, 323–34, 326; *See also* mestizo; *métis*
mobility, 178, 203, 323; immobility, 106,
322; polyvalent, 245, 256, 264; tactical,
251, 255
modernity, 63, 105, 107, 246–47, 273, 366;
and capitalism, 369; and liberalism,
248; colonies as laboratories of, 213;
ruins of, 357
Monde, Le, 289, 300
Monde Diplomatique, Le, 136, 153, 156, 181
Monroe Doctrine, 51n27, 199
Montag, Warren, 69, 120

toward, 154; rights in, 18; ruins in, 360, 364; surveillance of, 323. *See also* Gaza; Occupied Territories; *The Question of Palestine*

Papon, Maurice, 152, 153n99

Paris, 20n28, 67n67, 83, 97, 100n77, 101, 112, 136n38, 157, 159, 270, 280, 293–94, 308, 311, 315, 377; Commune of 1871, 81n28; *exposition coloniale* in, 158. *See also banlieue*

passé composé, 45, 155, 348

penal colony (*colonies pénitentiaires*), 71, 77, 81n28, 84, 91–97, 100–103, 107–12, 115–16, 119–20

Philippines, 41, 51, 104, 188, 198, 341; U.S.-Philippine War, 179

pieds-noirs (former colonials), 280, 293. *See also* Algeria

Plato, 246

political concepts, 24, 46, 60, 66, 70, 72, 75–77, 117–20, 210, 231, 252, 256, 261, 308, 341. *See also* concept-work

political rationalities, 13, 15, 117, 224, 239

politics of comparison, 39n3, 54, 61, 319–20

poor whites, 60, 159, 223–24, 231, 253, 370, 372

Port Arthur, 115

Portugal, 103, 128, 243, 293, 295, 358

postcolonial, 63, 129, 131, 133, 163, 166, 257, 260, 302, 311–12, 336, 358, 378; as distinguished from (post)colonial, ix; condition, 33, 40, 238; disorders, 3, 352n36; Edward Said, 47; intellectuals, 154n106; Palestine, 50; Pierre Bourdieu, 137; sex regimes, 308, 317; studies, 39, 48n21, 53, 55, 57; 132, 138–39, 146–47, 192, 343–46; temporality, 4, 30, 62, 124. *See also* colonial studies; (post)colonial studies

(post)colonial studies, 14, 17, 39–42, 46–47, 50–57, 58n46, 64–67, 132n27, 146, 175, 178, 180, 190, 205, 238, 305, 315, 324, 342, 345, 351–52, 378; as distin-

guished from postcolonialism, ix; Edward Said, 55; Palestine/Israel, 11, 37, 44, 61; Subaltern Studies, 56; temporality, 4, 25, 134. *See also* colonial studies; postcolonial

postcolony, 4, 40, 320, 378

postmodernism, 206, 254, 257, 302

power, 27, 198, 201, 211, 239, 244, 246, 251, 253–54, 265, 306, 309–10, 312–13, 362; allocation of, 70; analytic of, 349; biopolitical, 31; biopower, 164, 247; configurations of, 42, 197, 245; constitutive, 182; distribution of, 120, 241; forms of, 28, 198; fragility of, 347; imperialist, 137, 182, 310; implementation of, 192; implied, 194; network of, 44; regenerative, 84, 114; relations of, 8, 55, 87, 229, 238, 248, 252, 256, 283; sovereign, 197; structures of, 149, 169; technology of, 30

Prakash, Gyan, 50, 210, 212

Pratt, Mary Louise, 139–40

precarity, 3, 72, 119, 263, 305, 318, 323–24, 326, 359, 366

preserved possibility, 177, 248

Price, Richard, 36n58, 115, 355; *Convict and Colonel*, 63

Project Hostile Intent, 331

proletariat, 50n24, 137; proletarian flow, 159

prostitution, 98, 129, 310, 314–15, 333

Provincializing Europe (Dipesh Chakrabarty), 53

psychoanalysis, 253

Puerto Rico, 14, 41, 105n93, 194–96, 320

punctum, 95

Question of Palestine, The (Edward Said), 37, 42, 44, 46, 50, 53, 55, 57

Rabinow, Paul, 19n23, 32n49, 75, 79, 92, 107, 223, 330

race, 13, 69n2, 122, 133, 135–36, 145, 156–57, 163–66, 225, 228–29, 245, 247–48,

race (continued)
258n62, 261–62, 275–76, 279–80, 302;
analytics of, 321; and imperialism, 312,
371; and intelligence, 239; and sex, 309,
315; borderlands of, 222; categories of,
237; concepts of, 237, 241, 250–52; 259;
dynamics of, 238; elisions of, 137; epistemologies of, 16, 123, 224, 237, 243–44,
263; etymologies of, 243; folk theories of,
258; in science, 209, 244; mobile essentialisms of, 240; polyvalent mobility of,
256, 264; permeability of racial categories, 244; protean qualities of, 16, 222;
racecraft, 249, 256, 263; race making,
210; racial contamination, 169, 261; racial formations, 22, 135, 189, 238–39, 241,
257, 263, 309; racial grammar, 239, 309;
racial kinds, 209, 238; racial ontologies,
369; racial truth, 170, 237, 243, 250, 260;
recursive genealogies of, 238; resilience
of, 274, 303; social distortions of, 141
Race and the Education of Desire (Ann L.
Stoler), 28, 237
racism, 28, 31, 157, 163, 166, 189, 200–201,
235, 239–41, 243–44, 247–49, 251–52,
256, 259–64, 269, 274, 276–79, 284,
286, 303; across Europe, 55, 156; and
Rebublicanism, 142; and social reform,
83, 111; and xenophobia, 165; anti-
French, 282–83; biological, 238; cold
racism, 139; colonial, 6, 16, 170, 238,
242, 257; end of, 275; in France, 151,
163; environmental, 351; intellectual,
139, 238; new, 238, 242, 245, 253, 257; of
the state, 30, 139, 155, 164, 255, 258, 295,
377; universalism and, 246
Radio Le Pen, 289
Raj, The (British), 191, 195
Ramallah, 38
Rancière, Jacques, 138–39, 214, 273
Rao, Vyjayanthi, 366
rape, 307, 309, 316n37, 317, 328, 333, 360;
and sexual violation, 308, 317, 327; and
sexual violence, 318, 332, 334, 359

rationality, 214, 216, 246–47; and Max
Weber, 229; European rationalism, 215;
hyper-rationalized technologies, 234;
irrationality, 216, 229, 285; political, 13,
15, 65, 76, 117, 205, 217, 224, 239; behavior, 256; choice, 257; knowledge, 207,
211, 220–21, 225–26, 229; rationale for
torture, 235; rationale for Islamophobia, 316; scientific, 209–10, 220
Reagan, Ronald, 181
reason, 141, 175, 212, 214, 220, 229–30,
285; Age of Reason, 207; architectonics
of, 217; calculus of, 217; colonialist, 13,
226, 235; commitment to, 207–8; cunning of, 210; déraison (unreason), 168,
230, 233–35; Enlightenment Reason,
219, 222; failures of, 227; force of, 216;
historiographies of, 21; ideology of,
225; reasons of state, 231; refusal of,
206n4; rule of, 207–8, 210, 215; scientific, 210; supremacy of, 13, 205, 221,
118, 236; underside of, 232; universal,
205, 210–11, 215. *See also* rationality
recognition, 5, 33, 52, 60 72, 123, 133,
156, 194, 233, 241, 244, 260; of
concepts, 68; of refusal, 151; of race,
165, 247n23; of ruins, 364; refusal of,
176. *See also* misrecognition; refusal;
self-determination
recursion, 3, 6, 22, 27–28, 33, 52, 77, 107,
114, 120, 250, 302; analytics, 26, 30;
genealogies, 238; histories, ix, 24, 32,
35, 40, 42, 189, 263; movement, 169;
recalibrations; 56, 72
refugee, 3, 138, 156, 304, 332; environmental, 337
refugee camp, 24, 37, 57, 77, 81, 116,
291n31, 325, 329, 365
refusal, 4, 8, 13, 23, 50n4, 60, 72, 98, 119,
143, 152, 154, 169, 206n4, 278, 310, 347;
of white supremacy, 359; 379; recognition of, 151; strategies of, 39
république coloniale, 145, 324
réseau (network), 110, 319. *See also* dispositif

www.ingramcontent.com/pod-product-compliance
Lightning Source LLC
Chambersburg PA
CBHW050329270326
41926CB00016B/3368